LANDSCAPES

LEAVING CERTIFICATE GEOGRAPHY
CORE UNITS AND HUMAN ELECTIVE

DECLAN FITZGERALD & P.J. WHITE

GILL EDUCATION

Gill Education
Hume Avenue
Park West
Dublin 12

www.gilleducation.ie

Gill Education is an imprint of M.H. Gill & Co.

© Declan Fitzgerald and P.J. White 2019

ISBN: 978-0-7171-71187

Design: Liz White Designs
Layout: Jen Patton, Liz White Designs
Illustrations: Andriy Yankovskyy

All rights reserved. No part of this publication may be copied, reproduced or transmitted in any form or by any means without written permission of the publishers or else under the terms of any licence permitting limited copying issued by the Irish Copyright Licensing Agency.

At the time of going to press, all web addresses were active and contained information relevant to the topics in this book. Gill Education does not, however, accept responsibility for the content or views contained on these websites. Content, views and addresses may change beyond the publisher or author's control. Students should always be supervised when reviewing websites.

For permission to reproduce photographs, the authors and publisher gratefully acknowledge the following:

© Alamy: 21BL, 21BR, 26BL, 52, 66B, 75BR, 78, 83L, 93T, 93B, 98, 107, 116, 119, 120, 121, 128, 129, 130T, 131, 134, 137, 139T, 142, 152, 156, 157, 158, 159T, 161, 166B, 199R, 203, 240C, 256, 260, 276R, 283B, 285BR, 286T, 291, 297, 298, 306, 311, 323T, 341, 342, 344, 345, 346, 347, 350L, 351, 352, 355, 356, 366, 367CL, 367CR, 370, 372, 374, 375, 376TL, 376TR, 378, 382, 383T, 390B, 392, 393, 394B, 395, 396, 399, 400B, 402, 409, 410, 419, 420, 436, 442, 443, 444, 445B, 447, 450T, 461TR, 461B, 467, 469T, 469C, 476, 481, 482T, 485, 486, 500B, 501CT, 501CB, 502T, 504, 505, 507T, 507B, 508, 509B, 510, 511T, 511C, 512, 516, 520T, 525T, 525C, 528, 529, 532T, 533T; © Alexey Seleznev: 371B; © Barrow/Coakley: 140, 200, 201T, 204, 205, 207, 209, 274, 494, 502B, 525B; © Basilicata Turistica: 354; © Ben Deck: 332C; © Brian Gratwicke: 161; © CCAFS: 445T; © CNN: 26TR; © Collections École Polytechnique/Jérémy Barande: 325; Courtesy of O'Mahoney-Pike Architects: 523B; © David Nance, ARS: 451; © Digital Vision/Getty Premium: 271; Courtesy of Dublin City Library: 509T; © E+/Getty Premium: 108, 132, 143, 290, 405T; © European Photo Services Ltd: 523T; Courtesy of Failte Ireland: 278, 305; Courtesy of Irish Farmers Journal: 465T; © Getty Images: 14, 26BR, 66T, 73, 74T, 76TL, 76B, 79, 89, 91B, 98, 113, 243, 339, 459, 473B, 474, 519, 520BL, 520BR; © INPHO/Morgan Treacy: 390T; Courtesy of Inter Trade Ireland: 389; © Irish Times: 501T; © iStock/Getty Premium: 1, 18B, 21T, 22, 35, 38, 40, 45, 46, 53, 57, 59, 61, 62, 67T, 71, 75BL, 76TR, 82, 88, 93C, 95, 96, 98, 101, 109, 135B, 147, 151C, 161, 164, 228, 240, 247, 265, 267, 270, 277, 285T, 301, 307, 312, 316, 319, 322, 323B, 326, 330, 332T, 332B, 343, 348, 349, 350R, 360, 363, 365, 367TR, 367BR, 368, 371T, 388, 389, 417, 435, 440, 452T, 453, 468, 469B, 470, 482B, 487B, 501BR, 506, 511B, 514, 527, 532C, 533T, 535T, 535CB, 539; © Jean-Christophe Benoist: 112; © Joseph King: 77; © Joe O'Shaughnessy/The Connacht Tribune: 90; © John Kelly Photography: 139B; © John Heroitt/Ireland Aerial Photography: 67B, 507C, 515; © Jon Sullivan: 484B; © Lonely Planet/Getty Images: 130B, 138; © Madhav Pai: 450B; © Mick Knapton: 161; © Moment/Getty Premium: 29, 286B; © NASA: 21C, 25, 117, 118, 218, 219, 220, 221, 222, 379; © NPS Photo: 160; Courtesy of Ocean Exploration Trust: 19; © PA Images: 92; © Peter Bijsterveld: 151T; © Richard Webb: 159C; © Robert Linsdell: 523C; © Rolling News: 521, 530B; © RTE: 530T; © Shutterstock: 72, 74B, 91T, 125, 154, 166T, 170, 198, 199L, 201B, 202, 241B, 242T, 257, 269, 276L, 285BL, 292, 294, 303, 304, 324, 337, 340, 361, 362, 367TL, 376B, 377, 381, 383B, 424, 434, 461TL, 477, 484T, 487T, 493, 500, 526, 532B, 534, 535CT, 535B; Courtesy of TG4: 400T; © USGS: 18T, 26TL, 159B; © The Image Bank/Getty Images: 24; Courtesy of Tourism Ireland: 389; Courtesy US Department of Water Resources: 115; Courtesy of Wild Irish Seaweeds Ltd: 299; © William Murphy: 283T, 501BL, 522.

Ordnance Survey Ireland Permit No. 9200
© Ordnance Survey Ireland/Government of Ireland

The authors and publisher have made every effort to trace all copyright holders, but if any have been inadvertently overlooked we would be pleased to make the necessary arrangement at the first opportunity.

CONTENTS

Introduction vi

CORE UNIT 1

PATTERNS AND PROCESSES IN THE PHYSICAL ENVIRONMENT viii

Chapter 1 Plate Tectonics 1
- The Earth's Structure
- Continental Drift
- Sea-Floor Spreading
- The Pacific Ring of Fire
- Plate Boundaries
- Examination Questions
- *Revision Summary*

Chapter 2 Volcanic Activity 14
- Volcanic Activity on the Earth's Surface
- Life Cycle of a Volcano
- Extrusive 'Volcanic' Features
- Intrusive 'Plutonic' Features
- Human Interaction with Volcanoes
- Examination Questions
- *Revision Summary*

Chapter 3 Earthquake Activity 29
- Components of an Earthquake
- Where Earthquakes Occur
- Earthquake Recording
- Earthquake Prediction
- The Impact of Earthquakes
- Examination Questions
- *Revision Summary*

Chapter 4 Folding and Faulting Activity 45
- Rock Structures Formed by Tectonic Forces
- Examination Questions
- *Revision Summary*

Chapter 5 Rocks 57
- Rock Classification
- Active and Passive Plate Margins
- Human Interaction with the Rock Cycle
- Examination Questions
- *Revision Summary*

Chapter 6 Weathering Processes and Landforms 71
- Factors Affecting the Rate of Weathering
- Mechanical Weathering Processes
- Chemical Weathering Processes
- Biological Weathering Processes
- Distinctive Irish Landscapes Formed by Weathering
- Examination Questions
- *Revision Summary*

Chapter 7 Mass Movement 88
- Influences on Mass Movement
- Classification of Mass Movement
- The Impact of Human Activity on Mass Movement
- Examination Questions
- *Revision Summary*

Chapter 8 River Action 101
- River Drainage Patterns
- River Processes
- Youthful Stage – Upper Valley
- Mature Stage – Middle Valley
- Old Age Stage – Lower Valley
- Examination Questions
- *Revision Summary*

Chapter 9 The Sea at Work 125
- Waves
- Coastal Erosion
- Transport by the Sea
- Coastal Deposition
- Human Interaction with Coastal Areas
- Examination Questions
- *Revision Summary*

Chapter 10 Glaciation and Glacial Processes 147
- Pleistocene Glaciation
- The Glaciations of Ireland
- Glacial Ice Formation
- Types of Glaciation
- Examination Questions
- *Revision Summary*

Chapter 11 Isostasy 164
- How Glaciation Causes Isostatic Movement
- The Impact of Isostasy on Fluvial Processes
- Landscape Development
- Examination Questions
- *Revision Summary*

CORE UNIT 2

GEOGRAPHICAL INVESTIGATION AND SKILLS ...169

Chapter 12 Ordnance Survey Maps ...170
- Ordnance Survey Ireland
- Direction
- Measuring Distance
- Calculating Area
- Relief on OS Maps
- Drawing Skills: Sketch Maps and Cross-Sections
- Interpreting OS Maps
- Examination Questions
- *Revision Summary*

Chapter 13 Aerial Photographs ...198
- Types of Aerial Photography
- Interpreting Aerial Photographs
- Comparing OS Maps and Aerial Photographs
- Direction on an Aerial Photograph
- Examination Questions
- *Revision Summary*

Chapter 14 Weather Maps and Satellite Imagery ...212
- Weather Maps
- Satellite Imagery
- Examination Questions
- *Revision Summary*

Chapter 15 Graph Skills ...228
- Types of Graph
- Examination Questions
- *Revision Summary*

Chapter 16 Geographical Investigation ...240
- Stage 1: Introduction
- Stage 2: Planning
- Stage 3: Gathering Information
- Stage 4: Results, Conclusions and Evaluation
- Stage 5: Organisation and Presentation of Results
- *Marking Scheme for Geographical Investigation: Summary*

CORE UNIT 3

REGIONAL GEOGRAPHY ...246

Chapter 17 The Concept of a Region ...247
- Climatic Regions
- Geomorphological Regions
- Administrative Regions
- Cultural Regions
- A Region of Industrial Decline
- Urban Regions
- Socio-Economic Regions
- Examination Questions
- *Revision Summary*

Chapter 18 A Core Irish Region – The Greater Dublin Area ...265
- Physical Processes
- Primary Economic Activities
- Secondary Economic Activities
- Tertiary Economic Activities
- Human Processes
- Examination Questions
- *Revision Summary*

Chapter 19 A Peripheral Irish Region – The Western Region ...290
- Physical Processes
- Primary Economic Activities
- Secondary Economic Activities
- Tertiary Economic Activities
- Human Processes
- Examination Questions
- *Revision Summary*

Chapter 20 A Core European Region – The Paris Basin ...316
- Physical Processes
- Primary Economic Activities
- Secondary Economic Activities
- Tertiary Economic Activities
- Human Processes
- Examination Questions
- *Revision Summary*

Chapter 21 A Peripheral European Region – The Mezzogiorno ...337
- Physical Processes
- Primary Economic Activities
- Secondary Economic Activities
- Tertiary Economic Activities
- Human Processes
- Examination Questions
- *Revision Summary*

Chapter 22 A Continental/Subcontinental Region – India ...360
- Physical Processes
- Primary Economic Activities
- Secondary Economic Activities
- Tertiary Economic Activities
- Human Processes
- Examination Questions
- *Revision Summary*

Chapter 23 The Complexity of Regions I 388
- The Interaction of Economic, Political and Cultural Activities in a Region
- The Interaction of Different Cultural Groups and Political Regions
- The Future of Europe and the European Union
- Challenges to the Economic Union
- Sovereignty
- Examination Questions
- *Revision Summary*

Chapter 24 The Complexity of Regions II 399
- Changes in the Boundaries and Extent of Language Regions
- Urban Growth and the Expansion of Cities
- Changes in Political Boundaries and Their Impact on Cultural Groups
- The Development of the European Union
- EU Policy Development
- EU Enlargement
- Factors That Have Influenced EU Development and Enlargement
- Examination Questions
- *Revision Summary*

ELECTIVE UNIT 5

PATTERNS AND PROCESSES IN THE HUMAN ENVIRONMENT 416

Chapter 25 Population Changes Over Time and Space 417
- Population Distribution
- Population Density
- Global Population Growth Patterns
- The Demographic Transition Model
- Population Structure
- The Impact of Fertility Rates on Population Structure
- The Impact of Mortality Rates and Life Expectancy on Population Structure
- Examination Questions
- *Revision Summary*

Chapter 26 Population and Human Development 440
- The Impact of Resource Development on Population
- The Impact of Society and Culture on Population
- The Impact of Income Levels on Population
- The Impact of Technology on Population
- The Impact of Population Change on Rates of Human Development
- The Impact of Population Growth on Human Development
- Examination Questions
- *Revision Summary*

Chapter 27 Migration 459
- Migration and Donor Regions
- Migration and Host Regions
- Changing Migration Patterns in Ireland
- Rural-to-Urban Migration in the Developed World
- Rural-to-Urban Migration in the Developing World
- European Union Immigration Policies
- Asylum Seekers and Refugees in the European Union
- The European Migrant Crisis
- Issues That Can Arise from Migration
- Examination Questions
- *Revision Summary*

Chapter 28 Settlement 481
- Development of Settlements
- History of Settlement in Ireland
- Rural Settlement Patterns
- Rural Planning
- Urban Functions
- Changing Functions and Services of an Urban Centre
- Central Place Theory
- Examination Questions
- *Revision Summary*

Chapter 29 Urban Land Use and Planning 500
- Land Use Zones
- Urban Land Use Theories
- Social Stratification in Cities
- Changes in Land Use
- Planning Issues Arising from Changes in Land Use
- Land Values in Cities
- How Land Values Influence Land Use in Modern Cities
- Expanding Cities and the Pressure on Rural Land Use
- Examination Questions
- *Revision Summary*

Chapter 30 Urban Growth Problems 519
- Traffic Flow and Congestion
- Urban Sprawl
- Heritage in Urban Areas
- Environmental Quality in Urban Areas
- Urban Planning and Renewal
- Cities in the Developing World
- The Future of Urbanism
- Examination Questions
- *Revision Summary*

Examination Guide 539
Index 557

INTRODUCTION

Landscapes: Core Units and Human Elective covers the three core units of the Leaving Certificate Syllabus as well as the Human Elective:

- **Core Unit 1:** Patterns and Processes in the Physical Environment
- **Core Unit 2:** Regional Geography
- **Core Unit 3:** Geographical Investigation and Skills
- **Elective Unit 5:** Patterns and Processes in the Human Environment.

Putting the Core and your preferred Elective together allows for **better integration of the topics** through cross-referencing, and means Ordinary Level students only require one book.

A **detailed examination guide** at the back gives advice on answering questions, sample answers and SRP hints and tips.

This book is written using headings and text that follows the **language of the examination**.

Clear and concise **diagrams** are in line with examinations and are easy for students to reproduce.

Key to Features

Learning Intentions unpack the learning into manageable focused lessons for students, letting them know what they should be able to do, know or understand by then end of the topic.

Relevant and interesting **Case Studies** put concepts in context and allow for further investigation.

Important **definitions** are highlighted in boxes to focus learning and revision.

Exam Tips let students know the important ways to get top marks when answering questions.

Check Your Learning questions appear after each topic to allow for assessment for learning.

Note boxes provide additional relevant information to enhance the topic.

Skills Activities focus on bringing theory and skill together in preparation for examination questions.

Examination Questions at the end of every chapter include Ordinary and Higher Level Part One and Part Two questions with up-to-date marking schemes.

Did You Know? material brings interesting facts into the classroom to engage students in the learning.

Syllabus Link: 1.1, 1.2	**Syllabus Links** refer to the Leaving Certificate Geography Curriculum to allow for teacher preparation and planning.
KEYWORDS	**Keywords** at the start of topics provide geoliteracy opportunities and assist with revision.
Chapter 1: Plate Tectonics	**Chapter Links** show students where other areas of the course may be relevant to the learning, helping them to make connections and see Geography in its wider context.
Revision Summary	**Revision Summaries** complete the topics, allowing students to check their achievement of the Learning Intentions.
EXAM LINK (OL) **EXAM LINK (HL)**	*Landscapes* includes unique features to allow for maximum exam focus. **Exam Links** provide relevant examination questions and marking schemes beside the text, putting the learning in context.

For the Teacher

Landscapes is accompanied by comprehensive **PowerPoints** on **www.gillexplore.ie**, our easy-to-use digital resources website.

The PowerPoints for every chapter include:
- content to enhance teaching and learning;
- sample answers and marking schemes for every question (Check Your Learning, Exam Link and end-of-chapter Examination Questions);
- revision test material with marking schemes;
- relevant weblinks.

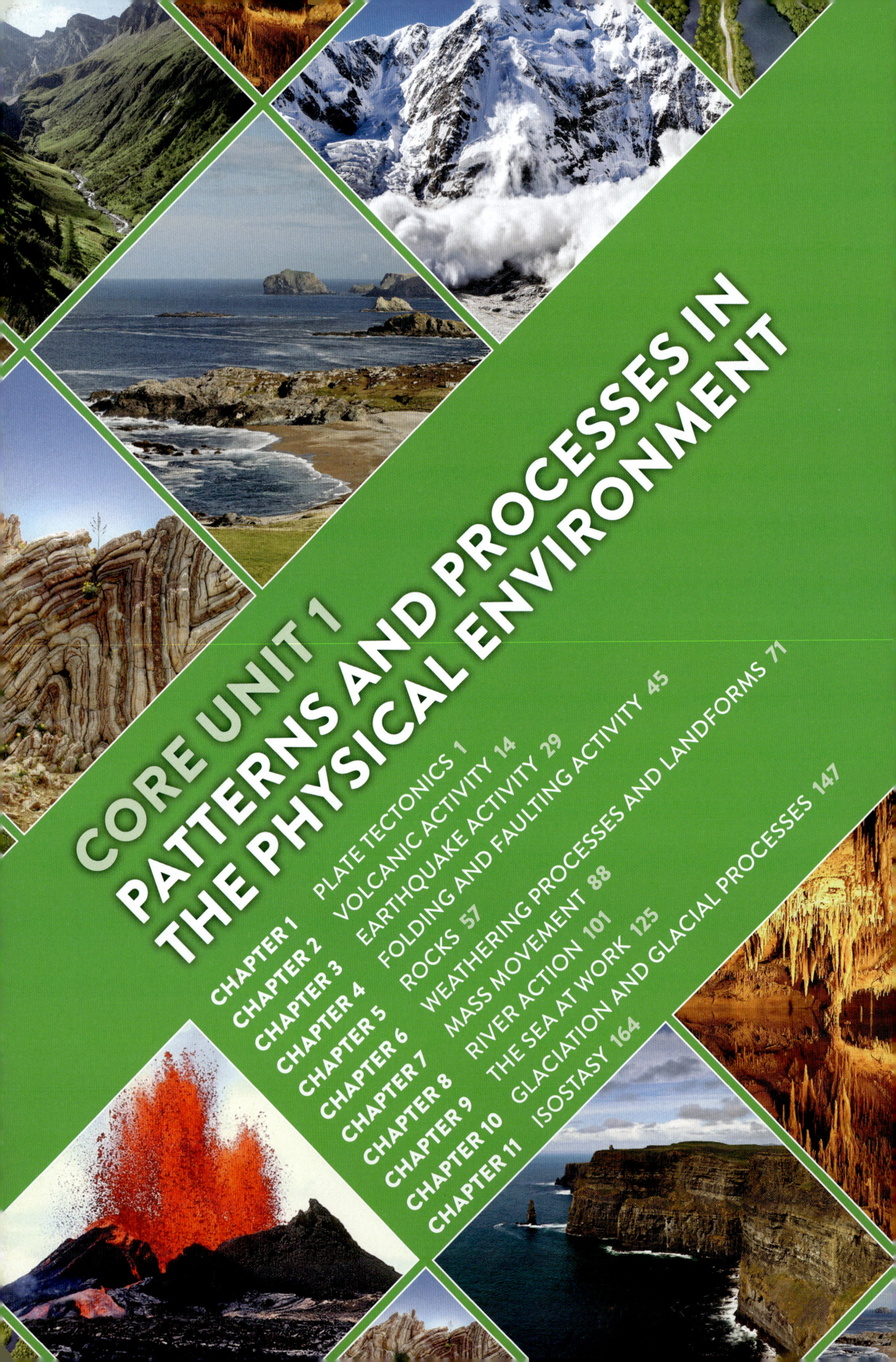

CORE UNIT 1
PATTERNS AND PROCESSES IN THE PHYSICAL ENVIRONMENT

CHAPTER 1 PLATE TECTONICS 1
CHAPTER 2 VOLCANIC ACTIVITY 14
CHAPTER 3 EARTHQUAKE ACTIVITY 29
CHAPTER 4 FOLDING AND FAULTING ACTIVITY 45
CHAPTER 5 ROCKS 57
CHAPTER 6 WEATHERING PROCESSES AND LANDFORMS 71
CHAPTER 7 MASS MOVEMENT 88
CHAPTER 8 RIVER ACTION 101
CHAPTER 9 THE SEA AT WORK 125
CHAPTER 10 GLACIATION AND GLACIAL PROCESSES 147
CHAPTER 11 ISOSTASY 164

1 PLATE TECTONICS

LEARNING INTENTIONS
Syllabus Link: 1.1, 1.2, 1.3

By the end of this chapter I will be able to:
- identify each part of the earth's structure from a diagram;
- describe the key elements of each part of the earth's structure;
- name and locate all of the earth's main plates;
- explain Alfred Wegener's theory of continental drift and its proofs;
- explain Harry Hess's theory of sea-floor spreading and its proofs;
- describe the theory of plate tectonics;
- describe the processes at work at each plate boundary and their impacts on the landscape.

KEYWORDS

earth	mantle	outer core	tectonic plate
continental crust	lithosphere	inner core	mesosaurus
oceanic crust	asthenosphere	continental drift	sea-floor spreading
Moho	convection currents	Pangaea	magma

The Earth's Structure

The **crust** is the earth's outer layer. It has two zones, each made of solid rock (**Fig. 1.1(a)**).

- **Continental crust** comprises the continents and continental shelves, covering approximately 40% of the earth's surface. Its older, lighter rocks (e.g. **granite**) contain high quantities of two minerals – silica and alumina **(SIAL)**. It varies in thickness from 25 km to 70 km.

- **Oceanic crust** covers 60% of the earth's surface. Its heavier, denser rocks (e.g. **basalt**) contain high quantities of silica and magnesium **(SIMA)**. It varies in thickness from 3 km to 10 km.

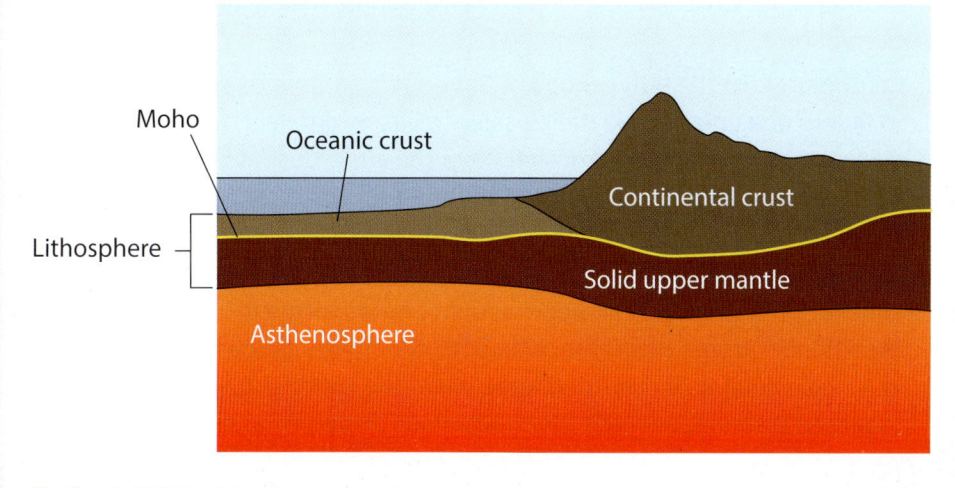

Endogenic forces: Forces within the earth's crust which cause the earth's surface to move horizontally and vertically.

The **Moho** is a boundary found in the lithosphere which divides the upper mantle and the crust. It was named after Andrija Mohorovicic (1857–1936), the seismologist who discovered the feature.

↑ **Fig. 1.1(a)** The lithosphere and asthenosphere.

Landscapes

> The **Lithosphere** is broken down into sections called **tectonic plates**. There are eight major plates and many more small ones.

> **Convection currents:** Currents that move through liquids. They move lighter, less dense liquids away from the heat source. They move heavier, more dense liquids towards the heat source.

The **mantle** is the thickest layer of the earth (over 75% of its volume) and is divided into three sections (**Fig. 1.1(b)**).

- The **solid upper mantle** is connected to the outer crust. Combined they form the **lithosphere**, the earth's rigid outer layer, which varies in thickness from 50 km to 200 km in places.
- The **semi-molten upper mantle**, known as the **asthenosphere**, is approximately 100 km thick.
- The **lower mantle**, comprised of molten material, is the hottest part of the mantle. This is the largest section and **convection currents** operating here move the plates of the earth's outer crust.

The **outer core** consists of hot liquid rock. Temperatures can reach 4,000°C. Rock present in this layer has a high percentage of iron and small amounts of nickel.

The **inner core** is largely made up of solid nickel and iron. This layer has the highest temperatures, ranging from 5,000°C to 6,000°C.

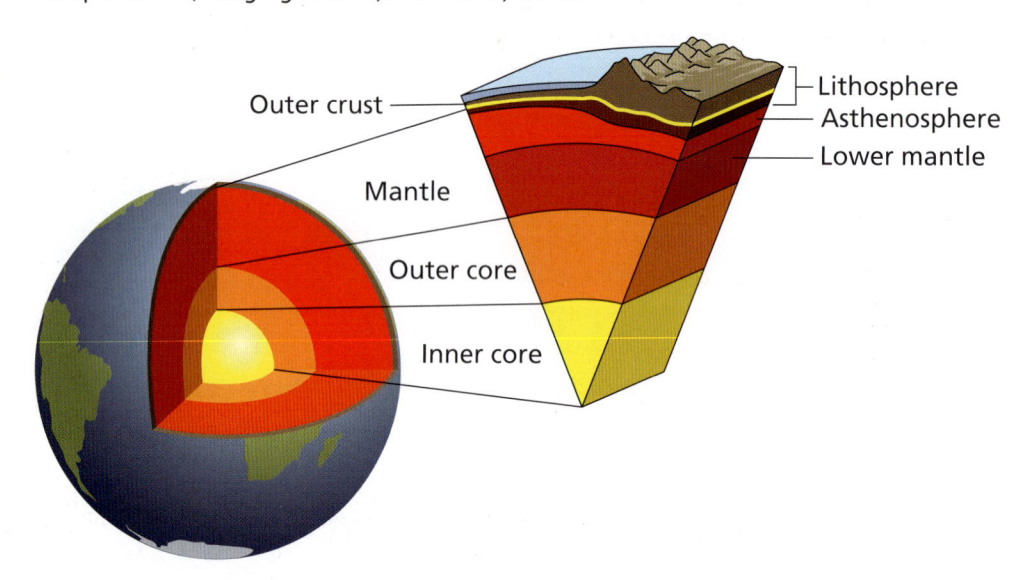

→ **Fig. 1.1(b)** The structure of the earth.

> **Continental shelf:** Gently sloping area at the edge of continents under shallow water.
>
> **Pangaea:** Means 'all lands', referencing the theory that all continents were originally joined.

Continental Drift

In 1912, Alfred Wegener proposed that the earth's continents were once joined together forming a single supercontinent called **Pangaea**, or Pangea (**Fig. 1.2**). Approximately 200 million years ago, however, the earth's outer crust fractured very slowly. The newly formed **tectonic plates** that hold our continents drifted apart across the earth's surface to the positions they occupy today – hence the name, **continental drift**. Wegener based his 'groundbreaking' theory on four key observations:

1. **Continental fit:** The outer shape of the earth's continents would allow them to fit into one another like the pieces of a jigsaw puzzle. This is especially evident when the continental shelves of the east coast of South America and the west coast of Africa are placed together.

2. **Fossil similarity:** Fossil remains such as those of the ancient freshwater reptile **mesosaurus** were discovered on both the African and South American continents. This species of reptile couldn't have existed in or swum across the Atlantic Ocean. Its presence on both continents suggests that it existed in a single habitat of rivers and lakes when the continents were once joined together. Wegener believed the species was dispersed to different continents when Pangaea broke apart and the continents drifted away from one another.

> Wegener believed the movement of the plates could be attributed to the rotation of the earth.

3. **Matching rocks and mountain ranges:** The mountain ranges of the east coast of the USA (e.g. **Appalachian mountains**) and north-western Europe (i.e. Connacht, Ulster, Scotland and Scandinavia) have similar features and are more than likely related. Formed during the **Caledonian** mountain building period, these mountain ranges have a similar rock type (granite) and directional trend (south-west to north-east).

4. **Ice sheets once covered areas that today are very warm:** Places such as India, Australia and South Africa couldn't support an Ice Age based on their current latitude. Lying close to the equator, the remains of the ice sheets found here suggest that these areas once existed at different latitudes before being moved by continental drift.

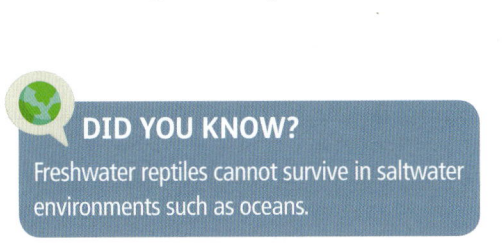

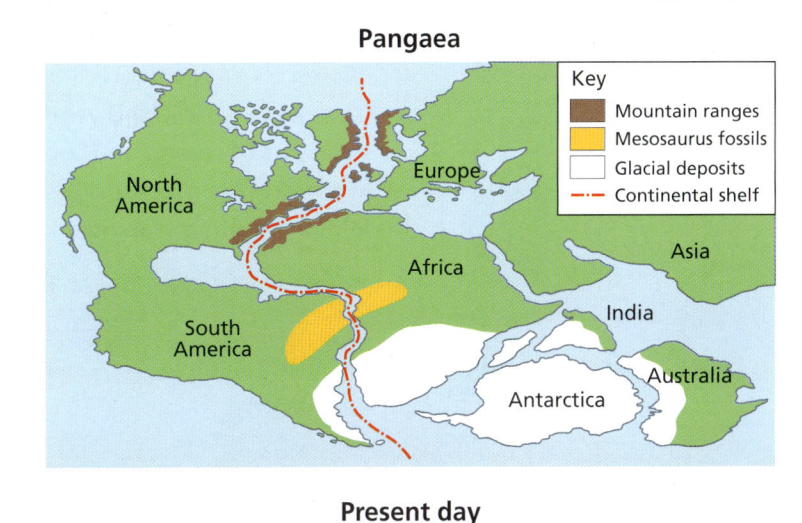

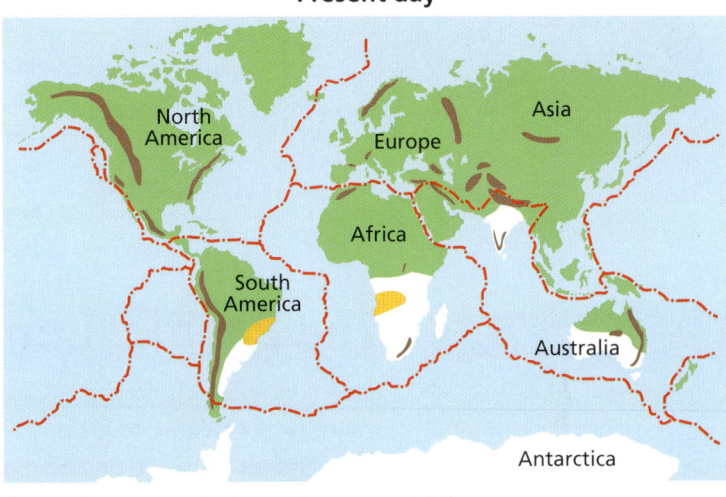

> **DID YOU KNOW?**
> Freshwater reptiles cannot survive in saltwater environments such as oceans.

↑ **Fig. 1.2** Wegener's theory of continental drift.

CHECK YOUR LEARNING

1. What are endogenic forces?
2. Which layer of the earth is the hottest?
3. Suggest one reason why this layer is the hottest.
4. Which layer of the earth is the thickest?
5. Who proposed the theory of continental drift?
6. What do the abbreviations SIMA and SIAL stand for?
7. What was Pangaea?
8. Explain two pieces of evidence that back up the theory of continental drift.

Sea-Floor Spreading

Most scientists only accepted Wegener's continental drift theory after Harry Hess discovered **sea-floor spreading** at the Mid-Atlantic Ridge. In 1960, Hess, a professor at Princeton University in the United States, noticed that:

- the age of the rock on the sea floor is youngest along mid-ocean ridges;
- rocks get progressively older and deeper the further one moves from this point (**Fig. 1.3**).

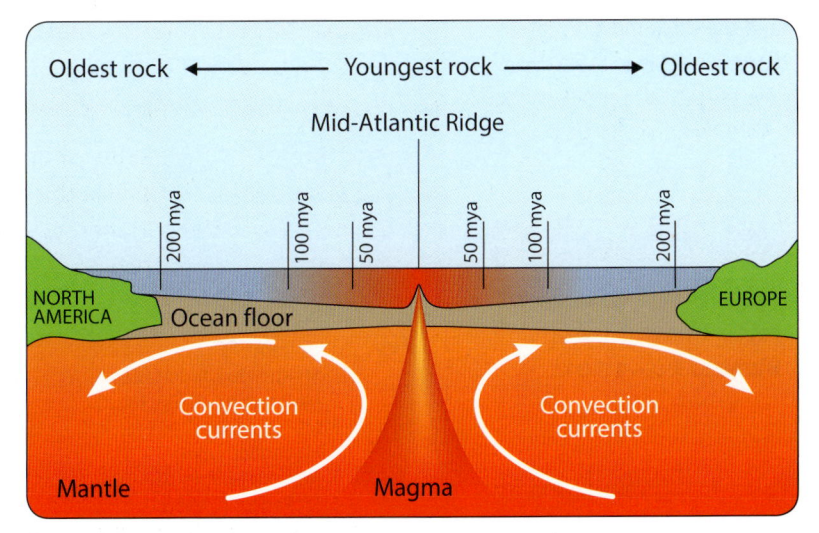

↑ **Fig. 1.3** Sea-floor spreading – crust gets progressively older moving away from the mid-ocean ridge.

Landscapes

Plate boundary: Zone where plates collide, separate or slide past one another.

- Using these observations, Hess proposed that the earth's plates float on heavier, semi-molten rock (**magma**) beneath them in the mantle. Convection currents at work in this layer move the plates like a conveyor belt, causing the sea floors to spread and continents around the world to collide with, separate from and slide past each other. Known as **plate tectonics**, this process causes **folding, faulting, earthquake** and **volcanic activity** at plate boundaries.

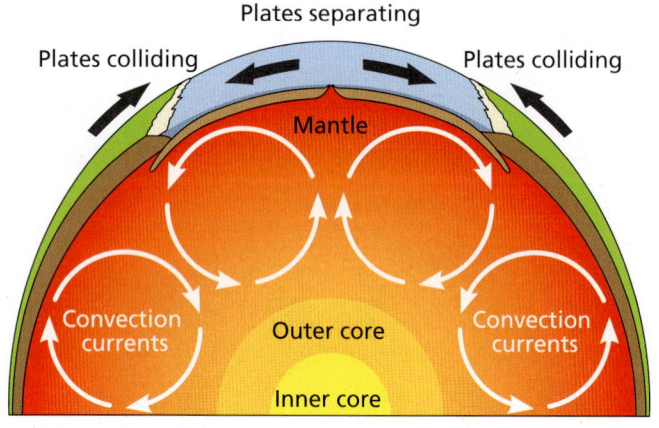

The theory of thermal convection which causes plate movement

Molten rock (magma) in the mantle is heated by energy from the earth's core. This causes the magma to expand and rise away from the source of the heat towards the earth's surface, which is cooler. As it reaches the top of the mantle it moves sideways, carrying the lithosphere with it (**Fig. 1.4**). Magma also transfers some of its heat energy to the lithosphere, causing it to become denser. The magma then sinks back down towards the core for the process to repeat itself again.

↑ **Fig. 1.4** Convection currents cause plate movements.

EXAM TIP (HL)

A good understanding of plate tectonics is vital, as it has appeared in association with the global distribution of volcanoes, earthquakes and fold mountains in the past.

SKILLS ACTIVITY

Draw a labelled diagram of the Pacific Ring of Fire. Include all the plates in contact with the Pacific Plate, three active volcanoes and the three most recent earthquakes (see **Fig. 1.5**).

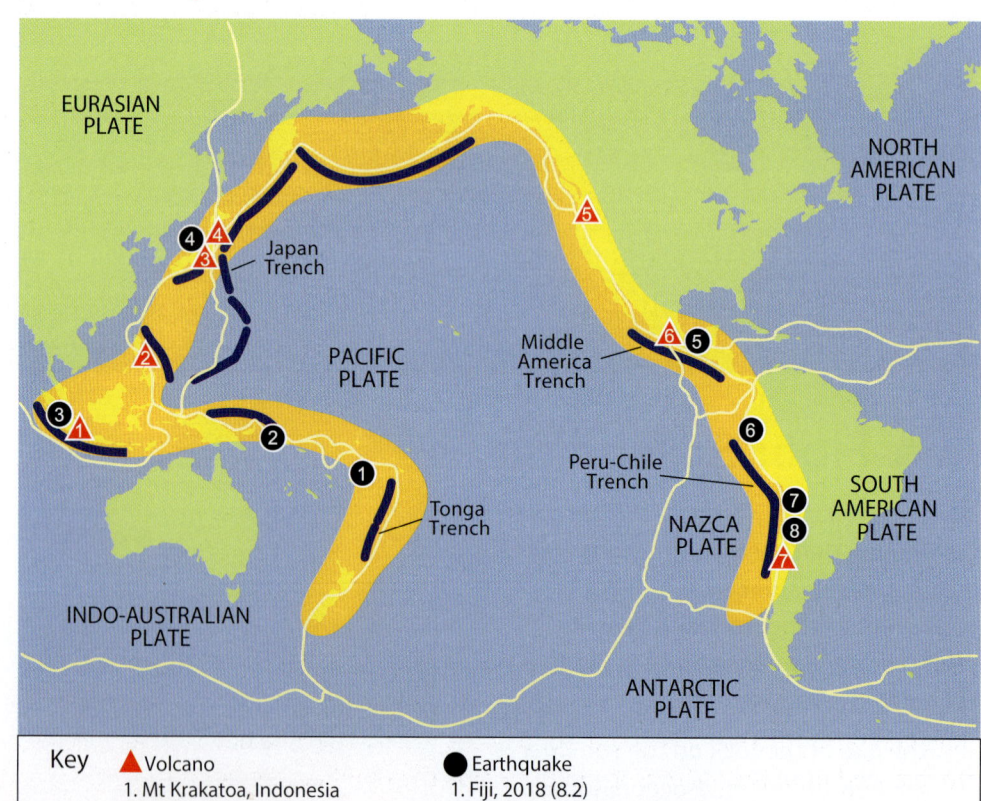

EXAM TIP

Diagrams must be **labelled**, have a **title** and have a **frame** to receive marks.

→ **Fig. 1.5** Volcanic and earthquake activity along the edge of the Pacific Plate.

The Pacific Ring of Fire

Each year, about 80% of the world's most **destructive earthquakes** and the vast majority of **volcanic eruptions** take place around the rim of the Pacific Ocean. This area, known as the Pacific Ring of Fire, is where the edges of many large crustal plates meet (**Fig. 1.5**).

Key
▲ Volcano
1. Mt Krakatoa, Indonesia
2. Mt Pinatubo, Philippines
3. Mt Fuji, Japan
4. Mt Sendai, Japan
5. Mt Saint Helens, USA
6. Mt Parícutin, Mexico
7. Mt Santiago, Chile
— Ocean trench

● Earthquake
1. Fiji, 2018 (8.2)
2. Solomon Islands, 2013 (8.0)
3. Sumatra, Indonesia, 2012 (8.6)
4. Honshu, Japan, 2011 (9.0)
5. Chiapas, Mexico, 2017 (8.2)
6. Ecuador, 2016 (7.8)
7. Tarapaca, Chile, 2014 (8.2)
8. Coquimbo, Chile, 2015 (8.3)

CHECK YOUR LEARNING

1. Who discovered sea-floor spreading?
2. List one piece of evidence that supports the theory of sea-floor spreading.
3. What are convection currents?
4. Explain how convection currents move plates.
5. Name three active volcanoes that can be found in the Pacific Ring of Fire.
6. What percentage of destructive earthquakes occurs at the Pacific Ring of Fire?

Plate Boundaries

Folding, faulting and earthquake and volcanic activity occur at boundaries where plates collide (**converge**), separate (**diverge**) or slide past one another (**transform**) (**Fig. 1.6**).

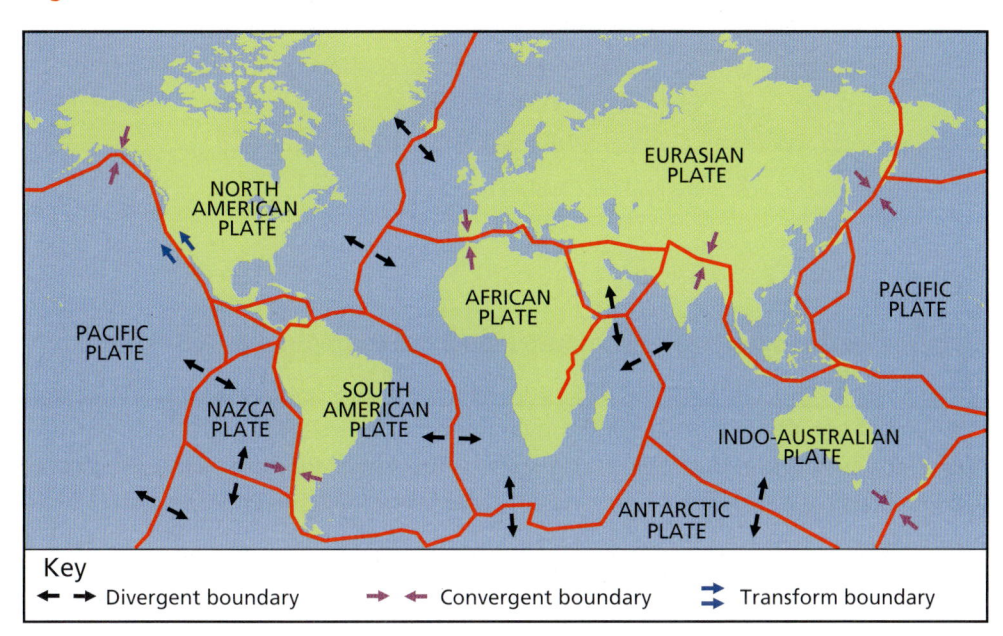

KEYWORDS

constructive
convergent
destructive
divergent
earthquake
fault line
fissure
island arc
mid-ocean ridge
plate boundary
subduction
transform

← **Fig. 1.6** Map of the earth – main plates and boundaries highlighted.

Convergent plate boundaries (destructive)

Convection currents in the mantle cause plates to collide in zones known as **convergent plate boundaries**. **Powerful earthquakes are common** as the rough edges of rocks at either side of the boundary lock in position. Stress builds up as convection currents continue to push both plates towards each other. Earthquakes are generated when the rocks eventually break, allowing the plates to move forward very suddenly.

Three types of convergent plate boundary can be identified: where two oceanic plates collide; where two continental plates collide; and where an oceanic plate collides with a continental plate.

Two oceanic plates collide

Example: Pacific Plate collides with Eurasian Plate (Fig. 1.7)

The heavier, denser plate subducts into the mantle. As convection currents drag the plate downwards, an arc-shaped **ocean trench** is formed at the **subduction zone (Japan Trench)**. Fluids (water) and gases (carbon dioxide and sulphur dioxide) are released from the crust as it sinks towards the mantle. Temperatures in the area rapidly increase, causing the sinking crust to melt. A silica and gas-rich magma is formed from the destroyed crust. As it rises, the new magma burns a path through the overlying, lighter oceanic crust. An **explosive volcanic eruption** occurs on the sea floor once the magma reaches the surface of the earth. As volcanic activity continues, a chain of volcanic islands known as an **island arc** forms parallel to the oceanic trench (e.g. the **Japanese islands**).

Subduction: The edge of one of the earth's crustal plates sinks downwards into the mantle beneath another plate.

Subduction zone: An area where two crustal plates come together and subduction occurs.

Ocean trench: A steep-sided depression in the ocean floor marking the zone where an oceanic plate has subducted.

Landscapes

Oceanic plate: A tectonic plate with oceanic crust at the boundary in question.

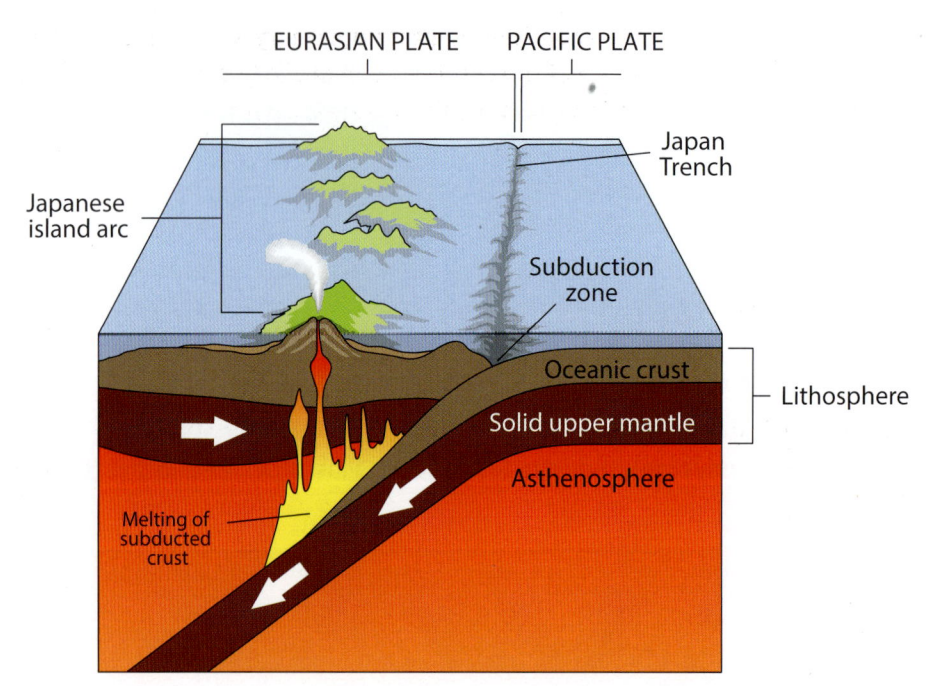

↑ **Fig. 1.7** Convergent (destructive) plate boundary – oceanic plate colliding with an oceanic plate.

Two continental plates collide

Example: The Eurasian Plate collides with the African Plate (Fig. 1.8)

There is very little subduction at this zone, as both plates tend to be similar in age, weight and density. Instead of moving down, the two plates buckle upwards slowly, creating **fold mountain ranges** such as the **Alps**. Magma can intrude into gaps created between layers of rock as they fold upwards. This magma cools slowly creating new rock under the surface of the earth.

Continental plate: A tectonic plate with continental crust at the boundary in question.

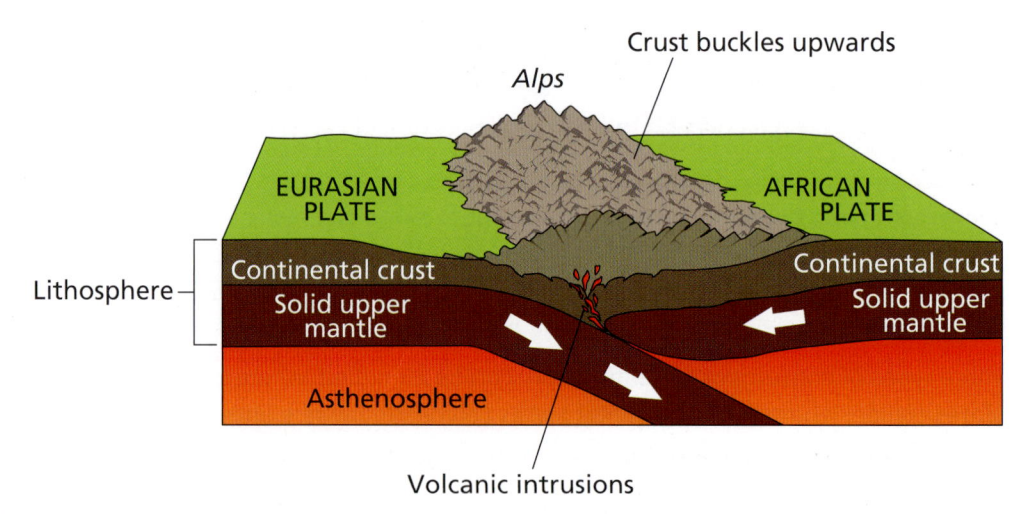

↑ **Fig. 1.8** Convergent plate boundary – continental plate colliding with a continental plate.

An oceanic plate collides with a continental plate

Example: The Nazca Plate collides with the South American Plate.

The heavier, denser oceanic plate subducts under the lighter continental plate. As convection currents drag the plate downwards, a deep arc-shaped **ocean trench** forms at the **subduction zone**. Crust in the oceanic plate melts, creating a hot silica and gas-rich magma. This less dense magma burns a path to the surface of the continental plate, leading to a powerful **volcanic eruption**. Over time, a **chain of volcanic mountains** form parallel to the subduction zone (**Andes volcanic arc**).

Destructive plate boundary: Crust is destroyed at convergent plate boundaries when an oceanic plate is one of the plates in collision.

Constructive plate boundary: Crust is created at divergent plate boundaries.

Stress also builds at the **continental plate boundary** as the plates collide. This causes rocks at the edge of the continental plate to buckle upwards, forming a range of **fold mountains**, such as the **Andes** in South America.

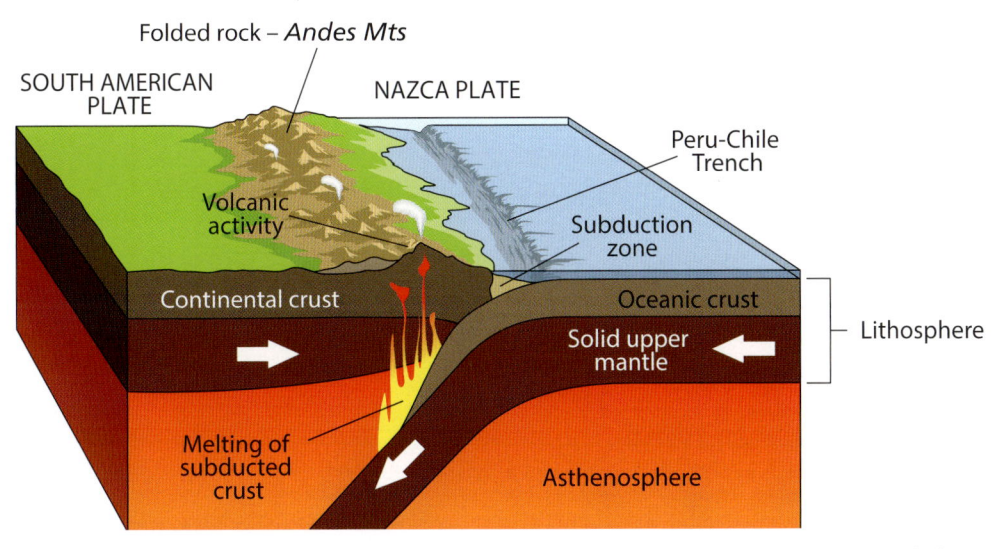

↑ **Fig. 1.9** Convergent (destructive) plate boundary – oceanic plate colliding with a continental plate.

EXAM TIP

A Significant Relevant Point, or SRP, is a piece of factual information relevant to the question being asked. It may be a term and brief explanation, a relevant statistic, or further information that develops or explains the topic in question.

Fully labelled diagrams with a frame and a title will receive 1 SRP. If additional information to the text is included, it may also be awarded (max. 2) SRPs.

EXAM LINK (HL)

Plate Tectonics (30 marks)
Describe and explain destructive plate boundaries.
2018, Q3B & 2014, Q3B

Marking Scheme:
Examples = 3 × 2 marks
Relevant labelled diagram = 1 SRP × 2 marks
Description and explanation of destructive plate boundaries = 11 SRPs × 2 marks

EXAM TIP (HL)

When attempting a Higher Level 30-mark question, each SRP is worth 2 marks.

Students have approximately 13 minutes in which to answer a 30-mark question at Higher Level.

EXAM LINK (OL)

Plate Tectonics (30 marks)
Describe and explain what happens at plate boundaries.
2014, Q3C & 2011, Q3C

Marking Scheme:
10 SRPs × 3 marks

EXAM TIP (OL)

When attempting an Ordinary Level 30/40-mark question, each SRP is worth 3 marks.

Students have approximately 12 minutes in which to answer a 30-mark question and 16 minutes to answer a 40-mark question.

Divergent plate boundaries (constructive)

New land is created at **divergent plate boundaries** where currents in magma cause **oceanic plates to separate** and **continental plates to split**.

Sea-floor spreading

The **Mid-Atlantic Ridge** has formed at a boundary where the oceanic plate margins of the North and South American plates are slowly separating from the Eurasian and African plates respectively (Fig. 1.10). As the plates diverge, their crusts get thinner and large cracks called **fissures** form along the boundary. Magma rises to the surface of the earth through these fissures, whereupon it cools quickly on contact with the cold ocean waters to form solid rock (new crust). The new rock builds up to form a **mid-ocean ridge**, whose peaks often rise above sea level to create **volcanic islands** such as **Iceland**.

The Mid-Atlantic Ridge runs for 16,000 km in a north-south direction.

Landscapes

→ **Fig. 1.10** Divergent (constructive) plate boundary – the formation of the Mid-Atlantic Ridge.

> **EXAM TIP (OL)**
>
> With the exception of 2014, a question on the **'formation of landforms'** appeared every year from 2011 to 2018.
>
> **Marking Scheme:**
> Landform named = 3 marks
> Example = 2 marks
> Description of its formation = 5 SRPs × 3 marks

Fault lines: Fractures on the earth's surface where rocks on either side of the crack slide past one another.

Transform plate boundary: This type of boundary can also be referred to as a **'conservative'** or **'passive'** plate boundary.

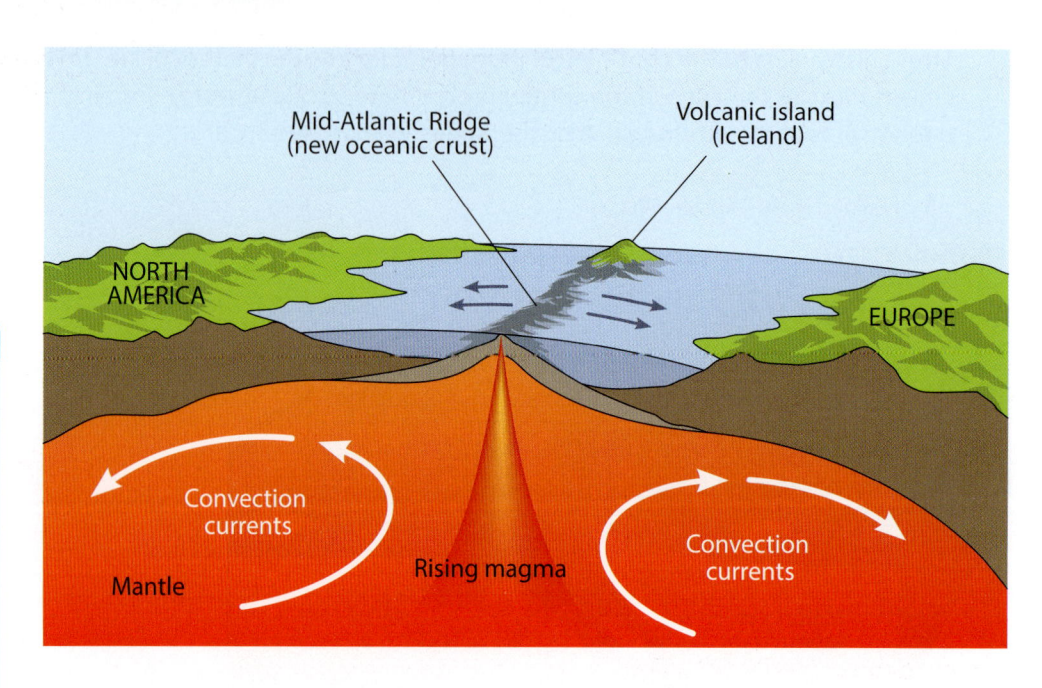

Continental splitting

Rising **magma plumes** have caused the continental African crust to stretch and split. Magma rises through **fissures** in the crust forming **volcanoes** (new crust) on the earth's surface such as **Mount Kilimanjaro** in an area known as the East African Rift Valley.

Transform plate boundaries

Transform plate boundaries occur where two plates slide past one another. While **land is neither created nor destroyed**, rocks at the edge of both plates can lock in position. Stress builds up at the boundary as convection currents continue pushing the plates laterally past each other. **Earthquakes** are generated when rocks at the boundary eventually break, allowing the plates to move forward very suddenly.

Along the **San Andreas Fault** line, the Pacific and North American plates are both moving north-west, but at different speeds (**Fig. 1.11**). Earthquakes occurring here are particularly violent, as the focus of the quake tends to be close to the surface of the earth's crust.

→ **Fig. 1.11** Transform plate boundary – the Pacific and North American plates slide past one another.

8

1 Plate Tectonics

CHECK YOUR LEARNING

1. On which plate boundary is Ireland located?
2. What does the term 'subduction' mean?
3. What is an ocean trench?
4. List three types of convergent plate boundary.
5. Name two plates separating from each other at the Mid-Atlantic Ridge.
6. Name a volcanic island formed at the Mid-Atlantic Ridge.
7. How has Mt. Kilimanjaro been formed?
8. What happens at a transform plate boundary?
9. Why are earthquakes so violent at the San Andreas Fault?

EXAM LINK (HL)

Plate Boundaries (30 marks)

'Plate boundaries are places where land is both created and destroyed.' Examine this statement, with reference to examples you have studied.

2007, Q1B

Marking Scheme:
Name one constructive and one destructive plate boundary = 2 × 2 marks
Discussion regarding both creation and destruction = 7 SRPs × 2 marks (creation or destruction) + 6 SRPs × 2 marks (destruction or creation)

CASE STUDY: IMPACT OF TECTONIC ACTIVITY ON THE IRISH LANDSCAPE

The impact of millions of years of plate tectonic activity can be observed in our natural landscape today.

- Around 850 mya, Ireland was divided into two sections (**Fig. 1.12(a)**).
  - North-west Ireland existed as part of the North American Plate, just south of the equator.
  - South-east Ireland existed over 60° south of the equator as part of a landmass which also contained England and Wales.
- 400 mya, the two landmasses merged about 20° south of the equator. The collision of the two landmasses led to:
  - the closure of the **Lapetus Sea**, which had separated the two landmasses. A scar on the landscape stretching from Clogherhead (Co. Louth) on the east coast to Dingle (Co. Kerry) on the west coast marks the line where the two landmasses merged;
  - the formation of the **Caledonian** fold mountain range. This range has a south-west to north-east directional trend, reflecting the line along which the plates collided;
  - **faulting** in the north of the country, with the various fault lines also taking south-west to north-east directional trends;
  - **volcanic activity**, which resulted in the formation of **granite** in the **Leinster Batholith**.

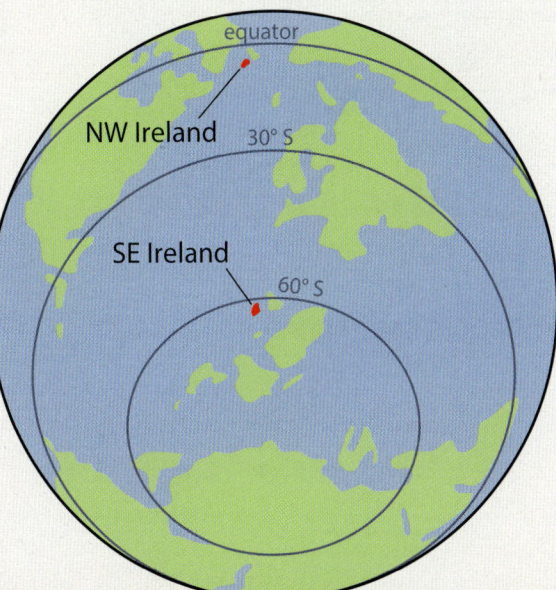

mya = million years ago

↑ **Fig. 1.12(a)** Ireland approximately 850 mya.

Landscapes

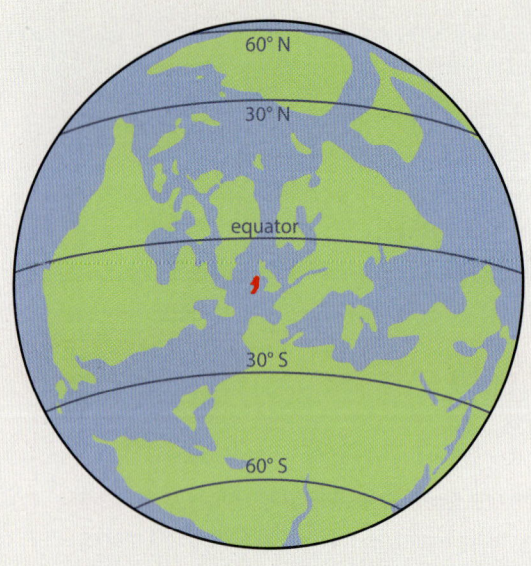

↑ Fig. 1.12(b) Ireland approximately 380 mya.

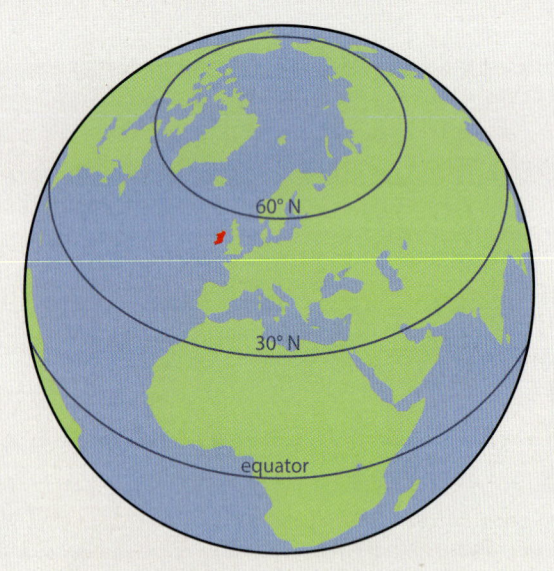

↑ Fig. 1.12(c) Present-day location of Ireland.

- Approximately 380 mya, Ireland had moved to a position just south of the equator (Fig. 1.12(b)). **Sandstone** was laid down at this time, as Ireland experienced a desert climate.

- Approximately 300 mya, sea levels had risen and Ireland lay under a warm, calm sea close to the equator. **Limestone** was formed over thousands of years at this location as the bones and shells of fish and other sea creatures accumulated on the sea floor.

- About 250 mya, Ireland had moved to a location 20° north of the equator. The **Armorican fold mountain range** was formed in Munster (e.g. **Macgillicuddy's Reeks** and **Caha Mountains**) when the Eurasian and African plates collided. As the greatest force came from the south, these folds have an east to west directional trend. **Sandstone** was brought above sea level during this folding period while the **Munster ridge and valley landscape** was also formed.

- Approximately 65 mya, Ireland experienced the impact of **sea-floor spreading**. The Eurasian and North American plates separated with water rushing in to create the Atlantic Ocean. As the plates moved apart, lava poured out of fissures created on the earth's crust in the north-east of the country. The lava cooled quickly on the earth's surface creating the **Antrim–Derry Plateau** and the distinctive six-sided columns of basalt at the **Giant's Causeway** (Fig. 1.13).

DID YOU KNOW?
Ireland is currently moving north at a rate of approximately 4 cm per year.

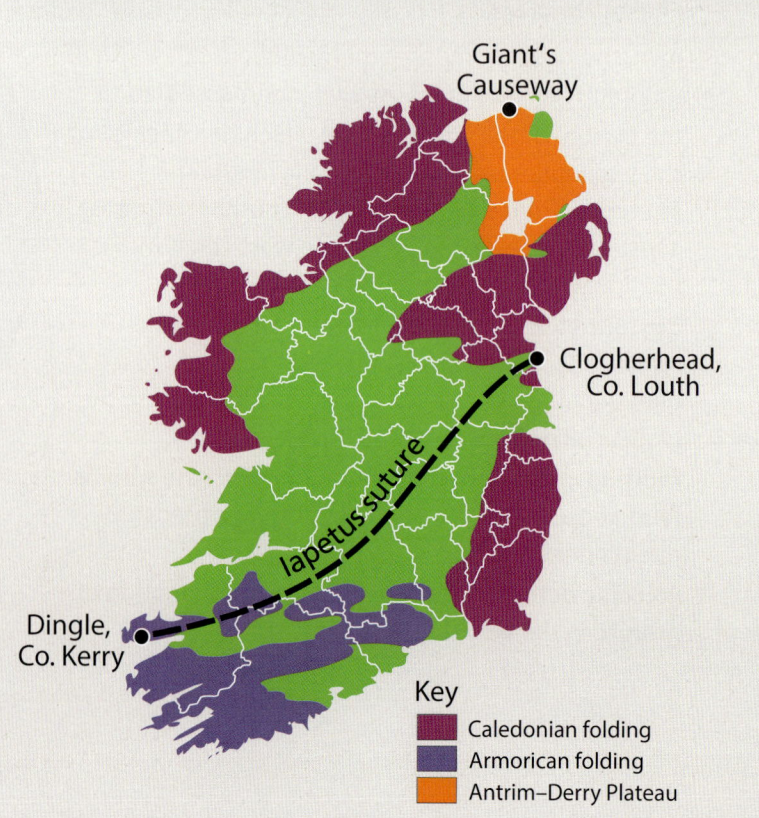

→ Fig. 1.13 Features of the landscape formed by tectonic activity in Ireland.

Key
- Caledonian folding
- Armorican folding
- Antrim–Derry Plateau

EXAMINATION QUESTIONS
ORDINARY LEVEL

Short Questions

1. Layers of the Earth

Examine the diagram which shows the different layers of the earth and answer each of the following questions.

(i) Match each of the letters A, B, C and D with the correct layer in the table.
4 × 2 marks

Layer	Letter
Outer core	
Crust	
Inner core	
Mantle	

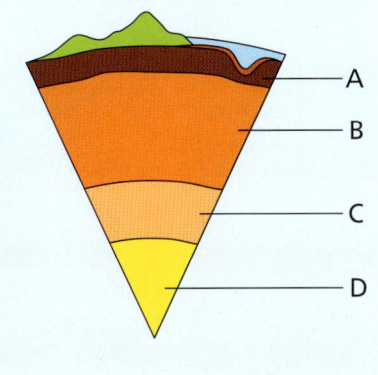

(ii) What is the term given to the molten rock found in the mantle? *2 marks*

2017, Part One, Q1 (10 marks)

Long Questions

2. Plate Boundaries

Examine the diagrams and answer each of the following questions.

(i) In your answer book, match each of the plate boundaries named with the type of plate movement from the list below most associated with it: *3 × 4 marks*
- Plates pushing together
- Plates sliding past each other
- Plates pulling apart.

(ii) State what is meant by the term 'plate'. *3 marks*

(iii) Explain briefly how plates move. *2 SRPs × 3 marks*

(iv) At which of the plate boundaries named on the diagram do ocean ridges form? *3 marks*

(v) At which of the plate boundaries named on the diagram do fold mountains form? *3 marks*

(vi) Name one example of an ocean ridge or name one example of a range of fold mountains. *3 marks*

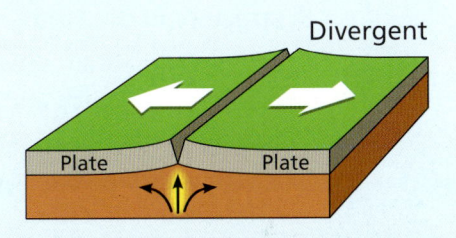

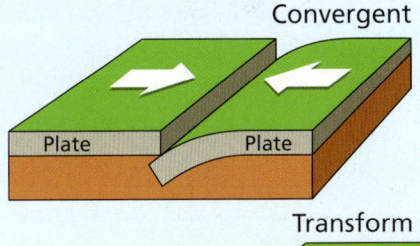

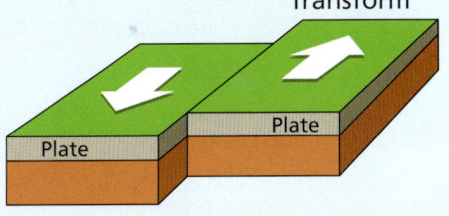

2018, Part Two, Section 1, Q2A (30 marks)

HIGHER LEVEL

Short Questions

3. Plate Tectonics

Examine the map and answer each of the following questions.

(i) Name each of the plates labelled A and B. *2 × 1 mark*

(ii) Name the two plates that converged to form the Andes mountain range. *2 × 1 mark*

(iii) What is the name given to the area X where earthquakes and volcanic eruptions occur? *2 marks*

(iv) Name the type of plate boundary at Y. *2 marks*

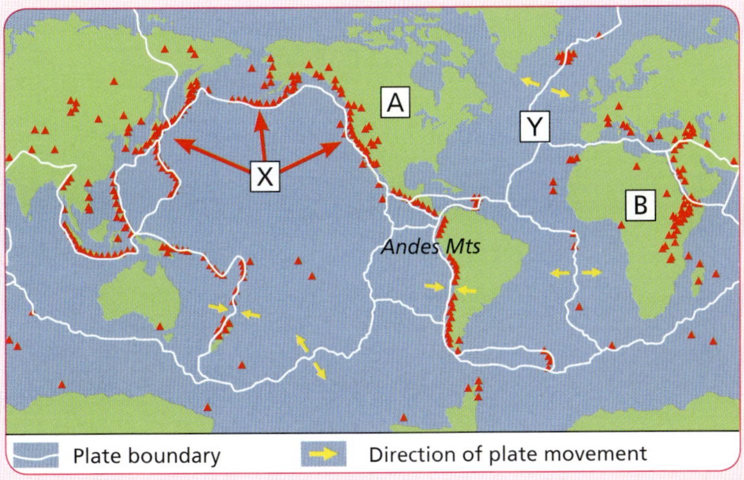

2018, Part One, Q6 (8 marks)

11

Landscapes

4. The Tectonic Cycle

Examine the diagram and answer each of the following questions.

(i) Match each of the letters A, B, C, D, E and F with the feature that best matches it in the table below.
          6 × 1 mark

(ii) Indicate whether the following statement is true or false, by circling the correct option.

Plutonic igneous rocks are formed at C.
True / False   2 marks

2016, Part One, Q1 (8 marks)

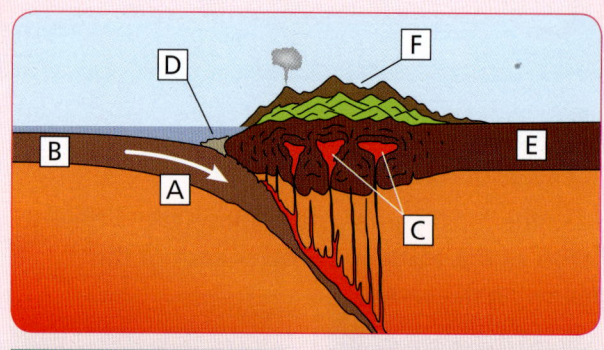

Feature	Letter
Continental crust	
Ocean trench	
Mountain range	

Feature	Letter
Oceanic crust	
Subduction zone	
Magma chamber	

Long Questions

5. Structure of the Earth

Examine the diagram showing the internal structure of the earth and answer the following questions.

(i) Name each of the layers of the earth labelled A, B and C.   3 × 2 marks

(ii) Name the two main minerals found in the core.   2 × 2 marks

(iii) What is the name given to the boundary between the crust and the mantle?   2 marks

(iv) Explain briefly how plates move.
     2 SRPs × 2 marks

(v) Explain briefly what is meant by endogenic forces.   2 SRPs × 2 marks

2018, Part Two, Section 1, Q2A (20 marks)

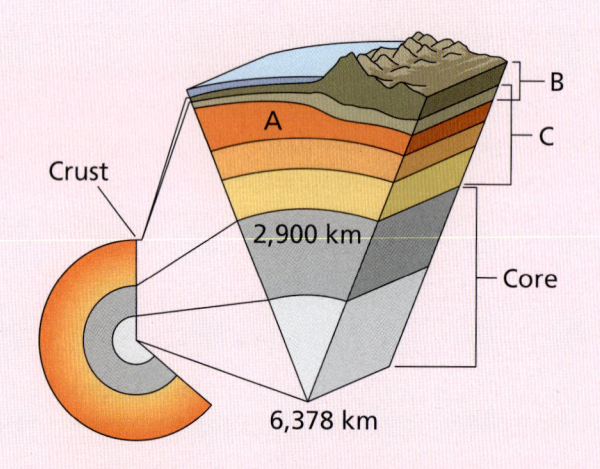

6. The Internal Structure of the Earth

Examine the diagram showing the internal structure of the earth and answer the following questions.

(i) Name each of the layers of the earth A, B, C, D, E and F.
     6 × 2 marks

(ii) Describe briefly the main difference between the composition of layer C and layer D.   2 SRPs × 2 marks

(iii) Explain briefly why plates move.   2 SRPs × 2 marks

2014, Part Two, Section 1, Q2A (20 marks)

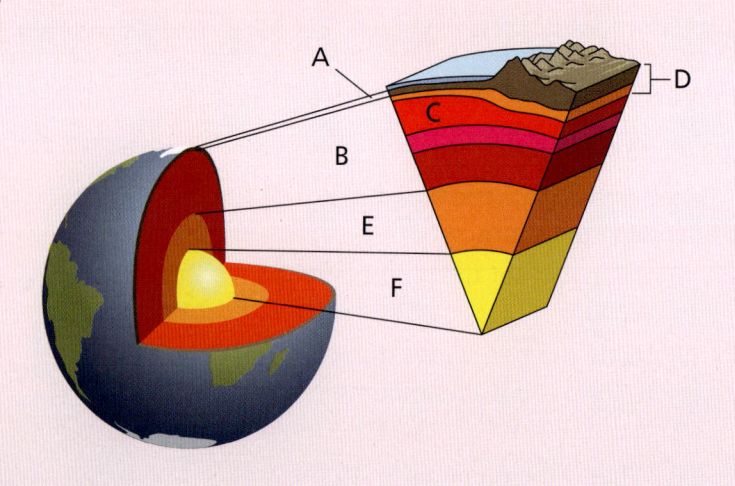

12

Revision Summary

Earth's structure

- Outer crust – continental crust (silica and alumina) and oceanic crust (silica and magnesium)
- Mantle – magma – thickest layer
- Outer core – hot liquid rock – 4,000°C
- Inner core – solid nickel and iron
- Lithosphere – rigid layer made of outer crust and solid upper mantle
- Asthenosphere – semi-molten part of upper mantle
- Pacific Ring of Fire – tectonic activity

Continental drift

- Alfred Wegener 1912
- Supercontinent – Pangaea
- Continental fit – continental shelves of Africa and South America fit together
- Fossil similarity – mesosaurus
- Matching rocks and mountain ranges – Caledonian folding, south-west to north-east directional trend
- Remains of ice sheets – India and Australia – current location couldn't support an Ice Age

Sea-floor spreading

- Harry Hess 1960
- Youngest rocks at mid-ocean ridges
- Get progressively older and deeper with distance from mid-ocean ridges
- Plates float on heavier, semi-molten magma beneath them in the mantle
- Plates moved by convection currents
- Plate tectonics – plates collide with, separate from and slide past each other
- Results in folding, faulting, earthquake and volcanic activity at plate boundaries

Convergent plate boundaries

Two oceanic plates converge

- Pacific Plate and Eurasian Plates collide
- Older, heavier, denser plate subducts
- Trench forms at boundary – e.g. Japan Trench
- Subducted plate melts
- Volcanic eruptions at weak point of younger, lighter plate – line parallel to subduction zone
- Volcanic arc of islands forms – e.g. Japan

Two continental plates converge

- Eurasian Plate and African Plate
- Plates similar in age, weight and density
- Plates push up and create fold mountains – e.g. Alps

Oceanic and continental plates converge

- Nazca Plate and South American Plate
- Heavier, denser oceanic plate subducts into the mantle and melts
- Trench forms at boundary
- Volcanic eruption at weak point of lighter continental plate
- Plates colliding – stress on continental plate – buckles and folds – e.g. Andes

Divergent plate boundaries

- Two oceanic plates diverge
- Sea-floor spreading
- North American Plate and Eurasian Plate – magma released through fissure – cools and hardens quickly – forms volcanic islands – Iceland on Mid-Atlantic Ridge
- Continental splitting
- Convection currents – continental African crust = stretched – magma released – volcanoes formed – Mount Kilimanjaro

Transform plate boundaries

- North American and Pacific Plates
- Plates slide past each other
- Land neither created nor destroyed
- Fault line created – San Andreas
- Earthquakes common – stress is released

The impact of plate tectonics on Ireland

- 850 mya: Ireland divided into two sections
- 400 mya: Ireland created – two landmasses collided and joined – Caledonian folding
- 380 mya: desert climate – sandstone formed
- 300 mya: limestone formed
- 250 mya: Armorican folding
- 65 mya: Eurasian and North American plates separated – Atlantic Ocean and Antrim–Derry Plateau formed

2 VOLCANIC ACTIVITY

KEYWORDS
extrusive
intrusive
volcano
magma
plutonic
eruption
hotspot
extinct
active
dormant

LEARNING INTENTIONS
Syllabus Link: 1.1, 1.2, 1.3

By the end of this chapter I will be able to:
- identify each part of a volcano's structure from a diagram or photograph;
- identify all volcanic features from a diagram or photograph;
- explain the global distribution of volcanoes;
- explain the three stages of a volcano's life;
- examine the processes involved in the formation of volcanic landforms;
- explain how volcanic activity can be predicted;
- describe, using examples, the positive and negative results of volcanic activity.

Magma: Hot liquid rock and metals.

Volcanic: A term used to describe extrusive features.

Plutonic: A term used to describe intrusive features.

DID YOU KNOW?
About 80% of the earth's surface, above and below sea level, originated because of volcanic activity.

Volcanic activity results in the formation of **extrusive** and **intrusive** features.
- Extrusive features form on the earth's crust when lava cools and solidifies quickly (Fig. 2.1).
- Intrusive features form within the earth's crust when magma and gases cool and solidify slowly.

Volcanic Activity on the Earth's Surface

1. Island arc (subduction zone)
2. Hotspot
3. Mid-ocean ridge (sea-floor spreading)
4. Volcanic arc (subduction zone)
5. Rifting

Mantle
Convection currents

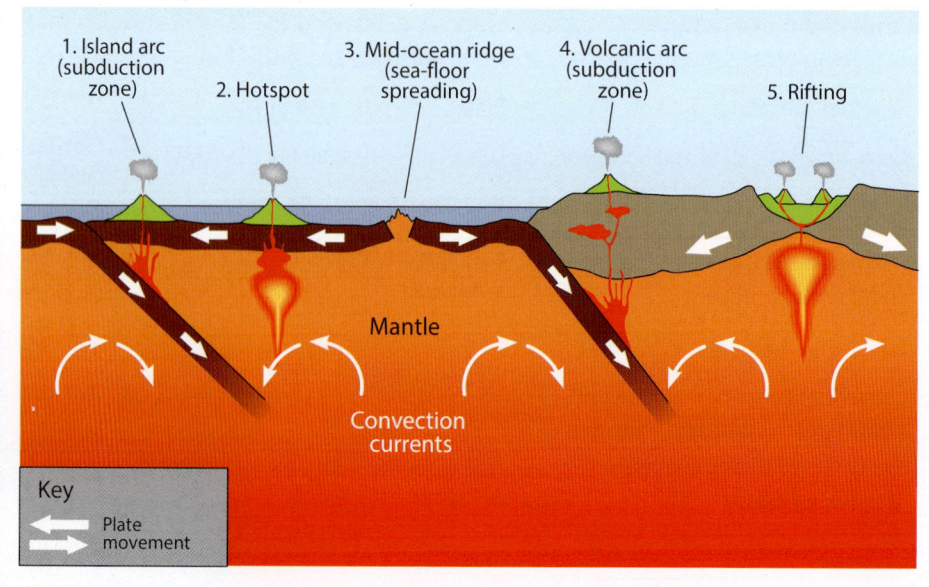

Key
Plate movement

↑ **Fig. 2.1** Extrusive volcanic features and the locations where they form.

14

Volcanoes form at subduction zones of convergent plate boundaries

When an oceanic plate collides with another tectonic plate, the heavier, denser plate subducts beneath the lighter plate. Fluids (water) and gases (carbon dioxide and sulphur dioxide) are released from the crust as it sinks towards the mantle. These fluids and gases raise the surrounding temperatures which melt the sinking crust. The silica and gas-rich magma formed from the melting crust rises and burns a path through the overlying crust. An **explosive volcanic eruption** occurs close to the subduction zone once the magma reaches the surface of the earth.

- A chain of volcanic islands known as an **island arc** forms at the subduction zone of two oceanic plates. The Japanese island arc was formed by the collision of the Pacific and Eurasian plates.

- A chain of volcanic mountains known as a **volcanic arc** forms at the subduction zone of colliding oceanic and continental plates. The **Andes volcanic arc** has formed where the oceanic crust of the Nazca Plate subducts beneath the continental crust of the South American Plate.

Volcanoes form at constructive plate boundaries

- Where two oceanic plates separate, magma rises through a **fissure** created on the earth's crust. Coming in contact with the cold ocean water, the lava quickly turns to solid rock. Over time, this builds up to form a **mid-ocean ridge** of volcanic mountains. The Eurasian and North American plates separate to form the **Mid-Atlantic Ridge**, which includes the island of Iceland.

- Rising **magma plumes** have caused the continental African crust to stretch and split. Magma rises through fissures in the crust forming volcanoes on the earth's surface such as **Mount Kilimanjaro**.

EXAM LINK (HL)

Vulcanicity (30 marks)

Explain how the study of plate tectonics has helped us to understand the global distribution of volcanoes.

2008, Q2B

Chapter 1: Plate Tectonics

Marking Scheme:
Global examples = 2 × 2 marks
Plate tectonics examined = 13 SRPs

Volcanoes form at hotspots

A **volcanic island chain** is formed at a **hotspot**. Hotspots are regions of the earth's mantle where the magma is hotter than the magma in the mantle surrounding it. The hotspot is located at a **fixed point** in the mantle while the earth's crustal plates move over it. When a weak area of the earth's crust moves over the hotspot, **plumes** (columns) of hot magma rise from the mantle to the surface and a **volcano** is formed. Over time, the volcano will become **extinct** as the earth's crustal plate continues moving, pushing it away from the hotspot. This process is repeated with each volcanic mountain getting progressively older as it moves away from the hotspot. An example of this is the **Hawaiian island chain**, which formed over a hotspot in the Pacific Ocean (**Fig. 2.2**).

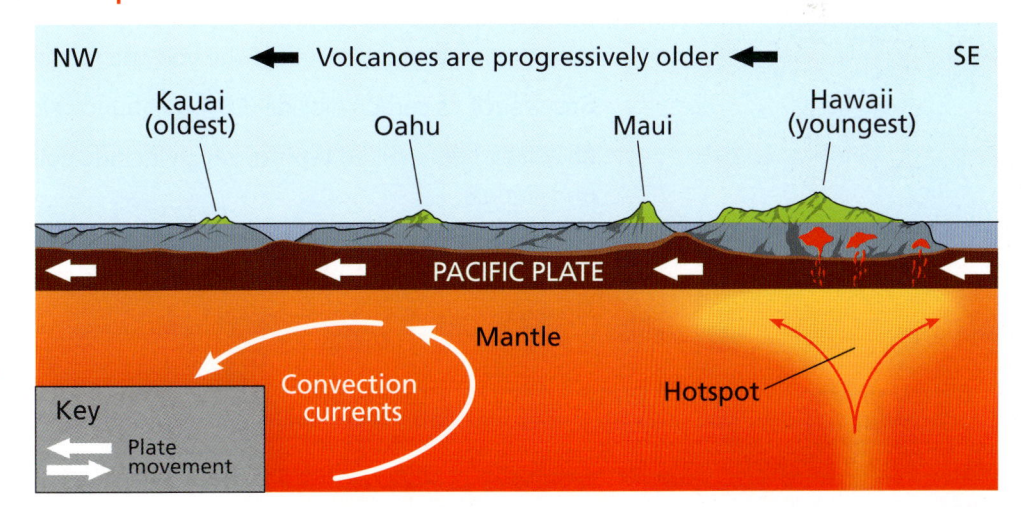

↑ **Fig. 2.2** The Hawaiian islands were formed as the Pacific Plate moved over a 'hotspot'.

Landscapes

Life Cycle of a Volcano

- **Active** volcanoes erupt regularly. **Mount Etna** in Sicily is one of the world's most active volcanoes.
- **Dormant** (sleeping) volcanoes have not erupted in a long time but scientists believe they could erupt again (e.g. **Parcutin, Mexico**).
- **Extinct** volcanoes have not erupted in historic times (over 2,000 years) and are not expected to erupt again, as they no longer have a magma supply. **Lambay Island**, located off Ireland's east coast, was formed by a now extinct volcano.

Pyroclastic flow: A mixture of hot steam, dust, ash and cinders.

Cinders: Small volcanic bombs.

CHECK YOUR LEARNING

1. Explain the difference between 'intrusive' features and 'extrusive' features.
2. What is magma?
3. List each of the locations volcanoes form on the earth's surface.
4. What is a hotspot?
5. Using an example, explain what an active volcano is.
6. What is the difference between a dormant and an extinct volcano?

KEYWORDS
acidic lava
basic lava
black smokers
caldera
central vent
composite volcano
fissure eruption
geyser
magma chamber
plateau
pyroclastic flow
shield volcano
silica

Extrusive 'Volcanic' Features

Volcanic activity can lead to the formation of many features on the earth's crust such as central vent volcanoes, lava plateaus, and geysers.

Vent eruptions

Central vent volcanoes are formed when volcanic materials are emitted from an opening in the earth's crust called a **central vent**. Three forms of material are emitted from the erupting volcano:

- **Lava**, the name given to magma once it reaches the earth's surface. This can be either basic or acidic and the type of lava will determine the magnitude of the eruption and the shape of the volcano formed.
- **Gases** such as carbon dioxide (CO_2), sulphur dioxide (SO_2), nitrogen and chlorine.
- Rock fragments called **tephra**, which include volcanic dust, volcanic ash and cinders.

Types of central vent volcano

Shield volcano

Example: Mauna Loa, Hawaii

Shield volcanoes are the largest on earth. Their slopes are very gradual, as they are formed from the buildup of successive **basic lava** flows. They are usually found at **divergent plate boundaries** or over **hotspots** (Fig. 2.3).

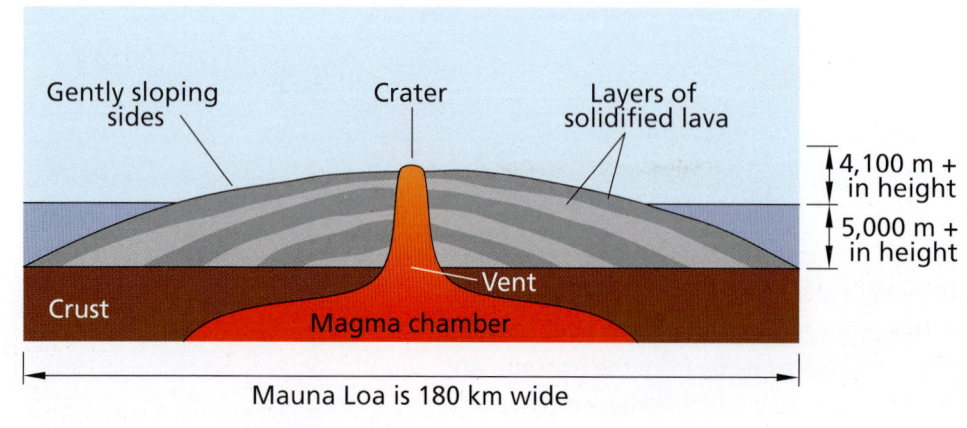

↑ **Fig. 2.3** Mauna Loa is a shield volcano.

2 Volcanic Activity

Characteristics of basic lava
- Low **silica** content (approximately 50%)
- Temperatures around 1,100°C
- Can travel long distances
- Cools and hardens slowly
- Quiet eruptions

DID YOU KNOW?
There are approximately 500 active volcanoes above sea level, of which 50–60 erupt each year.

Composite volcanoes: Volcanoes that are composed of different materials.

Composite volcano/stratovolcano

Examples: Mount Fuji, Japan; Mount Rainier, Washington, USA

Composite volcanoes are steep-sided conical-shaped volcanoes built from alternating layers of **acidic lava**, tephra and volcanic ash. They are usually found at **convergent plate boundaries** (Fig. 2.4).

Characteristics of acidic lava
- High silica content (approximately 70%)
- Temperatures of around 900°C
- Thick substance, only travels a short distance
- Cools and hardens quickly
- Violent eruptions

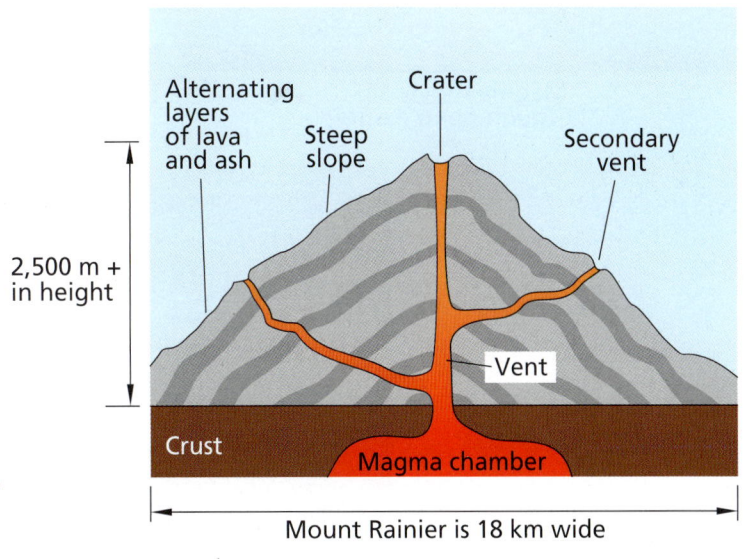

↑ **Fig. 2.4** Mount Rainier is a composite volcano.

Calderas

Example: Crater Lake, Oregon, USA

Calderas are formed by **violent eruptions** at **composite volcanoes**. The explosive eruption removes huge volumes of magma from the **magma chamber** and fractures the overlying rock that forms the roof of the magma chamber. The fractured rock collapses into the emptied chamber, producing a **large depression** on the earth's surface called a caldera (Fig. 2.5).

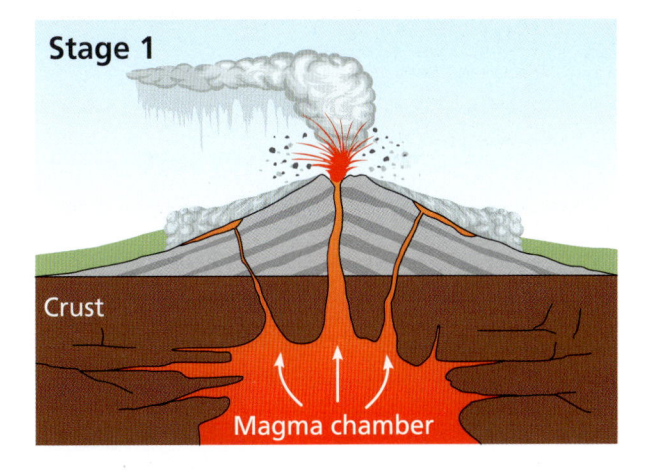

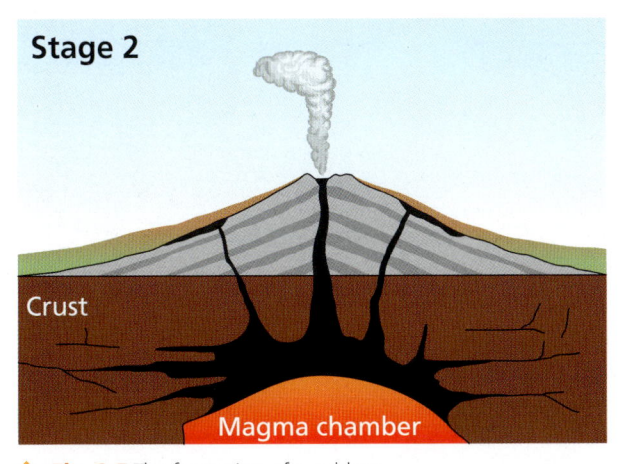

↑ **Fig. 2.5** The formation of a caldera.

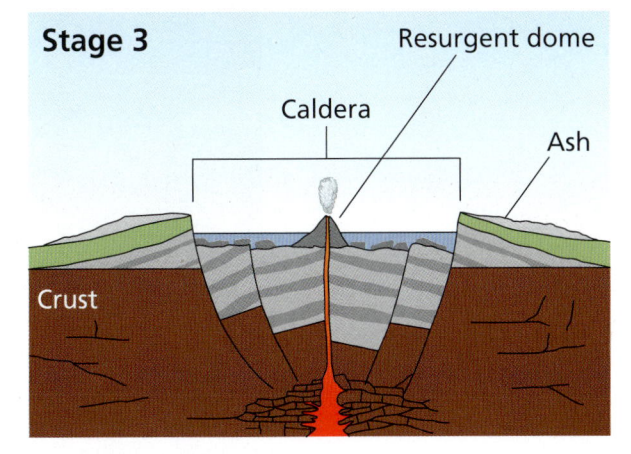

17

Landscapes

Molten lava / Basic lava spreads out slowly / Lava plateau / Previous lava flows / Magma moves up through open fissure

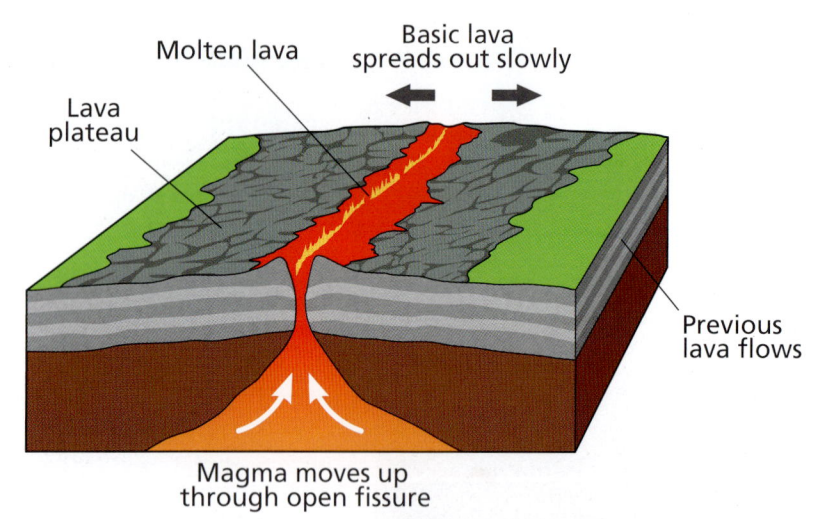

↑ **Fig. 2.6(a)** A fissure eruption.

Fissure eruptions

Example: Antrim–Derry Plateau

A **fissure eruption** occurs when **basic lava** flows quietly from a linear crack in the earth's crust (**Fig. 2.6(a)**). Fissures can be up to 50 metres in width, having been widened by the force of the rising magma. The lava spreads out slowly over a large area, often more than 50 km from the fissure (**Fig. 2.6(b)**). Repeated lava flows will result in the formation of a **lava plateau**.

→ **Fig. 2.6(b)** Basic lava flows from fissures.

Hydrothermal vents

Geysers

Example: Old Faithful, Yellowstone National Park, Wyoming, USA

Geysers are springs which eject hot water with great force at frequent intervals. Water descends to the lower crust, where it is heated by the surrounding hot rock. Pressure builds as the water boils. Eventually a spray of hot water and steam explodes onto the earth's surface.

→ **Fig. 2.7** Old Faithful – Yellowstone National Park contains about half of the world's geysers.

Black smokers

Example: Mid-Atlantic Ridge

Black smokers are chimney-like vents commonly found at depths below 3,000 metres near mid-ocean ridges (**Fig. 2.8**). The superheated water they release contains particles of dissolved minerals, including high levels of sulphur.

↑ **Fig. 2.8** A black smoker.

Intrusive 'Plutonic' Features

During periods of **folding** and **faulting**, cracks appear in the internal rock structure of the earth's crust. At times these cracks can stretch to the mantle, where molten magma is stored under great pressure. The magma is released and intrudes into the crust, where it cools and hardens, forming various intrusive features called **plutons** (**Fig. 2.9**). Some of these features include:

- **Batholith**: Large masses of intrusive igneous rocks formed when magma solidified slowly at the base of the mountain.
- **Dyke**: Magma vertically intruded, cooled and solidified within the earth's crust.
- **Sill**: Magma horizontally intruded into a bedding plane of sedimentary rock, before cooling and solidifying within the earth's crust.
- **Laccolith**: Magma pushed its way into the bedding plane of a sedimentary rock forcing the overlying **strata** upwards, forming a small **dome-shaped** structure.
- **Lopolith**: Magma pushed its way into the bedding plane of a sedimentary rock forcing the overlying strata downwards, forming a small **inverted dome-shaped** structure.

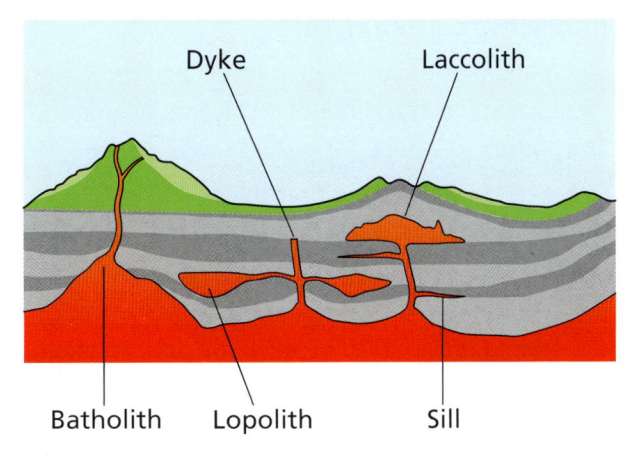

↑ **Fig. 2.9** Intrusive plutonic features.

---

2 Volcanic Activity

EXAM LINK (OL)

Volcanoes (40 marks)

(i) Define and name an example of each of the volcano types listed below:
- Active volcano
- Dormant volcano
- Extinct volcano

Marking Scheme:
Three volcano types: 6 marks + 5 marks + 5 marks

Each volcano:
Definition = 3 marks
Example = 3 or 2 marks

(ii) Explain in detail how volcanoes occur.

Marking Scheme:
Explanation = 8 SRPs × 3 marks = 24 marks

2015, Q3B

KEYWORDS

batholith   lopolith
dyke   plutons
faulting   sill
folding   strata
laccolith

Volcanic activity in Ireland resulted in the formation of:
- the Antrim–Derry Plateau, formed 65 million years ago (see basalt rock formation, page 58);
- Leinster batholith Lugnaquilla, whose peak is 925 metres above sea level (see granite rock formation, page 59).

19

Landscapes

CHECK YOUR LEARNING

1. List three gases released as part of a volcanic eruption.
2. What is tephra?
3. What is a pyroclastic flow?
4. List two differences between shield and composite volcanoes.
5. List three differences between acidic and basic lava.
6. Name and give examples of two types of hydrothermal vent.
7. What is a batholith?

KEYWORDS
geothermal energy
global cooling
lahar
Mount St Helens
Mount Vesuvius
nuée ardente
Pompeii
weather patterns

Human Interaction with Volcanoes

Predicting volcanic eruptions

The destructive nature of volcanic eruptions has led to greater study and investment in new technologies to predict when they will occur. Experts use a number of indicators to help them with their predictions:

Historic patterns

The best way to discover the future behaviour of a volcano is to study its past behaviour. **Volcanologists** look at historical data to predict how often a volcano erupts and the size of the eruption. **Geologists** examine sequences of layered deposits and lava flows from around volcanoes to discover the pattern and nature of volcanic eruptions.

Cone temperature

Rocks close to the surface of active vents get hotter, as magma rises prior to an eruption. **Infrared heat sensors** placed at the surface can detect temperature changes and send images to satellites to warn of an impending eruption.

Gas measurements

Volcanologists regularly collect samples of gases such as **sulphur dioxide (SO_2)** and **carbon dioxide (CO_2)** from active vents. Changes in their composition or increases in the rate at which they are emitted can indicate that a volcano is closer to erupting.

> **DID YOU KNOW?**
> Japan has about 110 active volcanoes – 75% of the world's total – but only half of these can be monitored intensively and constantly.

Changes in ground level

Sensitive instruments called **tiltmeters** record changes in the shape and steepness of active volcanoes. A bulge is created at the side of a volcano as pressurised magma builds up in its chamber. As the magma rises to the surface, the volcano deflates and returns to its original shape.

Changes to groundwater

Volcanologists monitor water levels and temperatures in local wells to identify any changes in the behaviour of a volcano. As magma moves into a volcano it can cause:

- a rise or fall in the water table;
- an increase in the temperature of groundwater.

Seismic activity

As magma moves into the reservoir prior to an eruption it ruptures already solidified magma in its way. This creates ground movements which can be detected by **seismographs** placed on the surface of the volcano.

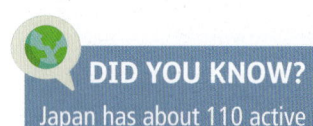

However, volcanic eruptions are still difficult to predict. Both Mount St Helens (1980) in the USA and Nevado Del Ruiz (1985) in Colombia erupted without warning. On the other hand, warnings were issued of impending volcanic eruptions in Italy in 1985 and New Zealand in 1995, but neither eruption happened!

Negative impacts of volcanic activity

- Lives can be lost as a result of a volcanic eruption. When **Mount Vesuvius** erupted in AD 79, over 20,000 people lost their lives in the towns of **Pompeii** and Herculaneum (**Fig. 2.10**).

- In 2010, air traffic was disrupted all over Europe following an eruption in Iceland. Flights were cancelled for two weeks as clouds of volcanic ash, which can damage jet engines, moved across Europe (**Fig. 2.11**).

- **Weather patterns** can be significantly altered following volcanic eruptions. Thick clouds of ash emitted from a volcano can block the sun's rays, causing a **global cooling**. On the other hand, **global warming** can result if the erupting volcano fills the atmosphere with greenhouse gases.

- Man-made and natural landscapes can be changed and destroyed forever. When **Mount St Helens** erupted in 1980, its summit was reduced by 401 m. The eruption also triggered a landslide which travelled at speeds of nearly 200 km per hour, destroying 600 km² of trees and killing over 7,000 wild animals, including deer, elk and bears (**Fig. 2.12**).

↑ **Fig. 2.10** Preserved remains at Pompeii.

↑ **Fig. 2.11** Satellite image of Icelandic volcano eruption.

↑ **Fig. 2.12** Mount St Helens before and after it erupted in 1980.

Landscapes

Fig. 2.13 A nuée ardente.

- When snow-capped volcanic mountains erupt, **lahars** (volcanic mudflows) are formed from the ash, mud and melting snow. These can devastate villages and towns in their path.
- Clouds of hot ash and poisonous gases called **nuées ardentes** ('glowing clouds') can be ejected from erupting volcanoes. These can travel long distances at speeds of up to 200 km per hour (**Fig. 2.13**).

Positive impacts of volcanic activity

- **New land:** New land is forming along the coastline of Iceland due to continuing volcanic eruptions. The lava cools quickly once it comes in contact with the cold ocean waters, forming solid rock which builds up over time to form new land. Surtsey, an island off the southern coast of Iceland, was formed by a volcanic eruption which lasted from November 1963 to June 1967.
- **Building materials:** Granite forms when magma cools slowly under the earth's surface. Granite from the Wicklow Mountains was used to construct buildings such as the General Post Office in Dublin. It is also used for headstones, grave chippings and table tops in kitchens.
- **Fertile soils:** The lava and ash deposited during an eruption breaks down to provide valuable nutrients creating rich, fertile soils. Lava cools to form basalt, which also weathers to a mineral-rich, fertile soil. Rich volcanic soils are common in Brazil, the world's leading coffee producer, and Italy, where they are cultivated to produce fruit and vegetables.
- **Mineral deposits:** Volcanoes directly or indirectly produce or hold deposits of diamonds, gold, silver, lead, zinc, copper and bauxite. Gold was discovered in California in 1848. Over the next seven years, over 300,000 people travelled to North America's west coast in search of their fortune, leading to the growth of cities such as San Francisco.
- **Jobs:** The dramatic scenery created by volcanic eruptions attract large numbers of people creating jobs in the tourist industry. Mount Vesuvius, which erupted in AD 79, covering the town of **Pompeii** in ash, is a popular tourist attraction, as are the volcanic **Hawaiian Islands**. Volcanic features, such as the **Old Faithful geyser** at Yellowstone National Park in Wyoming and the **Blue Lagoon** in Iceland, are also major tourist attractions.

> **DID YOU KNOW?**
> Brazil exports approximately 33 million bags of coffee beans per annum.

> **DID YOU KNOW?**
> Yellowstone National Park had 4.25 million visitors in 2017.

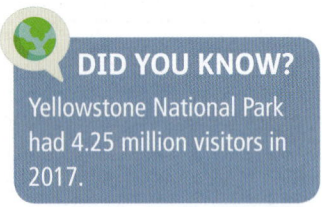

CHECK YOUR LEARNING

1. List and explain three ways experts attempt to predict volcanic activity.
2. How can erupting volcanoes impact on weather patterns?
3. Describe two ways the volcanic eruption at Mount St Helens impacted on the local area.
4. What is a lahar?
5. What is a nuée ardente?
6. How does volcanic activity benefit soil fertility?
7. List two volcanic tourist attractions.

2 Volcanic Activity

CASE STUDY: GEOTHERMAL ENERGY PRODUCTION IN ICELAND

By the mid-20th century, Iceland was one of the poorest countries in Europe, relying on energy derived from imported coal and local peat to develop its economy. Threats to supply (e.g. **World Wars**), the financial cost of importing coal and the environmental cost of burning fossil fuels (e.g. **air pollution**) led Icelanders to search for an alternative. With its high concentration of volcanoes (200) and hot springs (600) due to its location on the **Mid-Atlantic Ridge**, Iceland had excellent natural advantages for the generation of geothermal energy.

Geothermal energy

Power stations use pipes to carry cold water deep underground, where it is superheated using the heat from volcanic rocks. When it returns as steam to the earth's surface, it moves turbines connected to generators, producing electricity.

Magma close to the earth's surface superheats nearby water which stays as a liquid due to the pressure of overlying rocks. This hot water is piped directly to homes, commercial businesses and industries, satisfying their hot water and space heating needs (**Fig. 2.14**).

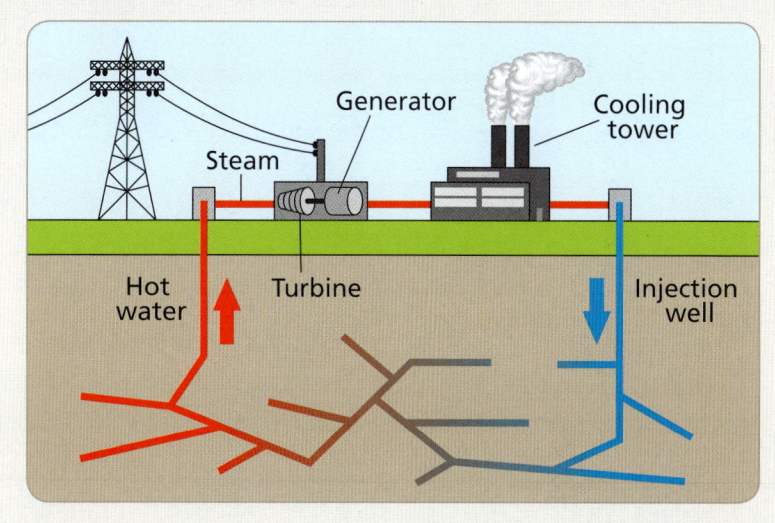

↑ **Fig. 2.14** Geothermal energy production.

Background to geothermal energy production

While geothermal heated water has been used since the 1930s, the first geothermal power plant wasn't built until 1969. The oil crisis of 1973 accelerated the need for Icelanders to become more self-sufficient and today Iceland leads the way in geothermal energy production which supplies 65% of its primary energy needs.

- **Geothermal heating** meets all necessary heating and hot water needs for approximately 87% of the country's buildings, including over 150 public swimming pools. Government officials believe that costs would be five times higher and CO_2 emissions would be up 40% greater if Icelanders were still dependent on fossil fuels for home heating instead of geothermal energy.
- Seven major **geothermal power plants** provide 30% of Iceland's electricity. Producing **low-cost, emission-free energy**, geothermal power plants have improved Iceland's energy security and boosted economic growth.

Economic benefits of geothermal energy production

- Despite the cool temperatures and short growing season, Iceland is **self-sufficient in food production**, with crops such as tomatoes, cucumbers and green peppers grown in geothermal greenhouses. Geothermal energy heats the greenhouses, geothermal steam is used to boil and disinfect the soil, while electric lighting has created a year-round growing season.
- **Geothermally heated water** is being used to create optimum temperatures for the growth of salmon, trout and arctic char in 20 of Iceland's 70 fish farms.
- Low-cost green electricity and a reliable transmission system has driven **rapid industrial development** over the last 25 years.

EXAM LINK (HL)

Volcanoes (30 marks)

Discuss the positive impacts of volcanic activity.

2018, Q1C & 2011, Q1B

Marking Scheme:
Positive impacts identified = 2 × 2 marks
Discussion = 13 SRPs

DID YOU KNOW?
Reykjavik is home to the largest district heating system in the world. Geothermal water is even used to keep pavements and car parks snow-free during the winter season.

Landscapes

EXAM TIP

An examination of 'Human interaction with geothermal energy' has appeared as:
- a Higher Level 30-mark question in 2006, 2007, 2009, 2010, 2011, 2013, 2015 and 2018 (15 SRPs);
- an Ordinary Level 30-mark question in 2007, 2010, 2013, 2014, 2016, 2017 and 2018 (10 SRPs).

- **Three aluminium smelters** located in Iceland use up to 70% of the geothermal energy produced in the country.
- The **data centre industry** is rapidly growing. Data servers use large amounts of energy and also benefit from Iceland's cool climate.
- Iceland's most famous tourist destination, the **Blue Lagoon**, was formed in 1976 during operations at the nearby geothermal power plant. Over the years, people have seen the health benefits of bathing in its mineral-rich water and applying the silica mud to their skin (Fig. 2.15).

↑ **Fig. 2.15** The Blue Lagoon with the geothermal power station in the background.

Future challenges

Icelandic officials are looking for more ways to develop their country using their natural geothermal resources.

- Ambitious plans are in place to build the world's largest underwater connector to allow Iceland to export clean geothermal electricity to the UK. The so-called 'Icelink' will help the UK to meet its renewable energy goals.
- Researchers are also working on a method of using geothermal electricity to split hydrogen from water. The hydrogen fuel cells would then be used to power the country's vehicles and fishing trawlers.

Between 1990 and 2014, Iceland's geothermal energy production grew by 1,700%.

EXAM LINK (OL)

Human Interaction with the Rock Cycle (30 marks)

Discuss how humans interact with the rock cycle with reference to geothermal energy production.

2018, Q2C

Marking Scheme:
Description/explanation = 10 SRPs × 3 marks

EXAM LINK (HL)

Human Interaction with the Rock Cycle (30 marks)

Humans interact with the rock cycle in a number of ways. Describe and explain how this interaction with the rock cycle takes place, with reference to geothermal energy production.

2018, Q3B

Marking Scheme:
Description/explanation = 15 SRPs × 2 marks

CHECK YOUR LEARNING

1. List three reasons Iceland started developing geothermal energy.
2. Explain how geothermal energy is produced.
3. How has Iceland's environment benefitted from the production of geothermal energy?
4. How has geothermal energy benefitted the production of food?
5. What impact has geothermal energy had on industrial development?
6. What is the Blue Lagoon?

EXAMINATION QUESTIONS
ORDINARY LEVEL

Short Questions

1. Volcanoes

Examine the diagram of a volcano and answer each of the following questions.

Feature	Letter
Crater	
Secondary volcanic cone	
Magma chamber	
Vent	

(i) Match each of the letters A, B, C and D with the feature that best matches it in the table. *4 × 2 marks*

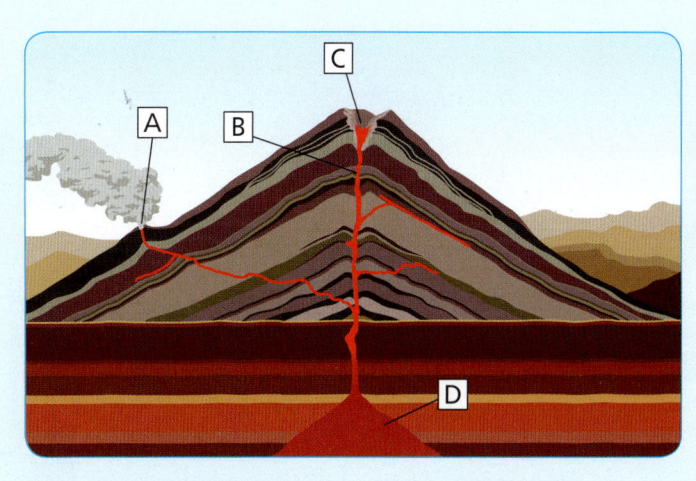

(ii) What name is given to a volcano that has not erupted in many hundreds of years but may erupt again? Tick the correct box. *2 marks*

Dormant ☐   Active ☐

2016, Part One, Q4 (10 marks)

Long Questions

2. Volcanoes

Volcanoes – Earth's Fiery Power

Most volcanoes exist along the edges of tectonic plates. About 90 per cent of all volcanoes exist within the Pacific Ring of Fire.

About 1,900 volcanoes on Earth are considered active, meaning they show some level of activity and are likely to explode again. Many other volcanoes are dormant while others are considered extinct.

A large eruption can be extremely dangerous for people living near a volcano. Flows of lava can be released, burning everything in its path. Boulders of hardening lava can rain down on villages. Mud flows from rapidly melting snow can strip mountains and valleys bare and bury towns.

Ash and toxic gases can cause lung damage and other problems. Scientists estimate that more than 260,000 people have died in the past 300 years from volcanic eruptions and their aftermath.

Amended from *National Geographic*

Read the extract above and answer the following questions.

(i) What percentage of volcanoes exist within the Pacific Ring of Fire? *3 marks*
(ii) State what is meant by the Pacific Ring of Fire. *3 marks*
(iii) Name two materials that are emitted into the air when volcanoes erupt. *2 × 3 marks*
(iv) Briefly explain what is meant by the term extinct volcano. *2 SRPs × 3 marks*
(v) List two negative effects of volcanoes. *2 negative effects × 3 marks*
(vi) Explain briefly one positive effect of volcanoes. *2 SRPs × 3 marks*

2017, Part Two, Section 1, Q2A (30 marks)

Landscapes

HIGHER LEVEL

Short Questions

3. Volcanic Activity

Examine the photographs and answer each of the following questions.

(i) Match each of the photographs A, B, C and D with the feature or process that best matches it in the table below.

4 × 1 marks

Feature / Process	Letter
Pyroclastic flow	
Lava fissure eruption	
Ash cloud	
Lava vent eruption	

(ii) Indicate whether each of the following statements is true or false, by circling the correct option in each case.

(a) Basic lava has a very high silica content. *2 marks*

True False

(b) Lava with a high silica content is most associated with explosive eruptions. *2 marks*

True False

2016, Part One, Q2 (8 marks)

4. Structure of a Volcano

Examine the diagram and answer each of the following questions.

(i) Match each of the letters A, B, C and D with the feature that best matches it in the table below.

4 × 1 mark

(ii) Indicate whether plutonic processes or volcanic processes are most associated with each of the features, by ticking the correct box in the table below.

4 × 1 mark

Feature	(i) Letter	(ii) Plutonic	(ii) Volcanic
Sill			
Pyroclastic sediment			
Dyke			
Lava flow			

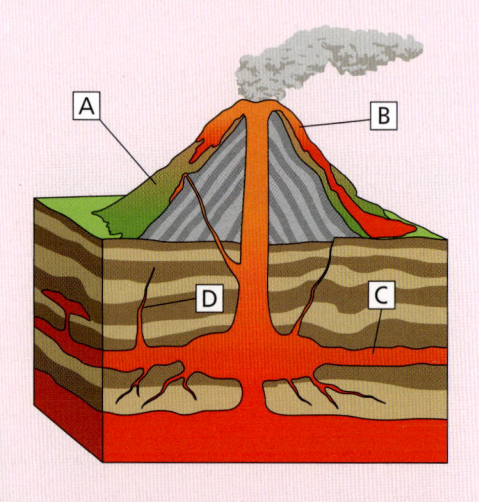

2015, Part One, Q1 (8 marks)

26

2 Volcanic Activity

Long Questions

5. Volcanoes

Examine the map and legend showing the extent of the materials deposited as a result of the eruption of the Mount St Helens volcano and answer the following questions.

(i) What were the most extensive deposits as a result of the eruption? *4 marks*

(ii) What was the direction of the pyroclastic flow deposits? *4 marks*

(iii) What distance did the pyroclastic flow deposits extend to? *4 marks*

(iv) Name two examples of pyroclastic materials. *2 × 2 marks*

(v) Explain briefly why some volcanoes erupt violently. *2 × 2 marks*

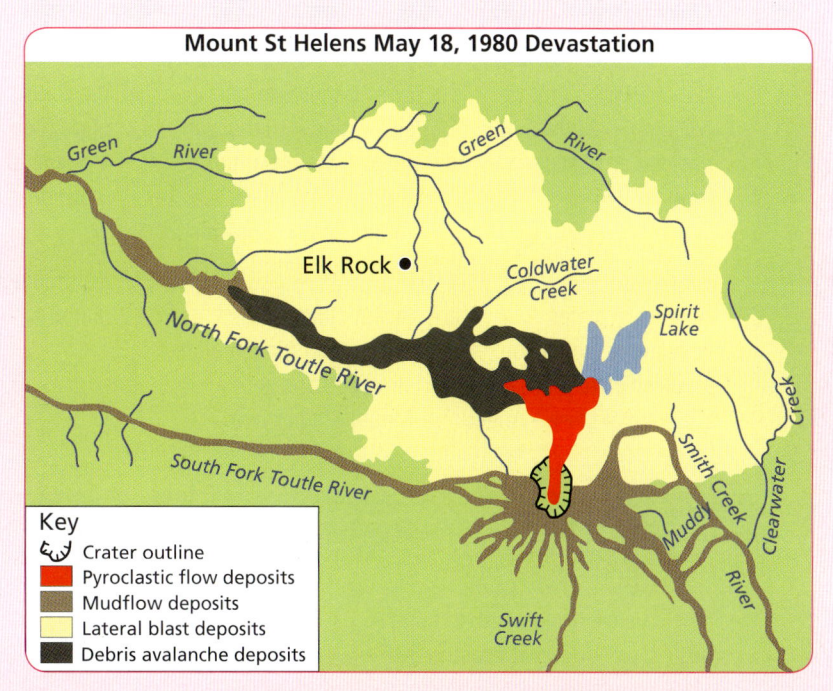

Mount St Helens May 18, 1980 Devastation

Key
- Crater outline
- Pyroclastic flow deposits
- Mudflow deposits
- Lateral blast deposits
- Debris avalanche deposits

2013, Part Two, Section 1, Q3A (20 marks)

6. Volcanoes

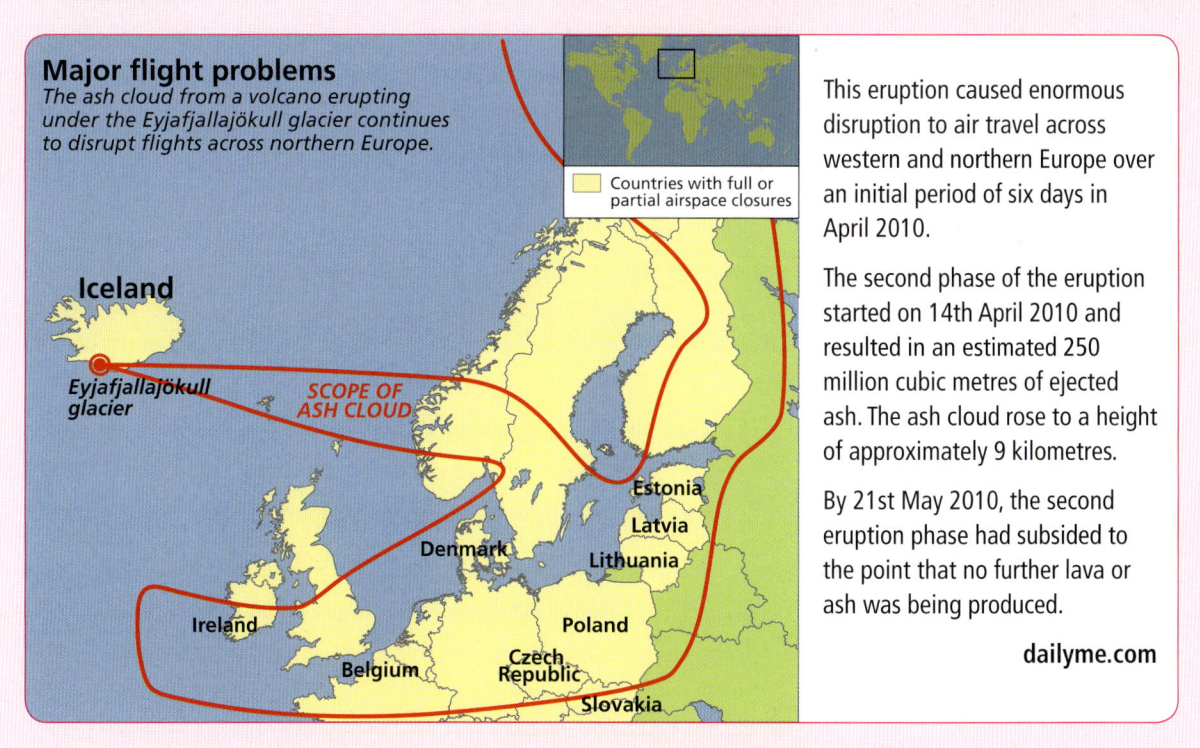

Major flight problems
The ash cloud from a volcano erupting under the Eyjafjallajökull glacier continues to disrupt flights across northern Europe.

Countries with full or partial airspace closures

SCOPE OF ASH CLOUD

This eruption caused enormous disruption to air travel across western and northern Europe over an initial period of six days in April 2010.

The second phase of the eruption started on 14th April 2010 and resulted in an estimated 250 million cubic metres of ejected ash. The ash cloud rose to a height of approximately 9 kilometres.

By 21st May 2010, the second eruption phase had subsided to the point that no further lava or ash was being produced.

dailyme.com

Examine the data above relating to the Eyjafjallajökull volcano which erupted in April 2010 and answer the following questions:

(i) What approximate height did the volcanic ash cloud rise to? *4 marks*

(ii) How many cubic metres of ash were ejected by the volcano? *4 marks*

(iii) Name **two** countries not named on the map which had full or partial airspace closures. *2 × 4 marks*

(iv) Briefly explain why volcanic activity occurs in Iceland. *4 marks*

2011, Part Two, Section 1, Q3A (30 marks)

27

Revision Summary

Location of volcanoes

Convergent plate boundaries

- Two oceanic plates colliding – subduction – island arc – Japanese islands
- Oceanic (Nazca) and continental (South American) plates colliding – subduction – volcanic arc forms on continental plate – Andes

Divergent plate boundaries

- Two oceanic plates separating – mid-ocean ridge – Mid-Atlantic Ridge where North American and Eurasian plates separate
- Rising plume – continental African plate stretched and split – Mount Kilimanjaro

Hotspots

- Weak part of oceanic plate (Pacific) moves over a plume of hot magma = eruption
- Volcano becomes extinct as it moves away from plume
- Chain of islands form – get older with distance from hotspot – Hawaiian Islands

Stages of a volcano

- **Active** – erupts regularly – Mt Etna, Italy
- **Dormant** – (sleeping) hasn't erupted in a long time – Parcutin, Mexico
- **Extinct** – hasn't erupted in historic times – Lambay Island, Ireland

Extrusive 'volcanic' features

Central vent eruptions

- Shield volcanoes – gently sloping – basic lava – found at constructive plate boundaries or over hot spots – Mauna Loa, Hawaii
- Composite volcanoes – steep-sided – acidic lava – found at convergent plate boundaries – Mount St Helens
- Calderas – depression formed by violent volcanic eruption – Crater Lake, Oregon, USA

Fissure eruption

- Crack on earth's surface – basic lava – cools quickly – Antrim–Derry Plateau

Hydrothermal vents

- **Geysers** – eject hot water and steam at frequent intervals – Old Faithful
- **Black smokers** – chimney-like vents – release superheated water and dissolved minerals with high levels of sulphur – Mid-Atlantic Ridge

Intrusive 'plutonic' features

- **Batholith** – magma fills a large vacuum within the crust and cools to form rock
- **Dyke** – rock structure formed by a vertical intrusion into the crust
- **Sill** – rock structure formed by a horizontal intrusion into a bedding plane
- **Laccolith** – small dome-shaped structure in the crust
- **Lopolith** – small inverted dome-shaped structure in the crust

Negative impacts of volcanic activity

- Lives lost – Pompeii – AD 79
- Ash cloud – Iceland – 2010
- Global cooling – ash blocks sun's rays
- Global warming - increased greenhouse gases
- Damaged landscape – Mount St Helens – 1980
- Lahars – volcanic landslide – Nevado del Ruiz
- Nuée ardente – clouds of hot poisonous gases

Positive impacts of volcanic activity

- New land formed – Iceland
- Building materials – Wicklow granite used to build GPO
- Fertile soils – lava, ash and basalt create mineral-rich soils – Brazil = world's largest coffee producer
- Mineral deposits – diamonds, gold, silver, lead, zinc, copper and bauxite – Californian Gold Rush
- Jobs – Pompeii, Hawaii, Yellowstone National Park

Geothermal energy production in Iceland

- Iceland – historically reliant on fossil fuels
- Natural advantages – 200 volcanoes + 600 hot springs
- Power stations create electricity from superheated water
- Natural hot springs provide hot water for homes, industry, etc.
- Oil crisis 1973 – accelerated need to be energy self-sufficient
- Geothermal energy supplies 65% of primary energy needs
- Costs would be five times higher and CO_2 emissions 40% greater if Icelanders were still dependent on fossil fuels
- Seven geothermal power plants provide 30% of Iceland's electricity
- Low-cost, emission-free energy = improved energy security and boosted economic growth
- Greenhouses – self-sufficient in food production
- Growth in aquaculture
- Growth in industry – aluminium smelters + data centres
- Tourism – Blue Lagoon
- Icelink

3 EARTHQUAKE ACTIVITY

LEARNING INTENTIONS
Syllabus Link: 1.1

By the end of this chapter I will be able to:
- recognise the different elements of an earthquake from a diagram;
- explain where earthquake activity occurs;
- describe how earthquakes can be predicted and measured;
- explain the factors which determine how destructive an earthquake can be;
- explain how human actions can limit the impacts of earthquakes;
- describe the causes and effects of an earthquake in both a developed and less developed country.

KEYWORDS
earthquake
focus
epicentre
seismic wave
aftershock
magnitude
tsunami
San Andreas Fault

An **earthquake** is a vibration of the earth's surface caused by the sudden release of energy beneath the crust. Around 8,000 earthquakes occur on average each year, of which approximately 1,000 are strong enough to be felt. About 40 of these result in major damage and, on average, 8,000 people are killed by their effects.

Components of an Earthquake

Focus: This is the point inside the earth's crust where the earthquake originates. The focus can be shallow, intermediate or deep:

- **Shallow focus** earthquakes occur close to the earth's surface, 0–70 km in depth. All things being equal, these are the most dangerous type of earthquake, as the shock waves have less distance to travel to reach the surface of the earth.

- **Intermediate focus** earthquakes occur between 70 and 300 km under the surface.

- **Deep focus** earthquakes occur over 300 km below the surface of the earth. These usually occur where oceanic and continental plates collide at convergent boundaries.

Epicentre: This is the point on the earth's surface directly above the focus, where the earthquake is strongest.

Seismic waves (tremors): These are shock waves that radiate from the focus. Their strength declines with increased distance from the epicentre.

Fault line: This is a fracture in the earth's crust, formed when two plates move.

Aftershocks: This is seismic activity that occurs after the initial earthquake.

Seismology: The study of earthquakes.

DID YOU KNOW?
Earthquakes have been responsible for about 13 million deaths in the past 4,000 years.

↓ **Fig. 3.1** Earthquake zones.

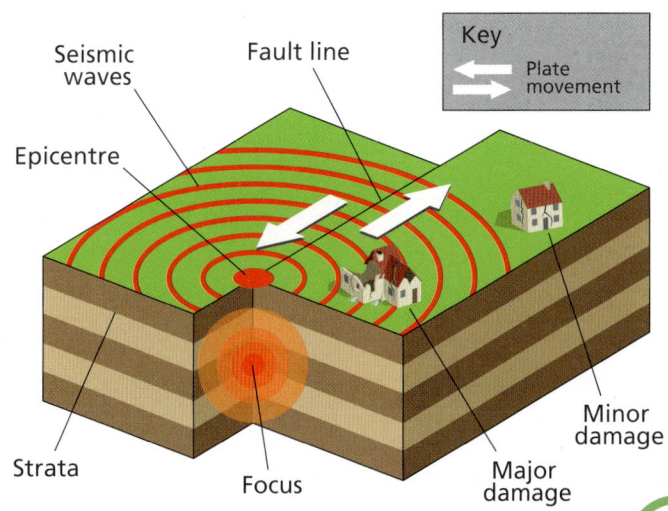

29

Landscapes

> Megathrust earthquakes occur at subduction zones at destructive convergent plate boundaries, where one tectonic plate is forced underneath another. These interplate earthquakes are the planet's most powerful, with magnitudes that can exceed 9.0.

Tsunami: Energy released by earthquakes under the ocean floor pushes the seawater upwards creating massive waves which can be very destructive to coastal areas.

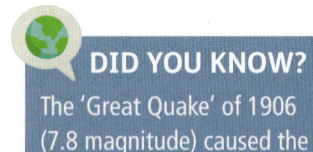

DID YOU KNOW?
The 'Great Quake' of 1906 (7.8 magnitude) caused the San Andreas Fault to slip by six metres.

Where Earthquakes Occur

Earthquakes occur at convergent, divergent and transform plate boundaries. (Fig. 3.2)

Convergent plate boundaries

The deepest, most powerful earthquakes occur where plates collide.

Massive friction is caused between layers of rock at **subduction zones** when an oceanic plate is in collision with another tectonic plate. As the heavier, denser oceanic plate sinks into the mantle, the rough edges of rocks at either side of the boundary lock in position. Stress builds up as convection currents continue to push both plates towards each other. Earthquakes are generated when the rocks eventually break, allowing the plates to move forward very suddenly. In 2011, the Pacific Plate (oceanic) converged with and subducted under the Eurasian Plate (continental). This led to a shallow focus megathrust earthquake 72 km off the coast of Japan, which in turn caused a devastating **tsunami**.

Earthquakes are common where **two continental plates** collide and rocks at the plate boundary lock in position. Convection currents continue to push the plates towards each other, causing stress to build up close to the earth's surface. In April 2015, an earthquake measuring 7.8 on the Richter scale occurred in **Nepal** when the Indian Plate slipped under the Eurasian Plate, releasing a large build-up of energy.

Divergent plate boundaries

Earthquakes also occur along the fractures that appear as two plates separate from one another. Many earthquakes occur along the **Mid-Atlantic Ridge**, for example, but their movements often go unnoticed, as no lives are lost and no property is damaged.

Transform plate boundaries

When two plates slide past one another, rocks at the edge of both plates lock in position. Stress builds at the boundary as convection currents try to push the plates past each other. Powerful earthquakes have been recorded at the **San Andreas Fault**, which runs along the western edge of California, when this energy has been released. Here, the Pacific Plate (travelling at a rate of 5 cm per year) slides laterally past the North American Plate (travelling 1 cm per year). Earthquakes produced at this boundary tend to be powerful, as the focus tends to be close to the earth's surface.

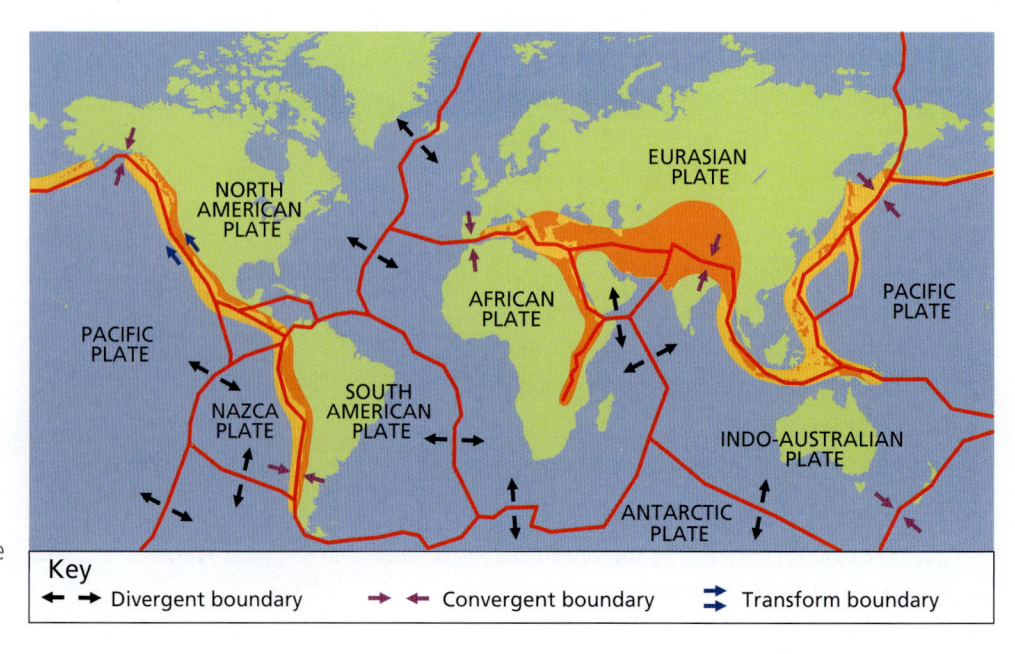

→ **Fig. 3.2** Major earthquake zones are located at plate boundaries.

Volcanic earthquakes can also result from stress changes in solid rock caused by the movement of magma. Earthquakes are produced when rock collapses into spaces created by the withdrawal of magma or by the injection of magma into the surrounding rock. A 5.1 magnitude earthquake occurred during the Mount St Helens eruption of 1980, triggering a massive landslide on the north face of the volcano.

EXAM LINK (HL)

Earthquakes (30 marks)

Explain, with reference to examples that you have studied, how the theory of plate tectonics helps to explain the distribution of earthquakes around the world.

2012, Q1C

Marking Scheme:
Global examples of earthquakes = 2 × 2 marks
Discussion = 13 SRPs

Earthquake Recording

Chapter 1: Plate Tectonics
Chapter 2: Volcanic Activity

KEYWORDS

seismograph	Richter scale
intensity	logarithmic scale
primary wave	Mercali scale
secondary wave	subjective scale
surface wave	

Seismograph

Seismologists use an instrument called a **seismograph** to detect and record earthquake activity (Fig. 3.3). Seismographs measure the **intensity** of seismic waves which can shake and displace the land on the earth's crust both horizontally (sideways) and vertically (up and down). They generate a graph called a **seismogram**.

Seismologists: Scientists who study the causes and effects of earthquakes.

Seismometer: Another word for seismograph.

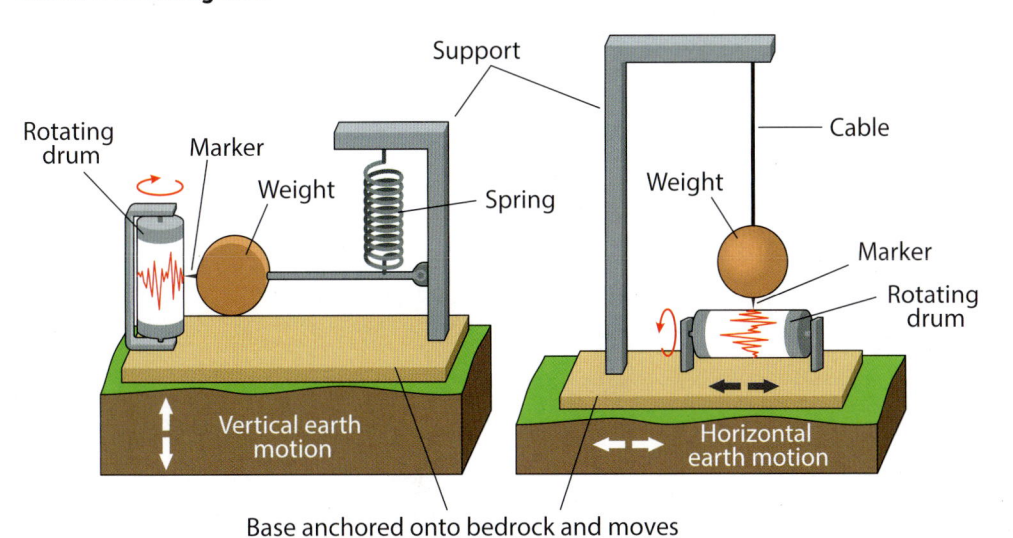

↑ **Fig. 3.3** Seismographs record the vertical and horizontal movement of the earth's crust.

31

Landscapes

There are two categories of seismic wave:
1. **Body waves:** Two types of body wave travel through the earth's inner layers, arriving at different times.
   a. **Primary waves (P-waves)** are the first wave of an earthquake to arrive. These are the fastest travelling seismic waves and they move through solid rock, liquids and gases.
   b. **Secondary waves (S-waves)** are the second wave of an earthquake. Travelling at medium speeds, they can only move through solid rock. Secondary waves cause the ground to move perpendicular to the direction the wave itself travels.
2. **Surface waves** are the last to arrive and travel at the slowest speed. Moving along the surface of the earth like ripples on water, they're responsible for most of the damage caused by earthquakes (Fig. 3.4).

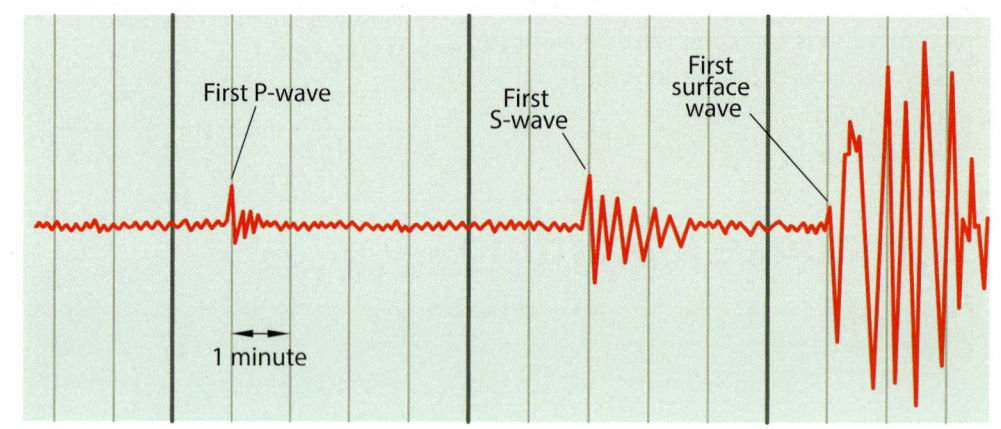

→ **Fig. 3.4** P-wave, S-wave and surface wave readings on a seismogram.

The Richter scale

Developed by Charles Richter in 1935, this scale allows **seismologists** to accurately record the **magnitude** of seismic activity (Table 3.1). The **Richter scale:**

- uses **seismograph readings** to calculate one internationally-accepted magnitude for each earthquake;
- is an **open-ended scale** – the highest earthquake magnitude recorded is the highest number on the scale;
- is a **logarithmic scale** – each full number on the scale represents ground movements 10 times greater than the number before it – magnitude 7 earthquakes are 10 times stronger than magnitude 6 earthquakes and 100 times stronger than magnitude 5 earthquakes, etc.

Earthquake magnitude: The amount of seismic energy released by an earthquake.

A quake is considered major when it registers 7.0 magnitude or greater on the Richter scale. Earthquakes measuring 1 or 2 on the scale are very common, happening on a daily basis in places like San Francisco. Too small to be felt by people, they're only picked up by a seismograph.

Rank	Location	Date	Magnitude
1	Valdivia, Chile	22 May 1960	9.5
2	Sumatra, Indonesia	26 December 2004	9.3
3	Alaska, USA	27 March 1964	9.2
=4	Pacific Ocean, Japan	11 March 2011	9.0
=4	Kamchatka, USSR	4 November 1952	9.0
=4	Arica, Chile	13 August 1868	9.0

↑ **Table 3.1** The most powerful earthquakes recorded on the Richter scale.

SKILLS ACTIVITY

Using graph paper, draw a suitable graph to illustrate the data presented in Table 3.1.

The Mercalli scale

Developed by Giuseppe Mercalli in 1912, the **Mercalli scale** measures the **intensity** of an earthquake from a **table of events**. This scale is based on the impact the earthquakes has on people, structures and the natural environment. It ranges from:

- intensity I – an event felt by very few people; to
- intensity XII – an extreme event with catastrophic effects.

Its **subjective scale** is less accurate than the Richter scale, as local conditions such as population density, geology and building standard can impact on the degree of destruction as much as the magnitude of the earthquake.

Subjective scale: A scale based on opinion rather than fact.

DID YOU KNOW?
The 2004 Indian Ocean earthquake lasted nearly 10 minutes, making it the longest on record.

CHECK YOUR LEARNING

1. Explain the term 'focus'.
2. Explain the term 'epicentre'.
3. What is happening at the San Andreas Fault that causes earthquakes?
4. What is a seismograph?
5. What are seismic waves?
6. How do P-waves differ from S-waves?
7. The Richter scale is a logarithmic scale. What does this mean?
8. What are the limitations of the Mercali scale?

Earthquake Prediction

While we know a lot about earthquakes, we still don't have a reliable way of predicting the epicentre location, magnitude or the exact time they will occur. Probabilities for potential future earthquakes are based on the following indicators:

Dating patterns

Seismologists study previous earthquake activity along fault lines in order to predict the likelihood, magnitude and intensity of a future earthquake. They look at patterns of activity, seismic gaps and both the magnitude and effects of previous earthquakes.

Electromagnetic fields

Changes in electromagnetic fields near fault lines can indicate an impending earthquake. **Satellite laser beams** and other sensors placed within the earth's crust can pick up these magnetic changes.

Changes to the earth's crust

- **Seismographs** may pick up an increasing number of vibrations in the earth's crust. This can indicate a build-up of stress that could possibly lead to a larger earthquake.
- **Strainmeters** are installed in boreholes about 200 metres under the ground. They detect rock deformation, which can indicate stress on the earth's crust near active faults.

KEYWORDS

dating pattern
seismologists
satellite
strainmeters
tiltmeters
radon gas
animal behaviour

- **Tiltmeters** can detect the slightest changes in the level of the land surface. Rising land levels can indicate increasing stress levels at the boundary of a tectonic plate.
- **Creepmeters** electronically measure the amount of displacement at a fault line over a specific period of time.

> The **US Geological Survey** are the leading experts in the monitoring of seismic activity worldwide.

Gas emissions

Rising levels of **radon gas** can be a good indicator of an impending earthquake. Radon is a radioactive gas produced by all rocks and soils. It can be released shortly before an earthquake when subterranean movements release it from cavities beneath the earth's crust. As a gas it rises quickly to the surface, where it is easily detected with sensitive instruments.

Animal behaviour

Unusual **animal behaviour** has been observed as a precursor to earthquake activity in the past. Numerous records indicate how animals, birds and insects have changed their behaviour when they sensed tectonic plate movements. Livestock have refused to go into barns, while other animals have come out of hibernation or escaped from underground habitats shortly before an earthquake.

The Impact of Earthquakes

KEYWORDS
intensity
subduction zone
depth
geology
secondary effects
architecture
developed countries
developing countries
planning procedures
early warning systems
cross-brace

Factors that determine the destructiveness of earthquakes

Earthquakes can strike suddenly, violently and without warning. Their effects will be determined by:

- **Intensity:** The more energy an earthquake has, the more destructive it tends to be. The most destructive earthquakes generally occur at **subduction zones**.
- **Depth:** Shallow focus earthquakes are more destructive than deep focus earthquakes, when all other factors are equal.
- **Location:** Urban areas have denser populations and taller buildings, putting more people in harm's way.
- **Time of day:** More people are likely to get trapped in their homes if an earthquake strikes at night.
- **Local geology:** Vibrations from earthquakes cause greater damage where the surface material at the epicentre is **unconsolidated** – loose, sandy, soggy soil can liquefy (**liquefaction**).
- **Secondary effects:**
  (a) Vibrations from a 7.8-magnitude earthquake caused major landslides and avalanches in the mountainous Nepal region in April 2015. Landslides blocked the Kali Gandaki River, flooding vast areas, while 19 people were killed in an avalanche on Mount Everest.
  (b) On 26 December 2004, a magnitude 9.3 earthquake on the sea floor off the coast of north-west Sumatra was recorded. It was not the earthquake that caused so much damage in the region, but the Indian Ocean tsunami it triggered.

> **Liquefaction:** Saturated or partially saturated soil loses strength and acts like a liquid after it is placed under stress by an earthquake.

- **Architecture:** While the strongest buildings may not survive a high intensity earthquake, the chances of building damage increase with poor construction and unenforced building regulations. In **developed countries** (which have well-developed economies and infrastructure, e.g. the USA), the quality of materials and engineering used in construction is likely to be of a higher standard than **developing countries** (which have poorly developed economies and infrastructure, e.g. Nepal). As a result, they are less likely to collapse if an earthquake strikes.
- **Technological advancement:** Sophisticated emergency and rescue services can reduce loss of life and the amount of damage caused. Developed countries are also more likely to maintain emergency supplies of food and water, while public information programmes show people how to respond to an earthquake.

Reducing the effects of earthquakes

While earthquakes can't be prevented, the dangers of serious injury or loss of life can be reduced by identifying hazards ahead of time and enforcing good **planning procedures**.

- Installing **early warning systems** such as seismographs can highlight the onset of earthquakes. This could be supported by putting effective communication and alarm systems in place for the public.
- Regular **earthquake drills** can familiarise people with what to do in times of an emergency.
- **Water, gas and electricity pipelines** should be placed deep underground, with automatic shut-off valves installed to turn off water, gas and electricity if an earthquake hits.
- **Power stations** (especially nuclear power plants) should be constructed away from fault lines.
- Building regulations should promote more **earthquake-proofing of buildings** (Fig. 3.5). Regulations could require people to:
  - develop buildings on **solid rock foundations**;
  - build structures that can **move with the ground** and still remain standing during an earthquake. While the base will move with the ground, the use of Teflon™ pads, enormous rollers or coiled springs can reduce the movement to the rest of the building;
  - **cross-brace buildings** to minimise the effect of shearing forces during earthquakes;
  - **retrofit older buildings and bridges** with steel-reinforced concrete frames (Fig. 3.6).

→ **Fig. 3.5** The Transamerica building in San Francisco was designed to absorb the energy of an earthquake and to withstand the movement of the earth.

Landscapes

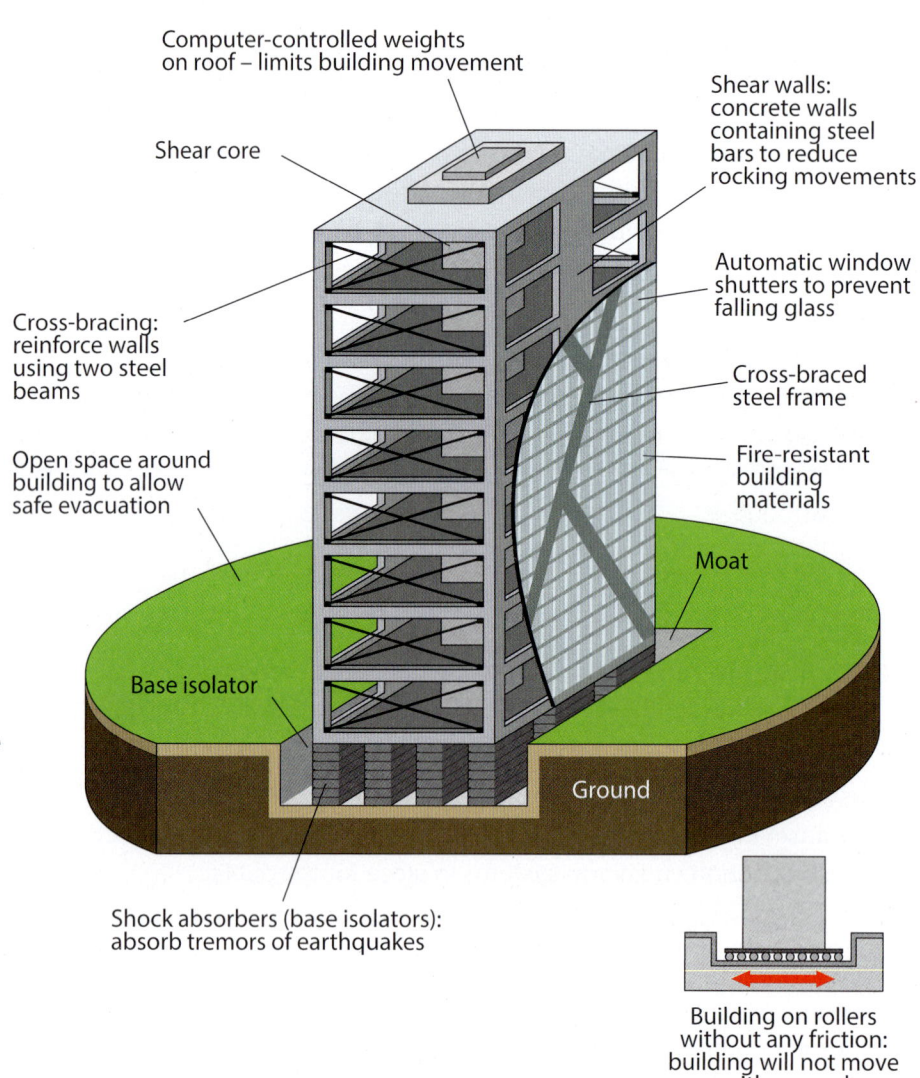

Computer-controlled weights on roof – limits building movement
Shear core
Shear walls: concrete walls containing steel bars to reduce rocking movements
Cross-bracing: reinforce walls using two steel beams
Automatic window shutters to prevent falling glass
Open space around building to allow safe evacuation
Cross-braced steel frame
Fire-resistant building materials
Moat
Base isolator
Ground
Shock absorbers (base isolators): absorb tremors of earthquakes
Building on rollers without any friction: building will not move with ground

→ **Fig. 3.6** Engineering methods used to limit the effects of earthquakes.

EXAM TIP

Exam candidates should be able to describe the causes and effects of earthquake activity in both a developed country and a developing country.

EXAM LINK (HL)

Seismic Activity (30 marks)

Explain how the occurrence of seismic activity can be predicted and its effects reduced.

2017, Q3C

Marking Scheme:
Reference to prediction of seismic activity = 2 marks
Reference to reducing impacts of seismic activity = 2 marks
Explanation = 13 SRPs

CHECK YOUR LEARNING

1. In studying dating patterns, what do seismologists look for?
2. Explain two ways in which changes to the earth's crust can indicate the onset of an earthquake.
3. How has animal behaviour been used to predict earthquake activity?
4. What organisation leads the way in earthquake monitoring?
5. Where do the most destructive earthquakes occur?
6. What is liquefaction?
7. Describe one way utilities could be protected from damage caused by earthquakes.
8. List three regulations that could be imposed on the construction of new buildings that would limit the damage caused by earthquakes.

3 Earthquake Activity

CASE STUDY: THE HAITI EARTHQUAKE

Background

Haiti, part of a large Caribbean island called Hispaniola, was one of the poorest countries in the world in 2010.

- Over 70% of the 10 million population lived under the poverty line.
- It ranked 149 out of 182 countries in the UN Human Development Index (HDI).

The Dominican Republic lies to the east of Haiti, covering over half of the island. Both countries lie on a transform plate boundary where the Caribbean and North American plates slide past one another in an east–west direction at a rate of 20 mm per year. Despite being built upon a major **fault line**, Haiti had very few **building regulations**, meaning there was little to ensure buildings were safe from earthquakes.

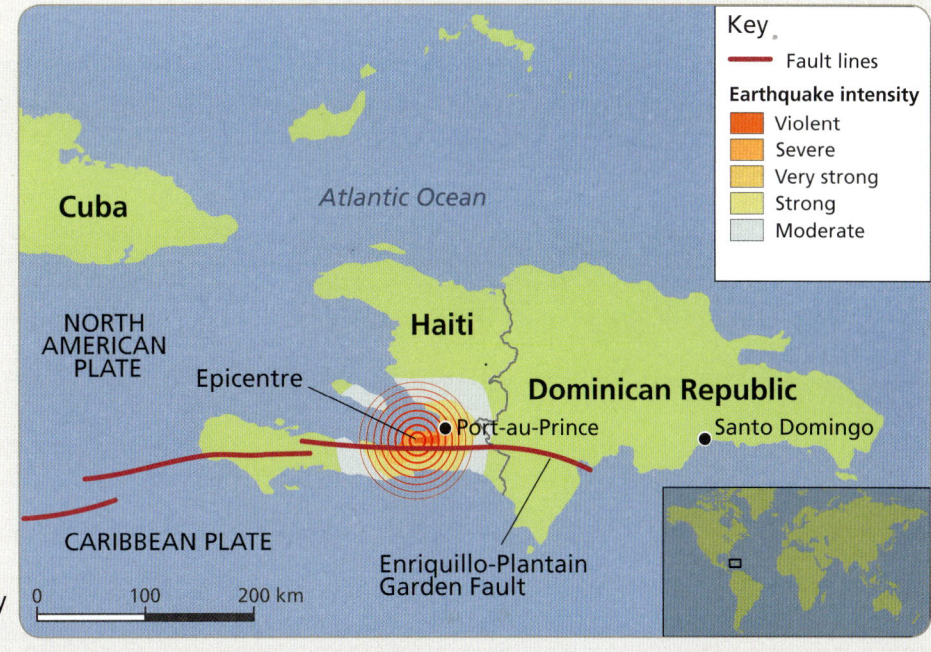

↑ **Fig. 3.7** Map showing the Haiti earthquake zone.

Earthquake

At 16:53 local time on Tuesday, 12 January 2010, a **7.0-magnitude earthquake** struck Haiti. Stress that had built up at points along the fault line (boundary) was suddenly released, causing a strong movement on both sides of the fault (**Fig. 3.7**). The **epicentre** was approximately 25 km west of Port-au-Prince, Haiti's capital city. As it was a shallow focus earthquake with a depth of just 13 km, the energy released was very close to the surface of the earth, making it more destructive. By 24 January, at least **52 aftershocks** measuring 4.5 or greater on the Richter scale had been recorded.

Short-term effects

- Over 3.5 million people were affected by the earthquake, with an estimated 230,000 deaths. A further 300,000 people suffered injuries as a result of the disaster.
- Approximately 250,000 homes were destroyed or severely damaged. Approximately 1.5 million people (20% of the population) were left homeless, living in camps with limited services (**Fig. 3.8**).
- There was a shortage of clean water, as river supplies were contaminated by decaying matter.
- Rescue and aid efforts were hampered because the airport control tower, the seaport, major roads and other communication links were all damaged beyond repair.
- Damage to hospitals meant that those that could cater for patients were badly overcrowded.
- There was an outbreak of looting and violence, as 4,000 inmates escaped from the National Penitentiary at Port-au-Prince, which was also destroyed.

Landscapes

Fig. 3.8 Damage caused by the Haiti earthquake.

Long-term effects

- Contaminated drinking water led to an outbreak of cholera that claimed almost 6,000 lives.
- Many children and badly injured people were left with nobody to care for them.
- Unemployment rose to 20%, as damage to 30,000 commercial buildings resulted in the collapse of industries such as textiles.
- Damage to 60% of government buildings affected the administration of government business.
- Damage to hotels, transport and communications, along with the increased threat of unrest, saw tourist numbers to the region plummet.
- Landmark buildings such as the Presidential Palace, the National Assembly building and Port-au-Prince Cathedral were significantly damaged or destroyed.

CASE STUDY: THE JAPANESE EARTHQUAKE AND TSUNAMI

Background

Japan, a chain of volcanic islands located in the Pacific Ocean, was one of the richest countries in the world in 2011. It ranked 12 out of 187 countries in the UN Human Development Index (HDI) and had the world's third-largest economy.

Due to its location on the Pacific Ring of Fire, Japan has a history of earthquake activity, many resulting in destructive tsunami. Its most devastating earthquake occurred in 1923 when 140,000 people were killed.

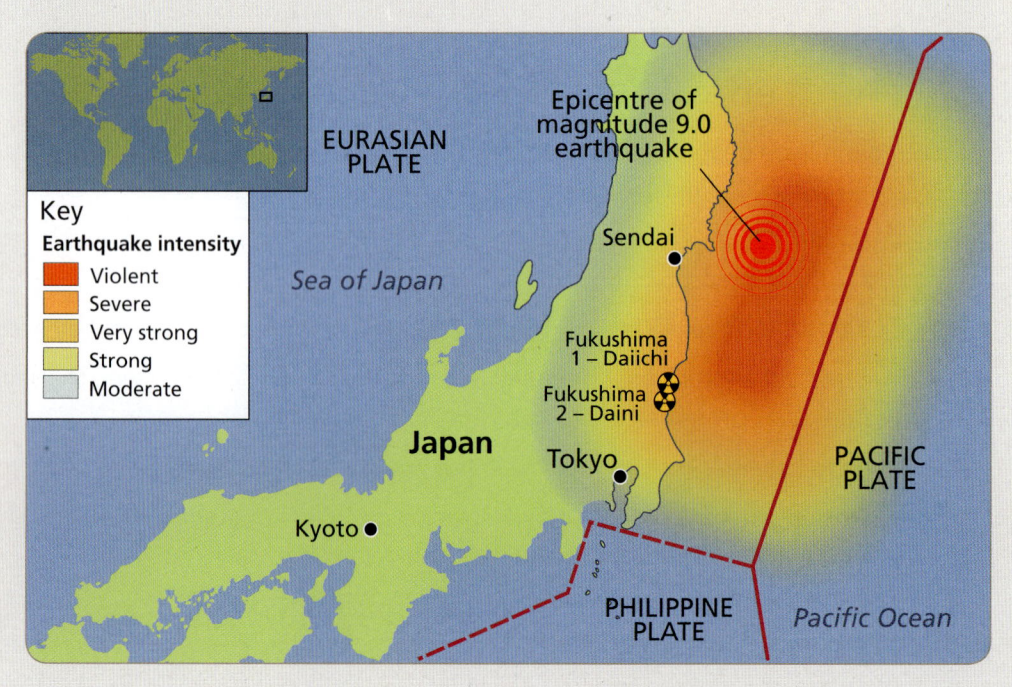

> This is referred to as the '*Tohoku*' or '**Great East Japan earthquake**'. It was the most powerful earthquake ever recorded in Japan.

Fig. 3.9 Map showing the Japanese earthquake zone.

Earthquake and tsunami

On 11 March 2011, a **9.0-magnitude earthquake** lasting approximately six minutes was recorded 72 km off the coast of Japan (**Fig. 3.9**). The earthquake occurred at the **fault line** where the Pacific Plate converges with the Eurasian Plate. As the two plates collided, the lighter continental Eurasian Plate rose over the heavier, denser Pacific Plate which was subducting. A **shallow, megathrust earthquake** with a **focus** 24 km under the Pacific Ocean bed followed. This caused the ocean floor of the Pacific Plate to rise more than 10 metres (**Fig. 3.10**). Billions of tonnes of seawater were driven upwards creating a powerful tsunami which flowed away from the fault in a series of waves, travelling at **speeds up to 500 km/hr**. As the waves reached the shallow waters off the Japanese coastline, they compressed and **rose up to 40 metres in height**. Giant waves overtopped and destroyed protective tsunami seawalls at several locations before travelling up to 10 km inland. The **tsunami** flooded approximately 561 km^2, causing massive damage, while the succeeding outflow of water also caused destruction (**Fig. 3.11**).

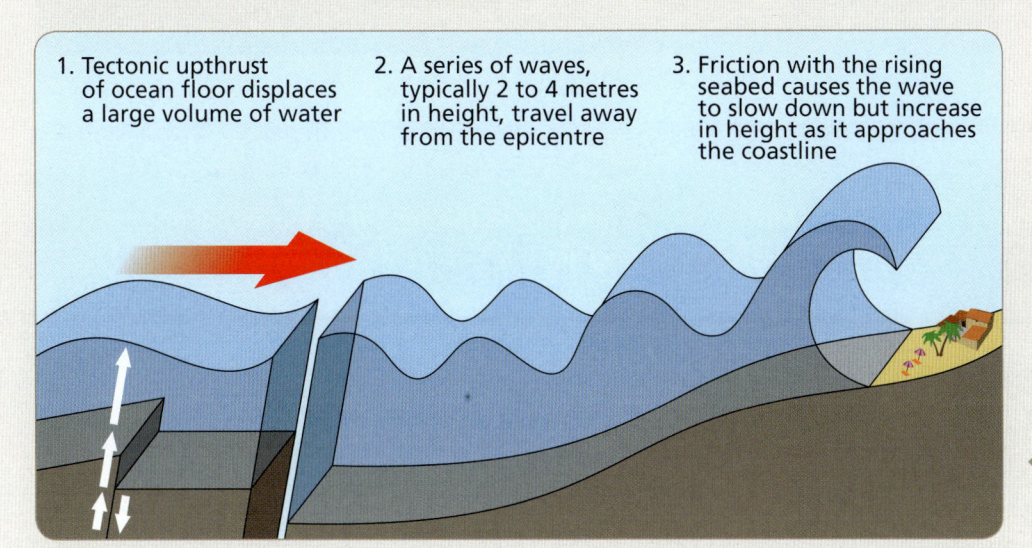

1. Tectonic upthrust of ocean floor displaces a large volume of water
2. A series of waves, typically 2 to 4 metres in height, travel away from the epicentre
3. Friction with the rising seabed causes the wave to slow down but increase in height as it approaches the coastline

← **Fig. 3.10** Formation of a tsunami by a megathrust earthquake.

Short-term effects

- Approximately 16,000 people died as a result of the tsunami, over 90% resulting from drowning.
- 25,000 people were injured, with many of those caught in the tsunami believing they were on high enough ground to be safe.
- Water pipes burst and contaminated water supplies, leaving 1.5 million people without access to 'safe' water.
- Nearly 4.4 million households were left without electricity.

The World Bank estimated that the economic cost of the disaster was US$235 billion, making it the costliest natural disaster in history.

Long-term effects

- 2,500 people are still considered missing.
- Over 125,000 buildings totally collapsed, with a quarter of a million people losing their homes.
- Transport and communication links were destroyed, but they were rebuilt very quickly.
- The impact of the tsunami was also responsible for explosions at three reactors in the Fukushima Daiichi Nuclear Power Plant Complex, where the cooling system failed due to the loss of electrical power. Following the explosions, residents within 20 km of the plant had to be evacuated from their homes due to a massive release of radiation. Even though evacuation orders have been lifted for many areas within the exclusion zone, very few people have returned home. People won't buy food produced in the region so farmers have been hugely affected.

Landscapes

Fig. 3.11 Tsunami hitting the coast of Japan.

CHECK YOUR LEARNING

1. Why are earthquakes likely to happen in Haiti?
2. Of the two countries (Haiti and Japan), which is more developed? Explain your answer.
3. What caused the Haiti earthquake of January 2010?
4. List three reasons the Haiti earthquake caused major destruction.
5. Explain one short-term and one long-term impact of the Haiti earthquake.
6. What caused the Japanese earthquake?
7. How did this lead to a tsunami?
8. What was the economic cost of the tsunami?
9. What impact did the tsunami have at Fukushima Daiichi?
10. In your opinion, which country suffered greater devastation? Explain why.

EXAMINATION QUESTIONS
ORDINARY LEVEL

Short Questions

1. Earthquakes

	Largest Earthquakes		Deadliest Earthquakes		
Year	Magnitude	Region	Magnitude	Fatalities	Region
2012	8.6	Northern Sumatra	6.7	113	Philippines
2011	9.0	Japan	9.0	20 896	Japan
2010	8.5	Chile	7.0	316 000	Haiti
2009	8.1	Samoan Islands	7.5	1117	Southern Sumatra

Amended from www.usgs.gov

Examine the table above and answer each of the following questions.
(i) What was the magnitude of the earthquake in Southern Sumatra in 2009? *2 marks*
(ii) In which year was the largest earthquake? *2 marks*
(iii) Where was the earthquake with the greatest number of fatalities? *2 marks*

(iv) What is the name given to the point on the earth's surface directly above the focus of an earthquake? *2 marks*

(v) Indicate whether the statement below is true or false, by ticking the correct box.

Earthquakes occur where plates collide.   True ☐   False ☐   *2 marks*

2015, Part One, Q4 (10 marks)

Ordinary Level Long Questions

2. Earthquakes

> **Nepal Earthquake, 2015**
>
> The death toll in Nepal from a severe earthquake and intense aftershocks has risen to over 8,000 people and left thousands injured.
>
> The original quake, with a magnitude of 7.9, struck before noon and was most severely felt in the capital Kathmandu, as well as the densely populated Kathmandu Valley. Its epicentre was some 80 km east of Nepal's second largest city, Pokhara. The quake occurred at a shallow depth (approximately 15 km), intensifying the amount of energy released over a relatively small area.
>
> As a consequence, houses collapsed, centuries-old temples were levelled and avalanches were triggered in the Himalayas. The earthquake also shook several cities across northern India and was felt as far away as Lahore in Pakistan and Lhasa in Tibet.
>
> Amended from www.irishtimes.com

Read the newspaper extract above and answer each of the following questions.

(i) What was the magnitude of the earthquake in Nepal?   *3 marks*

(ii) At what depth (in kilometres) did the earthquake occur?   *3 marks*

(iii) State what is meant by the term 'aftershock'.   *3 marks*

(iv) List three effects of earthquakes referred to in the newspaper extract above.
 3 effects × 3 marks

(v) State two ways that the effects of earthquakes could be reduced.   *2 ways × 3 marks*

(vi) Explain briefly the term 'epicentre'.   *2 SRPs × 3 marks*

2016, Part Two, Section 1, Q3A (30 marks)

3. Earthquakes

(i) Name two examples of different locations where earthquakes have occurred.
 2 locations × 3 marks

(ii) Name a scale used to measure the force of an earthquake.   *4 marks*

(iii) Explain how earthquakes occur and describe their main effects.
 Explanation/description = 10 SRPs × 3 marks

2017, Part Two, Section 1, Q3B (40 marks)

Landscapes

HIGHER LEVEL

Short Questions

4. Earthquakes

(i) Match each of the letters A, B, C and D on the diagram with the correct feature in the table.

4 × 1 mark

Feature	Letter
Focus	
Epicentre	
Seismic waves	
Fault line	

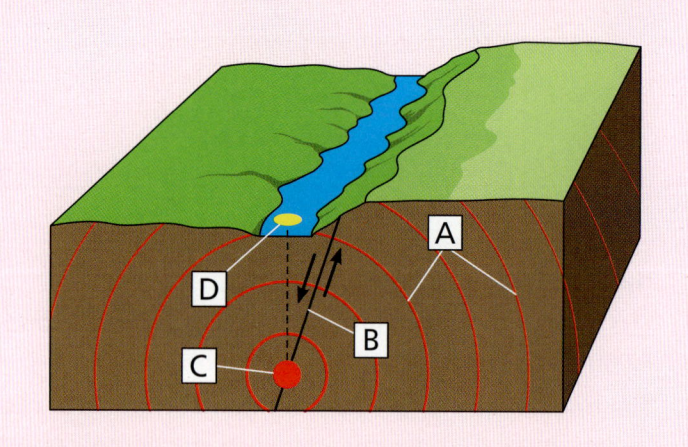

(ii) Explain briefly each of the following terms. *2 × 2 marks*

Seismologist

Seismometer

2013, Part One, Q2 (8 marks)

Long Questions

5. Earthquakes

Examine the diagram and answer each of the following questions.

(i) What was the magnitude of the earthquake in Nepal in 2015? *2 marks*

(ii) The movement of which two plates resulted in the earthquake in Nepal? *2 × 2 marks*

(iii) What type of plate boundary is shown? *2 marks*

(iv) Name two other types of plate boundaries. *2 × 2 marks*

(v) Explain briefly what is meant by the term epicentre. *2 × 2 marks*

(vi) Explain briefly one way of reducing the impact of earthquakes. *2 × 2 marks*

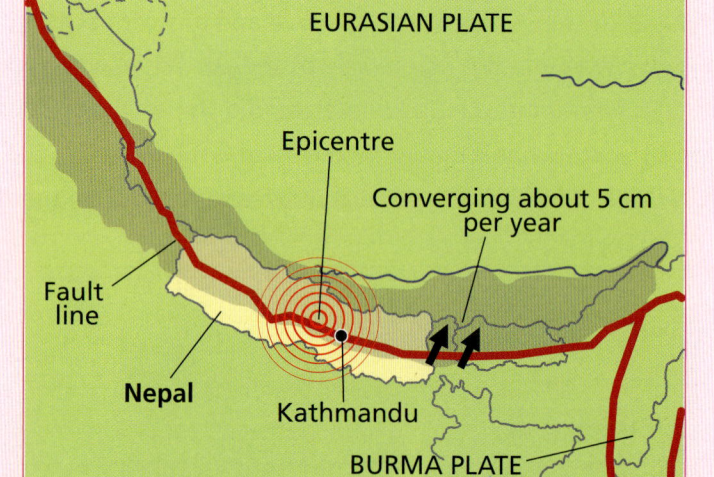

Nepal Earthquake, 25 April 2015, Magnitude 7.8

2016, Part Two, Section 1, Q2A (20 marks)

42

Revision Summary

Components of earthquakes	Where earthquakes occur
• Shallow focus • Intermediate focus • Deep focus • Epicentre • Seismic waves (tremor) • Fault line • Aftershock	**Convergent plate boundaries** • Oceanic plate collides with another tectonic plate – 2011 shallow megathrust earthquake 72 km off Japanese coast – Pacific Plate (**oceanic**) converged with and subducted under the Eurasian Plate (**continental**) – earthquake lead to a tsunami • Two continental plates collide – April 2015 – 8.1 magnitude earthquake in Nepal – Indian Plate collided with and slipped under Eurasian Plate releasing a large build-up of energy **Divergent plate boundaries** • Earthquakes where two plates separate – Mid-Atlantic Ridge – movements often go unnoticed, as no lives lost and no property damaged **Transform plate margin** • San Andreas Fault in California – Pacific and North American plates slide past one another – lock in position, stress builds up – earthquakes occur when energy released – focus tends to be close to the earth's surface

Earthquake measurement

Seismograph	Richter scale	Mercali scale
• Measures the intensity of seismic waves – vertically and horizontally • Creates graphs called seismograms • Primary waves – fastest wave • Secondary waves – slower • Surface waves – cause most damage	• Developed by Charles Richter in 1935 • Open-ended scale • 9.5 in Chile 1960 = highest recorded • Logarithmic scale – full number increase on scale = earthquake 10 times larger	• Developed by Giuseppe Mercalli in 1912 • Subjective scale – table of events • Scale ranges from 1–12 • External factors impact on the level of damage caused

Earthquake prediction	Factors determining the destructiveness of earthquakes	Reducing the effects of earthquakes
• Dating patterns • Electromagnetic field changes • Seismographs • Strainmeters • Tiltmeters • Creepmeters • Gas emissions • Animal behaviour	• Intensity – magnitude • Depth of focus – shallow or deep • Location – urban or rural • Time – day or night • Local geology – liquefaction • Secondary effects – landslides, tsunami, etc. • Architecture – quality of construction • Technological advancement	• Early warning systems • Effective communication systems • Earthquake drills • Bury pipes and gas deep underground • Install shut-off valves • No power stations built near fault lines • Improve building regulations

Landscapes

The Haiti earthquake	The Japanese earthquake and tsunami
Background and earthquake • Haiti – on Caribbean island of Hispaniola – 149 on the Human Development Index • Conservative plate boundary – Caribbean and North American plates • On fault line, but very few building regulations • 12 January 2010 a 7.0-magnitude earthquake struck • Epicentre approx. 25 km west of Port-au-Prince • Shallow focus earthquake – depth of 13 km = more destructive • By 24 January – 52 aftershocks of 4.5 or greater were recorded	**Background and earthquake** • Japan – chain of volcanic islands in the Pacific Ocean – 12 on the HDI in 2011 • Has a history of earthquake activity and tsunami • 11 March 2011 a 9.0-magnitude earthquake struck 72 km off coast of Japan • Eurasian Plate rose over subducting Pacific Plate • Shallow focus earthquake 24 km under the sea floor – caused it to rise 10 m – created tsunami travelling at 500 km/h • At coast rose to 40 m in height – travelled 10 km inland
Short-term effects • Over 3.5 million affected – 230,000 deaths, 300,000 injured • Approx. 1.5 million left homeless – living in camps • 250,000 dwellings destroyed or severely damaged • Water shortages – contaminated by decaying matter • Damaged communications hampered rescue and aid efforts • Damage to hospitals led to overcrowding • Outbreak of looting and violence – 4,000 prison inmates escaped	**Short-term effects** • Approximately 16,000 deaths – 90% from drowning • 25,000 people were injured • Burst water pipes – contaminated water supplies left 1.5 million without access to safe water • Nearly 4.4 million households were left without electricity
Long-term effects • Outbreak of cholera = 6,000 deaths • Many children and badly injured left with nobody to care for them • Unemployment up 20% – 30,000 commercial buildings damaged • Damage to 60% of government buildings affected the administration of government business • Damage to hotels, transport & communications + increased threat of unrest = tourist numbers fell • Landmark buildings significantly damaged or destroyed	**Long-term effects** • 2,500 people are still considered missing • Over 125,000 buildings totally collapsed • 250,000 people lost their homes • Transport and communication links were destroyed • Tsunami was responsible for explosions at three reactors in the Fukushima Daiichi Nuclear Power Plant Complex. The cooling system failed due to the loss of electrical power. Following the explosions, residents within 20 km of the plant had to be evacuated from their homes due to a massive release of radiation

4 FOLDING AND FAULTING ACTIVITY

LEARNING INTENTIONS
Syllabus Link: 1.3

By the end of this chapter I will be able to:
- identify each of the tectonic forces from a diagram;
- identify the various elements of a folded structure from a photograph or diagram;
- describe the folding process and the impact of different folding periods on Irish and international landscapes;
- identify the various types of fault from a diagram;
- describe how faulting occurs and the features formed at different fault margins using Irish and international examples.

KEYWORDS
tectonic forces
tension
compression
shearing
folding
faulting
anticline
syncline
limb
simple fold
asymmetrical fold
overfold
recumbent fold
overthrust fold

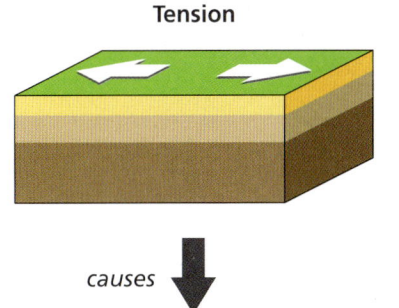

The rock structure of the earth's crust can change due to the stress exerted by three **tectonic forces**. (Fig. 4.1)

1. **Tension** happens where plates separate at divergent plate boundaries. Rocks lengthen through elasticity or break apart.
2. **Compression** happens where plates collide at convergent plate boundaries. Rocks are squeezed and shortened, causing them to fold or fracture.
3. **Shearing** happens where plates slide past one another at transform plate boundaries. The forces exerted act parallel to each other but in opposite directions.

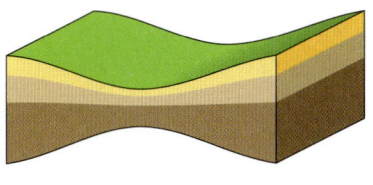

↑ **Fig. 4.1** Tectonic forces.

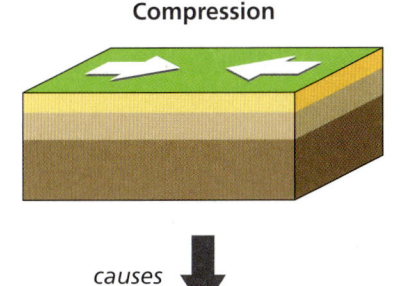

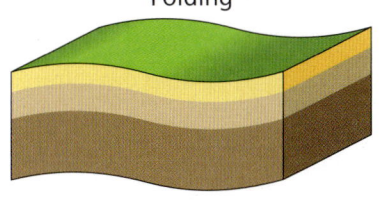

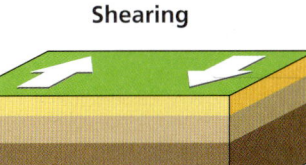

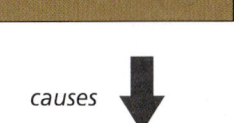

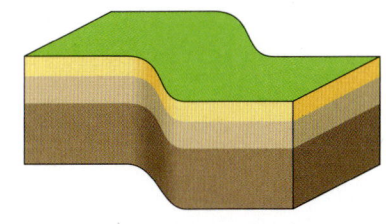

Landscapes

Rock Structures Formed by Tectonic Forces

Rocks deform in different ways depending on the type and strength of the tectonic force exerted on them. These forces lead to the formation of **folded** and **faulted** rock structures.

Folded structures

Fold mountains occur at the edge of continents, along **convergent plate boundaries**. The continental plate (in collision with either a continental or oceanic plate) is compressed by the forces exerted from both sides. The flat body of rock in the continental crust buckles or folds as it is squeezed. It doesn't fracture as it is uplifted for two reasons:

- the plates are more flexible, as the collision occurs at depths where the rocks are subjected to high temperatures;
- the process happens over a long period of time, allowing the rocks to adjust to their new position slowly without breaking.

Chapter 1: Plate Tectonics

Elements of a fold

The extent to which the rock surface has been compressed will determine the type of fold.

- The layers of rock that fold upwards form an **anticline**, which looks like an arch.
- The layers of rock that fold downwards form a **syncline**, which looks like a trough.
- The sides of a fold that join an **upfold/anticline** to a **downfold/syncline** are called the **limbs**. (Fig. 4.2)

→ **Fig. 4.2(a)** Elements of a fold.

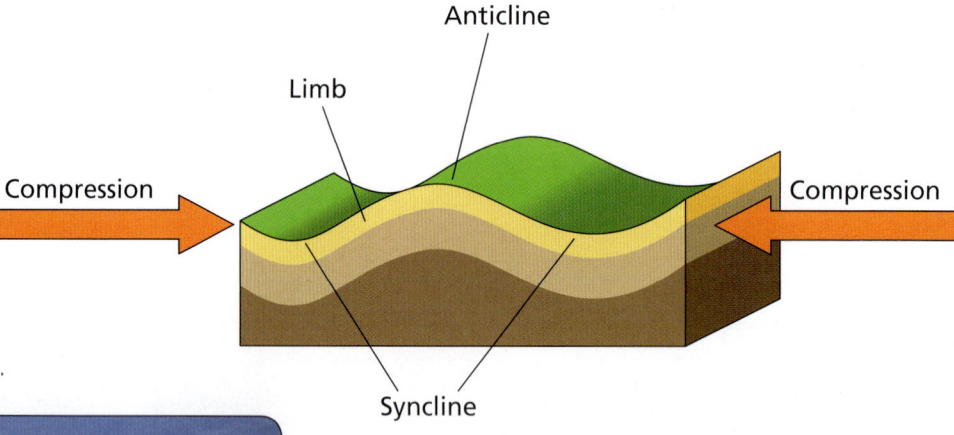

↓ **Fig. 4.2(b)** A folded rock structure.

Types of fold

- **Simple (symmetrical) fold:** The limbs on either side of the fold have the same steepness and length. Equal pressure has been applied from both sides.
- **Asymmetrical fold:** The limbs on either side of the fold are different in steepness and length. One limb is steeper and shorter than the Other, as more pressure has been applied from one side than the other.

46

- **Overfold:** Both limbs are moving in the same direction with one limb pushing over on top of the other. This is caused when more pressure has been applied from one side than the other.
- **Recumbent (overturned) fold:** Both limbs are moving in the same direction and horizontal.
- **Overthrust fold:** The pressure is so great that a fracture occurs in the rock structure and one limb is pushed over the other. The strata are no longer aligned. (Fig. 4.3)

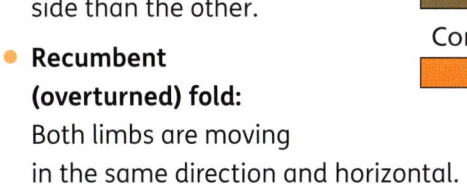

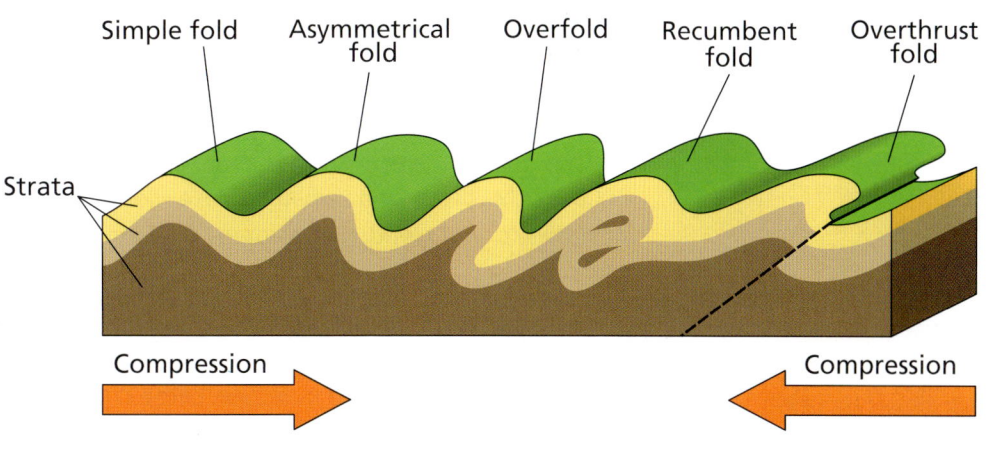

↑ **Fig. 4.3** Types of fold.

CHECK YOUR LEARNING

1. What type of stress is tension and at what type of plate boundary is it found?
2. What type of stress is compression and at what type of plate boundary is this found?
3. What type of stress is shearing and at what type of plate boundary is it found?
4. Why do some rock structures not crack while they are being folded?
5. At what type of plate boundary does folding occur?
6. What are anticlines and synclines?
7. What impact does the amount of pressure applied have on the limb of a folded structure?
8. Draw a diagram of the various types of fold.

Folding movements

Fold mountains can be dated to one of three major folding movements: **Caledonian**, **Armorican** and **Alpine** (Fig. 4.4). While the Caledonian and Armorican movements did impact on the Irish landscape, the Alpine is not represented here.

KEYWORDS

Caledonian folding
Armorican folding
Alpine folding
orogeny
upfolds
downfolds

Orogeny: A mountain building period caused by folding or faulting.

Trend: A general direction in which something is developing.

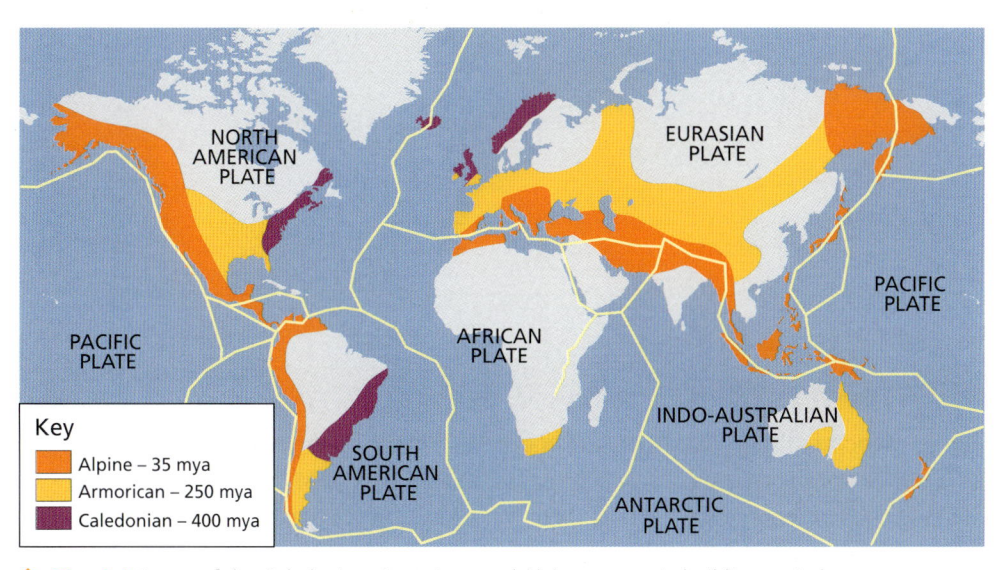

Key
- Alpine – 35 mya
- Armorican – 250 mya
- Caledonian – 400 mya

↑ **Fig. 4.4** Extent of the Caledonian, Armorican and Alpine mountain building periods.

Landscapes

> **EXAM TIP (OL)**
>
> A question on the formation of two landforms has appeared every year from 2011 to 2018, except for 2014. Each landform is worth 20 marks and the answer requires:
> - the landform being named (3 marks);
> - a named example (2 marks);
> - a description of its formation (5 SRPs × 3 marks).

Chapter 1: Plate Tectonics
Chapter 2: Volcanic Activity

> **DID YOU KNOW?**
> The Caledonian folding period is named after Caledonia, the Latin name for Scotland.
>
> The Scottish Highlands, the Scandinavian Mountains and the Appalachian Mountains in the USA were also formed during the Caledonian folding period.

→ **Fig. 4.5** Mountain ranges in Ireland formed during the Caledonian and Armorican folding movements.

> **DID YOU KNOW?**
> The Armorican folding period is named after the Armorica region in north-west France.
>
> The Hartz Mountains in Germany and the Pyrenees in France were also formed during this folding period.

Caledonian folding

The Caledonian folding movement occurred about **400 million years** ago when the Eurasian and North American plates converged. The ocean floor subducted under the two continents and sediments on the sea floor buckled up creating mountains in Connacht, Ulster and Leinster. These mountains have a **south-west to north-east directional trend**, as the forces of compression came from the north-west and south-east.

Magma also intruded into gaps in the **upfolds** during the folding process. This magma cooled slowly to form igneous rocks, such as granite, and metamorphic rocks, such as marble and quartzite. Large crystals of minerals such as mica and feldspar were formed in the rocks as the volcanic gases cooled slowly.

Mountains formed during this period originally stood higher than any that currently exist worldwide. Years of weathering and erosion have worn them down, however, and today they aren't even the tallest mountains in Ireland. Fold mountains from this period can be found in three of the four provinces:

- Nephin Beg in Connacht;
- the Derryveagh and Mourne Mountains in Ulster;
- the Wicklow Mountains in Leinster (**Fig. 4.5**).

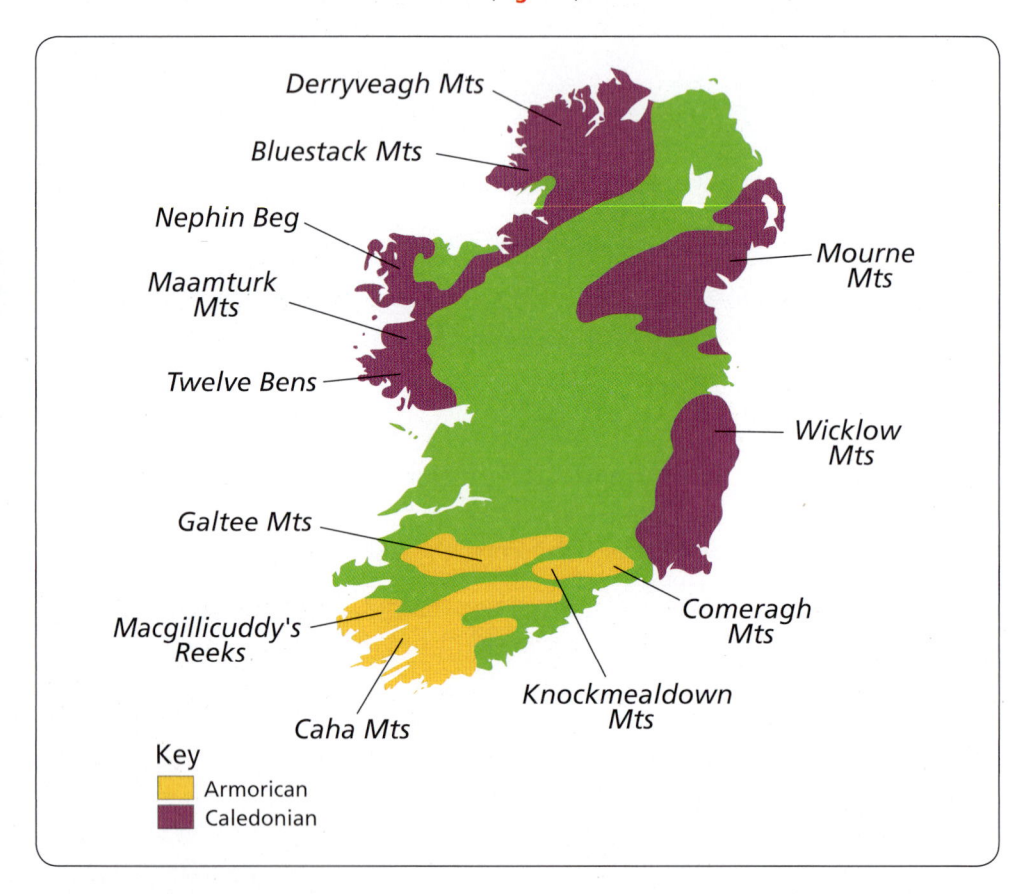

Armorican folding

The Armorican folding period occurred around **250 million years ago** when the Eurasian and African plates converged. The mountains of Munster including the Macgillicuddy's Reeks and Galtees were formed during this period. Their folds have an **east-to-west directional trend**, as the greatest force came from the south. Mountains formed during this period never reached the altitudes of those formed during the Caledonian period, as the folding took place much further away from the point of collision.

48

Stretching from the Caha Mountains in the west to the Comeragh Mountains in the east, the **Munster ridge and valley landscape** was formed during the Armorican movement (Fig. 4.5). Limestone rock, formed when Ireland existed under a warm shallow sea close to the equator, was brought to the surface as the plates collided. The upfolded limestone created ridges, which were subsequently weathered (freeze-thaw action) and eroded (rivers and glaciers). This exposed the underlying sandstone that caps the mountain ridges today. The **downfolded** limestone wasn't weathered to the same degree. Today, rivers including the Blackwater, Lee and Bandon flow in a west-to-east direction through valleys covered in limestone rock.

Alpine folding

Alpine folding, the last of the major mountain building periods, reached its peak around **30 million years ago**, when the African Plate moved north and converged with the Eurasian Plate. While subduction didn't occur, as both were continental plates, sediments in the Mediterranean Sea were uplifted to form the Alps and Apennines. The Himalayas, Rockies and Andes were also formed during this period. These mountain ranges are the highest that exist on earth today, as they haven't undergone the same degree of denudation as older mountains.

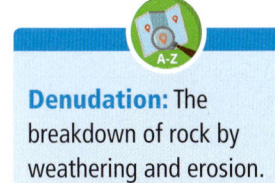

Denudation: The breakdown of rock by weathering and erosion.

EXAM LINK (HL)

Folding (30 marks)
Explain how the study of plate tectonics has helped us to understand the global distribution of fold mountains.
2010, Q2B

Marking Scheme:
Global examples of fold mountains = 2 × 2 marks
Discussion = 13 SRPs × 2 marks

EXAM LINK (OL)

Fold Mountains (30 marks)
With the aid of a diagram(s), describe and explain how fold mountains are formed.
2017, Q2C

Marking Scheme:
Named example of fold mountain = 3 marks
Diagram = 3 items × 2 marks
Explanation = 7 SRPs × 3 marks

CHECK YOUR LEARNING

1. Explain the term 'orogeny'.
2. Which plates collided during the Caledonian orogeny?
3. What directional trend do these mountains have and why?
4. Explain how granite was formed during the formation of the Wicklow Mountains?
5. How long ago did the Armorican orogeny take place?
6. How did the sandstone ridges and limestone valleys form on the Munster landscape?
7. Why do the rivers in County Cork typically flow eastwards towards the sea?
8. Explain why the Alpine folding period is represented by the highest mountain ranges on earth.

Landscapes

KEYWORDS
- normal fault
- graben fault
- reverse fault
- thrust fault
- block mountain
- tear (slip) fault
- dome structures
- horizontal structures
- uniclinal structures

Fault line: A fracture in the earth's surface.

Fault plane: The plane along which the faulted block of rock moves upwards or downwards.

Fault scarp: A step/cliff or cliff-like feature on the earth's surface caused by faulting.

Faulted structures

Faulting occurs when rocks are put under stress at divergent, convergent or transform plate boundaries. Compression, tension and shear forces lead to fractures/fault lines forming along a line of weakness in the surface rock of the earth's crust. A flat body of rock is then laterally displaced, sunken or lifted up, relative to the surrounding terrain. This can be recognised on sedimentary rock surfaces where the **strata are displaced** at the fault line. Fault lines can run for hundreds of miles or they can be very short, only affecting a small area.

Faults resulting from tension

Normal fault

A normal fault is formed at a **divergent plate boundary** when tension in the earth's crust causes it to stretch and become thinner. When the crust eventually fractures, one block of land will be displaced, moving downwards (**Fig. 4.6**).

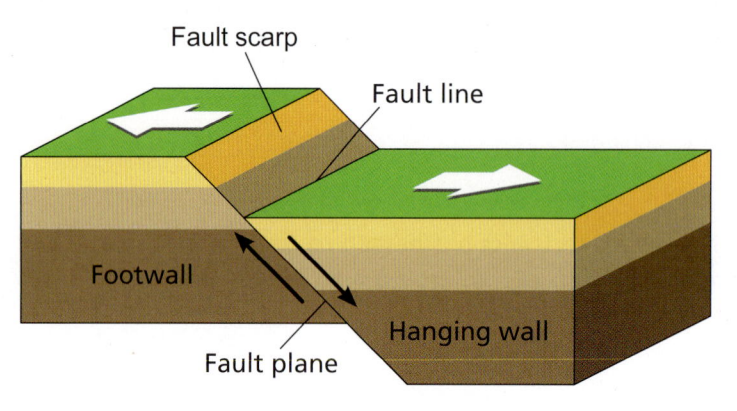

Normal fault: tension force – one section of the crust slips downwards

↑ **Fig. 4.6** Normal fault.

Graben fault

When tension causes two parallel faults, the large block of land in between may slip downwards. A **rift valley** is formed, with steep escarpments at either side. Death Valley in California and the Rhine Rift Valley in Germany are examples of this type of fault (**Fig. 4.7**).

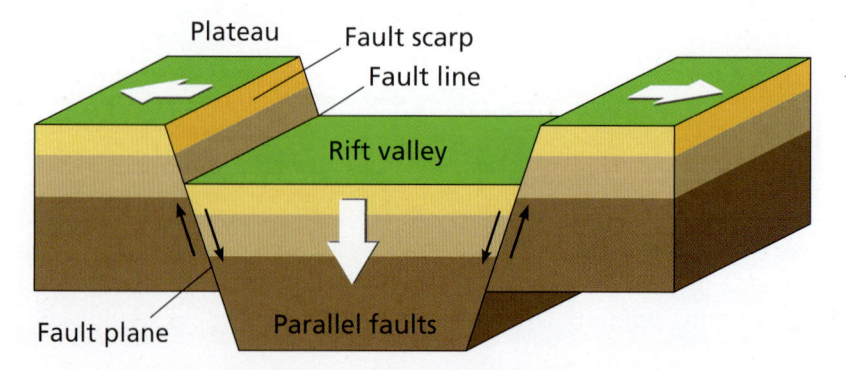

Graben fault: tension force – central block of crust sinks

↑ **Fig. 4.7** Graben fault.

4 Folding and Faulting Activity

CASE STUDY: EAST AFRICAN RIFT VALLEY

Background

The East African Rift Valley has formed as a result of faulting on the landscape. Created over the last 20 million years, it stretches approximately 4,800 km from Syria to the Zambezi River (Fig. 4.8). The movement of convection currents in a magma plume under the earth's crust caused the African continent to bulge, stretch and split. Two normal faults were created by the forces of tension and the centre portion of land slipped into the earth's crust forming a flat-floored rift valley. The land subsided to such an extent that some places in the rift valley lie more than 153 m below current sea level. The rifting process continues with the valley widening at a rate of 4 mm per year. Unless this stops, it is likely that the continent of Africa will eventually split apart. A number of features have formed in the valley as a result of the rifting process:

- volcanoes such as Mount Kilimanjaro formed as magma forced its way through fissures on the earth's surface;
- numerous lakes such as Lake Tanganyika have also been created on the floor of the rift valley.

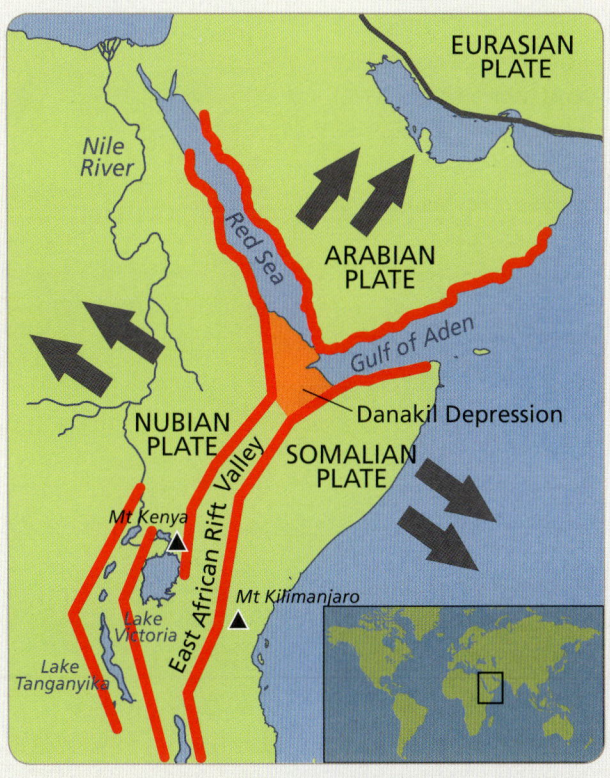

↑ **Fig. 4.8** East African Rift Valley.

Chapter 1: Plate Tectonics
Chapter 2: Volcanic Activity

Faults resulting from compression

Reverse fault

A reverse fault is formed at a **convergent plate boundary** when compression in the earth's crust causes the crust to fracture and one block of land moves upwards (Fig. 4.9).

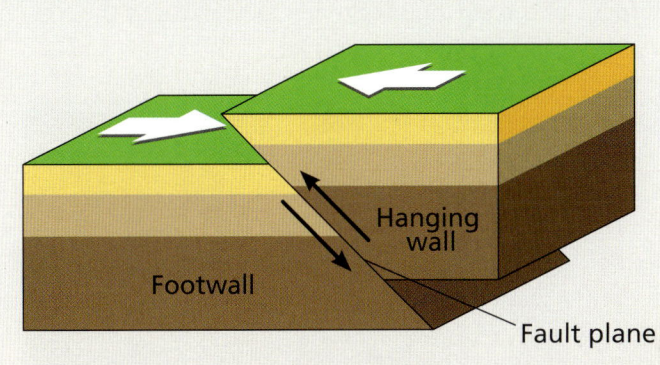

← **Fig. 4.9** Reverse fault.

Reverse fault: compression force – one section of crust is uplifted

↓ **Fig. 4.10** Thrust fault.

Thrust fault

A thrust fault is a type of reverse fault commonly found in areas where one plate is being subducted under another (e.g. **Japan**). The fault plane is inclined at an angle equal to or less than 45° (Fig. 4.10).

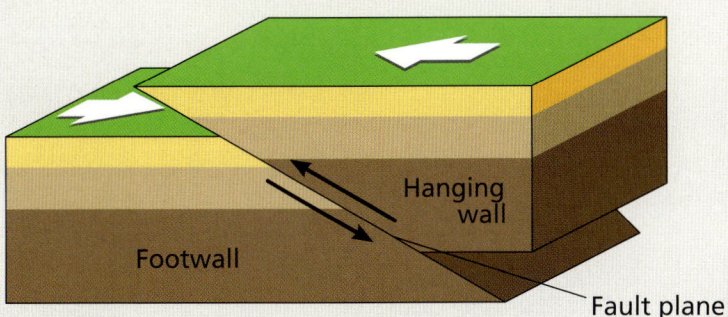

Thrust fault: compression force – angle of fault is equal or less than 45°

51

Landscapes

SKILLS ACTIVITY

Draw diagrams explaining the formation of a rift valley and a block mountain. Remember, all diagrams must have a **title** and a **frame**, and be **fully labelled**.

Block mountain

Also known as a **horst**, a **block mountain** is formed when compression creates two parallel faults and the large block of land in-between is pushed upwards, forming a hill or mountain (**Fig. 4.11**). The upthrown block is the horst. Block mountains in Ireland include the Ox Mountains in County Sligo.

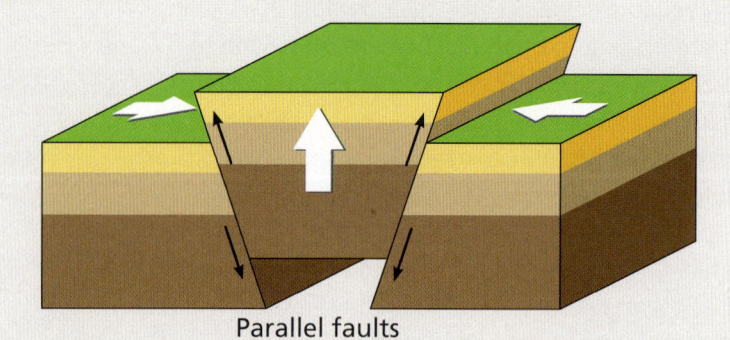

Parallel faults

Block mountain: compression force – central block of crust is uplifted

↑ **Fig. 4.11** Block mountain.

Slip fault: Another term for a tear fault.

Faults resulting from shearing

Tear fault

A tear fault is caused by lateral movement at **transform plate boundaries**. While crust is neither created nor destroyed, rocks at the edge of both plates can lock in position. Stress builds up at the boundary as convection currents continue pushing the plates laterally past each other. Earthquakes are generated when rocks at the boundary eventually break, allowing the plates to move forward very suddenly (**Fig. 4.12(a)**).

Along the San Andreas Fault line, the Pacific and North American plates are both moving north-west but at different speeds (**Fig. 4.12(b)**). Earthquakes occurring here are particularly violent, as the focus of the earthquake tends to be close to the surface of the earth's crust.

EXAM LINK (HL)

Landform Development (30 marks)

Explain how one of the following influences the development of landforms: Folding / Faulting.

2015, Q3B

Marking Scheme:
Landform identified = 2 marks
Examination = 14 SRPs × 2 marks

Tear fault: shear force – crust is horizontally displaced

↑ **Fig. 4.12(a)** Tear fault.

↑ **Fig. 4.12(b)** The San Andreas fault.

Other structures

Tectonic forces also formed some other rock structures of the Irish landscape.

Dome structures

When layers of rocks arch upward to form a circular type structure it is referred to as a **dome**. They can be formed in one of two ways:

- when compressional force is exerted on a plate;
- when rising magma raises rock upwards.

The oldest rocks become exposed at the centre of the dome when it is worn down by years of denudation. Dome structures formed in Ireland include the Slieve Bloom Mountains in Laois and Offaly.

Horizontal structures

Some rock structures are gently uplifted without any tilting, folding or faulting taking place. This can be recognised in sedimentary rock structures where the strata remain in a horizontal line such as Loop Head, County Clare.

Uniclinal structures

Some rock structures are uplifted on one side more than the other. This can be seen on Ben Bulben in County Sligo, where a slight tilt on the uplifted landscape is clearly visible (**Fig. 4.13**).

↑ **Fig. 4.13** Ben Bulbin.

CHECK YOUR LEARNING

1. List each of the forces that result in faulting.
2. In which rock structures are faults most easily recognised?
3. A normal fault is formed at which type of plate boundary?
4. A reverse fault is formed at which type of plate boundary?
5. What is another name for a block mountain?
6. What two plates are associated with the San Andreas Fault?
7. Why are earthquakes so severe in California?
8. How are dome structures formed?

Landscapes

EXAMINATION QUESTIONS
HIGHER LEVEL

Short Questions

1. Faulting

Examine the images and answer each of the following questions.

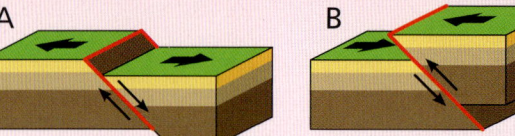

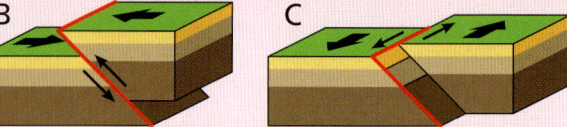

(i) Match each of the images A, B, and C with the type of fault in the table below that best matches it. *3 × 1 mark*

(ii) Indicate, by ticking the correct box, whether each of the types of fault named in the table below is most associated with compression, tension or shearing. *3 × 1 mark*

(iii) State whether the following statement is true or false. Horsts and grabens are features associated with faulting. *2 marks*

(i) Letter	Type of fault	(ii) Compression (✓)	Tension (✓)	Shearing (✓)
	Reverse fault			
	Transform fault			
	Normal fault			

2018, Part One, Q8 (8 marks)

2. Folding

(i) Match each of the diagrams A, B, C and D with the type of fold that best matches it in the table. *4 × 1 mark*

Type of fold	Letter
Asymmetrical fold	
Unfolded strata	C
Overthrust fold	
Symmetrical fold	

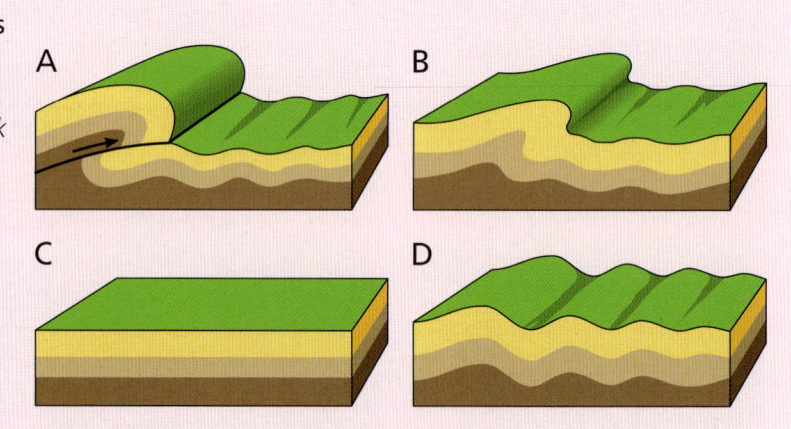

(ii) Name two periods of fold mountain building that shaped the Irish landscape over the last 400 million years. *2 × 2 marks*

2017, Part One, Q1 (8 marks)

Long Questions

3. Faulting and Landforms

Examine the diagrams and answer the following questions.

(i) Name the type of fault at A and the type of fault at B. *2 × 4 marks*

(ii) Explain briefly what causes the type of faulting at A or at B. *2 SRPs × 2 marks*

(iii) Name the landform at C and the landform at D that result from faulting. *2 × 4 marks*

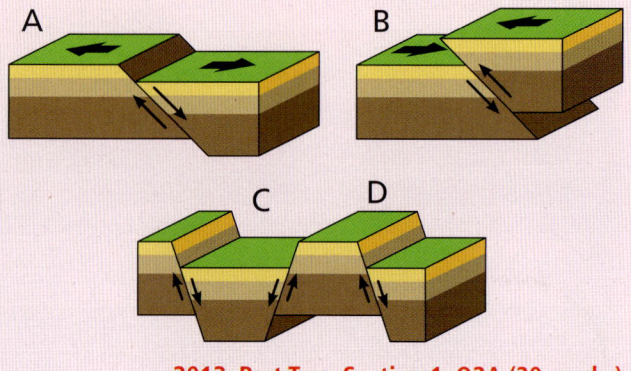

2013, Part Two, Section 1, Q2A (20 marks)

Revision Summary

Tectonic forces

- **Tension**: Rocks lengthened – divergent plate boundaries
- **Compression**: Rocks shortened – convergent plate boundaries
- **Shearing**: Sliding plates – transform plate boundaries

Other structures of deformation

- **Dome structures**: Slieve Bloom Mts
- **Horizontal structures**: Loop Head, Co. Clare
- **Uniclinal structures**: Benbulben, Co. Sligo

Folded structures

How folding occurs

- Edges of continents – convergent plate boundaries
- Plate folds as it is squeezed
- Rock doesn't fracture during uplift – collision at great depths, high temperatures = more flexible – process over a long period – rocks can adjust slowly

Elements of a fold

- **Upfold/anticline**: an arch
- **Downfold/syncline**: a trough
- **Limb**: joins upfold/anticline to a downfold/syncline

Types of a fold

- **Simple fold**: Limbs same steepness and length
- **Asymmetrical fold**: Limbs different steepness and length
- **Overfold**: Limbs moving in the same direction, one limb pushing over on top of the other
- **Recumbent (overturned) fold**: Limbs moving in the same direction and horizontal
- **Overthrust fold**: Fracture in rock structure – one limb pushed over the other – strata no longer aligned

Folding periods

Caledonian Period

- 400 mya
- Eurasian and North American plates
- Mountains in Connacht (Nephin Beg), Ulster (Mourne Mts) and Leinster (Wicklow Mts)
- South-west to north-east trend
- Magma intruded into upfolds – formed igneous (granite) and metamorphic rocks (marble and quartzite)
- Minerals (mica and feldspar) formed as volcanic gases cooled slowly
- Originally stood higher than any that currently exist – worn down by years of weathering and erosion

Armorican Period

- 250 mya
- Eurasian and African plates
- Mountains of Munster such as the **Macgillicuddy's** Reeks and Galtees
- East-to-west trend
- Smaller when formed than those of the Caledonian Period – folding further away from the point of collision
- Munster ridge and valley landscape
- Caha Mountains to the Comeragh Mountains
- Upfolded limestone created ridges – weathered and eroded
- Underlying sandstone exposed
- Blackwater, Lee and Bandon flow in a west-to-east direction through valleys covered in limestone rock

Alpine Period

- Most recent – peaked 30 mya
- African and Eurasian plates
- No subduction – both were continental plates
- Sediments in the Mediterranean Sea uplifted forming Alps and Apennines
- Himalayas, Rockies and Andes were also formed
- Highest mountain ranges on earth today – haven't undergone the same levels of denudation as older mountains

Faulting

Faults resulting from tension

- **Normal fault:** Divergent plate boundary – tension – earth's crust stretches, become thinner and eventually fractures – one block of land displaced – moves downwards
- **Graben fault:** Tension – two parallel faults – large block of land in-between slips downwards – forms rift valley with steep escarpments – Death Valley in California and the Rhine Rift Valley in Germany

Faults resulting from compression

- **Reverse fault:** Convergent plate boundary – compression – earth's crust fractures – one block of land moves upwards.
- **Thrust fault:** Type of reverse fault – plane is inclined – angle equal to or less than 45°
- **Block mountain (horst):** Compression – two parallel faults – block of land in-between pushed up forming a hill or mountain – Ox Mountains in Co. Sligo

Faults resulting from shearing

- **Tear fault:** Lateral movement – transform plate boundary – San Andreas Fault in California – Pacific and North American plates moving horizontally – no land created or destroyed but earthquakes common – violent, as focus tends to be close to the surface of the earth's crust

East African Rift Valley

- Created by faulting in the last 20 million years – stretches for over 4,800 km from Syria to the Zambezi River
- Convection currents – two normal faults created by tension – centre portion of land slipped – formed a flat-floored rift valley
- Rift valley lies more than 153 m below sea level in places
- Volcanoes (Mount Kilimanjaro) and lakes (Tanganyika) have formed on the floor of the rift valley
- Rift valley is widening by 4 mm per year – continent of Africa will eventually split apart if the rifting process continues

5 ROCKS

LEARNING INTENTIONS
Syllabus Links: 1.2, 1.3

By the end of this chapter I will be able to:
- understand and describe the rock cycle;
- recognise each rock type from a photograph;
- identify the location of each rock type;
- describe the formation of two rock types from the three rock groups found on the Irish landscape;
- explain how humans interact with the rock cycle through quarrying.

KEYWORDS
origin
minerals
texture
density
hardness
shape
rock cycle
lithification
compaction
cementation

Rocks are solid materials occurring in the earth's crust, composed of one or more **minerals**. They vary according to their:

- **origin:** where and how they were created;
- **mineral content:** rocks are composed of one or more minerals, natural substances such as calcite, quartz and gypsum formed by geological processes;
- **texture:** how rough or smooth the rock is on feeling it;
- **density:** the amount of rock comparative to the space it takes up (air may fill gaps in porous rocks);
- **hardness:** resistance to weathering and erosion;
- **shape:** how they were laid down, for example, limestone in strata and basalt in hexagonal shapes.

The **rock cycle** describes the earth's natural processes that cause **igneous**, **sedimentary** and **metamorphic** rocks to be formed, changed, destroyed and recycled (Fig. 5.1). These ongoing processes include:

- the cooling of magma/lava into solid rock;
- the melting of rock into magma during **subduction** (endogenic – internal forces);
- the breaking down of rock into sediments by the elements of weathering and erosion;
- the reformation of solid rock through the process of **lithification** (exogenic – external forces);
- the changing of a rock's structure by heat and pressure.

Lithification: Sediments are compacted and cemented together to form solid rock.

Compaction: Sediments are squeezed together by the weight of overlying layers, including water.

Cementation: Water evaporates from dissolved minerals, creating crystals that glue sediments together.

Chapter 1: Plate Tectonics
Chapter 2: Volcanic Activity

→ **Fig. 5.1** The rock cycle.

Landscapes

KEYWORDS
basalt   granite
crystals   igneous

Rock Classification

Different rock types are classified into three rock groups depending on their formation. The three main groups of rock are **igneous**, **sedimentary** and **metamorphic**.

Igneous: Comes from the Latin word *ignis*, meaning fire.

Magma: Hot, liquid rock, formed when the earth's crust is subducted and broken down in the mantle.

Plutonic rocks: Rocks formed deep beneath the earth's surface, also known as 'intrusive' rocks.

Volcanic rocks: Rocks formed on or near the earth's surface, also known as 'extrusive' rocks.

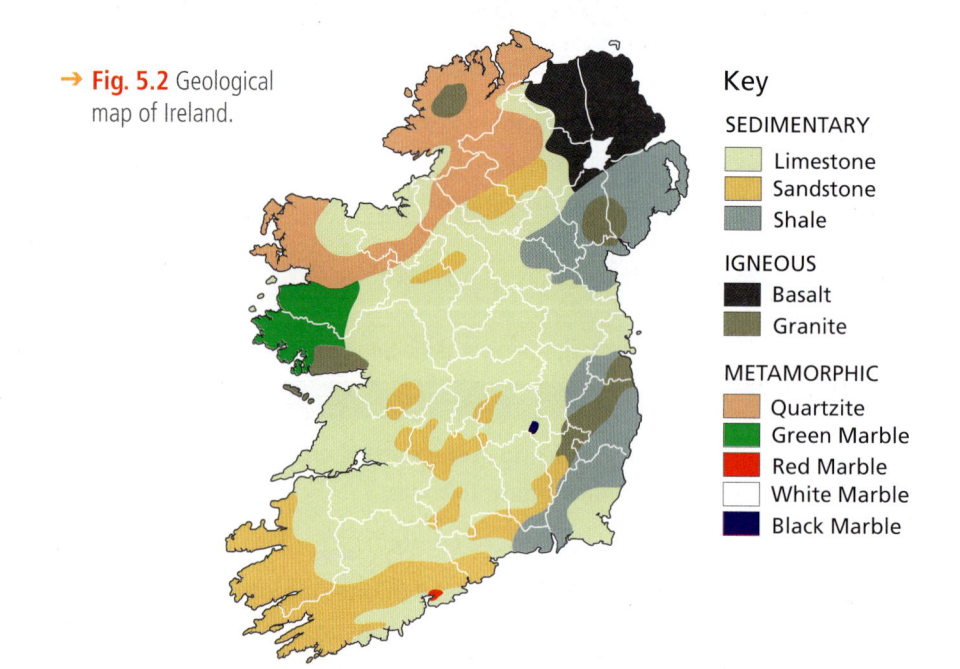

→ **Fig. 5.2** Geological map of Ireland.

Key
SEDIMENTARY
- Limestone
- Sandstone
- Shale

IGNEOUS
- Basalt
- Granite

METAMORPHIC
- Quartzite
- Green Marble
- Red Marble
- White Marble
- Black Marble

CHECK YOUR LEARNING

1. List three minerals found in rocks.
2. Rocks vary in shape. Explain this statement.
3. What processes break down rock?
4. What is Ireland's most common rock type?
5. Name the two counties in which green marble is most commonly found.
6. Explain the difference between 'plutonic' and 'volcanic' rocks.

Igneous rocks

Igneous rocks are formed when magma from the mantle cools and solidifies either within the earth's crust **(intrusive)** or on the earth's surface **(extrusive)** (Fig 5.3).

Acidic igneous rocks have a silica content of more than 55%.

Basic igneous rocks have a silica content of less than 55%.

Basalt

Irish example: *The Giant's Causeway; The Antrim–Derry Plateau* **(Fig. 5.2)**

The Antrim–Derry Plateau was formed by a number of lava flows cooling on top of one another.

Characteristics: Typically black to dark grey in colour, basalt is a smooth-textured hard rock.

Formation: Basalt is a **volcanic** (extrusive) rock formed at **divergent plate boundaries**. Approximately 65 million years ago, the Eurasian and North American plates separated, creating the Atlantic Ocean. As the plates moved apart, fissures were created on the earth's crust, allowing lava with a low silica content to pour out slowly onto the earth's surface. The lava cooled and hardened rapidly, forming a **basic** igneous rock. The rapid cooling of the lava directly affected

↑ **Fig. 5.3** Formation of intrusive and extrusive igneous rocks.

58

the rock being formed: only fine **crystals** of **quartz** had time to form in the rock. At the Giant's Causeway, the basalt contracted and cracked into **hexagonal (six-sided) columns**. Because the rock had a uniform mineral content, the cracks followed a geometric pattern (**Fig. 5.4**).

Economic value: Cut basalt is used as floor tiles and building veneer. Crushed basalt is used as road chippings and railroad ballast.

Granite

Irish example: Wicklow Mountains (Fig. 5.2)

Characteristics: Granite formed in Ireland is typically grey, but variations in colour can occur depending on the proportions of various minerals – such as potassium and quartz – found in the rock. It has a coarse-grained texture and is a hard, durable rock (**Fig. 5.5**).

Formation: Granite is a **plutonic** (intrusive) rock formed at **convergent plate boundaries**. Approximately 400 million years ago, the Eurasian and North American crustal plates collided, forming the Wicklow Mountains. During the folding process, molten magma with silica content close to 70% intruded into a large space in the upfolds beneath the earth's surface. The magma cooled slowly, as it was protected from the elements of weather by overlying layers of slate and quartzite. Over time, it formed a large, domed mass of granite known today as the **Leinster Batholith**. Large crystals of minerals, such as **feldspar**, **quartz** and **mica**, were formed in the granite – a direct result of the volcanic gases cooling slowly. The Leinster Batholith has become exposed, as the overlying rock has been worn down over millions of years by the processes of weathering and erosion.

Economic value: Granite is used in the construction of buildings and bridges. Polished granite is used in countertops and floor tiles.

↑ **Fig. 5.4** Giant's Causeway, Co. Antrim.

Granite rocks make up about 75% of the earth.

↑ **Fig. 5.5** Granite.

Chapter 1: Plate Tectonics
Chapter 2: Volcanic Activity
Chapter 4: Folding and Faulting Activity

EXAM LINK (HL)

Igneous Rocks (30 marks)
Explain the formation of igneous rocks with reference to Irish examples.
2014, Q1B and 2011, Q3B

Marking Scheme:
Two igneous rocks named = 2 × 2 marks
Examination = 13 SRPs × 2 marks

CHECK YOUR LEARNING

1. When can igneous rock be classified as 'acidic'?
2. At what type of plate boundary is basalt formed?
3. What impact did the cooling process have on the formation of crystals in basalt?
4. Why did the magma cool slowly under the Wicklow Mountains?
5. List three minerals found in granite.
6. How was the granite of the Leinster Batholith exposed?

EXAM TIP

Your answers must focus on the formation of rocks and how this influences their characteristics. Unless you are asked specifically, you won't get any marks for describing the uses of rocks.

Landscapes

Sedimentary rocks

KEYWORDS			
sedimentary	inorganic	fossil	coal
strata	limestone	joints	shale
bedding planes	chalk	permeable	conglomerate
organic	carboniferous	sandstone	breccia

Sedimentary: From the word 'sediment', which means 'small particle'.

Sedimentary rocks make up 8% of the earth's surface.

Sedimentary rocks are formed from particles of animals, sea creatures, plant life and broken down rocks. Sedimentary rocks are stratified; the sediments are laid down in **strata** (layers) and separated by horizontal gaps in the rock called **bedding planes**. They generally form on the beds of rivers, lakes or oceans, where the sediments are **lithified** (Fig. 5.6). Sedimentary rocks may be divided into two groups:

- **Organic sedimentary rocks** are formed from once living things or decayed vegetation.
- **Inorganic sedimentary rocks** are formed from the broken down sediments of other rocks.

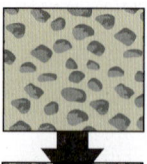

A. Deposition
Particles deposited as loosely packed sediment

B. Cementation
Over time, natural minerals (silica/calcium carbonate) glue the particles together

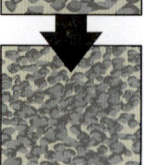

C. Compaction
The weight of the water and overlying layers squeeze the sediments together

→ Fig. 5.6 Formation of sedimentary rocks.

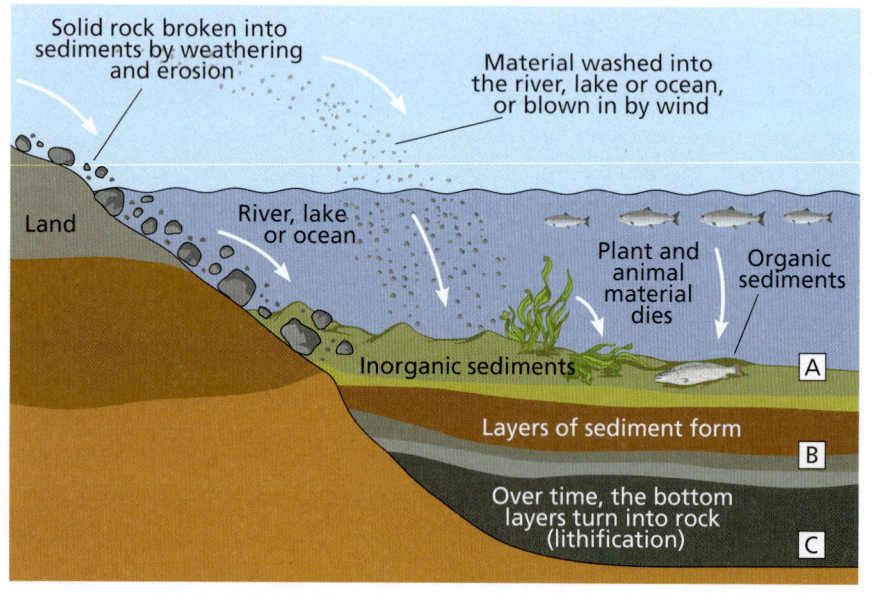

Limestone

Irish example: The Burren, Co. Clare (Fig. 5.2)

Characteristics: Different types of limestone can be identified by their colour and hardness.

- **Chalk** is a pure limestone, white in colour and very easily eroded.
- **Carboniferous limestone** is over 50% calcium carbonate. This gives it a grey colour and makes it more resistant to erosion.

Formation: Limestone, the most common rock formed in Ireland, is an organically-formed sedimentary rock. It began forming 300 million years ago, when Ireland lay under a warm, shallow sea close to the equator. Over time, the bones and shells of fish and other sea creatures built up on the sea floor. When rivers deposited sand and mud particles on top of it, the weight of these sediments compacted the dead marine matter together, pushing the seawater out of the pore spaces between the different bodies and pieces of dead matter. **Calcium carbonate** in the bones and shells of the marine life then cemented the compacted remains together. The preserved remains of sea creatures form **fossils** in the rock (Fig. 5.7(a)).

Limestone was formed in different periods with each period represented by **strata** – horizontal layers of limestone. The lower down in the earth's crust a stratum is, the older it is. Strata are separated from one another by horizontal **bedding planes**. Limestone also contains vertical cracks, or **joints**, which were formed when earth movements folded and split the rock. As a result, limestone is a **permeable** rock; water passes through the joints and bedding planes but is not passed through the body of the rock itself (Fig. 5.7(b)).

↑ **Fig. 5.7(a)** Fossil remains in limestone rock.

Economic value: Limestone is used in the making of cement and glass. Farmers use crushed limestone (lime) as a soil conditioner, as it neutralises acidic soils.

SKILLS ACTIVITY

Draw a diagram explaining the structure of limestone.

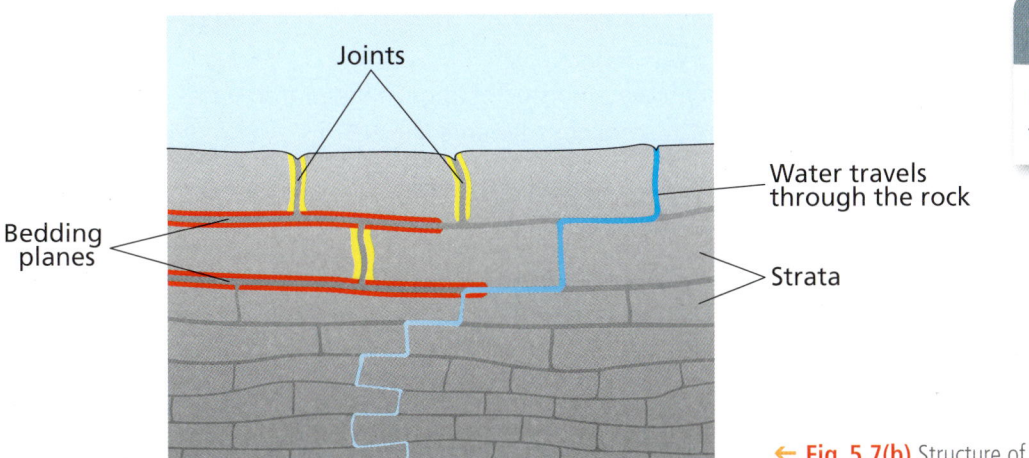

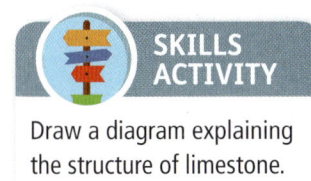

← **Fig. 5.7(b)** Structure of limestone.

Sandstone

Irish examples: The Caha Mountains; Macgillicuddy's Reeks (Fig. 5.2)

Characteristics: Old red sandstone, the most common type of sandstone found on the Irish landscape, has a reddish-brown colour due to the presence of iron oxide. It varies in hardness depending on how densely it was compacted and how much cementing agent (iron and silica) was used (Fig. 5.8).

Formation: Sandstone, the second most common rock formed in Ireland, is an inorganic sedimentary rock. Old red sandstone was formed approximately 380 million years ago, when the location of the continental plates meant Ireland was south of the equator and experienced a desert climate. Only the mountains of the north-west (Derryveagh Mountains), formed during the Caledonian folding period, were present above water. Rocks broken down by weathering and erosion were transported from the region by flash floods. Later, the sediments of fine sand were deposited in **strata** (layers) on the bed of a shallow sea. Over time, the sand was compressed by the weight of its own material and the weight of the seawater on top of it. This pushed any water out of the pore spaces before **calcium carbonate**, **iron** and **silica** cemented the sand grains together, forming a solid sandstone rock. In some instances, the preserved remains of sea creatures are seen as **fossil** remains in the rock.

↑ **Fig. 5.8** Old red sandstone.

Landscapes

Chapter 1: Plate Tectonics
Chapter 4: Folding and Faulting Activity

Folding during the Armorican movement caused the sandstone mountains of Munster to rise above sea level and occupy the position they currently hold.

Economic value: Sandstone is used as a decorative stone in sculptures, headstones or as paving stones.

Other sedimentary rocks

Coal, another organically-formed sedimentary rock, can be found in Arigna, County Roscommon. It is formed when dead vegetation is compacted by deposits of sand, silt and clay before it has decayed.

Shale, an inorganic sedimentary rock, can be found on the summit of Slieve Elva, the highest point of the Burren. It is formed when thin layers of mud and clay are deposited and lithified at the bottom of lakes and seas. Typically dark grey in colour, it contains minerals of **clay**, **quartz** and **calcite**. Fossil remains also commonly occur in this rock.

Conglomerates are coarse-grained sedimentary rocks composed of rounded fragments that have been compacted and cemented together by smaller, sand-sized sediments.

Breccia is a sedimentary rock composed of large, angular fragments, compacted and cemented together by smaller sediments (**Fig. 5.9**).

EXAM LINK (HL)

Sedimentary Rocks (30 marks)

Explain the formation of sedimentary rocks with reference to Irish examples.

2015, Q2B and 2009, Q2B

Marking Scheme:
Two sedimentary rocks named = 2 × 2 marks
Examination = 13 SRPs × 2 marks

EXAM LINK (OL)

Rocks (40 marks)

(i) Name two examples of sedimentary rocks.
(ii) State two different locations where sedimentary rocks are found.
(iii) Describe and explain how sedimentary rocks are formed.

2017, Q1B

Marking Scheme:
Two sedimentary rocks named = 2 × 3 marks
Two Irish locations named = 2 × 2 marks
Formation described = Two sedimentary rocks × 5 SRPs × 3 marks

Sand → COMPACTION/CEMENTATION → Sandstone
Mud/Clay → COMPACTION/CEMENTATION → Shale
Rounded fragments → COMPACTION/CEMENTATION → Conglomerate
Angular fragments → COMPACTION/CEMENTATION → Breccia

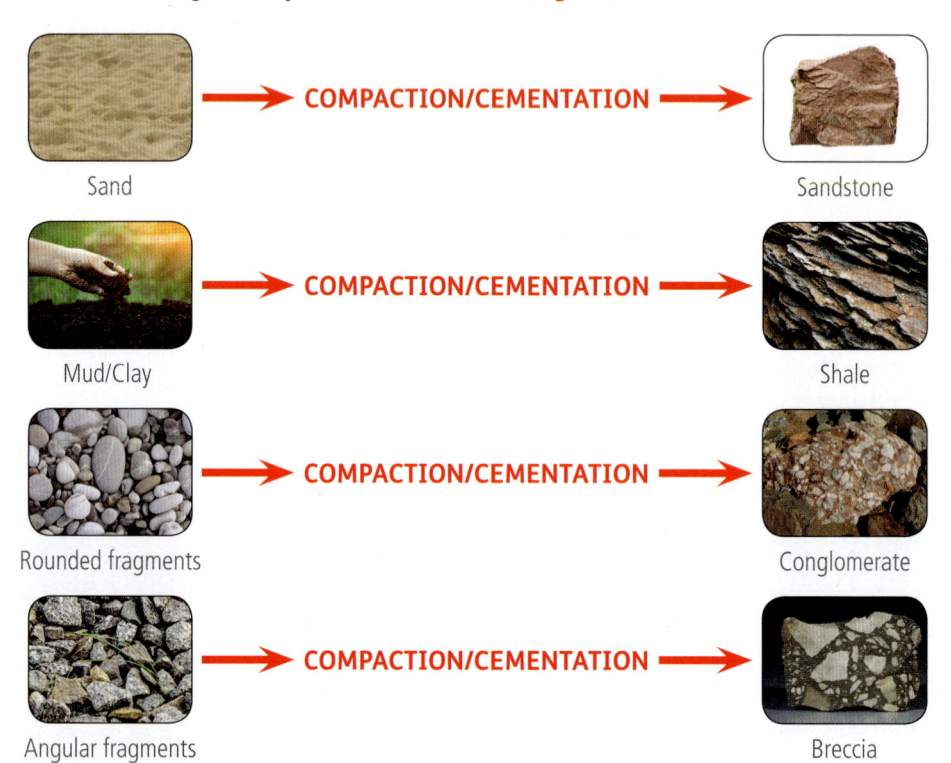

↑ **Fig. 5.9** Sandstone, shale, conglomerate and breccia are formed on the basis of parent material and particle size.

CHECK YOUR LEARNING

1. Explain how 'organic' and 'inorganic' sedimentary rocks differ from each other.
2. Explain the term 'lithification'.
3. What is a fossil?
4. What does 'permeable' mean?
5. List two types of limestone and explain two differences in their characteristics.
6. How is coal formed?
7. List three cementing agents found in sandstone.
8. List three minerals typically found in shale.

Metamorphic rocks

Metamorphic rocks are formed when igneous or sedimentary rocks are subjected to great heat and/or pressure. As it changes form the new metamorphic rock is compacted into a smaller volume, while many low temperature minerals are also transformed into high temperature minerals. This makes it denser and more resistant to weathering or erosion than the original rock.

Metamorphic rocks are formed in one of two ways.

- **Regional metamorphism (dynamic)**: Friction at convergent plate boundaries creates great heat and pressure which change the composition and texture of rocks over a large area, for example, a **zone of subduction**.
- **Contact metamorphism (thermal)**: Rising molten magma changes the composition and texture of rocks in a small surrounding area, for example, a **volcanic intrusion**. (Fig. 5.10)

KEYWORDS

regional/dynamic metamorphism
contact/thermal metamorphism
marble
gneiss
quartzite

Chapter 1: Plate Tectonics
Chapter 2: Volcanic Activity

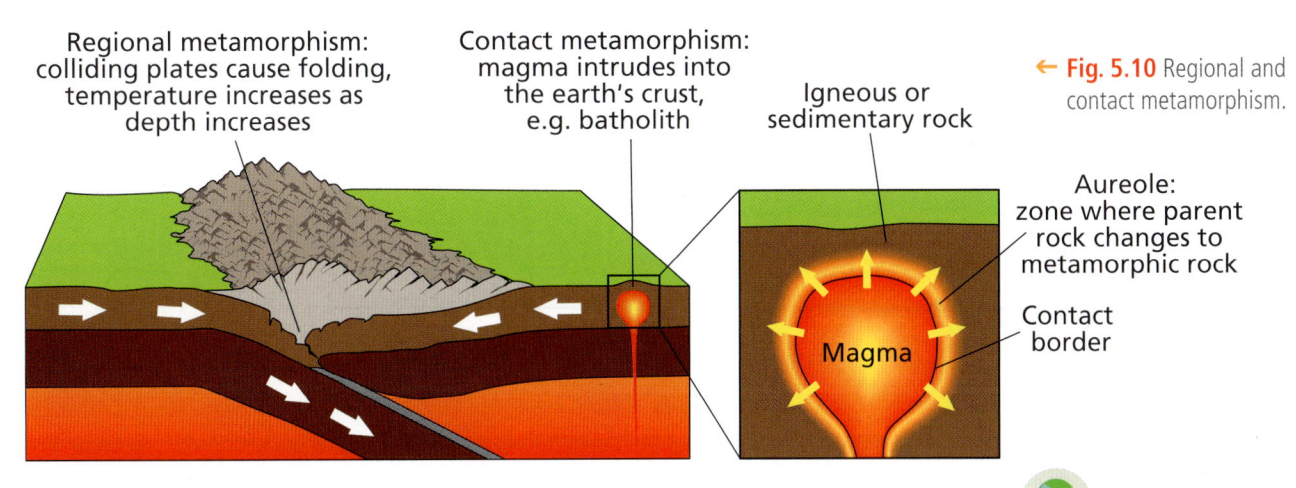

Regional metamorphism: colliding plates cause folding, temperature increases as depth increases

Contact metamorphism: magma intrudes into the earth's crust, e.g. batholith

Igneous or sedimentary rock

Aureole: zone where parent rock changes to metamorphic rock

Contact border

Magma

← Fig. 5.10 Regional and contact metamorphism.

Marble

Irish example: Connemara; Kilkenny; Cork (Fig. 5.2)

Characteristics: Marble is a coarse-grained hard rock, commonly polished to give it a smooth texture.

Formation: Marble is a crystalline rock, formed when limestone or chalk changes form as a result of **regional (dynamic) metamorphism** (Fig. 5.11). It is formed at convergent plate boundaries, where the **limestone** is changed due to the great heat and pressure caused by the friction of two colliding plates. During metamorphosis, **calcite** minerals in limestone are re-crystallised creating a denser rock composed of interlocking calcite crystals. Greater levels of metamorphosis produce larger calcite crystals.

Pure white marble, such as that found in Carrara, Italy, is formed from pure limestone with no impurities. Impurities in limestone react in different ways to the intense heat, resulting in varying colours of marble. For example, serpentine in limestone gives Connemara marble a green colour, while carbon gives Kilkenny marble a black colour. The red marble found in Cork is due to the presence of iron oxide (rust) found in the original limestone.

Economic value: Marble is highly valued as a decorative stone in building or as an ornamental stone for sculptures.

DID YOU KNOW?

Gneiss is most commonly formed from granite, but can also be formed from sandstone and shale at very high temperatures.

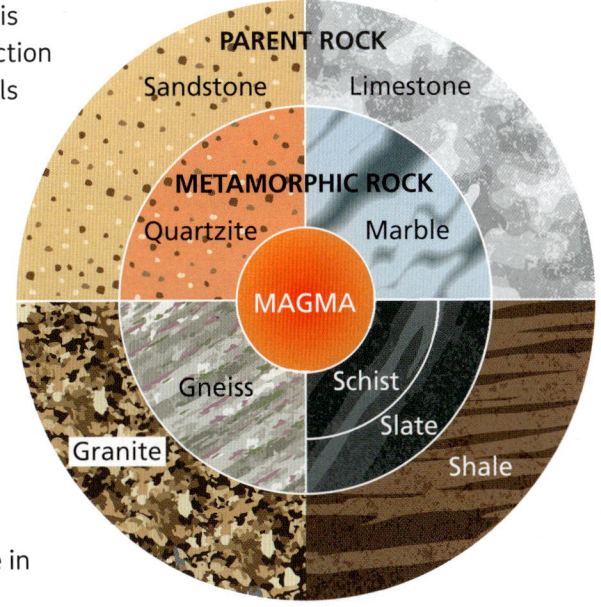

PARENT ROCK
Sandstone | Limestone
METAMORPHIC ROCK
Quartzite | Marble
MAGMA
Gneiss | Schist
Granite | Slate
Shale

↑ Fig. 5.11 Metamorphic rocks and their associated parent rocks.

63

Landscapes

> Metamorphism occurs at temperatures between 250°C and 850°C.
>
> Larger crystals are formed on the new metamorphic rock.

Metamorphic: From the Greek words '*meta*', meaning change, and '*morphe*', meaning form.

Chapter 1: Plate Tectonics
Chapter 2: Volcanic Activity

Quartzite

Irish example: Errigal, Co. Donegal; Hill of Howth, Co. Dublin (**Fig. 5.2**)

Characteristics: Quartzite is a medium-grained hard rock that exists in a variety of colours.

Formation: Sandstone is the parent rock of quartzite, a metamorphic rock formed as a result of **contact (thermal) metamorphism** (**Fig. 5.11**). It was formed approximately 400 million years ago, when the Eurasian and North American plates collided during the Caledonian folding period. During the folding process, molten magma intruded into spaces in the upfolds beneath the earth's surface and came into contact with sandstone. As the porous sandstone grains were superheated and pressurised, they chemically changed to **quartz**. At the same time, spaces between the grains were filled with **silica**, cementing the rock. The extreme heat and pressure in the surrounding region then caused the new non-porous and harder quartzite rock to form.

Economic Value: Polished quartzite is increasingly being used as countertops. Crushed quartzite is used to surface roads and in railway ballast.

EXAM LINK (HL)

Metamorphic Rocks (30 marks)

Explain the formation of metamorphic rocks with reference to Irish examples.

2013, Q1B and 2010, Q1C

> **Marking Scheme:**
> Two metamorphic rocks named = 2 × 2 marks
> Examination = 13 SRPs × 2 marks

EXAM LINK (OL)

Rocks (30 marks)

(i) Name one example of an igneous rock and state one location where it can be found.
(ii) Name one example of a metamorphic rock and state one location where it can be found.
(iii) Describe how igneous rocks are formed OR Describe how metamorphic rocks are formed.

2018, Q1B

> **Marking Scheme:**
> Igneous/Metamorphic rock named = 3 marks + 3 marks
> Irish location named = 3 marks + 3 marks
> Formation described = 6 SRPs × 3 marks for chosen rock

CHECK YOUR LEARNING

1. What does 'metamorphic' mean?
2. How does the structure of a rock change when it becomes a metamorphic rock?
3. What impact does this have on the rock's resistance?
4. Explain the term 'regional metamorphism'.
5. Explain the term 'contact metamorphism'.
6. What is the parent rock of marble?
7. List three colours of marble and explain how the marble got these colours.
8. Outline two uses of marble.
9. What is the parent rock of quartzite?
10. Explain how quartzite was formed in Ireland.

Active and Passive Plate Margins

Igneous and metamorphic rocks are both formed at **active plate margins**. This is evident along the west coast of the North American continent, where an oceanic plate (Pacific Plate) is subducting under a continental plate (North American Plate). Igneous rocks were formed when magma cooled above and below the earth's surface, while metamorphic rocks formed due to thermal or regional metamorphism at the plate boundary. Active plate margins are usually marked by earthquakes, folding and volcanic mountain belts on the continental plate.

Sedimentary rocks are typically found at **passive plate margins** which are found in the interior of a continental plate, away from crustal boundaries. Sedimentary rocks form here when deposits of other rock sediments or vegetation have been compressed and cemented together (Fig. 5.12).

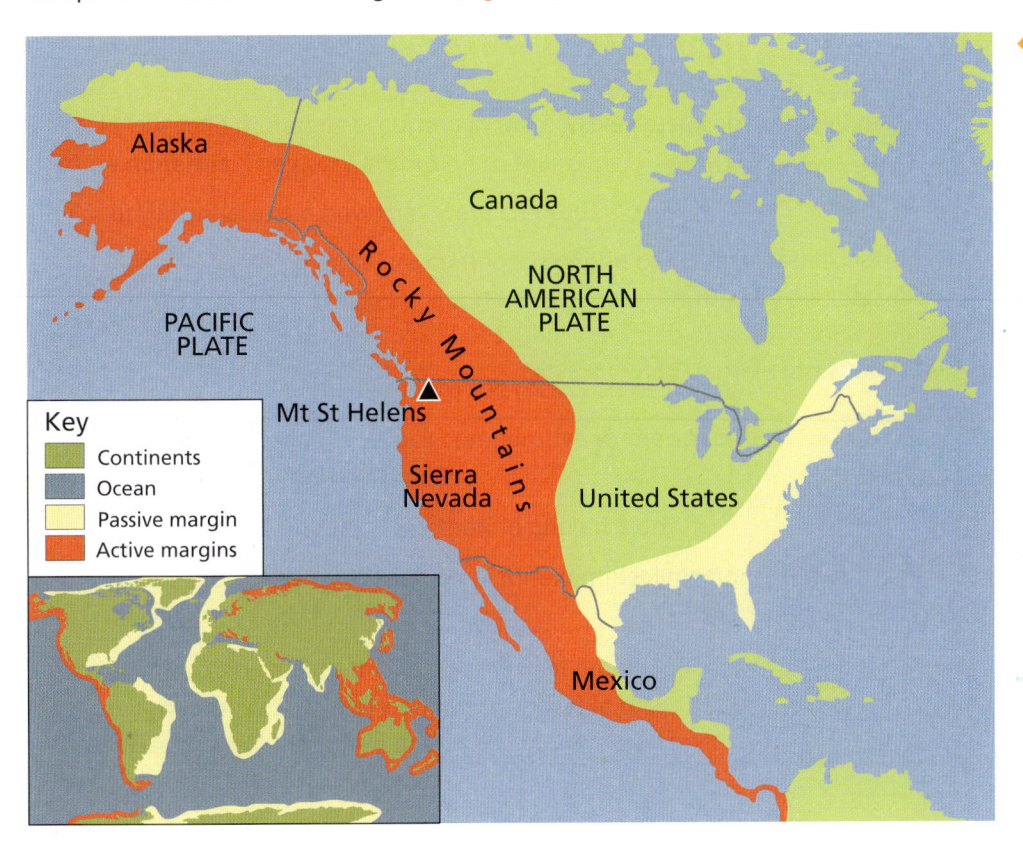

KEYWORDS
plate margin
active plate margin
passive (trailing)

Chapter 1: Plate Tectonics
Chapter 2: Volcanic Activity

← **Fig. 5.12** Active and passive plate margins in North America.

Trailing plate margins: Another term for passive plate margins.

Human Interaction with the Rock Cycle

Humans interact with the rock cycle in many different ways, notably through the processes of exploration and mining.

- **Oil and gas exploration:** Oil and gas are non-renewable resources formed over millions of years when plants and animals decomposed under great heat and pressure beneath the sea floor. Humans extract this oil and gas from underground rock reservoirs to use as a source of energy.
  The Kinsale gas field was discovered in the Celtic Sea in 1971, while the Corrib gas field was discovered 70 km off the Mayo coastline in 1996. Gas exploited from these fields is used to supply a great deal of Ireland's home heating and electricity needs.
- **Shaft mining:** This is the extraction of valuable minerals such as gold, silver, iron ore and coal, which were created in **seams** beneath the earth's surface. Vertical tunnels called **shafts** are dug from the earth's surface down to the seam and the minerals are extracted.

EXAM TIP

An examination of 'Human interaction with Quarrying / The Extraction of Building Materials' has appeared as:
- a 30-mark Higher Level question in 2006, 2007, 2009, 2010, 2011, 2013, 2015 and 2018 (15 SRPs);
- a 30-mark Ordinary Level question in 2007, 2010, 2013, 2014, 2016, 2017 and 2018 (10 SRPs).

KEYWORDS
oil and gas exploration
shafts
mining
mineral seam
quarrying
channelling
plug and feather
explosives

Landscapes

CASE STUDY: QUARRYING – THE EXTRACTION OF BUILDING MATERIALS

The extraction of rock from quarries on the earth's surface has provided building material in Ireland for over 7,000 years.

Quarries are also referred to as 'opencast mines' or 'pits'. In the New Stone Age (Neolithic Period), quarried rock was used to build stone walls and megalithic monuments such as passage graves and portal dolmens. The Normans used quarried rock to build castles, town walls, roads and bridges, as it was stronger than the timber structures built by previous generations.

Quarry operators today use several methods to remove rock depending on the type involved and whether it's going to be used as a **dimension stone** or as an **aggregate**.

Dimension stone, which is used in wall covering (veneer), sills, curbing or flagstone, is removed by:

- **levering:** Open fractures or weak planes are expanded using levers and large blocks of rock are removed. This method works best in sedimentary rocks, as joints and bedding planes provide natural planes of weakness.
- **channelling:** Channelling, or **carving**, is commonly used to remove large slices (20–30-ton blocks) of rock such as marble and granite. Wire saws with diamond- and tungsten-tipped cutting heads slice through rock, like a giant cheese-cutting wire.
- **splitting:** This method works best in quartz-rich rocks such as granite which have preferred splitting directions defined by microfractures in the quartz. New fractures are created using hammering, heating, blasting or a wedging method called **plug and feather**.

↑ Fig. 5.13(a) Plug and feather method.

Plug and feather method: The metal wedge (the plug) and two shims (the feathers) are inserted into pre-drilled holes with the 'ears' of the feathers facing the direction of the desired split (**Fig. 5.13**). The plugs are struck in sequence until a crack appears along the line that was scored on the surface and the stone splits apart allowing it to be levered away. Once the rock is removed, guillotines cut it into particular shapes and sizes depending on its intended use (**Fig 5.14**).

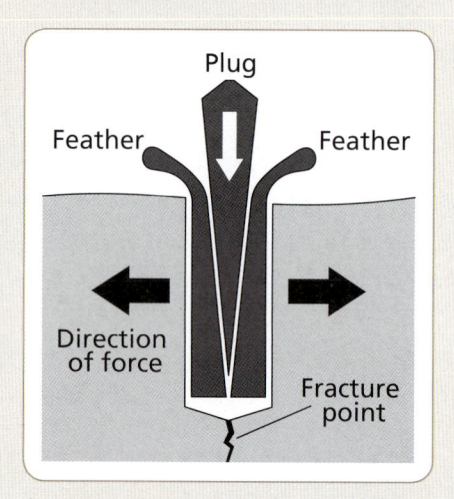

↑ Fig. 5.13(b) Plug and feather method.

Aggregates such as sand, gravel and stone are also quarried for the construction industry. Quarries are typically located close to highly populated areas due to the high cost of transporting the low value product.

> **DID YOU KNOW?**
> Aggregates are the most mined minerals in the world.

Crushed stone is usually made of granite, basalt, limestone or gneiss. During extraction, explosives are placed in pre-drilled holes and a large block is 'blasted'. The rock pile is broken into smaller pieces in a crushing machine and then it's washed. Finally, the material is screened into different sizes, shapes and types of stone to create distinct product stockpiles. Afterwards the crushed stone is used in ready-mixed-concrete, concrete blocks, bricks, road building materials such as asphalt, and ballast for railroads (**Fig. 5.16**).

↑ Fig. 5.14 Slab of rock being cut with a guillotine.

Positive impacts of quarrying

- Quarrying benefits the Irish economy:
  - Direct employment is created in the operation and maintenance of quarries. Indirect employment opportunities are also created for hauliers, mechanics, etc.
  - Quarrying provides a secure supply of raw materials, free of price fluctuations, for local industries such as cement, concrete and glass.
- Development contributions to local councils are used to improve local amenities such as roads.

Fig 5.15 The GPO in Dublin was rebuilt after the 1916 Rising using granite from the Glencullen quarry.

Negative impacts of quarrying

- Noise, dust and heavy goods traffic generated by quarries can damage people's quality of life.
- Quarries and their rusting machinery take from the beauty of the rural landscape.
- Quarry lakes formed by seasonal flooding are safety hazards if local people decide to swim in them.

→ **Fig. 5.16** Irish cement use crushed stone from its own quarry in Limerick as one of its major ingredients in the production of cement.

EXAM LINK (OL)

Human Interaction with the Rock Cycle (30 marks)

Discuss how humans interact with the rock cycle with reference to quarrying.

2018, Q2C

Marking Scheme:
Description/explanation = 10 SRPs × 3 marks

EXAM LINK (HL)

Human Interaction with the Rock Cycle (30 marks)

Humans interact with the rock cycle in a number of ways. Describe and explain how this interaction with the rock cycle takes place, with reference to the extraction of building materials.

2018, Q3B

Marking Scheme:
Description/explanation = 15 SRPs × 2 marks

CHECK YOUR LEARNING

1. What is an 'active' plate margin and where can one be found?
2. What is a 'passive' plate margin and where can one be found?
3. What did Ireland's first settlers use quarried rock for?
4. What did the Normans use quarried rock for?
5. Why did they decide to use rock for this purpose?
6. Explain the 'plug and feather' method of quarrying rocks.
7. What type of rock is 'channelled'?
8. List one use of rock that has been quarried using explosives.
9. Explain one positive impact of quarrying.
10. Explain one negative impact of quarrying.

Landscapes

EXAMINATION QUESTIONS
ORDINARY LEVEL

Short Questions

1. Rock Cycle

Examine the diagram of the rock cycle and answer each of the following questions.

(i) Match each of the letters on the rock cycle A, B and C with the stage in the rock cycle in the table most associated with it. *3 × 2 marks*

(ii) State whether each of the following statements is true or false.

(a) Marble is an example of a metamorphic rock. *2 marks*

(b) Fossils can be found in sedimentary rocks. *2 marks*

2018, Part One, Q1 (10 marks)

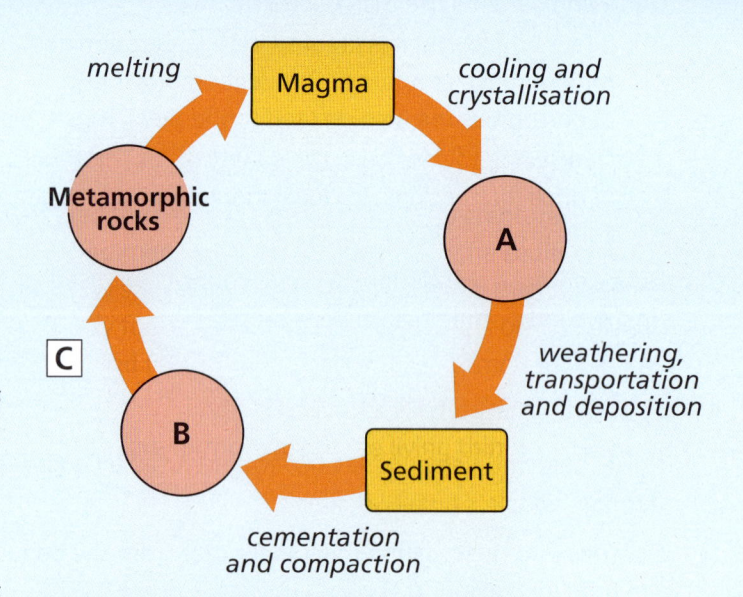

Stage in rock cycle	Letter
Heat and pressure	
Sedimentary rock	
Igneous rock	

HIGHER LEVEL

Short Questions

2. Rocks

(i) The list below contains a number of source materials from which rocks are formed and a number of metamorphic rocks.

Sand   **Marble**   **Shells and fish bones**   **Gneiss**   **Magma**   **Quartzite**

Complete the table by inserting the correct terms from the list, to match each of the rocks named in the table with: (a) the source material most associated with it and (b) the metamorphic rock most associated with it. *6 × 1 mark*

Rock name	Source material	Metamorphic rock
Sandstone		
Limestone		
Granite		

(ii) Name the rocks most associated with each of the following Irish locations. *2 × 1 mark*

(a) The Antrim Plateau   (b) The Burren

2016, Part One, Q4 (8 marks)

3. Rocks

The table contains information on rocks regarding their name, category, location in Ireland and the name of the metamorphic rock they can become following metamorphosis. Complete the table by inserting the correct term from the list in its correct position in the table. One row of the table is completed for you. *8 × 1 mark*

68

5 Rocks

Sedimentary	Central Plain of Ireland	Sandstone	Gneiss
Igneous	Marble	Wicklow Mountains	Granite
Mountains of Munster	Quartzite	Sedimentary	Limestone

Name of rock	Category of rock	Location in Ireland	Metamorphic rock
Limestone	Sedimentary	Central Plain of Ireland	Marble

2013, Part One, Q12 (8 marks)

Revision Summary

Igneous rocks

Basalt

- Volcanic (extrusive) rock – divergent plate boundaries
- 65 mya – Eurasian and North American plates separated
- Fissures created – low silica lava poured out
- Cooled and hardened rapidly – 'basic' igneous rock
- Rapid cooling = small crystals of quartz
- Giant's Causeway = hexagonal columns
- Black to dark grey in colour
- Smooth-textured, hard
- Cut basalt = floor tiles and building veneer
- Crushed basalt = road chippings and railway ballast

Granite

- Plutonic (intrusive) rock - convergent plate boundaries
- 400 mya – Eurasian and North American plates collided – Caledonian folding = Wicklow Mountains
- Magma intrusion – silica content approximately 70%
- Cooled slowly – protected by overlying slate and quartzite
- Formed domed mass of granite = Leinster Batholith
- Cooled slowly – minerals formed = feldspar, quartz, etc.
- Granite exposed by weathering and erosion
- Typically grey, variations in colour depending on minerals
- Coarse-grained texture, hard, durable
- Construction of buildings and bridges
- Polished granite is used in countertops and floor tiles

Sedimentary rocks

Limestone

- Organically-formed sedimentary rock
- 300 mya – Ireland under warm, shallow sea near equator
- Remains of fish and sea creatures collected on sea floor
- Rivers deposited sand and mud particles on top
- Seawater pushed out of the pore spaces
- Cementing agent = calcium carbonate
- Fossil remains
- Strata – a horizontal layer of limestone
- Bedding planes = horizontal gaps
- Joints = vertical cracks formed by folding
- Permeable rock
- Types = chalk/carboniferous limestone
- In cement and glass; as a soil conditioner

Sandstone

- Inorganic sedimentary rock
- 380 mya – old red sandstone formed
- Desert-type climate – south of equator
- Mountains of the north-west (e.g. Derryveagh Mountains)
- Rocks broken down by denudation
- Sand deposited in strata on shallow seabed
- Compressed by own weight and seawater
- Sand grains cemented by iron and silica
- Armorican folding = mountains of Munster
- Reddish-brown colour – iron oxide
- Hardness depends on compaction and cementation
- Decorative stone in sculptures, headstones; paving stones

Metamorphic rocks

Marble

- Coarse-grained hard rock - polished for smooth texture
- Crystalline rock – limestone/chalk changes by regional (dynamic) metamorphism – convergent plate boundaries
- Heat and pressure – friction of two colliding plates
- Calcite minerals re-crystallise forming denser rock
- Pure white marble – no added impurities – Carrara, Italy
- Green marble – serpentine – Connemara
- Black marble – carbon – Kilkenny
- Red marble – iron oxide – Cork
- Decorative building stone; ornamental stone

Quartzite

- Medium-grained hard rock that exists in a variety of colours
- Sandstone changed – contact (thermal) metamorphism
- 400 mya – Eurasian and North American plates collided – Caledonian folding
- Volcanic intrusion during folding
- Porous sandstone grains chemically changed to quartz
- Spaces between the grains filled with silica
- Extreme heat and pressure = new non-porous and harder quartzite rock
- Polished = countertops; crushed = surface roads

Human interaction with the rock cycle – Quarrying and extraction of building materials

History

- Neolithic Period – stone walls, megalithic monuments, etc.
- Norman Period – castles, town walls, roads and bridges

Dimension stone

- Veneer, sills, curbing, flagstone
- Levering = joints and bedding planes
- Channelling = carving with wire saws
- Splitting = plug and feather
- Cut by guillotine – shapes and sizes

Aggregates

- Sand, gravel, stone
- High transport costs/low value
- Blasted, crushed, washed
- Screened into size, shape, type
- Concrete, blocks, bricks, asphalt, etc.

Positive impact

- Direct and indirect employment
- Secure supply of raw materials – free of price fluctuations
- Development contributions – improve local amenities

Negative impact

- Pollution + congestion = damaging effect on quality of life
- Quarries and rusting machinery = destroys rural landscape
- Quarry lakes due to seasonal flooding = safety hazards

6 WEATHERING PROCESSES AND LANDFORMS

LEARNING INTENTIONS
Syllabus Links: 1.2, 1.4

By the end of this chapter I will be able to:
- explain the differences between erosion and weathering;
- examine the factors that influence the rate at which weathering occurs;
- recognise each of the weathering processes and the features they form on the landscape from a diagram or photograph, or from an Ordnance Survey (OS) map;
- describe each of the weathering processes that shape the landscape;
- explain how weathering can form distinctive rock landscapes;
- describe the formation of a surface and/or sub-surface feature from a karst region.

KEYWORDS

weathering
denudation
mechanical
chemical
biological

Weathering occurs when rocks, soils and minerals on the earth's surface are broken down by natural forces, including weather, climate, plants and animals. Weathered particles are not removed from the area in which they are broken down. There are three types of weathering:

- **Mechanical weathering** typically occurs in areas with extremes of temperature. While the rock is physically broken down into smaller pieces, its chemical composition is not altered.
- **Chemical weathering** is associated with wet and humid conditions. Rocks decay or dissolve as their chemical composition is altered.
- **Biological weathering** is the breakdown of rock by the actions of plants and animals.

Denudation: The collective name for the weathering and erosion of rocks on the earth's surface.

Erosion: When rocks are broken down and removed by agents such as wind, water or ice. The broken down rock is then transported to a new location by the agent that broke it down.

Physical weathering: Another name for mechanical weathering.

Factors Affecting the Rate of Weathering

Rock type: Each rock type is composed of different minerals. Rocks containing soft minerals, such as feldspar, calcite, and iron, weather more rapidly than rocks containing harder minerals, such as quartz.

Surface area: Rocks with a large surface area weather at a faster rate. Smaller pieces of rock and more porous rocks have a larger surface area exposed to the elements, therefore accelerating the actions of weathering.

Climate: Weathering is accelerated in areas with high levels of precipitation and wide temperature ranges.

Vegetation: Bare surfaces are weathered more rapidly than surfaces covered by vegetation.

Human activity: Pollution accelerates the weathering process. When fossil fuels such as coal, oil and gas are burned, carbon dioxide and other gases are released into the air. These gases dissolve in the rainwater, forming acid rain, which dissolves minerals in rocks, weathering them.

Landscapes

CHECK YOUR LEARNING

1. What is denudation?
2. What is the difference between weathering and erosion?
3. What is the most basic difference between mechanical and chemical weathering?
4. What is biological weathering?
5. How can rock type affect the rate at which weathering occurs?
6. List three other factors that affect the rate at which weathering occurs.

KEYWORDS

freeze-thaw action
scree (talus)
exfoliation (onion peeling)
diurnal temperature range
salt crystallisation
honeycomb
pressure release (unloading)

Mechanical Weathering Processes

Freeze-thaw action

Example: *Croagh Patrick, Co. Mayo*

Freeze-thaw action commonly occurs in mountainous areas where **temperatures fluctuate above and below the freezing point of water**. Mountainous areas have high precipitation levels, mainly due to relief rainfall and snowfall. Water from the rain and melting snow gathers in the joints of rocks, where it freezes when temperatures drop below 0°C at night. As the water changes to ice, its volume expands approximately 9%, widening the joint in the rock. During the day, temperatures rise above 0°C, allowing the ice to melt and the water to go further into the rock. As freeze-thaw action repeats itself over time, the cracks in the rock increase in size until the rock eventually cracks along its joints. Sharp angular pieces of rock called **scree** break away and move down slope under the influence of gravity (Fig. 6.1).

Freeze-thaw action: Also referred to as 'frost action' or 'frost shattering'.

Scree: Also known as 'talus'.

Joints: Cracks or fissures in the rock.

→ **Fig. 6.1(a)** Freeze-thaw action.

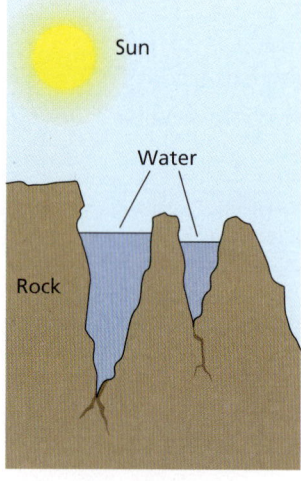

Daytime temperature 10° Celsius

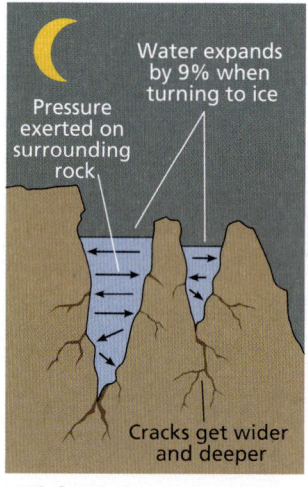

Night-time temperature −3° Celsius

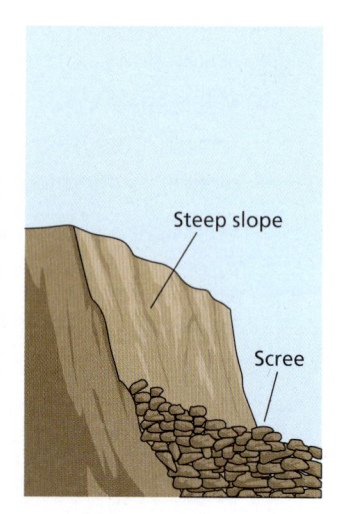

→ **Fig. 6.1(b)** Scree slope at Croagh Patrick.

Exfoliation

Example: Sonoran Desert

Exfoliation occurs in hot desert regions which have a **large diurnal temperature range**. Clear skies and long hours of sunshine during the day bring very high temperatures. This causes the outer layer of rock to get extremely hot and to expand. At night, a lack of cloud cover allows heat to escape and temperatures to fall, causing the rocks outer layer to cool and contract. Repeated expansion and contraction exerts stress on the rock, eventually causing it to crack. Over time, the cracks join up and a thin outer sheet peels away, similar to peeling the layers off an onion (Fig. 6.2).

While temperature changes are the main cause of exfoliation, moisture has also been found to enhance thermal expansion in rock.

> **Exfoliation:** Removing the outer layer of an object. It is sometimes referred to as 'onion peeling'.
>
> **Diurnal temperature range:** The difference between the highest and lowest temperatures in a 24-hour period.

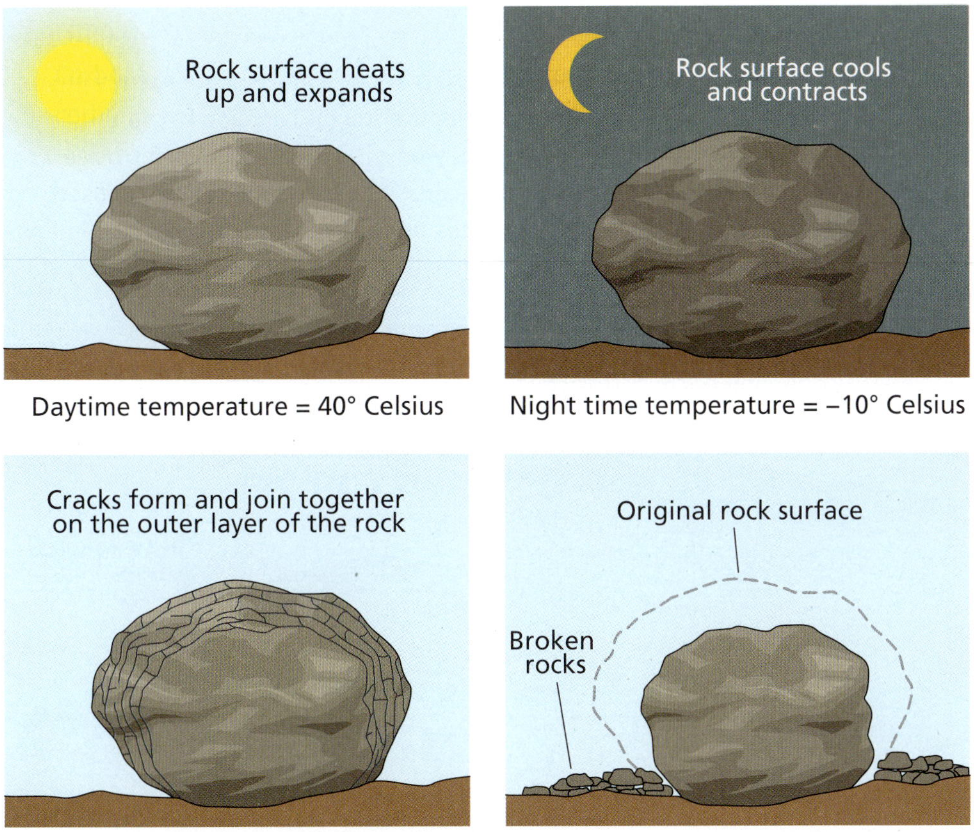

Rock surface heats up and expands
Daytime temperature = 40° Celsius

Rock surface cools and contracts
Night time temperature = −10° Celsius

Cracks form and join together on the outer layer of the rock

Original rock surface
Broken rocks

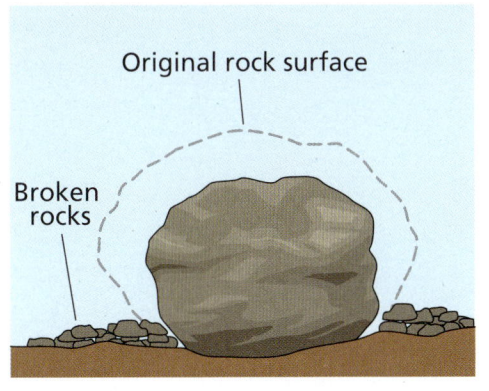

← Fig. 6.2(a) Exfoliation.

← Fig. 6.2(b) Exfoliated rock.

Landscapes

Salt crystallisation

Example: *California coastline*

Salt crystallisation takes place in areas with **dry climates** and **salt solutions**. It is commonly found in coastal areas, where salt water can seep into cracks and joints in rocks. High temperatures cause the water to evaporate leaving the salt crystals behind. The crystals expand with heat, exerting pressure on the rock which causes it to break down. Salt crystallisation can lead to the formation of **'honeycomb'** on sea walls constructed of granite, sandstone and limestone (**Fig. 6.3**).

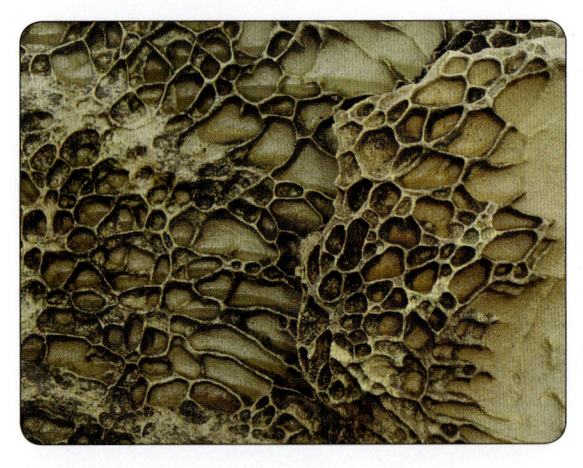

↑ **Fig. 6.3** Honeycomb formed by salt crystallisation.

Pressure release

Example: *Granite in the Wicklow Mountains*

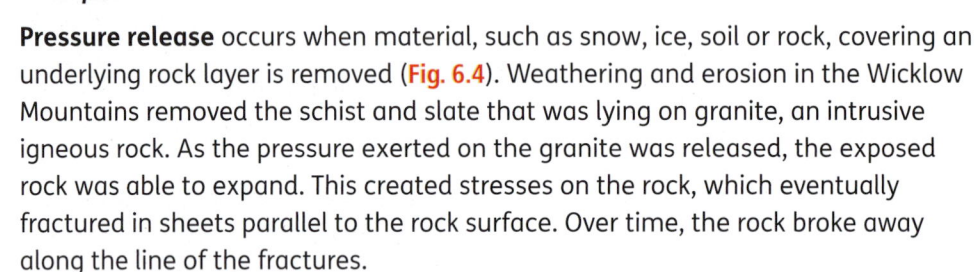

Pressure release occurs when material, such as snow, ice, soil or rock, covering an underlying rock layer is removed (**Fig. 6.4**). Weathering and erosion in the Wicklow Mountains removed the schist and slate that was lying on granite, an intrusive igneous rock. As the pressure exerted on the granite was released, the exposed rock was able to expand. This created stresses on the rock, which eventually fractured in sheets parallel to the rock surface. Over time, the rock broke away along the line of the fractures.

Haloclasty: Another word for salt crystallisation.

Pressure release: Also known as 'unloading' or 'sheeting'.

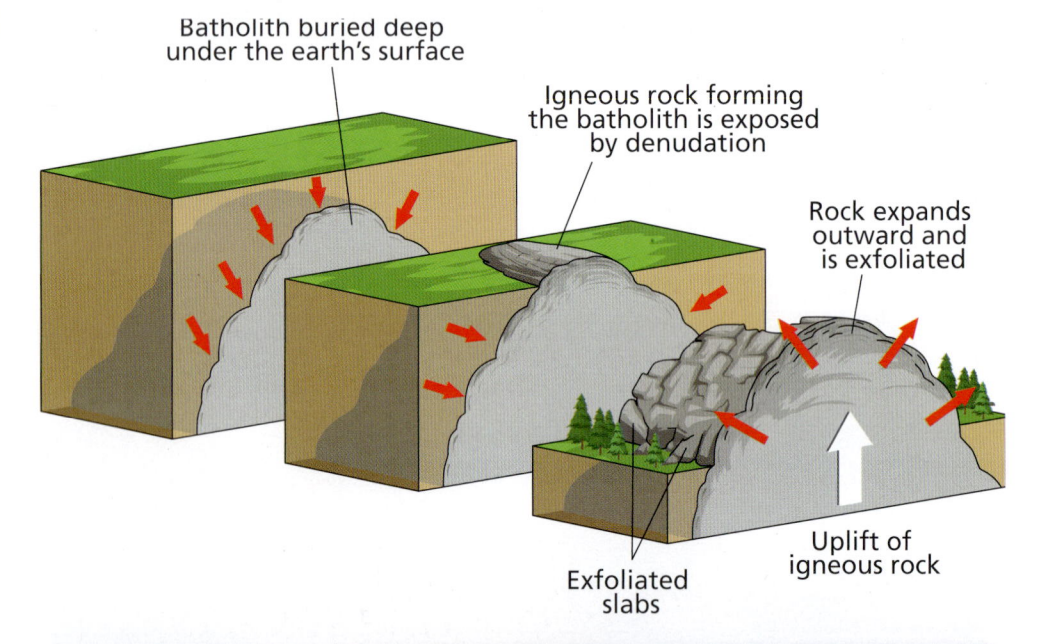

→ **Fig. 6.4(a)** Pressure release.

→ **Fig. 6.4(b)** Pressure release on rock at Yosemite National Park.

6 Weathering Processes and Landforms

> **CHECK YOUR LEARNING**
>
> 1. Identify the weather conditions needed for freeze-thaw action to occur.
> 2. Why is freeze-thaw action more common in upland areas?
> 3. What is scree?
> 4. List two reasons why exfoliation most commonly occurs in the desert.
> 5. Explain why exfoliation is also called 'onion peeling'.
> 6. Name one rock type exposed by the process of pressure release and its location in Ireland.
> 7. Where are the results of salt crystallisation commonly found?
> 8. What is another word for salt crystallisation?

Chemical Weathering Processes

Carbonation

Example: The Burren, Co. Clare

Limestone rock was formed when **calcium carbonate** in the bones and shells of marine life cemented their compacted remains together on the sea floor. As rainwater falls through the sky it absorbs carbon dioxide forming a weak **carbonic acid**. On the surface of the earth, carbonic acid reacts with calcium carbonate, the cementing agent in limestone. Soluble **calcium bicarbonate** is formed and carried away in solution.

The **carbonation** process is made easier, as limestone is a **permeable** sedimentary rock. It was laid down in strata with tiny horizontal cracks, called **bedding planes**, and vertical cracks, called **joints**. As limestone is permeable, carbonic acid can flow through and attack the cracks, opening them up wider.

Oxidation

Example: Colorado Plateau (Fig. 6.5)

Oxidation occurs when oxygen combines with minerals such as **iron** in rock. The iron mixes with oxygen creating a red/orange-coloured **iron oxide** that crumbles easily, weakening the rock.

Hydration

Soil forming minerals in rock such as **gypsum** do not contain any water. When it rains, they absorb water, causing them to expand and become soft before breaking apart (Fig. 6.6). **Shale** is one type of rock that is affected by **hydration**.

KEYWORDS

carbonation
carbonic acid
calcium bicarbonate
permeable
oxidation (rusting)
hydration
hydrolysis
feldspar
kaolin

Chemical formula for carbonic acid: water (H_2O) + carbon dioxide (CO_2) → H_2CO_3

Oxidation: Commonly referred to as 'rusting'.

↑ **Fig. 6.5** Colorado Plateau in the Rocky Mountains.

↑ **Fig. 6.6** The effects of hydration on rock.

75

Landscapes

Hydrolysis: To split using water.

Hydrolysis

Example: *Cleopatra's Needle, New York (***Fig. 6.7***)*

Hydrolysis takes place when **hydrogen** in water reacts with minerals in the rock creating a chemical reaction. **Feldspar**, which holds granite together, crumbles when it comes in contact with rainwater. This reaction leads to the formation of **kaolin**, a type of clay used in pottery.

DID YOU KNOW?
Quartz is a chemically resistant mineral, therefore it is not affected by hydrolysis.

↑ **Fig. 6.7** Before and after effects of hydrolysis on Cleopatra's Needle, New York.

EXAM LINK (HL)

Weathering (30 marks)
Explain one process of physical weathering and one process of chemical weathering.
2016, Q1C

Marking Scheme:
Physical and chemical processes named = 2 marks + 2 marks
Explanation of physical/chemical weathering = 6 SRPs × 2 marks + 7 SRPs × 2 marks

---

Biological weathering widens the joints in rocks. This allows water to penetrate further into the rock, which can lead to further weathering processes such as carbonation.

Biological Weathering Processes

Animals or **plant roots** can widen the spaces within or between rocks, causing them to break down. Animals such as rabbits can widen the crack in a rock through their burrowing, while plant roots push open the cracks making them wider and deeper as they grow bigger. Eventually the rock will weaken to the point where pieces will break away (**Fig. 6.8**).

→ **Fig. 6.8** Biological weathering.

6 Weathering Processes and Landforms

CHECK YOUR LEARNING

1. How is carbonic acid formed?
2. What makes limestone permeable?
3. Explain the process of 'carbonation'.
4. How does 'oxidation' occur?
5. How is shale affected by the process of hydration?
6. How is kaolin formed?
7. Name one mineral that is not affected by hydrolysis.
8. What part do animals play in biological weathering?

Distinctive Irish Landscapes Formed by Weathering

Granite landscapes

Example: *Three Rock Mountain* (Fig. 6.9)

Granite found in the Wicklow Mountains was formed during the Caledonian mountain building period approximately 400 million years ago. During the folding process, molten magma intruded into a large space in the upfolds under the earth's surface. Protected from the elements of weather by overlying layers of slate and quartzite, it cooled slowly to form a hard rock with large crystals of quartz, feldspar and mica. Over time, the granite became exposed as the overlying rock was worn down by weathering and removed by rivers and ice.

The removal of the overlying rock reduced the pressure exerted on the newly exposed granite allowing it to expand. This created stresses on the rock which led to the formation of joints and bedding planes. Water was then able to penetrate into the rock, leading to further weathering by **freeze-thaw action** and **hydrolysis**. The continuation of these processes over millions of years has led to the formation of rounded hills with **tors** at the summit.

↑ **Fig. 6.9** Three Rock Mountain.

KEYWORDS

tors
karst landscape
Burren
limestone pavement
grikes
clints
karren
fluting
swallow hole
disappearing stream
resurgence
dry valley
doline
turlough
dripstone
ailwee caves
percolation
evaporation
salcite
stalactite
stalagmite
pillar
curtain
cavern

Chapter 5: Rocks

Tor: A large block of rock that has been weathered more slowly than its surroundings.

77

Landscapes

Karst: From the Slovenian word *kras*, which means bare, stony ground.

Karst landscapes

Example: *The Burren, Co. Clare*

The Burren is an extensive area of bare rock that covers over 360 km² of north Clare and south Galway (**Fig. 6.10**). The Burren has numerous cliffed and terraced hills and an extensive underground drainage system. It has been forming since limestone was first laid down during the carboniferous geological period approximately 300 million years ago. Over thousands of years, the bones and shells of fish and other sea creatures accumulated on the sea floor where they were lithified into strata. During the Armorican folding movement, the limestone was uplifted and fractured, creating joints in the rock. Evidence of this folding can be found at Mullaghmore.

Evidence of the last glaciation can be seen in a number of places:

- Granite erratics are found in the northern part of the Burren.
- The Caher River (the only river in the region) flows through a valley covered by deposited boulder clay.
- Shale and sandstone lying at the top of Slieve Elva (345 m), the highest point of the Burren, provide evidence of the types of rocks covering the region prior to glacial erosion.

The Burren's fragile landscape is best known for the surface and underground features formed predominantly by the process of carbonation.

Chapter 1: Plate Tectonics
Chapter 4: Folding and Faulting Activity
Chapter 5: Rocks

DID YOU KNOW?
The Burren is a region whose geological heritage is internationally important. Along with the Cliffs of Moher, it has been afforded the title of Geopark by UNESCO. The Burren also includes archaeological sites (e.g. the Poulnabrone portal dolmen), small birds, and delicate Alpine flowers not usually found in Ireland.

↑ **Fig. 6.10** The Burren, Co. Clare.

CHECK YOUR LEARNING

1. What are tors?
2. List three weathering processes involved in the formation of tors.
3. What is a karst landscape?
4. How long has the Burren landscape been forming?
5. Apart from limestone, what evidence of other rocks can be found in the Burren?
6. Why do you think the Burren has been afforded the title of Geopark?

Surface features formed in karst regions: the Burren, Co. Clare – Figs 6.11 and 6.12

Limestone pavement

Limestone pavements are extensive areas of flat limestone rock.

Formation: First the soil cover must be removed. In the Burren, this happened about 10,000 years ago, when glaciers scoured large amounts of soil from the region's surface. As the glaciers melted, runoff caused soil erosion. Later, vast areas of woodland were removed so the land could be farmed. With no roots to hold it in place, the loose soil was easily eroded.

The exposed limestone is then chemically weathered by **carbonation**. Rainwater mixes with carbon dioxide, forming a weak carbonic acid. When this falls on the exposed limestone, it dissolves the calcium carbonate that cements the rock together. Percolating through the permeable limestone, the carbonic acid attacks **joints** in the rock. The joints are widened and deepened creating large gaps in the limestone called **grikes**. Blocks of limestone called **clints** remain on the surface of the landscape, separated by the grikes.

When carbonic acid settles on the surface of the clint, small depressions called **karren** are formed. During periods of heavy rainfall, a process called **fluting** can shape the sides of the clint. Carbonic acid overflows the edge of the clint, forming channels as it runs down the side.

Carbonic acid: A mixture of rainwater and carbon dioxide.

Percolation: The downward movement of water through soil or rock.

Soil is deposited in the grikes, providing a home for plant life, including hazel and ash trees, and exotic plants.

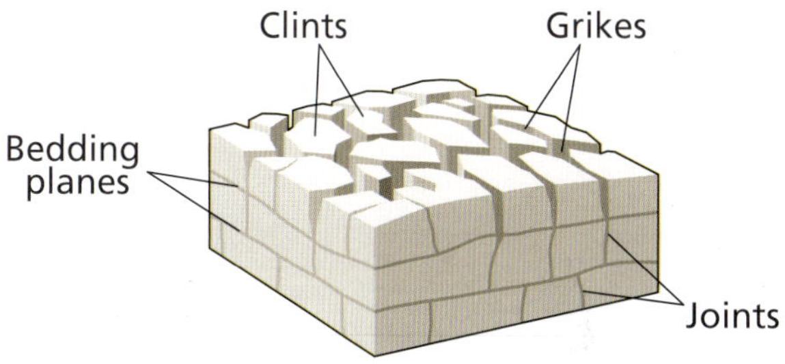

↑ **Fig. 6.11(a)** Limestone pavement.

← **Fig. 6.11(b)** Limestone pavement in the Burren.

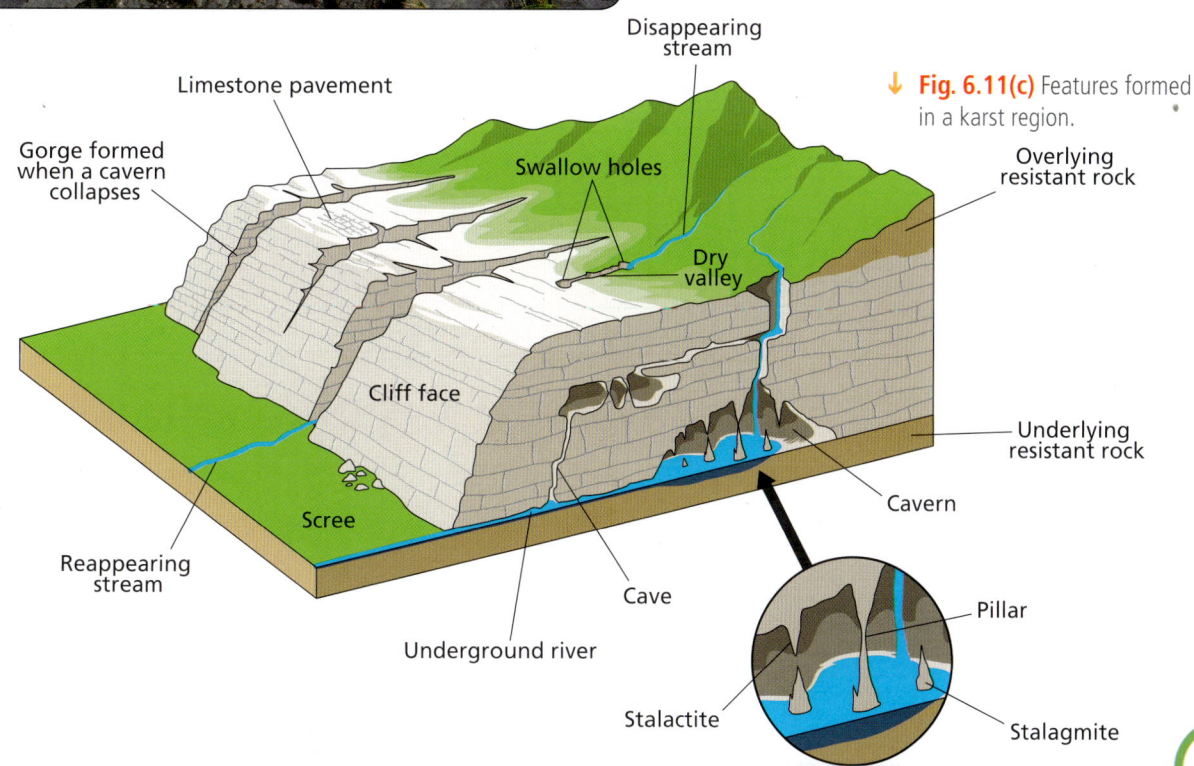

↓ **Fig. 6.11(c)** Features formed in a karst region.

Landscapes

Swallow holes

Example: *Pollnagollum, the Burren*

Swallow holes are large openings formed in the bed of rivers in limestone areas. Streams can erode the vertical joints/grikes in the permeable limestone using the processes of **solution, hydraulic action** and **abrasion**. Over time, grikes in the limestone are widened and eventually a number of them join to form a hole big enough to allow the stream to go underground.

Disappearing stream

Disappearing stream is the name given to a stream or river that instantly disappears underground through a **swallow hole**. Once underground, they often play a large part in the formation of **caves** and **caverns**.

Dry valleys

Dry valleys can form in one of two ways:

- After the river disappears underground, the valley downstream has no flowing water in it, unless the underground passage floods. Dry valleys can increase in length where more swallow holes are formed further upstream.
- Dry valleys could also have been formed by a postglacial stream as the glacier melted. When the glacier melted, the water disappeared.

Dolines

Dolines are deep hollows on the surface of the ground, formed when the roof of a cave collapses. When a limestone cave grows upwards, the layers of rock supporting the cave can become too thin to support itself.

Turloughs

Example: *Gort, Co. Galway*

Turloughs are depressions found on the surface of limestone areas. During long, wet spells of weather, they fill up and become seasonal lakes. As the weather improves, the water table drops and they dry up as the water slowly percolates underground.

> **River of resurgence:** A river that reappears further downslope having previously disappearing underground. It is sometimes referred to as a 'reappearing stream'.

> Dolines are also known as 'sluggas' or 'sinkholes'.

→ **Fig. 6.12** Karst features on an OS map extract of the Burren.

A swallow hole can be identified by the word 'Poll' or 'Poul', which means 'hole', e.g. Poulaphuca.

It is difficult to identify where the disappearing streams (e.g. Castletown River) disappear underground as neither the contours nor spot heights indicate the direction any of them are flowing.

The lake identified as a turlough lies in a depression with no supply from a river or stream. It is unnamed, which indicates it is a seasonal lake rather than a permanent one.

A cave can be identified by the word cave, e.g. Glencurran Cave. The surrounding area also has an absence of surface water, increasing the likelihood of underground streams.

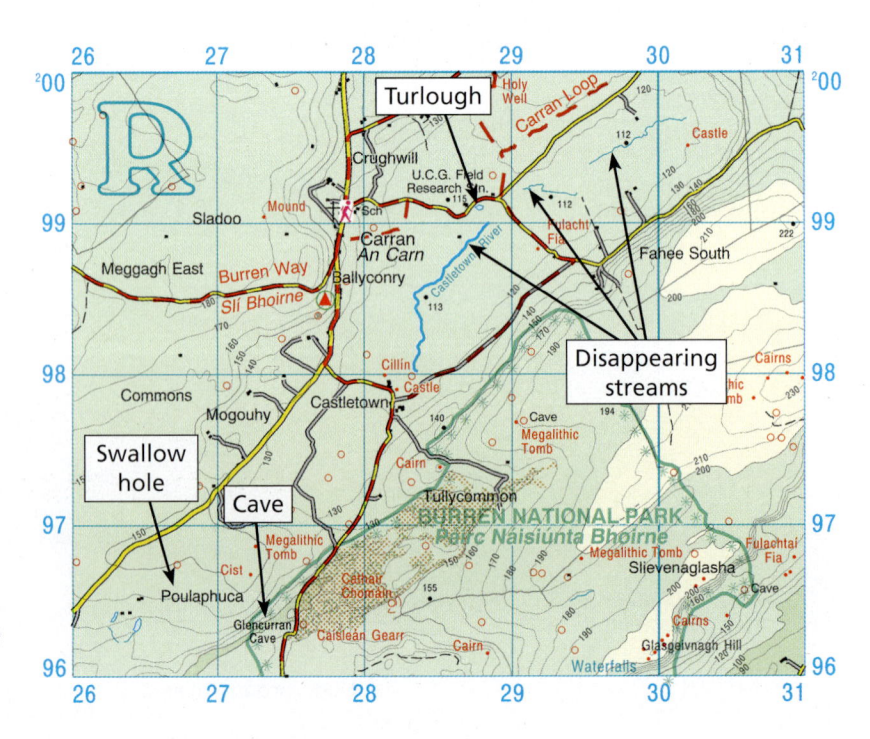

CHECK YOUR LEARNING

1. How are grikes formed?
2. What are clints?
3. What are karren and how are they formed?
4. Explain the term 'fluting'.
5. What is a swallow hole?
6. How does a dry valley form?
7. What is a river of resurgence?
8. What is a turlough?

Underground features formed in karst regions

Dripstone features

Example: Ailwee Cave, the Burren; Mitchelstown Caves

A number of processes play a role in the formation of **stalactites**, **stalagmites**, **pillars** and **curtains**:

- **Carbonation:** When rainwater mixes with carbon dioxide, it forms a weak carbonic acid. When this falls on limestone, it dissolves the calcium carbonate that cements the rock together. Soluble calcium bicarbonate is formed and carried away in solution.
- **Percolation:** The soluble calcium bicarbonate percolates through the joints and bedding planes of the permeable limestone to the roof of the cave.
- **Evaporation:** Water and carbon dioxide in the soluble calcium bicarbonate evaporates when it meets warmer air temperatures in the cave.
- **Deposition:** A small ring of **calcite** (calcium carbonate) is deposited and solidifies around a crack in the ceiling.

Stalactites

Straw-shaped **stalactites** grow downwards from the ceiling of the cave as more and more calcite is deposited. Sometimes the narrow inner tube of the straw stalactite solidifies when blocked by grit. When this happens, calcium bicarbonate is forced to flow down the outside of the tube forming carrot-shaped stalactites. They grow in thickness and anywhere between one-quarter to one full inch in length each century.

Stalagmites

Evaporation also affects soluble calcium bicarbonate which falls from stalactites onto the cave floor. The calcite left behind accumulates over time forming **stalagmites** that grow upwards. Stalagmites tend to be stronger than stalactites, as their bases and general areas are usually larger.

Pillars

Pillars, or columns, are formed when stalactites and stalagmites grow so large that they meet and join together.

Curtains

Curtains are formed when calcite deposits form a continuous, narrow but solid structure hanging from the roof of the cave. They grow downwards with age.

Evaporation: The process by which a liquid, such as water, is turned into a gas, such as water vapour.

Zone of saturation: The ground below the water table.

EXAM TIP (HL)

'Describe the formation of an underground karst feature.' In describing the formation of a pillar, one also has the opportunity to describe the processes behind the formation of stalactites and stalagmites.

EXAM LINK (HL)

Chemical Weathering (30 marks)

With the aid of a labelled diagram(s), explain how chemical weathering has shaped one of the following:

The surface karst landscape

OR

The underground karst landscape.

2017, Q2B

Marking Scheme:
Labelled diagram = 4 marks
Explanation = 13 SRPs × 2 marks

Landscapes

Caves and caverns

Example: *Ailwee Cave, the Burren; Mitchelstown Caves*

Underground passages called **caves** (Fig. 6.13) and underground chambers called **caverns** can be found in karst regions. They are formed by the erosive action of underground streams and are most commonly found at or below the **zone of saturation**. The underground stream forms caves and caverns using three processes:

- **Solution:** Carbonic acid in the stream reacts with calcium carbonate, the cementing agent in the limestone rock. The calcium carbonate is dissolved to form soluble calcium bicarbonate which is carried away in solution by the underground stream, making the caves and cavern wider and deeper.

↑ **Fig. 6.13** Caves can be found in karst regions.

- **Hydraulic action:** The force of the moving water in underground streams can widen and deepen both caves and caverns. At times of heavy rainfall, more water percolates underground, increasing the erosive power of the underground stream with its larger volume and increased speed of flow.

- **Abrasion:** The underground stream can pick up sediment or rock that it has eroded or that has fallen from the ceiling. It can use this load as a tool of erosion to widen and deepen caves and caverns.

EXAM LINK (OL)

Karst Landscapes (40 marks)
  (i) Name one example of a karst landscape.
  (ii) Explain, with the aid of a labelled diagram, how one surface feature in a karst landscape was formed.
  (iii) Explain, with the aid of a labelled diagram, how one underground feature in a karst landscape was formed.

2018, Q3B

Marking Scheme:
(i) Karst landscape named = 4 marks
(ii)–(iii) for each:
Feature named = 2 marks
Diagram(s) with two aspects = 2 × 2 marks
Formation explained = 4 SRPs × 3 marks

EXAM LINK (HL)

Landscape Development (30 marks)
Examine how different rock types produce distinctive landscapes.

2016, Q3B

Marking Scheme:
Two rocks and associated landscapes named = 2 + 2 marks
Examination = 13 SRPs

CHECK YOUR LEARNING

1. Explain the term 'percolation'.
2. What happens when a straw stalactite gets blocked by a piece of grit?
3. How are stalagmites formed?
4. What is another name for a column?
5. What affect do higher sub-surface temperatures have in forming sub-surface features?
6. What is the difference between a cave and a cavern?
7. What is the zone of saturation?
8. List and explain the three processes used in the formation of a cave or cavern.

6 Weathering Processes and Landforms

EXAMINATION QUESTIONS
ORDINARY LEVEL

Short Question

1. Karst Landscape

Examine the diagram of a karst landscape and answer each of the following questions.

(i) Match each of the letters A, B and C in the diagram with the landform that best matches it in the table below.

3 × 2 marks

Landform	Letter
Pillar/column	
Clint	
Stalactite	

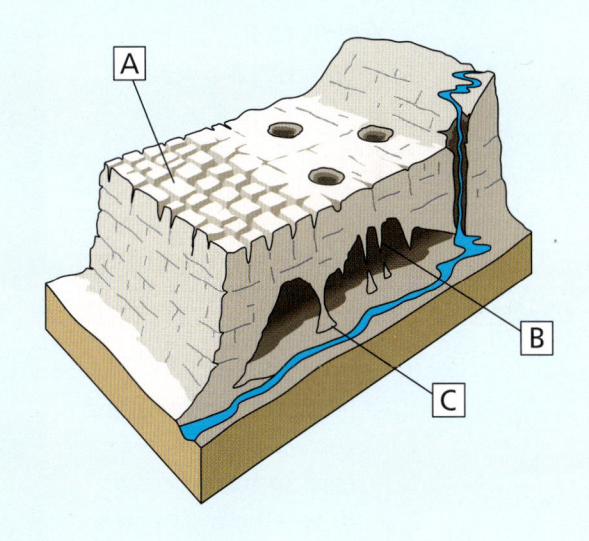

(ii) Indicate whether each of the statements below is true or false, by ticking the correct box.

(a) The Giant's Causeway is an example of a karst landscape. True ☐ False ☐ *2 marks*

(b) Permeable rock allows water to pass through it easily. True ☐ False ☐ *2 marks*

2015, Part One, Q3 (10 marks)

Long Question

2. Weathering

(i) Match each of the photographs A and B with the weathering process most associated with it from the list below:
 Carbonation
 Freeze-thaw action

(ii) With the aid of a diagram(s), explain how rocks are weathered by freeze-thaw action.

2016, Part Two, Section 1, Q2C (30 marks)

Marking Scheme:
(i) 3 marks + 3 marks
(ii) Explanation = 6 SRPs × 3 marks
 Diagrams = 2 SRPs × 3 marks

83

Landscapes

HIGHER LEVEL

Short Questions

3. Weathering

Examine the photographs and answer each of the following questions.

(i) Match each of the photographs A, B, C and D with the process of weathering that best matches it in the table below. 4 × 1 mark

(ii) Indicate, by ticking the correct box, whether each of the processes of weathering named in the table below is most associated with chemical weathering or mechanical weathering. 4 × 1 mark

		Q3(ii)	
Letter	**Type of fault**	**Chemical Weathering** (✓)	**Physical/Mechanical Weathering** (✓)
	Oxidation		
	Carbonation		
	Exfoliation/Onion Weathering		
	Freeze-thaw action		

Q3(i)

2017, Part One, Q4 (8 marks)

4. Weathering

(i) Identify the weathering agent active at A.

(ii) Is this agent an example of mechanical or chemical weathering?

(iii) Which of the following best describes temperatures at A:
   (a) Always below freezing point.
   (b) Varying above and below freezing point.
   (c) Never under freezing point.

(iv) What name is given to the rock particles (B) that gather at the foot of the slope?

4 × 2 marks

2006, Part One, Q1 (8 marks)

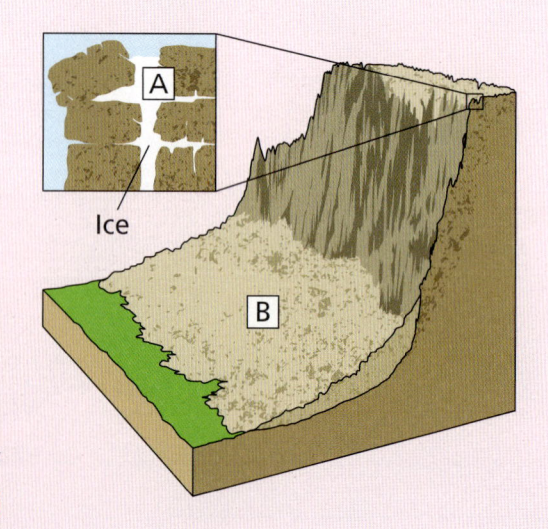

Long Questions

5. Karst Landscape (20 marks)

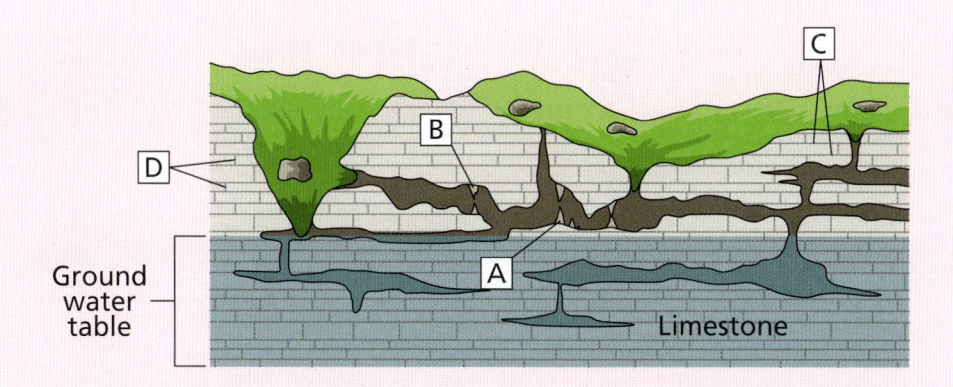

Examine the diagram above and answer each of the following questions.
- (i) Name each of the features labelled A and B.   *2 marks + 2 marks*
- (ii) What is the term given to the horizontal lines at C found in limestone?   *2 marks*
- (iii) What is the term given to the vertical lines at D found in limestone?   *2 marks*
- (iv) Name any two processes of chemical weathering.   *2 marks + 2 marks*
- (v) Explain briefly one of the processes of chemical weathering named by you above.   *2 SRPs × 2 marks*
- (vi) Explain briefly what is meant by the ground water table.   *2 SRPs × 2 marks*

2018, Part Two, Section 1, Q1A

6. Karst Landscapes (20 marks)

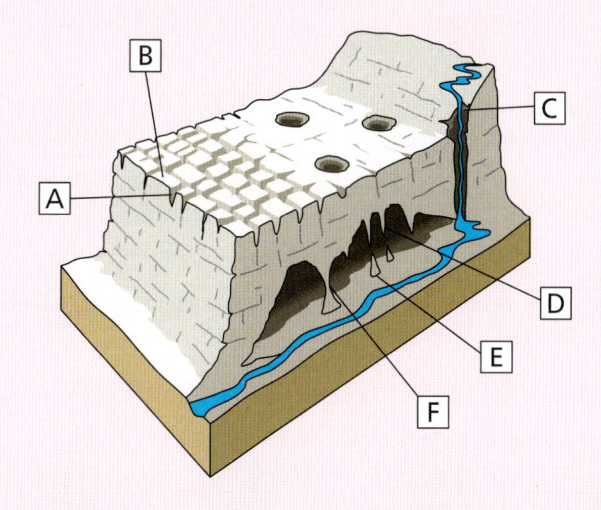

Examine the diagram above and answer each of the following questions.
- (i) Name each of the landforms A, B, C, D, E and F.   *6 × 2 marks*
- (ii) Name any two processes of chemical weathering.   *2 marks + 2 marks*
- (iii) State what is meant by the term permeable rock and name an example of a permeable rock.   *Any valid statement = 2 SRPs*

2015, Part Two, Section 1, Q1A

85

Revision Summary

Factors that affect the rate of weathering

- **Rock type** – rocks containing softer minerals (feldspar, calcite and iron) weather more rapidly than rocks containing harder minerals such as quartz
- **Surface area** – larger surface areas = more weathering
- **Climate** – high precipitation and wide temperature ranges – more weathering
- **Vegetation** – bare surfaces weather faster than those covered by vegetation
- **Human activity** – pollution accelerates weathering process – acid rain

Biological weathering processes

- Animals (rabbits burrowing) – plant roots (growing)
- Widen the spaces within or between rocks = more easily broken down

Mechanical weathering processes

Freeze-thaw action

- Mountainous areas – Croagh Patrick
- High precipitation levels
- Water gathers in rock joints
- Below 0°C = water freezes – expands by 9% – cracks widen – rock breaks
- Above 0°C = ice melts
- Scree
- Chemical weathering processes

Exfoliation

- Hot desert regions – Sonoran Desert
- Large diurnal temperature range
- High temperatures – outer layer of rock expands
- Cloud cover at night = cooler temperatures – outer layer contracts
- Repeated stress – cracks
- Rock layers peel away like an onion

Salt crystallisation

- Dry climates and salt solutions – Californian coastline
- Coastal areas
- High temperatures – water evaporates – salt crystals
- Crystals expand with heat
- Rock breaks down
- 'Honeycomb' forms on granite, sandstone and limestone sea walls

Pressure release

- Wicklow Mountains
- Overlying quartzite, schist and slate removed
- Underlying granite exposed and able to expand
- Joints and bedding planes form due to stress
- Rock broke away along the line of the fractures

Granite landscapes

- 400 mya – Eurasian and North American plates collided – Caledonian folding = Wicklow Mountains
- Magma intrusion – silica content approximately 70%
- Cooled slowly – protected by overlying slate, schist and quartzite = feldspar, quartz, etc. formed
- Formed domed mass of granite = Leinster Batholith
- Granite exposed by weathering and erosion
- Reduced pressure exerted on granite allowing it to expand
- Led to formation of joints and bedding planes
- Water penetration – freeze-thaw action and hydrolysis
- Rounded hills with tors at the summit

Karst landscapes

- The Burren – over 360 km^2 of Clare and Galway
- Landscape forming since Carboniferous period – 300 mya
- Remains of fish and sea creatures lithified into strata
- Armorican orogeny = limestone uplifted and fractured – creates joints in the rock – Mullaghmore
- Glacial evidence = granite erratics in the north Burren
- Caher River = only river in the region, flows through a valley covered by deposited boulder clay
- Shale and sandstone lie on top of the limestone at Slieve Elva
- Best-known characteristics are the surface and sub-surface features – mainly formed by carbonation

Chemical weathering processes

Carbonation	Oxidation	Hydration	Hydrolysis
• The Burren, Co. Clare • CO_2 + rainwater = weak carbonic acid • Dissolves calcium carbonate • Soluble calcium bicarbonate • Widens joints/bedding planes in limestone	• Colorado Plateau • Oxygen + minerals in rock • Iron + oxygen = iron oxide • Weakens rock	• Soil forming minerals (gypsum) + water = expand and weaken • Shale is affected	• Cleopatra's Needle, NY • Hydrogen + minerals in rock • Feldspar + water = kaolin

The Burren: surface features

- Limestone pavement – bare limestone surface
- Clints – blocks of limestone
- Grikes – gaps between blocks of limestone
- Karren – depressions on surface of limestone
- Swallow hole – grike widens and river disappears underground
- Disappearing stream – river that goes underground
- Dry valley – valley remaining after river goes underground
- River of resurgence – river reappears further downhill
- Doline – hollow formed by cave collapsing
- Turlough – depressions with seasonal lakes

The Burren: sub-surface features

- Stalactites – calcite grows down from ceiling
- Stalagmites – calcite grows up from the ground
- Pillars/columns – stalactite and stalagmite joins
- Curtains – calcite grows from crack in ceiling
- Carbonation – carbonic acid dissolves calcium carbonate
- Percolation – calcium bicarbonate passes through ground
- Evaporation – water evaporates in the cave
- Deposition – calcite deposited once water evaporates
- Caves – underground tunnels
- Caverns – underground rooms
- Solution / hydraulic action / abrasion

7 MASS MOVEMENT

KEYWORDS

regolith
gradient
water
vegetation
tectonic
human activity
soil creep

LEARNING INTENTIONS

Syllabus Links: 1.5, 1.7

By the end of this chapter I will be able to:
- understand the factors that influence the rate at which mass movement occurs;
- identify each type of mass movement and the features they form from a photograph or a diagram;
- indicate the main causes of each type of mass movement;
- describe in detail the processes involved in at least two forms of mass movement;
- explain the impact human activities have on mass movement processes.

Regolith: Loose rock, soil, snow and mud that is moved down a slope.

Chapter 2: Volcanic Activity
Chapter 3: Earthquake Activity

Mass movement, the movement of **regolith** down a slope in response to the pull of gravity, is influenced by **natural processes**, **natural disturbances** and **human activities**.

Influences on Mass Movement

The rate at which mass movement takes place is influenced by the following factors:

Natural process

Gradient: The steeper the slope, the more likely mass movement will take place and the faster the mass movement will be should it occur.

Water content: The more water there is, the faster the mass movement that will take place. The water acts as a lubricant, while also adding weight to the regolith.

Vegetation: This slows down mass movement, as it binds the particles of the soil together. Vegetation also helps to absorb rainfall that might make the slope unstable.

Slope material: If the slope material is consolidated, as in the case of solid rock, it is less likely that mass movement will take place. Unconsolidated material such as boulder clay is more likely to move down a slope.

Natural disturbance

Tectonic activity: This can speed up mass movement by weakening or shifting the slope surface material:
- volcanic activity can lead to a large movement of material down a slope (e.g. lahars);
- earthquakes can loosen the surface material on the sides of hills and mountains making it more likely to move down the slope.

Human activity

Human activity: This can speed up mass movement by weakening the slope surface material or increasing the gradient of the slope. It includes:
- the undercutting of hillsides for road, railway line and wind farm construction;
- over-cropping, overgrazing and deforestation of farm land;
- quarrying for rock into hillsides.

Classification of Mass Movement

Mass movement is classified according to:
- the speed at which it occurs;
- the type of material being moved;
- the condition of the material being moved – wet or dry.

Slow mass movement

Soil creep

Soil creep, the slowest form of mass movement, takes a long time to have a visible impact on the landscape. Soil and regolith are moved slowly downhill under the influence of gravity. Soil creep is also influenced by:

- **periods of heavy rainfall:** The underlying rock on a slope can become heavily saturated, to the point that water can no longer pass through the rock. The overlying soil particles then expand and push away from one another at a right-angle to the slope as they take on more water (hydration). When the weather gets warmer and drier, the soil will dry out (dehydration) and fall slightly downhill as it contracts.

- **frost heave:** This occurs during freeze-thaw action, common on higher slopes. As temperatures go below 0°C, the water in the soil particles freezes and expands. Soil particles are pushed upwards and away from one another. When the temperatures go above 0°C, the frozen particles thaw, contract and fall downhill.

As it happens at a rate unnoticeable to the naked eye, soil creep is identified by the long-term effects it can have on surface objects on weathered mountain slopes (**Fig. 7.1**). These effects include:

- the formation of **terracettes** when the surface soil moves downslope due to cycles of freezing and thawing, or hot and cold temperatures;
- telegraph poles and gravestones tilting backwards, facing downhill;
- fence posts tilting or breaking;
- tree trunks curving: the lower part of the trunk is tilted downhill, while the curve allows the upper part of the tree to grow towards the sun;
- cracks developing in roads parallel to the slope, as they are stretched due to gravity;
- soil moving downhill sometimes builds up behind a wall, causing it to bulge or break.

> **EXAM TIP**
>
> A question describing one mass movement process appeared as a Higher Level 30-mark question every year from 2010 to 2018, except 2014. In 2014, students had to describe two mass movement processes.
>
> A question describing two mass movement processes appeared on the Ordinary Level paper every year from 2011 to 2018.

↑ **Fig. 7.1(a)** Curved tree trunks are a result of soil creep.

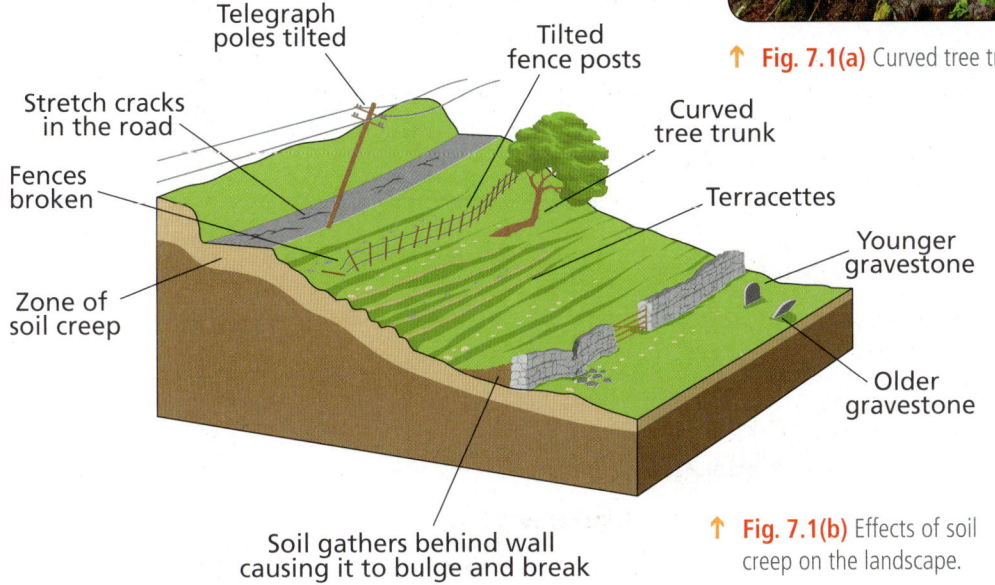

↑ **Fig. 7.1(b)** Effects of soil creep on the landscape.

Terracettes: Small terraces or ridges that form at the side of a hill.

Permafrost: Ground (rock, soil or sediment) that remains frozen (below 0°C) for two or more consecutive years.

89

Landscapes

Solifluction

Solifluction is a type of slow mass movement that occurs on higher altitudes with an underlying layer of permafrost. In summer, the upper layer of soil can become saturated if water is unable to percolate into the permafrost layer underneath. This allows the saturated soil to flow downhill, creating folds.

CHECK YOUR LEARNING

1. What is 'mass movement'?
2. What impact does water have in causing mass movement?
3. Vegetation slows mass movement. Explain.
4. How do we classify different types of mass movement?
5. What are terracettes?
6. Explain the part freeze-thaw action plays in soil creep.
7. List three ways humans can identify that soil creep is happening on the landscape.
8. At which time of year is solifluction most likely to occur?

KEYWORDS

bogburst
lahar
landslide
slumping
avalanche
rockfall
mudslide

Fast mass movement

Bogburst

Bogbursts can vary in speed from slow to fast. They occur when peat in blanket bogs covering hill and mountain slopes moves downslope due to gravity. Bogbursts most commonly occur in the autumn and winter when periods of dry weather are followed by periods of continuous heavy rain (Table 7.1; Fig. 7.2). They can also occur:

- when land is overgrazed by sheep with heather and upland plants no longer able to bind the soil;
- when machinery is involved in peat removal just before, or during, wet spells;
- when land is being drained for agriculture;
- when wind farms are being developed.

Date	Location	Main trigger
August 2008	Lyreacrompane, Co. Kerry	Heavy rainfall, wind turbine construction
October 2003	Derrybrien, Co. Galway	Heavy rainfall, wind turbine construction
September 2003	Pullathomas, Co. Mayo	Heavy rainfall, overgrazing by sheep

→ **Table 7.1** A number of major bogbursts have affected the Irish landscape.

→ **Fig. 7.2** October 2003, bogburst in Galway.

90

Mudflow

Mudflows can travel at speeds in excess of 100 km/h. They occur in areas with steep slopes, deep soils and an impermeable layer of underlying rock. During periods of heavy rainfall, the regolith becomes saturated, creating a mixture of soil and water with a consistency of wet concrete that can move rapidly downslope (Fig. 7.3).

Lahars

Lahars are **volcanic mudflows** that occur when snow-covered volcanic mountains erupt. The heat from the erupting volcano and the materials it emits cause the snow to melt rapidly. The resulting meltwater moves at speeds up to 100 km/h down the mountain, mixing with lava, ash, soil and rock.

↑ **Fig. 7.3** After-effects of a mudflow.

Chapter 2: Volcanic Activity

CASE STUDY: NEVADO DEL RUIZ, 1985

On 13 November 1985, the Nevado del Ruiz volcano erupted in Colombia after being dormant for 69 years. A pyroclastic flow melted the mountain's snow cap and glaciers, creating four thick lahars which travelled at average speeds of 60 km/h downhill. Despite many warnings from volcanological organisations, towns and villages in the area around the volcano were never evacuated prior to the eruption. Devastatingly, the lahar covered the town of Armero, killing over 20,000 people – two-thirds of the town's population. Around 3,000 people from neighbouring towns also died (Fig. 7.4).

↑ **Fig. 7.4(a)** Nevada del Ruiz.

← **Fig. 7.4(b)** Armero after the lahar.

CHECK YOUR LEARNING

1. At what time of year are bogbursts most likely to occur and why?
2. List two ways humans can trigger a bogburst.
3. What is a lahar?
4. List two impacts of the Nevado del Ruiz lahar.

Landslides kill approximately 8,000 people every year.

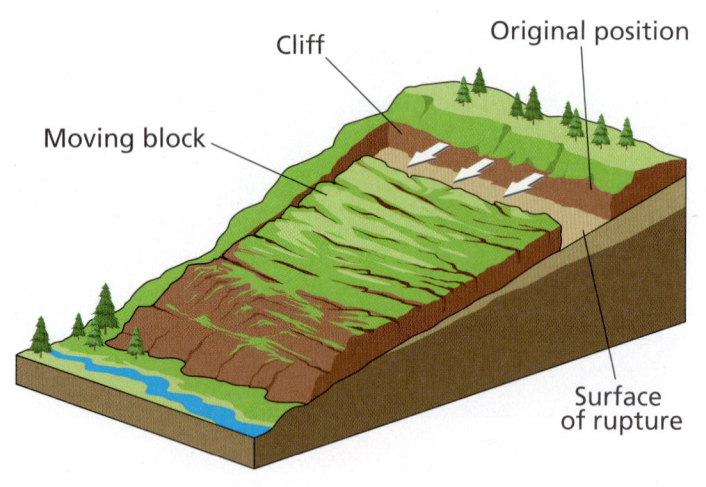

Landscapes

Fig. 7.5 Landslide.

Fig. 7.6 June 2017 landsides, Co. Donegal.

DID YOU KNOW?
In 2015, a 7.8-magnitude earthquake triggered approximately 4,000 landslides in Nepal.

In 2008, an 8.0-magnitude earthquake hit the Sichuan region of China, leading to 15,000 landslides and 20,000 deaths from landslides.

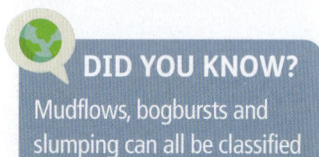

DID YOU KNOW?
Mudflows, bogbursts and slumping can all be classified as forms of landslide.

Rapid mass movement

Landslide

Landslides are a rapid form of mass movement which commonly occur in mountainous areas and along coasts (Fig. 7.5). Rock, earth and debris move rapidly down a slope. While most landslides are a result of natural factors, they can also be accelerated by human activities.

Natural factors causing landslides include:

- **rainfall:** Landslides most commonly occur after periods of heavy rainfall when the heavy rain lubricates the soil making it easier to move downslope (Fig. 7.6). The increased water content on the slope material also causes it to gain weight, which encourages it to move downslope.

- **weathering:** If the slope material (soil or rock) is weak or fractured by by weathering processes such as **freeze-thaw action**, it is more likely to move downslope.

- **earthquakes**: When earthquakes occur on areas with steep slopes, the vibrations can cause the soil to slip downhill.

- **strata:** Different layers of soil or rock may have different strengths and stiffness, contributing to the instability of slopes.

- **erosion:** The erosive action of moving water on coastal or river cliffs can cause a block of unconsolidated surface material to collapse.

Human activities contributing to landslides include:

- **loading:** The addition of heavy materials to a slope increases the downward force (gravity) placed on it. The increased load caused by wind farm developments has led to numerous landslides on slopes composed of unconsolidated material. The use of large machinery on steep slopes before, during or after very wet spells can have a similar impact. Dam construction increases the weight of water in a lake, causing the rock strata underneath to depress and become unstable.

- **undercutting:** Undercutting slopes during road or rail line construction increases the steepness of the gradient.

- **deforestation:** Clear-cutting forestry from hill or mountain slopes removes the surface vegetation, the roots of which stabilise soil particles.

- **mining and quarrying:** Operations that use blasting techniques cause vibrations under the soil, encouraging sliding in surrounding areas.

- **removing retaining walls:** This can destabilise slopes, especially ones that have been previously modified.

Slump rotational slide (slumping)

Slumping occurs where unconsolidated material, such as boulder clay, slips downward along a **curved surface** (Fig. 7.7). A **crescent-shaped cliff** forms with an abrupt end called a **scarp** at the top end of the slope. The material gathered at the foot of the slope is called a **slump**. Note, that there can be more than one scarp down the slope.

Avalanche

The rapid flow of snow down a slope is called an **avalanche** (Fig. 7.8). Avalanches occur mainly on steep slopes in the months of January, February and March, when heavy snowfall causes the weight of snow to become too much for the slope to hold. Other factors which can contribute to the occurrence of an avalanche include:

- snow foundations being loosened by spring rains or warm, dry winds;
- deforestation making the slope unstable, for example, the development of new ski runs;
- vibrations caused by earthquakes, artillery, blasting, thunder or noise from off-piste skiers.

Avalanches can cause death or serious injury. They can destroy buildings in their path as well as blocking roads and railway lines. Due to the extent of the devastation they can cause, a number of strategies have been developed in an effort to manage them. These include:

- predicting when they are likely to occur using historical data, weather information and information on the type and volume of snow on the mountainside: most avalanches happen in the Alps between January and March, a period known as 'avalanche season';
- avalanches are deliberately started using explosives in areas under threat of a large snow build up: this is managed in ways that there is no threat to human life;
- information on the risk of avalanches is very well displayed in all ski villages, while areas considered too dangerous to ski on are sealed off.

Rockfall

Rockfalls are heavily influenced by gravity and the steepness of the slope. They occur when loosened blocks of solid rock fall freely to the base of a slope forming an irregular pile of rock, called a **talus slope**. Rockfalls are most common in rocks which are characterised by the presence of vertical cracks in their structure (Fig. 7.9). They occur because of a number of factors such as:

- a period of freeze-thaw action;
- earthquake activity;
- undercutting by rivers and waves;
- plant-root wedging.

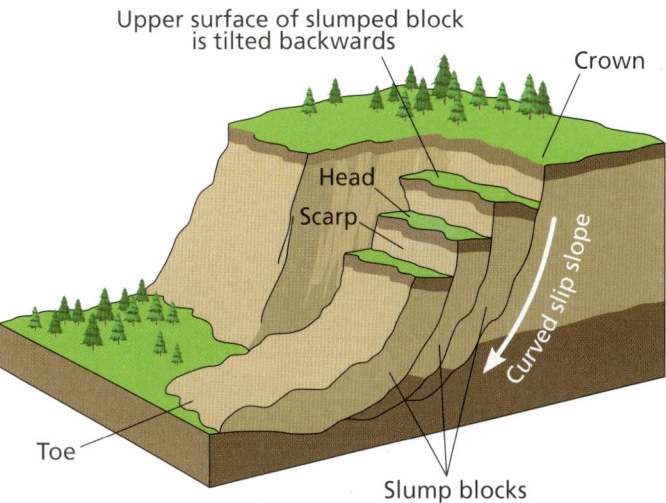

↑ **Fig. 7.7(a)** Slump rotational slide.

↑ **Fig. 7.7(b)** Slump rotational slide.

↑ **Fig. 7.8** Avalanche.

↑ **Fig. 7.9** Rockfall.

Landscapes

> Liquefied materials behave like a liquid, meaning the effects of the earthquake are reduced, as sheer stress does not travel through liquids.

Chapter 3: Earthquake Activity

Liquefaction

When loose sediment becomes oversaturated with water, the individual grains lose their grain-to-grain contact as the water gets between them (Fig. 7.10). This occurs at three main times:

- after periods of heavy rainfall;
- when there is rapid melting of snow or ice;
- strong vibrations from high magnitude earthquakes can force water upwards from several metres underground. If the solid surface of the ground cracks, saturated sand/soil will rise to the surface.

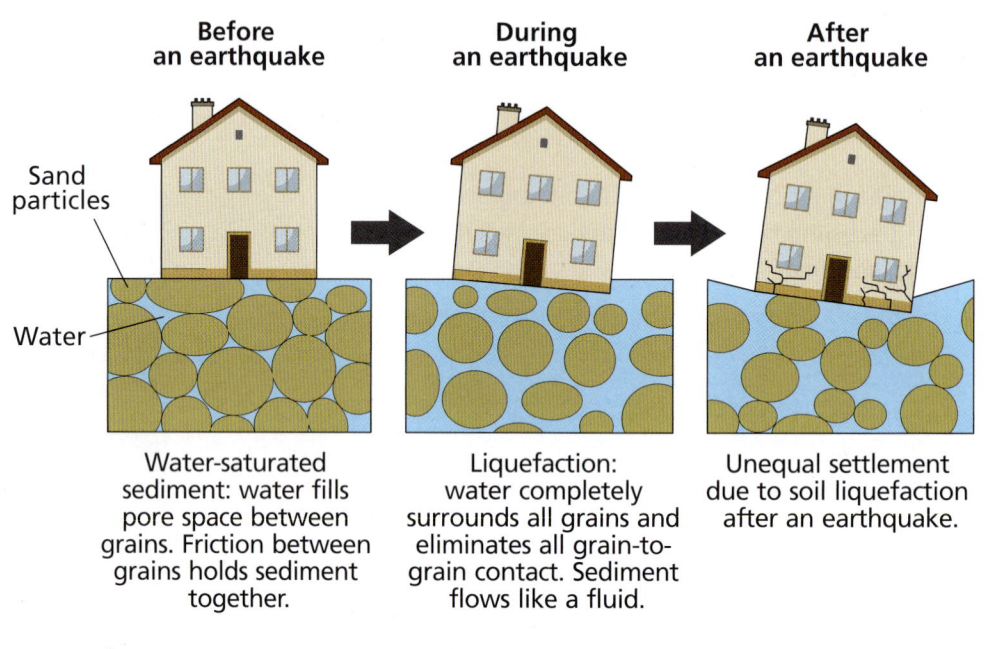

Before an earthquake
Water-saturated sediment: water fills pore space between grains. Friction between grains holds sediment together.

During an earthquake
Liquefaction: water completely surrounds all grains and eliminates all grain-to-grain contact. Sediment flows like a fluid.

After an earthquake
Unequal settlement due to soil liquefaction after an earthquake.

↑ Fig. 7.10 Liquefaction.

EXAM LINK (HL)

Surface Processes (30 marks)

Describe and explain the factors governing the operation of any one mass movement process that you have studied.

2017, Q3B

> **Marking Scheme:**
> Mass movement identified = 2 marks
> Examination = 14 SRPs × 2 marks

EXAM LINK (OL)

Landform Development (40 marks)

Describe and explain any two processes of mass movement.

2018, Q2B

> **Marking Scheme:**
> 2 processes × 20 marks each. For each process:
> Process stated = 2 marks
> Description/explanation = 6 SRPs × 3 marks

CHECK YOUR LEARNING

1. Explain two natural factors that can cause landslides.
2. Describe two human factors that can cause landslides.
3. List two factors that can trigger an avalanche.
4. Outline two ways humans attempt to manage avalanches.
5. Using your study of rocks, what type of rock is most commonly associated with rockfalls?
6. What is liquefaction?

The Impact of Human Activity on Mass Movement

CASE STUDY: OVERGRAZING IN THE WEST OF IRELAND

Cause

When Ireland joined the EU in 1973, farmers took advantage of measures introduced as part of the Common Agricultural Policy to boost their incomes.

- **Headage Payments Scheme** – farmers received payments based on the number of animals they had in stock.
- **Intervention** – farmers were guaranteed a minimum price for certain farm produce, such as meat, sold on the open market.

> Sheep numbers in Ireland grew from 3.3 million in 1980 to 8.8 million in 1991. Stock rates were five times higher than the UK.

Impact

These measures saw the number of sheep grow rapidly in peripheral mountainous areas (Fig. 7.11). In West of Ireland areas, such as the Connemara uplands (Co. Galway) and the Mweelrea Mountains (Co. Mayo), sheep numbers greatly exceeded the carrying capacity of the land. The soil structure of the land was damaged by:

- **overgrazing**, which removed much of the grass and heather binding the soil together (Fig. 7.12). As the soil became loose, it became unstable, making it easier to transport downslope under the influence of gravity;
- the repeated trampling of the soil by large numbers of sheep led to the soil being **compacted** and this led to faster runoff of surface water.

Approximately 30% of upland areas suffered serious soil erosion. This led to numerous localised landslides that damaged property, polluted rivers and lakes and blocked roads.

Fig. 7.11 Mountain ranges of the West of Ireland. The Connemara uplands includes the Twelve Bens and Maumturk mountains.

Fig. 7.12 Overgrazing by sheep has led to soil erosion in the West of Ireland.

Landscapes

CASE STUDY: DEFORESTATION IN THE AMAZON BASIN

DID YOU KNOW?
Ireland and the UK combined would fit into the Amazon rainforest approximately 17 times!

Parts of the Amazon rainforest can be found in Brazil, Bolivia, Peru, Ecuador, Colombia, Venezuela, Guyana, Suriname and French Guiana.

↑ **Fig. 7.13** Deforestation in the Amazon.

Cause

The Amazon rainforest covers 5.5 million square kilometres of South America, making it the largest tropical rainforest worldwide. Nearly two-thirds of the Amazon rainforest is found in Brazil and decisions made by government officials, farmers and loggers have led to vast areas being **deforested** (Fig. 7.13).

Infrastructural development

- Government supported infrastructure projects in the 1960s caused a great deal of deforestation. Roads such as the Trans-Amazonian Highway were built to improve accessibility for industry and support resettlement projects.
- This was accelerated further in 2001 when the government announced 'Advance Brazil', a $40 million development plan to replace rainforest with 10,000 km of new roads, railways, power lines, gas pipelines, reservoirs and hydroelectric dams, canals and industry.

Agriculture

- An increased demand for soy, beef and leather, especially from growing economies such as China, has resulted in 15% of the Brazilian Amazon rainforest being cleared for farming since the 1960s.
- Cattle ranching has been responsible for approximately 70% of deforestation in the Amazon as 350,000 km^2 of rainforest has been turned into pasture lands. Increasing market prices for beef has supported a growth in the Brazilian cattle population from 25 million in 1990 to over 90 million in 2018.
- Soy bean production accounts for 25 million hectares of Brazilian land, most of which was once forested as part of the Amazon rainforest. Brazil is now the second largest producer of this valuable commodity which can be eaten directly, used as an animal feed, or used to produce biodiesel.

Logging

Logging is responsible for almost 3% of deforestation with 30 million cubic metres of logs taken by legal and illegal means from the Amazon rainforest each year. The timber is used to produce paper, furniture and plywood for the construction industries in the US, Japan and Europe.

Mining

The Amazon rainforest has a rich supply of precious metals such as copper, tin, bauxite, iron and gold. The development of mining infrastructure such as roads, railways, airports and worker accommodation has led to large-scale deforestation.

Impact

Deforestation has removed the protective cover that prevents soil erosion in many areas of the Amazon rainforest.

- Trees act as an obstacle to rainwater as it flows downhill (runoff), slowing it down long enough to allow it to soak into the ground.
- They establish strong root systems which stabilise slopes, as they bind the soil in position. They act as a protective shield against the force of rainfall before it hits the soil, therefore reducing its ability to erode.
- Furthermore, leaf fall in autumn decomposes to provide a rich layer of organic matter which increases water infiltration and the strength of soil.

Lack of vegetation has left the soil loose and exposed. Water from heavy downpours, common in tropical regions, now acts as a lubricant to this loose, exposed soil. As a result, mudslides and landslides are becoming more common in areas that were once covered in thick forest.

EXAM LINK (HL)

Human Interaction with Surface Processes (30 marks)
Examine the impact of human activities on mass movement processes.
2017, Q1C

Marking Scheme:
Impact on process identified = 2 marks
Examination of impact on process = 14 SRPs × 2 marks

EXAM LINK (OL)

Human Interaction with Surface Processes (30 marks)
Examine how humans interact with mass movement processes.
2018, Q3C

Marking Scheme:
Interaction identified = 3 marks
Description/explanation = 9 SRPs × 3 marks

EXAM TIP (OL)

A question on human interaction with mass movement processes came up every year from 2009 to 2018.

CHECK YOUR LEARNING

1. When did Ireland join the EU?
2. What EU policy impacted Irish agriculture?
3. What impact did overgrazing have on the mountains of the West of Ireland?
4. List one piece of information that describes the vast size of the Amazon rainforest.
5. Explain one factor that led to large-scale deforestation in the Amazon Basin.
6. How has deforestation led to mass movement in the Amazon Basin?

Landscapes

EXAMINATION QUESTIONS
ORDINARY LEVEL

Long Questions

1. Mass Movement

Examine the photographs and answer each of the following questions.

(i) Match each of the photographs A, B, C and D with the type of mass movement from the list below that best matches it.
4 × 3 marks

Soil creep	Avalanche
Rock fall	Mudflow

(ii) Name one example of a fast mass movement process and one example of a slow mass movement process. *3 + 3 marks*

(iii) Explain briefly how slope affects the rate of mass movement. *2 SRPs × 3 marks*

(iv) Explain briefly how water affects the rate of mass movement. *2 SRPs × 3 marks*

2018, Part Two, Section 1, Q1A (30 marks)

HIGHER LEVEL

Short Questions

2. Mass Movement

Examine the photographs and answer each of the following questions.

(i) Match each of the letters A, B, C and D with the process that best matches it in the table below. *4 × 1 mark*

Process	Letter
Rotational slump	
Soil creep	
Landslide	
Mudflow	

(ii) Name any two factors that influence the operation of mass movement processes. *2 × 1 mark*

(iii) Name one example of a very rapid mass movement process and name one example of a very slow mass movement process. *2 × 1 mark*

2015, Part One, Q6 (8 marks)

Long Questions

3. Landform Development

Describe and explain two processes of mass movement that you have studied.

2014, Part Two, Section 1, Q2B (30 marks)

Marking Scheme:
Two processes named = 2 + 2 marks
Examination of process 1 = 6 or 7 SRPs × 2 marks
Examination of process 2 = 7 or 6 SRPs × 2 marks

98

Revision Summary

7 Mass Movement

Influences on mass movement

- **Gradient** – steeper slope = faster mass movement
- **Water content** – water = lubricates + adds weight
- **Vegetation** – slows mass movement = binds soil particles together + absorb rainfall
- **Slope material** – consolidated/unconsolidated
- **Tectonic activity** – earthquakes, volcanic activity = lahars
- **Human activity** – weakens slope surface material/increases gradient

Slow moving mass movement

- Soil creep
- Heavy rainfall – hydration/dehydration
- Frost heave
- Terracettes
- Telegraph poles/gravestones tilt downhill
- Fence posts = tilted/broken
- Curved tree trunks
- Cracks on roads parallel to slope
- Soil build up = walls bulge or break
- **Solifluction** – permafrost – folds

Fast moving/wet conditions

Bogburst

- Saturated peat in blanket bogs moves downslope
- Common in autumn and winter
- Dry weather followed by continuous heavy rain
- Overgrazing by sheep – loosens soil
- Heavy machinery removing peat
- After land is drained
- Development of wind farms

Mudflow (Mudslide)

- Speeds in excess of 100 km/h
- Steep slopes, deep soils and an impermeable layer of underlying rock
- Heavy rainfall – regolith becomes saturated

Lahars

- Volcanic mudflows
- Heat from erupting volcano causes snow to melt rapidly
- Meltwater moves rapidly downslope mixing with lava, ash, soil and rock
- 13 November, 1985 – Nevado del Ruiz volcano (Colombia)
- Was dormant for 69 years
- Pyroclastic flow melted the mountains snow cap and glaciers
- Four thick lahars created
- Travelled at average speeds of 60 km/h downhill
- Area around volcano not evacuated prior to eruption
- Lahar covered town of Armero, killing over 20,000 people
- 3,000 people from neighbouring towns also died
- **Liquefaction** – loose sediment becomes oversaturated

Fast moving/dry conditions

Avalanche

- Rapid flow of snow down a slope
- Occur on steep slopes in January, February or March
- Heavy snowfall – weight too much for the slope to hold
- Also caused by: spring rains – warm, dry winds – deforestation (new ski runs) – vibrations (earthquakes, artillery, etc.)
- Cause death, serious injury, destruction of buildings
- Prediction – historical data of weather, snow type + volume
- Avalanches managed to prevent threat to human life
- Information on avalanche risk displayed/ski runs closed

Rockfall

- Influenced by gravity and steepness of slope
- Loosened blocks fall freely – form talus slope
- Most common in rocks with vertical cracks in their structure
- Occur because of: freeze-thaw action – earthquake activity – undercutting by rivers and waves – plant-root wedging

Fast moving/wet conditions

Landslides

- Common in mountain areas and along coasts
- Rotational slides (slumping) – curved surface
- Natural factors causing landslides include: rainfall – weathering (freeze-thaw) – earthquakes (vibrations) – strata – erosion (river and sea)
- Human activities that contribute to landslides include: loading (machinery, dams, etc.) – undercutting (steeper gradient) – deforestation (soil destabilised) – mining and quarrying – removing retaining walls

Landscapes

Human activities that can result in mass movement processes

Overgrazing in the West of Ireland	Deforestation in the Amazon Basin
Causes • Common Agricultural Policy = boosted incomes • Headage payments scheme • Intervention **Impact** • Sheep numbers grew rapidly in peripheral mountainous areas • West of Ireland = Connemara uplands + Mweelrea Mountains • Sheep numbers exceeded carrying capacity of land • Overgrazing removed grass and heather binding the soil • Soil became loose and unstable = moved downslope • Soil was compacted = faster runoff of surface water • 30% of upland areas suffered serious soil erosion • Led to localised landslides = damaged property, blocked roads, polluted rivers and lakes	**Causes** • Infrastructural development – 'Advance Brazil' • **Agriculture** – cattle population grew from 25 million to 90 million • **Logging** – over 30 million m^3 of logs taken each year • **Mining** – minerals such as copper, nickel, gold **Impact** • Protective cover preventing soil erosion removed • Trees slow runoff, water soaks into ground • Trees root systems stabilise slopes – bind soil particles • Trees are protective shield against force of rainfall = reduces its ability to erode • Decomposed leaves = rich layer of organic matter – increases water infiltration and the strength of soil • Heavy rainfall = mudslides and landslides

8 RIVER ACTION

LEARNING INTENTIONS
Syllabus Links: 1.5, 1.7

By the end of this chapter I will be able to:
- describe each of the river processes;
- identify features of the landscape formed by rivers from an Ordnance Survey (OS) map, a photograph and a diagram;
- indicate the stage at which each feature is formed and the dominant process(es) at play during its formation;
- describe the formation of at least one feature of both river erosion and river deposition using Irish and/or international examples;
- explain how human activities can impact on the operation of river processes.

KEYWORDS
source
tributary
confluence
mouth
estuary
drainage basin
watershed
course
fluvial
dendritic
trellis
radial
parallel
deranged
gradient
erosion
transportation
deposition
hydraulic action
cavitation
abrasion
attrition
solution
suspension
saltation
traction

Rivers play a very important role in shaping the natural landscape. They also influence the living patterns and economic activities of people.

Along their course, rivers gain water from other sources (precipitation, springs, streams) and have many distinctive characteristics, elements or components (Fig. 8.1). These include:

- **source:** the place where a river begins, usually on high ground;
- **tributary:** a stream or river that joins a larger one;
- **confluence:** the junction where two rivers join;
- **mouth:** the place where a river enters the sea or a lake;
- **estuary:** found at the mouth of the river where the river's current and the sea's tide meet – has a mixture of fresh and salt water;
- **drainage basin:** the entire area of land drained by a river and its tributaries;
- **watershed:** an area of high ground that separates one river basin from another;
- **course:** the distance the river travels from its rising at the source to its entry into the sea at its mouth.

Fluvial: Refers to the processes associated with rivers and streams and the deposits and landforms created by them.

EXAM TIP
Students are often asked to identify river drainage patterns in Section 1 – the Short Questions section.

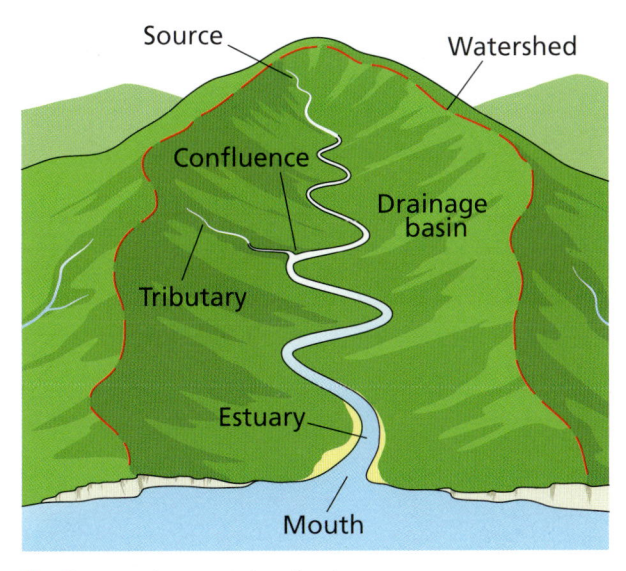

↑ **Fig. 8.1** Characteristics of a river system.

101

River Drainage Patterns

Dendritic

NOTE: Dendritic is the most common drainage pattern in Ireland.

The **dendritic** drainage pattern may be likened to the branches on a tree, as a large number of tributaries join the stream in a random fashion (Fig. 8.2). It's mainly found on upland areas, where the slope causes tributaries to join at an acute angle. The underlying unconsolidated material or rock can be easily eroded in all directions. The main river has the widest and deepest valley, as it has the greatest volume of water.

→ **Fig. 8.2(a)** Dendritic drainage pattern. Notice the way the streams look like the branches of a tree.

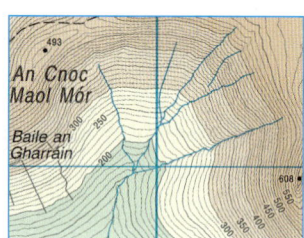

← **Fig. 8.2(b)** Dendritic drainage pattern on an OS map.

Trellis

The **trellis** drainage pattern displays a large number of right-angled confluences (Fig. 8.3). It can be found where folding has occurred or in places where the hardness of the rock varies. The rivers Bandon, Lee and Blackwater developed in valleys, where the softer limestone which occupied the anticlines was eroded, leaving the more resistant sandstone anticlines standing out.

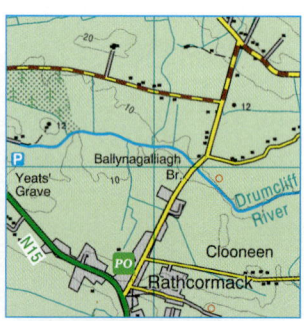

→ **Fig. 8.3(a)** Trellis drainage pattern.

↑ **Fig. 8.3(b)** Trellis drainage pattern on an OS map. Notice the right-angled confluences.

Radial

The **radial** drainage pattern sees rivers running off a conical hill or mountain. It gives a drainage pattern resembling the spokes on a wheel, radiating from the centre to the outer edges (Fig. 8.4). The individual rivers can later form a **dendritic** pattern as they move away from the hill.

↑ **Fig. 8.4(a)** Radial drainage pattern.

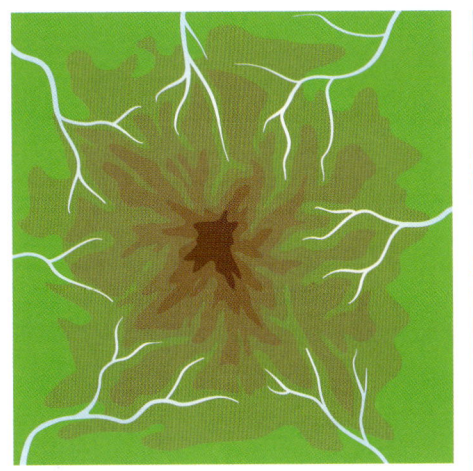

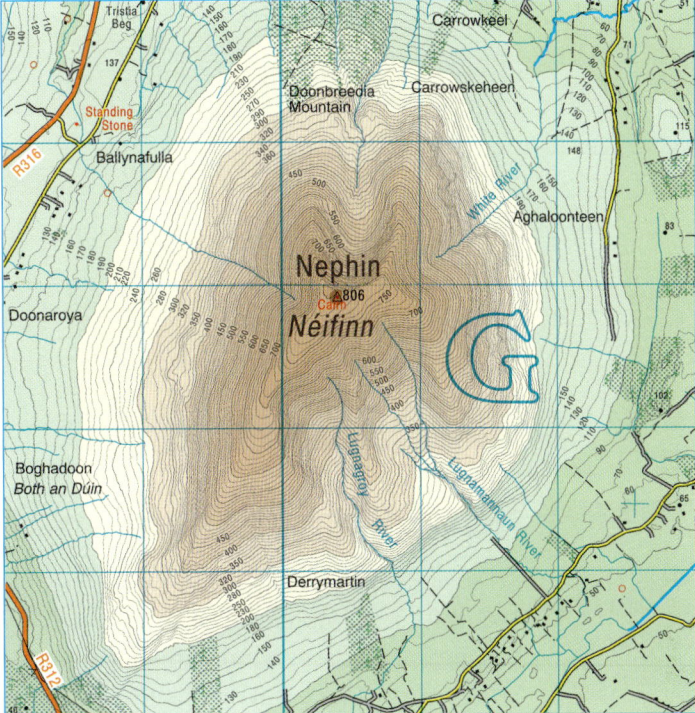

→ **Fig. 8.4(b)** Radial drainage pattern on an OS map.

Parallel

Commonly found in Cork and Waterford, these rivers flow **parallel** to each other due to the shape and structure of the land (Fig. 8.5). They run across the valleys created between fold mountains. Most rivers run from west to east, but all eventually run into the sea or lake without ever joining.

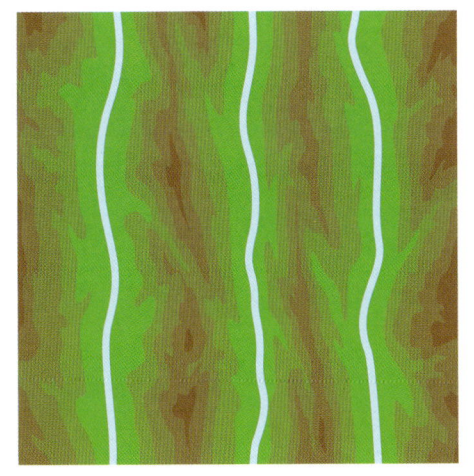

↑ **Fig. 8.5(a)** Parallel drainage pattern.

↑ **Fig. 8.5(b)** Parallel drainage pattern on an OS map. Notice the parallel river channels.

Deranged

When the pattern is **deranged**, streams flow in no particular direction. It is common in lowland areas which have been subjected to glacial deposition. Glacial deposits such as drumlins impede the establishment of any regular pattern and the rivers flow in a confused pattern through the area (**Fig. 8.6**).

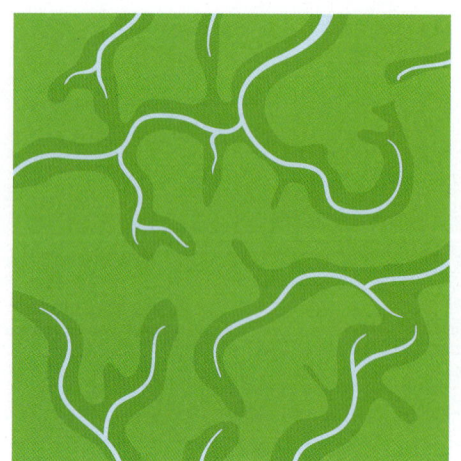

← **Fig. 8.6(a)** Deranged drainage pattern.

↓ **Fig. 8.6(b)** Deranged drainage pattern on an OS map.

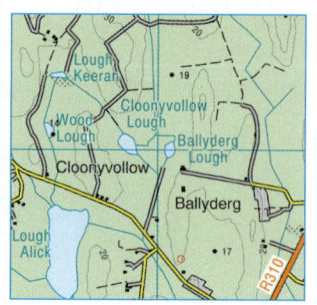

> Rivers carry a greater volume of water in winter than summer due to higher precipitation and lower evaporation rates.

> **Cavitation:** This is a process of hydraulic action, where bubbles of air collapse in the water creating shock waves that spread out. These shock waves weaken the banks of rivers, especially those composed of sand and clay, causing them to be broken down.

River Processes

The gradient and valley profile of a river changes as it flows from its source in its youthful stage/upper valley to its mouth in its old age stage/lower valley. Rivers shape our landscape through **erosion** (wearing it down), **transportation** (carrying the load downstream) and **deposition** (dropping the load).

Processes of river erosion

Hydraulic action: The riverbed and riverbank is eroded by the force of the moving water in its channel. Joints of rocks are enlarged, while loose fragments get swept away.

Abrasion/Corrasion: Material (**load**) picked up by the moving river is used as a tool of erosion against the bed and banks of the river.

Attrition: Rocks and pebbles (load) rub against one another as they are moved by the river. This causes their rough edges to be worn down leaving them smaller, smoother and rounder.

Solution/Corrosion: Soluble rocks in the river channel are dissolved by acids in the water, for example, limestone in the bed and bank of the river is dissolved by carbonic acid in the water.

The rate of river erosion depends on:
- **the volume of water of the river**. Rivers in flood erode at a faster rate than rivers in their normal state, as they have more energy.
- **the speed/velocity of the river**. Rivers erode at a faster rate when they flow quickly. The speed of flow is influenced by the:
  - **gradient**: steeper gradients create a faster flow of water, leading to greater rates of erosion;
  - **wetted perimeter**: friction caused by the flowing water, coming in contact with the riverbed and riverbank leads to a loss of energy and lower rates of erosion. Narrow, deep river channels have a smaller wetted perimeter, therefore the river flows faster, leading to greater rates of erosion (**Fig. 8.7**).
- **the hardness of the rock**. Softer, less resistant rocks (e.g. **sedimentary rocks**) are more easily eroded than harder, more resistant rocks (e.g. **metamorphic rocks**).

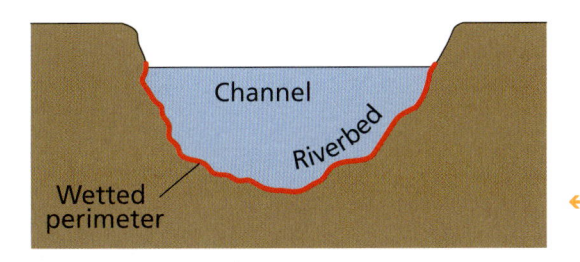

Fig. 8.7 The wetted perimeter of a river channel.

Wetted perimeter: The area of the riverbed and bank that comes into contact with water.

Processes of river transportation

Rivers transport material once they have eroded it (Fig. 8.8). This transportation takes place through:

- **solution:** dissolved rocks such as limestone are carried in a solution (this requires least energy);
- **suspension:** light materials such as sand and clay are carried by the moving water as a **suspended load**; this is commonly seen in times of flood when they turn the water a muddy brown colour;
- **saltation:** small, light rocks/pebbles are bounced along the riverbed;
- **traction:** heavy materials are rolled/dragged along the riverbed (this requires most energy).

River deposition

Rivers deposit their loads when:

- **their volume decreases.** A river's volume decreases when:
  - there is a dry season or it enters a hot, dry region with high evaporation rates;
  - permeable rocks such as limestone allow water to pass through them;
  - flood waters recede;
  - water is taken from the river for agricultural, industrial or domestic use.
- **their speed decreases.** The speed of a river decreases when:
  - it enters a sea, lake or a gently sloping plain;
  - there is an increase in the roughness of the channel.

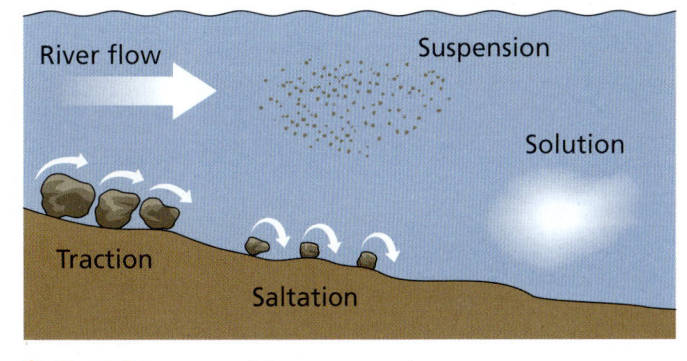

Fig. 8.8 Processes of river transportation.

CHECK YOUR LEARNING

1. Where is the source of a river found?
2. What is the tidal point of the river's mouth called?
3. How would you recognise a 'dendritic' drainage pattern on an OS map?
4. Where would you expect to find a 'radial' drainage pattern?
5. Glacial deposits have a big impact on the formation of what type of drainage pattern?
6. Explain the process of 'cavitation'.
7. Name one rock type that can be eroded by the process of solution and explain how this occurs.
8. Explain why a river may be brown in colour when in flood.

Landscapes

KEYWORDS

youthful stage
vertical erosion
bedload
headward erosion
differential erosion
V-shaped valley
potholes
interlocking spurs
less resistant
more resistant
waterfall
overhang
gorge
rapids

EXAM TIP

Students must be prepared to identify all river landforms from an OS map, a photograph or a diagram in Section 1 (short questions) OR in Part A questions (20 marks) in Section 2.

Youthful Stage – Upper Valley

Characteristics

Located near the river source, the river flows through a steep-sided and narrow valley, as it:

- exists in an upland area with few tributaries and therefore has a small volume of water;
- has a steep gradient, causing it to flow quickly and carry out **vertical erosion** (Fig. 8.9).

Weathered material, such as large rocks and angular stones, can be seen in the river channel. Known as the **bedload**, it is used as a tool of erosion (abrasion) when it is moved by traction and saltation.

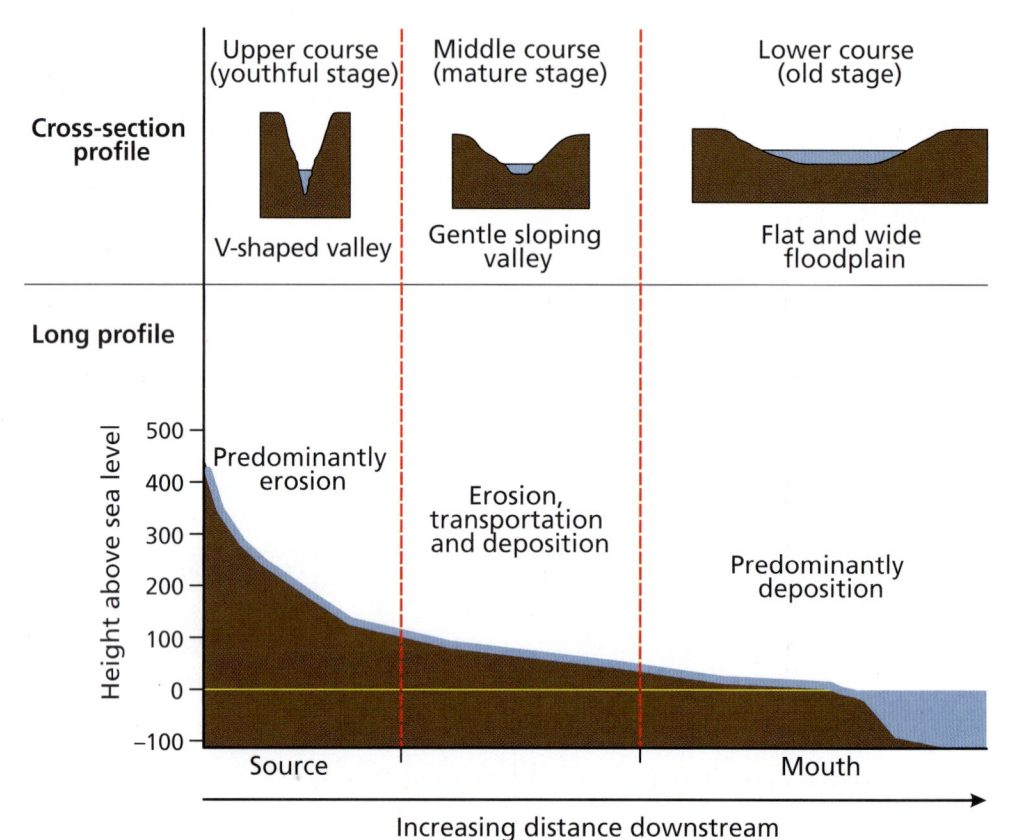

↑ **Fig. 8.9** Cross-section and long profile of a river valley from source to mouth.

→ **Fig. 8.10** Vertical and headward erosion.

Vertical erosion: When the river erodes downwards into its bed. This typically occurs in the youthful stage (Fig. 8.10).

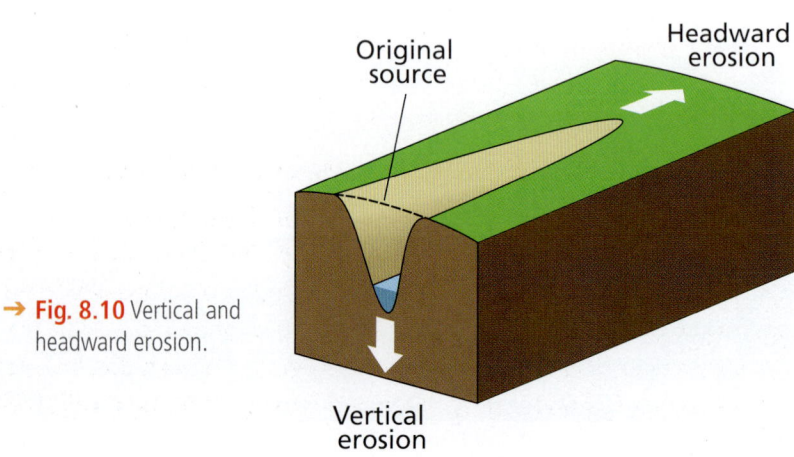

Landforms

V-shaped valley

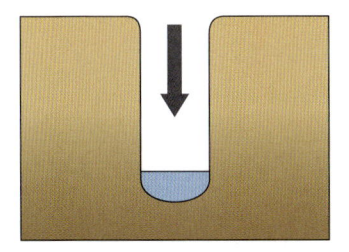

1. Vertical erosion Small volume of water uses its energy to erode downwards

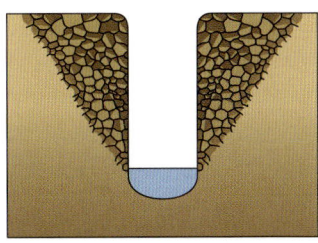

2. Weathering River is on high ground and valley sides are weathered by freeze-thaw action

3. Mass movement Loose material travels downslope under the influence of gravity, creating a bedload of large, angular rocks

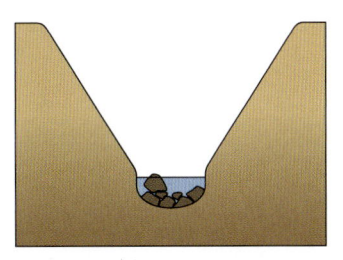

4. V-shaped valley Steep-sided, narrow valley is formed

← **Fig. 8.11(a)** Stages in the formation of a V-shaped valley.

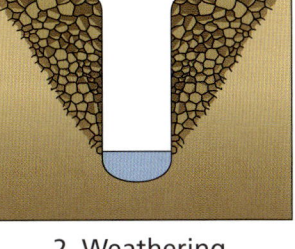

↓ **Fig. 8.11(b)** V-shaped valley: notice the steep slopes have formed a v-shape at either side of the river channel.

← **Fig. 8.11(c)** V-shaped valley on an OS map: as the river flows downhill, it flows through contours with an inverted V-shape.

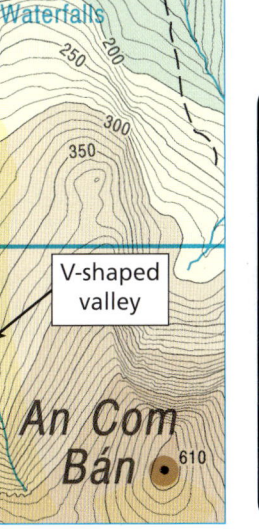

↑ **Fig. 8.12** Potholes in a river.

> The formation of **potholes** can also assist in the development of a V-shaped valley. Potholes are cylindrical holes formed in the bed of a river by swirling currents called **eddy** currents. The eddy currents can use the load carried by the river to erode the riverbed through abrasion. Over time, the potholes get bigger and bigger until they eventually join together, deepening the riverbed (Fig. 8.12).

Eddy currents: The swirling action of water, usually occurs as it enters a hole.

Chapter 6: Weathering Processes and Landforms
Chapter 7: Mass Movement

Irish examples: River Slaney; River Lee

Description: A **V-shaped valley** has a narrow floor and steep sides.

Formation: As the river flows quickly downhill from the source, its small volume of water is used to vertically erode the riverbed. The upland nature of the area brings high levels of precipitation, while temperatures are more likely to fluctuate above and below freezing point. As a result, the landscape on either side of the river channel is weathered by freeze-thaw action. The broken down material (scree) moves downslope under the influence of gravity, forming a valley with a 'V' shape (Fig. 8.11).

8 River Action

107

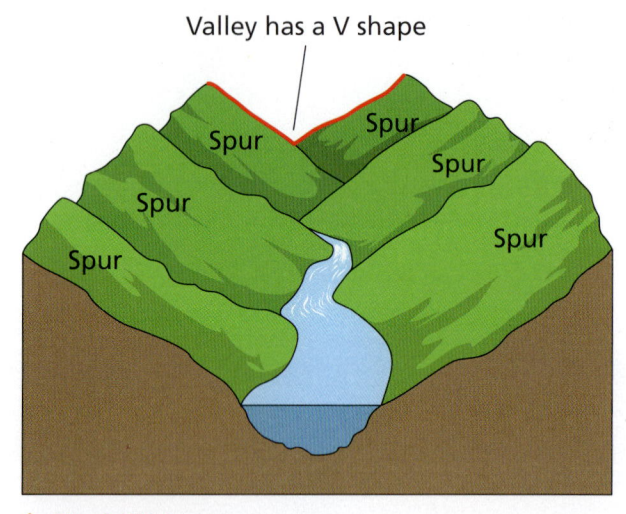

Landscapes

↑ **Fig. 8.13(a)** Interlocking spurs.

Differential erosion: Less resistant rocks are worn down at a faster rate than more resistant rocks, for example, chalk is worn down faster than granite.

→ **Fig. 8.13(c)** Interlocking spurs on an OS map: these are bends in a river as it flows downhill through a V-shaped valley.

→ **Fig. 8.13(b)** Interlocking spurs: notice how the spurs block the view of the river back upstream.

Waterfalls are also formed by:
- **tectonic activity:** when a river flows through an area where a block of rock is displaced, the fault created forces the river to plunge from a great height;
- **river rejuvenation:** when land rises, rivers renew the process of vertical erosion.

Interlocking spurs

Irish examples: *River Slaney; River Lee*

Description: Areas of high ground that lock into each other from either side of a young river valley.

Formation: In its youthful stage, the river flows quickly downhill with a small volume of water. As it cuts downwards into the riverbed, it erodes the unconsolidated material and softer, **less resistant** rock (**vertical erosion**). The young river hasn't enough energy to erode the harder, **more resistant** rocks at the same rate, however (**differential erosion**). Forced to find a path around the **truncated spurs** of harder rock at either side of the stream, the river develops a zigzag course (**Fig. 8.13**).

Waterfalls

Irish examples: *Torc Waterfall, Co. Kerry; Powerscourt Waterfall, Co. Wicklow*

Description: Water flows over a vertical drop in the bed of a young river.

Formation: Rivers undertake **vertical erosion** when they flow quickly downhill from upland areas. **Differential erosion** of the riverbed occurs where a band of soft, less resistant rock (e.g. **chalk**) lies downstream of a band of harder, more resistant rock (e.g. **granite**). A 'step' is created in the riverbed by the force of the moving water (**hydraulic action**) and the load that it carries (**abrasion**). The river increases its speed as it flows over the step due to a reduction in friction between the river and its channel. This further increases the river's ability to erode the softer rock, causing the step to deepen further. Over time, a small waterfall is created, as the harder rock is left elevated above the newly formed riverbed below.

As the river cascades over the small waterfall, a **plunge pool** is created at its base through **hydraulic action**, **abrasion** and **eddying** (the swirling action of the water).

8 River Action

An **overhang** of hard, resistant rock forms as the spray of the falling water erodes softer, less resistant rock found on the back wall of the waterfall (**solution**). Repeated undercutting of the overhang eventually causes it to collapse into the plunge pool under the force of its own weight (**gravity**). The energy of the material falling from the overhang causes further erosion of the plunge pool (**abrasion**) (Fig. 8.14).

Repeated undercutting and collapse results in the waterfall retreating upstream in a process called **headward erosion**. The volume of water in the river channel is reduced as the waterfall retreats upstream, reducing the rate of erosion. Below the waterfall, a narrow valley with steep sides called a **gorge** remains as evidence of the retreating waterfall. A gorge 11 km in length has been created as **Niagara Falls** on the Canada/USA border has retreated.

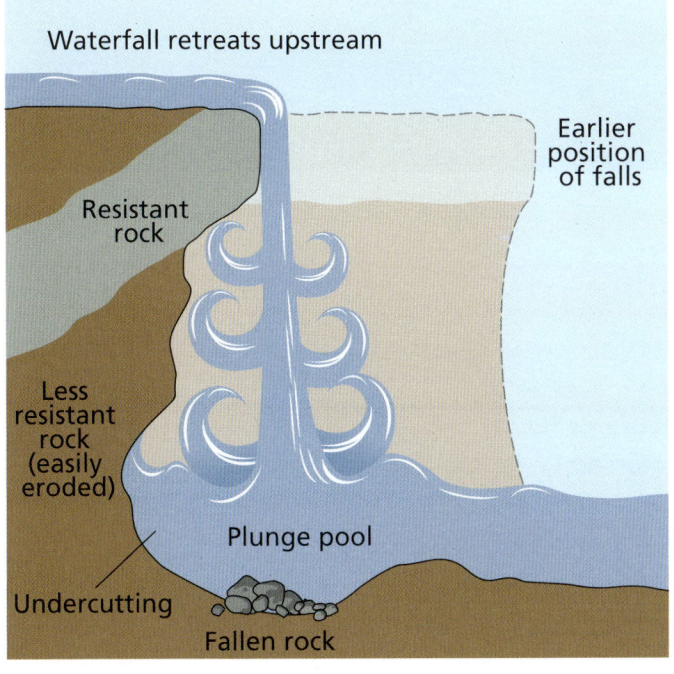

↑ **Fig. 8.14(a)** Formation of a waterfall.

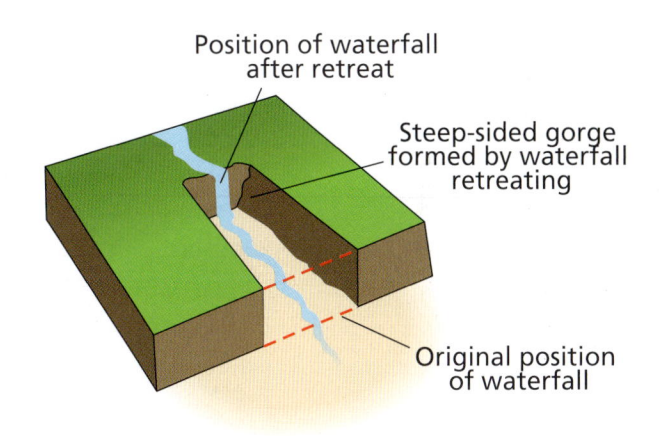

↑ **Fig. 8.14(b)** Formation of a waterfall: retreat.

← **Fig. 8.14(c)** Angel Falls on the Carrao River in Venezuela. At 979 m, this is the highest waterfall in the world.

↓ **Fig. 8.14(d)** Waterfalls will be labelled on an OS map using the word 'Waterfall' (or '*Eas*' if the map is from a Gaeltacht area).

Landscapes

Rapids: Rapids are formed in areas of the river where the gradient is steep and the hard, resistant rock is worn down at a slower rate than the softer, less resistant rock surrounding it. A drop is created in the river, increasing the speed and turbulence of the flowing water (**Fig. 8.15**).

↑ **Fig. 8.15** Rapids.

EXAM TIP

A relevant labelled diagram (optional) and a named example of the feature will be awarded 1 SRP each.

EXAM LINK (HL)

Surface Processes (30 marks)
Examine the impact of the processes of erosion on the formation of one fluvial landform that you have studied.
2015, Q1B

Marking Scheme:
Named processes = 2 + 2 marks
Named landform = 2 marks
Examination = 12 SRPs × 2 marks

EXAM TIP

Answering this question using a waterfall is recommended, as they're formed by a number of processes of erosion and have many associated features, each of which can be used to develop an SRP.
All processes mentioned should be explained and linked to the formation of the feature.

CHECK YOUR LEARNING

1. List the three stages of river development.
2. What transportation processes are most active in the youthful stage of the river?
3. Explain the terms vertical erosion and bedload.
4. List and explain three processes in the formation of a V-shaped valley.
5. What evidence in the photo tells you the river is at the youthful stage in Fig. 8.11(b)?
6. List and explain the process that forms potholes.
7. Explain the process of 'differential erosion'.
8. Explain the process of 'headward erosion'.
9. How does an overhang form?
10. Name two Irish and two international waterfalls.

110

Mature Stage – Middle Valley

Characteristics

The river has:

- a gentler gradient and smoother course which results in **reduced vertical erosion**;
- increased volumes of water, as tributaries have joined;
- a wider, flat-floored valley with gently sloping sides – this is a result of **lateral erosion**.

The load carried by the river is smaller and less angular, having been worn down by **attrition**. This lighter load is mainly transported by the process of **suspension**.

Landforms

Meanders

Irish examples: mature stages of the River Shannon; River Liffey

Description: Pronounced bends formed by the processes of erosion and deposition.

Formation: Meanders are initially found in the mature stage of a river, where **vertical erosion** of the youthful stage has been replaced by **lateral erosion**. The river channel is widened by:

- **hydraulic action** (the force of the moving water), a direct result of the increased volume of water due to added tributaries;
- **abrasion**, as the river is carrying a greater load following vertical erosion in the youthful stage.

In periods of dry weather or areas of permeable rock, the volume of water in the river will drop. This reduces its power, causing it to drop some of its **load** (silt and sand) on the riverbed. Up to this point, the river had a straight course, but now it is forced to swing from side to side as the water flows around the deposited bars of **sediment**. The shallow areas of the riverbed, where sediment has built up and the water travels slowly, are called **riffles**. The deeper areas of the riverbed, where the river flows quickly, are called **pools**. Gentle bends form over time as the river flows slowly around the riffles and quickly through the pools.

As the river flows around the outer bend, its strong current leads to erosion by the processes of **hydraulic action** and **abrasion**. The fast-flowing water and its load undercuts the riverbank, forming a **river cliff**. The river has to slow down to get around the narrow inner bank, causing it to deposit some of its load (silt and sand), forming a **point bar**. Meanders becomes more pronounced as they migrate downstream with the outer bends taking on a **concave** shape and the inner bends a **convex** shape (Fig. 8.17).

8 River Action

KEYWORDS

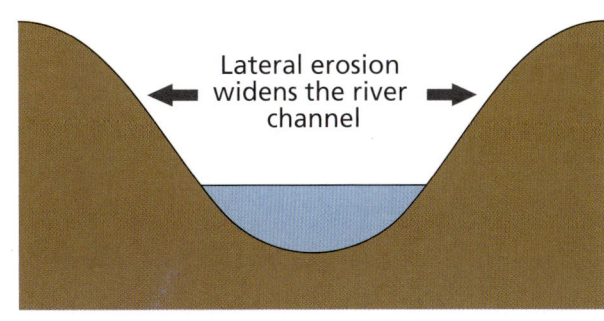

mature stage
lateral erosion
meander
sediment
riffles
pools
river cliff
point bar
concave
convex
alluvial fan
braided stream

↑ **Fig. 8.16** Lateral erosion.

Lateral erosion: When the river erodes sideways into its banks, widening the river channel. This is most commonly associated with the mature stage of a river (**Fig. 8.16**).

↓ **Fig. 8.17(a)** Formation of a meander.

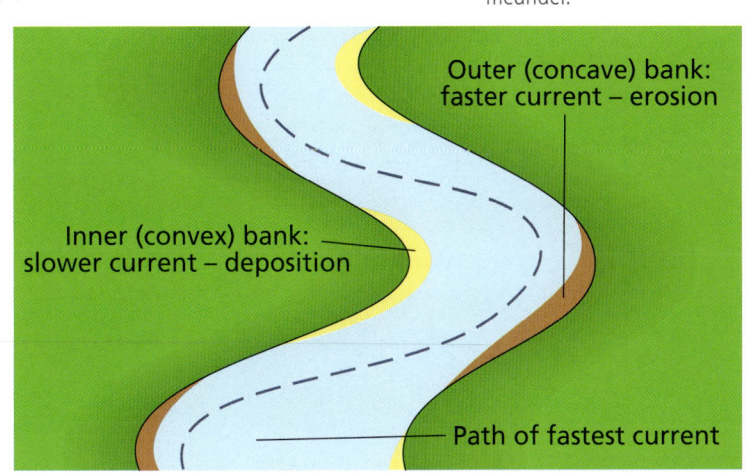

Outer (concave) bank: faster current – erosion

Inner (convex) bank: slower current – deposition

Path of fastest current

111

Landscapes

Point bar: This can also be referred to as a **slip-off slope** or a **river beach**.

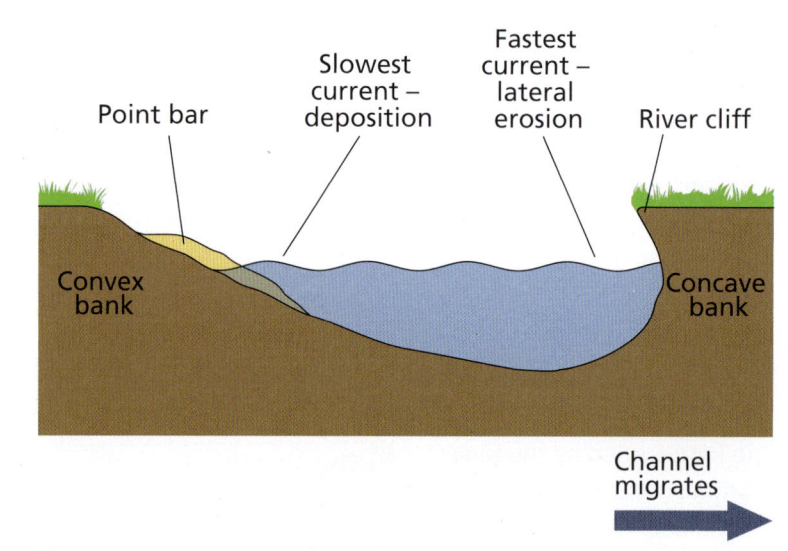

Fig. 8.17(b) Front profile of a meander being formed.

Labels: Point bar, Slowest current – deposition, Fastest current – lateral erosion, River cliff, Convex bank, Concave bank, Channel migrates

EXAM TIP (HL)

In the 2018 Higher Level paper, students were asked to describe the formation of a feature they could identify on the Ordnance Survey map extract accompanying the exam. Meanders can be identified on most OS map exam extracts, as they are typically taken from low-lying areas.

EXAM LINK (HL)

Possible exam question (30 marks)

Explain, with the aid of a labelled diagram(s), the formation of one landform created by both erosional and depositional processes.

Marking Scheme:
Named landform = 2 marks
Explanation = 14 SRPs × 2 marks

Fig. 8.17(c) Meander: notice the point bar on the inner bend and river cliff on the outer bend of the river.

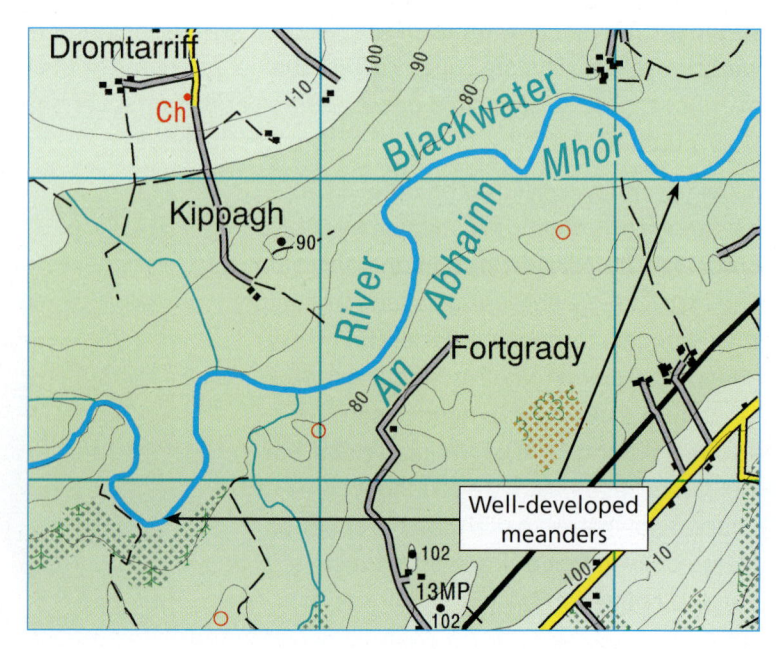

Fig. 8.17(d) Meanders (pronounced bends) on an OS map.

112

Alluvial fans and braided streams

As a river moves from higher ground onto a flatter plain, it loses energy. This causes the river to deposit the heaviest sediments of its load on the riverbed. As these sediments build up, they form **alluvial fans**, which can cause the river to split into more than one channel, forming a **braided stream** (Fig. 8.18).

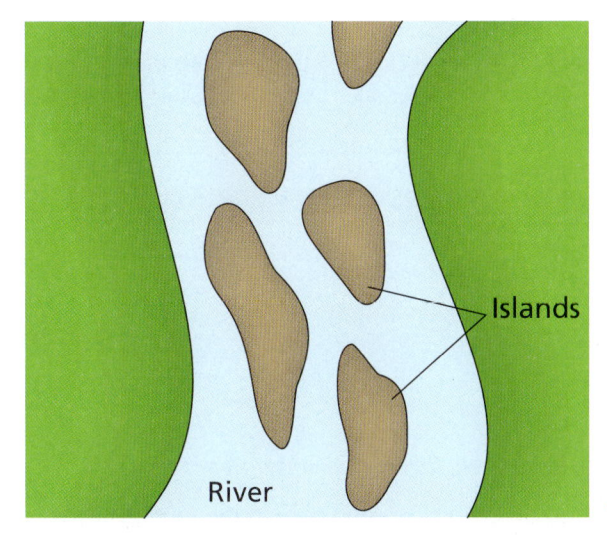

← Fig. 8.18(a) Braided stream.

↑ Fig. 8.18(b) Braided stream: notice the alluvial fans in the middle of the river.

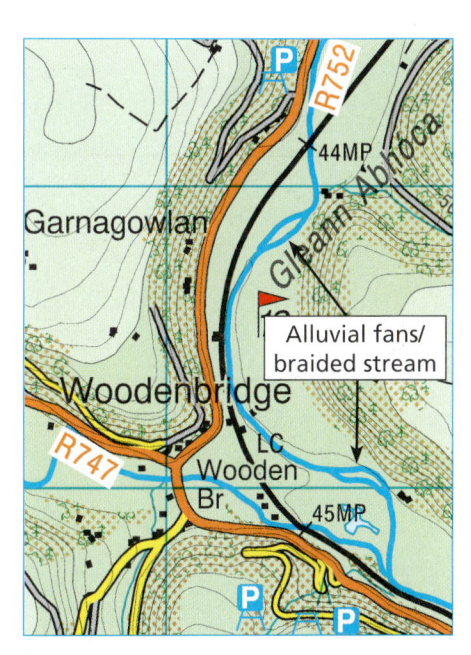

↑ Fig. 8.18(c) Braided stream: notice how the river has been divided into two streams before meeting again.

CHECK YOUR LEARNING

1. Explain the difference between vertical and lateral erosion.
2. Why does the river have an increased volume in the mature stage?
3. Explain the difference between 'bedload' and 'suspended load'.
4. List and explain two reasons deposition may occur on a river.
5. Describe what a meander looks like.
6. How does a river cliff form?
7. How does a point bar form?
8. What is a braided stream and how does it form?

Landscapes

KEYWORDS

old age stage
floodplain
alluvium
levee
back-swamp
bluff line
flooding
oxbow lake
mort lake
delta
lacustrine delta
topset bed
foreset bed
bottomset bed
arcuate delta
bird's foot delta

Old Age Stage – Lower Valley

Characteristics

- The river flows over land that has a very gentle gradient – it is almost level. As a result, the river moves slowly and has very little energy (power) to erode.
- This is the widest part of the river valley. It has a flat floor and gently sloping sides.
- The river carries large loads of small rounded material such as sand and silt.
- **Deposition** is common – finer material is deposited due to the rivers reduced energy.

Landforms

Floodplains

Irish examples: *River Shannon at Castleconnell; River Blackwater near Fermoy*

Description: A level area of land found on both sides of a river in its old age stage.

Formation: Volumes of water in the river channel are greatest in the old stage, as a number of tributaries have joined further upstream. The river also carries a large load as a result of upstream erosion – vertical erosion in the youthful stage and lateral erosion in the mature stage.

The gradient of the river is almost flat, meaning the river's ability to transport its load is reduced and instead it concentrates on **deposition**. Some of the load falls to the riverbed raising it up, causing water levels in the river channel to be raised also.

After heavy rain, the amount of water in the channel increases further causing the river to overflow its banks and flood the surrounding land. As the floodwaters spread out across the floodplain and away from the river channel, it loses its ability to carry its load and **deposition** occurs. The coarser, heavier material is deposited first on the banks of the river, as the river doesn't have the energy to carry it any further. Lighter sediments of sand and silt, which create a nutrient-rich **alluvium**, are carried further and deposited on the flat land of the floodplain (Fig. 8.19).

Repeated **flooding** and deposition of alluvium has two effects:

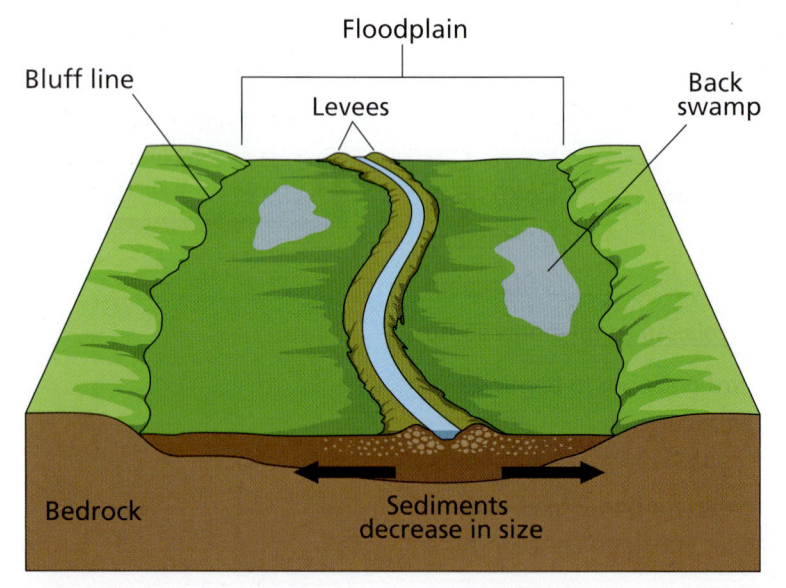

↑ **Fig. 8.19(a)** River floodplain.

1. The banks of the river are raised over the floodplain, forming **levees** which act as natural barriers against further flooding. Sometimes, the levees prevent floodwaters retreating back into the river, creating **backswamps** of infertile soil.
2. The flat land of the floodplain gradually increases in height, allowing floodwaters to spread further across the land. This causes the **bluff line**, which marks the end point of the floodplain and an increase in the height of the land, to be extended.

8 River Action

DID YOU KNOW?
Floodplains are very fertile areas of land, so are often used for agriculture and growing crops.

← **Fig. 8.19(b)** Floodplain: notice the levees (raised banks) and the flat land at either side of the river.

Flooding: Occurs when rivers are filled with too much water. The water breaks through the riverbanks and spreads over the surrounding land.

Artificial levees are sometimes constructed by engineers in or near urban areas in order to reduce a river's ability to flood businesses and homes.

← **Fig. 8.19(c)** Floodplain: notice there is no settlement on the floodplain due to the threat of flooding.

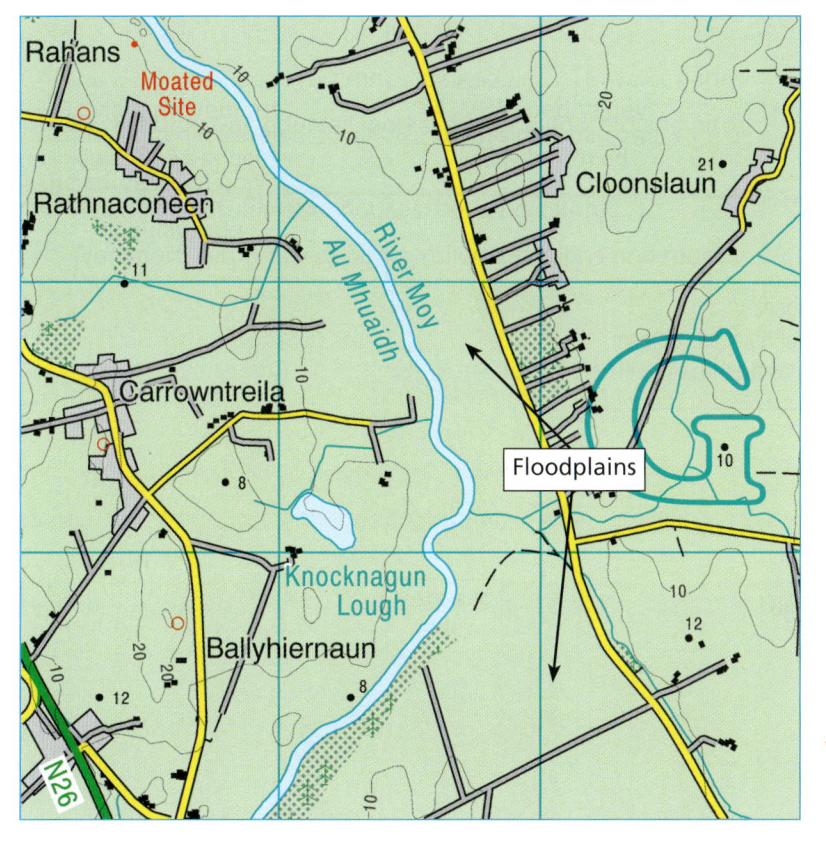

CHECK YOUR LEARNING

1. Why is the river 'slow moving' in its old age?
2. List two reasons why a river may overflow its banks.
3. What is 'alluvium'?
4. Explain the difference between natural and artificial levees.
5. How does a 'back-swamp' form?
6. What does a 'bluff line' indicate in a floodplain?
7. What evidence in Fig. 8.19(b) tells you the river is in the old stage/lower valley?
8. Floodplains are valuable agricultural land but unsuitable locations for development. Explain.

Landscapes

Mort lake: Over time, the oxbow lake will dry up, as it is not being supplied with water. It is then called a mort lake.

Oxbow lakes

Irish examples: *Inistioge on the River Nore, Co. Kilkenny; River Moy, Co. Mayo*

Description: A horseshoe-shaped lake found on the floodplain of a river in its old stage.

Formation: Rivers slow down in the older stage due to the gentle gradient of the land. As it slows, a river swerves from side to side, forming **pronounced meanders**. On the outer (concave) bank, the river flows quickly and **lateral erosion** takes place. On the inner (convex) bank, the river slows down to get around the narrower curve and **deposition** takes place. After a period of time, only a narrow neck of land separates the bend's inner banks. While in flood, the fast-flowing river cuts through this narrow neck of land, creating a straight river channel that allows water to move more efficiently. The flowing water gradually abandons the cut-off meander and sediment is deposited at the side of the river. Eventually, the cut-off meander becomes completely sealed off from the main river channel (**Fig. 8.20**).

↓ **Fig. 8.20(a)** Formation of an oxbow lake.

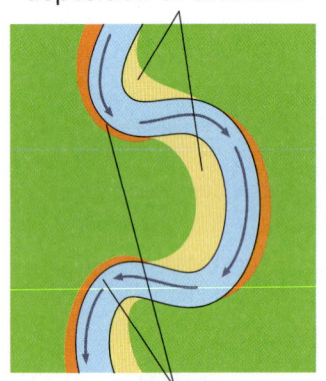

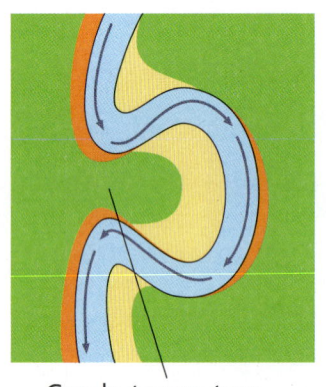

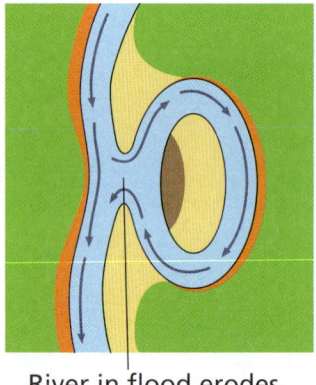

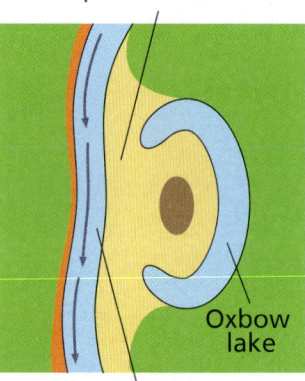

- Inner (convex) bank: slower current – deposition of sediment
- Outer (concave) bank: faster current – lateral erosion
- Gap between two meanders narrows
- River in flood erodes the narrow neck of land
- Following the flood, the river slows and deposition occurs
- River now flows on a straight channel
- Oxbow lake

Key
- Banks liable to erosion
- Newer deposits of sediment
- Older deposits of sediment
- → Current

↑ **Fig. 8.20(b)** An oxbow lake cut off from the main river.

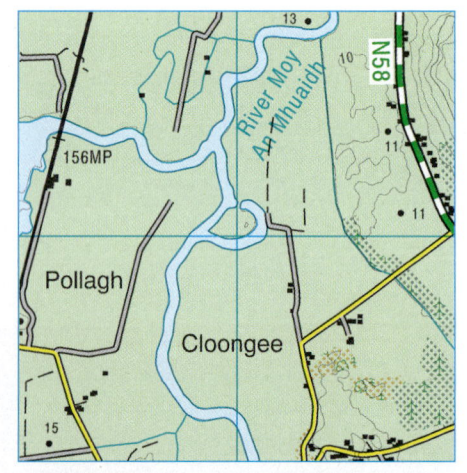

↑ **Fig. 8.20(c)** An oxbow lake being formed on the River Moy.

EXAM TIP (HL)

When answering a question based on the formation of a feature of river deposition, marks will only be awarded for the parts of your answer that deal with the process of deposition. Be careful not to spend time describing processes of erosion as you will not be awarded marks for this.

Deltas

Description: Deltas are deposits of sediment found in the mouth of a river. **Marine deltas** are formed where rivers flow into seas and **lacustrine deltas** form where rivers flow into lakes.

Formation: Rivers deposit large volumes of sediment in the mouth for two reasons:

1. Coming in contact with the sea causes the river to lose energy and slow down. This leaves it unable to carry the large suspended load it gathered during upstream erosion.
2. **Flocculation:** As fresh water (river) mixes with salt water (sea) a chemical reaction causes sediment particles to stick together and fall onto the riverbed, where they settle.

In some places, the currents and tides are weak and unable to carry away the deposited sediments. When this happens, sediments build up in layers called **beds**, forming new fertile patches of land called **deltas** (Fig. 8.21).

The largest and heaviest sediments are the first to be deposited as the river loses energy. They form the **topset bed** which extends the shortest distance out into the sea or lake.

Medium-grained sediments travel a little further before they are deposited on the **foreset bed**.

The finest/lightest sediments travel the furthest before they are deposited on the **bottomset bed**.

As the sediments build up, the river may be forced to split into a number of different channels called **distributaries**. Each of the three types of marine delta has a different shape, depending on how it was formed.

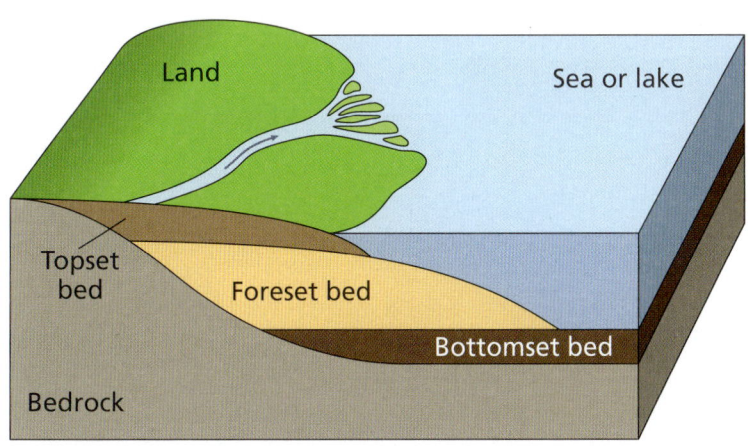

> **DID YOU KNOW?**
> The Yellow River in China deposits approximately 1.6 billion tonnes of sediment into its delta each year.

↑ **Fig. 8.21** Formation of a delta.

↑ **Fig. 8.22(a)** Arcuate delta.

Arcuate delta

Example: *Nile Delta, Egypt*

Arcuate deltas are **fan-shaped**, with the widest part of the fan facing the sea. They form where the river water is as dense as the sea water. Arcuate deltas are made of coarse materials such as gravel and sand and their distributaries form **dendritic** drainage patterns (Fig. 8.22).

→ **Fig. 8.22(b)** Satellite image of the Nile Delta.

Landscapes

> **EXAM TIP (OL)**
>
> With the exception of 2014, this question appeared every year from 2011 to 2018.

> **EXAM LINK (OL)**
>
> Landform Development (40 marks)
>
> Explain, with the aid of diagrams, the formation of any two landforms.
>
> 2018, Q2B
>
> **Marking Scheme:**
> Formation of any two landforms = 2 × 20 marks
> For each landform:
> landform = 1 mark
> diagram(s) = 2 aspects × 2 marks
> Formation explained = 5 SRPs × 3 marks. At least one SRP must explain a relevant process.

> **EXAM LINK (HL)**
>
> Landform Development (30 marks)
>
> Examine the impact of the processes of deposition on the formation of one fluvial landform that you have studied.
>
> 2016, Q1B
>
> **Marking Scheme:**
> Named landform = 2 marks
> Examination = 14 SRPs × 2 marks

> ⚠ A relevant labelled diagram (optional) and a named example of the feature will be awarded 1 SRP each.

Bird's foot delta

Example: *Mississippi Delta, USA*

A bird's foot delta is formed where the waves are weaker than the flow of the river. Sediment gathers along the edges of a small number of distributaries, giving the appearance of an out-stretched bird's claw (Fig. 8.23).

↑ **Fig 8.23(a)** Bird's foot delta.

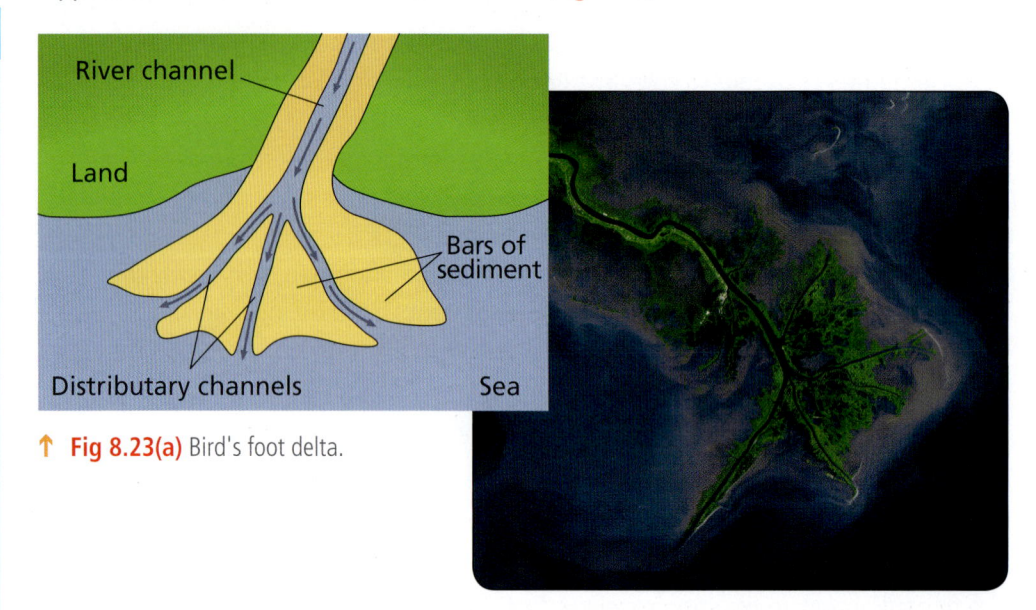

↑ **Fig 8.23(b)** Satellite image of the Mississippi Delta.

Cuspate delta

Example: *Tiber Delta, Italy*

Strong waves hit the river head-on, causing the deposited sediments to be spread in the shape of a tooth along a straight coastline (Fig. 8.24).

↑ **Fig 8.24(a)** Cuspate delta.

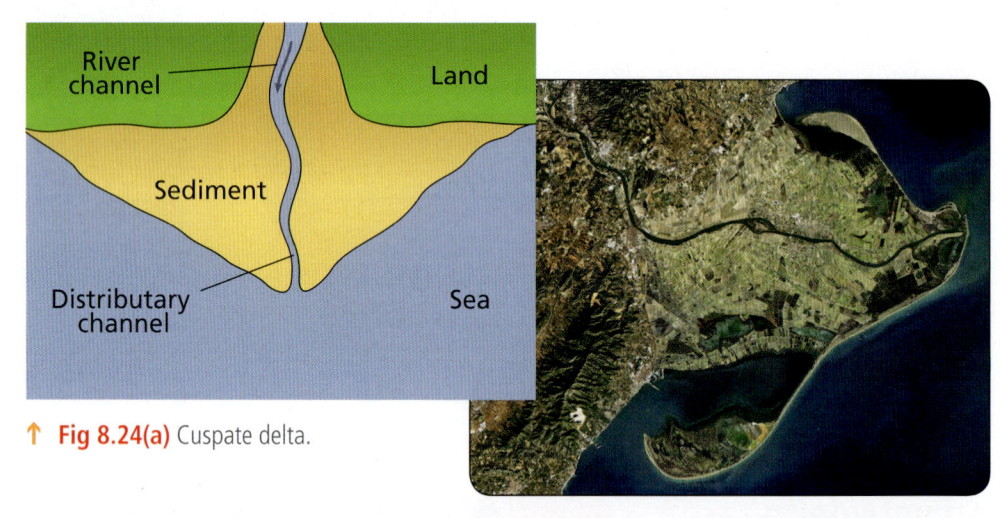

↑ **Fig 8.24(b)** Satellite image of the Ebro Delta

> **CHECK YOUR LEARNING**
>
> 1. Describe what an oxbow lake looks like.
> 2. How does a mort lake form?
> 3. List and explain two reasons sediment is deposited in the river mouth.
> 4. Describe two differences between the bottomset bed and the topset bed.
> 5. Explain the difference between a tributary and a distributary.
> 6. Where are lacustrine deltas formed? Give an example of where one can be found.

CASE STUDY: Mississippi River, USA

Background

The Mississippi River is the largest and longest river in North America. From its source in Minnesota, the Mississippi and its tributaries gather water from the whole of or parts of 31 states of the USA (Fig. 8.25). Flowing south for 3,734 km before entering the sea at New Orleans on the Gulf of Mexico, the Mississippi is worth over $400 billion to the US economy and supports approximately 1.3 million jobs.

The US Army Corp of Engineers is responsible for controlling the river. This includes:
- making sure navigation is safe;
- preventing major flooding.

Fig. 8.25 Drainage basin of the Mississippi River.

Navigation on the river

The Mississippi River and its tributaries are the backbone of a transportation system that feeds and fuels vast areas of the USA. Steamboats have been in use on the river since the 1830s, transporting goods (food, coal, gas, metals, timber, paper, etc.) to and from the world's largest port at New Orleans. This has led to the growth of many major cities (St Louis, Memphis, Minneapolis) and industries on its banks. Improving the river channel for shipping has been a major focus of river control efforts since the late 1800s.

DID YOU KNOW?
Barges move 300 million tonnes of goods each year on the Mississippi.

The Mississippi is used to transport 60% of US grain exports.

Upper course

29 **locks** and **dams** have been developed to support river navigation on the Upper Mississippi, where the valley gradient is steepest and the water level in the river channel is lowest (Fig. 8.26(a)). This has created lakes and a 2.7-metre deep channel which allows commercial barges and other small vessels to move up and down the river. As dams slowed the flow of the river, however, the natural process of erosion was interrupted and the river deposited material upstream that would normally be transported further downstream (Fig. 8.26(b)). This deprived agricultural land in floodplains downstream of fertile alluvial deposits.

Fig. 8.26(a) Sites of locks and dams on the upper Mississippi River.

Fig. 8.26(b) Barges on the Mississippi River.

Landscapes

Fig. 8.27 Concrete mat being used as revetment to prevent lateral erosion of the riverbank.

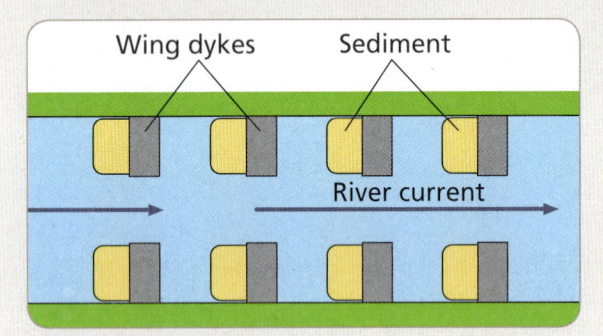

Fig. 8.28 Wing dykes.

Hydroelectric power stations were built in association with many of these dams to provide a source of clean, cheap, renewable electricity for the homes and businesses of the surrounding region. A great deal of the water stored in the dams was also used to serve other important functions: water treatment plants built beside the dams purify water for domestic and industrial use, and in the mid-west and southern states, very little rain falls from early June to late August, so irrigation is needed to support local agriculture.

Middle course

In the middle course of the Mississippi, lateral erosion on outer banks caused the river to move hundreds of feet unimpeded every year. This had major economic implications for towns and cities such as Rodney (Mississippi) which had grown up on the path of the Mississippi. As the river shifted, these towns were no longer on its path, meaning boats and barges no longer passed or docked, forcing many businesses to close. Initially, **revetments** using **stone facings** were built to prevent erosion of the riverbank and keep the river in place. Recent revetment programmes have seen **concrete mats** used for bank protection on almost 1,500 km of the river (Fig. 8.27).

More than 230,000 linear metres of **wing dykes** were also constructed on the middle stage of the Mississippi over the last 100 years (Fig. 8.28). Rocks and boulders were placed in the river channel at right angles to the bank at various locations to:

- slow the flow of water near the riverbank, reducing lateral erosion;
- force water into the faster flowing areas at the centre of the channel, reducing the rate of deposition.

The narrowing of the river channel led to an increase in velocity (speed) and erosion of the riverbed. Deeper channels were created, improving conditions for navigation.

Lower course

The lower Mississippi is approximately 15 metres deep, which allows large cargo ships to travel to inland ports such as Baton Rouge, Louisiana. The gentle gradient at this stage, however, causes the river to lose energy and slow down. Unable to carry its full suspended load, material is deposited on the riverbed forming sandbars which can damage the hull and propellers of large ships.

In problem areas, engineers **dredge** the riverbed to make it deeper and keep it navigable. Mud and other deposits are removed by dredging boats which scoop or suction material from the riverbed. Dredging is an expensive solution to this problem, however, and it has to be done annually due to high deposition levels.

Cut-offs have also been developed on all stages to improve navigation by eliminating dangerous winding channels. Over 243 km was taken off the distance of the river, which not only proved to be a commercial success, but also increased the speed of flow and reduced deposition on the riverbed in many problem areas.

Flood control

Throughout history, vast areas of the plain were flooded every spring when heavy rainfall and melting snow gathered by tributaries of the Mississippi caused the main stream to rise and frequently overflow its banks. If the flooding could be controlled, then it would be possible to farm the fertile alluvial floodplain, allowing settlements to grow up in the region.

Engineering

Two hundred and thirty **dams** were built on the upper Mississippi and its tributaries, controlling the flow of water downstream (Fig. 8.29). Large flood control reservoirs were created in areas where tributaries were likely to flood. During heavy rain, water is diverted into these reservoirs to prevent flooding and damage to surrounding areas. No dam can be built on the main channel, however, as the floodplain is too wide.

↑ **Fig. 8.29** Lock and dam on the Mississippi River.

DID YOU KNOW?
Over the past century, there has been one major flood of the Mississippi River approximately every seven years.

Artificial levee: Man-made embankment built to prevent a river from overflowing its banks.

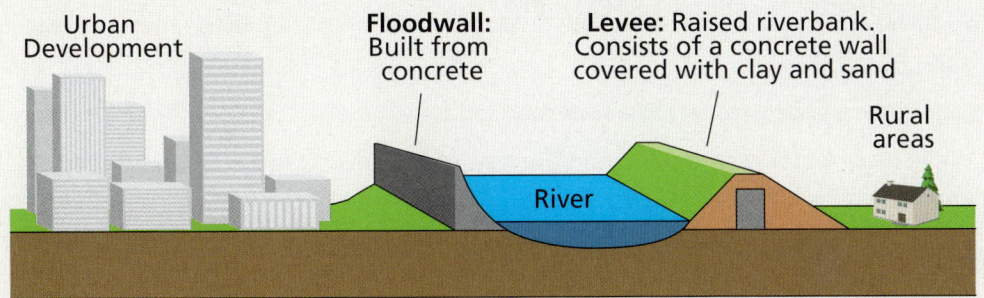

Over $20 billion has been spent on levees, floodwalls, gates and pumps in Greater New Orleans since Hurricane Katrina struck in 2005.

↑ **Fig. 8.30** Floodwalls and levees use materials that allow them to fit into the local landscape.

- Around 2,500 km of **artificial levees** have been built to hold back the water, protecting areas most in danger of floods. These levees consist of an impermeable concrete wall covered by earth materials, so they give a natural feel to the environment (Fig. 8.30). Natural levees already in place were also strengthened.

- Vast areas of land along the Mississippi River valley were **planted with forestry**. Forested areas absorb more rainfall, reducing the amount of surface runoff and sediment loads entering the river channel.

- **Diversion channels** were developed to divert large volumes of water around major cities such as New Orleans. This doubled the carrying capacity of the river during critical periods of heavy rainfall and high discharge.

- **Flood walls** made of reinforced concrete were built in cities, as they were stronger and took up less space in valuable urban land. Floodgates have been developed where the floodwalls cross roads, railways or waterways. They stay open for cars, trains and boat traffic but close during storm events.

- Under flood conditions, water is diverted into safe flood zones called **spillways** at critical points along the river's course. This reduces the speed of the river current and relieves pressure on local levees and floodwalls. Opened in 1931, the 7,200-acre Bonnet Carre Spillway has been used 12 times in total. Its 9 km course guides floodwaters into Lake Pontchartrain and on to the Gulf of Mexico (Fig. 8.31).

→ **Fig. 8.31** Map showing the extent of levee and spillway systems on the Mississippi River.

121

Landscapes

Effects on river processes

The flow of water along the Mississippi is more controlled and flooding now only affects 10% of the plain. The creation of man-made **artificial lakes** acting as reservoirs, however, means that farmland upstream has been lost to flooding.

Alluvial deposits on agricultural lands of the lower valley have also been greatly reduced as:

- **dam walls** act as obstacles to the suspended load in the youthful stage (Fig. 8.32);
- **revetment** works have successfully reduced the amount of lateral erosion in the mature stage.

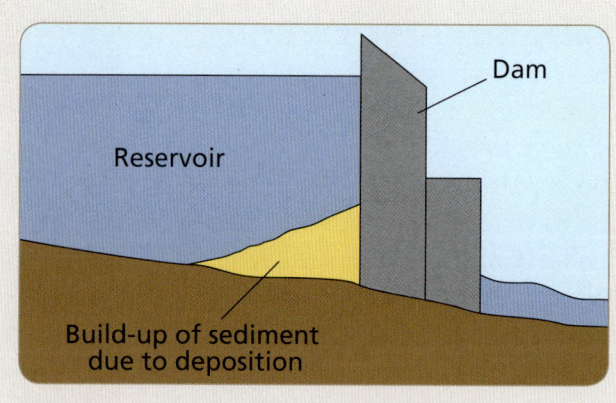

↑ **Fig. 8.32** Sediment being trapped behind a dam.

This has increased the cost of farming in the lower valley with farmers now having to purchase expensive fertilisers for their lands.

While more water is contained and the flow of water is more controlled, disasters are worse when the levees or walls break. Heavy winter snow and spring rains caused levees to burst on the Mississippi in 1993. Flooding caused $15 billion worth of damage with 10,000 homes completely destroyed. Hurricane Katrina brought thousands of deaths and widespread destruction in 2005. After this, a number of settlements that were built along the floodplain were abandoned, and new settlements were built on higher ground so as to avoid flooding.

EXAM LINK (OL)

Human Interaction with Surface Processes (30 marks)
Explain how humans interact with river processes.
2018, Q3C

Marking Scheme:
Interaction named: 3 marks
Description/explanation: 9 SRPs × 3 marks
Note: See Exam Tip on page 142.

EXAM LINK (HL)

Human Interaction with Surface Processes (30 marks)
Human activity impacts on surface processes. Examine this statement with reference to the impact of flood control measures on river processes.
2017, Q1C

Marking Scheme:
Impact on process identified = 2 marks
Examination of impact on process = 14 SRPs × 2 marks
Note: See Exam Tip on page 142.

EXAM TIP (OL)

With the exception of 2013, a question on human interaction with river processes has appeared on the exam paper every year from 2009 to 2018.

CHECK YOUR LEARNING

1. Why were dams built on the upper Mississippi?
2. What is 'dredging' and why was it carried out on the lower Mississippi?
3. What impact have wing dykes had on Mississippi navigation?
4. Explain why levees were built on the lower course of the Mississippi.
5. List and explain two steps carried out by engineers following the floods of 2005.
6. List three benefits of hydroelectric power (HEP).
7. Apart from the production of HEP, list and explain two other benefits of dam building.
8. Dam building causes problems for farmers. Explain.

8 River Action

EXAMINATION QUESTIONS
ORDINARY LEVEL

Short Questions

1. River Landforms

Examine the diagram showing river landforms and answer each of the following questions.

(i) Match each of the letters A, B, C and D with the landform that best matches it in the table below. *4 × 2 marks*

Landform	Letter
Levee	
Floodplain	
Meander	
Oxbow lake	

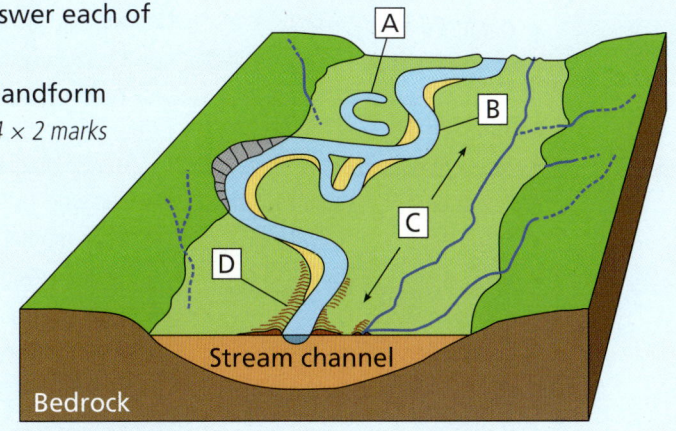

(ii) Indicate whether the landforms named above are most associated with the youthful stage of a river or the old age stage of a river, by ticking the correct box. *2 marks*

Youthful stage ☐   Old age stage ☐

2015, Part One, Q2 (10 marks)

HIGHER LEVEL

Short Questions

2. Pattern Recognition

Examine the diagrams showing fluvial drainage patterns. Match each of the letters A, B, C and D with the correct drainage pattern in the table. *4 × 2 marks*

Drainage pattern	Letter
Dendritic	
Deranged	
Trellis	
Radial	

2014, Part One, Q10 (8 marks)

Long Questions

3. Fluvial Landforms

Examine the diagram and answer each of the following questions.

(i) Name each of the fluvial landforms A, B, C, D, E and F. *6 × 2 marks*

(ii) Explain briefly what is meant by the term bedrock. *2 SRPs × 2 marks*

(iii) Explain briefly what is meant by the term alluvium. *2 SRPs × 2 marks*

2016, Part Two, Section 1, Q3A (20 marks)

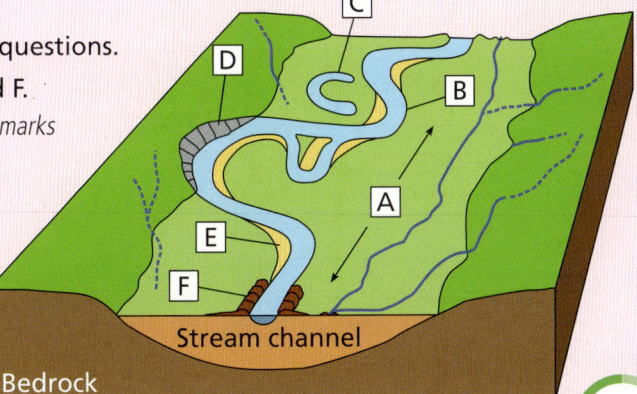

123

Revision Summary

Drainage patterns

- Dendritic – branches of tree
- Trellis – right-angled confluences
- Radial – spokes of a wheel
- Parallel – rivers side by side
- Deranged – no pattern

Processes

Erosion
- Hydraulic action
- Abrasion
- Attrition
- Solution

Transportation
- Solution
- Suspension – floating
- Saltation – bouncing
- Traction – dragging

Deposition
- Reduced volume – human use, evaporation, percolation
- Reduced speed – gradient almost flat

Youthful stage – upper valley

Characteristics
- Found in upland areas
- Few tributaries = small volume
- Steep gradient = fast-flowing
- Vertical erosion = steep-sided/narrow valley
- Weathering = large bedload

Features
- V-shaped valleys (River Lee)
- Interlocking spurs (River Slaney)
- Potholes and rapids
- Waterfalls (Torc; Powerscourt)
  - Youthful stage – steep gradient
  - Vertical erosion
  - Abrasion and attrition
  - Differential erosion
  - Step = less friction, faster flow
  - Cap rock – vertical fall
  - Plunge pool – falling water
  - Overhang formed – solution
  - Overhang collapse – gravity
  - Headward erosion = retreat
  - Gorge

Mature stage – middle valley

Characteristics
- Gentle gradient = less vertical erosion
- More tributaries = increased volume
- Lateral erosion = wider, flatter valley
- Smaller, less angular load – attrition
- Load transported by suspension

Features
- Alluvial fans and braided streams
- Meanders (River Shannon)
  - Pronounced bends
  - Erosion and deposition
  - Lateral erosion – wider channel
  - Hydraulic action – larger volume
  - Abrasion – larger load
  - Dry weather – reduced volume
  - Deposition on riverbed
  - Sediment build up – riffles
  - Deeper riverbed – pools
  - Outer bend – strong current
  - River cliff – concave shape
  - Inner bend – weaker current
  - River bar – convex shape

Old stage – lower valley

Characteristics
- Gradient almost flat – slow moving – little energy to erode
- Widest, flattest valley
- Rounded material – sand and silt – deposition – river's energy reduced

Features
- Oxbow lake (Inistioge on River Nore)
- Acruate delta (River Nile)
- Bird's foot delta (River Mississippi)
- Cuspate delta (River Tiber)
- Floodplain (River Blackwater)
  - Old age – flat valley
  - Large volume – tributaries
  - Large load – upstream erosion
  - Gentle gradient – reduced energy
  - Deposition raises riverbed
  - Heavy rainfall – overflows banks
  - Heaviest material first deposited
  - Lighter alluvium left on floodplain
  - Repeat flooding – levees
  - Backswamps
  - Bluff line – end of floodplain

Human interaction with river processes on the Mississippi River

Navigation
- Mississippi transportation system feeds and fuels vast areas of the USA
- Upper course
  - Steep gradient – low water levels
  - 29 locks and dams – 2.7 m deep channel
  - Dams slowed river flow – deposition upstream
  - Less alluvium downstream
- Middle course
  - Lateral erosion and deposition of riverbank
  - Bank protection using stone revetments
  - Concrete mats now on 1,500 km of riverbank
  - 230,000 m of wing dykes
  - Faster flowing, narrower channel
  - Erosion of riverbed, deeper channel = improved navigation
- Lower course
  - Deposition on the riverbed – sandbars
  - Riverbed deepened by expensive dredging
  - Cut-offs developed – navigation route shortened by 243 km

Flood prevention
- Seasonal rainfall and melting – flooding of the plain
- Flood control = allow settlements to grow on riverbank

Engineering
- 230 dams and large reservoirs on upper river and tributaries
- Volume of water downstream controlled
- 2,500 km of artificial levees built
- Forestry – absorbed water and reduced surface runoff
- Diversion channels increase carrying capacity – New Orleans
- Flood walls built in large urban areas
- Spillways developed at critical points

Effects on river processes
  - Flooding now only affects 10% of the plain
  - Reservoirs – farmland upstream lost to flooding
  - Upstream dams slowed river flow – deposition
  - Less alluvium for agricultural land downstream
- Major flooding in 1993, 2005 led to settlements being abandoned

9 THE SEA AT WORK

LEARNING INTENTIONS
Syllabus Links: 1.5, 1.7

By the end of this chapter I will be able to:
- describe each of the coastal processes;
- identify coastal landscape features from an Ordnance Survey (OS) map, a photograph and a diagram;
- indicate the dominant process(es) at work during the formation of each coastal feature;
- describe the formation of at least one feature of both coastal erosion and coastal deposition using Irish and/or international examples;
- explain how human activities can impact on the operation of coastal processes.

KEYWORDS
waves
swash
backwash
fetch
crest
constructive waves
spilling waves
destructive waves
plunging waves
wave refraction
hydraulic action
abrasion
attrition
solution
compression

The coast is a narrow zone where the land and sea meet. Its landscape is constantly being shaped by the actions of waves which erode, transport and deposit coastal material.

Waves

Waves are formed when wind moves over the surface of the sea. This movement causes the water to make a circular motion, which forms a wave shape. The wave moves in the direction of the coast, increasing in height and decreasing in width as it reaches shallower water at the coast. Eventually the wave breaks and white water rushes towards the shore (Fig. 9.1). The impact each wave has on the coastline depends on the:

- **swash**, the white foamy water that rushes up the shore following the breaking of a wave;
- **backwash**, the flow of water back down the shore and out to sea;
- **fetch**, the distance a wave travels from when it forms to when it breaks;
- **crest**, the highest point of a wave.

↑ **Fig. 9.1** The formation and breaking of a wave.

125

Landscapes

Types of wave

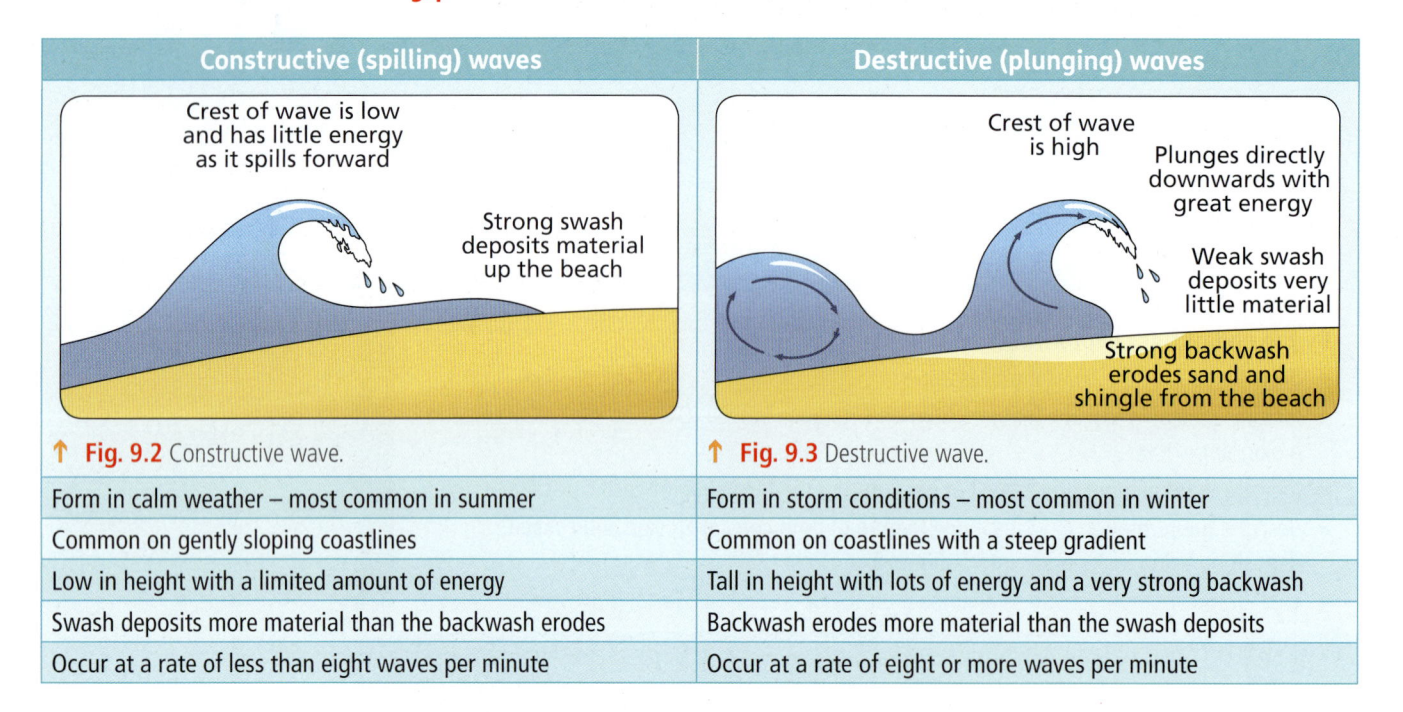

Constructive (spilling) waves	Destructive (plunging) waves
↑ **Fig. 9.2** Constructive wave.	↑ **Fig. 9.3** Destructive wave.
Form in calm weather – most common in summer	Form in storm conditions – most common in winter
Common on gently sloping coastlines	Common on coastlines with a steep gradient
Low in height with a limited amount of energy	Tall in height with lots of energy and a very strong backwash
Swash deposits more material than the backwash erodes	Backwash erodes more material than the swash deposits
Occur at a rate of less than eight waves per minute	Occur at a rate of eight or more waves per minute

Wave refraction

Close to the coast, as the water gets shallow, waves tend to slow down and bend (**refract**). Waves approaching the headland cause erosion, as they still move quickly, giving them more erosive power. Waves reaching the bay move through shallower water, causing them to slow down and deposit their load of eroded material (**Fig. 9.4**).

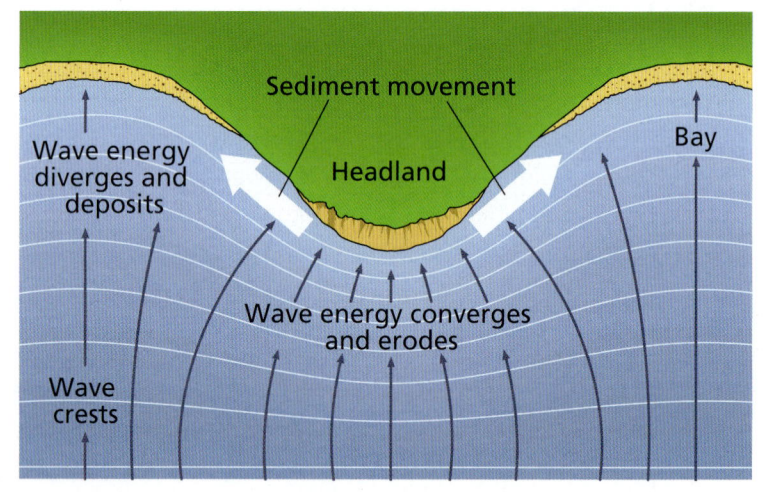

→ **Fig. 9.4** Wave refraction.

Coastal Erosion

Processes of coastal erosion

Hydraulic action: Material at the coastline is eroded by the force of the waves hitting against it. Joints of rocks are enlarged, while loose fragments get swept away.

Abrasion/Corrasion: The sea picks up material such as sand, stones and rocks (load). Waves lash this material against the coast, causing particles to be eroded.

Attrition: Rocks and pebbles rub against one another as they are moved by the swash and backwash. This causes their rough edges to be worn down, leaving them smaller, smoother and rounder.

Solution/Corrosion: Soluble rocks at the coastline are dissolved by acid in the seawater. For example, chalk and limestone coastal rocks, which are high in calcium carbonate, are dissolved by carbonic acid in the seawater.

Compression/Compressed air: Air is trapped in the cracks in the rocks. The pressure increases in the cracks, shattering the rocks.

The rate of coastal erosion depends on the following:

- **The power of the wave,** which is dictated by three elements:
    1. **strength of the wind** (stronger winds lead to stronger waves);
    2. **the length of time the wind is blowing** (the longer the wind is blowing, the stronger the wave);
    3. the **fetch** of the wave (the further the wave has travelled, the stronger it will be; Fig. 9.5).
- **The hardness of the rock.** Areas composed of soft materials, such as boulder clay, are more easily eroded than other areas composed of more resistant materials, such as granite. This process is called differential erosion.

↑ **Fig. 9.5** The fetch of a wave approaching the west coast of Ireland is far longer than waves approaching the east coast.

- **The slope of the beach.** Constructive waves are commonly found on gently sloping shores, where the waves break further offshore and lose their energy to erode. Destructive waves that cause coastal erosion are commonly found on coastlines with a steep slope.
- **The shape of the coast.** The rate of erosion is greater on irregular shaped coastlines, as more wave energy is focussed onto headlands due to wave refraction.
- **Rising sea levels.** Global warming is slowly melting the glaciers and ice sheets of the world, causing sea levels to rise. During the 20th century, sea levels rose by approximately 19 cm, and this figure is expected to increase significantly over the next 50 years. Coastal erosion and flooding will increase, while coastal defence mechanisms in many places will become outdated.
- **Human activity.** For hundreds of years, people lowered coastlines as they removed sand from beaches for construction, agricultural and recreational use. This has left the coast more open to wave erosion. However, humans also prevent coastal erosion when they put in place coastal defence mechanisms, such as rock armour and sea walls.

CHECK YOUR LEARNING

1. Explain the following terms: swash, backwash, fetch.
2. Explain two differences between constructive and destructive waves.
3. What does 'wave refraction' mean?
4. List and explain the five processes of coastal erosion.
5. List three factors which determine the power of a wave.
6. Explain how the rock type on the coastline has an effect on the rate of coastal erosion.
7. How does the slope of a beach affect rates of coastal erosion?
8. What impact will global warming have on coastal erosion?

Landscapes

KEYWORDS

headland
bay
cave
arch
stack
stump
blowhole
geo
cliff
wave-cut platform

Landforms of coastal erosion

Headlands and bays

Description: A headland is a high piece of land jutting out into the sea.

Irish examples: Mizen Head; Malin Head

Description: A bay is a large curved opening into the coast.

Irish examples: Dublin Bay; Galway Bay

Formation: Certain parts of the coastline consist of parallel bands of hard and soft material, placed perpendicular to the sea. Bands of hard, resistant rock (e.g. **granite**) are eroded at a slower rate than bands of softer, less resistant material (e.g. **boulder clay**). This process is called **differential erosion**. Sections of land left jutting out into the sea containing resistant rock are called **headlands**. Areas where the softer material has been eroded are called **bays** (Fig. 9.6).

EXAM TIP

Students must be prepared to identify all coastal landforms from an OS map, a photograph or a diagram in Section 1 (short questions) or in Section 2, Part A (20-mark question).

SKILLS ACTIVITY

Draw a labelled diagram describing the formation of headlands and bays.

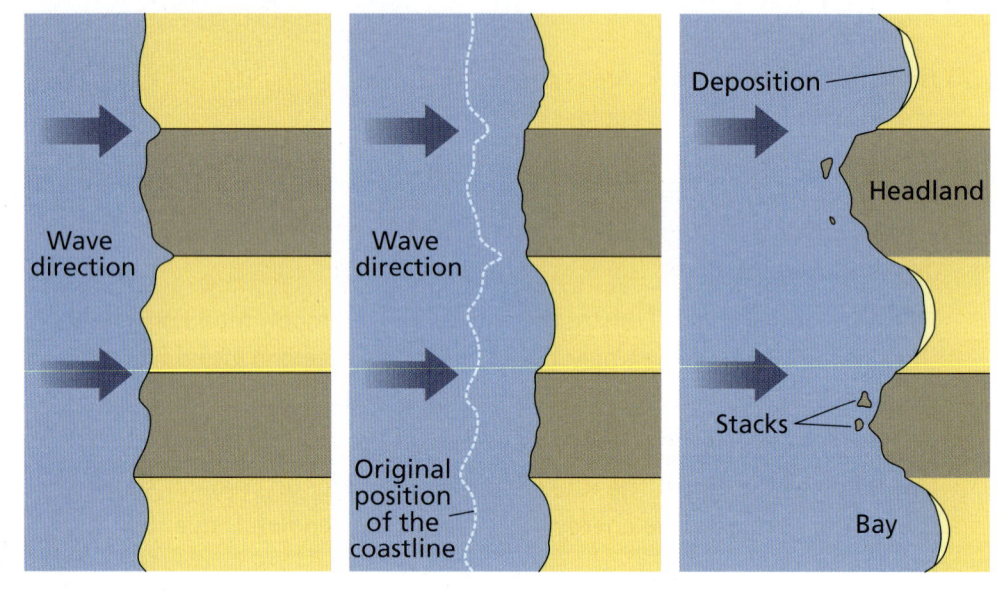

Key
Hard rock, e.g. granite
Soft rock, e.g. boulder clay

↑ **Fig. 9.6(a)** Stages in the formation of headlands and bays.

← **Fig. 9.6(b)** Headland and bay on the coastline.

↓ **Fig. 9.6(c)** Headlands and bays on an OS map. Headlands will be labelled on an OS map using the word 'Head' (or 'Ceann' if the map is from a Gaeltacht area).

128

Features of erosion formed on a headland

Headlands are eroded by wave refraction, leading to the formation of **caves**, **arches**, **stacks** and **stumps** (Fig. 9.7). These will also be eroded away over time.

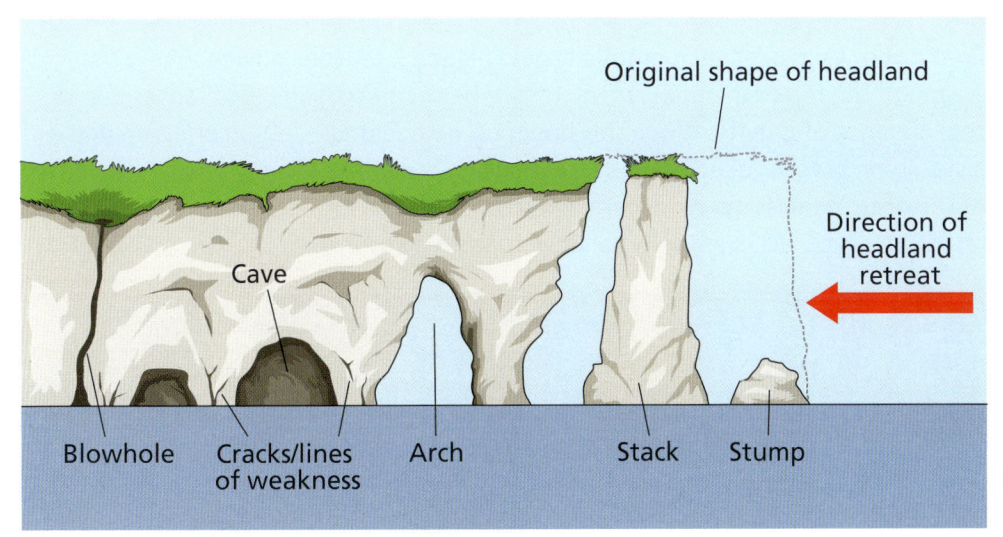

← **Fig. 9.7** Features formed on a headland.

Sea cave

Irish example: Ballyheigue, Co. Kerry

Description: Cylindrical tunnels or passages found at a cliff face or headland (Fig. 9.8).

Formation: Sea caves are formed when an area of softer, less resistant rock is eroded by **hydraulic action** (dominant process) and **compression**. Over time, a wave-cut notch is formed. As the notch increases in height and depth, it forms a cave, with **abrasion** playing a greater role.

← **Fig. 9.8(a)** Sea cave.

↓ **Fig. 9.8(b)** Caves will be labelled on an OS map using the word 'Cave' (or '*Pluais*' if the map is from a Gaeltacht area).

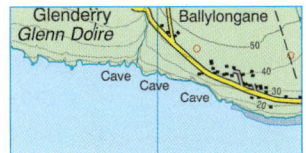

Sea arch

Irish example: The Bridges of Ross, Co. Clare

Description: An arch-shaped opening in a rocky headland (Fig. 9.9).

Formation: When a cave is formed in a headland, it may eventually break through to the other side forming an arch. An arch may also form when two caves at either side of a headland eventually join.

→ **Fig. 9.9** Sea arch. This feature cannot be identified on an OS map.

Landscapes

Wave-cut notch: A part of the headland between high and low tide levels which has been undercut by destructive waves.

Sea stack/Stump

Irish example: The Old Head of Kinsale, Co. Cork

Description: A sea stack is a pillar of rock jutting out of the sea near the coast (Fig. 9.10).

Formation: As the sea arch gradually gets bigger, it reaches a point where the weight at the top of the arch can no longer be supported, and it collapses due to the influence of **gravity**. When this happens, a headland is left on one side and a tall column of rock called a **sea stack** is left on the other. The stack will be attacked at the base in the same way that a **wave-cut notch** is formed. This weakens the structure which will eventually collapse to form a **stump**.

→ Fig. 9.10(a) Sea stack.

↑ Fig. 9.10(b) Sea stacks and stumps are found just off the coast on an OS map.

Blowhole

Irish example: Hook Head, Co. Wexford

Description: A pipe-like opening that links the surface of a headland to the roof of a sea cave (Fig. 9.11).

Formation: Blowholes are formed close to the cliff face when a joint between a sea cave and the land surface above the cave becomes enlarged. As water flows into the cave, air and seawater is expelled through the pipe-like joint, producing an impressive blast of spray that seems to emerge from the ground.

← Fig. 9.11(a) Blowhole.

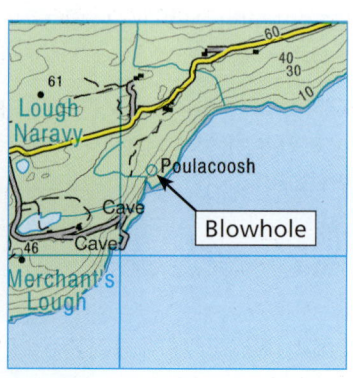

← Fig 9.11(b) Blowholes can be labelled on an OS map using the word 'Hole' (or '*Poll*' if the map is from a Gaeltacht area).

130

Geo

Irish example: The Old Head of Kinsale, Co. Cork

A **geo** is a small coastal inlet that forms when the roof of a sea cave collapses (Fig. 9.12).

← **Fig. 9.12(a)** A geo is an inlet on the coastline.

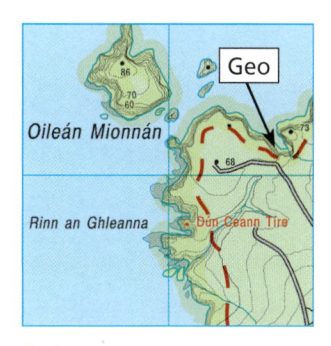

↑ **Fig. 9.12(b)** A geo (inlet) on an OS map.

Cliffs and wave-cut platforms

Irish example: Cliffs of Moher, Co. Clare

Description: Cliffs are vertical slopes found where the land and sea meet at the coastline (Fig. 9.13).

Formation: The greatest role in cliff formation is played by high-energy **destructive waves** which are most powerful in stormy conditions. They erode a **notch** at the coastline using the processes of coastal erosion.

- **Hydraulic action:** Lines of weakness are created between the high and low tide levels by the force of the destructive wave crashing against the coast.

- **Compression:** The destructive wave also forces air into cracks and joints of rock surfaces, where it is compressed. As the wave retreats, the air decompresses and rapidly expands, causing an explosion. Rocks are shattered into little pieces that fall into the sea, increasing the size of cracks and joints.

- **Abrasion:** The shattered pieces of rock are picked up by strong waves and used as another tool of erosion against the coastline.

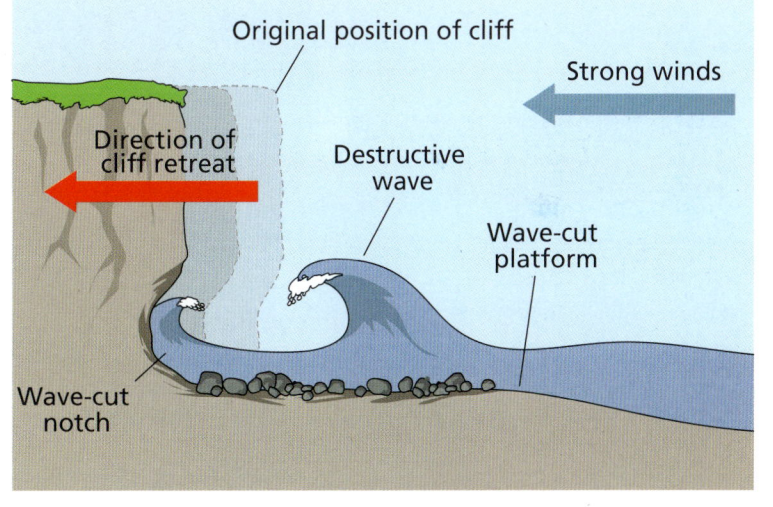

↑ **Fig. 9.13(a)** Formation of a cliff at the coastline.

As the notch gets bigger, the rock overhead is left overhanging and unsupported. Over time, the overhang becomes more vulnerable to the influence of **gravity**, until it eventually collapses under its own weight, forming a small cliff. **Destructive waves** continue the process of undercutting the coast, causing the cliff to **retreat inland**, getting taller each time. Acids in the sea (e.g. carbonic acid) also erode the cliff face through the process of **solution**.

Landscapes

> Gently sloping cliffs are formed from unconsolidated material, such as boulder clay, which is a soft rock that erodes quite quickly.
>
> Vertical cliffs are formed from consolidated material, such as sandstone, which is a more resistant rock that erodes slowly.

The collapsed rock debris is removed from the foot of the cliff by the **strong backwash** of the destructive waves. A gently sloping area of exposed rock called a **wave-cut platform** is left at the base of the cliff. Composed of more resistant rock and visible at low tide, the wave-cut platform is smoothened by **attrition**.

SKILLS ACTIVITY

Draw a labelled diagram describing the formation of a cliff and wave-cut platform.

← **Fig. 9.13(b)** Cliffs of Moher, Co. Clare.

← **Fig. 9.13(c)** Cliffs on an OS map: notice the dark black line at the coast, which is a result of contours being placed on top of each other.

EXAM TIP

A relevant labelled diagram (optional) and a named example of the feature will be awarded 1 SRP each.

EXAM LINK (HL)

Surface Processes (30 marks)
Examine the impact of the processes of erosion on the formation of one coastal landform that you have studied.
2015, Q1B

Marking Scheme:
Named processes = 2 + 2 marks
Named landform = 2 marks
Examination = 12 SRPs × 2 marks

CHECK YOUR LEARNING

1. Briefly explain how a cave is formed.
2. Describe how a cave can develop into a sea stack.
3. Name one place in Ireland where a blowhole can be found.
4. What is a geo?
5. Explain the role played by compression in cliff formation.
6. What is a wave-cut platform?
7. What does a gently-sloping cliff tell us about the type of rock it is made from? Why does it develop this way?
8. How would you recognise a cliff on an OS map?

Transport by the Sea

KEYWORDS		
transportation	baymouth bar	foreshore
longshore drift	tombolo	runnel
oblique angle	lagoon	ripple
deposition	beach	cusp
sand spit	undertow	berm
salt marsh	backshore	

The mud, sand, shingle, pebbles and stones found in the sea and carried along by waves is referred to as the waves load. These materials have been sourced a number of ways:

- they were eroded from the coast by **destructive waves** that were forming the features of coastal erosion;
- they were brought inland from offshore by **constructive waves**;
- they were **transported** along the coastline by **longshore drift**.

Longshore drift

Coastal materials such as sand and silt are transported along the coast by longshore drift. The prevailing wind causes waves to approach the coast at an **oblique angle**. The swash moves material up the shore, while the backwash brings it straight back out, following the slope of the shore. The sequence is repeated and in this way material is moved along the shore in a zigzag pattern (**Fig. 9.14**).

SKILLS ACTIVITY

Draw a labelled diagram describing the process of longshore drift.

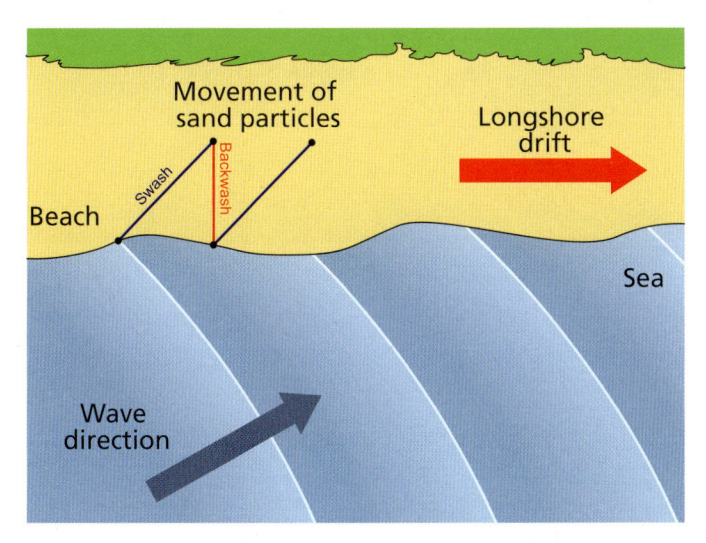

← Fig 9.14 Longshore drift.

Coastal Deposition

Just like a river in its 'old age', the sea deposits the load it has been carrying when it loses its energy. **Deposition** is carried out by **constructive waves** whose swash is stronger than their backwash.

Deposition is most likely to occur:

- in shallow waters, such as bays, where waves slow down due to **wave refraction**;
- when waves enter sheltered areas (bays/coves);
- in calm weather when there is little wind and the wave only has a limited amount of energy.

Landscapes

Landforms

Sand spit

Irish example: Inch Strand, Co. Kerry

Description: A ridge of sand, silt and at times small pebbles that extends from one end of a headland.

Formation: Sand, silt and small pebbles are moved along the coast by longshore drift. When the coastline changes direction, a spit can grow in shallow and sheltered water. More material is deposited than can be taken away by the currents and tides. The material is sorted as it is deposited with the heavier material deposited closer to the coast and the finer material at the furthest point from the coastline. As the spit grows, it may develop a curved end due to a change in wind direction. Vegetation can grow on the spit, allowing it to become stable and often fertile. As the spit grows, the water behind it can be sheltered from wind and waves, allowing a **salt marsh** to develop (Fig. 9.15).

Salt marsh: When waves cannot get past the spit, a sheltered area is created behind the spit. Silt can be deposited, creating a salt marsh.

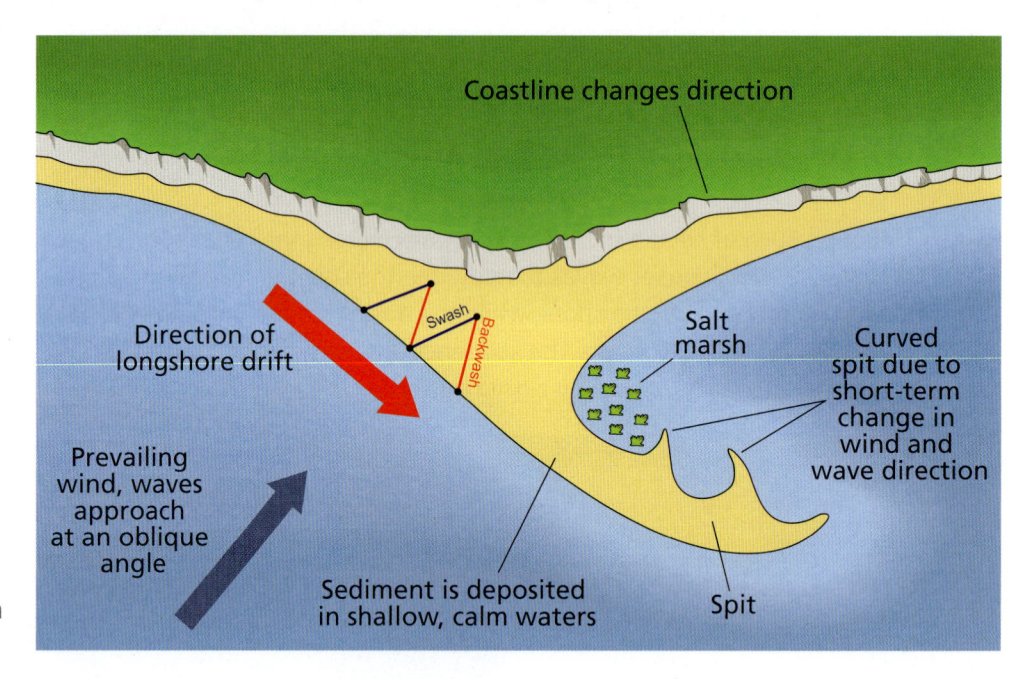

→ Fig. 9.15(a) Formation of a sand spit.

↑ Fig. 9.15(b) Sand spit growing from one side of a headland across a bay.

→ Fig. 9.15(c) Sand spit growing across Dingle Bay.

Sand bar

Irish example: *Kilkeran Lake, Co. Cork*

Description: This is a ridge of material that joins two headlands together cutting off a bay.

Formation: It can form in one of two ways:

1. A sand spit can extend across a bay, joining two headlands together, forming a **baymouth** bar. A shallow body of water separated from the sea called a **lagoon** forms behind the baymouth bar. This may develop into a **salt marsh** over time (Fig. 9.16).
2. A sand bar can develop offshore, parallel to the coastline. Known as an **offshore bar**, it can be moved towards the coastline by the waves and wind until it eventually joins the mainland.

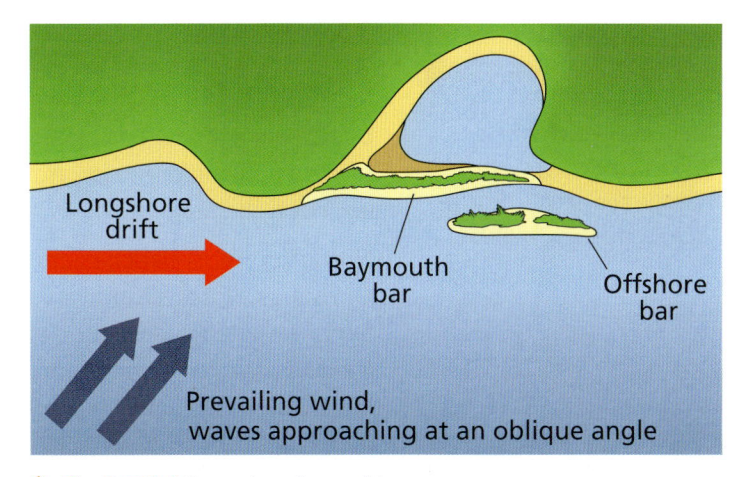

Tombolo

Irish example: *Sutton tombolo joins Howth to the mainland*

Description: A ridge of material that joins an island to the mainland.

Formation: This is formed by longshore drift, which moves material along the beach. The sheltered area between the island and mainland encourages deposition at the end of the beach. Over time, the beach extends outward from the mainland and links with the off-shore island (Fig. 9.17).

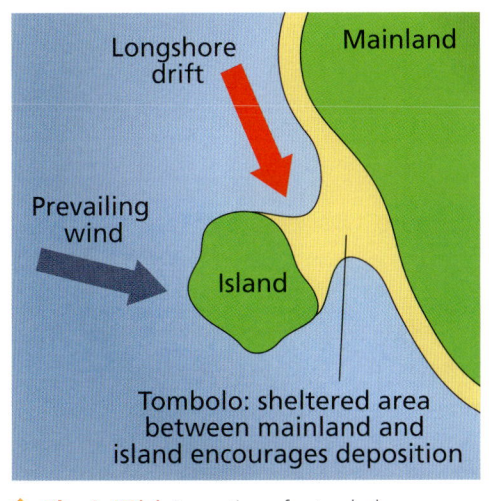

↑ **Fig 9.16(a)** Formation of a sand bar.

↑ **Fig 9.16(b)** Baymouth bar and lagoon.

← **Fig 9.16(c)** Baymouth bar and lagoon on an OS map.

↑ **Fig. 9.17(a)** Formation of a tombolo.

↑ **Fig. 9.17(b)** Tombolo: notice how the beach links the island to the mainland.

→ **Fig. 9.17(c)** Tombolo on an OS map.

CHECK YOUR LEARNING

1. List three ways the load carried by a wave is sourced.
2. Explain two reasons why the sea will start to deposit its load.
3. List and explain two reasons why some waves deposit rather than erode.
4. What is the difference between a sand spit and a baymouth bar?
5. Explain the following terms: lagoon, salt marsh.

Landscapes

Sand produces beaches with a gentle slope, while shingle and pebble beaches are steeper.

Undertow: A strong undercurrent flowing in a different direction from the surface current.

Foreshore: The part of the shore that lies between the low tide mark and the high tide mark.

Backshore: The part of the shore that lies between the high tide mark and the vegetation, only affected by waves during a storm.

Beach

Irish examples: *Inchidoney Co. Cork; Curracloe, Co. Wexford*

Description: A beach is formed from material that has been eroded at one point on the coastline before being transported and deposited between high and low tide level at a second point.

Formation: Most beaches are formed by **constructive waves** on gently sloping shorelines. More material is deposited by the powerful swash than is taken away by the **undertow** of the backwash. The weaker backwash sorts the material as it moves down the beach – the heavier material (stone and shingle) is left in the **backshore**, while the lighter material (fine sand) is carried to the lower **foreshore**.

Longshore drift contributes to the shape of the beach. The heaviest and largest volume of material is deposited on the side of the beach from which the prevailing wind comes from. Material deposited becomes smaller in size and volume the further across the beach one moves away from this point.

Pocket beaches are formed in small bays due to wave refraction. Oncoming waves concentrate their energy on the headland, while those travelling further into the bay slow down and deposit their load.

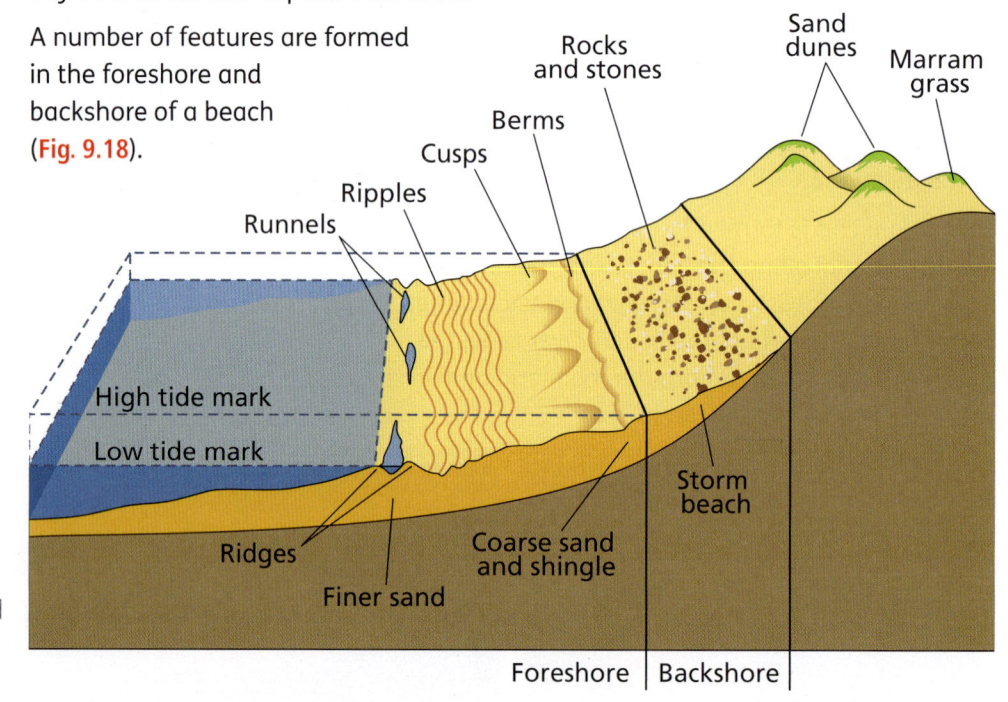

A number of features are formed in the foreshore and backshore of a beach (**Fig. 9.18**).

→ **Fig. 9.18(a)** A beach and its associated features.

Foreshore

- In the **lower** foreshore of sandy beaches, gently sloping ridges form parallel to the coastline. These ridges mark the points where constructive waves break. Depressions filled with water, called **runnels**, sometimes form between the ridges.

- In the **middle** foreshore, the incoming swash creates gentle lines in the sand called **ripples**.

- In the **upper** foreshore, constructive waves form temporary semi-circular depressions called **cusps** from coarse material. They generally occur in a row, are the same size and are spaced in a regular pattern.

- **Berms** form on the upper foreshore of shingle and stone beaches when small, low-energy constructive waves deposit material at the mean high tide mark.

136

9 The Sea at Work

← **Fig. 9.18(b)** Beach.

↓ **Fig 9.18(c)** Beach on an OS map. Notice the contour lines indicating the sand dunes at the back of the beach.

Backshore

- Stronger winds during storm periods create larger waves which push stones and pebbles to areas above regular high tide levels, before depositing them to form a **storm beach**.

- Onshore winds pick up grains of sand from the foreshore and carry them inland until they meet an obstacle such as a fence, a rock or vegetation. On hitting the obstacle, the sand grains lose momentum and settle, building up over time to form **sand dunes**.

EXAM LINK (OL)

Landform Development (40 marks)

Explain, with the aid of diagrams, the formation of any two landforms.

2018, Q2B

Marking Scheme:
Formation of any two landforms = 2 × 20 marks
For each landform:
- Landform named = 1 mark
- Diagram(s) two aspects = 2 × 2 marks

Formation explained = 5 SRPs × 3 marks (at least one SRP must explain a relevant process)

EXAM TIP (OL)

With the exception of 2014, this question appeared on the exam paper every year from 2011 to 2018.

EXAM LINK (HL)

Landform Development (30 marks)

Examine the impact of the processes of deposition on the formation of one coastal landform that you have studied.

2016, Q1B

Marking Scheme:
Named landform = 2 marks
Examination = 14 SRPs × 2 marks

EXAM TIP (HL)

Answering this question using a beach is recommended. Beaches are formed by deposition and have many associated features, each of which can be used to develop an SRP.

CHECK YOUR LEARNING

1. Explain the term 'sorting' in relation to the formation of a beach.
2. Explain the following terms: berms, ripples, runnels.
3. What part does longshore drift play in the formation of a beach?
4. What is a storm beach?
5. How are 'pocket beaches' formed?

EXAM TIP

A relevant labelled diagram (optional) and a named example of the feature will be awarded 1 SRP each.

137

Landscapes

Human Interaction with Coastal Areas

The sea plays a very important part in the way people live their lives. More than half of people worldwide live within 50 km of the sea, and this number is on the rise. People interact with the sea in many ways. The sea provides us with a food source in fish, while wave, tidal and wind energy are all generated in coastal areas. Oil and gas are drilled from under the seabed for use as fuel.

DID YOU KNOW?
There has been a 35% increase in the population of people living on the coasts since 1995.

KEYWORDS

rock armour	sea wall	groyne
hard engineering	marram grass	beach nourishment
soft engineering	gabions	

CASE STUDY: COASTAL PROTECTION AT LAHINCH, CO. CLARE

Lahinch is located in the Liscannor Bay area of Co. Clare. With its long sandy beach and excellent surfing conditions, it is a major tourist attraction. Since the early 19th century, humans have developed a number of hard structures to protect the local coastline, businesses and amenities from erosion and flooding.

A **hydro-dynamic sea wall** was constructed from concrete and re-enforced with steel. Its curved top:

- deflects the hydraulic power of the breaking wave back out to sea; having been deflected, it falls onto the next incoming wave, breaking its hydraulic power also;
- reduces the amount of seawater that gets over the wall.

Rock armour was placed at the base of local cliffs and in front of the curved sea wall. This prevents coastal erosion by breaking the hydraulic power of incoming waves before they reach the coastline (Fig. 9.19).

Hard engineering: This involves building structures to protect the coast – sea walls, rock armour, gabions, breakwaters and groynes.

Soft engineering: This involves working with nature by using natural materials. It tends to be less expensive than hard engineering options, while also being more sustainable, with less impact on the environment – beach nourishment and marram grass.

↑ **Fig. 9.19** Coastal defence at Lahinch.

One landmark in the area that is particularly vulnerable to coastal erosion is Lahinch Golf Club. Ranked in the top 30 worldwide, the club generates a lot of money for the region. Its course is built on sand dunes formed by coastal deposition. Both **soft and hard engineering** options have been used to prevent erosion of the golf course by **destructive waves**.

Marram grass has been planted on the vulnerable sand dunes to trap and stabilise sand that is blown inland. The marram grass also reduces the wind speed over the surface of the dune, while its strong underground root system allows sand to attach to it, holding the dune's sediments in place. Marram grass is salt-resistant and its long vertical roots allow it to store water that has travelled through the porous sand (Fig. 9.20).

Gabions (wire cages filled with stones) were placed in the upper part of the beach, in front of the sand dunes. They are flexible, porous structures that trap wind-blown sand and allow the growth of vegetation under favorable conditions.

Storm Darwin had a major impact on Lahinch in 2014. The original works proved inadequate, unable to prevent powerful storm waves from overtopping the defensive structures in place and causing over €6 million worth of damage (Fig. 9.21).

- Major damage was caused to buildings, wall cappings, footpaths and signage on the promenade (Fig. 9.22).
- Metal fencing along the shorefront collapsed.
- Sea water reached almost 500 m inland in places, leaving buildings adjacent to the car park under 1.5 m of water. Low-lying areas of Lahinch Golf Course were also flooded.

Major works aimed at protecting against similar future damage were completed in 2017, costing €2.85 million.

- The existing sea wall was strengthened with the addition of a new concrete apron and more rock armour.
- Gabions were removed from in front of the sand dunes and replaced by rock armour during coastal protection works that extended further along the coastline. The gabions were not sufficiently durable to withstand regular direct wave action. The rock armour will help to prevent future erosion by destructive waves, especially during big storm events, and will stabilise the disturbed dune system.

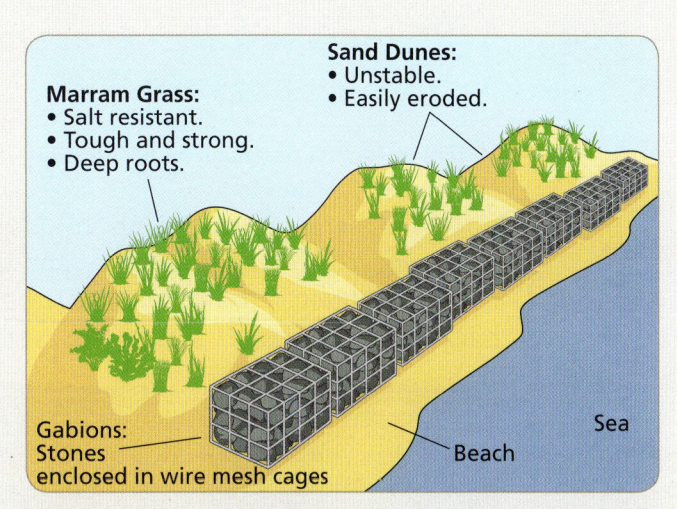

Fig. 9.20 Soft engineering methods, such as marram grass and gabions, protect sand dunes.

Fig. 9.21 Lahinch under attack from waves during Storm Darwin (2014).

Fig. 9.22 The after-effects of Storm Darwin in Lahinch (2014).

CHECK YOUR LEARNING

1. List four ways people interact with the sea.
2. Why are sea walls curved at the top?
3. What impact did Storm Darwin have on Lahinch?
4. Explain the difference between hard and soft engineering techniques for coastal protection.
5. Why were the gabions in Lahinch replaced?

Landscapes

CASE STUDY: HARBOUR DEVELOPMENT AT ROSSLARE

The construction of Rosslare Harbour began in 1867 to facilitate an increase in the volume of trade between Britain and Ireland. A pier was developed offshore and connected to the mainland by a viaduct so that longshore drift from the south could continue unaffected. The plan failed, however, as the viaduct provided shelter and large volumes of sediment built up in the harbour instead of moving northwards. The harbour had to be dredged in order to keep it navigable. The dredged material was deposited at sea, lost to the local beach system for good.

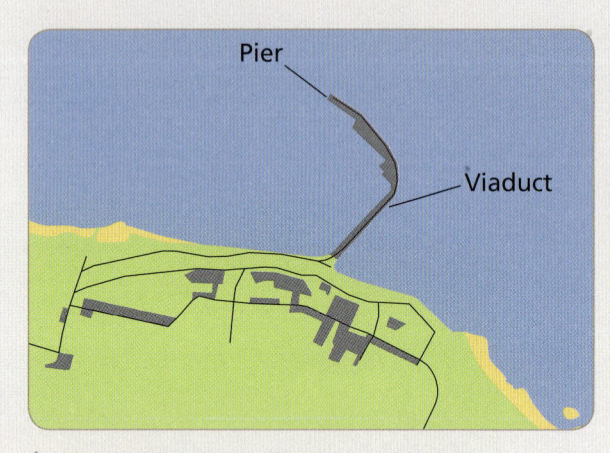

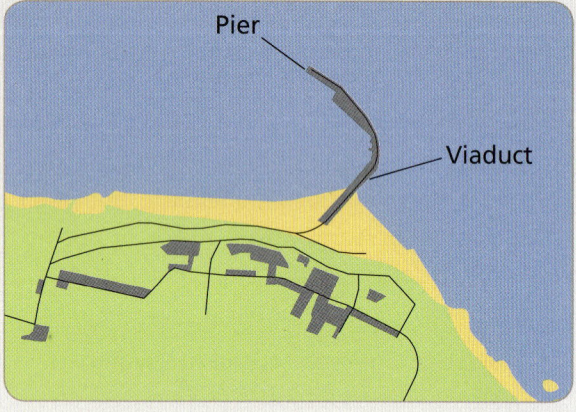

↑ **Fig. 9.23** Rosslare Harbour pier and viaduct – around 1900.

↑ **Fig. 9.24** Rosslare Harbour pier and viaduct – around 1940. Notice the build-up of sediment in the harbour.

Greater volumes of traffic, due to increased tourism and trade, lead to further developments at Rosslare Harbour. These were completed in the early 1980s (Figs 9.23–9.25).

- The viaduct was closed off to remove the need for further expensive dredging.
- A new pier was developed to cater for extra sea traffic.
- A **sea wall** was built to provide shelter for the ferry terminal.

The new developments had a major impact on the local coastline:

- With the viaduct closed off, the pier now acted as a huge **groyne**, trapping vast amounts of sand. This resulted in a new beach being formed on the leeward (southern) side of the pier.
- The newly built pier and sea wall caused **longshore drift** to be deflected offshore, where sand was deposited in deeper waters.
- Depositional features further north on the Wexford coast were deprived of the sand they needed to function, and started experiencing erosion as they were lowered.

Groynes: These are barriers (usually wooden) placed at right angles to the sea. They prevent beaches from losing sand through longshore drift. They can also build-up beaches which are a natural defence against coastal erosion.

DID YOU KNOW?
Wexford has a coastline of 264 km. Around 211 km of this consists of 'soft' coastline, i.e. dunes, cliffs and estuaries; 53 km consists of 'hard' coastline, mainly sea walls.

→ **Fig. 9.25** Aerial view of Rosslare Harbour (present day).

9 The Sea at Work

At Rosslare Strand, a major tourist and recreational attraction with Blue Flag status, the coastline was **retreating** almost 50 cm a year by the mid-1990s. Parts of the beach, sand dunes and golf course were being lost to the sea. In response, a **coastal protection scheme** was put in place from 1991–1995 to protect the local landscape and economy from erosion by the sea.

- **Rock armour**, **groynes** and **wooden breakwaters** were constructed on the beach to halt sediment loss by longshore drift and erosion (Fig. 9.26).

- A 275,000 cubic metre **beach nourishment** scheme was carried out. Sand was dredged from banks six kilometres offshore and deposited on the local beach system between the rock groynes. The sand created a gradual slope on the beach, causing the waves to break further from the coast. This slowed erosion, as water rushing up the beach lost its energy before reaching the coast (Fig. 9.27).

- Sand dunes were re-contoured and planted with marram grass so that they could be stabilised and strengthened.

- At Rosslare Golf Club, dunes were also strengthened and stabilised by the installation of **sand trap fences** and coastal protection **rock revetments**.

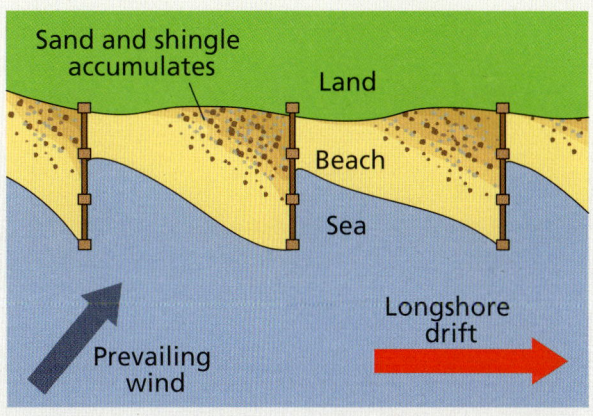

↑ Fig. 9.26 Groynes trap sand that is being transported by longshore drift.

Beach nourishment: The beach acts as a natural defence against erosion and coastal flooding. Sand is placed on a beach to replace sand that was lost through erosion or longshore drift. This allows the beach to maintain its natural look, while reducing the erosive impact of the waves. While this is a relatively inexpensive option, it requires constant maintenance to replace the beach material as it is washed away.

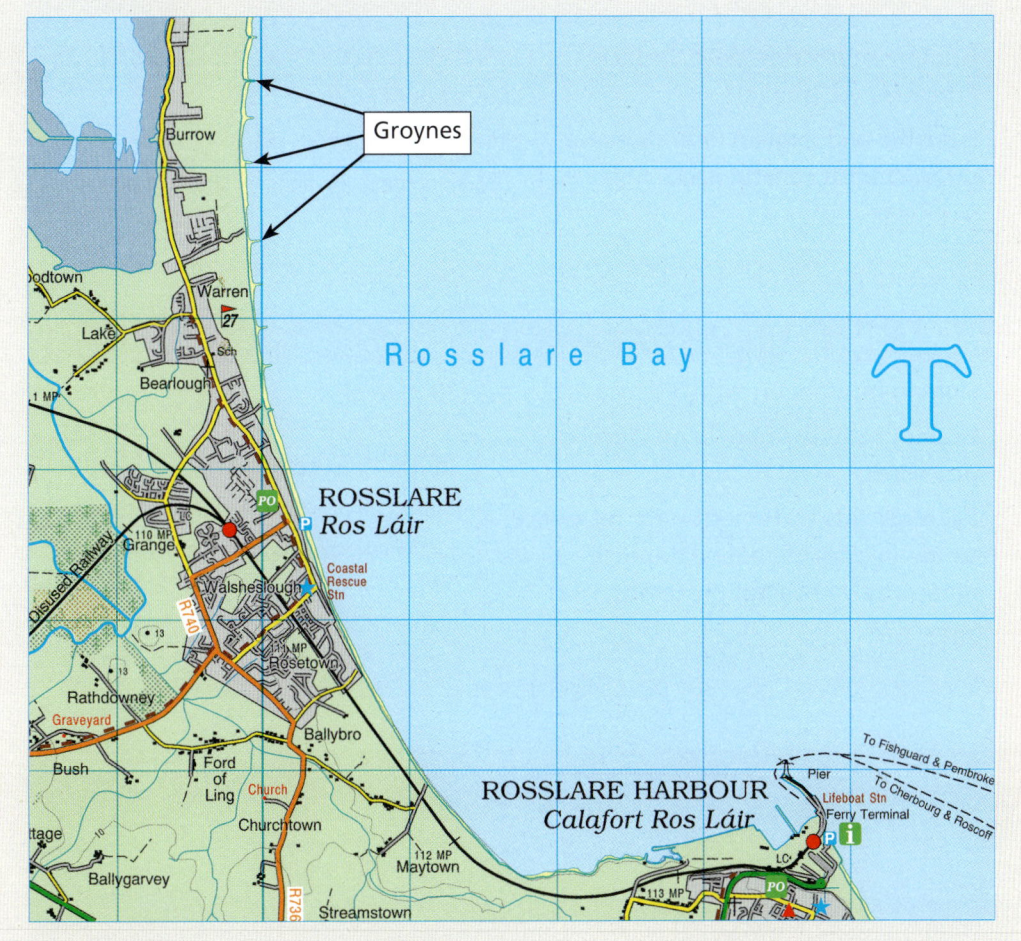

↑ Fig. 9.27 OS map of Rosslare Harbour. Notice the groynes that have been built on the coastline north of Rosslare.

141

Landscapes

Major revetment works were also carried out in 2007. Around 750 m of the coastline was strengthened with 20,000 tonnes of rock armour to prevent further erosion by destructive waves (Fig. 9.28).

→ **Fig. 9.28** Rock armour revetment works.

EXAM TIP

With the exception of 2013, this type of question appeared on the exam paper every year from 2009 to 2018.

EXAM TIP (OL)

Named example from examination = 1 SRP
Relevant labelled diagram = 1 SRP

EXAM LINK (OL)

Human Interaction with Surface Processes (30 marks)

Describe and explain how humans interact with coastal processes.

2018, Q3C

Marking Scheme:
Interaction named = 3 marks
Description/explanation = 9 SRPs × 3 marks

EXAM TIP (HL)

Named example from examination = 2 SRPs
Relevant labelled diagram = 1 SRP

EXAM LINK (HL)

Human Interaction with Surface Processes (30 marks)

Human activity impacts on surface processes.

Examine this statement with reference to the impact of coastal defence measures on coastal processes.

2017, Q1C

Marking Scheme:
Impact on process identified = 2 marks
Examination of impact on process = 14 SRPs × 2 marks

CHECK YOUR LEARNING

1. Why was a viaduct developed at Rosslare Harbour? Was the plan successful?
2. What developments were completed in Rosslare Harbour in the early 1980s?
3. What impact did these developments have on the local coastline?
4. Explain the beach nourishment programme at Rosslare Strand.
5. Why is marram grass suitable vegetation for planting sand dunes?

9 The Sea at Work

EXAMINATION QUESTIONS
ORDINARY LEVEL

Short Questions

1. Coastal Landforms and Processes

Examine the Ordnance Survey map extract above and answer each of the following questions.

(i) Match each of the letters A, B, C and D with the landform that best matches it in the table.

4 × 2 marks

Landform	Letter
Sea stack	
Beach	

Landform	Letter
Cliff	
Headland	

(ii) Which one of the landforms in the table above is formed as a result of coastal deposition?

2 marks

2017, Part One, Q2 (10 marks)

2. Coastal Landforms

(i) Examine the photograph showing coastal landforms and match each of the letters A, B, C and D with the landform that best matches it in the table below.

4 × 2 marks

Landform	Letter
Sea stack	
Sea arch	

Landform	Letter
Sea cave	
Sea cliff	

(ii) Indicate whether the statement below is true or false, by ticking the correct box.

All of the landforms named above are formed by coastal deposition.

TRUE ☐   FALSE ☐

2 marks

2015, Part One, Q1 (10 marks)

143

Landscapes

HIGHER LEVEL

Short Questions

3. Coastal Landscape

Examine the aerial photograph and answer each of the following questions.

(i) Match each of the letters A, B, C and D with the landform that best matches it in the table. 4 × 1 mark

Landform	Letter
Sand spit	
Tombolo	
Sand dunes	
Lagoon	

(ii) Name one process of coastal transportation associated with the formation of sand spits, lagoons and tombolos. *2 marks*

(iii) Name the coastal defence structures shown at X in photograph D. *2 marks*

2017, Part One, Q3 (8 marks)

4. Aerial Photograph

Examine the aerial photograph and answer each of the following questions.

(i) Match each of the letters A, B, C and D with the landform that best matches it in the table below. 4 × 1 mark

(ii) Indicate whether processes of coastal erosion or coastal deposition are most associated with the formation of each of the landforms, by ticking the correct box in the table below. 4 × 1 mark

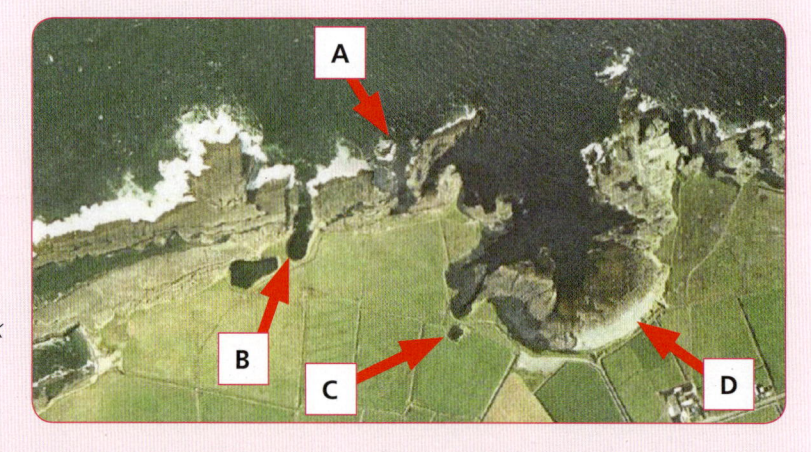

Landform	(i) Letter	(ii) Processes of coastal erosion	(ii) Processes of coastal deposition
Blowhole			
Sea stack			
Bay-head beach			
Geo			

2015, Part One, Q2 (8 marks)

144

Revision Summary

Waves	Processes of erosion	Rate of erosion
• Swash • Backwash • Fetch • Crest • Constructive • Destructive • Wave refraction	• Hydraulic action • Abrasion • Attrition • Solution • Compression	• Power of the wave • Hardness of the rock • Slope of the beach • Shape of the coast • Rising sea levels • Human activity

Longshore drift

- Incoming wave – oblique angle
- Deposits material – largest in volume and size first.
- Outgoing wave – follows slope of beach

Coastal erosion

Features and formation

- Headland – Malin and Mizen Head
- Bays – Dublin and Galway Bay
- Blowholes – Hook Head, Co. Wexford
- Caves – Ballyheigue, Co. Kerry
- Arch – The Bridges of Ross, Co. Clare
- Stacks and stumps – Old Head of Kinsale, Co. Cork
- Geo – Old Head of Kinsale, Co. Cork
- Cliffs – Cliffs of Moher
  - Destructive waves
  - Notch – hydraulic action
  - Gaps in rock – compression
  - Shattered rock – abrasion
  - Overhang grows – unstable
  - Collapses – gravity – small cliff
  - Coastal retreat – higher cliff
  - Cliff face eroded – solution
  - Destructive waves remove debris
- Wave-cut platform – resistant rock
- Visible at low tide
- Smoothed – attrition

Coastal deposition

- Occurs due to:
  - Wave refraction
  - Sheltered bays / coves
  - Calm weather

Features and formation

- Sand spit – Inch Strand, Co. Kerry
- Sand bar – Baymouth bar/lagoon – Kilkeran Lake, Co. Cork
- Tombolo – Sutton, Co. Dublin
- Beach – Curracloe, Co. Wexford
  - Material deposited between low and high tide
  - Constructive waves
  - Deposition greater than undertow
  - Sorting of beach material
  - Longshore drift
  - Wave refraction – pocket beaches
  - Gently sloping ridges – foreshore
  - Runnels – foreshore
  - Ripples – middle foreshore
  - Cusps – upper foreshore
  - Berms – shingle and stone beaches
  - Storm beaches
  - Sand dunes

Coastal Defence

Hard engineering

- Sea walls – Lahinch, Co. Clare – re-enforced concrete – curved tops to deflect waves' power
- Rock armour – Lahinch, Co. Clare – large boulders placed in front of cliffs, sea walls and dunes
- Groynes – Youghal, Co. Cork – barriers placed at right angles to the sea – stop longshore drift and trap sand

Soft engineering

- Beach nourishment – lost sand is replaced – inexpensive
- Gabions – Lahinch, Co. Clare – wire cages filled with stone – placed in front of dunes
- Marram grass – traps sand, stabilises dunes – strong, deep roots – salt-resistant

Human Interaction with Coastal Processes

- Lahinch in Liscannor Bay – sandy beach, good surf conditions
- Hard and soft structures to protect coastline, business, amenities, etc.
- Curved sea wall – deflect power of wave back to sea and reduces amount of sea water that gets over wall
- Rock armour – break the hydraulic power of the incoming wave
- Lahinch Golf Club – in the top 30 worldwide – vital to the local economy
- Marram grass – trap sand + stabilise and strengthen sand dunes
- Gabions – traps wind-blown sand, allows vegetation to grow
- Storm Darwin 2014 – over €6 million damage
- Buildings, wall cappings, signage and footpaths damaged
- Metal fencing collapsed
- Flooding – up to 500 m inland, low-lying areas of golf course
- €2.85 m programme
- Sea wall strengthened – new concrete apron and more rock armour
- Rock amour replaced gabions in front of sand dunes

- Construction of Rosslare Harbour began in 1867 – trade
- Pier developed offshore – connected by viaduct to mainland – longshore drift
- Plan failed – viaduct provided shelter – sediment built up in the harbour
- Harbour dredged – material deposited at sea – lost to local beach system
- 1970s and 1980s – more development due to increased tourism and trade
- Viaduct closed off to remove the need for further dredging
- Larger pier developed in deeper waters to cater for larger ships
- Sea wall built to provide shelter for the ferry terminal
- Viaduct closed off – pier acted as a huge groyne, trapping sand
- New beach formed on the leeward (southern) side of the pier
- Longshore drift deflected offshore – sand deposited in deeper waters
- Depositional features further north deprived of sand needed to survive
- Rosslare Strand 1990s – coastline retreating by 50 cm a year
- Parts of beach, sand dunes and golf course lost to the sea
- Coastal protection scheme – local landscape and economy
- Rock armour and wooden breakwaters – halt sediment loss
- 162,000 m^3 beach nourishment scheme
- Sand dunes re-contoured and strengthened with marram grass
- Sand trap fences and rock revetments at Rosslare Golf Club
- 2007 – major revetment works carried out to strengthen 750 m of the coastline

10 GLACIATION AND GLACIAL PROCESSES

LEARNING INTENTIONS
Syllabus Link: 1.5

By the end of this chapter I will be able to:
- describe the main glacial processes;
- identify features of the landscape formed by glaciation from an Ordnance Survey (OS) map, photographs and diagrams;
- identify the dominant processes at play in the formation of each feature;
- describe the formation of one feature of both glacial erosion and glacial deposition using Irish and/or international examples;
- describe the formation of one feature associated with fluvioglaciation using Irish and/or international examples.

KEYWORDS
Pleistocene
Munsterian
Midlandian
nunataks

Epoch: A subdivision of a geological period, ranging from 1 million to 10 million years.

Pleistocene Glaciation

The most recent geological time period, the Quaternary Period, began about 2.6 million years ago and continues to the present day. It is divided into two epochs: the **Pleistocene** and the **Holocene** (Fig. 10.1). A fall in global temperatures over 2.5 million years ago marked the start of the last great ice age, the Pleistocene. During this epoch, there were temperature variations; cold periods called **glacials** were followed by warmer periods called **interglacials**, when rising temperatures caused ice to melt and sea levels to rise above what they are today. When the Pleistocene Epoch ended about 12,000 years ago, the world entered an interglacial period called the Holocene Epoch.

→ **Fig. 10.1** European ice cover during the last glacial period of the Pleistocene Epoch.

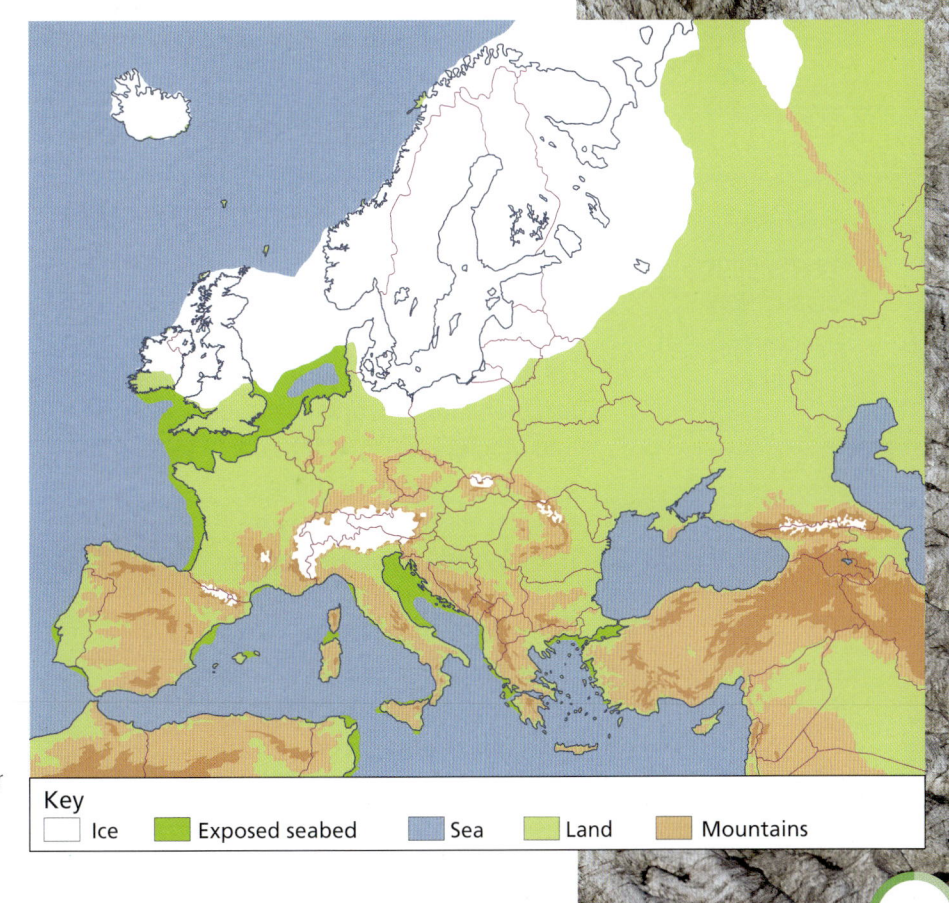

Key: Ice | Exposed seabed | Sea | Land | Mountains

147

Landscapes

> **DID YOU KNOW?**
> A geological period can span time frames ranging from 10 million to 100 million years.

Nunatak: Part of the landscape protruding above ice cover.

Terminal moraine: Material deposited in front of the ice sheets when the ice had reached its maximum advance.

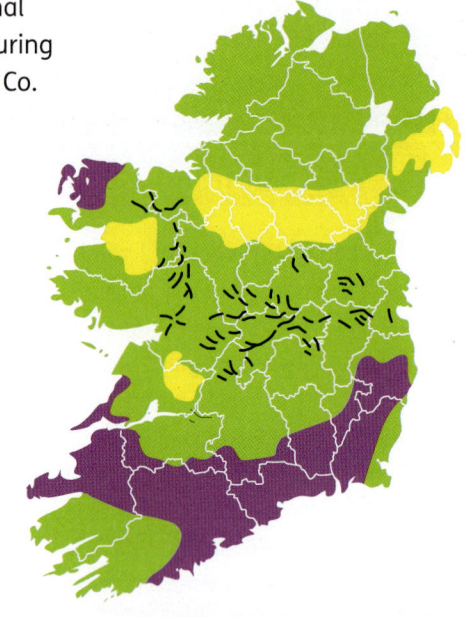

The Glaciations of Ireland

The Irish landscape has been affected by two major glaciations (Fig. 10.2). During the oldest, the **Munsterian** (300,000–130,000 years ago), all of Ireland was covered by ice up to 300 metres in thickness with only the highest mountains protruding to form **nunataks** (e.g. The Great Sugar Loaf, Co. Wicklow).

During the **Midlandian** glaciation (80,000–12,000 years ago), the advancing ice covered two-thirds of the country with the exception of the lowland areas of Munster. The terminal moraine marking the limit of ice advance during this glaciation extends from Co. Limerick to Co. Wicklow. Many examples of glacial landforms deposited during this glaciation – drumlins, eskers, moraines, etc. – can be found in the Midlands.

Key
- Midlandian glaciation
- Munsterian glaciation
- Drumlin swarms
- Eskers

→ **Fig. 10.2** The glaciations of Ireland.

CHECK YOUR LEARNING

1. When did the Pleistocene Epoch begin and end?
2. What name is given to the warmer periods during ice ages?
3. Name the two glaciations which Ireland experienced and describe the main characteristics of each.

KEYWORDS

mass balance
ablation
basal sliding
plastic flow
plucking
abrasion
freeze-thaw

Glacial Ice Formation

Ice advance–ice retreat

As falling snow accumulates, the increasing weight compresses the air from the underlying layers, changing it first into **granular ice**, then into **firn**, and eventually into **glacial ice** (Fig. 10.3). Low concentrations of air make this glacial ice blue in colour. It forms valley glaciers and ice sheets when glaciers coalesce on lowland areas. Today, valley glaciers occur in the Alps, while Greenland is covered by vast expanses of ice sheets.

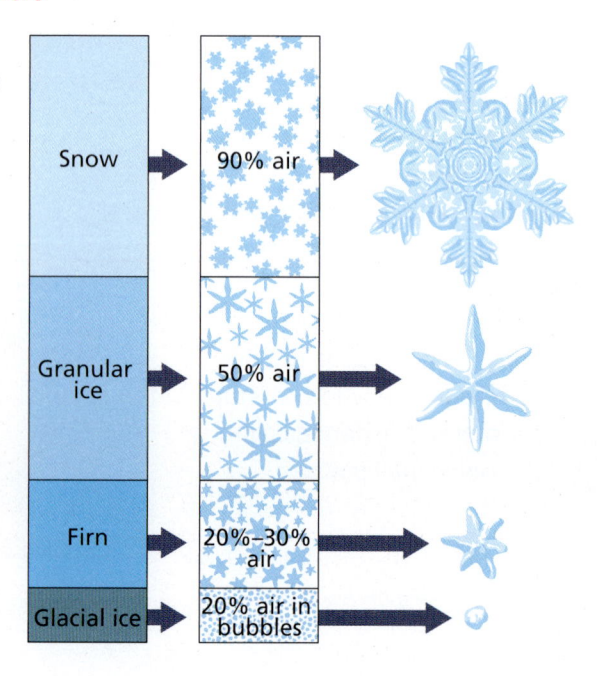

→ **Fig. 10.3** The formation of glacial ice.

Snow — 90% air
Granular ice — 50% air
Firn — 20%–30% air
Glacial ice — 20% air in bubbles

148

Glacier mass balance

Glacier **mass balance** is the difference between the amount of ice a glacier gains in winter and the amount it loses in summer.

A glacier with a **positive** mass balance gains more in winter than it loses in summer and is advancing, while one with a **negative** mass balance is losing more and is retreating. When loss and gain are in balance, the glacier is stationary.

Glaciers have two zones: one of **accumulation**, where snow falls and remains all year, and one of **ablation**, where winter snow melts during the summer. The boundary between the two is called the snow line (Fig. 10.4).

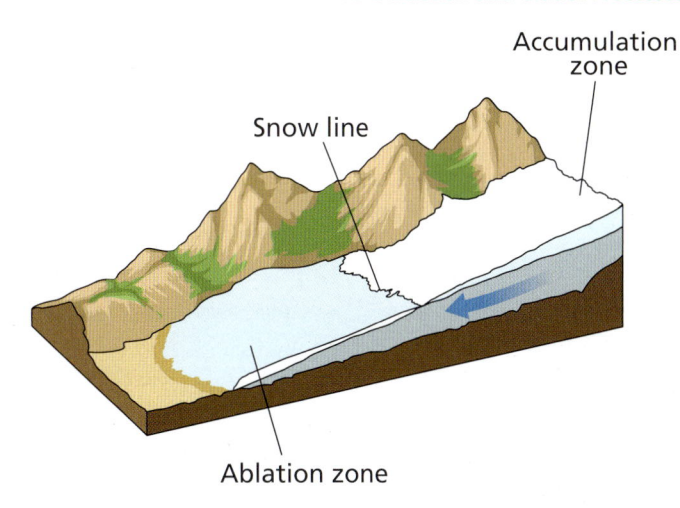

↑ **Fig. 10.4** Glacier zones.

Movement of ice

As ice formation continues, eventually the weight of the glacier, combined with the forces of gravit, cause the ice to flow downhill. Ice flow processes include:

Basal sliding: At the base of the glacier, friction caused by the weight of the ice pressing down on the bedrock causes melting to occur. This meltwater acts as a lubricant and the effect of gravity causes the glacier to move downhill. The rate of movement will depend on the steepness of the slope and the rate of ice accumulation.

Plastic flow/Internal flow: Within a glacier there are two zones: the upper zone, where the ice is brittle and breaks apart to from crevasses, and the lower zone, about 50 metres below the surface, where the ice is under steady pressure and is able to bend and change its shape without breaking.

Rate of flow: Due to friction with the bedrock and valley sides, the rate of flow at the base and sides is much slower than at the surface, while in the centre of the glacier the ice flows faster (Fig. 10.5).

Ablation: The loss of ice and snow from a glacier system through melting, runoff and evaporation.

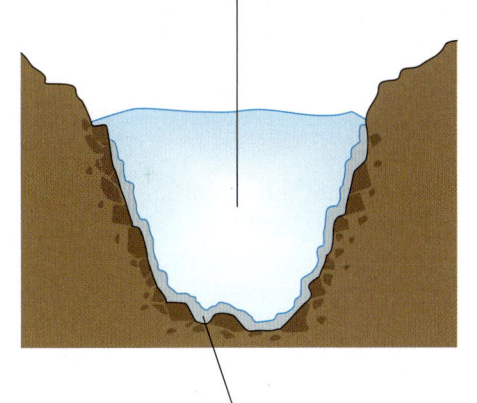

Glacial erosion

Plucking: As ice moves over rock or rock outcrops along the floor or sides of a valley, the pressure and friction causes the ice to melt. Sometimes this meltwater freezes the obstacle to the ice and carries it away. It can also seep into rock joints, where it refreezes, expands and splinters pieces from the bedrock through freeze-thaw action. The meltwater then freezes these pieces to the base and sides of the glacier (Fig. 10.6).

Abrasion: The rock particles along the sides and bottom of the glacier abrade the rocks over which the ice passes. They leave marks called **striae** on the rocks.

Freeze-thaw action: The expansion and contraction of ice causes fissures to develop in rock, allowing meltwater to penetrate further and rock particles called scree to break away.

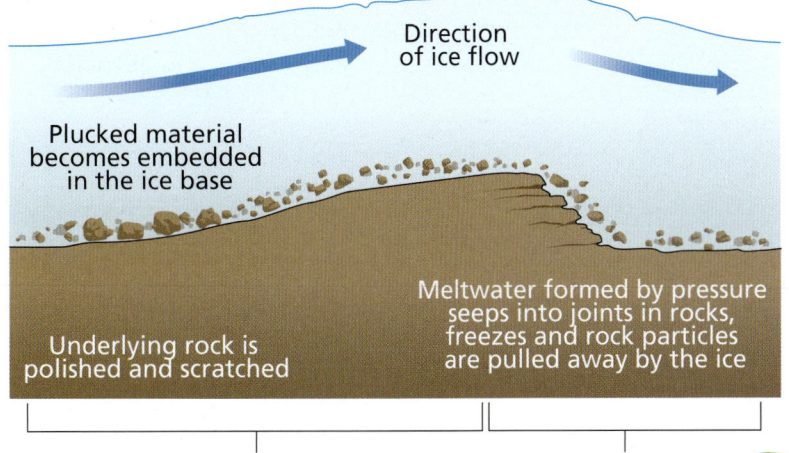

↑ **Fig. 10.5** Glacial friction.

→ **Fig. 10.6** Processes of glacial erosion.

Landscapes

The rate of glacial erosion is influenced by:
- the presence or absence of well-jointed bedrock;
- gradient – a steep gradient will result in a faster overall rate of erosion;
- the shape, size and amount of basal debris.

CHECK YOUR LEARNING

1. Explain the following terms: glacier mass balance, ablation.
2. Name two different types of ice flow.
3. In a glacier, where is ice flow slowest? Give one reason for this.
4. Name and explain two processes of glacial erosion.
5. What can affect the rate of glacial erosion?

KEYWORDS
upland
lowland
nivation
rotational slip
bergschrund
cirque
arête
pyramidal peak
hanging valley
U-shaped valley
differential erosion

EXAM TIP

Students must be prepared to identify all glacial landforms from an Ordnance Survey map, a photograph or a diagram in Section 1 (short questions) or in Section 2, Part A (20-mark question).

Types of Glaciation

Upland glaciation (Alpine) occurs in mountainous regions, is carried out by glaciers and produces mostly landforms of erosion. Examples of these occur in the uplands of Co. Kerry, while the Alps and Himalayas are two regions currently experiencing this type of glaciation.

Lowland glaciation (continental) is carried out by ice sheets and is associated with landforms of deposition. Examples of these can be found in Co. Kildare and Co. Offaly. Greenland is currently experiencing continental glaciation.

Landforms of glacial erosion

Cirque

Irish examples: Coomshingaun, Comeragh Mountains Co. Waterford; Lough Muskry, Galtee Mountains Co. Tipperary

Description: An armchair-shaped depression that forms on the east- or north-facing slopes of upland areas.

Formation: The process of **nivation** involves the weathering of rock under a snow patch by alternate freezing and thawing. Hollows on the mountain slope are deepened, allowing more snow to accumulate. Compression of the lower layers of snow form glacial ice and eventually a glacier (Fig. 10.7).

The ice moves under its own weight in a sliding motion called **rotational slip**, forming a crevasse – or **bergschrund** – within the ice. Scree particles loosened by freeze-thaw action fall into these gaps and, along with rock pieces plucked from the back and base of the hollow, are used by the glacier to over-deepen the hollow by abrasion. As the glacier grows, gravity causes it to move downslope. A terminal moraine often occurs at the cirque mouth. Today, some cirques contain lakes called **tarns**. **Coom** and **corrie** are two other names for this feature.

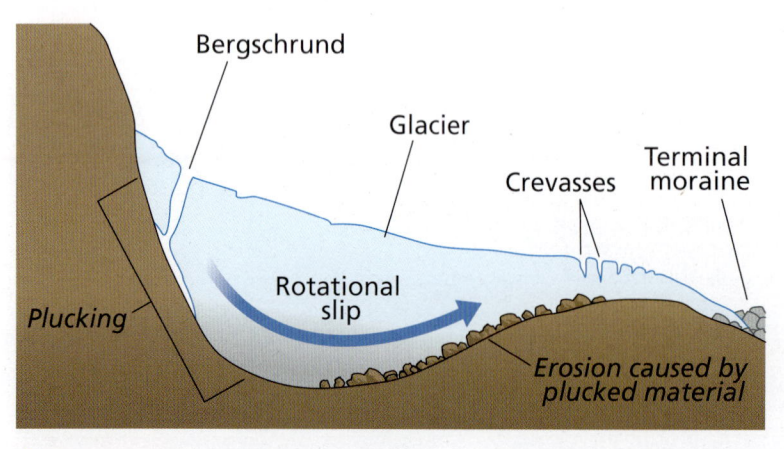

↑ Fig. 10.7(a) The formation of a cirque.

10 Glaciation and Glacial Processes

Fig. 10.7(b) A cirque on an OS map.
- Cirque: steep back and side walls
- Tarn lake

Fig. 10.7(c) A cirque with a tarn lake.

Arête

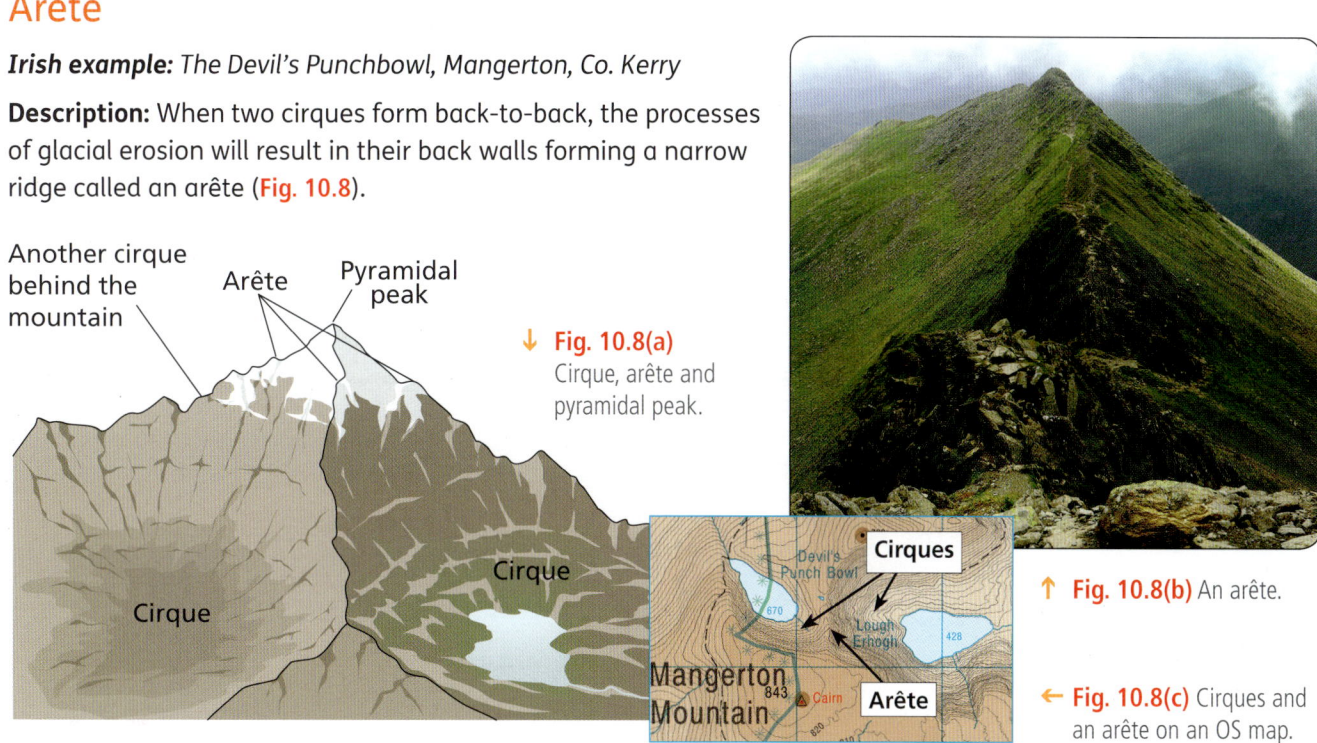

Irish example: The Devil's Punchbowl, Mangerton, Co. Kerry

Description: When two cirques form back-to-back, the processes of glacial erosion will result in their back walls forming a narrow ridge called an arête (**Fig. 10.8**).

Fig. 10.8(a) Cirque, arête and pyramidal peak.
- Another cirque behind the mountain
- Arête
- Pyramidal peak
- Cirque
- Cirque

Fig. 10.8(b) An arête.

Fig. 10.8(c) Cirques and an arête on an OS map.
- Cirques
- Arête

Pyramidal peak

Examples: Carrauntoohil, Co. Kerry; Matterhorn, Switzerland

Description: An angular, pointed mountain peak (**Fig. 10.9**).

Formation: Where three or more cirques form on a mountain, the processes of glacial erosion eroding the back walls will result in the formation of a pyramid-shaped peak or horn (**Fig. 10.8(a)**).

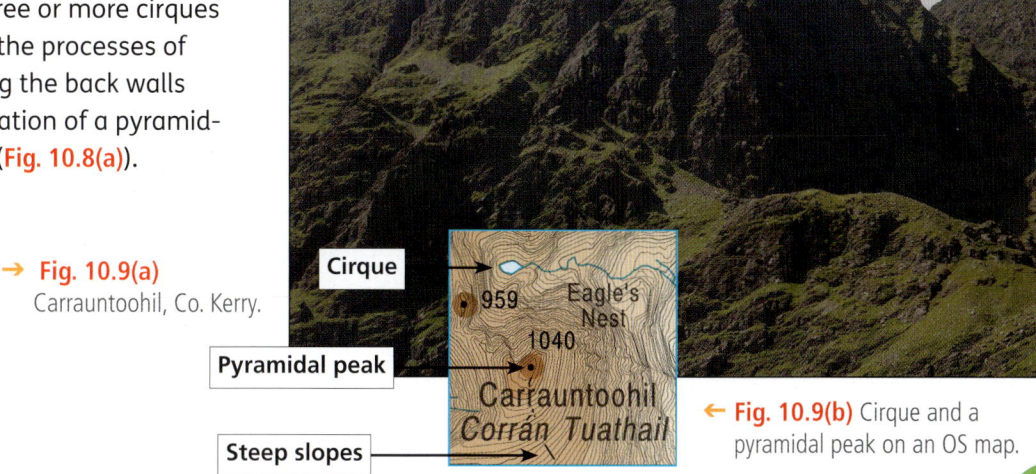

Fig. 10.9(a) Carrauntoohil, Co. Kerry.

Fig. 10.9(b) Cirque and a pyramidal peak on an OS map.
- Cirque
- Pyramidal peak
- Steep slopes

151

Landscapes

Fig.10.10(a) A U-shaped valley, with associated features.

→ **Fig.10.10(b)** A U-shaped valley, formed by glacial erosion.

← **Fig.10.10(c)** A U-shaped valley on an OS map.

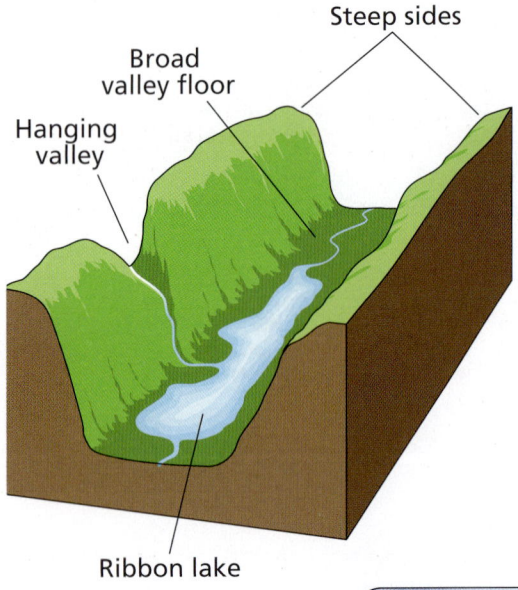

U-shaped valleys, hanging valleys, truncated spurs, ribbon lakes

Irish examples: Glendalough, Co. Wicklow; Glengesh, Co. Donegal

Description: Valley with steep sides and a broad, flat floor.

Formation: The **U-shaped valley** with its associated landforms (**hanging valley** and **truncated spurs**) is an example of a feature of glacial erosion. A number of processes of erosion are involved in the formation of this feature.

The process of **nivation** deepens depressions on mountain slopes, allowing glaciers to form. Moving downslope by gravity, the erosive power of the mass of the glaciers, combined with a number of erosion processes, forms U-shaped valleys – or **troughs** – with a number of associated landforms (Fig. 10.10).

EXAM TIP
A relevant labelled diagram (optional) and a named example of the feature will be awarded 1 SRP each.

- During glaciation, freeze-thaw action along the upper slopes of the valley causes **scree** to break away and fall both onto the glacier, and between it and the side of the valley.
- Friction at the base of the glacier melts the ice. When it refreezes, large pieces of the bedrock become stuck to the base of the glacier. When the ice moves, they are plucked and carried away.
- Glacial abrasion polishes the floor and sides of the valleys, leaving striae on outcropping rocks.
- Though plastic flow allows glaciers to bend and change shape, interlocking spurs are too great an obstacle for the ice to avoid. Instead, the force of the ice and the erosional processes erode them to form truncated spurs.
- **Differential erosion** of the valley floor (when areas of less resistant rock are plucked) forms hollows that become **ribbon lakes** (e.g. Lough NaFooey, Co. Galway; Fig. 10.11). The valley floors can also contain **misfit streams** that occupy only a small part of the valley floor, and could not have been responsible for the valley formation.

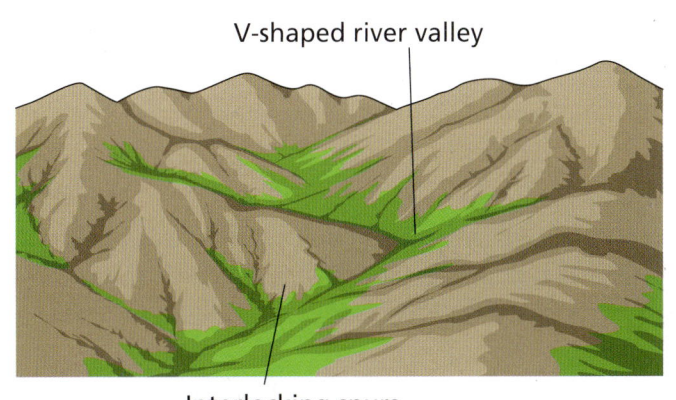

10 Glaciation and Glacial Processes

↑ **Fig.10.11(a)** Before glaciation.
(V-shaped river valley; Interlocking spurs)

↑ **Fig. 10.11(b)** During glaciation.
(Glaciers flow from cirques into the main valley; Tributary valleys contain smaller glaciers; Large glacier occupies the main valley)

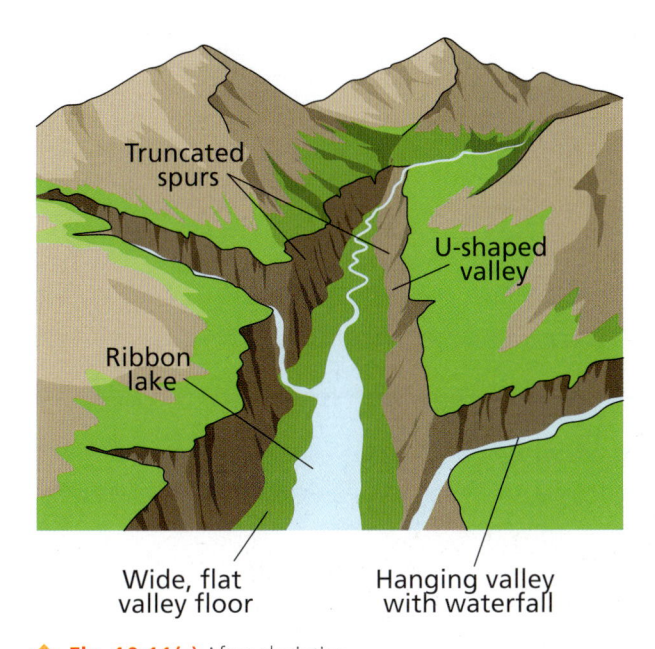

↑ **Fig. 10.11(c)** After glaciation.
(Truncated spurs; U-shaped valley; Ribbon lake; Wide, flat valley floor; Hanging valley with waterfall)

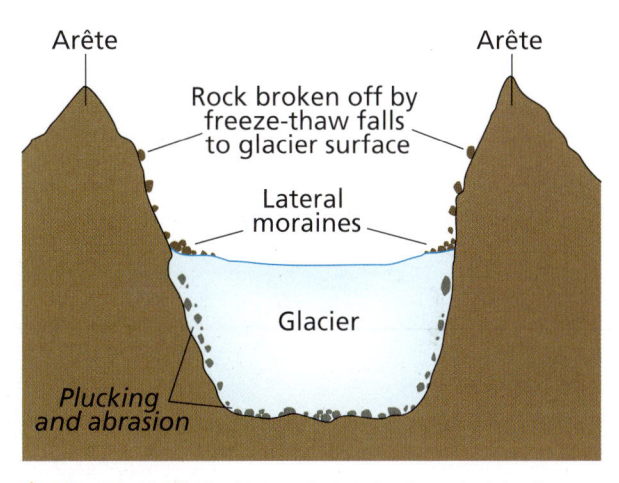

↑ **Fig. 10.11(d)** Plucking and abrasion in a glacial valley.
(Arête; Rock broken off by freeze-thaw falls to glacier surface; Lateral moraines; Glacier; Plucking and abrasion)

- Larger glaciers with greater erosive power occupy the main valley, while smaller glaciers fill tributary valleys. Being smaller, they are not able to erode their valleys to the same depth as the main valley. When the ice melts, these valleys are left **hanging** above the floor of the main valley.
- Streams flowing in these valleys create waterfalls when they enter the main valley (e.g. Glencar, Co Sligo). Deposited material from these rivers create alluvial fans that spread across the valley floor, like in Glendalough, where the alluvial fan divides the valley into two lakes.
- Glacial drift deposits, which form when the rocks and stones at the base of the ice are crushed by the sheer weight of the ice, occur on the floors of these valleys.

> **EXAM LINK (OL)**
> Landform Development (40 marks)
> **Explain, with the aid of diagrams, the formation of any two landforms.**
> 2017, Q2B
>
> **Marking Scheme:**
> Any two landforms at 20 marks each.
> For each landform:
> Landform named = 1 mark
> Diagram(s) = 2 aspects × 2 marks
> Formation explained = 5 SRPs × 3 marks

153

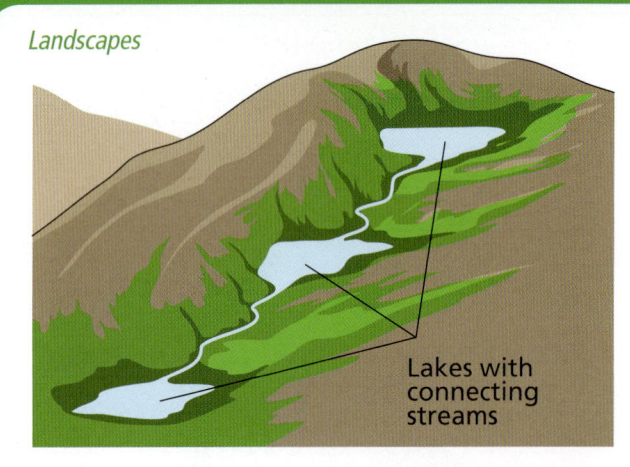

Landscapes

Fig. 10.12(a) Pater noster lakes.

Fig. 10.12(b) Pater noster lakes, on Brandon Mountain, Dingle Peninsula, Co. Kerry.

Fig. 10.12(c) Pater noster lakes on an OS map.

Pater noster lakes

Irish example: *Mount Brandon, Co. Kerry*

Description: A series of glacial lakes connected by streams (Fig. 10.12).

Formation: Differential erosion of the valley floor leads to the formation of depressions in areas of less resistant rock. These fill with water, often forming lakes linked by a river known as **pater noster** lakes. Sometimes waterfalls can occur between lakes.

EXAM TIP (HL)

In the 2018 Higher Level paper, students were asked to describe the formation of a feature they could identify on the Ordnance Survey map extract accompanying the exam.

EXAM LINK (HL)

Surface Processes (30 marks)
Examine the impact of the processes of erosion on the formation of one glacial landform that you have studied.
2017, Q3B

Marking Scheme:
Process of erosion named × 2 marks
Landform named × 2 marks
Examination = 13 SRPs × 2 marks

CHECK YOUR LEARNING

1. Describe the main characteristics of upland glaciation and lowland glaciation.
2. Explain the following terms: nivation, rotational slip.
3. What name is given to a lake occupying a cirque?
4. Draw a simple diagram to show the contour pattern for a cirque.
5. On which side of uplands do cirques form? Why?
6. Name an Irish example of (a) an arête and (b) a pyramidal peak.
7. Name four different processes involved in the formation of a U-shaped valley.

10 Glaciation and Glacial Processes

How ice transports material

The load of a glacier – consisting of rocks and boulders, sand and gravel – is transported in three different ways (Fig. 10.13):

1. **Onglacial:** Material loosened from the upper valley sides by freeze-thaw action or carried by landslides, debris slides or avalanches is carried on the surface of the glacier.
2. **Englacial:** Material found within the glacier that may have fallen onto it and melted its way downwards, fallen into a crevasse or that may have been raised from the valley floor to higher up within the ice.
3. **Subglacial:** Material found at the base of the glacier that may have been eroded by plucking or originated on the surface and made its way downwards through the ice.

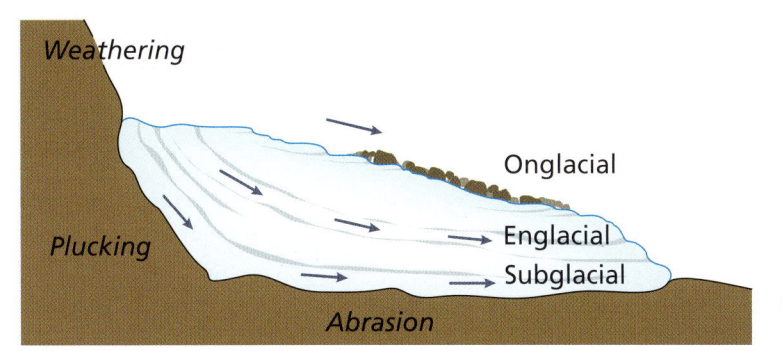

KEYWORDS
onglacial
englacial
subglacial

EXAM TIP (HL)
All processes mentioned should be explained and linked to the formation of the feature.

← **Fig.10.13** How glacial ice transports material.

Landforms of glacial deposition

Bedrock beneath glacial ice is crushed into either boulders, smaller rocks, pebbles, sand, silt or clay. When the ice melts, a mixture of all this material called **glacial drift** is left behind. There are two types of drift:

1. **Unstratified drift:** Deposited directly by the ice, this material consists of different sized particles all mixed together. It is more commonly known as **boulder clay** or **till**, and is the main component of **drumlins** and **moraines**. Boulder clay deposits cover much of the Irish landscape (e.g. the Golden Vale, Co. Limerick).
2. **Stratified drift:** deposited by meltwater from the ice. It is smooth, as a result of fluvial erosion, and was deposited in layers, with larger particles on the bottom and lighter material in the upper layers.

KEYWORDS
glacial drift
unstratified
drumlins
moraines
stratified
lateral
medial
terminal
recessional
erratic
drumlin
carrying capacity
friction

Moraines

Irish examples: Co. Kildare; Co. Limerick

Description: Accumulations of rock, earth, sand and gravel deposited by ice.

Formation: Moraines are composed of unstratified drift material of varying sizes deposited by glaciers and ice sheets. Onglacial, englacial and subglacial moraines are associated with existing valley glaciers (Fig. 10.14).

Valley glacier moraines are onglacial moraines formed from unstratified rock debris, loosened from the valley sides by freeze-thaw action and moved downslope by mass movement. These are found on the surface of existing glaciers.

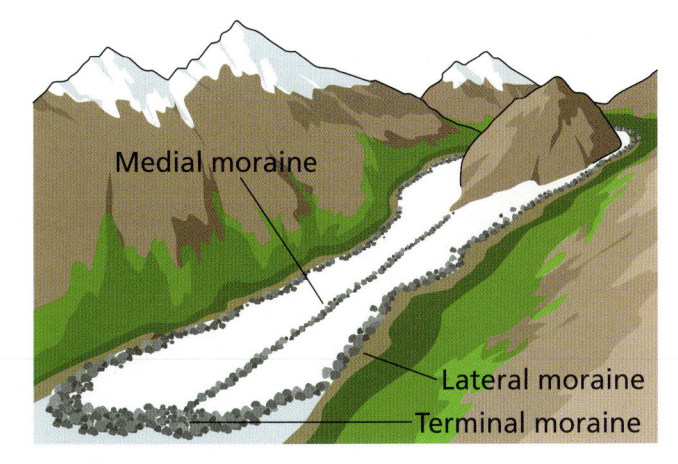

↑ **Fig.10.14(a)** Lateral, medial and terminal moraines during glaciation.

155

Lateral moraines occur along the sides of the glaciers, while **medial moraines** extending down the centre form when a tributary glacier joins a larger glacier. The rocks and stones in these moraines protect the underlying ice from melting, so they form ridges above the glacier's surface.

Terminal moraines occurring at the front or snout of the glacier mark the furthest advance of glaciers and ice sheets.

↑ **Fig.10.14(b)** Moraines, on Igdlorssuit Glacier, southern Greenland.

Moraines associated with post-glacial landscapes

Lateral moraines occur along the sides of U-shaped valleys (e.g. Glenmalure, Co. Wicklow).

A terminal moraine marks the maximum advancement of the glacier or ice sheet. In Co. Wicklow, a terminal moraine associated with valley glaciers occurs at Glendalough, while the terminal moraine associated with the Midlandian Ice Age extends from Co. Limerick through Tipperary and northwards along the western slopes of the Wicklow Mountains. Terminal moraines run parallel to glacier and ice sheet fronts.

Recessional moraines formed when the retreating glaciers and ice sheets halted and remained in a stationary position for a long time. In glacial valleys, they extend across the valley floors (Fig. 10.15).

Ground moraine is deposited on valley floors by retreating glaciers (e.g. Glendasan, Co. Wicklow), while retreating ice sheets deposit it on lowlands, creating gently rolling boulder clay plains (e.g. Co. Kildare).

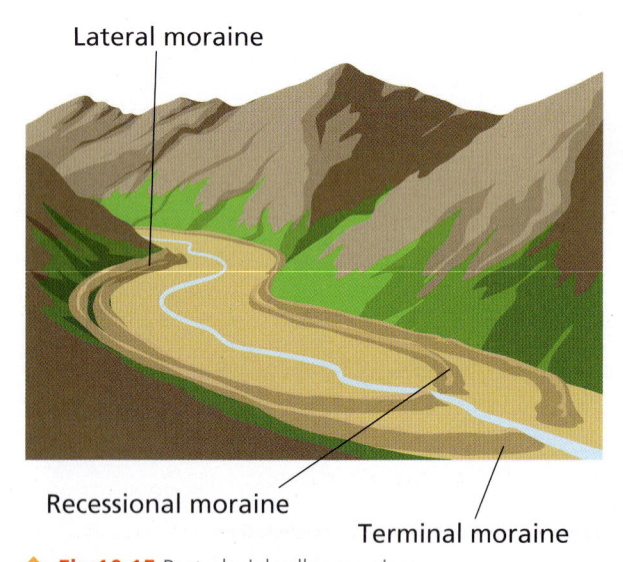

↑ **Fig.10.15** Post-glacial valley moraines.

Erratics

Irish example: Connemara granite, Inis Mór, Aran Islands

Description: A rock which differs in type and shape to its surroundings.

Formation: With the melting of the ice, transported load including rocks and boulders plucked by glaciers and ice sheets was deposited in areas where the bedrock was of a different composition (Fig. 10.16). An example of this can be seen in Connemara granite deposited on the limestone landscapes of the Aran Islands, Co. Galway.

← **Fig.10.16** Granite erratic, Aran Islands.

Drumlins

Irish examples: *Clew Bay, Co. Mayo; Scarriff-Sixmilebridge, Co. Clare*

Description: Drumlins are oval-shaped hills of boulder clay.

Formation: The **carrying capacity** of ice refers to its ability to transport material. When the ice becomes overloaded with sediment, the carrying capacity is reduced and deposition will occur.

Factors affecting carrying capacity include the **volume of sediment** and the **velocity of the ice flow**. Velocity can be reduced when the ice begins to melt, and when **friction** with the underlying rock occurs. The presence of rock cores in some drumlins suggest that they reduced the velocity of the ice, causing deposits to build up around them.

The reduced carrying capacity of the glacier causes the ice to deposit the transported material. The erosive action of the moving ice shapes and streamlines these deposits, giving the drumlins their characteristic shape. Some drumlins are elongated, which may be the result of faster ice movement around the deposits (Fig. 10.17).

> **EXAM TIP**
>
> A question on glacial landforms has come up every year since 2011.

↑ **Fig.10.17(a)** A drumlin in cross-section and plan.

↑ **Fig.10.17(b)** A drumlin near Strangford Lough, Co. Down.

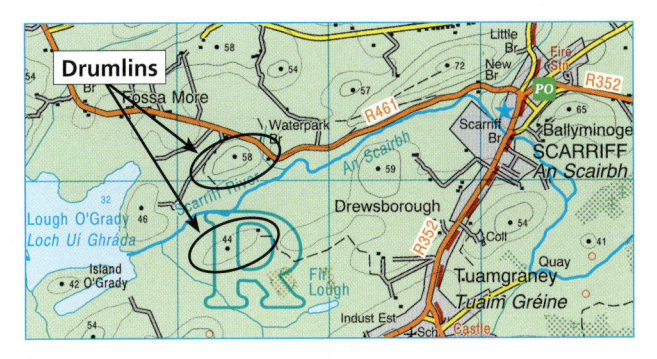

↑ **Fig.10.17(c)** Drumlins on an OS map.

Drumlins can be up to a kilometre long and 500 m wide with an average height of 50 metres. The orientation of drumlins is an indication of the direction of the ice flow; the steep end of a drumlin – the **stoss slope** – is the side that faced the approaching ice, while the **lee slope** faced away from it.

Drumlins occur in swarms and create a landscape called 'basket of eggs' topography. Precipitation drains down the slopes of the drumlins, but because the land at their base is also covered with impermeable boulder clay, drainage can be poor, leading to waterlogging and the formation of saturated gley soils.

The drumlin drift belt that extends from Strangford Lough, Co. Down to Clew Bay, Co. Mayo is an important example of a drumlin field. In both Strangford Lough and Clew Bay, post-glacial sea level rises have resulted in some of the drumlins being 'drowned' and forming islands.

> **EXAM LINK (HL)**
>
> Landform Development (30 marks)
>
> **Examine the impact of the processes of deposition on the formation of any one landform that you have studied.**
>
> 2016, Q2B
>
> **Marking Scheme:**
>
> Landform named = 2 marks
>
> Examination = 14 SRPs × 2 marks

CHECK YOUR LEARNING

1. Explain the following terms: stratified, unstratified.
2. Name three different types of moraine found in valley glaciers.
3. Name three types of moraines found on lowland areas.
4. What is an erratic?
5. List three steps in the formation of drumlins.

Landscapes

KEYWORDS
fluvioglaciation
spillway
pro-glacial lake
esker
kame
kettle hole
outwash plain

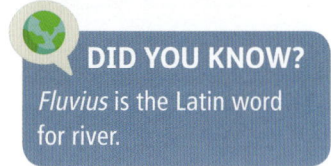

Landforms of fluvioglaciation

Fluvioglaciation is the process by which meltwater from glaciers and ice sheets was responsible for the creation of landforms of erosion and deposition. This process was most active when temperatures rose towards the end of the Pleistocene Epoch, releasing huge quantities of water. As water was the main agent involved, depositional features are all composed of stratified material with the heavier particles at the base of the feature.

Features of erosion

Glacial spillway

Irish examples: *Glen of the Downs, Co. Wicklow; Pass of Keimaneigh, Co. Cork*

Description: A valley formed by huge volumes of glacial meltwater.

Formation: A **pro-glacial** lake forms when meltwater becomes trapped between the ice and an upland area. The level of this lake continues to rise until the water reaches the lowest point of the upland and overflows (**Fig. 10.18**). The meltwater carries out vertical erosion by abrasion and hydraulic action, creating a river valley with its typical V-shaped profile. Established spillways are often occupied by misfit streams, and provide routes through upland areas.

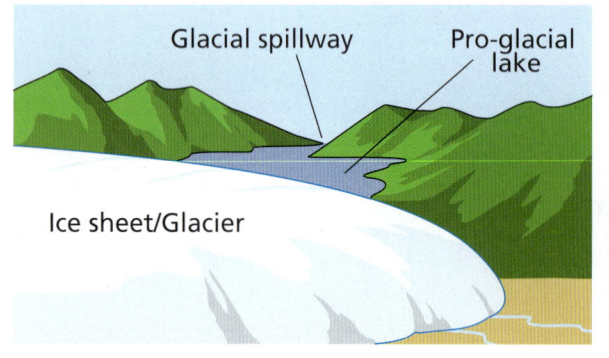

> **DID YOU KNOW?**
> *Fluvius* is the Latin word for river.

↑ **Fig.10.18(a)** The formation of a glacial spillway.

↑ **Fig.10.18(b)** Glen of the Downs, a glacial spillway in Co. Wicklow.

← **Fig.10.18(c)** A glacial spillway on an OS map.

> **DID YOU KNOW?**
> Esker derives from the Irish word *eiscar*, meaning ridge.

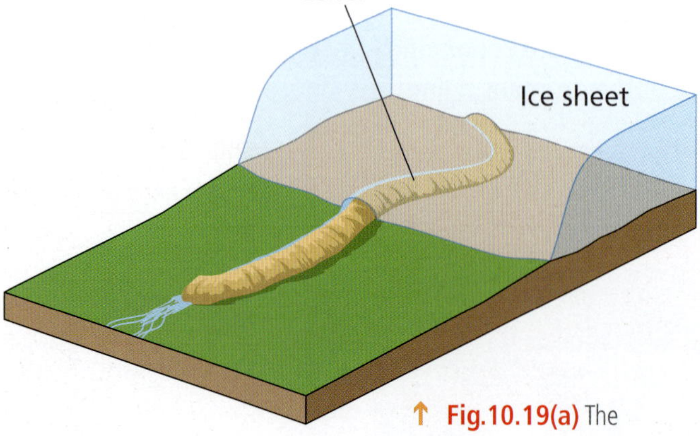

Features of deposition

Esker

Irish example: *Eiscir Riada, Clonmacnoise, Co. Westmeath*

Description: A long winding ridge of stratified glacial material.

Formation: Eskers form in tunnels under an advancing ice sheet where huge volumes of meltwater carry englacial material. The exits of these tunnels often get blocked by the build-up of material, stopping meltwater flow and causing

↑ **Fig.10.19(a)** The formation of an esker.

158

deposition. The material including boulders, sand and gravel is deposited in stratified layers (Fig. 10.19).

Eskers run perpendicular to terminal moraines. In the ancient past, they were used as routes, while today they supply commercial sand gravel pits.

Kame

Irish example: Co. Kildare

Description: A kame is a conical mound of stratified glacial drift, usually sand and gravel.

Formation: They form where hollows close to the edge of the melting ice fill with water which contains large amounts of sediments. These sediments are lowered through the melting ice and form a mound (Fig. 10.20).

↑ **Fig.10.19(b)** An esker in North Dakota.

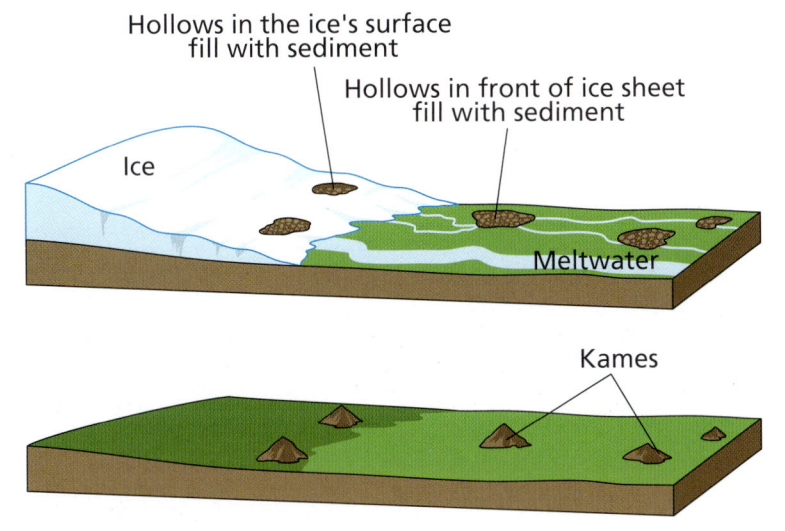

↑ **Fig.10.20(a)** The formation of kames.

↑ **Fig.10.20(b)** A kame in Wester Pearsie, Scotland.

Kettle holes

Irish example: Co. Westmeath

Description: Hollows, often filled with lakes.

Formation: As the ice age was ending, large pieces of ice sheets and glaciers broke away, leaving blocks of 'dead ice' in the fluvioglacial deposits. The melting ice formed depressions, called kettle holes, which can become lakes (Fig. 10.21).

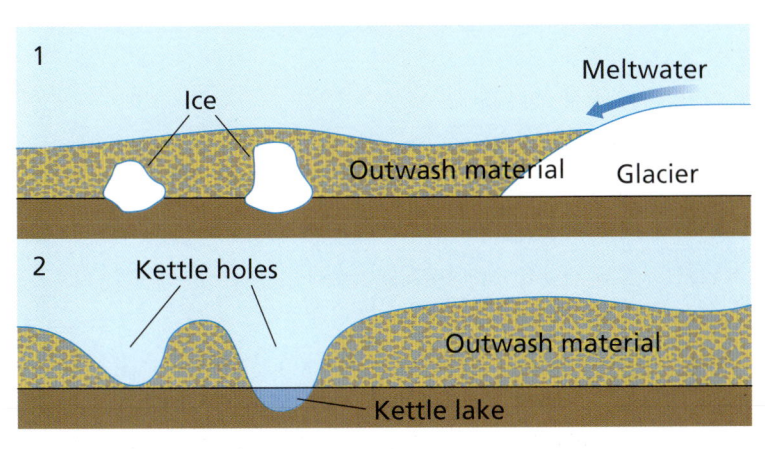

↑ **Fig.10.21(a)** The formation of kettle holes.

→ **Fig.10.21(b)** Kettle holes in Northwest Territory, Canada.

Landscapes

Outwash plain

Irish example: The Curragh, Co. Kildare

Description: A large area covered with meltwater deposits.

Formation: Meltwater flowing from glaciers and ice sheets deposits its load in front of the ice. In some cases, meltwater flowing through the terminal moraine removes material which is then deposited beyond the moraine to form an outwash plain (Fig. 10.22). The heavier gravel is transported the shortest distance, while lighter clays and sands are carried longer distances before they are deposited. Outwash deposits can be up to 50 m thick and extend over a wide area.

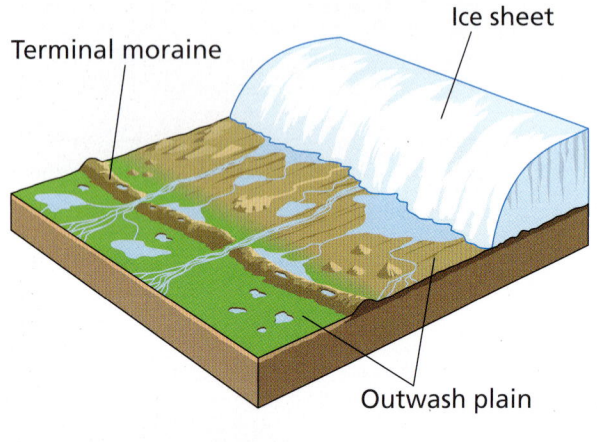

↑ **Fig.10.22(a)** The formation of an outwash plain.

→ **Fig.10.22(b)** An outwash plain, Alaska, USA.

CHECK YOUR LEARNING

1. What is fluvioglaciation?
2. Name and give an example of one erosional feature formed by fluvioglaciation.
3. Identify three depositional features formed by fluvioglaciation.
4. Match the landform to the correct letter on the diagram.

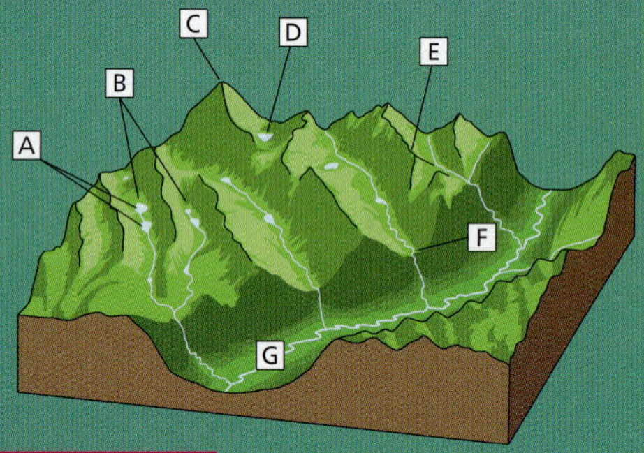

Landform	Letter
U-shaped valley	
Pyramidal peak	
Hanging valley	

Landform	Letter
Cirques	
Tarn	

Landform	Letter
Arête	
Pater noster lake	

5. Match the landform to the correct letter on the diagram.

Landform	Letter
Esker	
Drumlin	
Kettle holes	

Landform	Letter
Terminal moraine	
Kames	
Outwash plain	

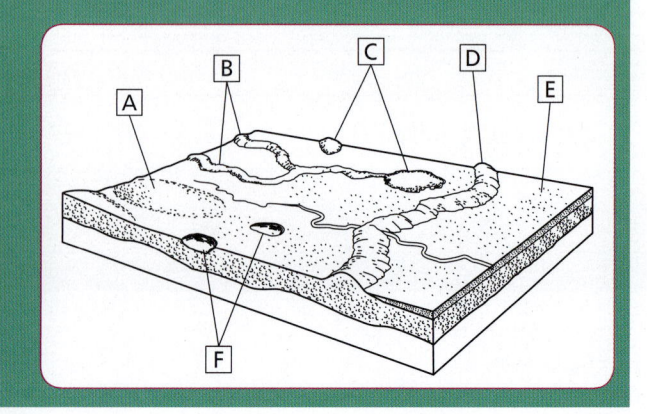

160

10 Glaciation and Glacial Processes

EXAMINATION QUESTIONS
ORDINARY LEVEL

Short Questions

1. Rivers and Glaciation

Examine the photographs and complete the table by answering each of the following questions. Some of the table has been completed for you.

(i) Match each of the photographs A, B and C with the landform that best matches it in the table below. *3 × 2 marks*

(ii) State whether each of the landforms named in the table is formed by river processes or glacial processes. *2 × 2 marks*

(i) Letter	Landform	(ii) River Processes / Glacial Processes
	Oxbow lake	River
D	U-shaped valley	
	Cirque/corrie/tarn	Glacial
	V-shaped valley	

2017, Part One, Q3 (10 marks)

HIGHER LEVEL

Short Questions

2. The Physical Environment

Examine the photographs and answer each of the following questions.

(i) Match each of the photographs A, B, C and D with the type that best matches it in the table below. *4 × 1 mark*

(ii) Indicate by ticking the correct box whether each of the types of lake named in the table below is most associated with glacial, fluvial or karst landscapes. *4 × 1 mark*

2017, Part One, Q2 (8 marks)

(i)   (ii)

Letter	Type of Lake	Glacial Landscape (✓)	Fluvial Landscape (✓)	Karst Landscape (✓)
	Pater noster lake			
	Oxbow lake			
	Tarn			
	Turlough			

161

Landscapes

3. Glaciation

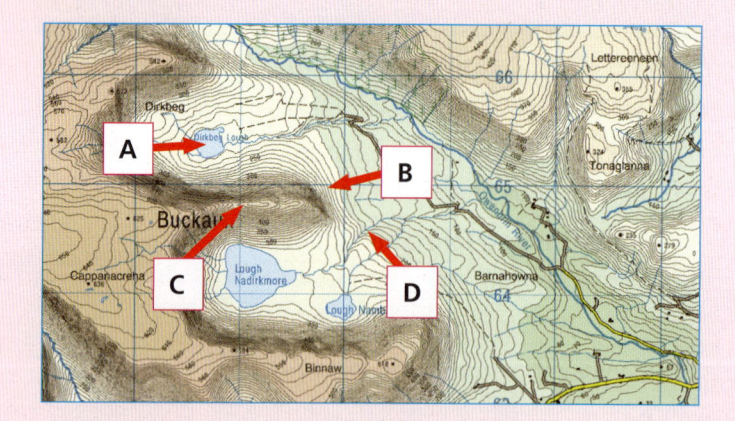

(i) Examine the Ordnance Survey map extract above and match each of the letters A, B, C and D with the correct feature in the table below.

4 × 1 mark

Feature	Letter
Hanging valley	
Arête	

Feature	Letter
Tarn	
Truncated spur	

(ii) Explain briefly each of the following terms:
- Plucking
- Abrasion

2 × 2 marks

2013, Part One, Q3 (8 marks)

Long Questions

4. Surface Processes

Examine the impact of the processes of erosion on the formation of one fluvial landform, coastal landform or glacial landform that you have studied.

2017, Part Two, Section 1, Q3B (30 marks)

Marking Scheme:
Process of erosion named = 2 marks
Landform named = 2 marks
Examination = 13 SRPs × 2 marks

10 Glaciation and Glacial Processes

Revision Summary

Pleistocene glaciation

- The most recent glaciation
- Glacial and interglacial periods in Ireland:
  - **Munsterian:** 300,000–130,000 years ago – ice covered all Ireland
  - **Midlandian:** 80,000–12,000 years ago – ice covered the Midlands
- Upland glaciation: Valley glaciers, features of erosion – Wicklow Mountains
- Lowland glaciation: Ice sheets features of deposition – Co. Offaly

Glacial ice formation: advance–retreat

- Process of ice formation: snow – granular ice – firn – glacial ice
- **Glacial mass balance:** The difference between the amount of ice accumulated during the winter and lost by melting during the summer
- **Positive:** Ice accumulation greater
- **Negative:** Ice loss is greater
- **Stationary:** Accumulation and loss in balance
- **Snow line:** The boundary for permanent snow
- **Ablation:** The loss of ice and snow due to melting

Glacial processes

Movement
- Rotational slip: Ice moves under its own weight
- Basal slip: Meltwater acts as a lubricant
- Plastic flow: Internal flow within the ice
- Rate of flow: Slower at valley sides due to increased friction

Erosion
- Plucking
- Abrasion
- Freeze-thaw action

Transportation
- Onglacial: On the surface of the ice
- Englacial: Within the ice
- Subglacial: Under the ice

Deposition
- **Stratified drift:** Material is sorted by glacial meltwater according to size and weight
- **Unstratified drift:** Material is not sorted

Fluvioglaciation

- Meltwater from glaciers and ice sheets eroded, transported and deposited.
- Stratified deposits: Heavier material carried short distances

Feature of erosion
- Glacial spillway: Glen of the Downs – meltwater trapped behind a ridge – overflowing water erodes a channel

Features of deposition
- Esker: Eiscir Riada, Co. Westmeath – form in tunnels under ice sheet – exits get blocked stopping meltwater flow and causing deposition – stratified layers
- Outwash plain: Curragh, Co Kildare – glacial meltwater washes out material from terminal moraines – heavy particles are carried shortest distances
- Kames: Co. Kildare – sediment deposits lowered through melting ice – form stratified mounds
- Kettle holes: Co. Westmeath – blocks of ice deposited in till melt – leave hollows that fill with water

Landforms of deposition

Glacial drift
- The Golden Vale
- Boulder clay/till

Moraines
- Co. Kildare, Co. Limerick
- Lateral – medial – terminal

Erratics
- Aran Islands

Drumlins
- Formation processes of drumlins:
  - Sediment: Clay, rocks, sand, gravel
  - Carrying capacity: How much sediment the ice can carry
  - Velocity: Reduced velocity reduces carrying capacity
  - Rock core: Around which sediment is deposited
  - Oval shape
  - Unstratified material
  - Saturated gley soils at base

Landforms of erosion

Cirque
- Coomshinguan, Comeragh Mountains
- Armchair-shaped hollow, north-facing slopes

Formation processes
- Nivation
- Freeze-thaw action
- Plucking
- Abrasion
- Rotational slip

Characteristics
- Bergschrund
- Moraine
- Tarn lake

Arête
- Devil's Punch Bowl, Co. Kerry
- Ridge between two cirques
- Freeze-thaw action

Pyramidal peak
- Carrauntoohill, Co. Kerry

U-shaped valley
- Glendalough, Co. Wicklow
- Formation processes:
  - Nivation
  - Freeze-thaw action
  - Plucking
  - Abrasion
  - Differential erosion

Characteristics
- Striae
- Steep sides
- Broad floor
- Truncated spurs
- Hanging valley
- Ribbon lakes
- Pater noster lake
- Mount Brandon, Co. Kerry

163

11 ISOSTASY

KEYWORDS
- isostasy
- long profile
- rejuvenation
- base level
- knick point
- incised meanders
- entrenched meanders
- ingrown meanders
- paired terraces

LEARNING INTENTIONS
Syllabus Link: 1.6

By the end of this chapter I will be able to:
- understand that over time different forces act to alter the balance of the lithosphere;
- explain how isostasy has impacted on fluvial processes;
- identify features of rejuvenation from Ordnance Survey maps, diagrams and photographs;
- describe the formation of one feature associated with rejuvenation, giving named examples;
- explain how isostasy has impacted on coastal landscapes;
- identify coastal features formed by isostasy from diagrams and photographs;
- understand how subaerial processes lead to the erosion of the landscape and the formation of peneplains;
- explain and be able to identify from diagrams the stages in the cycle of landscape formation.

Chapter 1: Plate Tectonics

Isostatic readjustment: The sinking downwards of land due to the weight of ice.

Isostatic rebound: When land moves upwards following the melting of ice sheets.

Isostasy refers to the adjustment the earth's crust undergoes as it either sinks into or rises up from the mantle.

How Glaciation Causes Isostatic Movement

During the ice ages, ice accumulated on the surface of the earth. The weight of the ice on the earth's crust caused the crust to sink into the mantle (Fig. 11.1(a)).

When the ice melted, the crust rose slowly upwards, a process called isostatic rebound (**Fig. 11.1(b)**). Rebound from the last ice age is ongoing today, for example, in the Gulf of Bothnia, Finland.

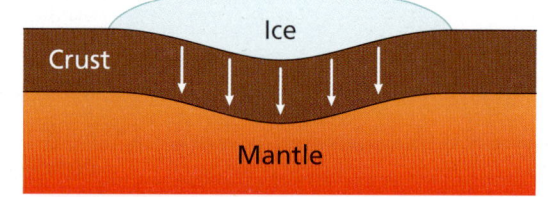

↑ **Fig. 11.1(a)** The crust sinks slowly into the mantle under the weight of glacial ice.

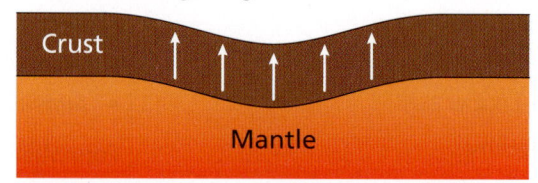

↑ **Fig. 11.1(b)** When the ice has melted, the crust rebounds.

The Impact of Isostasy on Fluvial Processes

The post-glacial upward movement of continents led to falling sea levels which impacted on fluvial processes. Sea level is generally regarded as being the base level for rivers and is the lowest level on a river channel to which erosion can occur. The **long profile** of rivers shows them as having steep gradients in the upper stage and gentle gradients in the lower stage. (Fig. 11.2(a))

↑ **Fig. 11.2(a)** The long profile of a river.

11 Isostasy

Post-glacial land rises led to a fall in sea level which increased the gradient in the lower stage, altering the long profile and increasing river velocity. Increased velocity led to increased erosive power, causing rivers in their old stage to behave like youthful rivers, they were **rejuvenated** (Fig. 11.2b).

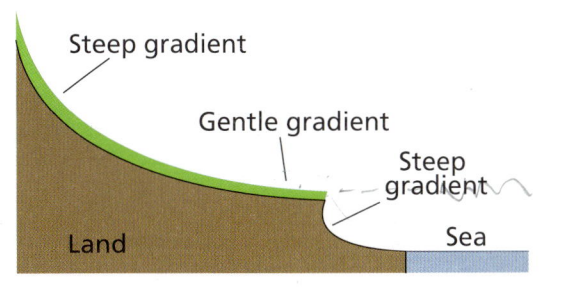

> Chapter 8: River Action

↑ **Fig. 11.2(b)** The impact of rejuvenation on the long profile of a river.

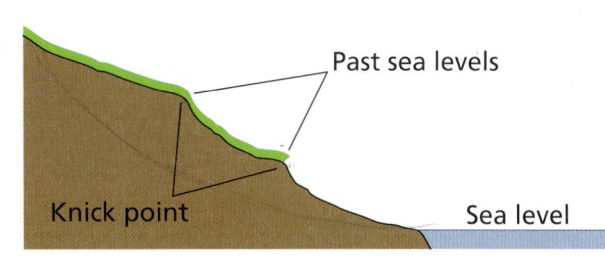

↑ **Fig. 11.2(c)** The long profile of a river with knick points.

Rejuvenation

Rejuvenation occurs when there is a change in sea level relative to the level of the land, caused either by falling sea level or rising land level. In order to adjust to its new **base level**, erosion of the river channel starts in the lower stage and continues back up along the channel until the new profile is complete. This process leads to the formation of a number of fluvial features (Fig. 11.2(c)).

Knick points

Irish example: *River Nore and River Barrow, Co. Kilkenny*

Description: Changes in slope along a river profile.

The river's adjustment to the new base level begins at the sea. A **knick point** marks the point of change in the river's profile. It occurs at a point between the old profile and the new one being created, in response to the changed base level. A very marked knick point will form a waterfall, but smaller, less steep ones marked by rapids can also occur. The change in river gradient increases its erosive power, leading to vertical erosion of the river channel.

Incised meanders

Irish example: *River Barrow, Co. Carlow*

Description: A meander that has been eroded deep into the landscape.

Meanders are features associated with the mature and old stages of rivers. When rejuvenation causes vertical erosion to occur along these meanders, they become incised (eroded) into the landscape.

There are two types of incised meanders:

- **entrenched meanders**: when vertical erosion is so rapid that there is not enough time for lateral erosion to take place. This results in the meander having steep slopes on both sides (Fig. 11.3).

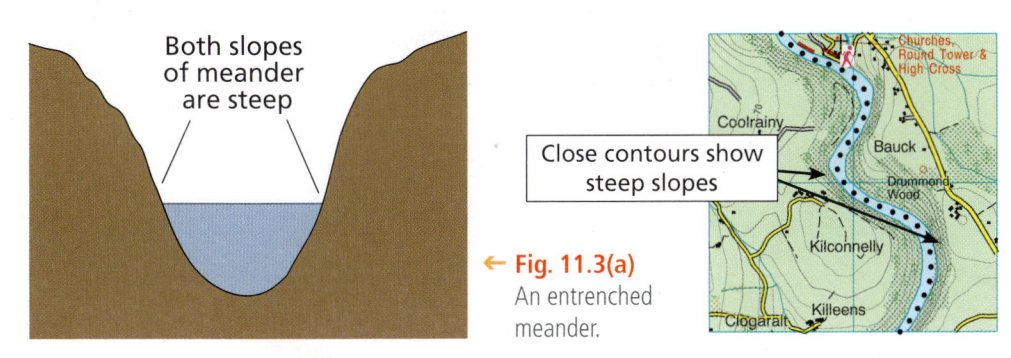

Rejuvenation: To become youthful again.

EXAM LINK (HL)

Fluvial Adjustment (30 marks)

Examine how changes in base level impact on geomorphic processes and landforms in a fluvial environment.

2016, Q2C

Marking Scheme:
Each SRP = 2 marks
Impact on processes identified = 1 SRP
Impact on landform identified = 1 SRP
Examination = 13 × SRPs

EXAM TIP

A relevant labelled diagram (optional) is worth 1 SRP, or 2 marks.

← **Fig. 11.3(a)** An entrenched meander.

← **Fig. 11.3(b)** An entrenched meander on the River Barrow.

Landscapes

- **ingrown meanders**: form when a slower rate of vertical erosion allows lateral erosion to occur resulting in one side, the outer bend, having a steep slope, while the inner bend has a gentle slip-off slope (Fig. 11.4).

Paired terraces: Terraces occurring at different levels above the current floodplain.

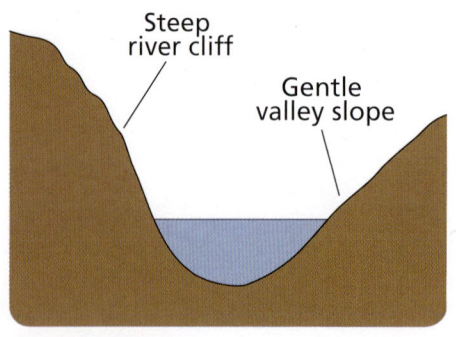

↑ **Fig. 11.4(a)** An ingrown meander.

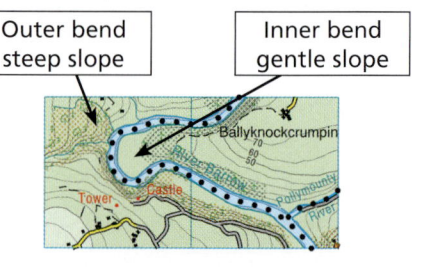

↑ **Fig. 11.4(b)** An ingrown meander on the River Barrow.

Paired terraces

Irish examples: River Dodder, Co. Dublin; River Barrow, Co. Kilkenny

In their mature and old stages, rivers develop floodplains. With rejuvenation, vertical erosion along the river channel incises it into the floodplain. Lateral erosion widens the river channel to create a new floodplain. The remains of the old floodplain forms paired terraces (Fig. 11.5).

↑ **Fig. 11.4(a) Fig. 11.5** Paired terraces, Central Asia.

The impact of isostasy on coastal landforms

Isostatic adjustment of the land in the past has led to coastal landforms being raised above sea level, forming **raised beaches**, **raised cliffs** and **raised sea caves**.

KEYWORDS
isostatic adjustment
raised beach
raised caves
raised cliff

Raised beach

Irish example: Ballyhillin, Malin Head, Co. Donegal

Description: A beach which is today above the level of high tides.

Eustatic movement: Change in sea level – it falls when water is 'locked up' as ice and rises when the ice melts.

During past glaciations, when water was locked into the ice, sea levels were lower than they are today. Marine processes of erosion and deposition were active along these coasts, and created landforms. With isostatic adjustment, the uplift of the land resulted in these features being raised above sea level, where today they form raised beaches, raised cliffs and relic caves (Fig. 11.6). While they are no longer affected by marine processes, they are still subjected to weathering.

↑ **Fig. 11.6(a)** Coastal features formed by isostasy.

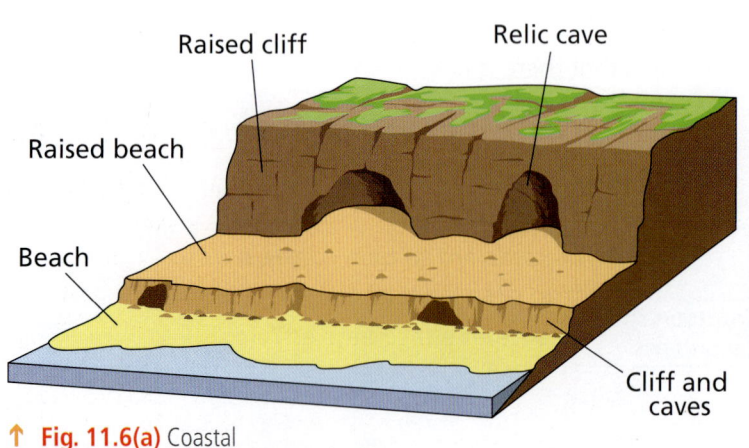

↑ **Fig. 11.6(b)** A raised beach, Ballyhillin, Malin Head, Co. Donegal.

CHECK YOUR LEARNING

1. Explain the term 'isostasy'.
2. Using diagrams, explain how glaciation influences isostasy.
3. Explain the term 'rejuvenation'.
4. Name three fluvial features formed by rejuvenation.
5. Name two coastal features formed by isostasy.

Landscape Development

The geographical cycle of erosion

In 1889, American geographer William Morris Davis developed a theory on landscape development. His cycle of erosion theory proposed that rivers and other agents of erosion acting on an uplifted landmass will eventually reduce it to a low, featureless plain called a **peneplain**. According to Davis, rock structure, physical processes and time are all factors that influence the cycle. The main assumptions he made were:

- that the cycle begins with tectonic uplift;
- that erosion only starts after the uplift has ceased.

The cycle has three stages.

1. Youth (Fig. 11.7(a)): The uplift has stopped and erosion begins. Consequent streams flowing over the surface erode their valley floors, forming deep V-shaped valleys. Headward erosion extends the river channels, leading to river capture. Fluvial features including rapids, **waterfalls,** gorges and lakes are formed during this stage.

2. Maturity (Fig. 11.7(b)): By this stage, the rivers have become graded, there is a balance between erosion and deposition. The landmass is now well drained by rivers that have dissected it, forming ridges and valleys. Vertical erosion is now overtaken by lateral erosion, and **meanders** and **floodplains** appear.

3. Old age (Fig. 11.7(c)): In this stage, rivers have reached their base level, are flowing slowly and have lost their erosive ability. Deposition is the main activity. The landscape has now been reduced to a **peneplain**.

Extending from Co. Cork to Co. Waterford, the South Ireland Peneplain has elevations ranging between 200 and 250 metres above sea level.

KEYWORDS

cycle of erosion
peneplain
tectonic uplift
headward erosion

↑ **Fig. 11.7(a)** Landscape development: youthful stage.

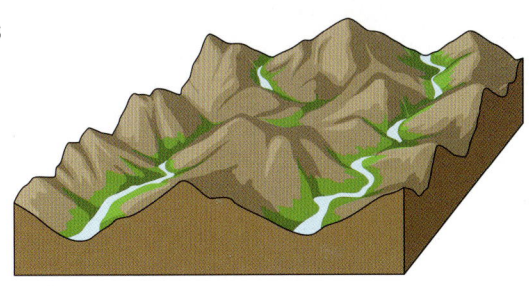

↑ **Fig. 11.7(b)** Landscape development: mature stage.

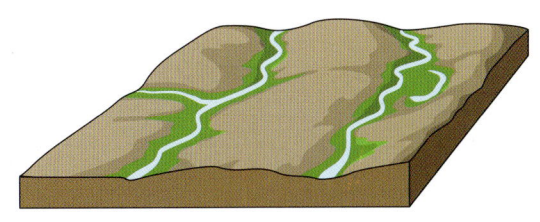

↑ **Fig. 11.7(c)** Landscape development: old age peneplain.

CHECK YOUR LEARNING

1. Identify the three stages of the geographical cycle of erosion.
2. Name a fluvial feature associated with each stage.
3. Give a brief description of each stage.
4. Explain the term 'peneplain'.

River capture: Headward erosion that extends a river upstream from its source diverts (captures) water from other rivers and streams into its own channel.

Landscapes

EXAMINATION QUESTIONS
HIGHER LEVEL

Long Questions

1. Landscape Development

Examine the diagram, which shows the stages in the cyclical development of a fluvial landscape, and answer each of the following questions.

(i) Name each of the stages A, B and C. *3 × 2 marks*

(ii) Name one fluvial landform from each stage. *3 × 2 marks*

(iii) Explain briefly what is meant by **peneplain**. *2 SRPs × 2 marks*

(iv) Explain briefly what is meant by **base level**. *2 SRPs × 2 marks.*

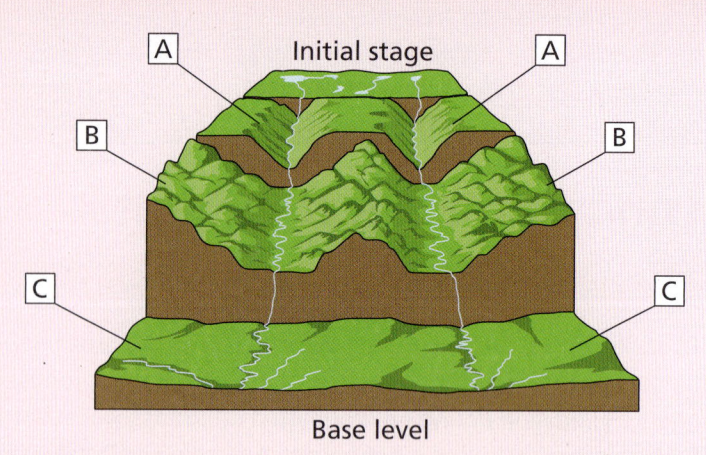

2014, Part Two, Section 1, Q3A (20 marks)

Initial stage — Base level (diagram labels A, B, C)

Revision Summary

Isostasy	Impact on surface structures	
	Fluvial environments	**Coastal environments**

Isostasy	Fluvial environments	Coastal environments

• Movement of the earth's crust caused by ice forming and melting during and after glacial periods.
• **Isostatic readjustment**: ice formed – weight caused earth's crust to sink into mantle
• **Isostatic rebound**: ice melted – reduced weight caused upward crustal movement
• Causes:
  – Weight of ice forces crust downwards
  – Melting of ice reduces pressure on crust, causing it to rise upwards
• Impacts:
  – Uplift of land
  – Causes sea level to fall
  – Changes the base level of rivers, leading to rejuvenation
	Rejuvenation
	• Sea level = base level for rivers
	• Changes to sea level rejuvenate rivers – rivers start eroding in lower stages
	• Erosion begins in old stage and moves back along river channel – new profile formed over time
	
	Features of rejuvenation
	• **Knick points**: mark boundary between old and new profiles
	• **Entrenched meanders**: steep slopes
	• **Ingrown meanders**: outer bend steep slope – inner bend gentle slope
	• **Paired terraces**: river channel eroded into floodplain – lateral erosion forms new floodplain – old plain forms paired terraces
		• Marine processes formed features of coastal erosion and deposition
		• Isostatic adjustment of the land resulted in these features being raised above sea level
		• Features:
		  – Raised cliffs
		  – Raised beaches
		  – Relic caves
		
		Cycle of erosion: landscape development
		• William Morris Davis, 1889
		• Uplifted landmass – subjected to processes of erosion – reduced to a peneplain
		• Three stages: youth – maturity – old

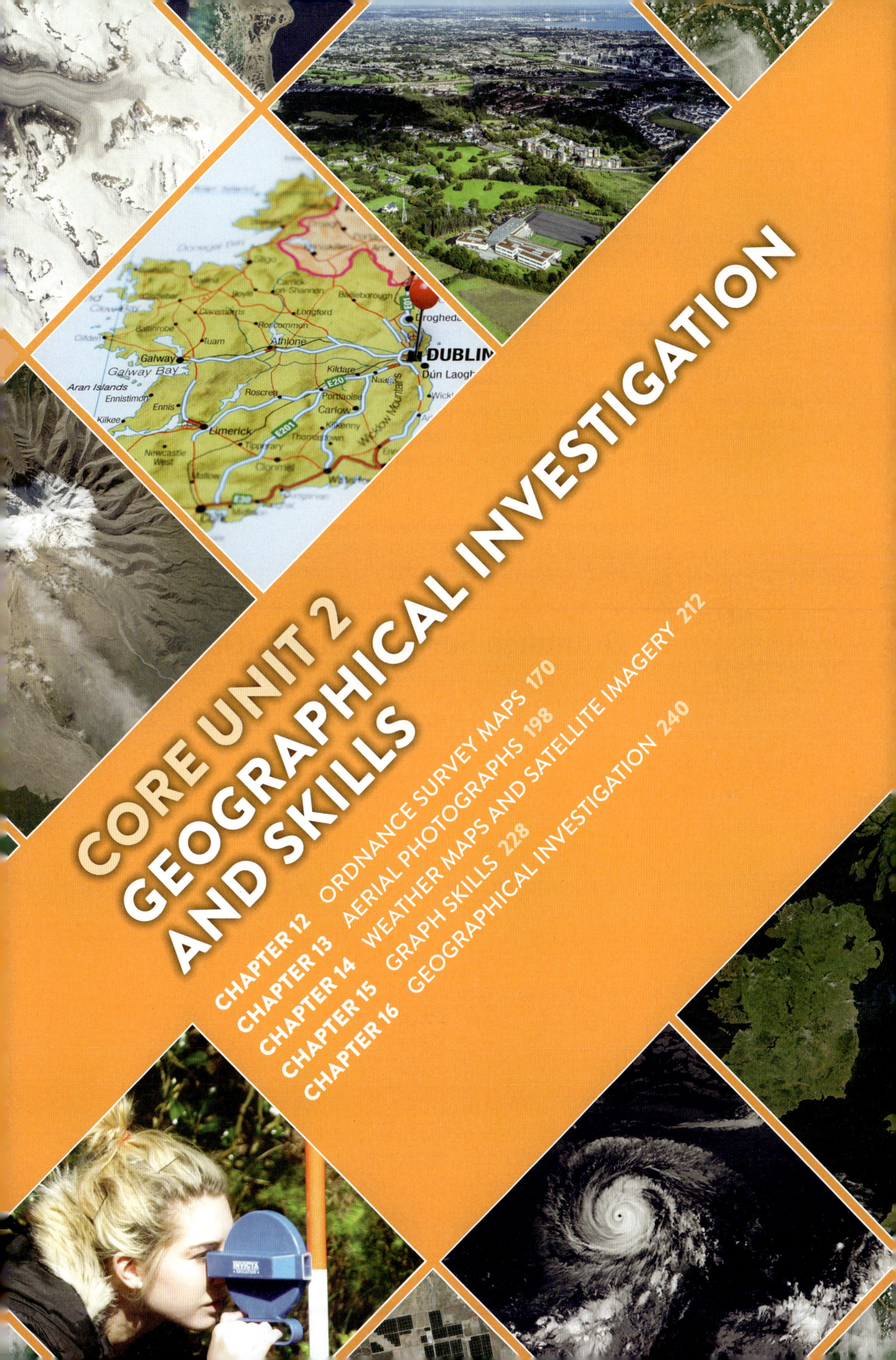

CORE UNIT 2
GEOGRAPHICAL INVESTIGATION AND SKILLS

CHAPTER 12 ORDNANCE SURVEY MAPS 170
CHAPTER 13 AERIAL PHOTOGRAPHS 198
CHAPTER 14 WEATHER MAPS AND SATELLITE IMAGERY 212
CHAPTER 15 GRAPH SKILLS 228
CHAPTER 16 GEOGRAPHICAL INVESTIGATION 240

12 ORDNANCE SURVEY MAPS

KEYWORDS

National grid
sub-zone
map legend
linear scale
representative fraction
statement of scale
grid reference
easting
northing
cardinal point
straight-line distance
curved-line distance
regular area
irregular area

LEARNING INTENTIONS

Syllabus Links: 3

By the end of this chapter I will be able to:
- use Ordnance Survey map reading skills to get location, direction, distance and area;
- draw and interpret sketch maps and cross-sections;
- recognise and interpret symbols and colours relating to the physical, human and economic landscape.

Ordnance Survey Ireland (OSI)

Maps are drawings of the earth's surface that show how things are related to each other by distance, direction and size. Ordnance Survey Ireland (OSI) draws and publishes 75 of these maps covering the entire landscape of Ireland as part of their Discovery Series.

The National Grid

The **National Grid** is used to give the location of places on Ordnance Survey (OS) maps of Ireland. It consists of 25 squares called **sub-zones** which cover the whole country and some of its sea areas. Each sub-zone measures 100 km in length and 100 km in width and is identified by a letter of the alphabet from A to Z. As there are 25 sub-zones, one letter of the alphabet is not used – the letter I. Sub-zone letters are illustrated in a blue colour (**Fig. 12.1(a)**).

A	B	C	D	E
F	G	H	J	K
L	M	N	O	P
Q	R	S	T	U
V	W	X	Y	Z

— Sub-zone N

↑ **Fig. 12.1(a)** The National Grid.

170

12 Ordnance Survey Maps

Map legend

All features shown on an OS map have a **label**, **symbol** or **colour**. The symbols and colours are explained on the legend that accompanies the OS map (**Fig. 12.1(b)**).

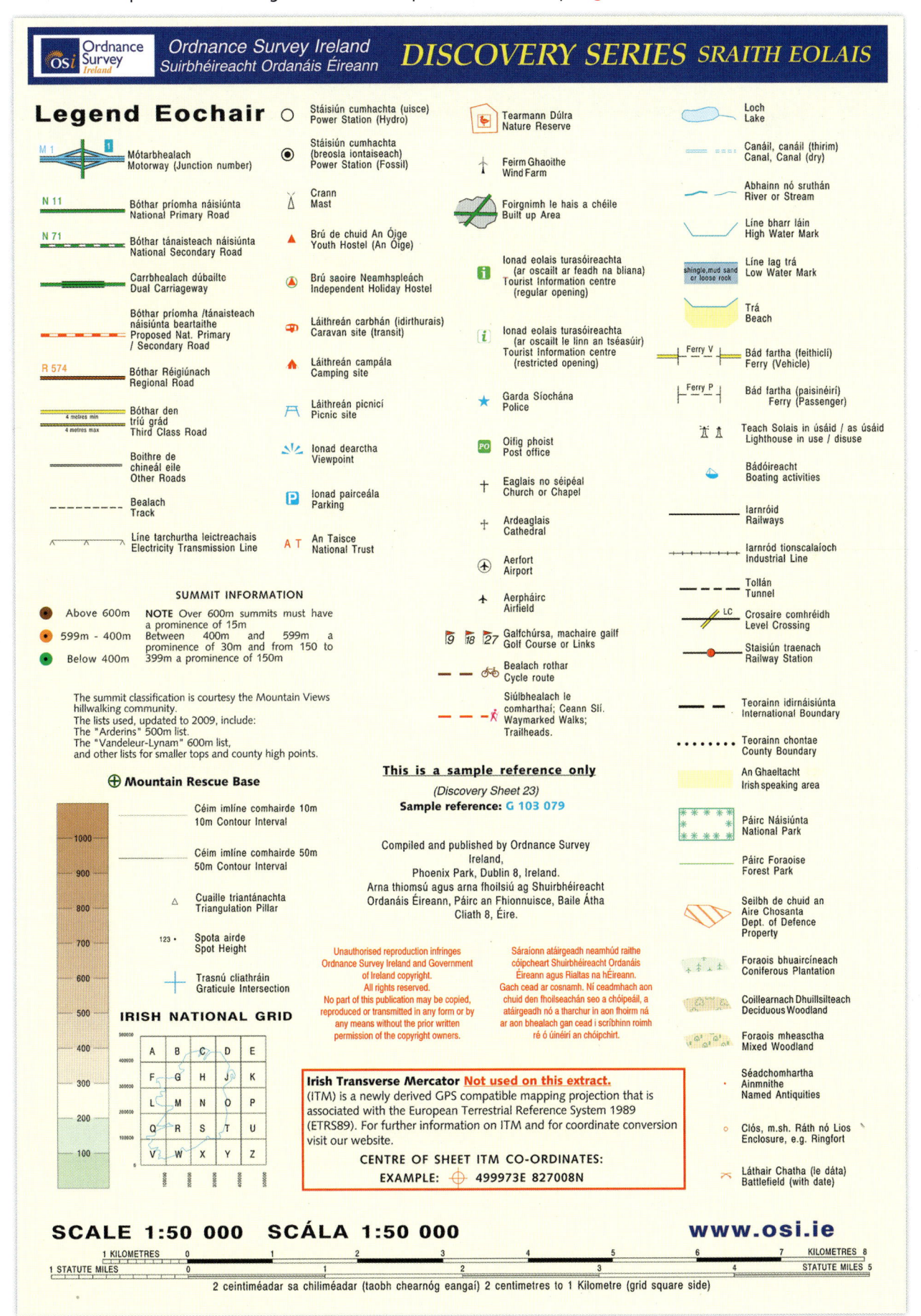

↑ **Fig. 12.1(b)** The OSI map legend released in 2016.

Landscapes

> Scale is displayed on the legend for OSI maps used in the Leaving Certificate.

Scale

Every OSI map has a scale. This is used to show the relationship between a certain distance on the map and the **real** distance on the ground (**Fig. 12.2**). Scale is described in three different ways.

- **Representative fraction:** The scale is written as a ratio: 1:50,000. 1 centimetre on the map represents 50,000 centimetres on the ground.
- **Linear scale:** The scale is shown on a line that is divided into kilometres.
- **Statement of scale:** The scale is stated, e.g. 2 centimetres to 1 kilometre.

Representative fraction (RF) — Linear scale

SCALE 1:50 000   SCÁLA 1:50 000
1 KILOMETRES 0   1   2   3   4   5   6   7
2 ceintiméadar sa chiliméadar (taobh chearnóg eangaí) 2 centimetres to 1 Kilometre (grid square side)

Statement of scale

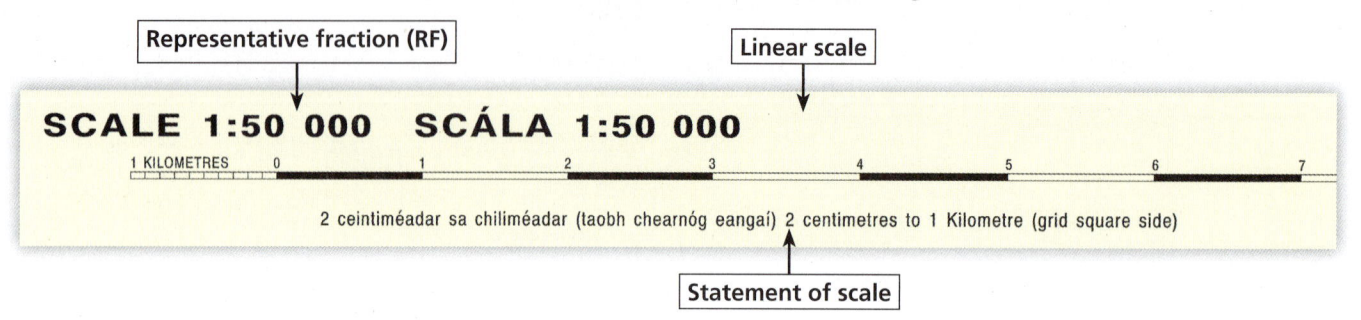

↑ **Fig.12.2** Scale showing representative fraction, linear scale and statement of scale.

The OS Discovery Series (1:50,000)

- Most maps are drawn to a scale of 1:50,000. On these maps, 2 cm represents 1 km.
- Each grid square on the map represents one square kilometre.
- Some features, like the width of roads and rivers, are not drawn to scale.
- The larger the scale, the greater the detail.

Grid reference

Grid references are used to accurately locate a feature on an OS map. Each sub-zone is divided by:

- 100 vertical blue lines called **eastings**, which increase in value as you move eastwards on the map – from left to right;
- 100 horizontal blue lines called **northings**, which increase in value as you move northwards on the map – from the bottom to the top.

Eastings and northings are numbered from 00 to 99.

Four-figure grid reference

> Four-figure grid references will get you within one square kilometre of a feature.
>
> Four-figure grid references may be used to show the location of:
> - a town
> - a lake
> - an island
> - an area of forestry.

The four-figure grid reference is used to give the location of an entire grid square or large feature on an OS map (**Fig. 12.3**). The grid reference should be recorded as follows: **Letter-Easting-Northing (LEN)**. The reference is gathered in the following way.

1. Highlight the grid square in question, e.g. draw a frame around it.
2. From the bottom left-hand corner of the highlighted grid square, draw a vertical line along the blue easting line to the bottom of the map and a horizontal line along the blue northing line to the left side of the map.
3. Record the sub-zone letter the highlighted grid square is in.
4. Record the easting number along the bottom of the map that has been linked to the highlighted grid square.
5. Finally, record the northing number along the left side of the map that has been linked to the highlighted grid square.

172

12 Ordnance Survey Maps

← **Fig.12.3** Sub-zones, eastings and northings; four-figure grid references: Golden S 01 38 and lake R 98 40.

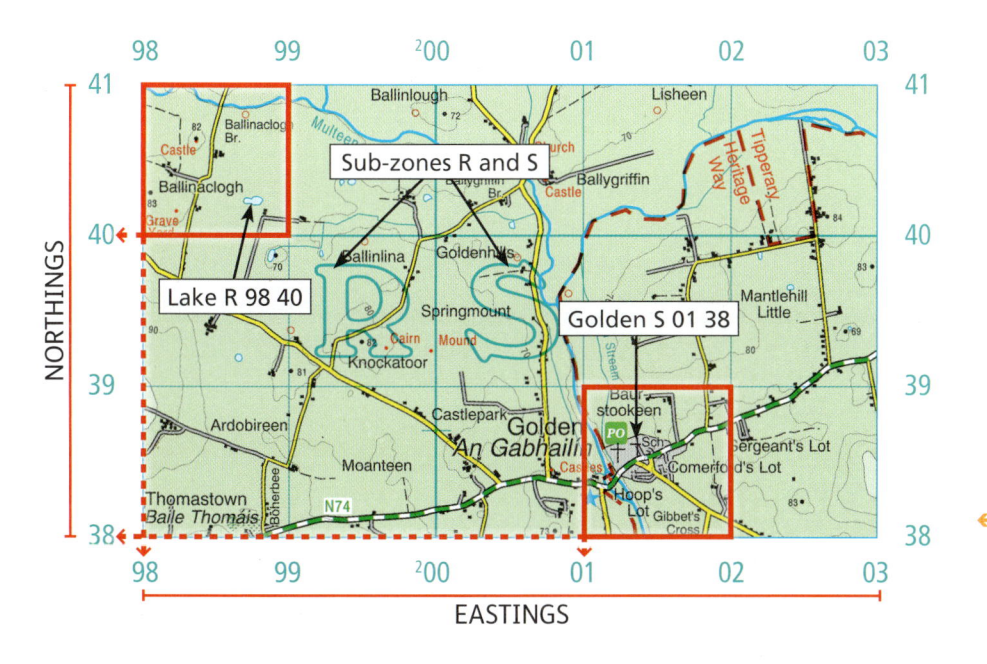

> **EXAM TIP**
>
> If there are two or more sub-zone letters on the map, then the boundary separating the two letters is the vertical or horizontal line that runs from 00 to 00. Draw a line from 00 to 00 to highlight the difference in sub-zones for grid referencing.

Six-figure grid reference

A six-figure grid reference is used to give a more exact location (**Fig. 12.4**). They are calculated in the following way.

1. Record the sub-zone letter and the four-figure grid reference, as shown previously.
2. Using a ruler, divide the horizontal line at the bottom of the grid square and the vertical line to the left of the grid square into 10 equal parts. On a 1:50,000 scale map, each space will be 2 mm.
3. Using a ruler and pencil, link the feature being recorded down to the horizontal line at the bottom of the grid square and left to the vertical line to the left of the grid square.
4. The third digit of the easting is the number of tenth parts across the horizontal line the feature is located.
5. The third digit of the northing is the number of tenth parts up the vertical line the feature is located.

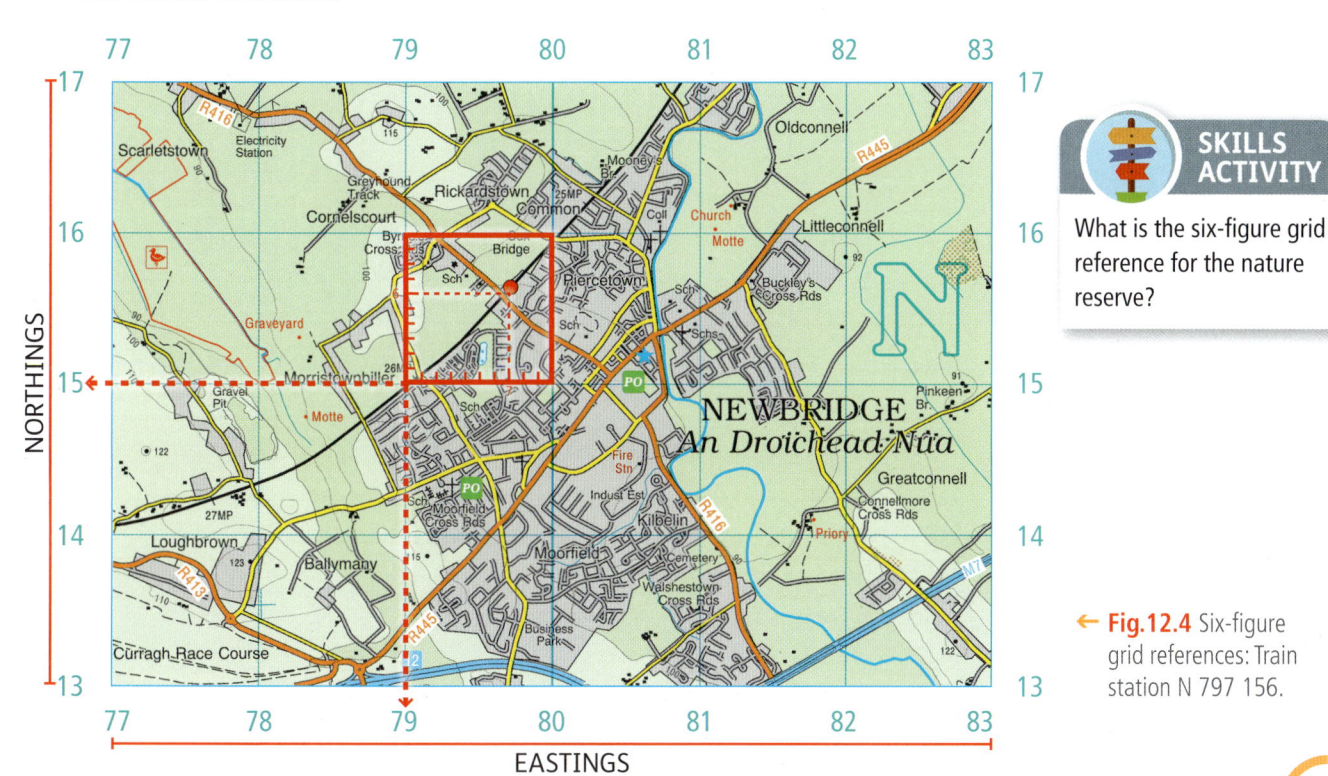

> **SKILLS ACTIVITY**
>
> What is the six-figure grid reference for the nature reserve?

← **Fig.12.4** Six-figure grid references: Train station N 797 156.

173

Landscapes

> **CHECK YOUR LEARNING**
>
> Examine the 1:50,000 Ordnance Survey map of Westport on page 191 and answer the following questions.
> 1. Give a four-figure grid reference for the following:
>   a. Roman Island
>   b. Kinlooey Lough
> 2. Give a six-figure grid reference for the following:
>   a. A tourist information centre at Westport
>   b. A train station at Westport
> 3. What are the names of the features found at the following four-figure grid references?
>   a. The lake at L 98 86
>   b. The island at L 92 84
> 4. What would you find at the following six-figure grid references?
>   a. L 971 856
>   b. L 987 853
>   c. M 023 850

Direction

Cardinal points: The four main points of the compass – north, south, east and west. It is vital to know all 16 points of the compass so one can indicate the exact direction required.

Directions on a map are given in the form of compass points (**Fig. 12.5(a)**).

1. Mark the starting point (**X**). Using a ruler and pencil, draw a straight line to the point you are asked to get the direction to (**Y**).
2. Draw a compass on **X** and see which point of the compass corresponds to the line you have drawn to **Y**.
3. Start with the four **cardinal points**, then the secondary points and so on.

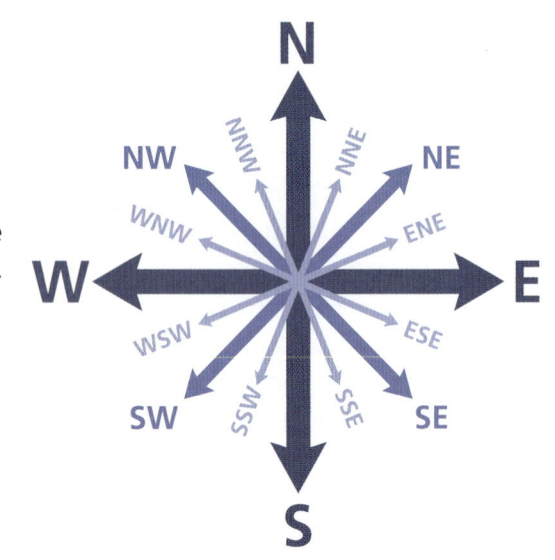

↑ **Fig.12.5(a)** Direction on a compass.

SKILLS ACTIVITY

What direction would you be travelling if you were going from the school in Curracloe (T 095 279) to the motte (T 086 264)?

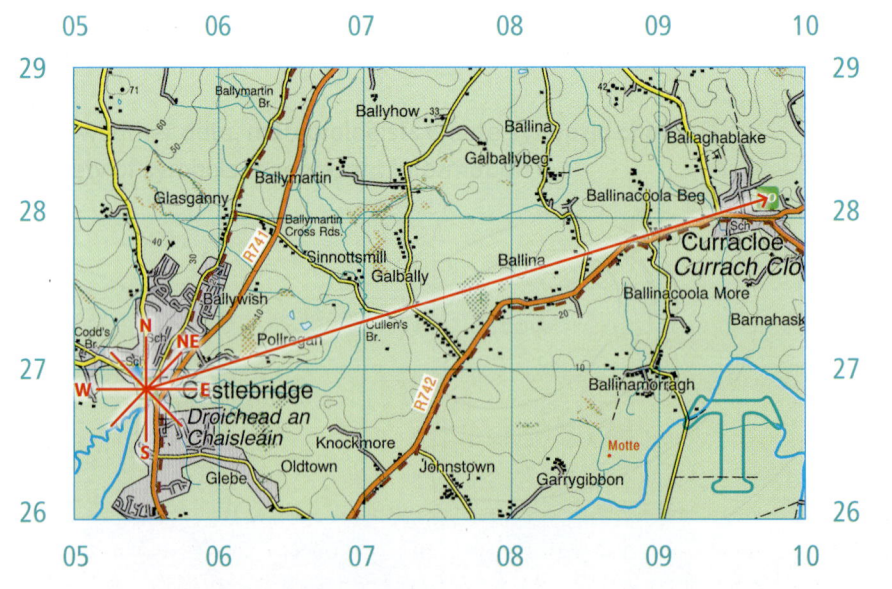

↑ **Fig. 12.5(b)** Direction on a map using a compass. The arrow is travelling in an East-North-East (ENE) direction.

174

Measuring Distance

Straight-line distance

The following method should be used to measure the straight-line distance on a map (**Fig. 12.6**).

1. Mark the two places being recorded X and Y and draw a straight line linking both places.
2. Place the straight edge of a piece of paper on the line linking X and Y on the map.
3. Mark the edge of the paper where it touches both X and Y at either end of the straight line.
4. Place the straight edge of paper against the OS map's **linear scale**, with the second mark (Y) placed at the last full kilometre that can be measured.

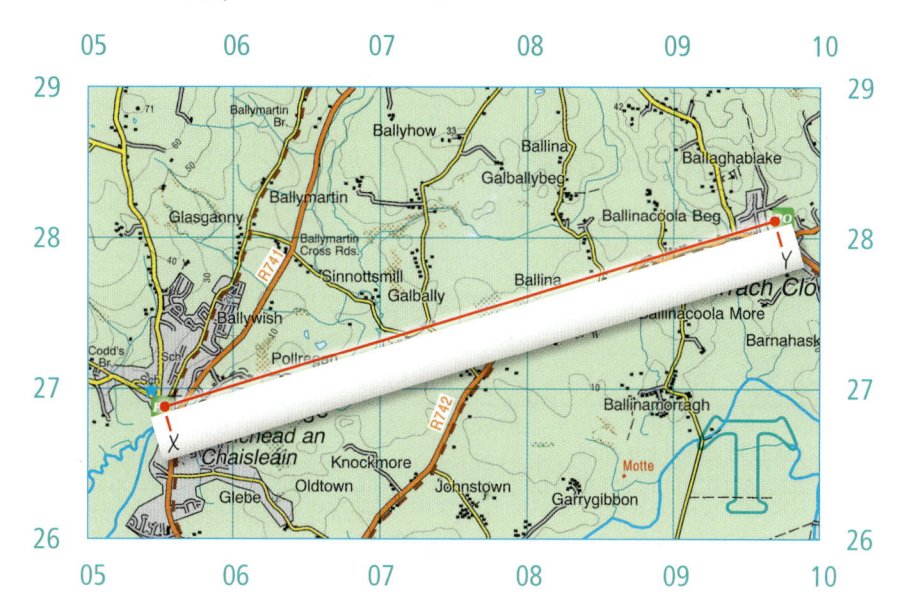

Straight-line distance: Also known as the distance 'as the crow flies'.

EXAM TIP

On 1:50,000 scale maps, a ruler can also be used to measure the straight line distance between two points. Measure the distance with the ruler, e.g. 12.4 cm. To calculate the distance in kilometres, divide by two, e.g. 12.4 cm ÷ 2 = 6.2 km.

SKILLS ACTIVITY

What is the distance from Castlebridge Post Office (X) to Curracloe Post Office (Y)?

← **Fig.12.6(a)** Measuring straight-line distance.

↑ **Fig.12.6(b)** Placing the Y at a whole number 4 allows a more accurate reading; you can use the broken line scale that comes before 0 to measure a part of a kilometre.

Curved-line distance

The following method should be used to measure the distance along a curved line (**Fig. 12.7**).

1. Place a straight-edged strip of paper at the starting point. Mark and number both the map and strip of paper (1).
2. Hold the edge of the strip of paper along the centre of the line being measured until the first turn is reached. Mark and number (2) the map and strip of paper at the point where they are no longer in contact.
3. Using the last mark (2) as the new starting point, hold the strip of paper along the centre of the line until the next turn. Again, mark and number (3) the map and strip of paper at the point where they are no longer in contact.
4. Repeat the process until the required distance is covered.
5. Place the straight-edged strip of paper against the map's **linear scale**, with the last mark placed at the last full kilometre that can be measured.
6. Record the distance between the two points in **kilometres** from the scale.

Curved-line distance: Typically a measurement along a road or railway line.

175

Landscapes

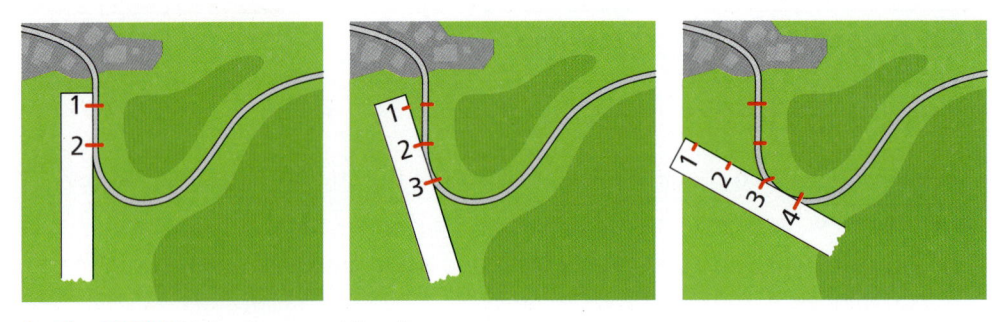

↑ **Fig. 12.7(a)** Measuring curved-line distance.

↑ **Fig. 12.7(b)** Use the broken line scale that comes before 0 to measure a part of a kilometre.

Calculating Area

Regular-shaped area

The following method should be used to calculate the area of a regular **area** (**Fig. 12.8**).

1. Number each full grid square across the base of the area being measured.
2. Number each full grid square along the side of the area being measured.
3. Multiply the number of squares across the bottom by the number of squares along the side. This will give you the area in square kilometres, as each square is 1 square kilometre.

Example (**Fig. 12.8**): 6 grid squares × 4 grid squares = 24 grid squares = 24 km^2.

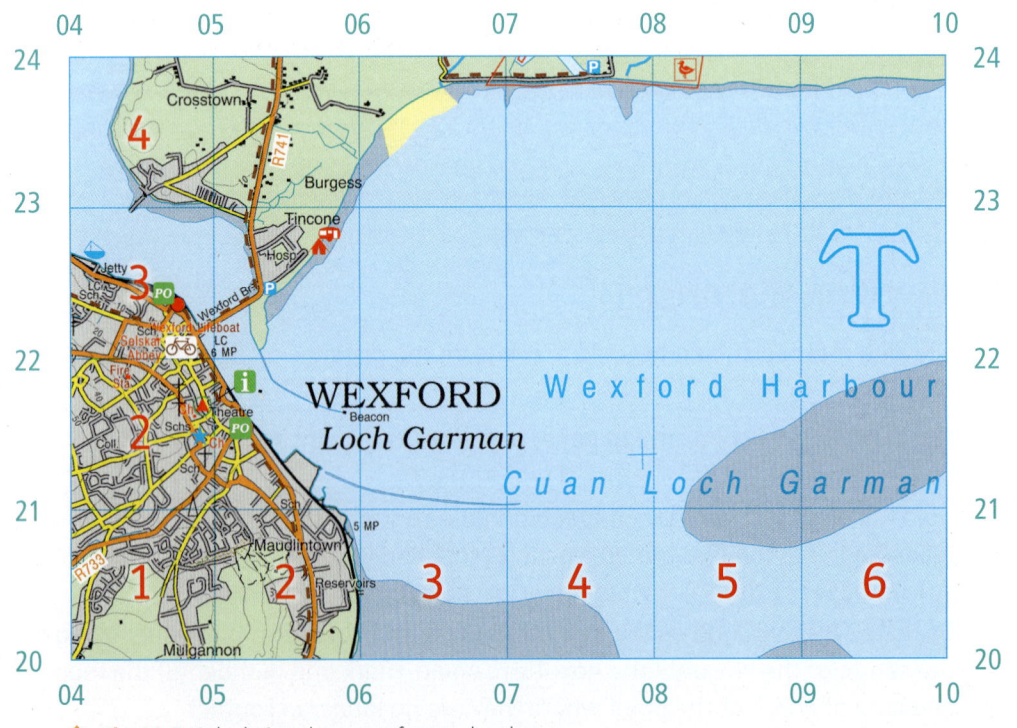

↑ **Fig.12.8** Calculating the area of a regular shape.

Irregular-shaped area

The following method should be used to calculate the area of an **irregular area** (Fig. 12.9).

1. Using a red pen, tick all of the squares that are at least half-filled by the feature being measured.
2. In cases where one is unsure whether the square is at least half-filled with the feature being measured, divide the square in half with a diagonal, vertical or horizontal line using a ruler and pencil.
3. Number the squares that have a red tick – this number represents the approximate area of the feature in square kilometres.

   Example (Fig. 12.9): 15 grid squares are more than 50% filled with water. Therefore, the area of the map covered by the sea is 15 km².

Irregular-shaped area: This is typically used to measure the area of:
- a town
- an island
- a body of water (sea or lake)
- an area of forestry
- an area of upland.

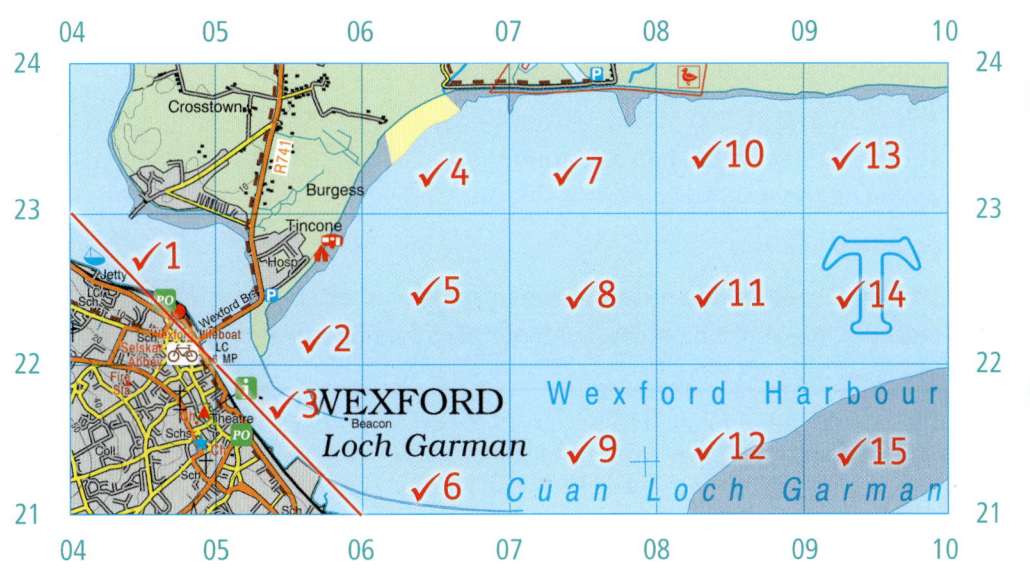

↑ **Fig.12.9** Calculating the area of an irregular shape. Notice how the grid square boxes numbered 1 and 3 have been divided using a diagonal line to clarify that over 50% of the grid square is filled with water.

EXAM TIP

Number each grid square being counted so as to avoid a mistake.

SKILLS ACTIVITY

What area of the map in **Fig. 12.9** is covered in land?

CHECK YOUR LEARNING

Examine the 1:50,000 Ordnance Survey map of Kenmare on page 194 and answer the following questions.

1. What direction would you be travelling if you went from:
   a. The post office in Kenmare to the car park at Moll's Gap?
   b. The post office in Kenmare to the post office in Assroe?
2. What is the straight-line distance from:
   a. The peak of Knocknaguish (V 919 768) to the peak of Derrygarriff (V 872 774)?
   b. The post office in Kenmare to the post office in Assroe?
3. What is the curved-line distance along the N71 from where it enters the map at V 940 684 to the point it crosses the Kenmare River at V 912 698?
4. What is the total area of the map?
5. What area of the map is covered by the Kenmare River?

Landscapes

KEYWORDS
contour lines
index contour
triangulation pillar
spot height
concave slope
convex slope
even slope
stepped slope
gradient

Relief on OS Maps

Interpreting height

Height on Irish maps is calculated from a point on Malin Head, Co. Donegal, known as **Ordnance Datum (OD)**. Measured in metres above sea level, height is shown four ways on OS maps (**Fig. 12.10**).

Colour layering

- Variations in colour are used to show changes in height.
- The colour changes every 100 m.

Contour lines

- These are imaginary lines drawn on OS maps that join places of equal height above sea level.
- Contour lines are drawn at 10 m intervals.
- The 50 m, 100 m, 200 m and 250 m heights are sometimes indicated by a stronger line called an **index contour**. Index contours always have heights shown on them.

Triangulation pillars

- Sometimes referred to as triangulation stations, these are concrete pillars placed at the summit of hills and mountains to mark their exact height above sea level.
- On OS maps, triangulation pillars are identified by a **black triangle** with a number placed beside it.

Spot heights

- Spot heights are used to indicate the height above sea level at various points on the map.
- They are identified by a **black dot** with a number beside it.

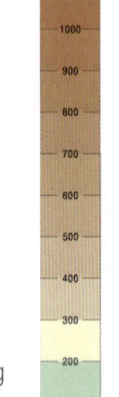

→ **Fig. 12.10(a)** Contour layering table from the OS legend.

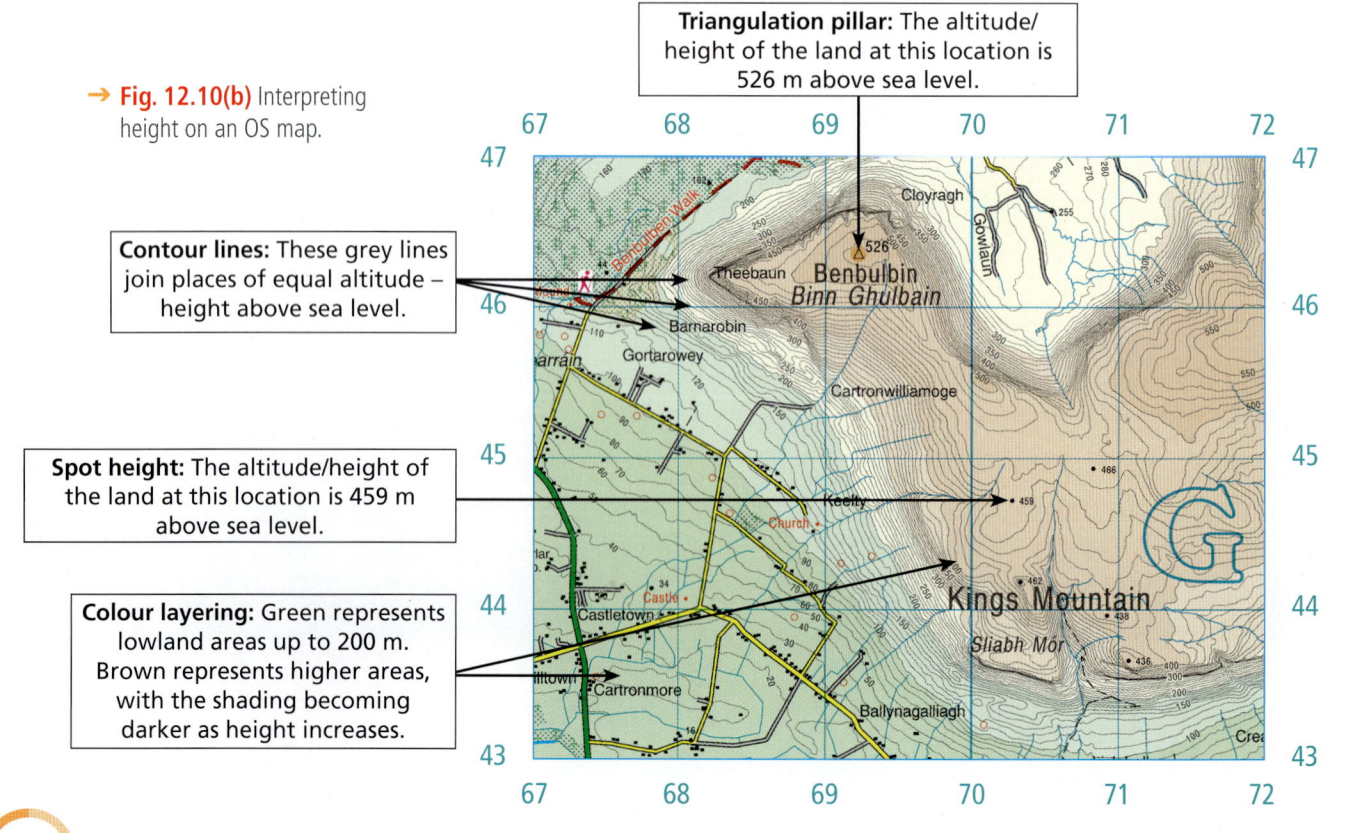

→ **Fig. 12.10(b)** Interpreting height on an OS map.

Contour lines: These grey lines join places of equal altitude – height above sea level.

Triangulation pillar: The altitude/height of the land at this location is 526 m above sea level.

Spot height: The altitude/height of the land at this location is 459 m above sea level.

Colour layering: Green represents lowland areas up to 200 m. Brown represents higher areas, with the shading becoming darker as height increases.

Slope

The amount or **degree** of slope on an OS map is indicated by the distance between the contours on the map (**Fig. 12.11**).

Gentle slopes are indicated by widely-spaced contours.

Cliffs are indicated by a heavy black line at the coastline. A number of contours have been placed on top of one another.

Flat land is indicated by an absence of contours.

Steep slopes are indicated by contours that are placed close to one another.

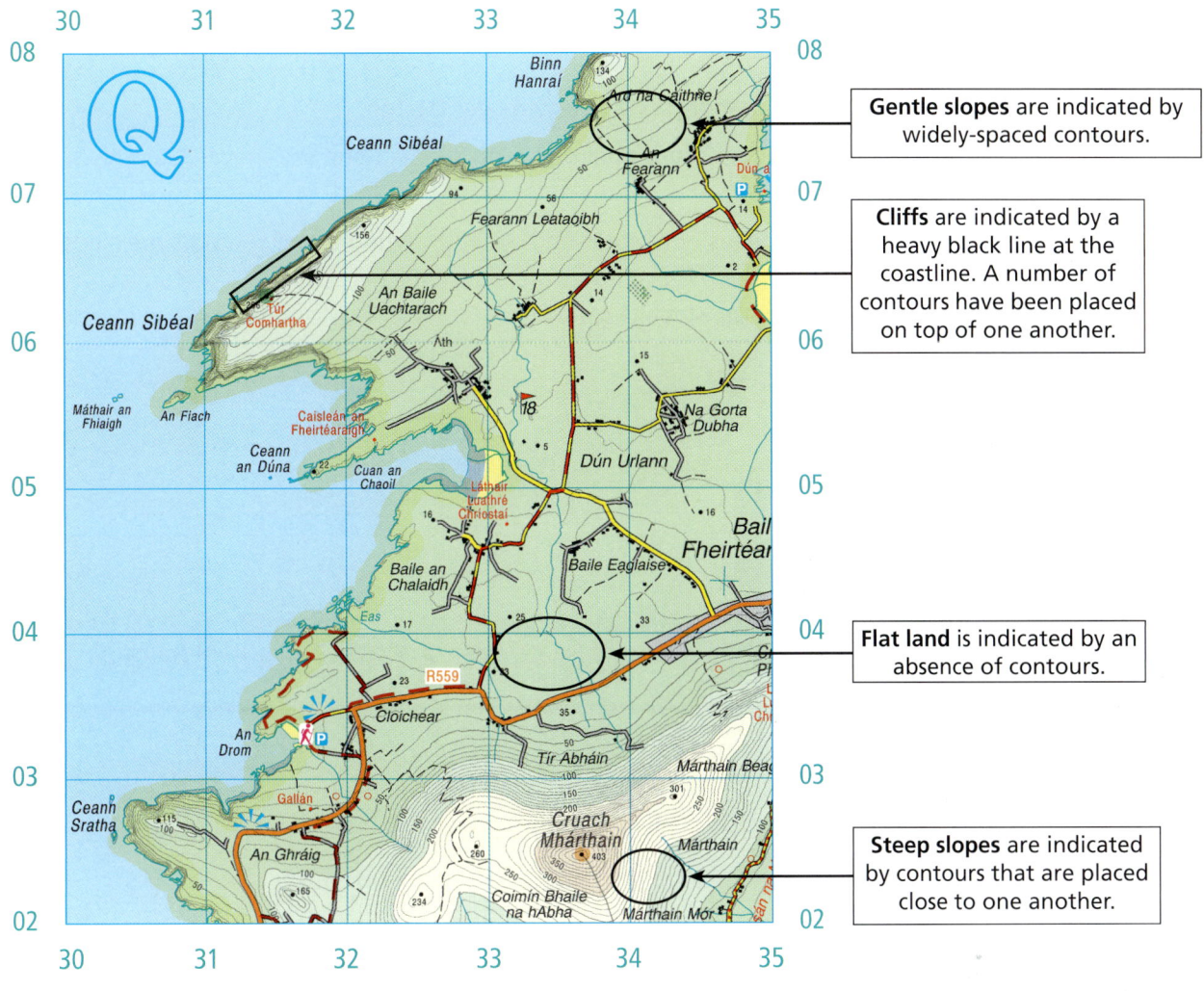

↑ **Fig. 12.11(a)** Ballyferriter OS map showing steep slopes, cliffs, gentle slopes and flat land.

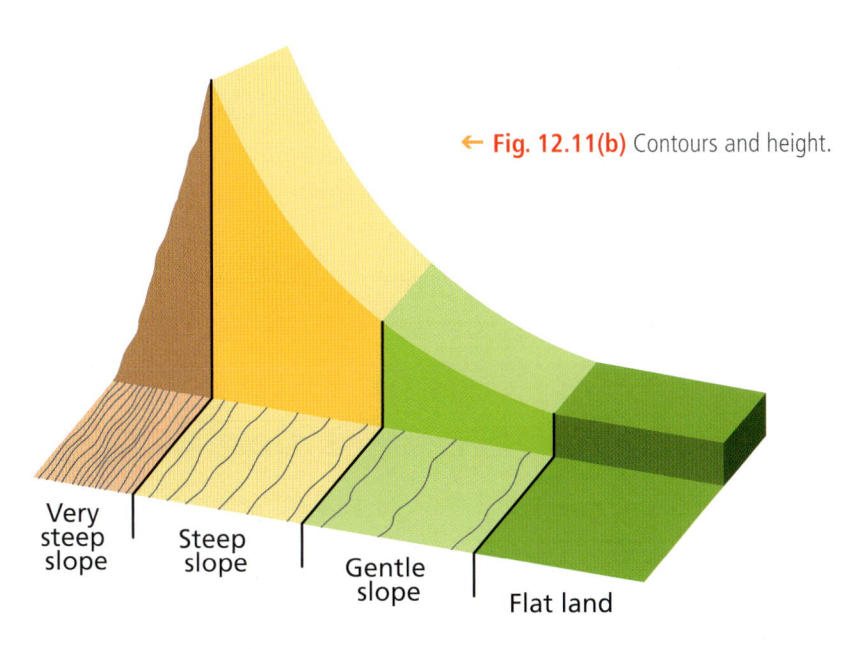

← **Fig. 12.11(b)** Contours and height.

Very steep slope | Steep slope | Gentle slope | Flat land

Landscapes

Slope type

- **Concave slopes** are gentle near the base but get steeper closer to the top. Concave slopes are represented on OS maps by contours that are widely spaced at the base and more closely packed near the top of the slope.
- **Convex slopes** are steep near the base but more gentle closer to the top (a **plateau**). Convex slopes are indicated by contours that are closely packed near the base but more widely spaced near the top.
- **Even or graded slopes** have an even gradient and are shown by evenly spaced contours.
- **Stepped slopes** have steps and plateaus. A number of contours are placed close together then contours are placed further apart. This pattern continues throughout the slope (Fig. 12.12).

Gradient: Gradient is the degree of slope between two points on an OS map.

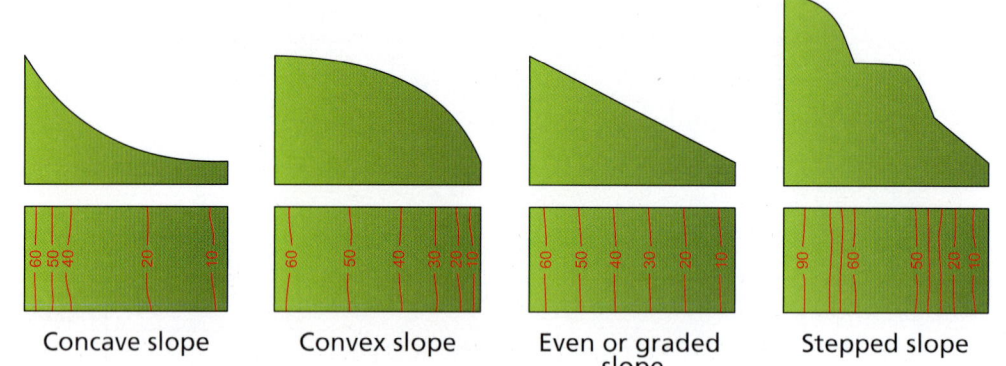

→ Fig. 12.12 Slopes and contour lines.

Concave slope   Convex slope   Even or graded slope   Stepped slope

Calculating average gradient

Gradient is the degree of slope between two points on an OS map. The gradient is expressed as a **ratio** such as 1:10. It can be calculated very accurately using the following formula:

$$\text{Average Gradient} = \frac{\text{Vertical Interval (Altitude 1 – Altitude 2)}}{\text{Horizontal Equivalent (Distance between the two locations)}}$$

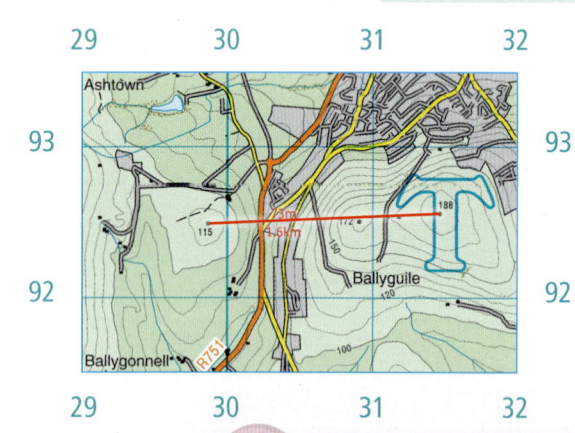

Example (Fig. 12.13):

$$\frac{188\text{ m} - 115\text{ m}}{1.6\text{ km}} = \frac{73}{1{,}600} = \frac{1}{21.9}$$

The gradient can be written as 1:21.9. This means there is a one-metre increase in the height of the land for every 21.9 metres travelled between the two points in question.

← Fig. 12.13 Calculating average gradient.

CHECK YOUR LEARNING

Examine the 1:50,000 Ordnance Survey map of Kenmare on page 194 and answer the following questions.

1. List two colours shown on the map extract and the heights they represent.
2. What is the total land area of the map over 200 m?
3. What is the height of the land at the following grid references?
   a. V 904 765
   b. V 857 771
   c. V 884 738
4. What type of slope is found south of Knocknaguish (V 919 768)?
5. Calculate the average gradient between the spot height at V 931 996 to V 914 680.

Drawing Skills: Sketch Maps and Cross-Sections

Sketch maps

The following method should be used to draw a sketch map of a given area (Fig. 12.14).

1. Use a pencil, ruler and graph paper.
2. Draw a rectangular frame half the size of the OS map. Allow one centimetre on the sketch for each grid square on the OS map.
3. Using a pencil and ruler, lightly divide both the OS map and the sketch map into nine equal segments that can be used as a guide when positioning features on the sketch map.
4. Above the frame of the sketch map, write in a title, e.g. 'Sligo Sketch Map'.
5. Mark the **north point** arrow into the sketch map to show direction.
6. If there is a coastline on the OS map, it must be drawn into the sketch whether it is asked for or not.
7. Insert any features required by the question.
   a. Most features can be represented by symbols.
   b. Use colours to shade in complete areas where requested e.g. the area of land over 200 m.
8. Explain the symbols on the sketch map using a key or legend. This should also have a title, e.g. 'Key for Sligo Sketch Map'.
9. Mark in the scale of the sketch map underneath the sketch map – typically 1 cm: 1 km.
10. There shouldn't be any writing on the OS map, except for the naming of a road.

12 Ordnance Survey Maps

KEYWORDS
- sketch map
- north point
- cross-section
- intervisibility

Note: OS Map of Sligo is on the next page.

EXAM TIP

Drawing a sketch of an OS map has appeared as:
- a 20-mark question in the Physical Section of the Higher Level paper every year from 2006 to 2018;
- a 30-mark question in the Physical Section of the Ordinary Level paper every year from 2006 to 2018.

Drawing a sketch of an OS map may also appear in the Elective section of the exam paper.

When answering these questions, use a hard pencil (HB), as these produce clean, sharp lines that are ideal for sketch maps.

EXAM TIP

If the OS map is 13 grid squares in width and 9 grid squares in length, then the sketch map should be 13 centimetres in width and 9 centimetres in length.

The frame of the sketch map must be the same shape as the frame of the OS map.

A sketch map drawn to half scale is actually one-quarter the size of the OS map.

EXAM LINK (HL) AND SAMPLE ANSWER

Sligo OS Map (20 marks)
Examine the 1:50,000 Ordnance Survey map of Sligo on page 182.
Draw a sketch map of the area shown to half scale. On it, correctly show and label each of the following:

(a) The entire course of the Drumcliff River
(b) Two named lakes
(c) The entire area of land above 300 metres south of northing 43.

2018, Q3A

Marking Scheme:
Sketch outline: 4 marks (graded 4/0)
4 features × 4 marks each:
  Shown = 3 marks (graded 3/1/0)
  Label = 1 mark

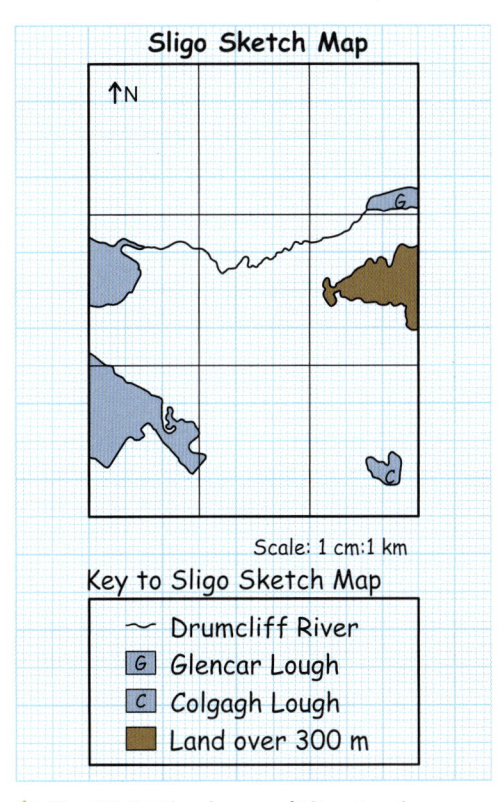

↑ **Fig. 12.14** Sketch map of Sligo. See the 1:50,000 OS map of Sligo on page 182. *Note:* This example is not drawn to scale, see **Exam Tip** to the right.

181

Landscapes

Sligo OS map

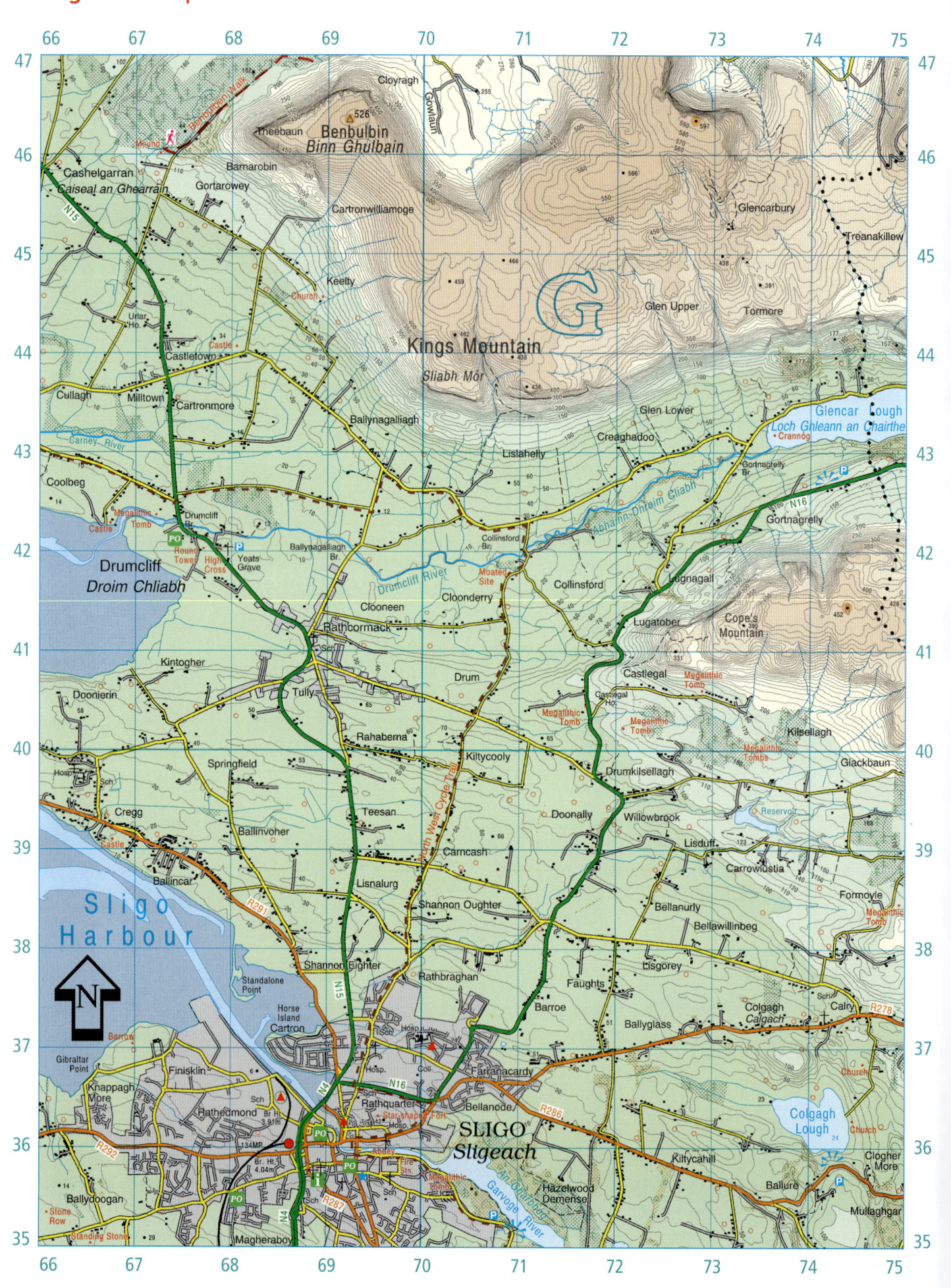

182

12 Ordnance Survey Maps

Cross-sections (Higher Level only)

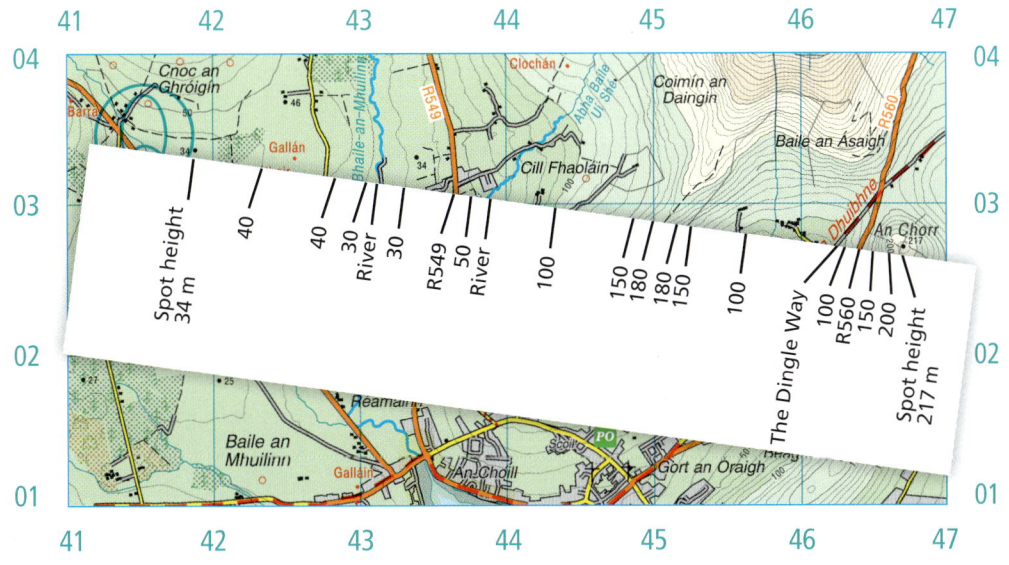

← **Fig. 12.15** Cross-section of Dingle OS map from spot height 34 m to spot height 217 m.

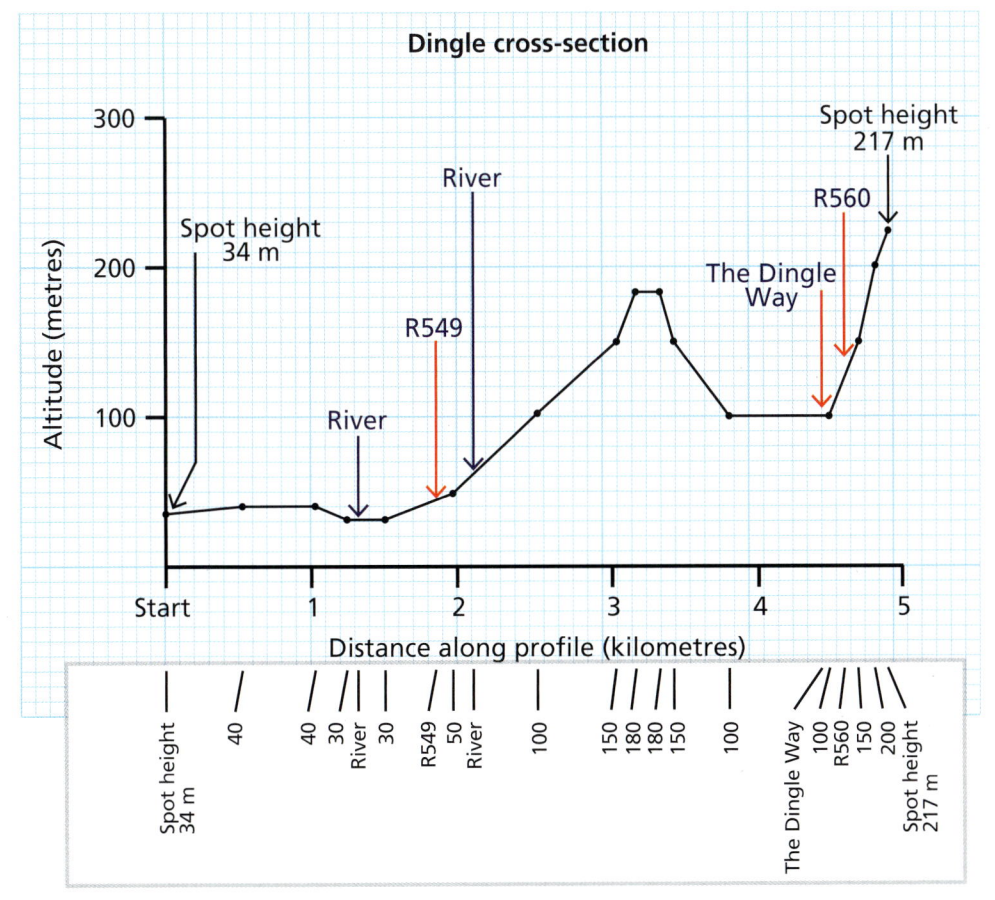

Dingle cross-section

SKILLS ACTIVITY

Draw a cross-section of the Kenmare OS map on page 194 from V 884 725 (205 m) to V 889 678 (95 m).

EXAM TIP (HL)

Cross-sections regularly appear in Part One – Short Questions, where students have to interpret information from a cross-section drawing already produced.

A **cross-section** is a side view of a section landscape on an OS map (**Fig. 12.15**). It also shows if there is **intervisibility** between two points on the map. The following method should be used to draw a cross-section.

1. Link the two grid references (the outer points of the cross-section) with a straight-edged strip of paper.
2. Mark the strip of paper where it touches the two outer points and note the height of the land at the starting point and finishing point.
3. Now mark the strip of paper where it touches each of the contours between the starting point and the finishing point. Note the height of the contour line at each mark made on the strip of paper.
4. Mark the edge of the paper where it touches any feature of the landscape, e.g. a river, a road.

Intervisibility: Whether one place can be seen from another, there may be high ground such as a mountain in between.

5. Using graph paper, draw a graph, marking the Y-axis in metres above sea level.
6. Give the cross-section a title, e.g. 'Dingle cross-section'.
7. Place the strip of paper on the X-axis and mark the point where each contour touches the X-axis. Then plot each point to the height on the graph that the contour corresponds to.
8. Join the points on the graph to show the height of the land.
9. Place the strip of paper onto the X-axis again and mark the location of each feature of the landscape recorded onto the graph, showing the height of the land.

> **KEYWORDS**
> altitude
> drainage
> aspect
> defence
> communications
> settlement
> dispersed
> linear
> nucleated
> antiquities
> urban functions

Interpreting OS Maps

Factors affecting the location of Irish settlements

Physical factors

- **Altitude:** Most people choose to live in low-lying areas, usually less than 200 metres above sea level. Mountainous areas repel settlers because:
  - the climate is cold, wet and windy;
  - construction is difficult and expensive;
  - there are fewer communication links, and those that do exist are usually poor in quality.
- **Drainage:** Many settlements initially grew around river valleys, as:
  - settlers were attracted to the water supply for drinking, transport, cooking, etc.;
  - they provided rich alluvial soils which were ideal for crop production.
  - Historically, settlers avoided floodplains and marshy land.
- **Aspect:** As Ireland is in the northern hemisphere, people prefer to build their homes on south-facing slopes, as:
  - more direct sunlight is received;
  - they're open to the warm southerly winds, while being protected from the cold northerly winds.
- **Coast:** Many people live at the coast in order to get access to the sea and coastal resources.

Defence

In the past, settlements grew around castles and army barracks, as defence was important.

Communications

Roads, railway lines and airports are typically built:

- on low-lying land – usually less than 200 m above sea level – as this is where the largest population densities are concentrated;
- on flat land, as construction is both easier and cheaper;
- away from floodplains, so as to avoid flooding;
- at narrow or shallow points of rivers known as bridging points (this doesn't apply to airports).

Many Irish settlements have grown at the bridging points of rivers, also known as 'fords' (**áth** in Irish). Settlements also developed where communication lines such as roads and railways intersect.

Historical evidence of settlement

Stone Age settlement: court cairns, megalithic tomb, stone circles.

Bronze Age settlement: dolmens, fulachta fia, standing stones, wedge tombs.

Iron Age settlement: crannóg, ogham stone, promontory fort, souterrain, togher. Place names featuring the words **caher/dún**, meaning stone fort; or **rath**, meaning timber-fenced fort; e.g. Cahirciveen, Dunboyne, Rathmore.

Early Christian settlement: abbey, graveyard, high cross, holy well, round tower, monastery. Place names featuring the word **kil/cill**, meaning church, or **monaster/mainistir**, meaning monastery, e.g. Kilmallock, Monasterevin.

Norman settlement: abbey, castle, tower house, town gate, town wall. Place names featuring the word **bally/baile**, e.g. Ballyhaunis and Baile Átha Cliath, were towns in Norman times.

Plantation settlement: demesne or manor. Place names featuring the landlord's name or a man-made feature followed by the word 'town', e.g. Paulstown, Castletown.

Rural settlement patterns

Absence of settlement: No settlements may be found in:
- Upland areas: Land over 200 metres above sea level. Climates tend to be colder and wetter, while communication lines such as roads are limited.
- Floodplains: People don't build houses here because of the possibility of flooding.

Dispersed (scattered/random) settlement: Buildings are spread out, forming no definite pattern. This type of settlement is found in rural areas where farmhouses or one-off houses are scattered.

Linear (ribbon) settlement: Buildings are found in a line such as along a roadway or a valley. This pattern is typically found leading to and from towns and villages.

Nucleated (clustered) settlement: Buildings occur in clusters at a small road junction or at the bridging point of a river.

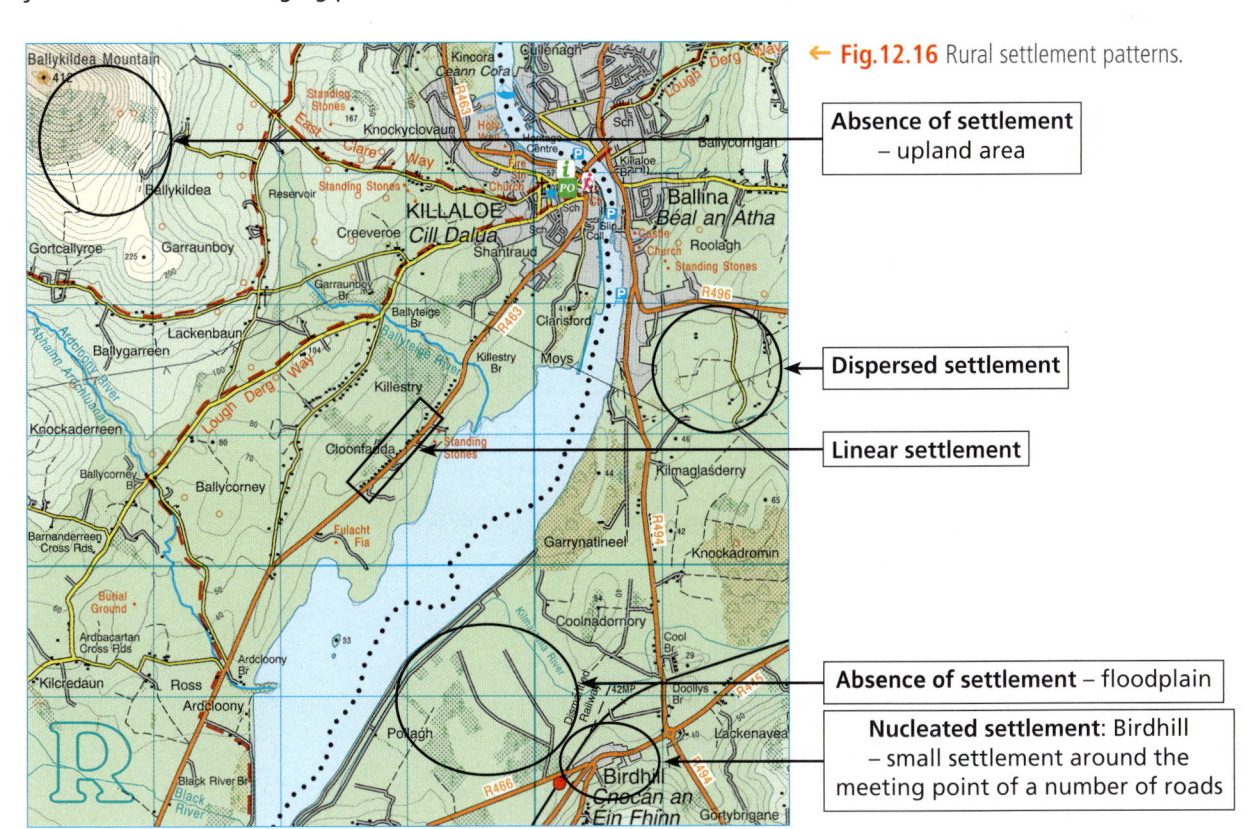

← **Fig.12.16** Rural settlement patterns.

- Absence of settlement – upland area
- Dispersed settlement
- Linear settlement
- Absence of settlement – floodplain
- **Nucleated settlement:** Birdhill – small settlement around the meeting point of a number of roads

Landscapes

Tourist attractions

Each of the following features can be recognised on an OS map and linked to tourist activities (**Fig. 12.17**).

- **Transport services**, such as railway stations, ports and national primary and secondary roads provide good access.
- **Tourist accommodation**, including campsites, caravan parks, independent holiday hotels and youth hostels mean that visitors can stay for multiple days.
- **Tourist information centres** offer advice on how to have the best tourist experience. They provide information on local activities, attractions, events and tours.
- **Coastal areas** (especially beaches) provide opportunities for activities such as children playing, fishing, picnics, sailing, sunbathing, surfing and swimming.
- The clean waters of Ireland's **lakes and rivers** provide opportunities for fishing, boating and swimming.
- **Mountains and hills** are attractive locations for people who wish to go hillwalking, mountain biking or orienteering.
- **Forests** attract those interested in bike trails, nature trails, orienteering and picnics.
- **Nature reserves and national parks** allow people to see flora and fauna in their natural habitat.
- **Recreational activities** such as golf courses and race courses attract a diverse range of visitors.
- People interested in the history and culture of an area will be attracted by any local **antiquities**.

SKILLS ACTIVITY

Recreation is highlighted as a function in three places on the OS map (**Fig. 12.17**). Name the activity that takes place at each location.

Urban functions

The purpose for which land is used in an urban area is referred to as its 'function'. Many features can be identified on OS maps which indicate current and former functions, including:

- **Educational:** schools, colleges and universities.
- **Industrial:** industrial estates.
- **Market:** urban areas usually offer a range of services, while well-drained lowlands would provide agricultural produce.
- **Medical:** hospital.
- **Port:** beacon, harbour, lighthouse, port and quay.
- **Recreational:** golf course, park, racetrack and stadium.
- **Religious:** cathedral, church and convent.
- **Residential:** housing estates.
- **Tourism:** see above.
- **Transport:** airport, car park, railway station and road.

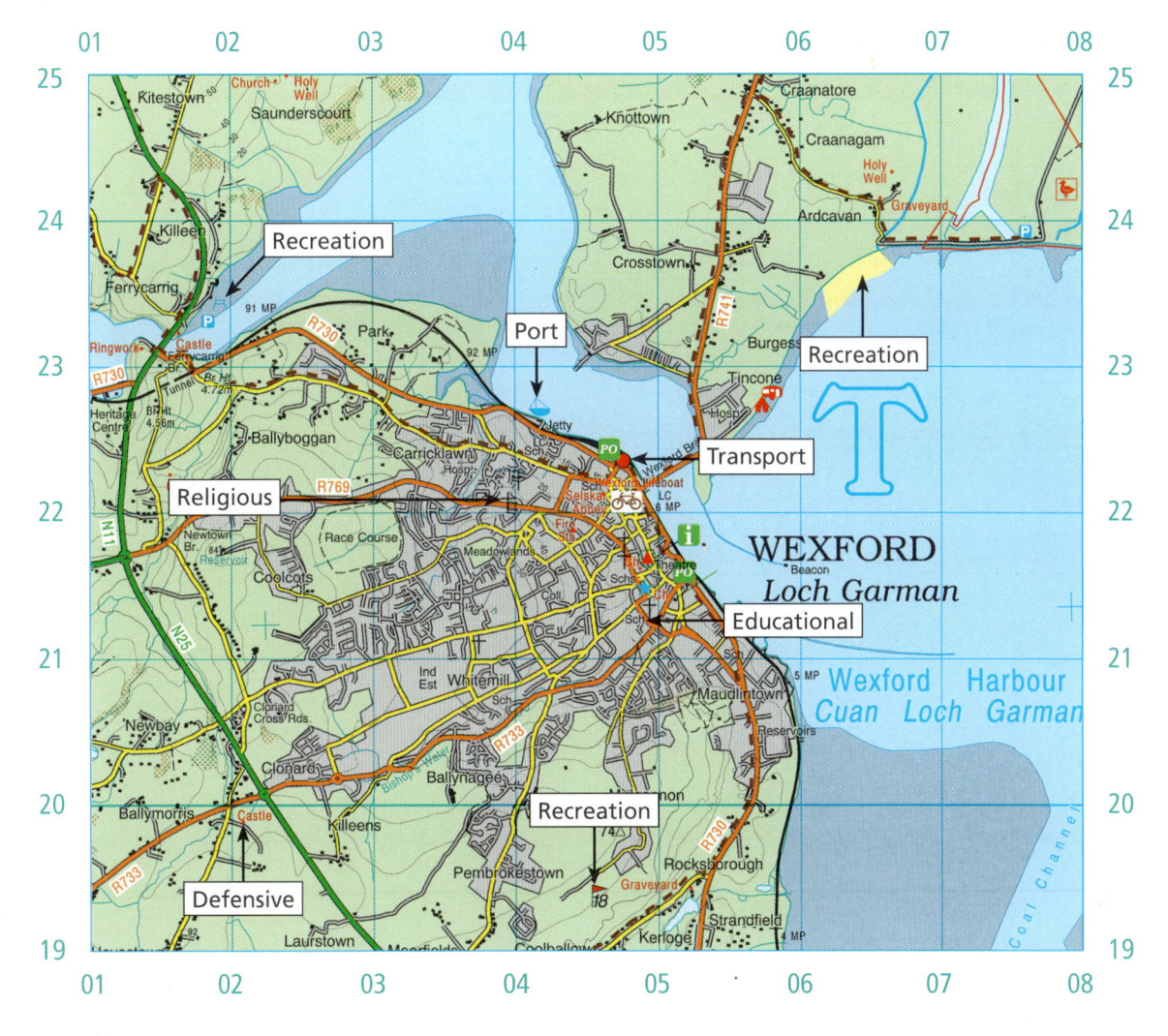

↑ **Fig.12.17** Some urban functions on an OS map.

Changing functions

The following features generally represent former functions of Irish settlements:

- **Defensive:** castle, military barracks and town wall.
- **Religious:** abbey and monastery.
- **Transport:** canals are now used for leisure rather than transporting goods.

CHECK YOUR LEARNING

Examine the 1:50,000 Ordnance Survey map of Westport on page 191 and answer the following questions.

1. Using six-figure grid references, list three pieces of historical evidence on the map and the approximate periods in time from which they come.
2. Using four-figure grid references, list three patterns of settlement visible on the map.
3. Using six-figure grid references, list three tourist attractions visible on the map.
4. Using six-figure grid references, list three functions of settlement in Westport.

Landscapes

EXAMINATION QUESTIONS

Macroom OS map

12 Ordnance Survey Maps

ORDINARY LEVEL

Short Questions

1. Macroom OS Map

Examine the 1:50,000 Ordnance Survey map of Macroom on page 188.

(i) What is the length of the R587 regional road, from where it enters the map at W 285 650 to where it meets the R584 regional road at W 296 703? Tick the correct box. *5 marks*

4.1 km ☐   6.7 km ☐

(ii) If a person travelled from the school in Dromleigh W 284 652 to the Garda Station in Macroom town, in what direction would they have travelled? Tick the correct box. *5 marks*

North ☐   North-east ☐

2017, Part One, Q5 (10 marks)

Long Questions

2. Macroom OS Map

Examine the 1:50,000 Ordnance Survey map of Macroom on page 188.

Draw a sketch map of the area shown on the OS map. On it, show and label each of the following:

(a) The entire area of the reservoir east of Lee Bridge (W 342 713)
(b) An area of land above 200 metres at Cill na Martra in the north-west of the map
(c) The Sullane River
(d) An area of coniferous plantation in the south-west of the map
(e) The built-up area of Macroom.

Marking Scheme:
Sketch outline:
  Frame = 1 mark
  Proportions = 2 marks
  Overall impression = 2 marks
Five features shown and labelled:
  Shown = 5 × 3 marks
  Labelled = 5 × 2 marks

2017, Part Two, Section 1, Q1A (30 marks)

HIGHER LEVEL

Short Questions

3. Macroom OS Map – Landscape Identification

Examine the 1:50,000 Ordnance Survey map of Macroom on page 188.

(i) Match each of the features with the grid reference that best matches its location on the OS map. *4 x 1 mark*

(a) A plateau surface between 160 metres and 167 metres   (c) A V-shaped valley
(b) River braiding   (d) A meander.

Grid Reference	Feature
W 29 69	
W 36 72	
W 34 72	
W 28 73	

(ii) What is the aspect of the slope at W 308 652 on the OS map? *2 marks*
(iii) Name any two river drainage patterns. *2 marks*

2017, Part One, Q6 (8 marks)

Landscapes

4. Macroom OS Map

Examine the 1:50,000 Ordnance Survey map of Macroom on page 188.

(i) Name the antiquity located at W 293 734. *2 marks*

(ii) What does the Ordnance Survey map symbol at W 328 712 represent? *2 marks*

(iii) Measure the length of the R618 road, in kilometres, from where it enters the map at W 370 718 to where it meets the N22 road at W 353 725. *2 marks*

(iv) Calculate the approximate area of the map which is to the north and east of the N22 road and to the east of easting 31 (in square kilometres). *2 marks*

2017, Part One, Q7 (8 marks)

5. Macroom OS Map – Elevation Profile

Locate point **X**, W 340 740, and point **Y**, W 340 680, on the 1:50,000 Ordnance Survey map of Macroom on page 188. Both points are on easting 34.

Figure 1 shows an elevation profile of the cross-section of the line between point **X** and point **Y**.

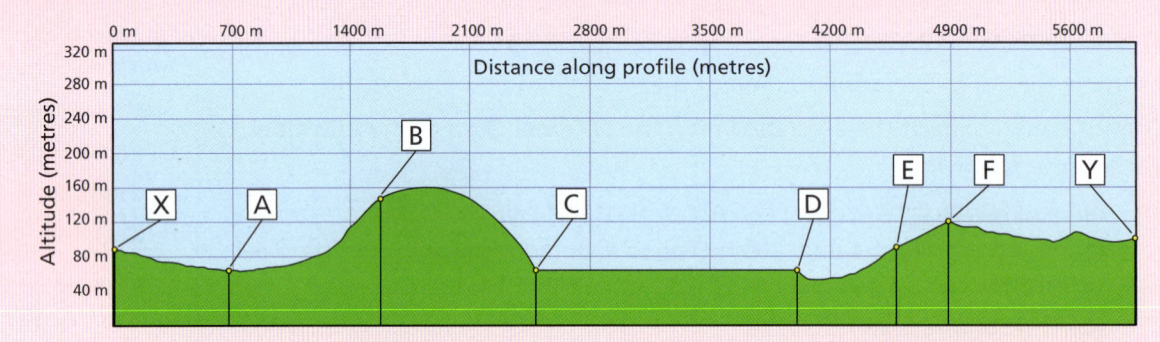

Note: This elevation profile is not to the same scale as the OS map

Using the 1:50,000 Ordnance Survey map of Macroom on page 188 and the elevation profile above, indicate whether each of the following statements is true or false, by circling the correct option in each case. *8 × 1 mark*

(i) The River Lee is located at A. True False
(ii) B is located in the Sleveen West townland. True False
(iii) The R584 regional road is located at C. True False
(iv) The slope between B and C is concave. True False
(v) Part of the built-up area of Macroom lies on a concave slope. True False
(vi) The slope of the cross-section between C and D is zero. True False
(vii) The height at F is 160 metres. True False
(viii) There is a constant or even slope between E and F. True False

2017, Part One, Q8 (8 marks)

Long Questions

6. Macroom OS Map

Examine the 1:50,000 Ordnance Survey map of Macroom on page 188.

Draw a sketch map of the area shown to half scale. On it, correctly show and label each of the following:

(a) The area of the reservoir west of Lee Bridge
(b) The course of the River Lee from W 250 667 to W 314 709
(c) The entire area of land above 200 metres at Cill na Martra
(d) The entire area of coniferous plantation at W 25 66.

Marking Scheme:
Sketch outline: 4 marks (4/0)
Four features × 4 marks each:
 Shown = 3 marks (graded 3/1/0)
 Label = 1 mark

2017, Part Two, Section 1, Q1A (20 marks)

Westport OS map

12 Ordnance Survey Maps

191

Landscapes

ORDINARY LEVEL

Short Questions

7. Westport OS Map

Examine the 1:50,000 Ordnance Survey map of Westport on page 191.

(i) What is the total area of the map? Tick the correct box. *5 marks*

99 km² ☐   108 km² ☐

(ii) The length of the N5 road, from where it enters the map at M 040 849 to where it meets the R330 road at L 998 845 is:

4.4 km ☐   2.9 km ☐

Tick the correct box. *5 marks*

2016, Part One, Q2 (10 marks)

Long Questions

8. Westport OS Map

Examine the 1:50,000 Ordnance Survey map of Westport on page 191.

Draw a sketch map of the area shown on the OS map. On it, show and label each of the following:

- Westport Bay
- The Owenwee River
- Two named lakes
- An area of coniferous plantation.

Marking Scheme:
Sketch outline:
  Frame = 1 mark
  Proportions = 2 marks
  Overall impression = 2 marks
Five features shown and labelled:
  Shown = 5 × 3 marks
  Labelled = 5 × 2 marks

2016, Part Two, Section 1, Q2A (30 marks)

HIGHER LEVEL

Short Questions

9. Westport OS Map – Landforms

Examine the 1:50,000 Ordnance Survey map of Westport on page 191.

(i) Match each of the following landforms with the grid reference that best matches its location on the Ordnance Survey map in the table below. *4 × 1 mark*

(a) V-shaped valley
(b) Cut-off meander
(c) Drumlin
(d) Lagoon

(ii) Indicate whether glacial processes or fluvial processes or coastal processes are most associated with the formation of each landform, by ticking the correct box in the table below. *4 × 1 mark*

Grid Reference	(i) Landform	(ii) Glacial Processes	(ii) Fluvial Processes	(ii) Coastal Processes
L 95 78				
L 93 78				
L 94 83				
L 92 85				

2016, Part One, Q5 (8 marks)

12 Ordnance Survey Maps

10. Westport OS Map

Examine the 1:50,000 Ordnance Survey map of Westport on page 191.
- (i) Calculate the approximate area, in square kilometres, of Westport Bay, south of northing 85 and west of easting 95. *2 marks*
- (ii) What is the aspect of the slope at M 037 784? *2 marks*
- (iii) Measure the straight-line distance, in kilometres, from the Post Office in Westport town to the Post Office at M 033 804. *2 marks*
- (iv) Give a six-figure grid reference for the Trailhead on the waymarked walk, in the south of the OS map. *2 marks*

2016, Part One, Q6 (8 marks)

11. Westport OS Map – Map Skills

Locate point **X**, L 936 781, and point **Y**, L 937 825, on the 1:50,000 Ordnance Survey map of Westport on page 191. Figure 1 shows an elevation profile of the cross-section of a line between point **X** and point **Y** on the Ordnance Survey map.

Using the 1:50,000 Ordnance Survey map on page 191 and the elevation profile here, answer each of the following questions.

- (i) Match each of the letters **A**, **B**, **C** and **D** on the elevation profile opposite, with the feature on the Ordnance Survey map that best matches it in the table below. *4 × 1 mark*
- (ii) Indicate whether each feature in the table below is part of the physical landscape or cultural landscape, by ticking the correct box. *4 × 1 mark*

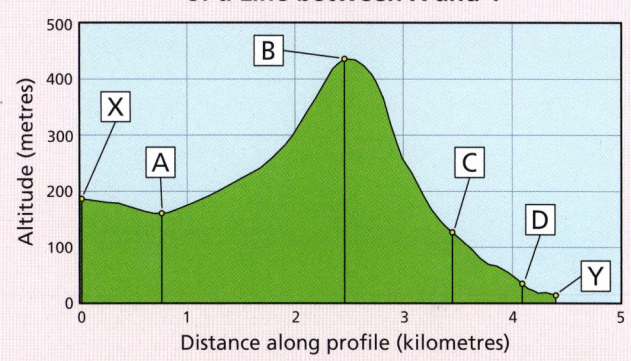

↑ **Figure 1** Elevation profile of the cross-section of a line between X–Y.

Feature on Ordnance Survey Map	(i) Letter	(ii) Physical Landscape	(ii) Cultural Landscape
R335			
Owenwee River			
Conical Peak			
Waymarked Walk			

2016, Part One, Q7 (8 marks)

Long Questions

12. Westport OS Map

Examine the 1:50,000 Ordnance Survey map of Westport on page 191. Draw a sketch map of the area shown to half scale. On it, correctly show and label each of the following:
- Westport Bay
- The entire course of the Owenwee River
- The entire area of Kilooey Lough at M 03 81
- The entire area of land above 200 metres in the south-west of the map.

2016, Part Two, Section 1, Q1A (20 marks)

Marking Scheme:
Sketch outline = 4 marks
Features = 4 × 4 marks:
  Shown = 3 marks (graded 3/1/0)
  Named = 1 mark

193

Landscapes

Kenmare OS map

12 Ordnance Survey Maps

ORDINARY LEVEL

Short Questions

13. Kenmare OS Map

Examine the 1:50,000 Ordnance Survey map of Kenmare on page 194.
Draw a sketch map of the area shown on the OS map. On it, show and label each of the following:

- (a) An area of natural woodland
- (b) An area of land above 400 metres
- (c) Dinish Island
- (d) The Kenmare River
- (e) A named lake.

Marking Scheme:
Sketch outline:
  Frame = 1 mark
  Proportions = 2 marks
  Overall impression = 2 marks
Five features shown and labelled:
  Shown = 5 × 3 marks
  Labelled = 5 × 2 marks

2015, Part Two, Section 1, Q1A (30 marks)

14. Kenmare OS Map

Examine the 1:50,000 Ordnance Survey map of Kenmare on page 194.

(i) Name the features which can be found at the following grid references:
  - (a) V 862 773
  - (b) V 918 718
  - (c) V 877 676
  - (d) V 909 706

4 × 2 marks

(ii) Indicate the rural settlement pattern found at V 898 719, by ticking the correct box.

Linear ☐   Dispersed ☐   Clustered/Nucleated ☐   *2 marks*

2015, Part One, Q6 (10 marks)

HIGHER LEVEL

Short Questions

15. Kenmare OS Map

Examine the 1:50,000 Ordnance Survey map of Kenmare on page 194.

(i) Measure the straight-line distance, in kilometres, from the 18-hole golf course at V 851 712 to the parking at V 862 773. *2 marks*

(ii) Calculate the approximate area of the Kenmare River west of Easting 88, shown on the map. *2 marks*

(iii) State one piece of evidence to show there may be permeable rock present at V 92 77. *2 marks*

(iv) Name one species of tree that may be found in the natural woodland at V 87 74. *2 marks*

2015, Part One, Q7 (8 marks)

16. Kenmare OS Map – Map Skills

Figure 1 shows a line **X–Y** along northing 76 on the Ordnance Survey map on page 194.
Figure 2 shows the elevation profile of the cross-section of the line **X–Y**.

Using the 1:50,000 Ordnance Survey map of Kenmare on page 194 and the elevation profile, answer each of the following questions.

(i) Name the road at A. *2 marks*

(ii) Name the waymarked walk at B. *2 marks*

(iii) Name the stream/river at C. *2 marks*

(iv) Calculate the difference in the altitude between the road at A on the Elevation Profile (Figure 2) and the triangulation pillar at Peakeen Mountain. *2 marks*

Landscapes

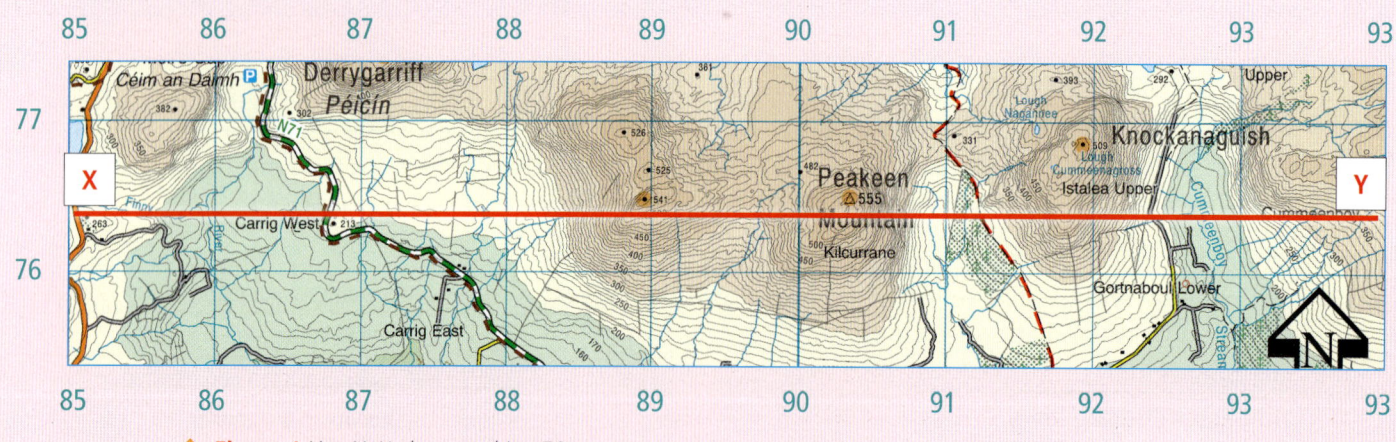

Figure 1 Line X–Y along northing 76.

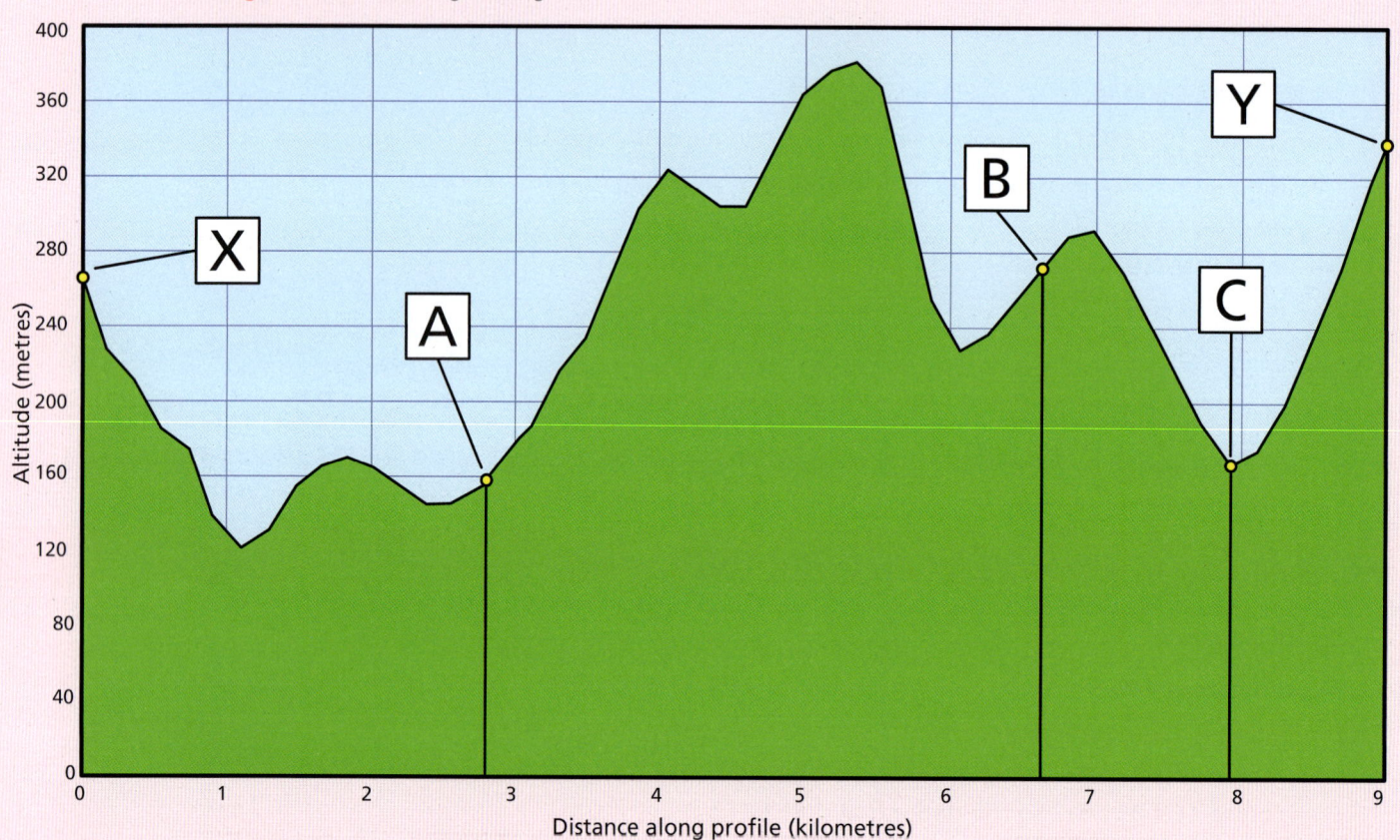

Figure 2 Elevation profile of the cross-section of the line X–Y.

2015, Part One, Q9 (8 marks)

Long Questions

17. Kenmare OS Map

Examine the 1:50,000 Ordnance Survey map of Kenmare on page 194.

Draw a sketch map of the area shown to half scale. On it, correctly show and label each of the following:

(a) The entire route of the waymarked walk called the Béara Way shown on the map
(b) The entire area of coniferous plantation at V 85 72
(c) The entire area of land above 300 metres at Letter South
(d) The entire area of the Kenmare River shown on the map.

Marking Scheme:
Sketch outline: 4 marks (4/0)
Four features × 4 marks each:
 Shown = 3 marks (graded 3/1/0)
 Label = 1 mark

2015, Part Two, Section 1, Q2 (20 marks)

196

Revision Summary

OSI maps
- Show relationship between distance, direction and size
- 75 maps
- 25 sub-zones – each identified by a letter
- Sub-zones – 100 km × 100 km

Scale
- Representative fraction
- Linear scale
- Statement of scale

Recording skills
- **Grid referencing:** four-figure – six-figure
- **Direction:** compass points
- **Distance:** straight and curved-line
- **Area:** regular and irregular areas
- **Gradient:** average slope

Relief on OS maps
- Colour layering
- Contour lines
- Triangulation station/pillar
- Spot height

Slope on OS maps
- **Concave:** gentle base – steep at top
- **Convex:** steep base – plateau at top
- **Even:** evenly spaced contours
- **Stepped:** steps and plateaus

OS map sketches
Instructions
- Use pencil, ruler and graph paper
- Frame = half size of OS map
- 1 cm allowed for each grid square
- Divide sketch and OS map into nine equal segments
- Give sketch a title
- Add north arrow
- Must mark in coastline
- Insert features with symbols
- Shade in areas of land over 200 metres
- Add key/legend with a title
- Mark in scale underneath sketch map

Cross-sections
- Intervisibility

Instructions
- Link outer points of the cross-section with straight-edged strip of paper
- Mark paper where it touches the outer points and any feature or contour
- Draw X and Y axes on graph paper
- Y-axis = height above sea level
- X-axis = plot outer points, contours and features onto this line
- Give the cross-section a title

Factors affecting the location of Irish settlements
- **Altitude:** high ground repels settlers
- **Drainage:** avoid floodplains
- **Aspect:** south-facing slopes preferred
- **Coast:** access to sea and coastal resources
- **Communications:** bridging points (áth) or intersection points of routeways
- **Defence:** settlements grew around castles and army barracks

Growth of a settlement
- **Stone Age:** court cairns, megalithic tomb, stone circles
- **Bronze Age:** dolmens, fulachta fia, standing stones, etc.
- **Iron Age:** crannog, ogham stone, promontory fort, souterrain, togher – place names with *caher/dún*
- **Early Christian:** abbey, graveyard, high cross, holy well, round tower, monastery – place names with *kil/cill* or *monaster/mainistir*
- **Norman settlement:** abbey, castle, tower house, town gate, town wall – place names with *bally/baile*
- **Plantation settlement:** demesne or manor – place names with *town*

Rural settlement patterns
- **Absence of settlement:** no settlements in upland areas, climate too cold in winter and limited accessibility – no settlements on floodplains, possibility of flooding
- **Dispersed settlement:** buildings form no definite pattern – rural areas
- **Linear settlement:** buildings are in a line – along a roadway or a valley
- **Nucleated settlement:** buildings occur in clusters – road junctions/bridging points

Tourist attractions
- **Transport services:** railway stations – roads
- **Tourist accommodation:** camping/caravan sites/hotels/hostels
- **Tourist information centres**
- **Coastal areas:** leisure – fishing – picnics – sailing – sunbathing – surfing – swimming
- **Rivers and lakes:** fishing – rowing – swimming
- **Mountains and hills:** hillwalking – mountain biking – orienteering
- **Forests:** bicycle/nature trails – orienteering – picnics
- **Nature reserves:** flora and fauna
- **Recreational activities:** golf courses & racecourses
- **Antiquities:** history & culture

Urban functions
- **Educational:** schools, colleges, universities
- **Industrial:** industrial estates
- **Market**
- **Medical:** hospital
- **Port:** beacon, harbour, lighthouse, port, quay
- **Recreational:** golf course, racetrack, park, stadium
- **Religious:** cathedral, church, convent
- **Residential:** housing estate
- **Tourism:** see opposite
- **Transport:** airport, car park, railway station, road

Changing functions
- **Defensive:** town wall, castle, military barracks
- **Religious:** abbey, monastery
- **Transport:** canals

13 AERIAL PHOTOGRAPHS

KEYWORDS
vertical photograph
oblique photograph
horizon
background
middleground
foreground
skyline
interpret
traffic management
land use
function

LEARNING INTENTIONS
Syllabus Links: 3

By the end of this chapter I will be able to:
- recognise the differences between vertical and oblique aerial photographs;
- understand and use aerial photograph reading skills;
- recognise and interpret information and patterns from aerial photographs.

Aerial photographs are pictures of the ground taken from elevated positions. In the past, planes, helicopters and hot-air balloons were commonly used, but today, drones provide a modern, cheaper alternative. Aerial photographs provide invaluable information on land uses and traffic management, along with building heights, shapes and quality.

Photographs are typically classified by their type.

Types of Aerial Photography

Vertical photographs

The camera is vertically overhead, pointing directly down onto the area being photographed. The resulting photograph has a uniform scale with rooftops, roads and other features of the landscape appearing in a flat, map-like image.

Vertical photographs should be divided into nine equal segments. The terms illustrated below should be used to provide the location of any feature when asked.

↑ **Fig. 13.1** Three types of aerial photographs can be produced depending on the camera angle.

↑ **Fig. 13.2(a)** Compass points are used to give a location on a vertical aerial photograph.

↑ **Fig. 13.2(b)** Location on a vertical aerial photograph may have to be altered depending on where the north arrow is pointing.

198

Oblique photographs

The camera is pointed at an angle to the ground when the picture is taken. The scale is not uniform as the field of vision is truncated, with objects in the lower part of the photograph (**foreground**) appearing larger than those at the top of the picture (**background**). There are two types of oblique photograph:

Low oblique photographs: The camera is pointing from a low angle, usually about 30 degrees from the vertical position. The area covered in the picture is smaller with **no horizon visible**, **only land**.

High oblique photographs: The camera is pointing from a high angle, usually about 60 degrees from the vertical position. The area covered in the picture is larger: both the **land surface and part of the horizon are seen**.

Oblique photographs should also be divided into nine equal segments in order to indicate the location of features on the photograph. The terms illustrated in each section should be used to provide the location of any feature when asked.

> In oblique photographs, the scale decreases as one moves from the foreground to the background.

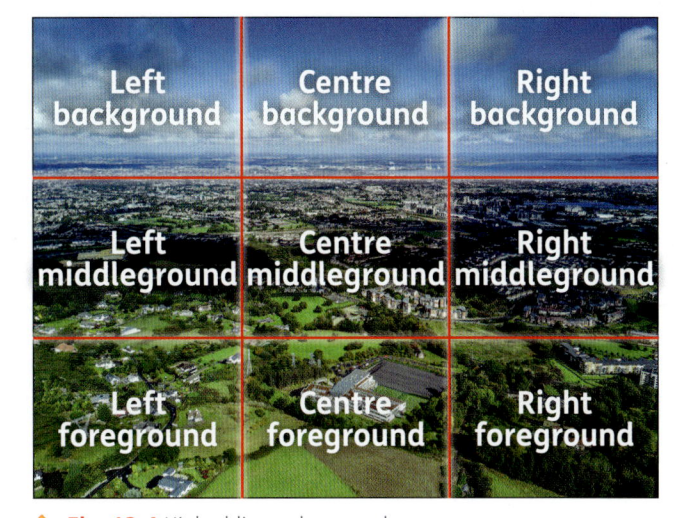

↑ **Fig. 13.3** Low oblique photograph.

↑ **Fig. 13.4** High oblique photograph.

Drawing a sketch map of an aerial photograph

The following method should be used to draw a sketch map of an aerial photograph.

1. Use a pencil, ruler and graph paper. Use a hard pencil (HB), as these produce clean, sharp lines, which are ideal for sketch maps.
2. Draw a rectangular frame half the size of the aerial photograph. The frame must be the same shape as the aerial photograph.
3. Divide both the aerial photograph and the sketch map into nine equal segments. The segments can be used as a guide when features are being placed onto the sketch map.
4. Above the frame of the sketch map, write in a title, e.g. 'Sligo Sketch Map'.
5. If there is a coastline or skyline on the aerial photograph, it must be drawn into the sketch, whether it is asked for or not.
6. Using different colours, insert the required features in their exact location. The shape and size of the features should be relative to the size of the sketch map. Do not insert any extra features.
7. Explain the colours used on the sketch map using a key/legend. This should also have a title, e.g. 'Key for Sligo Sketch Map'.

Landscapes

EXAM LINK (HL) AND SAMPLE ANSWER

Sligo OS Map (20 marks)

Draw a sketch map of the aerial photograph of Sligo, half the length and half the breadth. On it, correctly show and label each of the following:
- The river
- A large historical ruin in the middle ground
- Emergency services depot in the left background
- A carpark in the left foreground.

2018, Q10A

Marking Scheme:
Outline = 4 marks (graded)
Features = 4 × 4 marks
   Shown = 3 marks (graded 3/1/0)
   Named = 1 mark

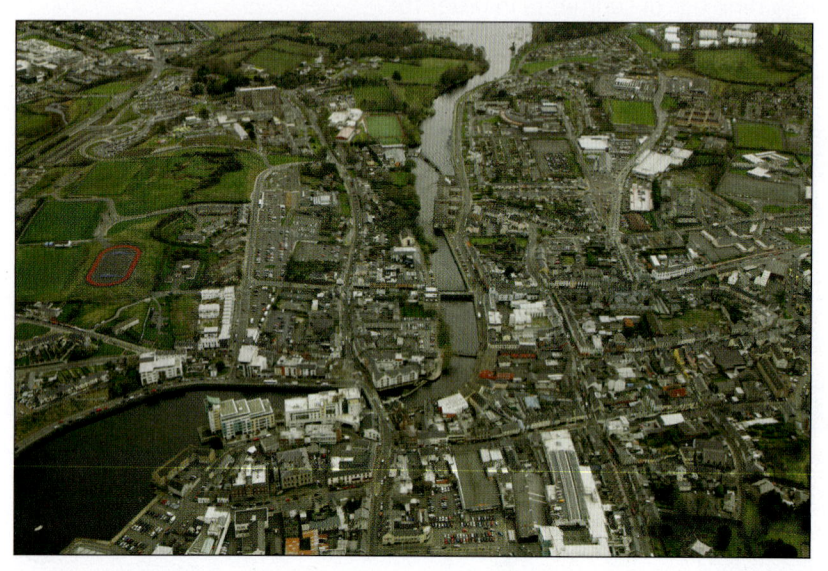

↑ **Fig. 13.5** Aerial photograph of Sligo.

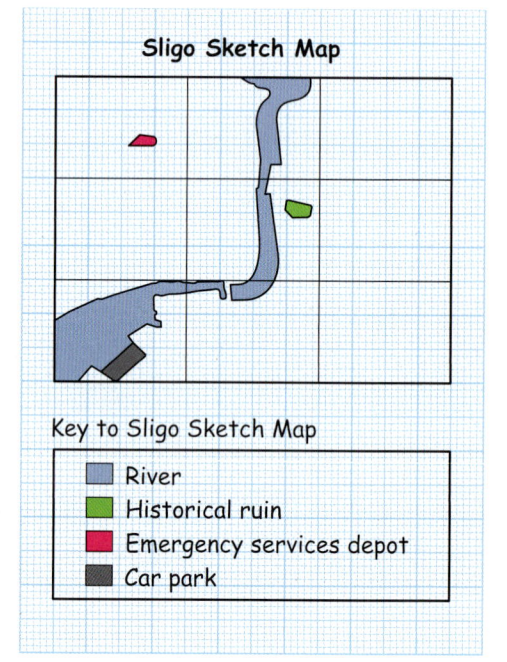

→ **Fig. 13.6** Sketch map of Sligo.

Sligo Sketch Map

Key to Sligo Sketch Map
- River
- Historical ruin
- Emergency services depot
- Car park

EXAM TIP

This question will come up in the Elective section of the course.

Questions where one is asked to interpret various aspects of an aerial photograph appear in Part One of the exam paper – the Short Questions section.

Interpreting Aerial Photographs

Colour and shading

It is possible to identify a number of features by interpreting colour and shading.

1. **Direction:** As most aerial photographs are taken at noon, shadows typically point to the north.
2. **Weather conditions:**
   a. Water may appear white and sunlit if the day is calm.
   b. On darker days, water may appear black, as the light isn't being reflected.
3. **Rivers** are usually dark blue or grey in colour.
4. **Roads** are usually grey in colour.
5. **Railway lines** are usually black in colour.
6. **Woodland** is usually dark green in colour.
7. **Agriculture:**
   a. Permanent grassland is green, which indicates pastoral farming.
   b. Fields that appear either yellow or brown in colour most likely indicate arable farming.
   c. Fields that are brown in colour have probably been recently ploughed.

Time of year

It is possible to figure out the time of year a photograph was taken by recognising a variety of features.

Spring	Summer
• Trees have a light covering of leaves. • Calves or lambs are close to their mothers.	• Deciduous trees and bushes are fully leafed. • Cereal crops appear ripe (yellow). • Hay or straw bales in fields. • Animals may be grazing. • Crowded beaches at the coast.
Autumn	**Winter**
• Leaves on trees have numerous shades – red, yellow, brown. • Fields are cleared of hay or straw bales.	• No leaves on trees. • No animals in the fields. • Recently ploughed fields. • Snow on the ground. • Chimney smoke indicates lower temperatures. • Rivers may be brown in colour following flooding.

← **Fig. 13.7(a)** An aerial photograph taken in summer.

← **Fig. 13.7(b)** An aerial photograph taken in autumn.

Landscapes

Traffic management

Fig. 13.8 Traffic management systems in an urban area.

SKILLS ACTIVITY

Identify three traffic management systems that are visible in **Fig. 13.8**.

Traffic congestion is a major problem in Irish urban areas. It has resulted from:
- increasing individual wealth and disposable income, which has supported the growth of car ownership;
- the growth of the Irish population, especially in urban areas.

It is possible to recognise places on aerial photographs where congestion is likely to occur. These include:
- junctions where a number of streets meet, especially at the bridging points of rivers;
- areas where large numbers of people gather: shopping centres, schools, churches, sports grounds, etc;
- areas where streets become narrow or have on-street parking;
- areas where lanes are closed for road or utility works.

Measures aimed at reducing traffic congestion can be seen aerial photographs. These include:
- **roundabouts**, which reduce delays at intersections;
- **'yellow-box' junctions**; which ease congestion where roads intersect and at entrances to important buildings;
- **filter lanes**, which allow traffic to move from different directions at an intersection;
- **traffic lights**, which control traffic flow at busy junctions;
- **one-way systems**, wherein all traffic moves in the same direction;
- **double yellow lines**, which prevent on-street parking;
- **car parks**, both off street and multi-storey;
- **cycle lanes**, which encourage more people to cycle;
- **quality bus corridors**;
- **pedestrianised streets**;
- **flyovers** at major junctions;
- **bypasses** and **ring-roads**, which reduce the volume of traffic passing through urban areas.

Rural land use

- **Agriculture:** Fields, animals, agricultural machinery.
- **Horticulture:** Greenhouses, tunnels used for growing, fruit, vegetables, herbs and flowers.
- **Forestry:** Large areas of deciduous or coniferous plantation.
- **Wind farms:** Wind turbines generating electricity are usually built on land not conducive to agriculture.
- **Mining:** Quarries.

Urban functions

- **Defensive (former function):** Castle, military barracks, towers, town wall.
- **Religious:** Cathedrals, churches, convents and graveyards. Abbeys and monasteries represent former functions.
- **Educational:** Schools, colleges, universities.
- **Industrial:** Industrial estates or stand-alone factories.
- **Market:** Market square, petrol station, shops.
- **Medical:** Hospitals.
- **Port:** Harbours, quays, cranes, boats, ships, container parks, warehouses.
- **Recreation:** Golf courses, parks, playgrounds, playing pitches, race tracks and tennis courts.
- **Residential:** Individual houses, housing estates.
- **Transport:** Airports, car parks, railway stations and roads.

↑ **Fig. 13.9** Agricultural land use.

Comparing OS Maps and Aerial Photographs

	Ordnance Survey maps	Aerial photographs
Location	Four- or six-figure grid references.	Varying terms depending on whether it is a vertical or oblique photograph.
Scale	OS maps are drawn to scale – allows accurate measurement of distance and area.	Vertical photographs have a uniform scale. Oblique photographs have a truncated field of vision so their scale is not uniform. Objects in the foreground appear larger than objects in the background.
Topography	OS maps use colour layering, contours, triangulation stations and spot heights to show the height of the land. The gradient of a slope can also be calculated.	The actual height of the land cannot be identified on photographs. Slope can be recognised on oblique photographs but not on vertical photographs.
Features	The features presented on an OS map are labelled or have a symbol/colour that can be identified in the legend.	There are no labels or symbols to identify features. It is, however, possible to identify the following: • rural and urban land use functions; • the size and shape of buildings; • the relative age and condition of buildings; • derelict sites; • the time of year the photograph was taken; • the width of roads and urban street patterns.

Landscapes

Direction on an Aerial Photograph

1. Draw a line through the centre of the photograph from the foreground (bottom) to the background (top). Place an arrow at the top of the line. This arrow represents the direction the camera was pointing when the photograph was being taken.
2. Identify two features on/following the line drawn. These features must be identifiable on the OS map also, e.g. a church, castle, bridge, railway or road.
3. Draw an arrow leading from the lower feature on the photograph to the upper feature on the photograph.
4. Identify the same two features on the OS map. Then draw an arrow on the OS map leading from the lower feature identified on the photograph to the upper feature identified on the photograph.
5. The direction the arrow is pointing on the OS map represents the direction the camera was pointing when the photograph was being taken. Record this direction using compass points.

Look at the example below, using an OS map extract and aerial photo from Sligo.

In the photograph, the **black arrow** represents the direction in which the camera was pointing when the photograph was taken. A **red arrow** has been drawn alongside that arrow, starting at the bridge in the centre foreground and travelling to the church in the centre background. The regional road leading from the bridge is on the left-hand side of the arrow, and the river is on the right-hand side of the arrow.

The bridge over the river and the church have been circled on the OS map (see centre of the OS map). Looking at the OS map, we can see that the arrow is pointing east, so we know that the camera was pointing east when the photograph was taken.

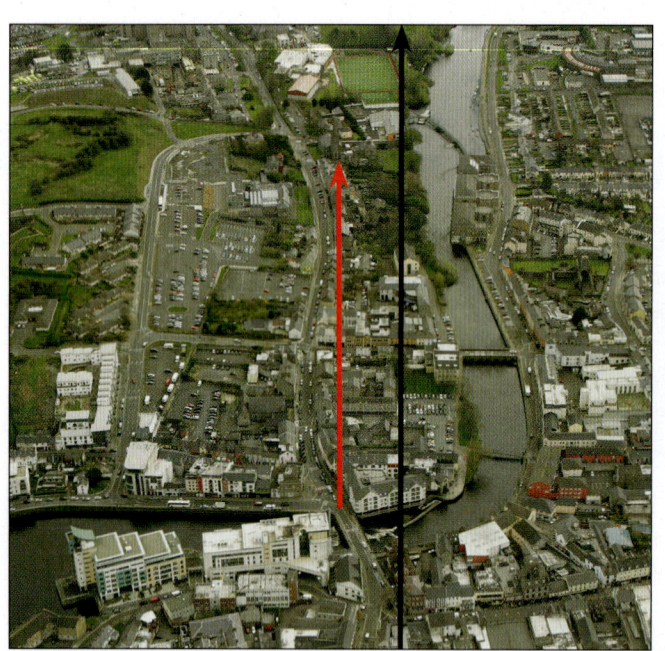

← ↑ **Fig. 13.10(a) & (b)** Aerial photo and OS map extract from Sligo.

→ Direction in which the photograph was taken.

→ Two features in line with the direction in which the photograph was taken.

CHECK YOUR LEARNING

Using the Westport aerial photograph on page 207, answer the following questions.

1. Is this a vertical, high oblique or low oblique aerial photograph?
2. What time of year was this photograph taken? Explain, using evidence from the photo.
3. Give the correct photographic location of the large GAA field in the photo.
4. Give the correct photographic location of a church in the photo.
5. Using the OS map on page 191, identify which direction the camera was pointing when this photograph was taken.

204

13 Aerial Photographs

EXAMINATION QUESTIONS

Macroom

ORDINARY LEVEL

Short Question

1. Aerial Photograph

Examine the aerial photograph of Macroom above. State whether each of the following statements is true or false. *5× 2 marks*

(i) There is a graveyard in the left background of the aerial photograph.	True False
(ii) There is a roundabout in the left foreground of the aerial photograph.	True False
(iii) The bridging point of the river is in the left middleground of the aerial photograph.	True False
(iv) The Central Business District (CBD) is in the centre middleground of the aerial photograph.	True False
(v) This aerial photograph is a vertical aerial photograph.	

2017, Part One, Q7 (10 marks)

Long Question

2. Aerial Photograph

Draw a sketch map of the area shown on the aerial photograph of Macroom above. On it, show and label each of the following:

- Two connecting streets
- The river
- The church in the left middleground
- An area of warehousing in the left foreground
- A recreational area.

Marking Scheme:

Sketch outline:
- Limits/frame = 1 mark
- Proportions = 2 marks (2/0)
- Overall impression = 2 marks (graded 2/1/0)

Features = 5 × 5 marks:
- Shown = 3 marks (graded 3/1/0)
- Labelled = 2 marks

2017, Part Two, Section 2, Q11A (30 marks)

205

Landscapes

HIGHER LEVEL

Short Question

3. Aerial Photograph – Location

Examine the aerial photograph of Macroom on page 205 and the street map below of part of the area covered by the aerial photograph.

Note: The orientation of the aerial photograph is different from the orientation of the street map below.

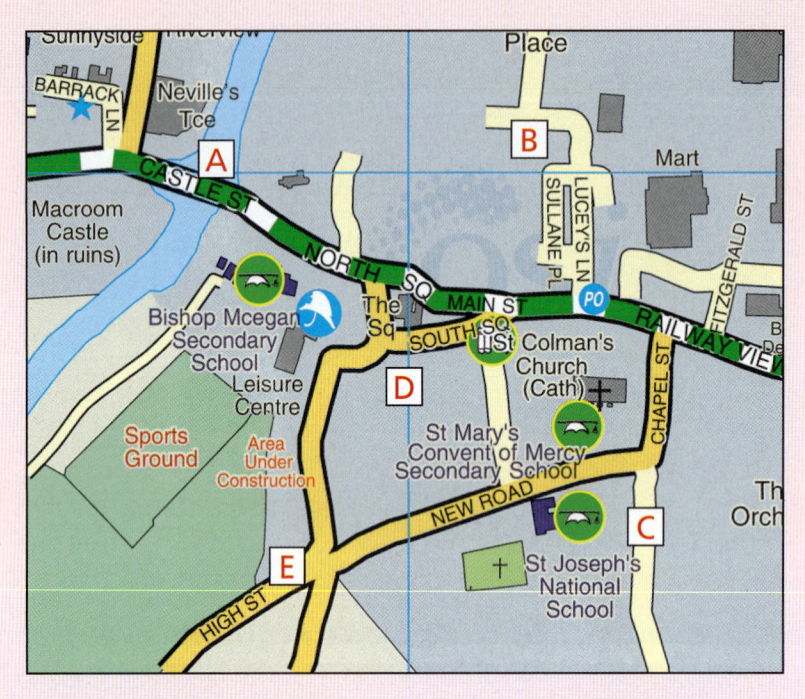

Locate each of the features labelled A, B, C, D and E above, on the aerial photograph on page 205. Using accepted notation, give the location of each of these features on the aerial photograph in the table below. One has been completed.

4 × 2marks

Feature on Street Map	Location on Aerial Photograph
A River bridge	Right middleground
B Terraced housing	
C St Joseph's Primary School	
D South Square	
E Road	

2017, Part One, Q9 (8 marks)

Long Question

4. Aerial Photograph

Draw a sketch map of the aerial photograph of Macroom on page 205, half the length and half the breadth. On it, correctly show and label each of the following:

- The river
- A large sports field
- The triangular street pattern in the centre middleground
- An ecclesiastical building in the left middleground.

Marking Scheme:
Outline = 4 marks graded.
Features = 4 × 4 marks:
   Shown = 3 marks (graded 3/1/0)
   Named = 1 mark

2017, Part Two, Section 2, Q10A (20 marks)

206

Westport

ORDINARY LEVEL

Short Question

5. Aerial Photograph

Examine the aerial photograph of Westport above.

(i) Indicate whether each of the following statements is true or false, by circling the correct option in each case. *4 × 2 marks*

  (a) There is a river meander in the right background.   True   False
  (b) There is a bridge crossing the river in the centre middleground.   True   False
  (c) There is a church located in the centre foreground.   True   False
  (d) There is a large playing field in the left foreground.   True   False

  (e) Indicate whether the aerial photograph is a vertical or an oblique aerial photograph, by ticking the correct box.

  Vertical ☐   Oblique ☐

2 marks
2016, Part One, Q1 (10 marks)

Long Question

6. Aerial Photograph

Draw a sketch map of the area shown on the aerial photograph of Westport above. On it, show and label each of the following:

- A bridge
- Two connecting streets
- A car park in the foreground
- An industrial area in the left middleground
- An area of waste ground in the background

Marking Scheme:
Sketch outline:
  Limits/frame = 1 marks
  Proportions = 2 marks (2/0)
  Overall impression 2 marks (graded 2/1/0)
Features = 5 × 5 marks:
  Shown = 3 marks (graded 3/1/0)
  Labelled = 2 marks

2016, Part Two, Section 2, Q7A (30 marks)

207

Landscapes

HIGHER LEVEL

Short Question

7. Aerial Photograph – Location

Examine the street map of Westport below and the aerial photograph on page 207.

N.B. The orientation of the aerial photograph accompanying this paper is different from the orientation of the street map below. The aerial photograph was taken from a point just north of the area shown on the street map, looking southwards across the town.

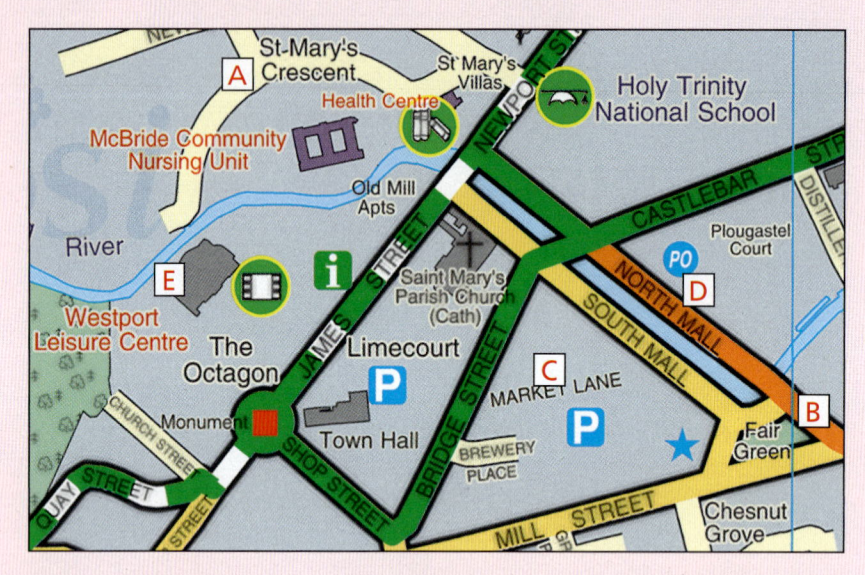

Locate each of the features A, B, C, D and E labelled above, on the aerial photograph on page 207. Using accepted notation, give the location of each of these features on the aerial photograph in the table below. One has been completed for you.

4 × 2 marks

Feature on Street Map	Location on Aerial Photograph
A Centre of St Mary's Crescent	Right foreground
B Fairgreen	
C Car Park	
D North Mall	
E Leisure Centre	

2016, Part One, Q8 (8 marks)

Long Question

8. Aerial Photographs

Examine the aerial photograph of Westport on page 207. Draw a sketch of the aerial photograph, half the length and half the breadth. On it, correctly show and label each of the following features:

- The river
- A bridge
- A large car park in the background
- The main road running from the centre foreground to the right background.

Marking Scheme:
Outline = 4 marks graded
Features = 4 × 4 marks:
   Shown = 3 marks (graded 3/1/0)
   Named = 1 mark
Required size is 14.2 cm × 8.7 cm (allow for ½ cm difference)

2016, Part Two, Section 2, Q11A

Kenmare

13 Aerial Photographs

ORDINARY LEVEL

Short Question

9. Aerial Photograph – Location

Examine the aerial photograph of Kenmare, and the sections taken from it to the right.

Indicate whether the descriptions of the locations of each of the sections from the aerial photograph are correct, by circling the correct option in each case.

One has been completed for you.   *5 × 2 marks*

2015, Part One, Q7 (10 marks)

Centre Background
(True)   False

Left Foreground
True   False

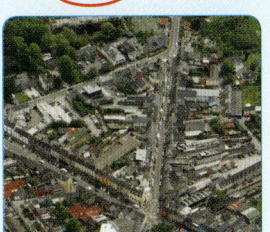

Centre Middleground
True   False

Right Middleground
True   False

Right Background
True   False

Left Background
True   False

209

Landscapes

Long Questions

10. Aerial Photograph

Draw a sketch map of the area shown on the aerial photograph of Kenmare on page 209. On it, show and label each of the following:

- An area of agricultural land
- Two connecting streets
- A roundabout
- A car park
- An area of waste ground.

> **Marking Scheme:**
> Sketch outline:
> Limits/frame = 1 mark
> Proportions = 2 marks (2/0)
> Overall impression = 2 marks (graded 2/1/0)
> Features = 5 × 5 marks:
> Shown = 3 marks (graded 3/1/0)
> Labelled = 2 marks

2015, Part Two, Section 2, Q7A (30 marks)

HIGHER LEVEL

Short Question

11. Aerial Photograph and Ordnance Survey Map

Examine the aerial photograph of Kenmare on page 209 and OS map on page 194 and answer each of the following questions. *4 × 2 marks*

(i) Give a six-figure grid reference for the large church located in the centre foreground of the aerial photograph.

(ii) In what direction was the camera pointed when the aerial photograph was taken?

(iii) Name the main road that runs through the aerial photograph from the centre background to the centre foreground.

(iv) State one piece of evidence, from the Ordnance Survey map or the aerial photograph, that indicates that Kenmare is a plantation town.

2015, Part One, Q8 (8 marks)

Long Question

12. Aerial Photograph

Examine the aerial photograph of Kenmare on page 209. Draw a sketch map of the aerial photograph, half the length and half the breadth. On it, correctly show and label each of the following:

- A car park
- The triangular street network in the middleground of the aerial photograph
- A large commercial/industrial building in the foreground of the aerial photograph
- An area of waste ground suitable for development.

> **Marking Scheme:**
> Outline = 4 marks (graded)
> Features = 4 × 4 marks:
> Shown = 3 marks (graded 3/1/0)
> Named – 1 mark

2015, Part Two, Section 2, Q8A (20 marks)

Revision Summary

Vertical aerial photograph
- Camera is vertically overhead
- Uniform scale
- Map-like image

Oblique aerial photograph

Low oblique
- Low angle camera position – 30° from ground
- Small area – no horizon

High oblique
- High angle camera position – 60° from ground
- Larger area – land and horizon in picture

Sketching aerial photographs
- Use a pencil, ruler and graph paper
- Frame = half the size of the aerial photograph
- Sketch and aerial photograph – 9 equal segments
- Sketch title
- Mark in coastline
- Shade in areas of required features
- Key/legend with a title

Finding direction of photography
- Line through centre of photo from foreground to background – direction camera was pointing
- Identify features on/near line drawn – church, castle etc.
- Identify same features on OS map – draw line on map corresponding to the line drawn on photo
- Use compass points to give direction the camera was pointing

Interpreting aerial photographs

Colour and shading
- **Direction:** shadows usually point north
- **Type of day:** water appears white and sunlit if the day is calm – water appears black on cloudy days – light isn't being reflected
- **Rivers:** usually dark blue/grey
- **Roads:** usually grey
- **Railway lines:** usually black
- **Woodland:** usually dark green
- **Agriculture:**
  - Pastoral farming – permanent grassland is green
  - Arable farming – fields yellow/brown
  - Recently ploughed fields – brown

Time of year

Spring
- Trees have a light covering of leaves
- Calves or lambs are close to their mothers

Summer
- Deciduous trees/bushes fully leafed
- Cereal crops appear ripe (yellow)
- Hay/straw bales in fields
- Animals grazing
- Crowded beaches

Autumn
- Leaves have numerous shades – red, yellow, brown
- Fields cleared of hay/straw bales

Winter
- No leaves on trees
- No animals in the fields
- Recently ploughed fields
- Snow on the ground
- Chimney smoke – lower temperatures
- Brown rivers – flooding

Rural land uses
- **Agriculture:** fields, animals, agricultural machinery
- **Horticulture:** greenhouses, tunnels
- **Forestry:** deciduous/coniferous plantation
- **Wind farms:** wind turbines
- **Mining:** quarries

Urban functions
- **Defensive (former function):** town wall, castle, towers, military barracks
- **Religious:** churches, cathedrals, convents and graveyards – monasteries and abbeys represent former functions
- **Educational:** schools, colleges, universities
- **Industrial:** industrial estates, stand-alone factories
- **Market:** shops, petrol station, market square
- **Medical:** hospitals
- **Port:** harbours, quays, cranes, boats, ships, container parks, warehouses
- **Recreation:** golf courses, race tracks, tennis courts, playing pitches, parks, playgrounds
- **Residential:** individual houses, housing estates
- **Transport:** roads, railway station, car parks, airports

Traffic management
- More wealth and disposable income – growth of car ownership
- Growing population – growth of car ownership
- Traffic congestions at street junctions, bridging points, shopping centres, school, churches, narrow streets or areas with on-street parking
- Measures aimed at reducing traffic congestion include roundabouts, 'yellow-box' junctions, filter lanes, one-way systems, double yellow lines, car parks, quality bus corridors, pedestrianised streets, flyovers, bypasses, ring-roads

14 WEATHER MAPS AND SATELLITE IMAGERY

KEYWORDS
meteorology
air mass
depression
polar front
altostratus
nimbostratus
warm front
cold front
synoptic chart
occluded front
hectopascals
millibars

LEARNING INTENTIONS
Syllabus Link: 3

By the end of this chapter I will be able to:
- list the elements that influence weather;
- identify the weather patterns associated with depressions and anticyclones;
- recognise the different symbols and weather patterns on synoptic weather charts;
- interpret weather data from synoptic weather charts;
- identify and interpret different graphical representations of weather data;
- recognise and link images to relevant descriptions based on the uses of satellite imagery such as physical feature identification, environmental damage and natural disasters;
- explain how GIS systems are used in the mapping process and describe their uses and limitations.

Weather Maps

Meteorology is the study of processes in our atmosphere and predicting and forecasting their likely weather outcomes.

Meteorologists study atmospheric pressure, temperature, moisture and wind and collect a variety of data which enables them to produce detailed synoptic weather charts.

Less detailed charts and maps can be found on mobile phone apps, websites and newspapers. Occupations and activities requiring weather information include pilots, fishermen, farmers and shipping. Local authorities monitor snow forecasts for gritting and salting roads and to organise flood protection during heavy rain spells, while power companies use forecasts to prepare for storm outages. Met Éireann is the Irish Metrological Service.

Understanding the weather

Weather refers to the state of the atmosphere at a particular time. There are a number of factors which have an influence on the weather we experience in Ireland including **air mass**, depressions and anticyclones.

14 Weather Maps and Satellite Imagery

Air mass

An **air mass** is a large body of air which has similar characteristics of temperature, humidity and pressure. During the course of a year, Ireland can come under the influence of different air masses, including Polar Maritime, Arctic Maritime, Polar Continental, Tropical Continental and Tropical Maritime. Each air mass results in different weather types being experienced (Fig. 14.1).

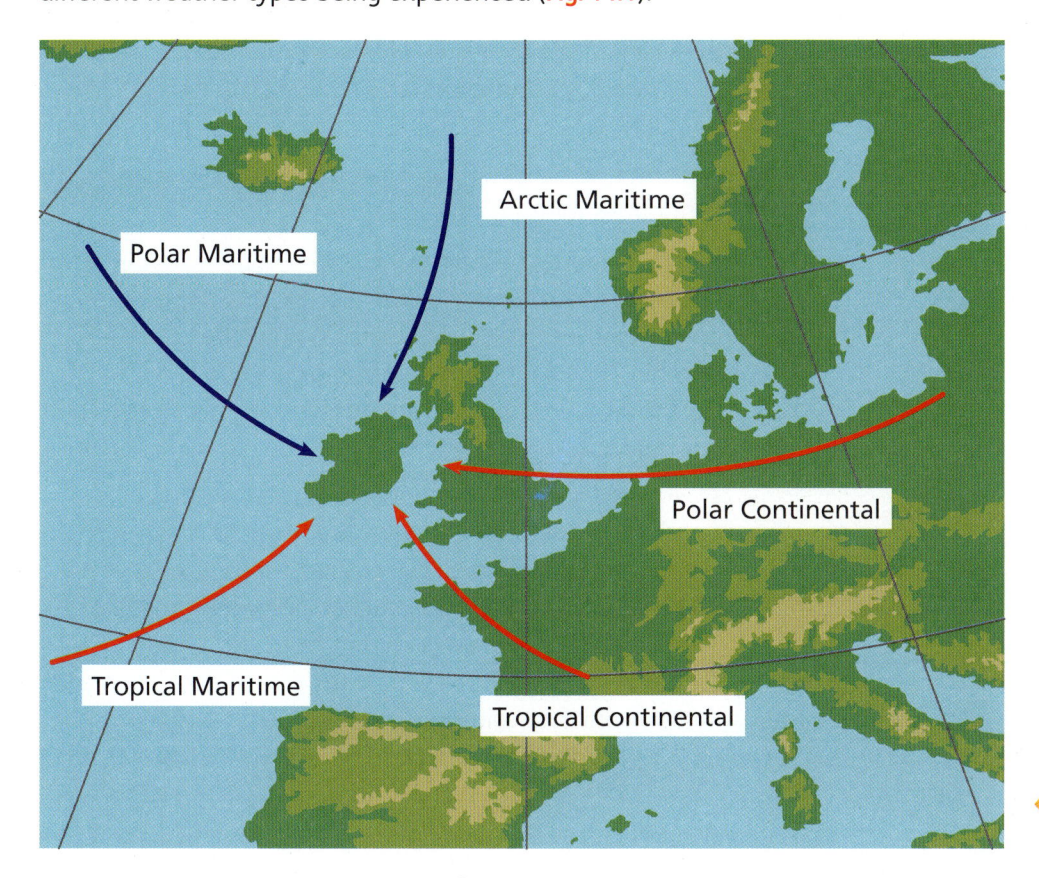

← Fig. 14.1 Air masses that influence Ireland's weather.

Depression

A **depression** is an area of low pressure which forms in the North Atlantic along the **polar front**. This is the boundary between warm, moist air moving northwards and colder, denser, drier air moving southwards. Composed of three different sectors, depressions generally move from west to east over Ireland; their overall wind direction is anticlockwise (Fig. 14.2).

Front: The boundary between different air masses.

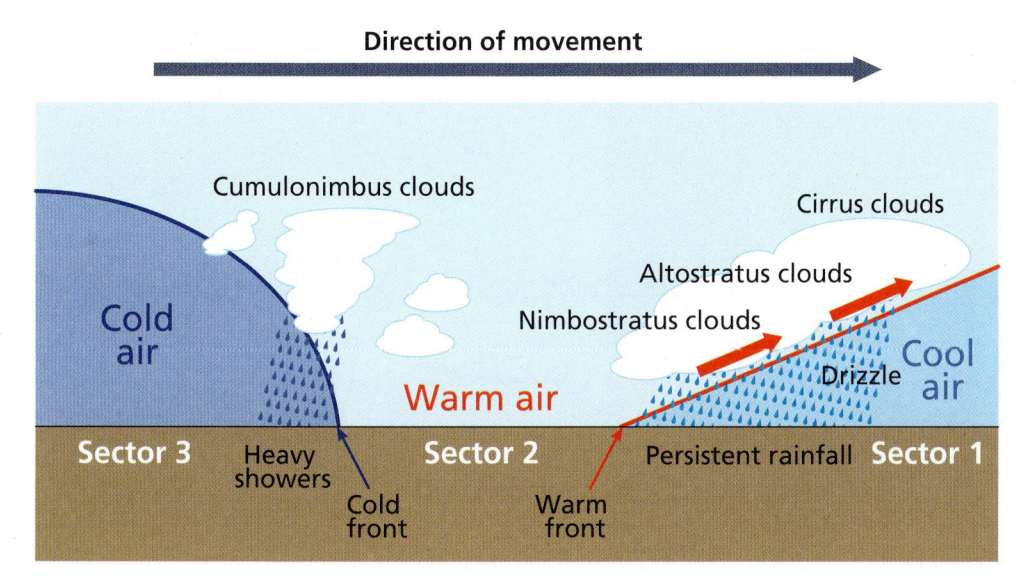

← Fig. 14.2 The structure of a depression.

213

Landscapes

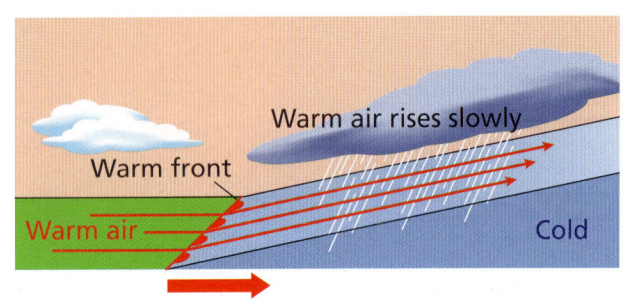

↑ **Fig. 14.3(a)** A warm front.

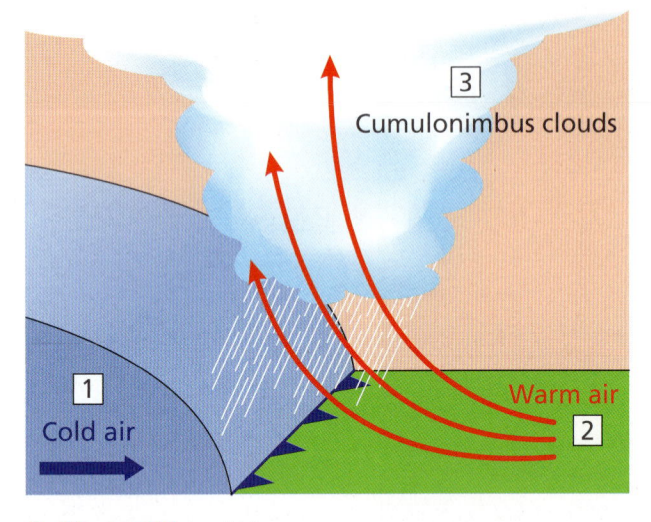

↑ **Fig. 14.3(b)** A cold front.

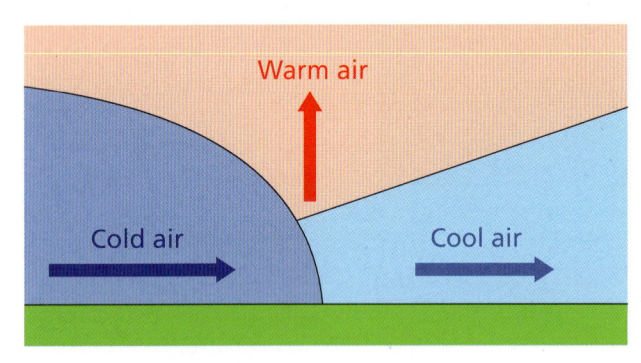

↑ **Fig. 14.3(c)** An occluded front.

The sequence of formation and weather associated with the approach and passage of a depression is as follows. (Refer to **Fig. 14.2**.)

Sector 1: The boundary between warm and cold air is called a **warm front** and along its length unstable, warm air is forced to rise slowly over stable, cooler, dense air. As it rises, it cools and condenses, leading to increasing cloud cover from **cirrus, altostratus and nimbostratus clouds**. Light rain is followed by prolonged steady rainfall (**Fig. 14.3(a)**).

Sector 2: This is the centre of the depression. Here the air is warm and moist. Generally, drizzle occurs here, though sometimes rain can stop.

Sector 3: Along the **cold front**, cold air **(1)** forces the warm air to rise upwards very quickly **(2)** (**Fig. 14.3(b)**). This rapid upward movement causes tall cumulonimbus clouds **(3)** to form. These bring heavy rain showers and sometimes thunder. When the cold front passes over, the skies clear leaving showers of rain associated with cumulus clouds.

In the final stage of formation, the faster moving cold front catches up with the warm front. There is now no warm air in contact with the ground, it has all been uplifted. This is called an **occlusion** and where the two fronts meet is called an **occluded front** (**Fig. 14.3(c)**). The rainfall associated with this is a mixture of heavy rain and lighter persistent rain.

Anticyclone

An anticyclone is an area of high pressure caused by air sinking downwards (**Fig. 14.4**). They bring settled conditions with clear skies, which in winter can result in frosty nights, while in summer they give clear sunny days. When an anticyclone is established over an area, it can block rain-bearing depressions, forcing them to track around it.

Weather charts

Using weather data, meteorologists create **synoptic charts** (**Fig. 14.5(a)**), which use a variety of symbols to represent information (**Fig. 14.5(b)**).

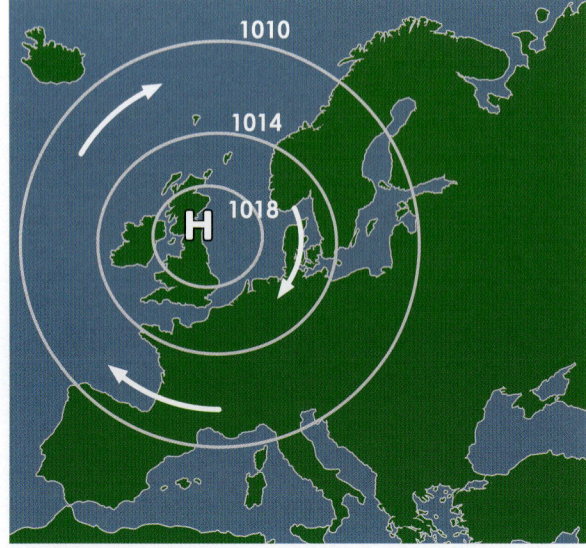

↑ **Fig. 14.4** An anticyclone.

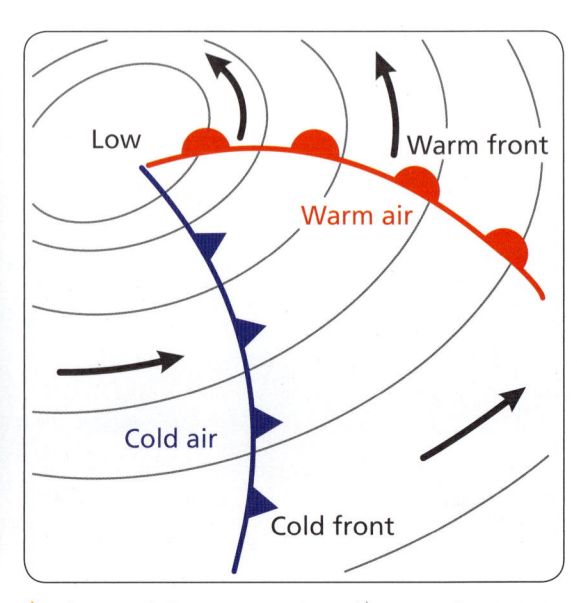

↑ **Fig. 14.5(a)** A synoptic chart showing a depression.

14 Weather Maps and Satellite Imagery

Warm front   Cold front   Occluded front

↑ **Fig. 14.5(b)** Synoptic chart symbols.

Pressure values, shown by **isobars**, are measured in **hectopascals**. They are usually shown at four-hectopascal intervals (Fig. 14.6).

Winds generally blow parallel to isobars. In a **depression** the overall wind direction will be anticlockwise. A pattern of close isobars indicates strong winds. The word **LOW** or the letter **L** marks the centre of a depression.

The wind pattern associated with an **anticyclone** is clockwise. The pattern of isobars is well-spaced, indicating little or no winds, which can result in fog. The word **HIGH** or the letter **H** identifies the centre of an anticyclone.

> Hectopascals are the agreed units of measurement for atmospheric pressure.
> 1 millibar (mb) = 1 hectopascal (hPa)

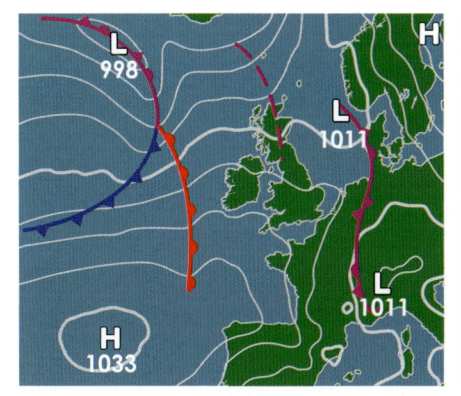

↑ **Fig. 14.6(a)** The chart shows a depression of 998 hectopascals, with an occluded front and associated warm and cold fronts to the west/north-west.

↑ **Fig. 14.6(b)** Note the bands of cloud associated with the fronts to the west.

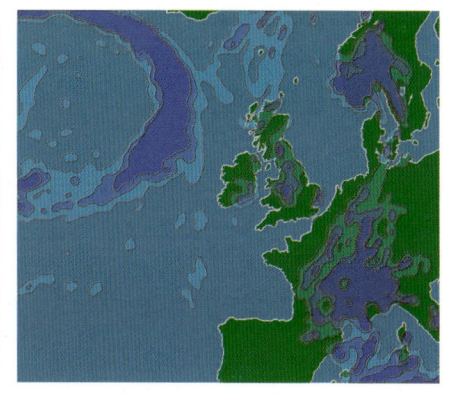

↑ **Fig. 14.6(c)** Rain associated with the warm front is shown in lighter blue, while a band of heavy rain (dark blue) associated with the cold front lies approaches from the west.

CHECK YOUR LEARNING

1. Name three occupations or activities which rely on weather forecasts.
2. Name three different types of fronts and draw the symbols used to represent each type.
3. What are isobars? What units are used to measure them?
4. Name two characteristics of an anticyclone?
5. Copy the chart below into your copybook and then match the correct number to the correct description

a. Stable weather conditions	i. Warm front
b. Warm air rising quickly	ii. Hectopascals
c. Heavy rain showers	iii. Well-spaced isobars
d. Light winds	iv Cold front
e. Measurement of pressure	v. Anticyclone

Synoptic chart: A weather chart showing information on atmospheric pressure patterns, wind, temperature and precipitation.

Isotherm: A line on a map joining places of equal temperature.

Isohyet: A line on a map joining places of equal precipitation.

Isotach: A line on a map joining places of equal wind speed.

Landscapes

Wind rose diagrams

Wind rose diagrams are created using wind speed and direction data. These circular diagrams show the frequency of wind direction and speed for a particular location for a given time period.

The spokes indicate the direction of the wind, and are colour-coded to indicate different wind speeds, while the concentric circles represent the frequency of each wind as a percentage of time.

The rose in Figure 14.7 shows that the westerly wind was most frequent, blowing approximately 18% of the time with its highest speed greater than 50 metres per second (m/s).

Creating a wind rose would be the first step in deciding the location of a runway, as planes take off into wind.

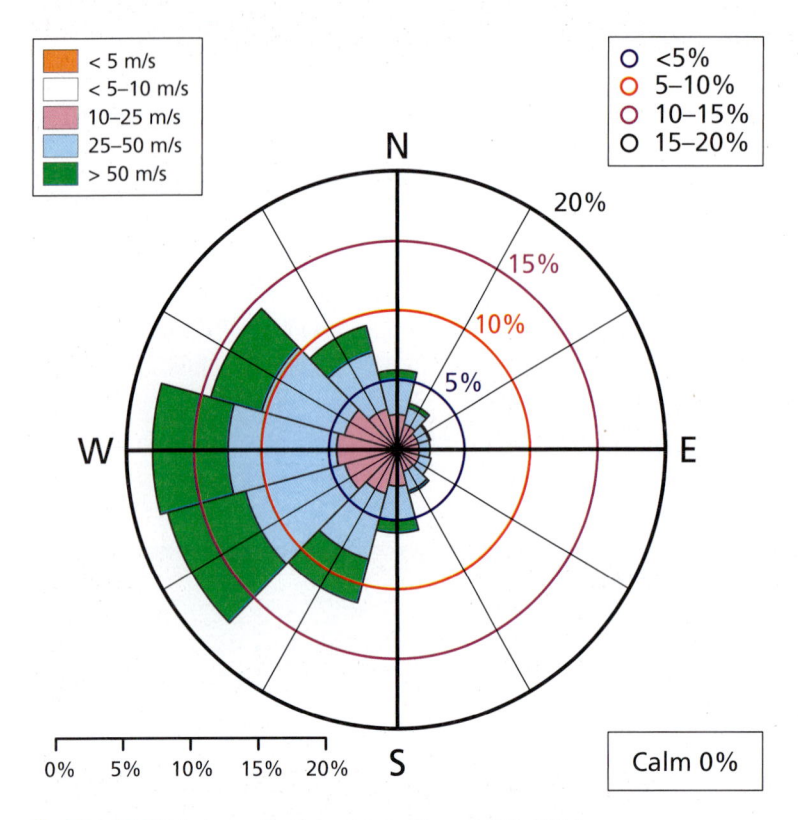

↑ **Fig. 14.7** Wind rose for Valentia, Co. Kerry, 1980–2010.

CHECK YOUR LEARNING

Study the wind rose diagram in Fig. 14.7 and answer the following questions.

1. What is the approximate percentage of time the wind blows from the north?
2. What is the maximum speed reached by this wind?
3. What is the frequency of the east wind at this station?
4. What percentage of the time was the speed of the west wind between 10 and 25 m/s?
5. What is the percentage calm?

Wind radar charts

The chart for each weather station has eight cardinal points, and shows (a) the direction the wind is blowing from and (b) its frequency. By measuring the length of each spoke against the scale of frequency, the percentage time for each wind can be calculated. Data at the centre of the charts records the percentage of calm.

The chart in **Figure 14.8** reveals the following:

- at Dublin Airport, the most frequent wind comes from the west, and blows for about 20% of the time;
- at Malin Head, the southerly wind is the most frequent, blowing for 18% of the time;
- at Claremorris, the north-easterly wind is the least frequent, blowing for 5% of the time.

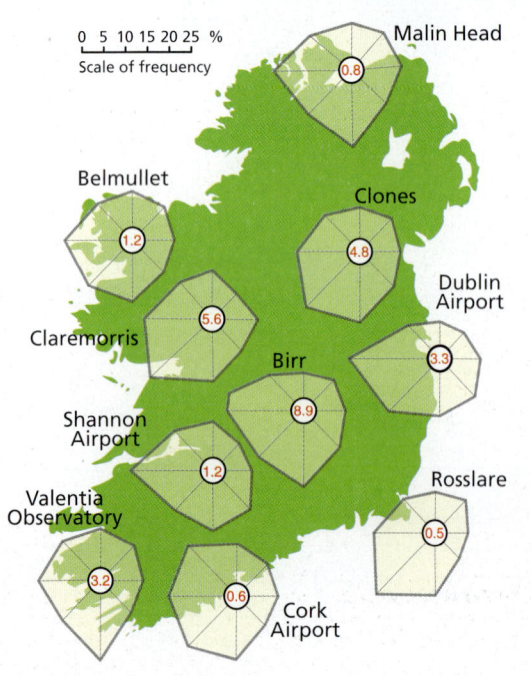

↑ **Fig. 14.8** Wind radar charts for Ireland (averages).

216

14 Weather Maps and Satellite Imagery

CHECK YOUR LEARNING

1. Use the data from the wind radar chart in Figure 14.8 to answer the following questions.
   a. Which is the least frequent wind at Dublin Airport?
   b. What is its percentage?
   c. What is the percentage calm at Birr?
   d. Which station has the lowest calm percentage?
   e. What is the most frequent wind at Shannon Airport?

Pressure charts

1 | 2 | 3

Cloud charts

A | B | C

2. Copy the table below into your copybook and, using the letters, match the correct cloud chart to the pressure chart.

Pressure chart	Cloud chart
1	
2	
3	

3. Study pressure charts 1, 2 and 3 and answer the following questions:

   Chart 1
   a. Give the pressure reading for the low-pressure area to the south-west of Ireland.
   b. What type of front is located over the east of Ireland?
   c. Is Ireland experiencing wet or dry weather? Explain your answer.

   Chart 2
   d. What is the barometric pressure for the anticyclone to north-west of Ireland?
   e. Identify the type of front located to the south of Ireland.

   Chart 3
   f. Are wind speeds high or low over Ireland? Give a reason for your answer.
   g. Is Ireland experiencing wet or dry weather? Explain your answer.

Landscapes

KEYWORDS

mapping
environmental impact
disaster response
Geographic information systems (GIS)

Satellite Imagery

Earth-orbiting satellites capture high-quality images of our planet which are transmitted back to earth where they are analysed and interpreted. While government agencies such as NASA and European agencies such as EUMETSAT play a huge role in this area, an increase in the use of satellite imagery has seen more commercial enterprises becoming involved. Apps such as Google Earth have led to the increased use of satellite imagery in our daily lives.

Uses of satellite imagery

Information gained from satellite imagery has many applications.

Physical landscape

Satellite images can provide us with unique views of features of the physical landscape.

↑ **Fig. 14.9** Glaciers, British Columbia, Canada.

↑ **Fig. 14.10** Lacustrine delta, River Don, Russia.

↑ **Fig. 14.11** Meanders, Amazon River, Peru.

↑ **Fig. 14.12** Mount Vesuvius and Naples.

218

14 Weather Maps and Satellite Imagery

Environmental impact of human activity

Images captured by satellites also provide evidence of the environmental impact of human activity.

← **Fig. 14.13** Toxic mud after dam collapse, Rio Doce, Brazil, 2015.

↓ **Fig. 14.14** Kiribati, Pacific Ocean, effects of rising sea level.

↑ **Fig. 14.15** Open-cast mining, Carajás, Brazil.

↑ **Fig. 14.16** Soil erosion due to rainforest removal, Indonesia.

Landscapes

Meteorology

In meteorology, satellite imagery is used to predict and track major weather events such as hurricanes.

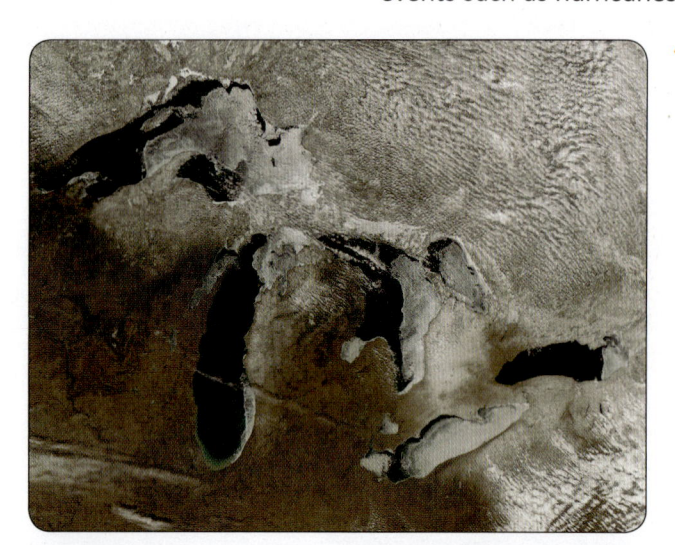

← **Fig. 14.17** Winter ice on the Great Lakes, USA.

↓ **Fig. 14.18** Hurricane Ignacio, 2015.

← **Fig. 14.19** Intense low-pressure system tracking towards Ireland.

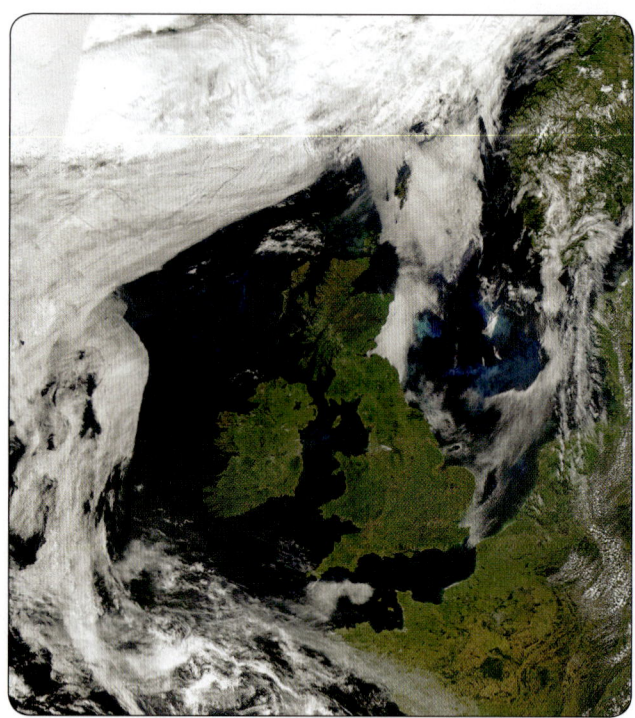

↓ **Fig. 14.20** Anticyclone over Ireland, 27 June 2018.

Human impact on the landscape

An important function of satellite images is to clearly show the impact humans have had on the natural landscape through various activities, including construction and agriculture.

→ **Fig. 14.21** Solar panels, California.

14 Weather Maps and Satellite Imagery

← **Fig. 14.22** Centre pivot irrigation, Saudi Arabia.

↓ **Fig. 14.23** Deforestation, Amazon Basin.

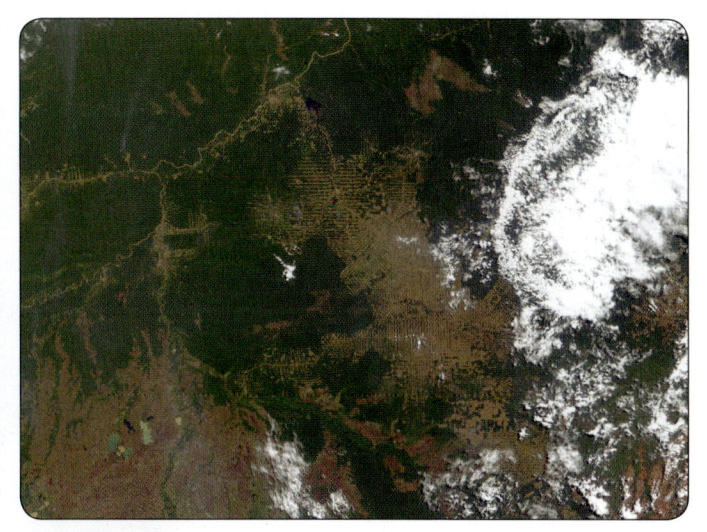

← **Fig. 14.24** Dallas/Fort Worth International Airport.

Natural disasters

Satellite imagery can provide real-time information to agencies responding to natural disasters. They can show the extent of earthquake damage to buildings, roads and bridges, as well as the extent of flooding and the progress of wild fires. This information helps to inform the type of response from these agencies, such as evacuations, use of helicopters and emergency shelter provision.

↓ **Fig. 14.26** Flooding on the River Elbe, Germany.

↓ **Fig. 14.25** Ash flow, Sinabung volcano, Indonesia.

221

Landscapes

↑ **Fig. 14.27** Landslide caused by earthquake, Nepal, 2015.

↑ **Fig. 14.28** Wildfires, California, 2018.

CHECK YOUR LEARNING

Study the images below and match them to the corresponding descriptions.

A B C D

E F G H

Description	Image
Sahara dust	
Deforestation	
Melting ice sheets	
Urban area	

Description	Image
The Alps and northern Italy	
Erupting volcano	
Open-cast mining	
Landslide	

Geographic information systems (GIS)

Geographic information systems are computer-based systems that store different types of data. The data can be collected from a variety of sources including satellite photographs, aerial photographs, maps, census data, environmental data and archaeological data. This data can be used to generate different data themes or layers, for example, streets, land use, topography or administrative areas, which are then combined to create a composite, layered map of specific areas (Fig. 14.29).

Hydrography: The study and plotting of rivers, lakes and seas.

Applications

The government is a major user of GIS. It uses them to, among other things, monitor land use and assist in urban planning. Retail outlets use GIS to access data on population to help decide on locations for new units, while utility companies that provide water, gas and electricity use GIS to monitor their networks and identify issues with supply.

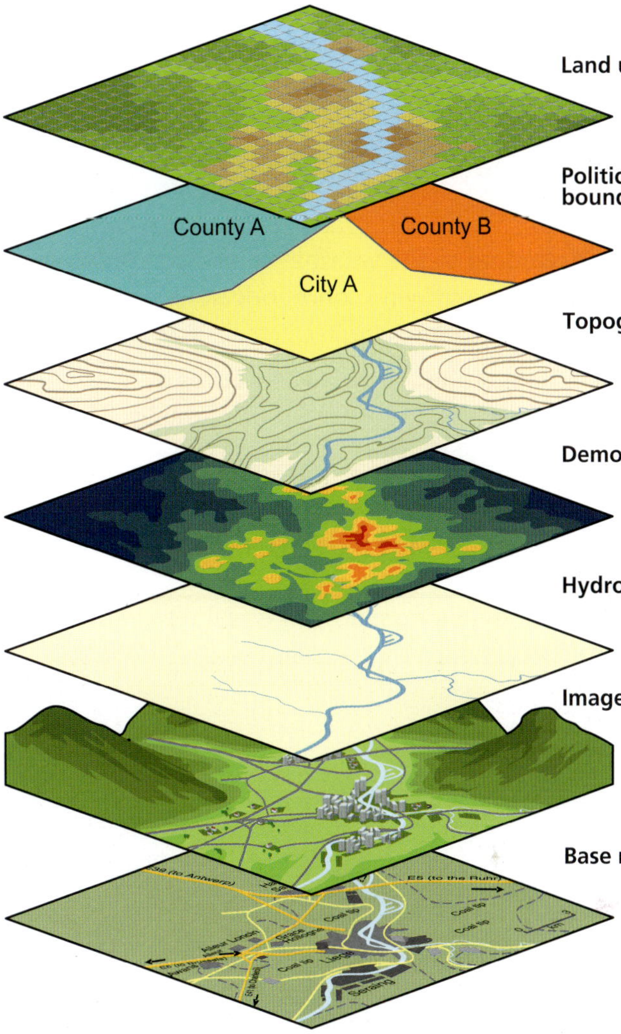
Land use
Political/administrative boundaries
County A
County B
City A
Topography
Demographics
Hydrography
Imagery
Base map

→ Fig. 14.29 A GIS map is created using different layers of data.

Advantages of GIS	Disadvantages of GIS
• Data can be easily updated, e.g. new census data. • Data is easily accessible: maps can be accessed on mobile devices such as smartphones.	• A large amount of data input can be needed for some tasks, which increases the possibility of input errors. • Due to the technical nature of the system, users may regard it as totally reliable and this can lead to results not being fully scrutinised.

GIS and Ireland

The Environmental Protection Agency (EPA) website (www.epa.ie) – contains GIS **mapping** that provides data on topics including protected areas, ground water quality and bathing water quality.

Myplan.ie is a mapping initiative of the Department of Housing, Planning and Local Government. It contains information on a variety of themes including administrative boundaries, planning, census population data and flood mapping.

Landscapes

EXAMINATION QUESTIONS
ORDINARY LEVEL

Short Questions

1. Weather

Examine the weather chart and answer each of the following questions.

(i) What is the barometric pressure (in hectopascals/millibars) to the north of Spain? *2 marks*

(ii) Draw the weather chart symbol for a warm front. *2 marks*

(iii) According to the weather chart, what type of wind conditions is Ireland experiencing? *2 marks*

(iv) Complete the following sentences by inserting the correct word from the list below in each case.

isotherms   isohyets

(a) Lines joining places of equal rainfall on a weather chart are called _____. *2 marks*

(b) Lines joining places of equal temperature on a weather chart are called _____. *2 marks*

2017, Part One, Q11 (10 marks)

2. Weather Charts

(i) Match each of the weather chart symbols with the feature of weather that best matches it, by writing the correct letter. *4 × 2 marks*

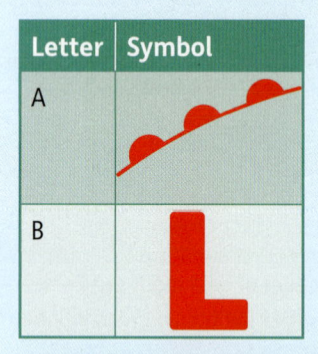

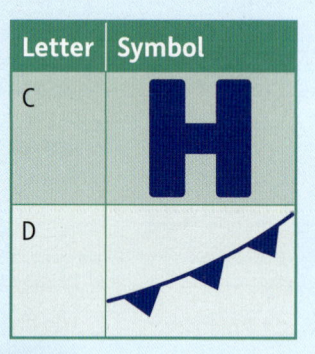

Letter	Symbol
A	(warm front symbol)
B	L

Letter	Symbol
C	H
D	(cold front symbol)

Feature of Weather	Letter
High-pressure system	
Cold front	
Low-pressure system	
Warm front	

(ii) Indicate whether the following statement is true or false, by circling the correct option.

Isotherms are lines that join places of equal temperature on a weather chart. *2 marks*

True   False

2016, Part One, Q7 (10 marks)

14 Weather Maps and Satellite Imagery

HIGHER LEVEL

Short Questions

3. Weather

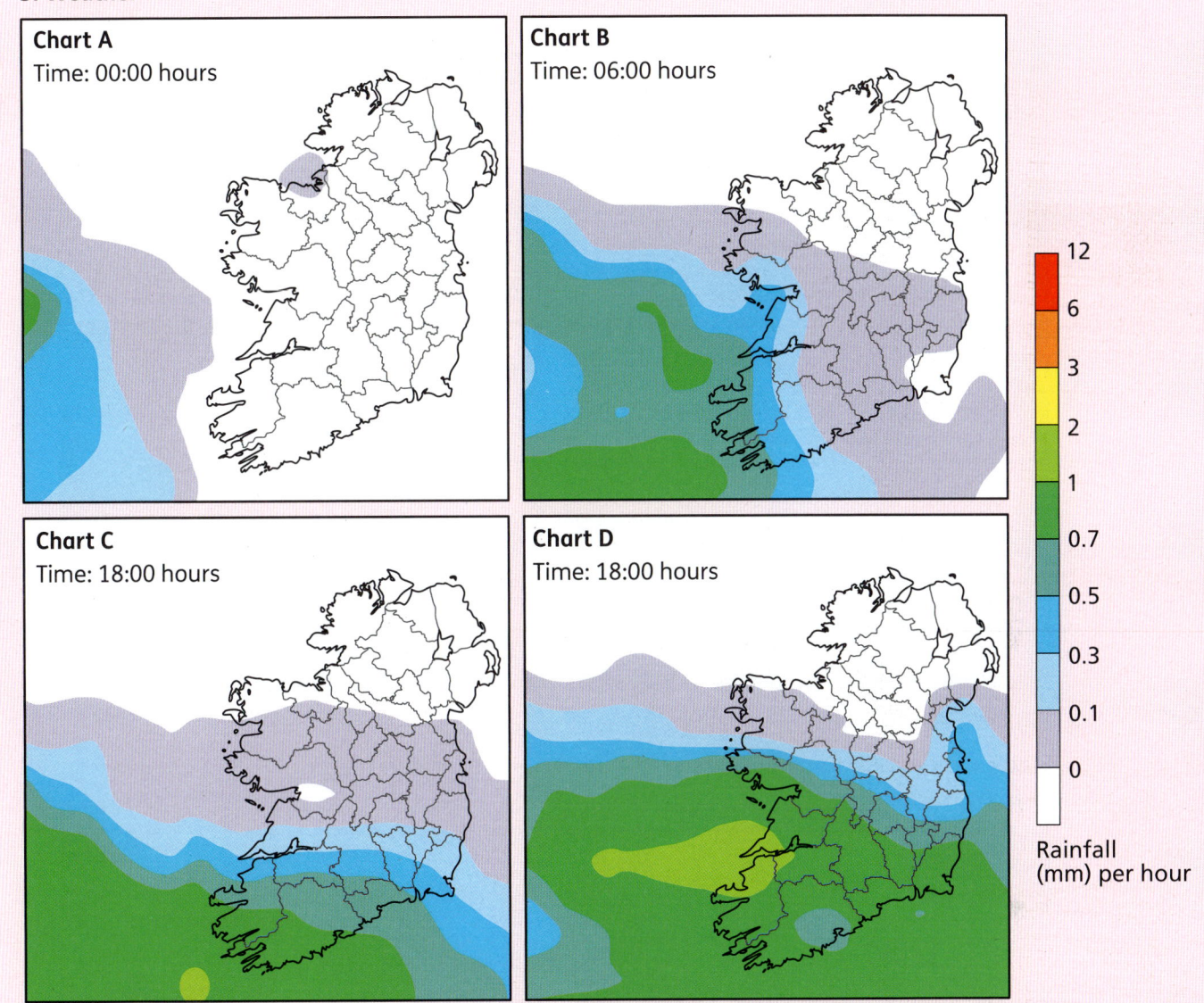

Chart A Time: 00:00 hours

Chart B Time: 06:00 hours

Chart C Time: 18:00 hours

Chart D Time: 18:00 hours

Rainfall (mm) per hour

Examine the rainfall forecast charts for a period from 00:00 hours to 18:00 hours and answer each of the following questions.

(i) Which province is forecast to receive the least amount of rainfall over the period?   *2 marks*

(ii) Indicate whether the following statement is true or false by circling the correct option.
 2 marks

   Rainfall is spreading from the south-east at 06:00 hours.   True   False   *2 marks*

(iii) Is rainfall most associated with anticyclones or depressions?   *2 marks*

(iv) What term is used to describe lines on a weather map joining places of equal rainfall?
 2 marks

2017, Part One, Q10 (8 marks)

225

Landscapes

4. Weather Charts

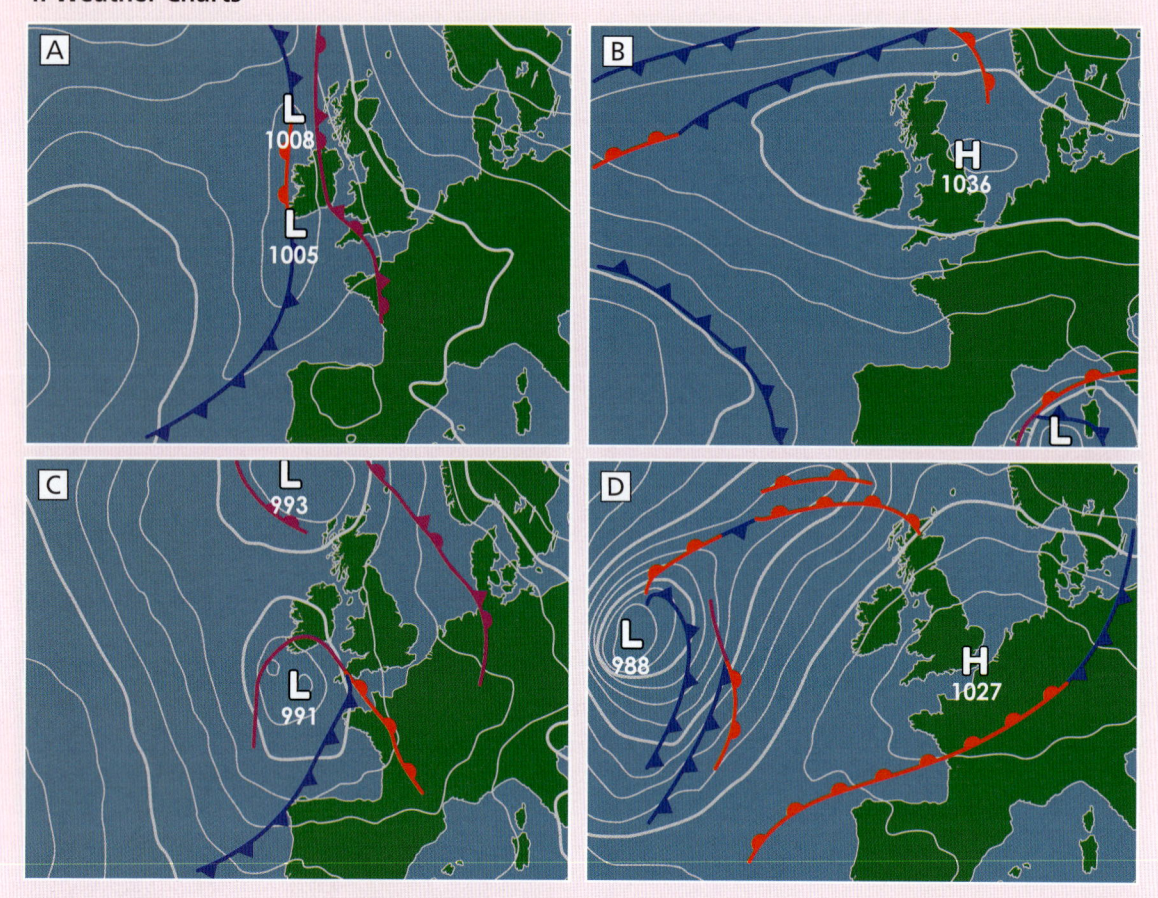

Examine the weather charts above and the cloud charts below.

Match each of the weather charts A, B, C and D with the cloud chart (i), (ii), (iii), (iv) most associated with it.

4 × 2 marks

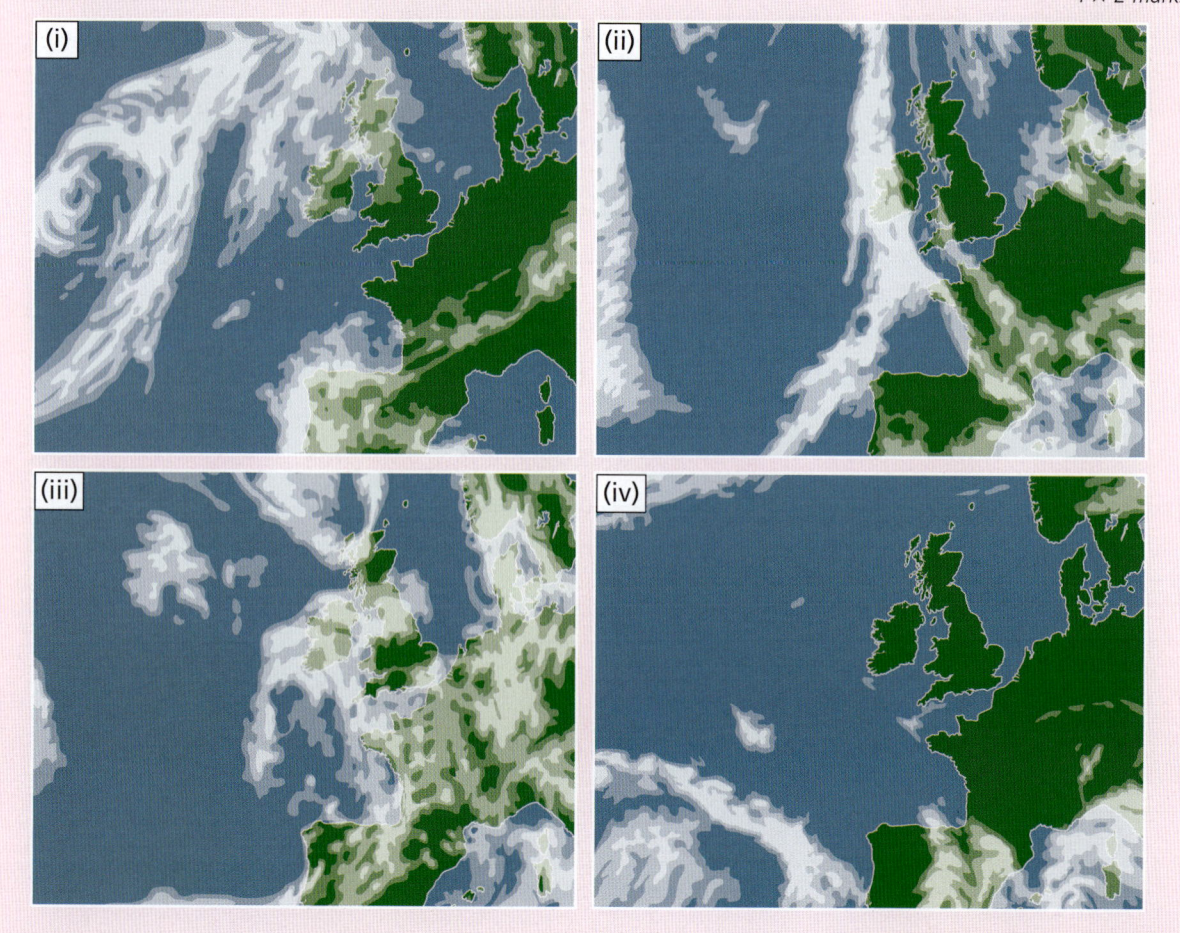

2016, Part One, Q9 (8 marks)

Revision Summary

Weather forecast

Necessity of forecasting
- Farmers, fishermen, pilots, shipping
- **Electricity companies:** prepare for power outages caused by storms
- **Local authorities:** flood protection, gritting and salting roads

Factors influencing Irish weather
- Air masses
- Depressions
- Anticyclones

Weather charts

Depression
- Forms along polar front
- Low pressure cell
- Moves from west to east
- Quick passage
- Wind direction anticlockwise
- Frontal rain
- SECTOR 1: Warm front
  - Cloud cover increases
  - Continuous rain
- SECTOR 2: Centre of depression
- SECTOR 3: Cold front
  - Heavy showers
  - Frontal rain
  - Occlusion
  - Occluded front

Anticyclone
- High pressure cell
- Stable, lasts many days
- Air sinking
- Clear skies
  - Summer: warm, dry weather
  - Winter: cold dry, weather – fog sometimes
- Well-spaced isobars indicate calm conditions

Synoptic charts
- Warm front symbol
- Cold front symbol
- Occluded front symbol
- Isobars: showing pressure – measured in hectopascals – four-hPa intervals
- Winds blow parallel to isobars
- Close isobar pattern indicates strong winds

Wind rose
- Frequency of wind direction
- Wind speed
- For a particular location
- For a given time period

Wind radar
- Direction wind is blowing from
- Most frequent winds
- Least frequent winds

Satellite imagery

Uses of satellite imagery
- Physical landscape: oxbow lakes
- Impact of human activities on the environment: open-cast mining
- Meteorology: hurricane paths
- Human impact on landscape: solar panels
- Natural disasters: California wildfires

Geographical information systems
- Computer based
- Using different sets of data sources: aerial and satellite photographs – census data – maps – administrative data – archaeological data – environmental data
- Layered maps created
- Uses: governments – commercial
- Advantage: Easy to update new data
- Disadvantage: Volume of data input can lead to errors

15 GRAPH SKILLS

KEYWORDS
bar chart
x-axis
y-axis
stacked bar chart
pie chart
trend graph
climograph
scatter graph
triangle graphs
choropleth maps

LEARNING INTENTIONS
Syllabus Link: 3

At the end of this chapter I will be able to:
- analyse and interpret data contained in graphs;
- create a graph from given data;
- apply graph skills in the presentation of data in a geographical investigation;
- understand that care and accuracy are important to ensure maximum marks are earned;
- ensure all graphs are constructed on graph paper.

When you're drawing a graph, remember to add SALT:
- **S** Is the **s**cale suitable?
- **A** Are the **a**xis intervals equal?
- **L** Are both axes **l**abelled?
- **T** Have you **t**itled the graph?

EXAM TIP
Poor and incorrect labelling of axes on the graph work was noted both in the Geographical Investigation Report and in the written examination paper and was identified as an area of weakness for many students.

Graphs are used to present data in visual form, making it easier to interpret. Graphs can illustrate many different types of data, show trends over time and allow data comparisons to be made.

Types of Graph

Bar chart

A **bar chart** displays data in separate columns (**Fig. 15.1**). It is the most frequently used method for answering examination questions requiring students to draw graphs to display data.

Guidelines for drawing a bar chart:
- they must be drawn on graph paper;
- always use a ruler to ensure straight lines;
- draw and label the **x and y axes**;
- plot the data, making sure that columns are straight and of equal width;
- columns can be coloured/shaded;
- give the chart a title based on the information it contains.

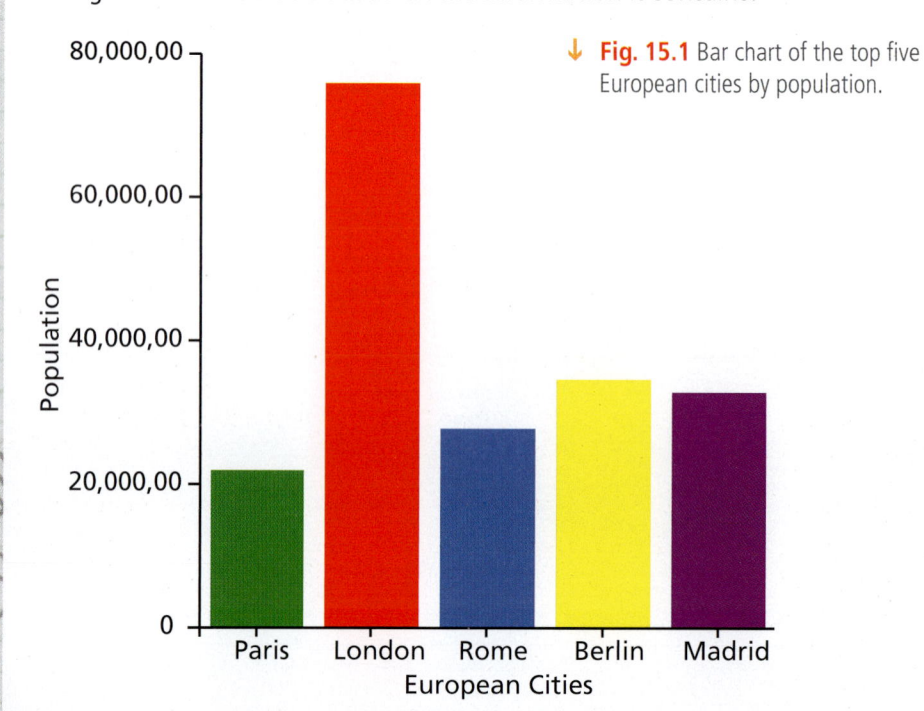

↓ **Fig. 15.1** Bar chart of the top five European cities by population.

228

Stacked bar chart

A **stacked bar chart** is used to display a variety of data, for example, energy consumption by sector, waste disposal by method or agricultural exports by type (**Fig. 15.2**). These graphs allow comparisons to be made between the different data parts. Too many categories, however, can make it difficult to identify patterns.

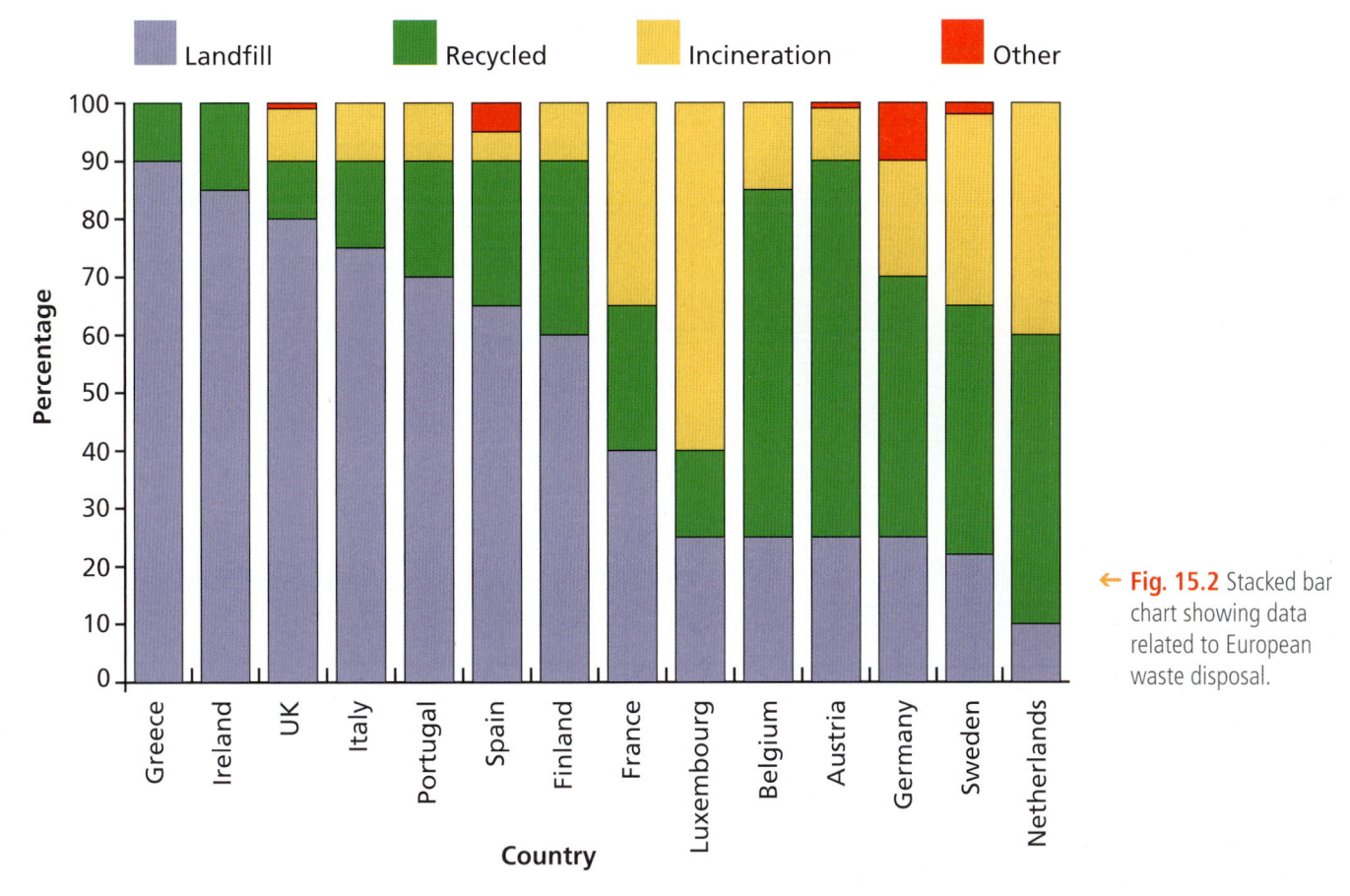

← **Fig. 15.2** Stacked bar chart showing data related to European waste disposal.

CHECK YOUR LEARNING

Examine the bar chart in Figure 15.2 above, which shows the methods used for the disposal of waste by a number of European countries, and answer the following questions.

1. Which country sent 60% of its waste to landfill?
2. Which country recycled the largest percentage of its waste? (Name the country and the percentage).
3. Which country incinerated the largest percentage of its waste? (Name the country and the percentage).

Pie charts

Pie charts are circular charts whose sectors show the proportions of a data set, for example, primary, secondary and tertiary economic activities.

How to construct a pie chart

Construction of pie charts involves calculating the number of degrees that are needed to represent the different data categories.

1. If the data is not already in percentage format, calculate the percentages.
2. Convert percentages into degrees by multiplying by 3.6. For example, if one segment of the chart was worth 90% of the total, the sum would be:
   90 × 3.6 = 324° (**Fig. 15.3**).

EXAM TIP

Remember, when using pie charts to present data in the Geographical Investigation, the compass perforation must show on the page in the report booklet.

Landscapes

3. Use a compass to draw a suitably-sized circle, and then use a protractor to mark out the degree segments for each category. Remember to shift the protractor to zero again after each segment!
4. Label each segment with the percentage data.
5. Colour or shade the separate segments as appropriate.

Example

The table below shows the proportions of energy consumed by different sectors in Ireland.

Type	%		Degrees
Transport	41		148
Residential	27	× 3.6 =	58
Industry	16		97
Services	14		50
Agriculture	2		7

To display the data in a pie chart format, the percentages must be converted to degrees. You multiply the value for each sector by 3.6 to give the number of degrees it will need on the pie chart.

The different values/sectors can then be transferred onto a circle to create a pie chart. (Fig. 15.4)

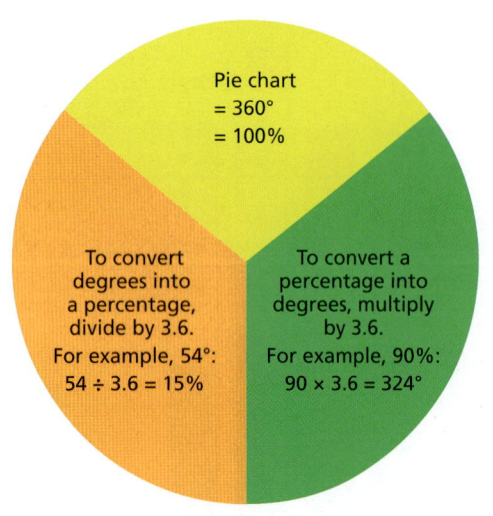

Pie chart
= 360°
= 100%

To convert degrees into a percentage, divide by 3.6. For example, 54°: 54 ÷ 3.6 = 15%

To convert a percentage into degrees, multiply by 3.6. For example, 90%: 90 × 3.6 = 324°

↑ **Fig. 15.3** Constructing a pie chart.

SKILLS ACTIVITY

Construct a pie chart to illustrate the data in this table.

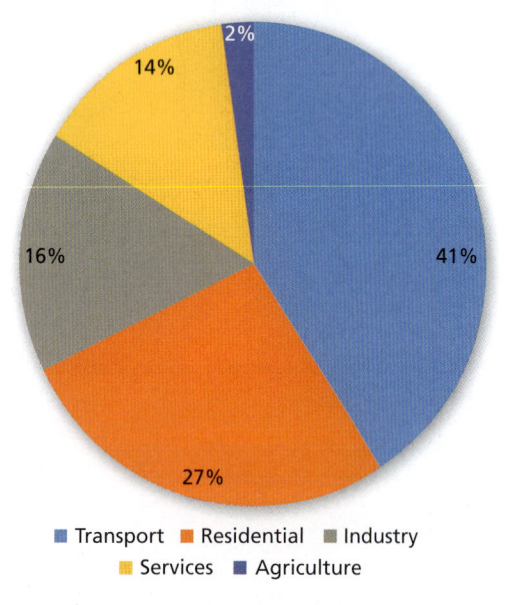

Overseas Visitors to Ireland 2016	
Source Area	**%**
Great Britain	42
Mainland Europe	35
North America	17
Rest of World	6

↑ **Fig. 15.4** Sample pie chart.

■ Transport ■ Residential ■ Industry
■ Services ■ Agriculture

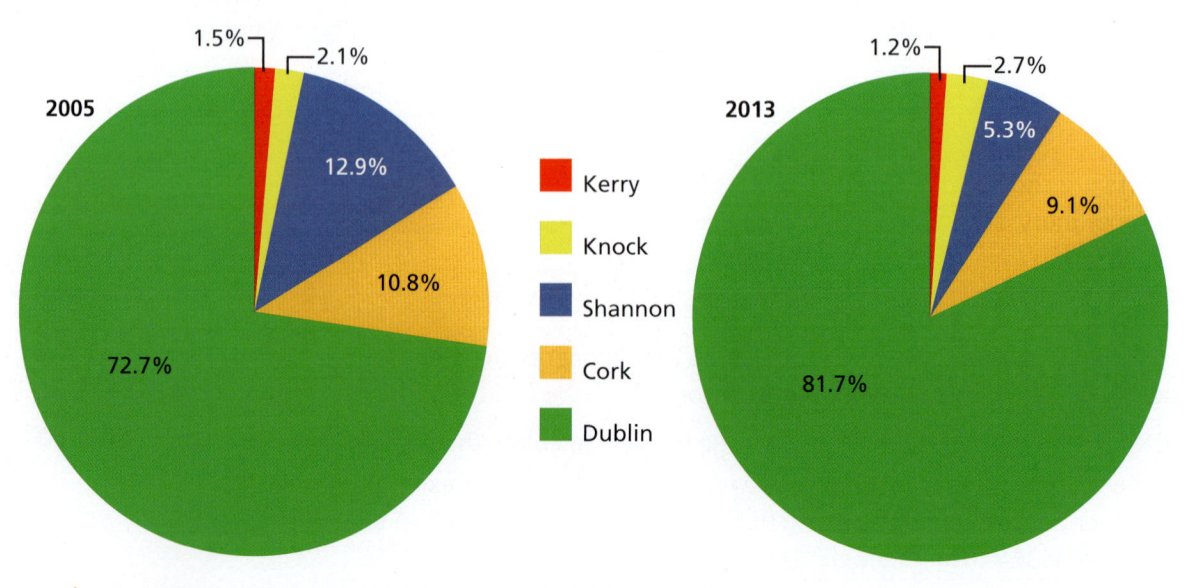

2005: 72.7%, 10.8%, 12.9%, 2.1%, 1.5%
2013: 81.7%, 9.1%, 5.3%, 2.7%, 1.2%

■ Kerry
■ Knock
■ Shannon
■ Cork
■ Dublin

↑ **Fig. 15.5** Percentage share of total passengers for Irish airports 2005 and 2013.

15 Graph Skills

CHECK YOUR LEARNING

Examine the pie charts in Figure 15.5 above showing the percentage share of total passengers by airport in Ireland in 2005 and 2013, and answer each of the following questions.

1. Which airport had the largest percentage share of total passengers in 2013?
2. Which airport had the second largest percentage share of total passengers in 2005?
3. Calculate the decrease in Shannon Airport's percentage share of total passengers between 2005 and 2013.
4. Explain briefly one economic effect of a decrease in passenger numbers at Shannon Airport on the Shannon Region.

Trend (line) graph

Trend – or line – graphs show patterns or trends in data over time. They can include a variety of categories, for example, population data: birth rates, death rates, life expectancy rates (**Fig. 15.6**).

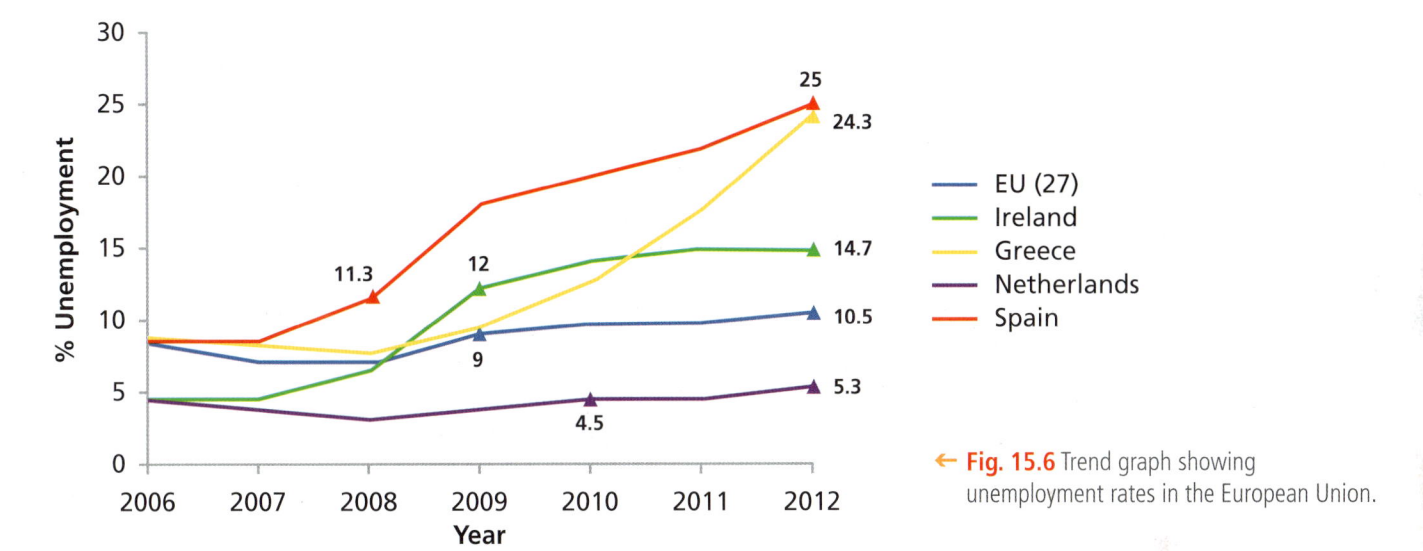

← Fig. 15.6 Trend graph showing unemployment rates in the European Union.

CHECK YOUR LEARNING

Examine the trend graph in Figure 15.6 above and answer each of the following questions.

1. Which country had the highest percentage unemployment between 2008 and 2012 and which country had the lowest percentage unemployment between 2008 and 2012?
2. Which country had the most significant increase in percentage unemployment between 2010 and 2012?
3. Name two countries where the percentage unemployment decreased between 2006 and 2007.
4. Calculate the increase in the percentage unemployment in the EU (27) between 2009 and 2012 and state one reason for this increase.

EXAM TIP

Answers to questions on graphs should include the data, e.g. in questions 1, 2 and 3 you should name the country **and** give the percentage.

Landscapes

Climograph

A **climograph** is a graph that combines precipitation and temperature data of a selected station for an extended period of time (**Fig. 15.7**). Precipitation is represented by a bar chart, while a line graph is used to represent temperature data.

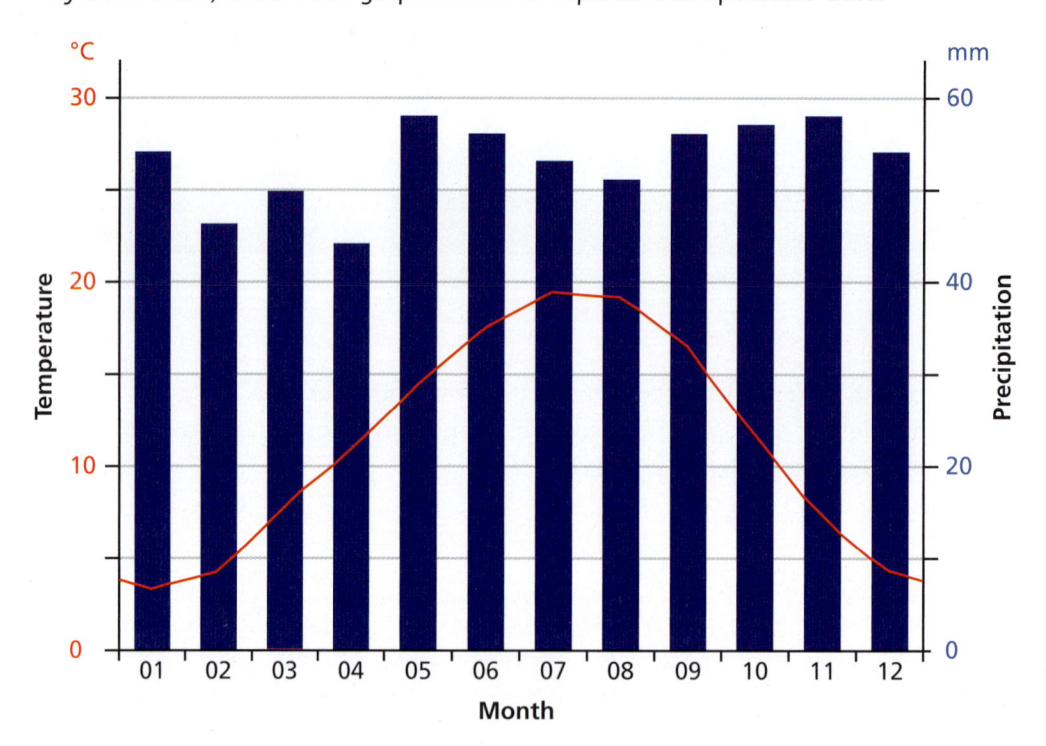

→ **Fig. 15.7** Climograph for Paris, 2015.

CHECK YOUR LEARNING

Examine the climograph in Figure 15.7 above and answer each of the following questions.

1. Which month recorded the lowest average temperature? (Name the month and state the temperature).
2. Which month recorded the highest average temperature? (Name the month and state the temperature).
3. What was the total annual rainfall amount for Paris for 2014?
4. What was the annual temperature range for 2014?
5. Which months recorded average temperatures above 15°C?

Temperature range: The difference between the highest and lowest recorded temperatures in a given data set.

Scatter graph

A **scatter graph** is used to show the relationship (correlation) between two data sets. A positive correlation sees both factors moving in the same direction, as in **Figure 15.8**. In the example, as the GDP (gross domestic product) per capita increases, so too does the life expectancy rate, suggesting a positive correlation. A negative correlation would see the values on the y-axis decrease as those on the x-axis increase.

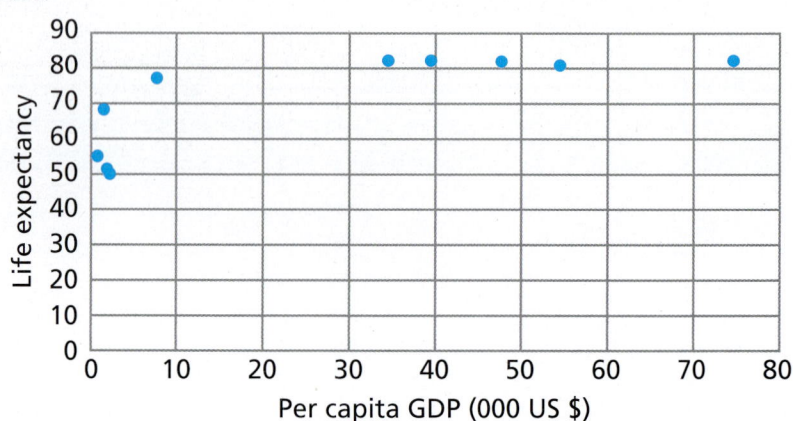

→ **Fig. 15.8** Scatter graph showing the relationship between GDP and life expectancy.

15 Graph Skills

Triangle graph

A **triangle graph** is used to show the relationship between three different components. It consists of three axes, divided into 100 intervals representing percentage values, forming an equilateral triangle. Lines are drawn at angles of 60° from each axis. This type of graph is usually used to show soil composition data (**Fig. 15.9**), but they have other applications including population analysis.

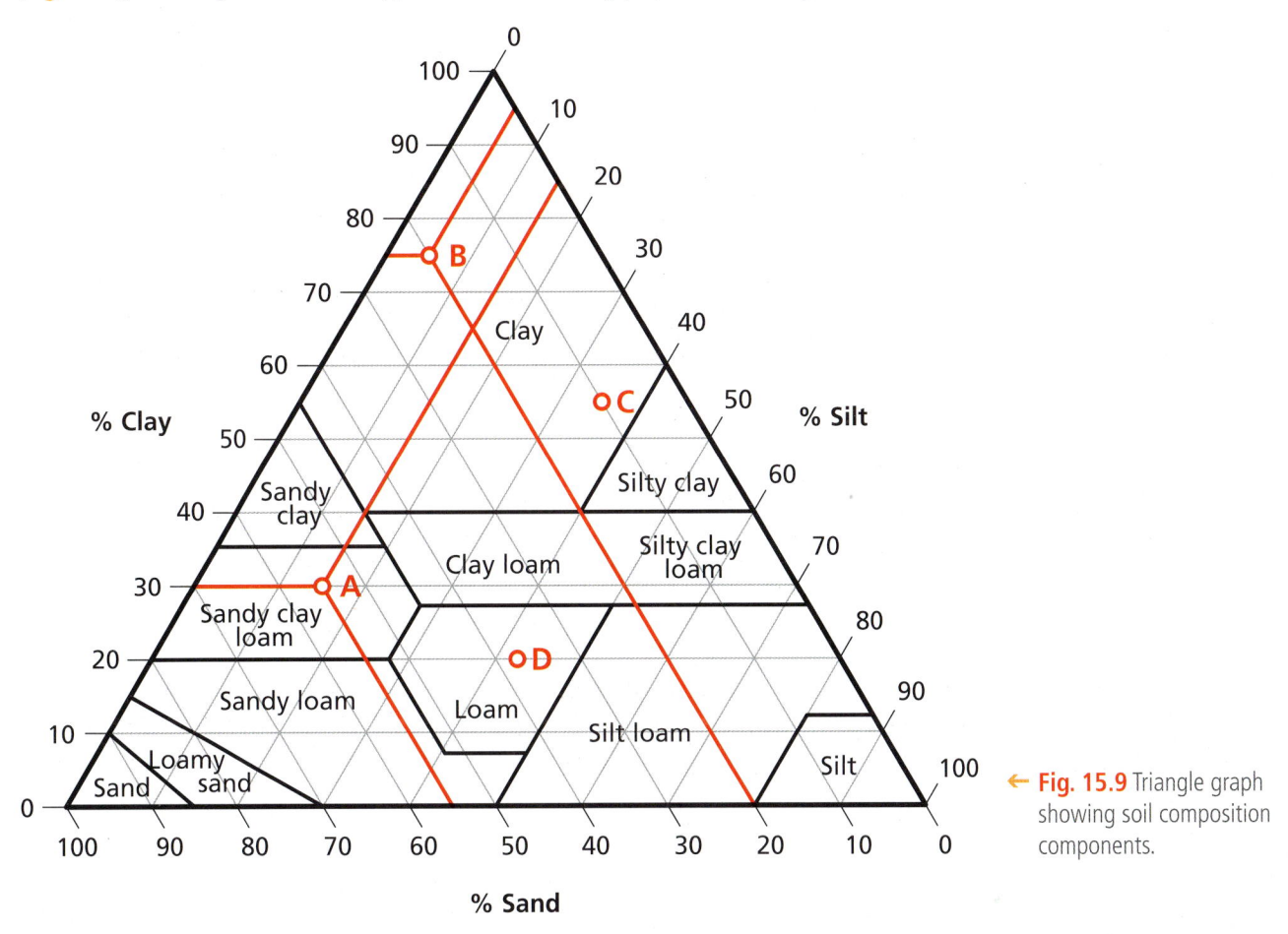

← Fig. 15.9 Triangle graph showing soil composition components.

To read triangle graphs: start with the left axis, find the value and then moving in an anticlockwise direction find the values along the other two axes. **Figure 15.9**, for example, shows the respective compositions of two soil samples, A and B.

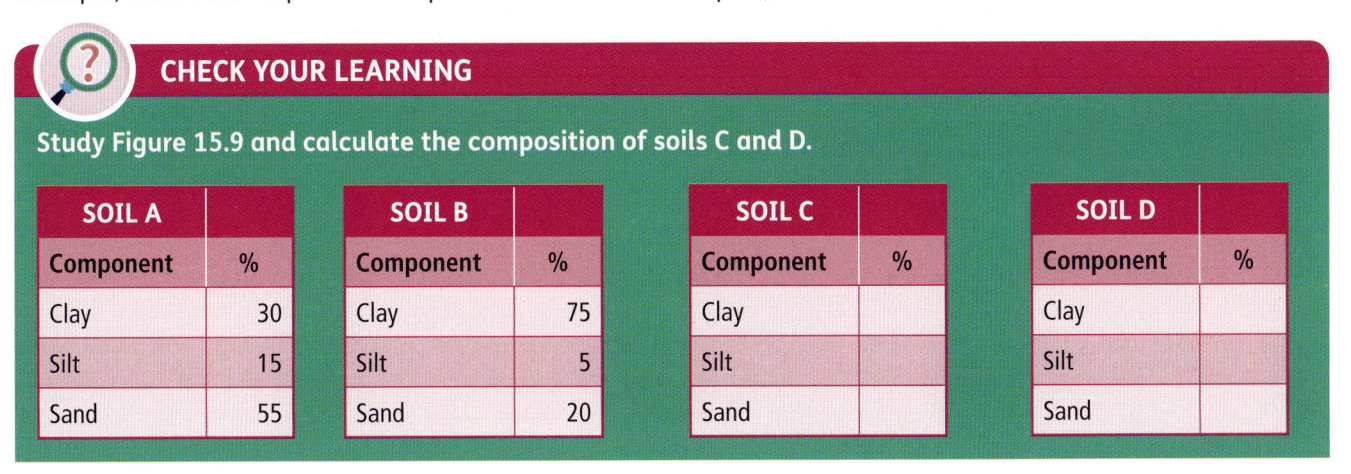

CHECK YOUR LEARNING

Study Figure 15.9 and calculate the composition of soils C and D.

SOIL A	
Component	%
Clay	30
Silt	15
Sand	55

SOIL B	
Component	%
Clay	75
Silt	5
Sand	20

SOIL C	
Component	%
Clay	
Silt	
Sand	

SOIL D	
Component	%
Clay	
Silt	
Sand	

233

Landscapes

EXAM TIP

The Chief Examiner's Report (2012) encourages teachers to provide opportunities for students to interpret and use information from various stimuli, for example, charts, diagrams, tables, maps of various scales, etc.

Choropleth maps

Choropleth maps use shading or colour to show variations in data. A legend or key provides information relating to the data. These maps are widely used in demographic studies where they show components of population change (**Fig. 15.10**).

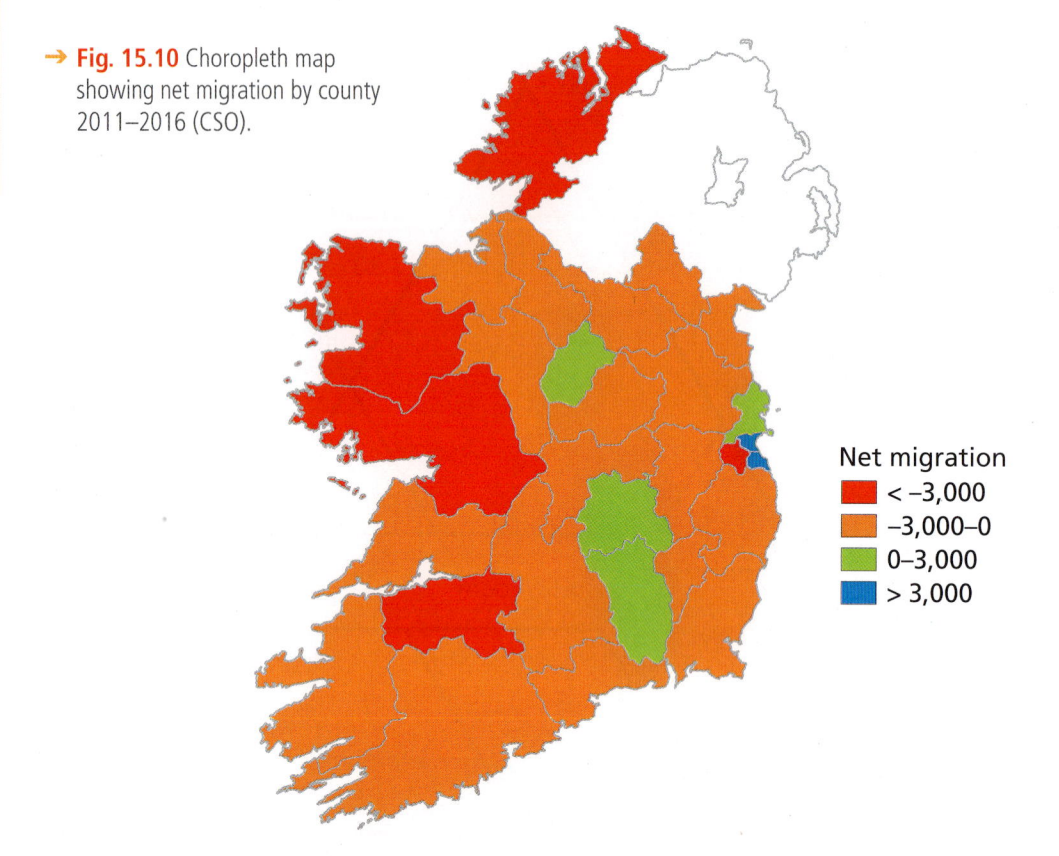

→ **Fig. 15.10** Choropleth map showing net migration by county 2011–2016 (CSO).

Net migration
- < –3,000
- –3,000–0
- 0–3,000
- > 3,000

CHECK YOUR LEARNING

Examine the map in Figure 15.10 above and answer each of the following questions.

1. Name any two counties that experienced net out-migration greater than 3,000 persons.
2. Name any two counties that experienced net in-migration.

234

EXAMINATION QUESTIONS
ORDINARY LEVEL

Short Questions

1. Economic Activities

Primary, Secondary and Tertiary Economic Activities in Ireland, Brazil and Nepal

Examine the chart and answer each of the following questions.

(i) Which country has the highest percentage of primary economic activities? *2 marks*

(ii) Calculate the total percentage of primary and secondary economic activities combined in Brazil. *2 marks*

(iii) Which of the three countries, Ireland, Brazil or Nepal, has the most developed economy? *2 marks*

(iv) State whether each of the following is an example of a primary, secondary or tertiary economic activity. *2 × 2 marks*

Teaching   Fishing

2016, Part One, Q9 (10 marks)

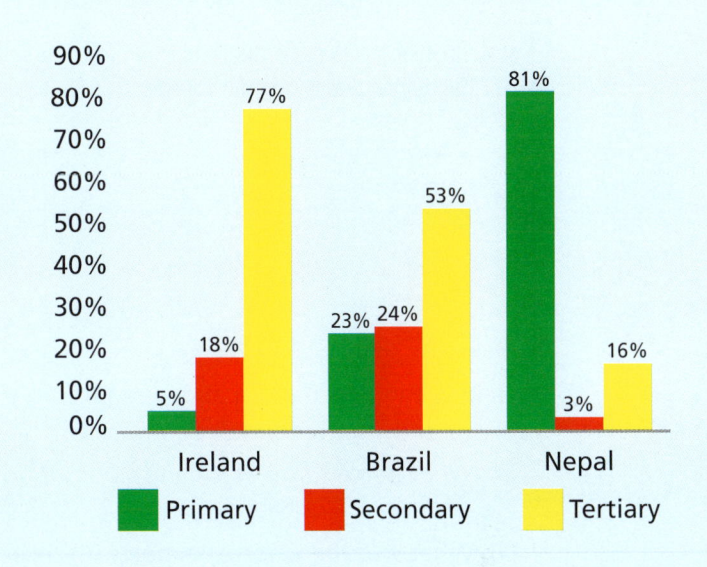

2. Symbol Recognition and Scale

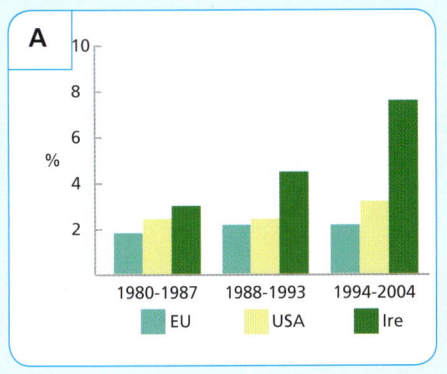

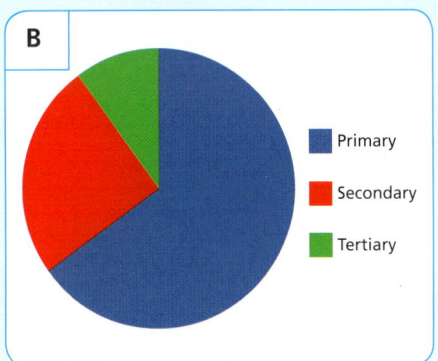

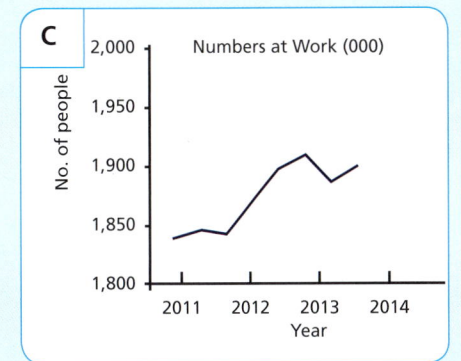

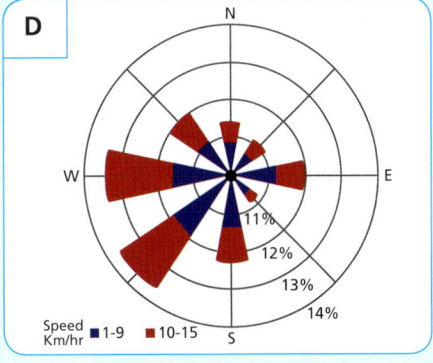

Title	Letter
Pie chart	
Wind rose	
Bar chart	
Trend graph	

(i) Match each statistical chart with the most suitable title in the table above, by writing the correct letter in each case. *4 × 2 marks*

(ii) State one advantage of using a graph to present information. *2 marks*

2015, Part One, Q11 (10 marks)

Long Questions

3. Agriculture in Ireland

Irish Agri-food and Drink Sector
- The agri-food and drink sector accounts for 12.3% of exports and 8.6% of employment.
- In 2015, agri-food and drink exports increased by an estimated 3% to €10.8 billion.
- 4.5 million hectares of land is use for agriculture and a further 730,000 hectares is used for forestry.

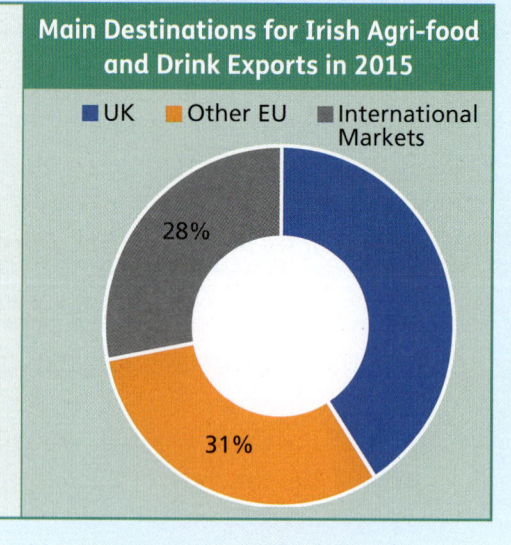

Main Destinations for Irish Agri-food and Drink Exports in 2015
- UK
- Other EU
- International Markets

28%, 31%

Examine the information above regarding the Irish agri-food and drink sector in 2015 and answer each of the following questions.

(i) What percentage of Ireland's population is employed in the agri-food and drink sector?
3 marks

(ii) What was the value of exports (€) from the Irish agri-food and drink sector in 2015? *3 marks*

(iii) Calculate **X**, the percentage of Irish agri-food and drink exported to the UK in 2015. *6 marks*

(iv) How many hectares of land is used for agriculture and how many hectares of land is used for forestry?
3 + 3 marks

(v) Explain briefly one advantage of European Union membership for Ireland's agri-food and drink sector.
2 SRPs × 3 marks

(vi) Explain briefly one disadvantage of European Union membership for Ireland's agri-food and drink sector.
2 SRPs × 3 marks

2017, Part Two, Section 1, Q5A (30 marks)

4. Tourism in Ireland

Examine the chart showing information regarding popular Irish tourist attractions in 2013 and answer each of the following questions.

- National Botanic Gardens: 550,000
- Book of Kells: 588,723
- National Gallery of Ireland: 641,572
- Cliffs of Moher Visitor Experience: 960,134
- Dublin Zoo: 1,026,611
- Guinness Storehouse: 1,157,900
- National Aquatic Centre: 858,031
- Tayto Park: 435,000
- National Museum of Ireland – Archaeology: 404,230
- Fota Wildlife Park: 365,396

(i) Name the two most popular Irish tourist attractions in 2013.
2 × 3 marks

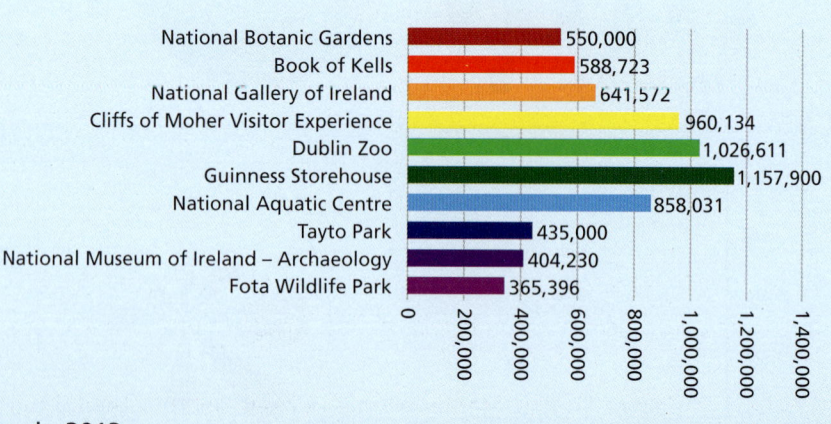

(ii) Name the tourist attraction with the least number of visitors and state how many visitors it received.
3 + 3 marks

(iii) Calculate the difference between the number of tourists that visited the National Botanic Gardens and the number that visited Tayto Park in 2013.
6 marks

(iv) Explain briefly one positive effect of tourism on Ireland.
2 SRPs × 3 marks

(v) Explain briefly one negative effect of tourism on Ireland
2 SRPs × 3 marks

2016, Part Two, Section 1, Q6A (30 marks)

15 Graph Skills

HIGHER LEVEL

Short Questions

5. Graphical Interpretation

Examine the chart, which shows the consumption of renewable energy in the European Union (EU) in 2011, and answer each of the following questions.

(i) What was the percentage of hydro power consumed? *2 marks*

(ii) Calculate X, the percentage of solar energy consumed. *2 marks*

(iii) Calculate B, the percentage of biomass generated from wood and wood waste. *2 marks*

(iv) Explain briefly what is meant by geothermal energy. *2 marks*

2014, Part One, Q12 (8 marks)

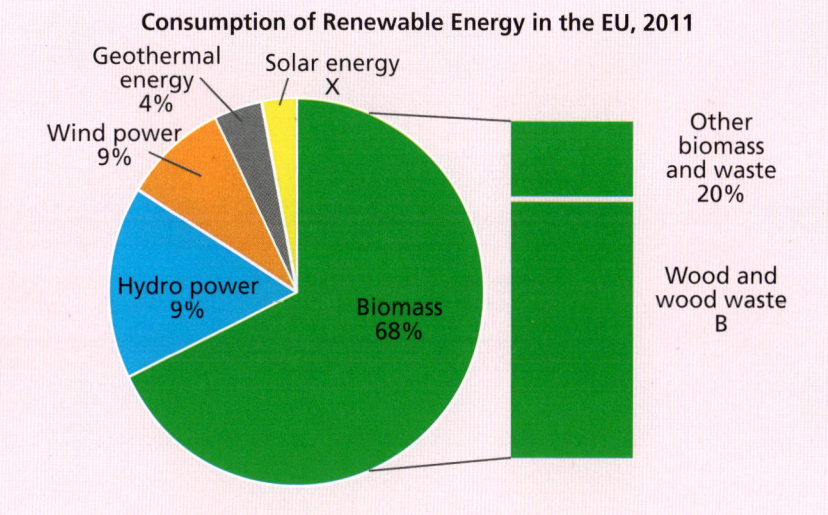

Consumption of Renewable Energy in the EU, 2011
- Geothermal energy 4%
- Solar energy X
- Wind power 9%
- Hydro power 9%
- Biomass 68%
  - Other biomass and waste 20%
  - Wood and wood waste B

6. Disposable Income of Irish Regions

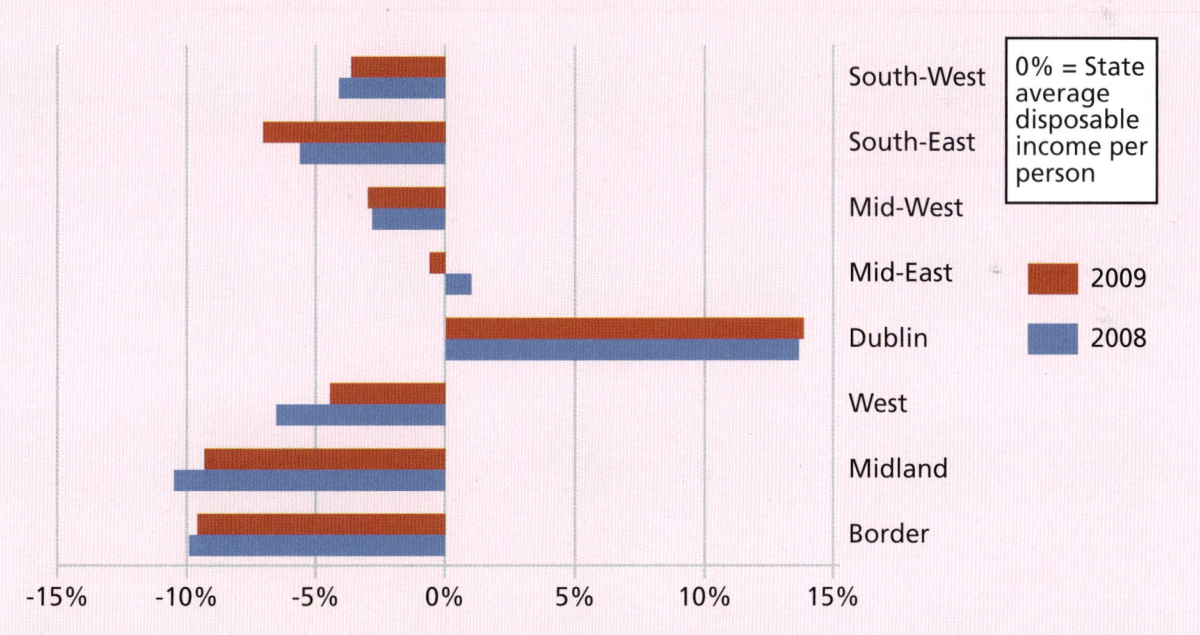

Disposable income per person – percentage deviation from state average

Regions: South-West, South-East, Mid-West, Mid-East, Dublin, West, Midland, Border

Legend: 2009 (red), 2008 (blue)

0% = State average disposable income per person

Examine the graph above and answer the following questions.

(i) How many regions had a disposable income per person below the State average in 2008? *4 marks*

(ii) Which region had a disposable income per person 10% below the State average in 2008? *4 marks*

(iii) Which region's disposable income per person was closest to the State average in both 2008 and 2009? *4 marks*

(iv) Which region had a disposable income per person above the State average in both 2008 and 2009? *4 marks*

(v) Explain briefly why this region had a disposable income per person above the State average in both 2008 and 2009. *2 + 2 marks*

2013, Part Two, Section 1, Q5A (20 marks)

Landscapes

Long Questions

7. European Union Population

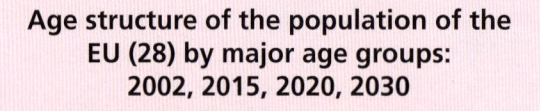

Age structure of the population of the EU (28) by major age groups: 2002, 2015, 2020, 2030

Legend: ■ 0–19 ■ 20–64 ■ 65–79 ■ 80 and over

Year	0–19	20–64	65–79	80 and over
2030	20.20%	55.90%	16.80%	7.10%
2020	20.70%	58.90%	14.60%	5.80%
2015	20.90%	x	13.60%	5.20%
2002	23.20%	60.80%	12.40%	3.60%

Examine the chart above showing the age structure of the population of the European Union (EU-28) in 2002 and 2015, and the projected age structure of the population in 2020 and 2030 and answer each of the following questions.

(i) Calculate X, the percentage of the EU (28) population aged between 20 and 64 years in 2015. *4 marks*

(ii) In which age group is the percentage of the population projected to almost double, from 2002 to 2030? State one reason for this projected increase. *2 + 2 marks*

(iii) In which two age groups is the percentage of the population projected to decline, from 2002 to 2030? *2 × 2 marks*

(iv) Explain briefly two challenges presented by the projected decline in the percentage of the population in these two age groups. *2 × 4 marks*

2017, Part Two, Section 1, Q6A (20 marks)

8. Economic Activity

Examine the charts showing the main aquaculture producers in the European Union (EU-28) in 1995 and 2012 and answer each of the following questions.

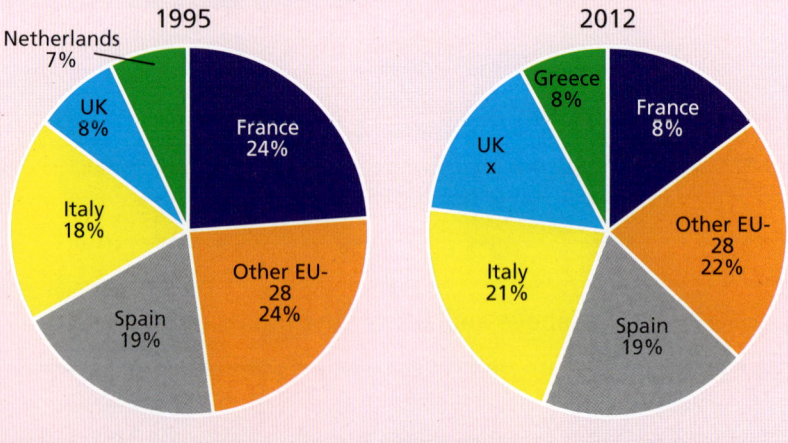

Main Aquaculture Producers in the European Union (EU-28) in 1995 and 2012

1995: France 24%, Other EU-28 24%, Spain 19%, Italy 18%, UK 8%, Netherlands 7%

2012: Other EU-28 22%, Italy 21%, Spain 19%, France 8%, Greece 8%, UK x

(i) Calculate X, the percentage of EU-28 aquaculture produced by the UK in 2012. *4 marks*

(ii) Which single country produced over one-fifth of EU-28 aquaculture production in 2012, and what percentage did that country produce in 1995? *2 + 2 marks*

(iii) With reference to the charts above, which country was no longer one of the main EU-28 aquaculture producers in 2012 and which country replaced it? *2 + 2 marks*

(iv) Explain briefly one positive impact of European Union policy on the fishing industry. *4 marks*

(v) Explain briefly one negative impact of European Union policy on the fishing industry. *4 marks*

2016, Part Two, Section 1, Q5 (20 marks)

Revision Summary

Bar chart	Pie chart
• Shows data in separate columns • **To construct:** Use graph paper – label axes – draw straight columns of equal width • Must include a relevant title **Stacked bar chart** • Columns are divided • Different data shown allows comparison • Limit to categories	• Shows data in percentages of a whole • **To construct:** Use a protractor – 1%= 3.6° – show percentages in each sector – colour or shade sectors • Use key for colour/shading • Must include a relevant title

Trend graph	Climograph
• Also known as a line graph • Used to show patterns or trends in data over time • **To construct:** Use graph paper – draw and label axes – plot data – connect plotted points • Must include a relevant title	• Used for climate data • Precipitation represented in bar chart format • Temperature represented in line graph format • Must include a relevant title

Scatter graph	Triangle graph
• Used to show the relationship between two data sets • **Positive correlation:** as values on x-axis increase, values on y-axis increase • **Negative correlation:** as values on x-axis increase, values on y-axis decrease • Must include a relevant title	• Usually used to compare soil compositions • Three different data sets – three labelled axes • To read, start with left axis and continue clockwise • Must include a relevant title
	Choropleth
	• Used in demographic studies • Shading/colouring show data variations • Key shows categories • Must include a relevant title

16 GEOGRAPHICAL INVESTIGATION

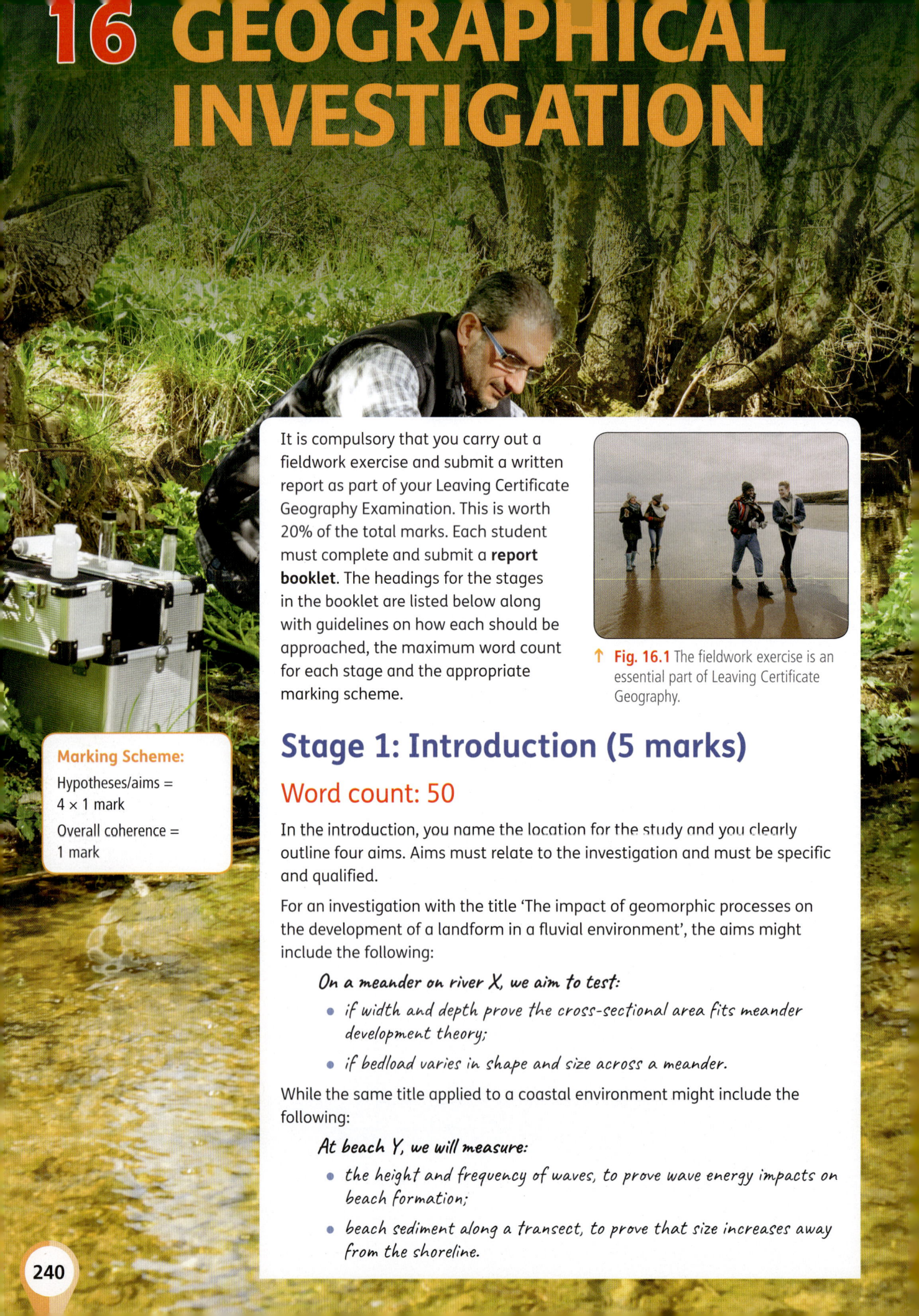

It is compulsory that you carry out a fieldwork exercise and submit a written report as part of your Leaving Certificate Geography Examination. This is worth 20% of the total marks. Each student must complete and submit a **report booklet**. The headings for the stages in the booklet are listed below along with guidelines on how each should be approached, the maximum word count for each stage and the appropriate marking scheme.

↑ **Fig. 16.1** The fieldwork exercise is an essential part of Leaving Certificate Geography.

Marking Scheme:
Hypotheses/aims = 4 × 1 mark
Overall coherence = 1 mark

Stage 1: Introduction (5 marks)

Word count: 50

In the introduction, you name the location for the study and you clearly outline four aims. Aims must relate to the investigation and must be specific and qualified.

For an investigation with the title 'The impact of geomorphic processes on the development of a landform in a fluvial environment', the aims might include the following:

On a meander on river X, we aim to test:
- *if width and depth prove the cross-sectional area fits meander development theory;*
- *if bedload varies in shape and size across a meander.*

While the same title applied to a coastal environment might include the following:

At beach Y, we will measure:
- *the height and frequency of waves, to prove wave energy impacts on beach formation;*
- *beach sediment along a transect, to prove that size increases away from the shoreline.*

Stage 2: Planning (5 marks)

Marking Scheme:
Statements relating to preparation = 4 × 1 mark
Overall coherence = 1 mark

Word count: 100

The planning section refers to the work done before the field study. The information to be gathered will be determined by the hypotheses or aims that have been set out.

Gathering

Identify **what** information will be gathered, **why** it is to be gathered, **how** it will be gathered and **how** it will be recorded.

Example:

> *The class divided into groups and we outlined the areas of the study we were going to undertake at each location, the type of data we would need to gather, how we were going to gather it, the equipment we needed for each task ...*

Practising how to use the equipment will make usage faster and more accurate in the field. A list of the equipment to be used can be included, but sketching the equipment is not likely to earn any marks.

Example:

> *I practised using a clinometer and ranging rods ...* (Fig. 16.2)

↑ **Fig. 16.2** A clinometer is used to measure angle of slope.

Revision

You will use secondary sources such as texts, film clips and maps. You must **qualify** each statement explaining why you used or accessed these sources. You must also state the title, author and chapter/pages for any texts used, any video clips used must also have a title and production details. For any material researched or downloaded from websites, give the author, website name and address.

Example:

> *I downloaded a Power's Roundness Scale (www.researchgate.net) to help me with the pebble roundness study ...*

Worksheet

You will need worksheets to record data collected in the field for analysis back in the classroom. The type of worksheet required will depend on the data to be collected. Each worksheet must be titled and have sufficient space for the relevant data. You can include a copy of one of your data sheets.

Example:

> *I designed charts to accurately record the following ...*

↑ **Fig. 16.3** Practise your sketching technique before doing your field work.

Viewfinder

You will make/acquire a viewfinder and practise sketching techniques in the school grounds or local area (Fig. 16.3).

Examples:

> *I made a viewfinder using a sheet of clear plastic, on which I had drawn a grid.*
> *We practised in pairs ...*

Landscapes

Fig. 16.4 Check the weather forecast and tide times before the trip.

Weather

Consulting the Met Éireann website (**www.met.ie**) just before the trip will help to decide whether it is safe to proceed with the fieldwork on the day and will also inform appropriate clothing and protection for data sheets (**Fig. 16.4**).

Examples:

I/we checked the weather forecast on Met Éireann ...

I/we checked tide times on the Tide Forecast (www.tide-forecast.com) to be sure we would be able to access all areas of the beach ...

Scoilnet

The Scoilnet website (**www.scoilnet.ie**) allows access to the OSI Discovery Map Series. You can use this to locate the study site and ensure that it is accessible, and record the grid references. The site also offers advice on conducting a safety audit before any field work. Plan for carrying out an on-site risk assessment on the day of the fieldwork.

> **Marking Scheme:**
> Methods = 2 × (9 SRPs × 2 marks)
> Overall coherence and conformity to prescribed length = 4 marks (graded 4/2/0)

Stage 3: Gathering Information (40 marks)

Word count: 450

This section describes the actual fieldwork. You are required to describe two methods. Each method can consist of a number of tasks. In a geomorphic investigation of a river feature, one method could be measuring the feature and the second method can be about measuring the processes. In a coastal environment, the two methods could be gathering of information to investigate whether deposition was taking place on the day of the study and determining the direction of longshore drift in the study area.

For each method, you need to include:

Measurements or recordings

In this section, you must clearly describe (using action words, e.g. I collected, measured, placed, drew, recorded) **how** and using **what** instruments you gathered or observed the gathering of information in the field. (**Fig. 16.5**)

Example:

*Cian and Marie measured out 10 metres in length along both sides of the river (A). Using mallets, Emma drove poles on one bank, and Ben did the same on the opposite banks (B-B) (C-C). Cian and Marie secured ropes between the poles, making a start and finish line (**Fig. 16.6**). Sean entered the river above the start line with three floats. Cian moved below the finish line. I had the stopwatch and I gave the signal to Sean, who dropped the float above the start line. As it passed the line, I started the stopwatch and stopped it when the float crossed the finish line. I called out the time and the others recorded it on their river velocity data sheets ...*

Fig. 16.5 Measuring and recording bedload size.

A labelled sketch

One SRP per task or method can be earned by including relevant labelled sketches/diagrams that are activity-based and illustrate the gathering process. The sketch(es) can be linked with the description of the gathering of information, as in the examples.

Example:

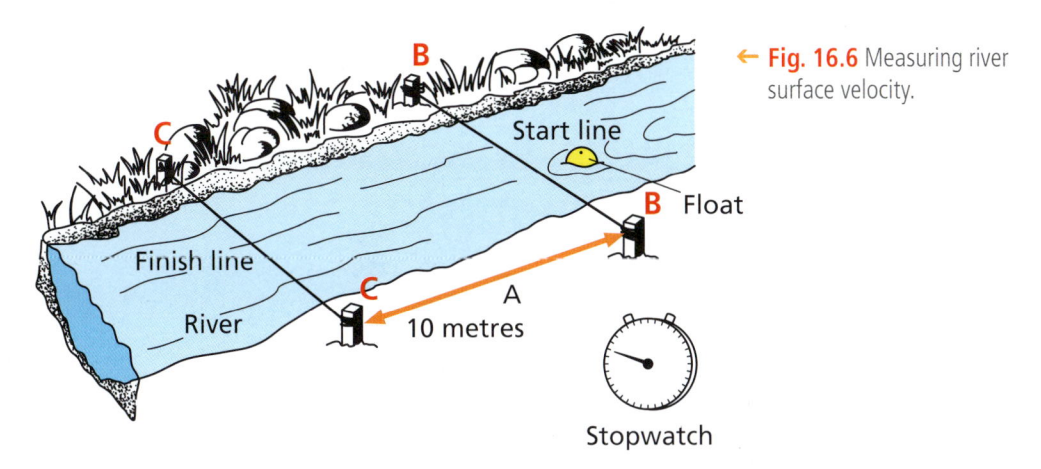

← **Fig. 16.6** Measuring river surface velocity.

I placed one end of a rope under a rock on the upper beach and walked down the lower beach where I placed the other end under another rock. This was my transect line. I then placed the quadrat on this line in the lower section of the beach. With my eyes closed, I randomly selected a sample from within the quadrat (Fig. 16.7). John and I examined the sample and consulted our Power's Index Chart to decide which of the classes 1–6 the sample best matched. I recorded the results on my data sheet …

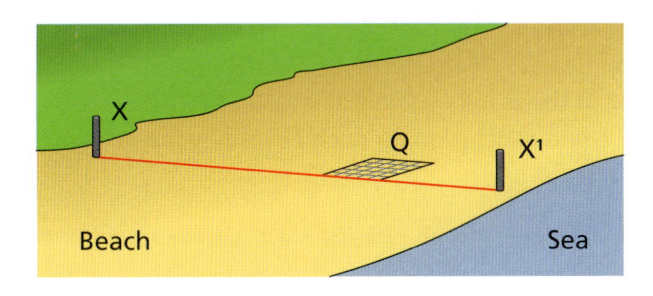

← **Fig. 16.7** Beach sediment analysis.

An observation

Describe something you observed at the study site on the day. Your statement must be **qualified** or explained.

Examples:

River study:
I observed:
- low volumes of water due to the recent prolonged dry spell;
- evidence of recent flooding had resulted in surface water on the floodplain.

Coastal study:
I observed:
- evidence of a small area of oil slick on the lower beach;
- large amounts of seaweed, which were deposited on the upper beach during recent storms.

↑ **Fig. 16.8** Record at least one observation you made on the day.

16 Geographical Investigation

Issue

Describe something which arose while doing the fieldwork. Your statement must be qualified.

Examples:

River study: Large boulders/storm debris blocking the float while trying to calculate river velocity caused ...

Coastal study: There was some difficulty agreeing which class some of the samples belonged to because ...

Stage 4: Results, Conclusions and Evaluation (30 marks)

Word count: 400

Results

In Stage 4 of your booklet, write the heading **Results**. Here you should present four or five results from your investigation. Each result should be clearly stated and the correct unit of measurement included.

Example:

River study: Site (1) The average bedload size was as follows: long axis 23 mm and short axis 14 mm.

Coastal study: Wind speed was recorded at 10 kilometres per hour and there was an average of four waves per minute.

Conclusions

After you have written up your results clearly, write the heading **Conclusions**. In this section, you need to look at the results you obtained and explain what they are telling you. You must have one conclusion for each of your hypotheses or aims.

Examples:

River study: Sample bedload increases in size across the meander from the inside to the outside ...

Coastal study: Deposition from constructive waves was occurring on the beach today. The four-wave-per-minute average is less than the minimum eight waves per minute required for erosion to take place ...

Evaluation

After you have written your conclusions, write the heading **Evaluation**. In this section, you are required to reflect on the fieldwork and its outcomes. You need to refer back to your aims and objectives, and to the activities in the field. Think about the following:

- Did you collect sufficient data?
- How accurate were your results?
- Were the results you got those you expected?
- How might you improve data collecting methods if you were to do the work again?
- Would collecting different data have improved your results?
- Did your results prove or disprove stated hypotheses?

The answers to the above and any other relevant questions need to be fully explained and expanded on. Vague or general answers will not earn any marks!

EXAM TIP

You are required to give four results, four conclusions and four evaluations, but it is recommended that you add an extra one in case the examiner decides that one is not relevant.

Marking Scheme:
4 SRPs × 2 marks

Marking Scheme:
4 SRPs × 2 marks

Marking Scheme:
4 SRPs × 2 marks
Overall coherence and conformity to prescribed length = 6 marks (graded 6/4/2/0)

Stage 5: Organisation and Presentation of Results (20 marks)

Results should be presented on the blank and graph pages in the **Results, Conclusions and Evaluation** section of the booklet. All graphs must be drawn on graph paper. Your data must be presented using at least two different formats from the following list: **bar chart, pie chart, line graph, chart or table, sketch or map**. Make sure that each graph is presented alongside the relevant results, for example, the bedload analysis chart should be on the page opposite the written result for bedload analysis.

Chapter 15: Graph Skills

Marking Scheme

Students must use a minimum of two of the following formats, each worth eight marks.

Bar chart:
Suitable title = 2 marks
Labelled axes = 2 marks
Plotted information = 2 × 2 marks

Pie chart:
Suitable title = 2 marks
Centred circle = 2 marks
Plotted information = 2 × 2 marks

Line graph:
Suitable title = 2 marks
Labelled axes = 2 marks
Plotted information = 2 × 2 marks

Chart or table:
Suitable title = 2 marks
Rows = 2 marks
Columns = 2 marks
Frame = 2 marks

Sketch or map:
Suitable title = 2 marks
Frame = 2 marks
Relevant information = 2 marks
Plotted information = 2 marks

Four marks are awarded for overall coherence, which refers to the quality and clarity of the overall presentation. If only one method is used, no marks will be awarded for overall coherence.

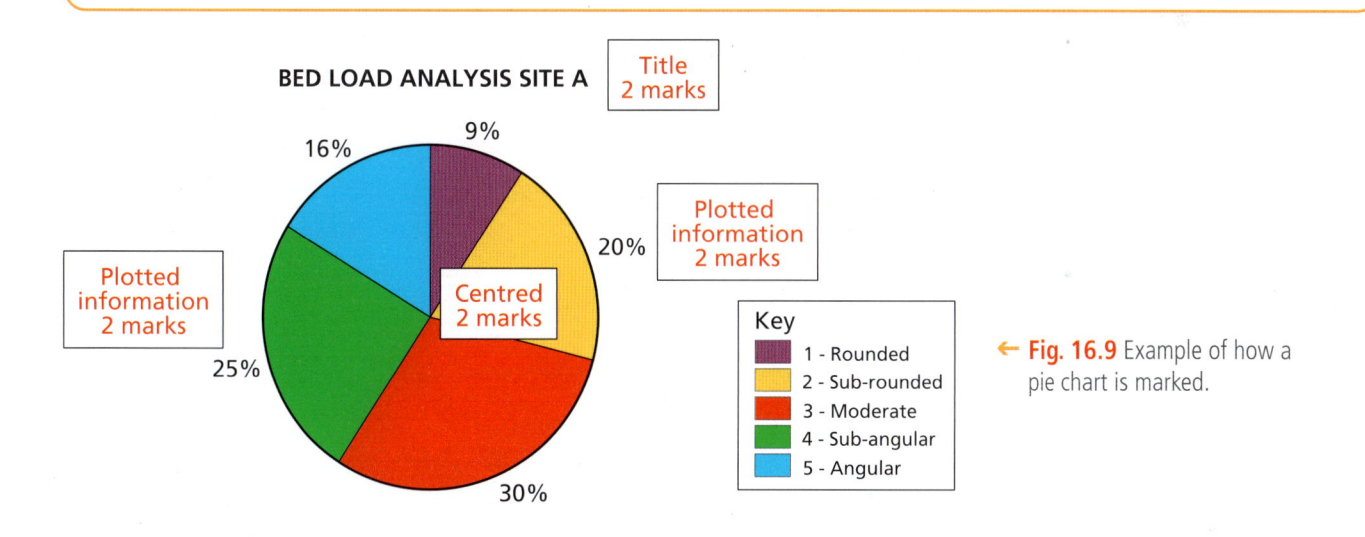

← **Fig. 16.9** Example of how a pie chart is marked.

Marking Scheme for Geographical Investigation: Summary

Stage 1	Stage 2	Stage 3	Stage 4	Stage 5
Introduction	**Planning**	**Gathering Information**	**Results**	**Organisation & Presentation of Results**
4 SRPs × 1 mark = 4 marks	4 SRPs × 1 mark = 4 marks	2 methods × 20 marks	4 SRPs × 2 marks = 8 marks	2 presentations × 8 marks
Overall coherence = 1 mark	Overall coherence = 1 mark	Each method:	Conclusions:	Each presentation:
		9 SRPs × 2 marks = 18 marks	4 SRPs × 2 marks = 8 marks	4 SRPs × 2 marks = 8 marks
		Overall coherence = 2 marks	Evaluation:	Overall coherence = 4 marks
			4 SRPs × 2 marks = 8 marks	
			Overall coherence = 6 marks	
Total = 5 marks	**Total = 5 marks**	**Total = 40 marks**	**Total = 30 marks**	**Total = 20 marks**

CORE UNIT 3
REGIONAL GEOGRAPHY

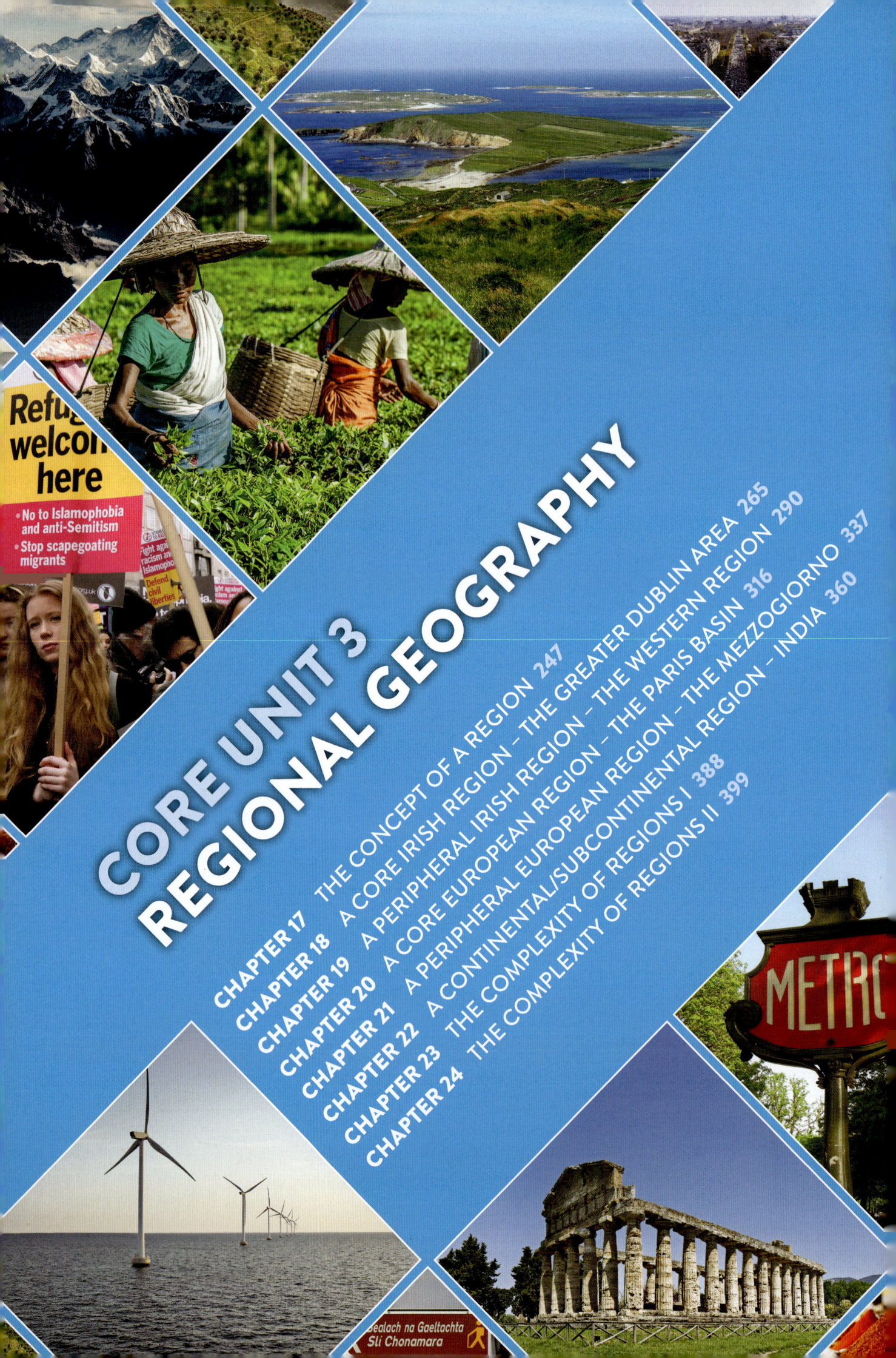

CHAPTER 17   THE CONCEPT OF A REGION 247
CHAPTER 18   A CORE IRISH REGION – THE GREATER DUBLIN AREA 265
CHAPTER 19   A PERIPHERAL IRISH REGION – THE WESTERN REGION 290
CHAPTER 20   A CORE EUROPEAN REGION – THE PARIS BASIN 316
CHAPTER 21   A PERIPHERAL EUROPEAN REGION – THE MEZZOGIORNO 337
CHAPTER 22   A CONTINENTAL/SUBCONTINENTAL REGION – INDIA 360
CHAPTER 23   THE COMPLEXITY OF REGIONS I 388
CHAPTER 24   THE COMPLEXITY OF REGIONS II 399

17 THE CONCEPT OF A REGION

LEARNING INTENTIONS
Syllabus Links: 2.1

By the end of this chapter I will be able to:
- link named types of region with specific named examples;
- describe the characteristics of each region type;
- give at least two examples of named region types;
- include relevant diagrams to support answers.

KEYWORDS
temperate
latitude
prevailing winds
relief rain
jet stream
depressions
frontal rain

A **region** is an area of the earth's surface. Characteristics used to differentiate regions include **climatic**, **geomorphological**, **administrative**, **cultural**, **socio-economic** and **urban**.

Climatic Regions

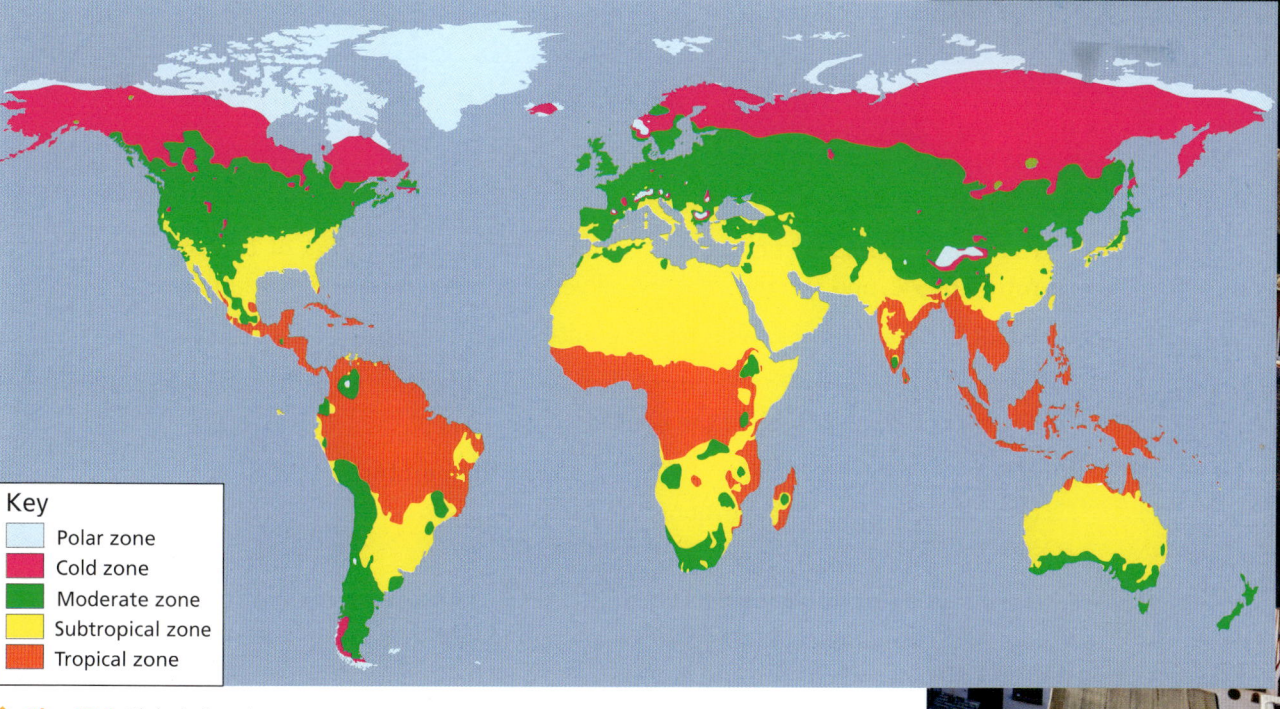

Key
- Polar zone
- Cold zone
- Moderate zone
- Subtropical zone
- Tropical zone

↑ **Fig. 17.1** Global climatic zones.

Figure 17.1 shows the variety and extent of climate types around the world. A variety of different factors combine to give these climates their temperature and precipitation characteristics.

247

Landscapes

CASE STUDY: THE COOL TEMPERATE OCEANIC CLIMATE

The **cool temperate oceanic** type of climate occurs in coastal regions along the western sides of continents. In north-western Europe, it is experienced in Ireland and in coastal areas extending from Norway to Spain (**Fig. 17.2**).

Chapter 18:
A Core Irish Region – The Greater Dublin Area
Chapter 19:
A Peripheral Irish Region – The Western Region

→ **Fig. 17.2** Areas influenced by the cool temperate oceanic climate in Europe.

Ireland's climatic characteristics are an average **summer temperature of 15°C**, an average **winter temperature of 5°C**, and rainfall occurring all year but with a winter maximum.

A number of factors influence the cool temperate oceanic climate. These include:

- **Latitude:** The climate is most commonly found along western coasts in **temperate latitudes** (40° to 65° north and south of the equator).

- **The sea:** The moderating effects of the sea **keep temperatures mild all year round**. The sea is also a source of moisture; evaporated water vapour is carried by south-westerly winds travelling over it towards land.

- **Prevailing winds:** The warm 'moist' **south-westerly winds** exert a major influence on this climate and are responsible for mild winters (**Fig. 17.3**). These winds are **moisture-laden** and give the region its characteristic high annual levels of precipitation. Where there are coastal uplands, as in the west of Ireland, **relief rain** will form, giving higher precipitation levels than are present in the eastern '**rain shadow**' area.

Relief rain: Precipitation that forms when moisture-laden winds are forced to rise over uplands.

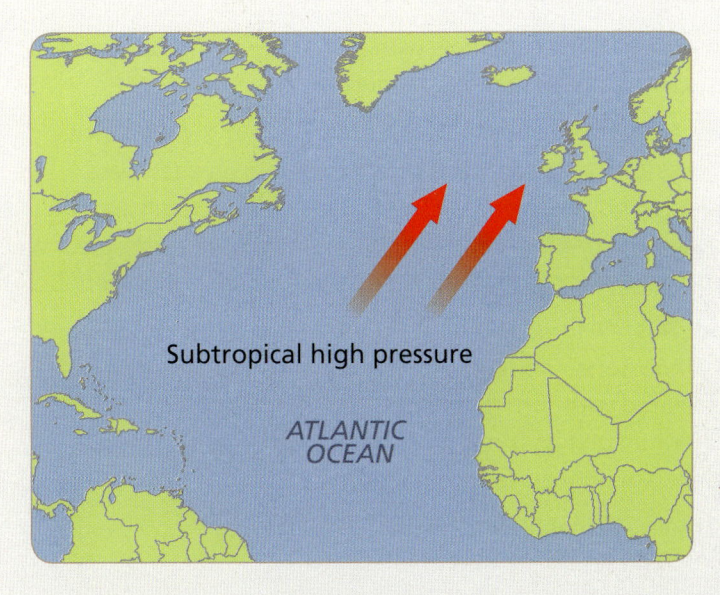

Fig. 17.3 Prevailing south-westerly winds are responsible for Ireland's mild winters.

- **Jet streams:** These **high-altitude, fast-moving currents of air** cause low-pressure **depressions** to track from west to east across the Atlantic Ocean, bringing **frontal rainfall**. They can travel to the north and or the south of Ireland. For much of June and July 2018, the North Atlantic jet stream was positioned to the north of Ireland, allowing high pressure to dominate, blocking depressions and resulting in clear skies, high temperatures and little rainfall (Fig. 17.4). Jet streams can also remain stationary, allowing depressions to move across Ireland, causing extended periods of rainfall that can cause flooding.

Frontal rain: Precipitation forms when a warm air mass rises over a cooler air mass.

- **Ocean currents:** Ocean currents are **movements of water in the sea** caused by global winds, temperature differences and the effects of the earth's rotation. The warm water associated with the **North Atlantic Drift** keeps winter temperatures in Ireland higher than they would be otherwise for these latitudes. It also increases the rate of evaporation into the warm south-westerly winds, contributing to high levels of precipitation.

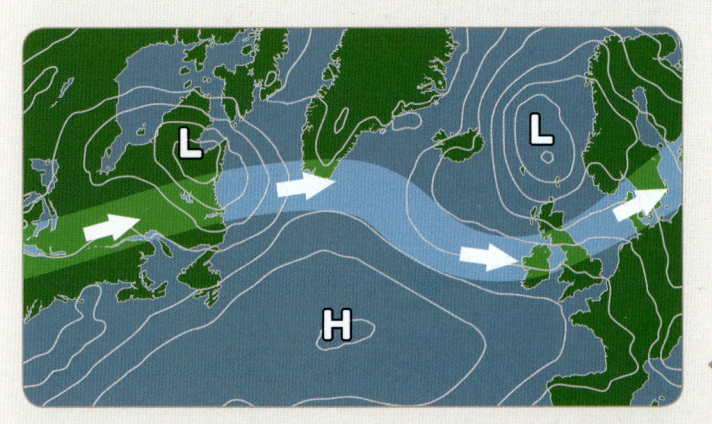

Fig. 17.4 The North Atlantic jet stream.

CHECK YOUR LEARNING

1. Describe the main characteristics of a cool temperate oceanic climate.
2. Name four countries that experience this type of climate.
3. Explain how the sea, the North Atlantic jet stream and ocean currents influence Ireland's cool temperate oceanic climate.
4. Give a possible reason why in 2018 Belmullet in County Mayo recorded 1,183 mm of precipitation, while County Dublin only recorded 709.4 mm.

Geomorphological Regions

Geomorphological regions are geological regions with distinctive landscapes and landforms. Examples of such regions include the following:

Munster Ridge and Valley, Ireland: This region was formed during the Armorican folding period. Strata of limestone over sandstone were folded in an east-west trend. Over time, the limestone has been eroded from the anticlines, exposing the sandstone, which forms ridges. Limestone remains on the floors of the syncline. Rivers such as the Bandon flow in the synclines, and have trellis drainage patterns.

The Central Plain, Ireland: This is a large low-lying region in the centre of Ireland. Underlain by sedimentary limestone, the region is covered in glacial drift and depositional features associated with the Midlandian glaciation. Drainage is dominated by the River Shannon and its tributaries. Numerous lakes and large areas of bogland are evidence of poor surface drainage.

The Burren, Ireland: This region is covered in *Chapter 6: Weathering Processes and Landforms*.

The North European Plain: This extensive lowland area covers much of France and extends through Belgium, the Netherlands, Germany, Poland and Scandinavia. Deposits from the Pleistocene glaciation including boulder clay, moraines, outwash plains and limon deposits are widespread. In some areas, poor surface drainage associated with glacial soils led to the formation of bogs and heathland. The area drained by a number of important rivers, including the Rhine, the Elbe and the Vistula. Alluvial soils deposited by these rivers and glacial boulder clay soils make this one of the most fertile regions in the world.

CHECK YOUR LEARNING
1. Name four different geomorphological regions.
2. List three characteristics of any one such region.

Administrative Regions

Administrative regions are created by governments for the efficient provision of local government services.

KEYWORDS			
regional assemblies	regions	*arrondissements*	county council
municipal districts	départements	communes	city council

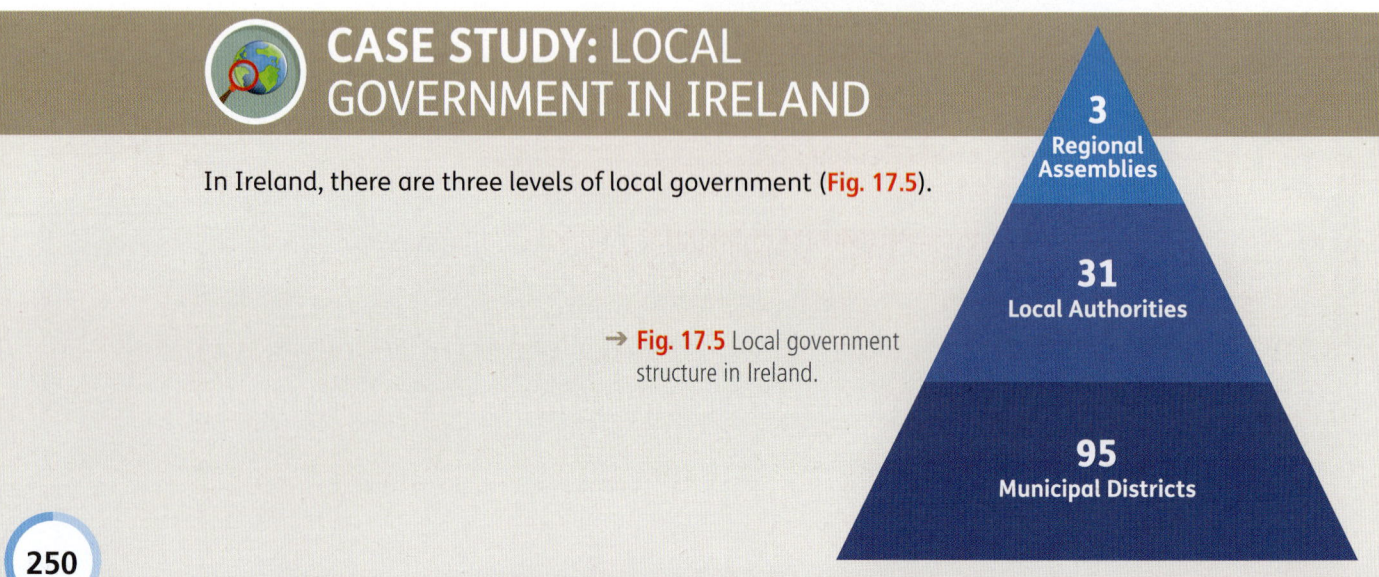

CASE STUDY: LOCAL GOVERNMENT IN IRELAND

In Ireland, there are three levels of local government (Fig. 17.5).

→ **Fig. 17.5** Local government structure in Ireland.

- 3 Regional Assemblies
- 31 Local Authorities
- 95 Municipal Districts

- **Level 1: Regional Assemblies.** The Northern and Western, the Southern, and the Eastern and Midland regions of Ireland are composed of elected members from the local authority areas within each region (**Fig. 17.6**).

← **Fig. 17.6** Irish counties and regions.

- **Level 2: Local Authorities.** There are 31 local authorities in Ireland, composed of:
    - 26 **county councils**;
    - two city and county councils (Limerick and Waterford);
    - three **city councils** (Dublin, Cork and Galway).
- **Level 3: Municipal Districts.** The 95 municipal districts (e.g. Castlecomer, Co. Kilkenny; Listowel, Co. Kerry) form the first level of local government. Councillors are elected simultaneously to both a municipal district and county council. These provide a forum where the views of the local community are represented.

Funding for local government in Ireland comes from a number of sources, including rates on commercial properties and the Local Government Fund.

CHECK YOUR LEARNING

1. List the three different levels of local government in Ireland.
2. Name one function of each level of local government in Ireland.
3. Identify in which regional assembly area the following counties are located: Waterford, Kerry, Donegal, Carlow, Monaghan, Sligo.

Landscapes

CASE STUDY: LOCAL GOVERNMENT IN FRANCE

Local government in France is based on three levels: regional, intermediate and local (**Fig. 17.7**).

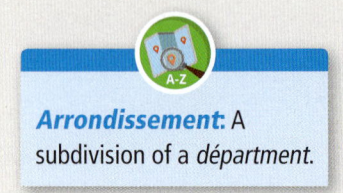

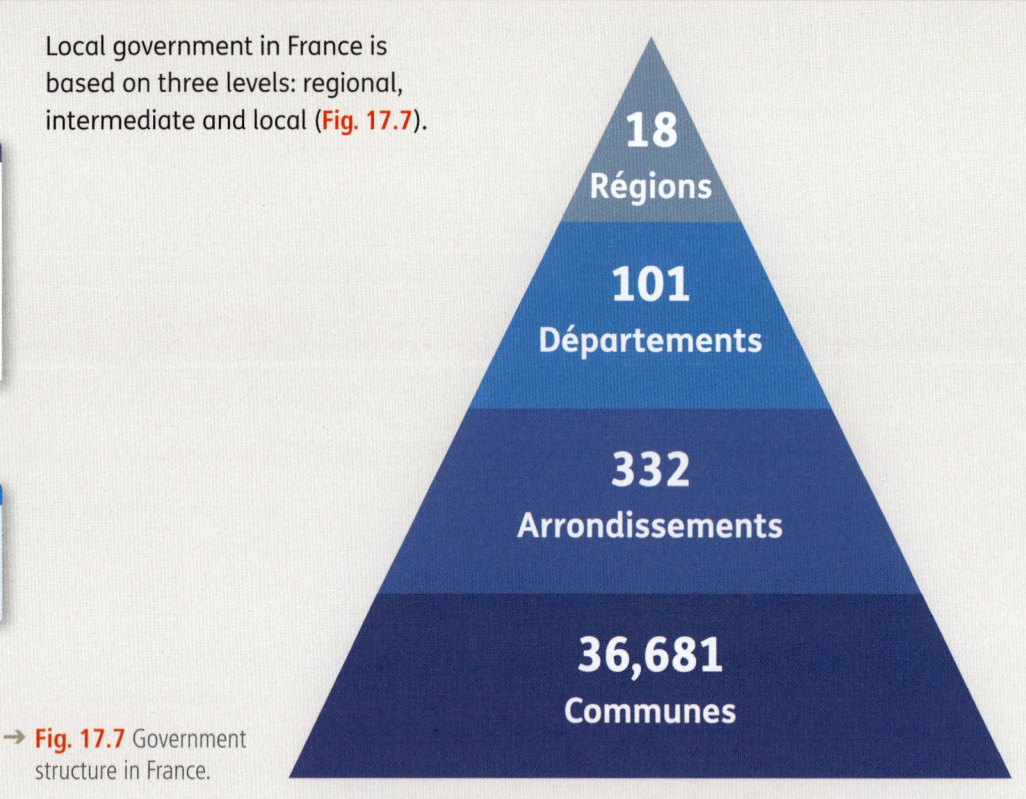

A reform of French local government on 1 January 2016 reduced the number of administrative units at all levels.

Arrondissement: A subdivision of a *département*.

- **18** Régions
- **101** Départements
- **332** Arrondissements
- **36,681** Communes

→ **Fig. 17.7** Government structure in France.

- **Regional level:** *régions*. Included in the 18 *régions* of France are the island of Corsica and **five overseas territories**. (**Fig. 17.8**). The administration of the *régions* consists of a regional council **elected for six years** and headed by a president. They receive funding from central government and can levy their own local taxes.

→ **Fig. 17.8** French *régions*.

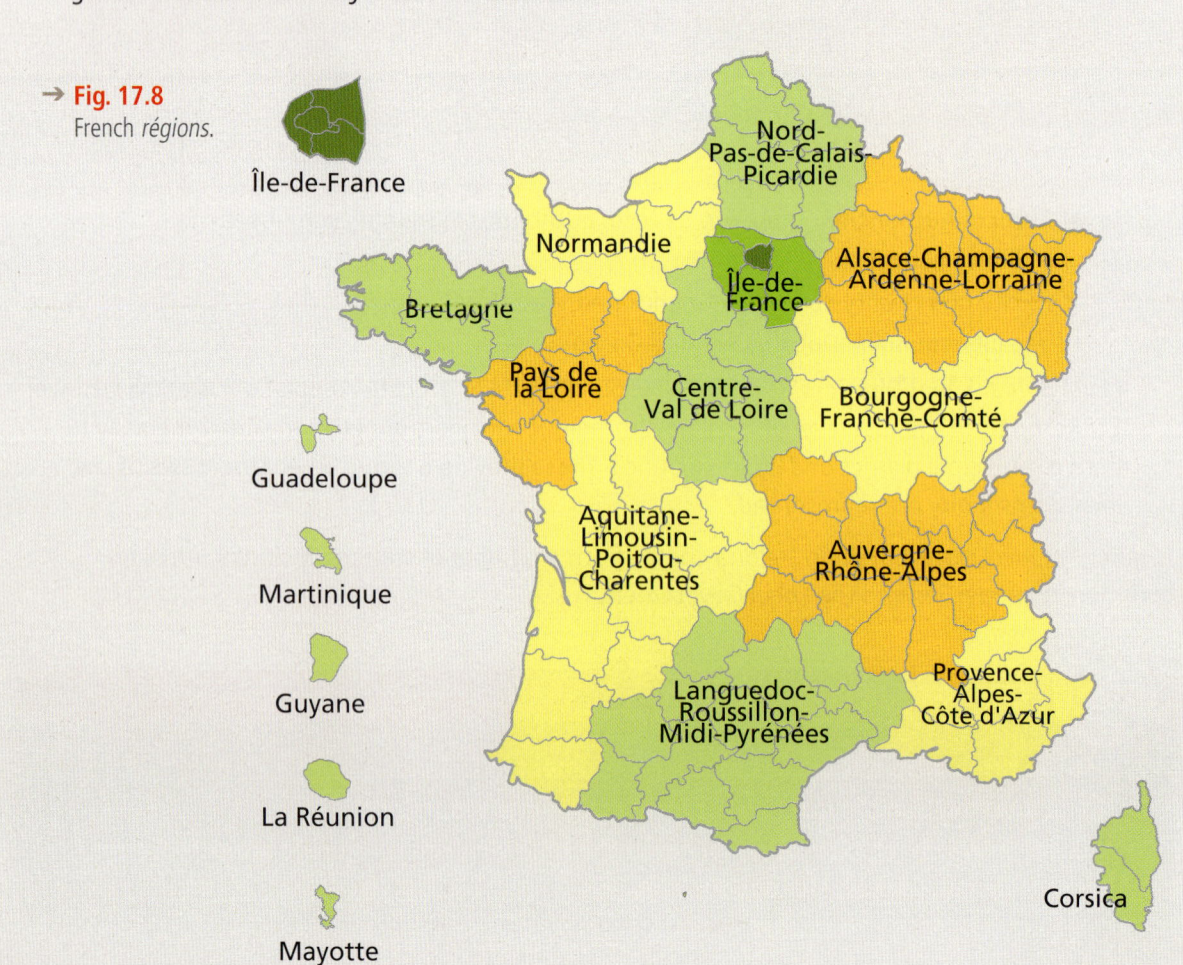

Île-de-France
Nord-Pas-de-Calais-Picardie
Normandie
Bretagne
Alsace-Champagne-Ardenne-Lorraine
Pays de la Loire
Centre-Val de Loire
Bourgogne-Franche-Comté
Guadeloupe
Aquitane-Limousin-Poitou-Charentes
Auvergne-Rhône-Alpes
Martinique
Guyane
Languedoc-Roussillon-Midi-Pyrénées
Provence-Alpes-Côte d'Azur
La Réunion
Corsica
Mayotte

252

- **Intermediate level: *départements*.** France has 101 ***départements***, of which five are overseas territories. They are further subdivided into 332 ***arrondissements***, which vary in size from Lozère in south-western France with around 75,000 residents, to Le Nord in north-east France, which has over 2.5 million residents. Funding comes from local taxation.
- **Local level: *communes*.** France has over **36,000 *communes***, varying in size but with an average population of about 400 people. Their functions include town planning and provision of local services.

CHECK YOUR LEARNING

1. Identify the three levels of local government in France.
2. Name three *régions* in mainland France.

Cultural Regions

Culture describes the way of life, the values and the beliefs of a group of people that is passed from one generation to the next. **Religion** and **language** are two key elements of a society's culture.

KEYWORDS		
fragmented	Údarás na Gaeltachta	TG4
declining	Wild Atlantic Way	Raidió na Gaeltachta
heritage	linguistic and cultural	summer courses

CASE STUDY: THE GAELTACHT, A LANGUAGE REGION IN IRELAND

The Gaeltacht is a region in Ireland where Irish (Gaeilge) is the main spoken language. It is geographically **fragmented**, but is mostly concentrated in the western counties of **Kerry**, **Galway**, **Mayo**, **Donegal** and parts of counties **Cork**, **Waterford** and **Meath** (**Fig. 17.9**). The Irish State, set up in 1922, formally established the Gaeltacht and defined its extent. Gaeilge was recognised in the Constitution of Ireland as the first official language of Ireland, and in 2005 it became one of the official languages of the EU. **The Department of Culture, Heritage and the Gaeltacht** is responsible for Gaeltacht affairs.

The Gaeltacht region is currently facing a number of challenges, many of which are contributing to the **declining** use of Irish. These include **migration** out of the region, which is leading to a reduced number of native Irish speakers.

The **peripheral location** of Gaeltacht areas, their **poor infrastructure** and their **low population densities** are major disadvantages when it comes to attracting **inward investment**. This results in **limited job opportunities**, higher rates of **unemployment** and net **out-migration**.

→ **Fig. 17.9** Gaeltacht areas.

Chapter 24: The Complexity of Regions II

Landscapes

Údarás na Gaeltachta: A regional state authority with responsibility for the economic, social and cultural development of the Gaeltacht.

Údarás na Gaeltachta has responsibility for economic development in the Gaeltacht and provides grants, advance factories and training programmes to attract inward investment.

Government-supported Irish-language summer courses in the Gaeltacht are important in the promotion of the language, while also contributing to the local economy.

While the Gaeltacht is defined by the usage of the Irish language, other aspects of Irish culture find expression in activities such as Gaelic sports and traditional Irish music, song and dance.

The development of the **Wild Atlantic Way** (a 2,500 km tourist trail along Ireland's north, west, south-west and south coasts) has led to the promotion of the unique **linguistic and cultural heritages** of Gaeltacht areas in counties Mayo and Galway. It is hoped that this will lead to an increasing regard for the language and the unique character it brings to Gaeltacht areas.

A wide variety of **government grants** for home improvements and new houses are available to people who live in Gaeltacht areas, though applicants will need to prove that Irish is the main language used in the home.

The introduction of Irish-language TV channel **TG4** and Irish-language radio station **Raidió na Gaeltachta** were seen as positive supports to the language. However, a 2015 report highlighted the serious decline in the use of the language in the community, so activists are now calling for more radical steps to be taken to promote and sustain the use of Irish in Ireland.

CHECK YOUR LEARNING

1. Name the main Gaeltacht areas in Ireland.
2. List two problems facing these areas.
3. Name three types of support Gaeltacht areas receive.

CASE STUDY: BELGIUM, A EUROPEAN LANGUAGE REGION

KEYWORDS
Flanders
Flemish
Wallonia
French
bilingual
communes à facilités

→ Fig. 17.10 Official languages in Belgium.

In 1830, two culturally different regions, Flanders and Wallonia, came together to form what we know today as Belgium. In 1920, part of Germany was annexed to the eastern part of Belgium, and today, Belgium has **four distinct language communities** within its borders (Fig. 17.10).

- **Flanders**, in the north, has **Flemish** as its official language.
- **Wallonia**, located in the south, has **French** as its official language.
- The **East Cantons** (Eupen-Malmedy) have **German** as their official language.
- **Brussels**, Belgium's capital city, is a designated **bilingual** area, where French and Flemish have equal status.

Following the formation of Belgium, French-speaking Wallonia was the richest and most industrialised part of Belgium, so French became the language of business and the professional classes such as doctors, lawyers and architects.

Within Belgium, local administration is based on **municipalities** (*communes*). In Flanders and Wallonia, all matters dealing with public administration are conducted in the language of that region, so in Flanders, Flemish is used, and in Wallonia, French is the language of choice.

Problems arise, however, if you are a French speaker living in a Flemish-speaking area. How do you interact with administration; pay your taxes or get a driving licence? In French-speaking areas, the official language in schools is French, so what do you do if you are a Flemish speaker? There appears to be a complete lack of willingness to give equal status to both languages throughout Belgium.

↑ **Fig. 17.11** French and Flemish street signs, Brussels.

However, in border areas between Flanders and Wallonia there are communes (*communes à facilités*) that, under law, must provide language facilities for the **minority language**: French in Flanders and Flemish in Wallonia. Here, citizens are entitled to services such as education and engagement with administration in their own language.

Brussels, the capital of Belgium, is officially a **bilingual city**, though more than 80% of its population speak French. Public administration must be carried out in both Flemish and French, and all official documentation and street signs must also be bilingual (Fig. 17.11).

In Brussels, urban sprawl has meant the city is expanding, leading to increasing numbers of French speakers moving into *communes* where Flemish is the official language, and where no provision is made for them. Demands for French speakers to be accommodated have been opposed by Flemish speakers who view it as a threat to their language, and tensions between the language groups have increased. To ensure impartiality, all disputes regarding language have to be decided by the National Courts.

Bilingual: A bilingual region is one where two different languages are in daily use.

Communes à facilités were created to cater for people who did not speak the official language of the region, e.g. French speakers in a Flemish language area.

CHECK YOUR LEARNING

1. List the different language regions in Belgium and identify the language associated with each.
2. Identify two problems caused by the language differences between regions.

CASE STUDY: NORTHERN IRELAND – A REGION ASSOCIATED WITH RELIGION

Chapter 23: The Complexity of Regions I

The 17th-century **Ulster Plantation** played a key role in religion becoming one of Northern Ireland's most important cultural elements. By granting land to Scottish Presbyterian and English Protestant settlers, a majority Protestant community was formed.

The **Government of Ireland Act 1920 established the six counties** of Northern Ireland (Antrim, Armagh, Down, Fermanagh, Londonderry and Tyrone) as a self-governing region within the United Kingdom. Broadly speaking, this new state contained two community groups: **Protestant Unionists**, who supported the union with the United Kingdom, and **Catholic Nationalists**, who wanted to be part of the new Irish Free State.

KEYWORDS

Unionist
Nationalist
civil rights
discrimination
segregated
intermarriage
Orange Order

Civil rights: The rights that all people are entitled to regardless of their race, religion, gender or age.

Nationalist: A supporter of a united Ireland.

Unionist: A person who wants to remain part of the United Kingdom.

Discrimination: The unfair treatment of people on the basis of their race, religion, gender or age.

From its formation, Catholics viewed Northern Ireland as a Protestant state whose institutions of government were designed to **discriminate** against them and keep power in Protestant hands. The civil service, the police force and major industries such as shipbuilding employed mostly Protestants. In 1961, Catholics made up only 12% of the Royal Ulster Constabulary police force.

In 1969, the **Civil Rights Movement** began to campaign for rights for members of the Catholic community. As Unionists were opposed to any loss of power, Northern Ireland became consumed by conflict. This was known as **the Troubles**, and lasted from **1969 until 1998** when the **Good Friday/Belfast Agreement** was signed. Over **3,600 people were killed** over the 30 years of unrest.

The Good Friday/Belfast Agreement marked a new beginning for politics and co-existence in Northern Ireland.

- The formation of a **power-sharing executive** meant Catholics could participate in the political process.
- Over 30% of the **Police Service of Northern Ireland** is now drawn from the Catholic community.
- The **Equality Commission for Northern Ireland** ensures that religious-based discrimination is not tolerated, and investigates all types of equality issues.
- **Power-sharing government:** The first and deputy first ministers (one Unionist and one Nationalist) hold joint office, while the ministerial cabinet is made up of members from both Unionist and Nationalist parties.

Today, while the political situation has changed, religion can still be a divisive issue in Northern Ireland.

- In Belfast, barriers called **Peace Walls** erected to separate Protestant and Catholic working-class areas during the Troubles are still in place (Fig. 17.12).
- The educational structure reflects the religious divide; over 90% of students still attend schools where students all have the same religion. This is called **segregation**.
- Rates of **intermarriage** between religions are still very low.
- The **Orange Order** is a political organisation composed mostly of Protestants. Every year on **12 July**, it commemorates King William of Orange's victory over the Catholic King James. Long-established parade routes though Catholic areas were – and still are – regarded by residents as displays of Protestant triumphalism. The **Parades Commission** was established to rule on parade routes, but many of their decisions have caused tensions among both communities (Fig. 17.13).

↑ **Fig. 17.12** A Peace Wall in Belfast.

↑ **Fig. 17.13** An Orange Order parade.

The changing demographics of the population has implications for the future as the percentage of Catholics in Northern Ireland increases. While Northern Ireland has made huge strides towards peace and democracy, religious differences will continue to have a big influence on the region.

CHECK YOUR LEARNING

1. Identify two examples of the discrimination experienced by Catholics following the creation of the Northern Ireland state.
2. What changes did the Good Friday/Belfast Agreement bring to the lives of Northern Irish Nationalists?
3. List three indications that a religious divide still exists in Northern Ireland.

CASE STUDY: THE ISLAMIC WORLD – A REGION ASSOCIATED WITH RELIGION

The Islamic religion was founded by the **prophet Muhammad** at the beginning of the 7th century AD. After his death in 632, disputes over his successor led to the formation of two separate Muslim sects: **Sunni** and **Shia**. Sunnis make up the majority of the **Islamic World** today. Islamic teaching permeates **all aspects of society**, from law to the economy and social issues. There are over 50,000 Muslims living in Ireland. Throughout the Islamic World, different **customs** and traditions have evolved due to the influence of local and regional influences.

KEYWORDS
Sunni
Shia
Islamic world
customs

The Kingdom of Saudi Arabia

Located in the Middle East, the Kingdom of Saudi Arabia is an Islamic country (**Fig. 17.14**). It is a **monarchy**, and follows a strict form of Islam associated with the **Wahhabi sect**. **Sharia law** forms the basis of the country's legal system; the religious police – the **Muttawa** – are charged with enforcing dress codes and ensuring strict separation of men and women in public places.

Islamic World: Refers to Muslims or followers of Islam and the societies where Islam is practised.

DID YOU KNOW?
Islam is the world's second largest religion (after Christianity). There are approximately 50,000 Muslims living in Ireland as of 2016.

← **Fig. 17.14** Map of Saudi Arabia.

Prayer: There are five occasions daily when prayers are offered. During prayers, many shops and restaurants close.

Dress: Saudi men are expected to wear clothing that covers their entire body. They also generally wear a chequered head cloth known as a **keffiyeh**. When Saudi women are in public, they are expected to wear a black overgarment called an **abaya** as well as a headpiece, the **niqab** (**Fig. 17.15**).

Food and drink: Alcohol is forbidden in Saudi Arabia as is the consumption of **pork** and pork products.

Gender roles: A combination of traditional customs and interpretations of Sharia law have resulted in women's rights being limited. All women are considered to have an **official male guardian**, usually their father, brother, uncle or husband. Major decisions such as getting a passport, going travelling, and getting married or divorced require the guardian's approval.

↑ **Fig. 17.15** Traditional clothing in Saudi Aradia.

257

Religious practice: Sunni Islam is the state religion, and any religious practices that contradict Sunni beliefs are not permitted in public. Christians, Jews and other religious minorities are allowed to practise their religion in the privacy of their own homes. The minority Shiite community faces major discrimination and isolation within the Kingdom.

Changes

Social and economic changes are slowly being introduced to the country. In 2015, women were given the right to vote and run for office in municipal elections. The ban on women driving alone was lifted in 2018, and is expected to result in women becoming more active in the workforce. At the time of writing, women made up only 22% of the working population.

EXAM LINK (OL)

Regions and Culture (30 marks)

The culture of a region can often be determined by the following factors:
- Religion
- Politics
- Sport/Games
- Language
- Music/Dance

Describe and explain the importance of culture in any region that you have studied.

2016, Q4C

Marking Scheme:
Description and explanation = 10 SRPs × 3 marks
Allow one SRP for a named region.
At least one SRP must be for explanation.

EXAM LINK (HL)

Concept of a Region (30 marks)

Examine how culture can be used to define regions, with reference to example(s) that you have studied.

2018, Q4B

Marking Scheme:
Aspect of culture identified = 2 marks
Example of a region defined by culture = 2 marks
Examination = 13 SRPs × 2 marks

CHECK YOUR LEARNING

1. Name the two main religious sects in the Islamic World.
2. Describe four ways in which religion influences daily life in Saudi Arabia.

A Region of Industrial Decline

KEYWORDS
competition · iron and steel · out-migration · contraction
coal · textiles · de-industrialisation · redevelopment
rivers · coastal steel plants · decline

The **Industrial Revolution** of the 18th century led to the growth and development of major industrial regions in Europe. However, by the mid-20th century, declining coal reserves, changing energy sources, increasing production costs and competition from other world regions brought some unwelcome changes. What were once important centres of manufacturing and employment were now areas of **industrial decline** with abandoned plants and high levels of unemployment.

CASE STUDY: THE SAMBRE-MEUSE VALLEY, BELGIUM

In the 19th century, **abundant coal deposits** that could be easily and cheaply transported from the main coalfields along the **River Meuse** made the Sambre-Meuse Valley in Belgium one of the major industrial regions in Europe (**Fig. 17.16**). Attracted by the coal, **iron and steel industries** formed the basis of a vast range of engineering industries in the area, and industrial towns such as **Liège** grew and prospered. Coal deposits also attracted the **textile industry** – Verviers developed as an important centre for the production of woollen cloth. The concentration of industry in the Sambre-Meuse Valley drew in huge numbers of workers, making Wallonia the dominant economic and cultural region in Belgium.

↑ **Fig. 17.16** Map of Belgium. The Sambre-Meuse Valley surrounds the two rivers, the Sambre and the Meuse, and is where most of the country's coalfields are located.

Decline
By the 1960s, the region had undergone major changes.

Contraction in coal mining
By the middle of the 20th century, many coal mines had become **exhausted**, while in others **mining costs increased** as pits went deeper. **Cheaper coal imports** from Poland and the USA, as well as **competition** from other energy sources such as oil and gas, led to **reduced demand**.

In the mid-1980s, when the last coal mines closed, an industry that once provided employment for over 100,000 people had completely disappeared.

Declining iron and steel production
Inland steel plants were forced to close due to competition from modern, lower-cost/higher-productivity **coastal plants**, e.g. Zelzate, which used imported coal and ore, and from lower-cost steel producers such as India.

The textile industry
Competition from low-cost producers in Asia, for example, Bangladesh, led to the decline of textile manufacturing.

Impacts
Socio-economic impact
The status of Wallonia as the centre of industry and employment in Belgium declined, and a region that once attracted migrants was now experiencing **net out-migration**. This movement of French speakers to non-French-speaking areas also impacted on the **language issue**.

Unemployment increased with the closure of coal mines and the decline of the iron and steel and textile industries.

The **de-industrialisation** of the region coincided with the growth of industries such as electronics and petrochemicals in Flanders. The lack of employment opportunities in the Sambre-Meuse Valley meant people now migrated to the new growth areas in Flanders, such as the city of Antwerp.

Landscapes

Environmental impact

The Sambre-Meuse Valley was littered with coal waste heaps and abandoned industrial plants (Fig. 17.17). A long history of industrial pollution and construction had resulted in an unattractive, depressed industrial region.

Redevelopment

By the mid-1980s, when the last coal mine closed, the economic regeneration of the region had become a priority for the Belgian government.

↑ **Fig. 17.17** A coal waste heap, Sambre-Meuse Valley.

The region was designated an **Objective 2** region under the **EU Regional Development Fund**. The traditional pattern of heavy industry was never going to reappear, so the Belgian government had to initiate strategies to redevelop the region. These strategies included:

- provision of **low-interest loans, grants and tax incentives** to attract investment;
- the **European Social Fund** supported the retraining of former miners;
- **new motorways** and **high-speed trains** linking the region to Brussels and Europe to reduce transport costs and improve trade routes;
- **industrial estates** and **technopoles** linked to nearby technological institutions, for example, **Liège Science Park**, were constructed;
- decaying buildings were cleared, coal waste heaps removed and the sites landscaped. Some elements of the industrial heritage have been preserved, while others have been restored and now have new functions (e.g. **Blegny-Mine**, a former coal mine that is now a museum).

Objective 2 region: The European Regional Development Fund classifies declining industrial regions as 'Objective 2' regions. The Fund will provide 50% of the finance for approved projects designed to stimulate socio-economic development in these regions.

Technopole: An industrial development with a focus on high-tech industries and businesses with access to educational and research and development facilities.

EXAM LINK (HL)

Industrial Decline (30 marks)

Examine the causes and impacts of industrial decline with reference to any region(s) that you have studied.

2015, Q4B

Marking Scheme:
Cause identified = 2 marks
Impact identified = 2 marks
Examination = 13 SRPs × 2 marks

CHECK YOUR LEARNING

1. Explain two reasons why the Sambre-Meuse Valley became a major centre of industry.
2. List two reasons why coal mining declined in the Sambre-Meuse Valley in the 20th century.
3. Name two reasons for the decline of the iron and steel industry in the Sambre-Meuse Valley.
4. List two impacts of industrial decline on the region.
5. Name four redevelopment strategies implemented in the Sambre-Meuse Valley region.

Urban Regions

Urban regions are also referred to as **nodal regions** or **cities**. They are built-up areas, usually with a high population density, and can include towns and suburbs.

Cities have developed and grown in all regions of the world. Economic and social factors resulted in rapid urban growth in the 20th and 21st centuries. By 2050, it is estimated that 66% – two-thirds – of the global population will live in cities.

Case studies on urban regions are examined in *Chapter 18: A Core Irish Region – The Greater Dublin Area*, *Chapter 20: A Core European Region – The Paris Basin*, and *Chapter 22: A Continental/Subcontinental Region: India*.

Nodal region: A centre with a concentration of population and a range of industrial and economic activities. It is connected to surrounding regions by transport and communication infrastructures.

City: A business and cultural centre with a network of suburbs and a large population.

Socio-Economic Regions

The characteristics of socio-economic regions are based on both economic and social factors. The interaction of these different factors, combined with the physical characteristics of the region in question, results in economically well-developed **core** regions and less well-developed **peripheral** regions.

Characteristics of core and peripheral regions

Core regions

Physical characteristics	Social characteristics	Economic characteristics
Favourable physical environment	High population density	Economically well-developed
No climate extremes	In-migration	Excellent infrastructure
Core location	Low dependency ratio	Variety of economic activities
Fertile soils	Pool of skilled labour	Well-developed market
Natural resources	Decision-making centres (government)	High income levels

Chapter 18: A Core Irish Region – The Greater Dublin Area
Chapter 20: A Core European Region – The Paris Basin

Peripheral regions

Physical characteristics	Social characteristics	Economic characteristics
Difficult physical environment	Low population density	Less economically developed
Extremes of climate	Out-migration	Poor infrastructure
Peripheral location	High dependency ratio	Dependent on primary activities
Poor soils	Lack of skilled labour	Poor local market
Lack of resources	Political neglect	Low income levels

Chapter 19: A Peripheral Irish Region – The Western Region
Chapter 20: A Peripheral European Region – The Mezzogiorno

EXAM LINK (HL)

The Concept of a Region (30 marks)

Explain three differences between the characteristics of core regions and the characteristics of peripheral regions, with reference to examples that you have studied.

2017, Q6C

Marking Scheme:
Core region named = 2 marks
Peripheral region named = 2 marks
Three differences explained = 13 × 2 marks

Dependency ratio: The ratio of the dependent sector (0–14 and 65+ years) to the active sector (15–64 years) in an economy.

Landscapes

EXAMINATION QUESTIONS
ORDINARY LEVEL

Short Questions

1. Regions

Match the description of a region with the example of the region that best matches it, by writing the correct letter in each case in the table below.

	Description of region	Example of region	Letter
A	A cultural region	The Greater Dublin Area	
B	A core region	Munster Ridge and Valley	
C	A geomorphological region	Cool temperate oceanic	
D	An administrative region in France	The Basque region	
E	A climatic region	Département	

2017, Part One, Q8 (10 marks)

HIGHER LEVEL

Short Questions

2. Regions

Complete the table by matching each of the examples of regions in the list below with the type of region most associated with it.

Wallonia   The Burren   Temperate oceanic region   Waterford County Council
Islamic World   Rotterdam   Pas-de-Calais Département   Northern European Plain

Type of region	Example of region
Geomorphological	
Geomorphological	
Cultural (language)	
Nodal	
Administrative	
Administrative	
Cultural (religion)	
Climatic	

2017, Part One, Q5 (8 marks)

262

Revision Summary

Climatic regions

- Global climate zones: Polar – Cold – Moderate – Subtropical – Tropical
- Cool temperate oceanic climate – between +/–40° and +/–65° latitude – includes NW Europe, from Norway to Northern Spain
- Ireland has cool temperate oceanic climate – winter av. 5°C – summer av. 15°C – relief and frontal rain all year – prevailing SW winds – North Atlantic Drift gives warmer water temperatures and winds – depressions carried (tracked) from the West by North Atlantic jet stream

Geomorphological regions

The Burren, Co. Clare
- See Chapter 6

Munster Ridge and Valley
- Armorican folding
- Anticline/Synclines

North European Plain
- Lowland
- Variety of soils
- Glacial: boulder clay, limon

Administrative regions

Ireland
- Regional Assemblies: 3
- Local authorities
  - County councils: 26
  - City and county councils: 2
  - City councils: 3
- Municipal districts

France
- Major reforms 2016
- Régions: 18
- Départements: 101
- Communes: 36,000

Socio-economic regions

- Core regions: Greater Dublin Area – Paris Basin
- Peripheral regions: Western Region of Ireland – Mezzogiorno

Cultural regions: language

Ireland
- Gaeltacht – a region where Irish is the main spoken language
- Peripheral location – poor infrastructure – low population densities – limited job opportunities
- Údarás na Gaeltacht – provides grants, advance factories, training programmes – attract inward investment
- Irish language summer courses – Gaelic sports – traditional Irish music – The Wild Atlantic Way – unique character of Gaeltacht areas
- Government grants for new houses, home improvements – applicants must prove Irish is main language at home
- TG4 and Raidió na Gaeltachta positive supports

Belgium
- Contains four language communities: Flanders, Flemish – Wallonia, French – Eupen-Malmedy, German – Brussels, Flemish and French
- Wallonia was the most industrialised region – French became the language of business and professionals
- Industrial decline of Wallonia mid-20th century – economic growth in Flanders – increasing status of Flemish
- In Flanders and Wallonia, public administration is in main language – *communes à facilités* must provide language facilities for minority language
- Brussels is bilingual – public administration, documents and street signs must be in Flemish and French – most speak French, so urban sprawl means more French speakers in Flemish areas – perceived threat to Flemish language

Cultural regions: religion

Ireland
- Ulster Plantation 17th century – majority Protestant community formed – The Government of Ireland Act 1920 – six counties of Northern Ireland a self-governing region within UK
- Two community groups – Protestant Unionists (majority) – Catholic Nationalists (minority)
- Civil service, the police force, major industries employed mostly members of Protestant community
- The Troubles 1969–98: 30 years of unrest – 3,600 people killed
- 1998 Good Friday/Belfast Agreement – power-sharing executive – Equality Commission
- Religion still divisive in Northern Ireland – peace walls – segregated education – low intermarriage rates – Orange Order and 12 July parade – recent resurgence of Nationalist violence

Saudi Arabia
- Islam the world's second largest religion – two sects, Sunni and Shia
- Kingdom of Saudi Arabia – state religion is strict form of Sunni Islam – Sharia law enforced
- Dress codes – prayer five times daily, shops and restaurants close – alcohol and pork products forbidden – strict segregation of sexes
- Limited rights and freedom for women – must have male guardian
- Religious practices contradicting Sunni beliefs are not permitted in public – minorities face discrimination and isolation
- Changes in recent years: 2015, women given right to vote and run for municipal office – 2018, ban on women driving alone lifted, hopes for more women in workplace
- In 2018, women were 22% of working population

Declining industrial region

Sambre-Meuse Valley – Belgium

- Easily accessible coal – major industrial region in 19th century – attracted iron and steel and engineering industries – industrial towns evolved
- Major centre of employment – Wallonia became the dominant economic and cultural region in Belgium (see Cultural regions: language)
- Decline in 20th century – coal mines exhausted – imported coal cheaper – reduced demand due to competition from oil and gas – over 100,000 mining jobs had disappeared
- Iron and steel decline – competition from modern coastal plants, lower-cost and higher productivity – using imported coal and ore
- Socio-economic impact – economy of Wallonia declined – unemployment – coincided with industrial growth in Flanders – out-migration
- Environmental impact – waste heaps – abandoned industrial plants – industrial pollution – unattractive
- Redevelopment – classified ERDF Objective 2 region – provision of low interest loans, grants and tax incentives to attract investment – retraining for former miners – new transport infrastructure – new industrial estates and technopoles linked to technological institutions – decaying buildings cleared, coal waste heaps removed, sites landscaped
- Some elements of industrial heritage preserved, others have been restored and have new functions, e.g. Blegny-Mine

18 A CORE IRISH REGION – THE GREATER DUBLIN AREA

Core region: An economically well-developed region.

LEARNING INTENTIONS
Syllabus Links: 2.2

By the end of this chapter I will be able to:
- draw an outline map of the Greater Dublin Area and show and name different types of features;
- explain how physical processes have shaped the landscape of this region;
- describe the factors that have influenced the development of primary, secondary and tertiary activities of the region;
- describe and explain the human processes that have influenced the population of the region;
- explain how the city of Dublin has developed.

KEYWORDS
cool temperate oceanic climate
frontal rainfall
relief rainfall
metamorphosis
brown earth
alluvial
podzol

The Greater Dublin Area (GDA) is part of the **Eastern and Midland Regional Assembly**. It comprises Dublin city, Fingal, South Dublin and Dún Laoghaire-Rathdown, along with counties Meath, Kildare and Wicklow (**Figs 18.1–18.2**).

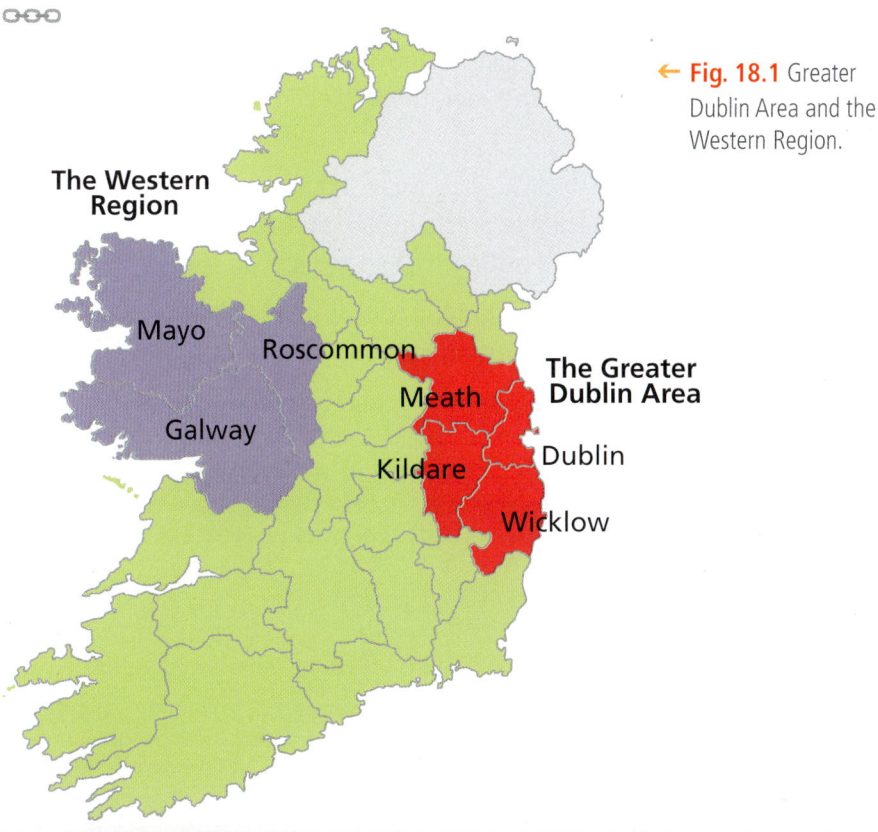

← Fig. 18.1 Greater Dublin Area and the Western Region.

Chapter 17: The Concept of a Region

SKILLS ACTIVITY

Draw a sketch map of Ireland. On it, show and label the following:
- a region you have studied;
- one named area of relief (upland or lowland) in this region;
- one named river in this region;
- one named road in this region;
- one named town or city in this region;
- an industrial area in this region;
- an agricultural area in this region.

Landscapes

Sketch Map of the Greater Dublin Area

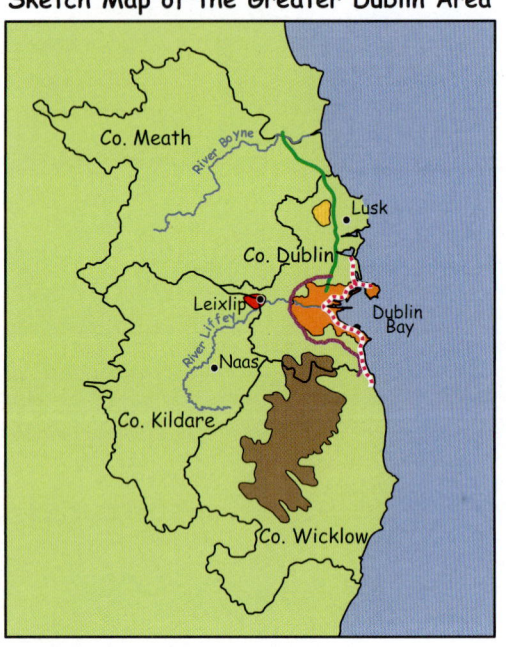

Key for Sketch Map of the Greater Dublin Area
- Agricultural area
- Industrial area
- Upland area: Wicklow Mountains
- Dublin city
- Urban centre
- M1
- M50
- DART

↑ **Fig. 18.2** Sketch map of the Greater Dublin Area.

↑ **Fig. 18.3** Relief map of the Greater Dublin Area.

> Grass grows only in soil with a temperature above 6°C.

SKILLS ACTIVITY

Using graph paper, draw a suitable graph to illustrate the precipitation data from January to June in **Table 18.1**.

Physical Processes

Climate

The GDA has a **cool temperate oceanic climate**. Its main characteristics include:

- warm summer temperatures averaging 15°C, and mild winter temperatures averaging 5°C;
- approximately 800 mm of precipitation annually – the lowest of any Irish region. Most precipitation comes in the form of **frontal rainfall**. While precipitation falls throughout the year, the wettest months are December and January;
- upland areas such as the Wicklow Mountains experience lower temperatures, while **relief rainfall** brings higher precipitation rates. Easterly winds in winter bring cold continental air across the Irish Sea, which can lead to snow;
- the average number of days with ground frost is much lower than that found in inland areas due to the **moderating influence** of the Irish Sea;
- an average of four hours of daily sunshine, and a **growing season** of approximately 285 days.

	Jan	Feb	Mar	Apr	May	Jun	Jul	Aug	Sep	Oct	Nov	Dec
Mean temperature (°C)	5.3	3.4	4.3	8.1	11.4	14.5	16.1	15.3	12.2	9.3	8.2	7.7
Total rainfall (mm)	93.1	36.9	100.0	68.9	19.1	4.8	40.0	48.0	43.8	42.6	131.2	81.0

↑ **Table 18.1** Climate data for Dublin Airport, 2018 (Met Éireann).

→ **Table 18.2** Total annual rainfall at Dublin Airport (Met Éireann).

2016	2017	2018
713.6 mm	660.7 mm	709.4 mm

Relief and drainage

To the north and west, lowlands are under-laid with permeable carboniferous limestone, ensuring **good surface drainage**.

To the south of the region are the Wicklow Mountains. Formed during the **Caledonian folding period** approximately 400 million years ago, they have a north-east to south-west directional trend. During the folding process, magma intruded and then cooled slowly to form granite. Pre-existing shales and sandstones experienced **old metamorphosis**, forming slate, schist and quartzite (e.g. the **Sugar Loaf Mountain**, Fig. 18.4).

Cooling volcanic gases also formed **minerals** such as lead, zinc, copper and gold deposits – the copper mine at Avoca was based on one of these large deposits.

The uplands were affected by **glaciation** with examples of glacial features including cirques (e.g. **Lough Nahanagan**) and U-shaped and hanging valleys (e.g. **Glendalough**).

The rivers Liffey, Tolka, Dargle and Boyne drain the region eastwards to the Irish Sea, while the River Barrow in Kildare flows southwards.

Chapter 4: Folding and Faulting Activity
Chapter 17: The Concept of a Region

Permeable: A permeable rock allows water to pass through it.

SKILLS ACTIVITY

Draw an outline map of Ireland showing and naming the following:
- two named urban centres;
- a named feature of relief (upland or lowland);
- a numbered road and one other communications link;
- two features of drainage.

↑ **Fig. 18.4** The Sugar Loaf Mountain in the Wicklow Mountains.

Soils

Fertile, well-drained **brown earth** soils are found on lowland areas. They have a high humus content, as they were formed under the deciduous forest that originally covered the GDA.

Alluvial soils are found on the flood plains of the major rivers draining the region (e.g. the rivers **Liffey** and **Boyne**), while sand has been deposited on the **brown earth** soils of North County Dublin, making them lighter and better-drained.

Glacial deposits of **boulder clay** are found in counties Kildare and Meath.

Podzol soils, which formed on the granite bedrock, and peaty soils, associated with blanket bogs, are both found in the Wicklow Mountains.

EXAM TIP

According to the Chief Examiner's Report (2012), the quality of students' sketch maps in the Regional Geography section was unsatisfactory. It recommended that students should practise the skill of drawing sketch maps of Ireland, European and continental/subcontinental regions.

You can always use the map of Ireland shown at the bottom of the OS map to assist you when drawing sketch maps of Irish regions.

CHECK YOUR LEARNING

1. List four characteristics of the climate experienced by the Greater Dublin Area.
2. Describe the relief of the GDA.
3. Name three features of glacial erosion found in the uplands of this region.
4. Describe the distribution of soils in the GDA.
5. Explain the following terms: podzol, frontal rainfall, metamorphosis.

Landscapes

KEYWORDS
fishing
forestry
energy
market gardening
growing season
pastoral
arable
fodder

Primary Economic Activities

In core regions, primary activities involving the extraction and use of the earth's land and sea resources are well-developed. They include **farming**, **fishing**, **forestry**, **mining** and **energy**.

Agriculture

Agriculture in the Greater Dublin Area is **well-developed** and **highly productive**. Its success is due to the interaction of a number of different factors.

Physical factors

Climate

- The GDA experiences **a cool temperate oceanic climate**, resulting in mild winters. Combined with the moderating influence of the sea, the risk of frost is reduced. This provides ideal conditions for **market gardening** (**horticulture**) with vegetables grown outdoors rather than under glass for most of the year, **reducing costs**. This in turn produces **higher profit margins** on horticultural crops such as cabbage and Brussels sprouts, grown in Rush and Lusk.

- The GDA has a long **growing season** of over 285 days, which supports **multi-cropping** of horticultural crops in North County Dublin.

- **Pastoral farming** is an important activity in the GDA. The long **growing season** contributes to the early growth of grass, allowing farmers to get the animals out onto pastures early in the year and so reduce the consumption of expensive **winter fodder**. **Beef cattle**, many of whom have been reared in the western region, are fattened on the fertile grasslands of County Meath, while dairy farming is carried on in County Kildare (**Fig. 18.5**).

- The **rain shadow effect** means the GDA receives much less rainfall than the west of Ireland. This means that the damp, humid conditions that contribute to potato blight are not so prevalent in the GDA. Counties Dublin and Meath are the main commercial potato-producing areas.

- Warm temperatures and moderate rainfall provide ideal conditions for **arable farming**. Crops such as wheat, barley and maize are cultivated throughout the region.

- Due to the harsher climate, **sheep farming** is an important pastoral farming activity on the **upper slopes** of the Wicklow Mountains.

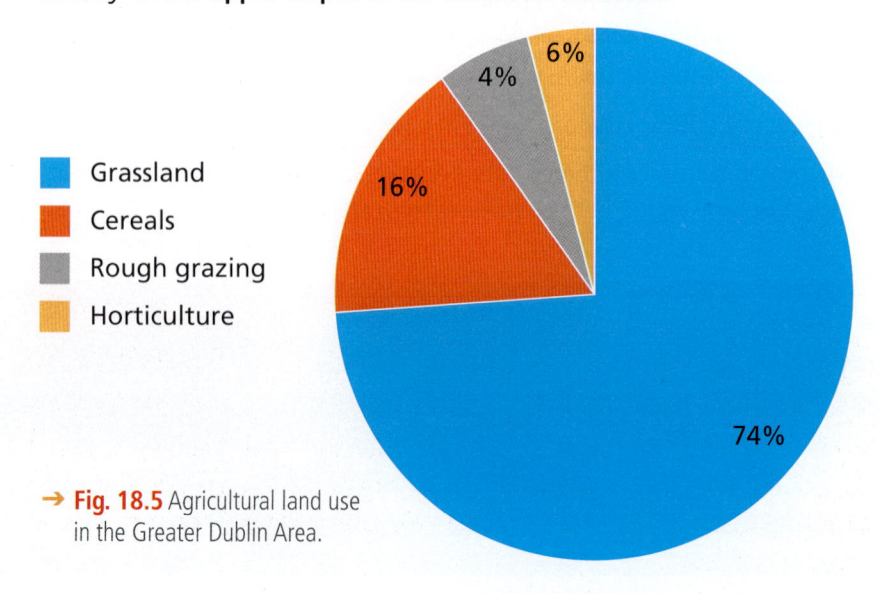

EXAM TIP
Answers to questions on Irish regions must refer to the region by name, and include places and economic activities specific to that region.

Rain shadow: The area on the landward side of mountains where rainfall is lower.

- Grassland — 74%
- Cereals — 16%
- Rough grazing — 4%
- Horticulture — 6%

→ **Fig. 18.5** Agricultural land use in the Greater Dublin Area.

Relief

- Much of the region consists of well-drained, gently undulating lowlands. The lowland relief supports the widespread use of machinery, and a well-developed **commercial arable farming** sector has evolved.

- Ploughing, sowing, and spraying of crops is efficiently carried out by single-driver-operated machinery, **reducing labour costs** and **increasing profits**. Large, gently-sloping fields are also suited to combine harvesters, resulting in the production of cereals such as wheat and barley. Lowland relief has also contributed to the large-scale production of **fodder crops**, such as rapeseed and maize, especially in County Meath.

- In the past, the lowland relief also facilitated the development of the **Royal and Grand Canals**, which were used to **transport agricultural raw materials** such as wheat to flour mills in Dublin.

- The low, flat land has enabled the development of an excellent **road transport infrastructure**, allowing for the movement of **agricultural raw materials** such as malting barley to Guinness and beef cattle to meat processing plants (e.g. **Kepak**).

- The sloping relief of the **Wicklow Mountains** cannot support commercial arable agriculture. **Sheep** are reared on the steep **upper slopes**, while **pastoral** farming of dairy and beef **cattle** is found on the **lower slopes**.

Soil

- Low levels of precipitation in most parts of the GDA have reduced the impact of **nutrient leaching**, thus maintaining soil fertility levels.

- **Light loam soils** – formed by the mixing of **marine sands** and **brown earth** soils – in North County Dublin are extremely fertile. These soils are ideal for **horticulture** when they warm up in spring.

- The high **calcium** content in soils covering the carboniferous limestone of County Kildare have encouraged **horse breeding**.

- Higher precipitation levels on the Wicklow Mountains due to relief rain cause **extensive leaching**, resulting in infertile **podzol** soils. It has also contributed to the formation of blanket bogs with infertile **peat** and **gley** soils. These poor soils support **rough grazing** for sheep, and also some **forestry**.

- Infertile **outwash sands** and **gravel** on the Curragh in County Kildare support **sheep rearing**.

> **Leaching:** Soluble minerals such as calcium are carried from the soil's A horizon to the B horizon by percolating water.
>
> **Gley soils:** Grey-coloured waterlogged soils with low oxygen levels. This slows down the rate that soil organisms break down organic matter.

Socio-economic factors

Efficient commercialised farms

Farm sizes within the GDA exceed the **national average of 32.5 hectares**. For example, the average size of a farm in **County Kildare is 44.1 hectares**. These farms tend to have large fields that facilitate the use of large, modern machinery (Fig. 18.6).

↑ **Fig. 18.6** Large fields and greenhouses, north County Dublin.

Approximately **two-thirds** of farmers in the GDA are aged between **35 and 64 years**. Younger farmers tend to engage in more progressive methods of farming, resulting in high crop yields and the introduction of high-milk-yielding breeds of dairy cows. The use of technology among younger farmers is also increasing. **Modern technology applications** for farming include weather apps, calving sensors and record-keeping software.

Feed for animals during winter is a huge expense for farmers. Farmers reduce the cost of winter feed by growing **outdoor forage crops** such as kale. This is fed to cattle during the early winter months, reducing the time animals need to be kept indoors (which is expensive). By reducing the amount of time animals are kept indoors, the **risk of infection and disease** being spread among the herd is also reduced.

As a result of these measures, **farm outputs are higher**, providing **average incomes of €52,000** – well above the national average of €36,000. This provides farmers with a decent standard of living and surplus cash to reinvest in their farms.

Markets and infrastructure

Markets stimulate and support commercial agricultural production, so proximity and good access across the country are vital. The GDA constitutes the **largest (1.9 million) and most affluent market** in the country. It supports:

- a large **horticultural** sector in North County Dublin (fruit and vegetables are produced for **farm shops** and **supermarkets** in local urban areas);
- a strong **beef farming** sector (cattle fattened on farms in Co. Meath and Co. Kildare are **processed in local plants** to supply a large number of butchers, supermarkets and restaurants);
- a variety of **food and drink processors** (e.g. **Largo Foods** in Meath, **Green Isle** in Kildare and **Guinness** in Dublin), which encourage commercial farming of their **raw materials**.

An excellent transport infrastructure links the agricultural hinterland to the large urban market and agri-food industries. This is important for two reasons: firstly, it **limits the cost of transporting agricultural produce**, and secondly, the faster perishable produce gets to the point of sale, the longer the **shelf life** will be, giving them a higher commercial value.

Dublin Port facilitates the export of agricultural produce to UK, European and global **markets**. In recent years, however, the impact of **Brexit** and the falling value of sterling have led to a reduction in exports from all parts of Ireland, including the GDA.

Political factors

EU support

The larger and more commercial farms of the GDA benefitted greatly from the Guidance Section of the EU's Common Agricultural Policy (CAP), which provided grants for farm improvements through investment in machinery and buildings. This has led to increased farm output and higher profits.

The **Rural Environmental Protection Scheme (REPS)** and its successor, the **Green, Low-Carbon, Agri-Environment Scheme**, provide payments to farmers who make an effort to farm in an environmentally-friendly way, protecting and preserving traditional hay meadows and animal habitats, and addressing carbon emissions from farming. EU membership also gives farmers access to the **European Single Market**, one of the largest markets in the world.

Fishing

Howth is the most important fishing port in the Greater Dublin Area, followed by the smaller port of Skerries further to the north (Fig. 18.7). In Howth, major **government and EU investment** led to improvements, including better harbour access, new piers, new boat-repair facilities and a new ice plant. The nearby urban market of Dublin and the **excellent transport infrastructure** throughout the region means fresh fish can be quickly delivered to fish markets, supermarkets and local food processing plants.

↑ **Fig. 18.7** Howth fishing port.

Reduced catches due to **overfishing** and the quotas associated with the EU's **Common Fisheries Policy** have impacted on the fishing industry, and fish landings have declined in terms of tonnage and value. This has resulted in reduction in fishing fleet size, and thus the number of people employed in the industry.

> High levels of pollution in coastal areas of the GDA have prevented the large-scale development of fish farming.

Forestry

Upland relief and **poor soils** limit agricultural land use in the Wicklow Mountains. However, conditions are suited to **forestry**, an important land use in the uplands. The mild climate encourages quick growth of **Sitka and Norway spruce**, the most common varieties of timber, so forests provide **employment** in logging and **sawmilling**. Rich in biodiversity, they are important recreational areas for the urban population of the Greater Dublin Area (e.g. the Vale of Clara forest walk), and thus provide even more **employment** opportunities in **tourism** and **maintenance**.

Most of the GDA forestry is **state-owned** and managed by Coillte, though **government** policy, higher premiums and EU grants have resulted in an **increase in private ownership** of forests in recent years.

> **DID YOU KNOW?**
> Co. Wicklow has the largest afforested land mass in the country with approximately 22% of the land covered in woodland.

Mining

Lead and zinc ore is mined at Tara Mines in Navan, Co. Meath.

Renewable energy

The **Arklow Bank Wind Park**, located on a shallow water sandbank off County Wicklow, is the **first offshore wind farm** in Ireland. It has a production capacity of 25 megawatts (Fig. 18.8). Proposals for further expansion of wind energy generation in the Irish Sea have been strenuously opposed by tourism and environmental interest groups, who are concerned about the scale of the proposed development and its visibility from the shore.

> **DID YOU KNOW?**
> Tara Mines employs almost 600 people and is Europe's largest lead and zinc mine. Concentrates from the mine are shipped through Dublin Port to smelters throughout Europe.

Hydroelectric power is generated at three locations on the River Liffey – **Golden Falls** and **Poulaphuca** in County Wicklow, and **Leixlip** in County Kildare. A station located at **Turlough Hill**, County Wicklow, uses off-peak electricity to pump water to a storage reservoir at the top of the hill. This water is then released at peak demand times to generate electricity.

Fig. 18.8 Offshore wind farms in the Irish Sea have been opposed by tourism and environment interest groups.

EXAM LINK (OL)

Agriculture in Ireland (40 marks)
(i) Name two types of farming in Ireland.
(ii) Explain how any two of the following factors influence the development of agriculture in an Irish region you have studied.
   Relief and soils   Markets   Climate

2016, Q4B

Marking Scheme:
(i) 2 × 2 marks
(ii) Each factor = 6 SRPs × 3 marks

Landscapes

> **EXAM LINK (HL)**
>
> Primary Economic Activity – Irish Region (30 marks)
>
> Examine the physical factors that influence the development of one primary economic activity in an Irish region that you have studied.
>
> 2017, Q4C
>
> **Marking Scheme:**
> Physical factors identified = 2 × 2 marks
> Examination = 13 SRPs × 2 marks
> Credit two specific examples of primary economic activities named as 2 SRPs

> **CHECK YOUR LEARNING**
> 1. Name three types of farming carried out in the GDA and name one area associated with each type.
> 2. Name three crops grown in the GDA.
> 3. Explain how any three socio-economic factors have influenced agricultural development in the GDA.
> 4. Describe two impacts the EU has had on the development of agriculture in the GDA.
> 5. Name two forms of renewable energy generated in this region.

KEYWORDS
raw materials
horticulture
workforce
quality of life
transport
markets
government
costs
corporation tax

Secondary Economic Activities

In core economic regions, secondary economic activities are very well-developed. This is due to the interaction of a number of factors.

Physical factors

Raw materials

The Greater Dublin Area's **cool temperate oceanic climate**, lowland relief and fertile soils support a wide variety of agricultural production. A range of **agri-food industries** using locally produced **raw materials** have developed in the region.

- **Malt barley** supports **brewing**, and is used by **Guinness** at St. James's Gate, Dublin. A number of new **distilleries** making Irish whiskey also use malting barley in the process.
- **Reservoirs** in the Wicklow Mountains provide an abundant supply of clean water to a variety of industries in the region, including **pharmaceutical** companies such as **Pfizer** at Grange Castle.
- **Milk** from dairy farming in the region supplies the **Cadbury** plant in Coolock, and is also used in the production of **crème liqueurs**.
- Meat processing plants (e.g. **Kepak** in Co. Meath and **Kildare Chilling Company** in Co. Kildare) are supplied by the **beef** farmers of the region.
- **Horticulture** supports the vegetable processing industry, supplying companies such as **Green Isle** in Naas and **potato crisp** manufacturers in North County Dublin.

Fish processing

Fish landed at Howth and Skerries are used to supply a number of plants throughout the region. These plants (e.g. **Oceanpath**, Howth) smoke and process a wide variety of seafood, including cod and mackerel.

Artisan foods

Small and medium-sized units throughout the region produce food items such as rapeseed oil and artisanal cheese (e.g. **Wicklow Farmhouse Cheese**).

Forestry

Sawmills process trees from Wicklow forests and produce a variety of products including construction timber, packaging timber, fencing products and decking (e.g. **Woodfab**, Aughrim).

Socio-economic factors

Labour force

- **Foreign Direct Investment (FDI)** has been attracted to the Greater Dublin Area by a young, well-educated and highly productive **workforce**. Local universities (Trinity College, University College Dublin, Dublin City University, National University of Ireland, Maynooth) and technological institutes (Blanchardstown, Tallaght, Dublin Institute of Technology) provide a skilled labour pool, which has attracted **technology companies** such as **Intel** in Leixlip, County Kildare (**Fig. 18.9**).

- **Research and development** activities at higher education institutions also support the **biotech, pharmaceutical and medical device industries**, which have become important elements in the industrial landscape (e.g. **Pfizer**, Newbridge).

- Many of the companies establishing themselves in the GDA are US **multinationals**. As the local workforce is **English-speaking**, American managers can easily communicate their needs and ideas with those developing and later working in these facilities.

- **Inward migration** from other EU states since the mid-1990s, and provision of language education in schools, means the workforce also has a **strong and diverse range of multilingual skills**. This is vital in the areas of global sales, distribution and technical support.

- The GDA also offers a **good quality of life** to employees. This is especially important for those who have to **relocate** themselves and, in some cases, their families.

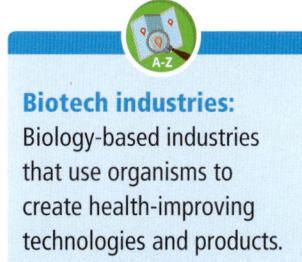

Biotech industries: Biology-based industries that use organisms to create health-improving technologies and products.

↑ Fig. 18.9 Dublin City University.

Transport

An efficient **transport infrastructure** allows goods manufactured in the GDA to access national, European and international **markets**. The **transport network** includes:

- **Dublin Airport**, Ireland's largest and busiest airport, which has direct passenger and freight connections with Europe and North America;

- **Dublin Port**, the largest port in the country, which is the main point of import and export for Irish trade. It has a large container port and roll-on roll-off freight and ferry services with the UK;

- plans for a new high-speed **roll-on roll-off (RoRo) ferry link** between Dublin, the Netherlands and Belgium, which will allow freight traffic to avoid travelling through the UK after it leaves the EU;

- **rail links** between Dublin and the rest of the country, which allow fast movement of raw materials and manufactured products to and from the region;

- the Irish **motorway network**, which radiates from Dublin and facilitates freight transport by HGV;

- **Dublin Area Rapid Transit (DART), Luas and Dublin Bus networks**, which provide transport for workers and residents within the region.

Landscapes

> **DID YOU KNOW?**
> The Greater Dublin Area is home to:
> - 9 of the top 10 global ICT companies;
> - 9 of the world's top 10 pharma companies;
> - 17 of the world's top 25 med-tech companies.

Unfortunately, most of the modern manufacturing plants are located along the **urban fringe** and are poorly serviced by **public transport** services, so workers are forced to use their cars to get to and from work. This has led to significant traffic **congestion** in the region, resulting in longer journey times for workers and increased transport **costs** for companies.

Markets

More than 1.9 million people live in the GDA, making it the **largest market in Ireland**, while **wages** in the region are **above the EU average**. Both of these factors support a wide range of local **consumer industries**, such as printing and publishing plants (e.g. **International News and Media**, Dublin) and food processing industries (e.g. **Tayto** in Oldcastle, Co. Meath).

Excellent **transport links** within Ireland allow access to a national market of over 2.5 million people, while road and rail connections with Northern Ireland allow access to a further market of 1.8 million.

Efficient **air and sea transport links** also allow products to move in an efficient and cost-effective way to access **markets** in Europe.

Ireland's membership of the EU opens up access to the **Single Market** of over 500 million people for any industry located in the GDA. This has been instrumental in attracting **foreign direct investment** to the region with many pharmaceutical and medical technology companies establishing manufacturing plants in the region to access this market.

> **SKILLS ACTIVITY**
> Study **Fig. 18.11** and identify some of the advantages the business park has as a location for industry. Use the aerial photography locations (left centre, right background, etc.) in your answer.

The **multiplier effect** creates markets among manufacturing industries in the region for products such as packaging.

Government agencies such as **Enterprise Ireland** help manufacturers source and develop new markets by providing support in the form of trade missions, grants and relevant contact information (**Fig. 18.10**).

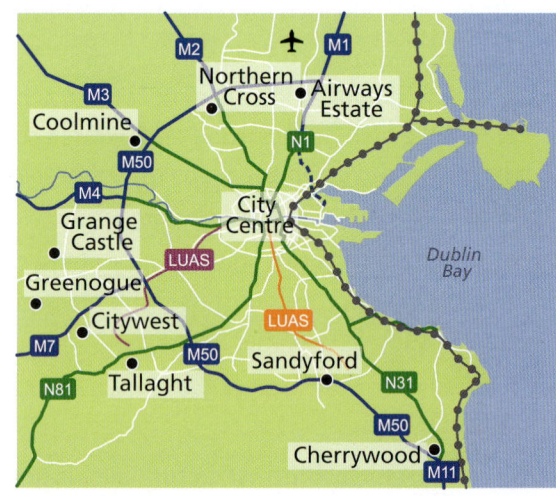

↑ **Fig. 18.10** Business and industrial parks on Dublin's urban fringe.

Political factors

Government support

> Economic activity in the GDA accounts for 47% of Ireland's GDP.

Ireland's low **corporation tax** rate of **12.5%** has helped to attract manufacturing to the GDA. The **Industrial Development Authority (IDA)** has developed fully-serviced industrial estates and technology parks on the outskirts of the city with excellent access to major **transport** routes (e.g. **Park West, Citywest, Sandyford Industrial Estate**; **Fig. 18.11**).

↑ **Fig. 18.11** Citywest Business Campus.

> **Gross Domestic Product (GDP):** the total value of all goods and services produced within a country within a specified time period.

Other IDA supports include training and capital grants, as well as the construction of advance factory units. **Enterprise Ireland** supports Irish entrepreneurs from innovation through start up and expansion.

Challenges facing manufacturing in the region

At present, just under half of Irish industry exports go to Britain. Since the UK decided to leave the EU, there are growing fears for the value of Irish goods on the British market as:

- the **value of sterling** has fallen significantly against the euro;
- a return to a hard border would likely see a re-introduction of **export tariffs**;
- greater **bureaucratic restrictions** would increase delivery times and **transport costs**.

Ireland's low **corporation tax rate** of 12.5% has become an issue for some member states of the European Union, who see it as giving unfair advantage to Ireland in terms of competition. Growing opposition and proposals to examine the **harmonisation of tax rates** throughout the EU could cause major problems for the GDA's future growth and development.

EXAM LINK (OL)

Secondary Economic Activity in an Irish Region (40 marks)

Answer each of the following with reference to an Irish region that you have studied.

(i) Name one example of a secondary economic activity in the region.
(ii) Describe the advantages that this region has for the development of this secondary economic activity.
(iii) Describe one challenge faced by this secondary economic activity in this region.

2018, Q4B

Marking Scheme:
(i) 4 marks
(ii) 9 SRPs × 3 marks
(iii) 3 SRPs × 3 marks

EXAM LINK (HL)

Secondary Economic Activity (30 marks)

Examine the impact of each of the following on the development of secondary economic activity in an Irish region that you have studied.

Raw materials   Markets

2018, Q5C

Marking Scheme:
Region named = 2 marks
Explanation:
Raw materials = 7 SRPs × 2 marks
Markets = 7 SRPs × 2 marks

CHECK YOUR LEARNING

1. Name three types of manufacturing in the GDA that rely on agriculture for raw materials.
2. List and explain three socio-economic factors that have influenced the development of manufacturing in the GDA.
3. Describe four ways in which the Irish government supports the development of the manufacturing industry.
4. Explain two ways the EU has impacted the development of manufacturing in the Greater Dublin Area.
5. Describe and explain one challenge facing the manufacturing industry in the Greater Dublin Area.

Landscapes

KEYWORDS
access
attractions
activities
government
accommodation
Brexit

Tertiary Economic Activities

Economic activity in the GDA is dominated by the tertiary sector with over **80% of the workforce** employed in sectors such as the civil service, health, education, banking, tourism and transport.

Tourism

In 2017, around nine million visitors generated income of more than €2.6 billion in the Greater Dublin Area, helping to stimulate growth and provide **employment** for over 170,000 people in the tourism sector.

The development of tourism in the Greater Dublin Area is the result of the interaction of a number of factors.

County	Overseas visitors	Value (€ m)	Domestic visitors	Value (€ m)
Dublin	5,936,000	1981	1,497,000	307
Kildare	211,000	91	286,000	36
Wicklow	275,000	73	319,000	49
Meath	162,000	44	223,000	44
Total	6,584,000	€2,189 m	2,325,000	€436 m

↑ **Table 18.3** Visitors and spend by county in the Greater Dublin Area, 2017.

Accessibility

The fact that almost 70% of overseas visitors to Ireland visited the Greater Dublin Area in 2017 shows how important **accessibility** is in promoting the region as a tourist destination.

Dublin Airport is Ireland's largest and busiest airport (**Fig. 18.12**). In 2018, around 31.5 million passengers passed through the airport.

Dublin Port has passenger ferry connections with the UK (via Holyhead) and France. In 2018, it handled 151 cruise ships carrying a total of over 250,000 passengers, who contributed over €60 million to the local economy. In 2019, cruise ship traffic is expected to increase to 173 ships (**Fig. 18.13**).

↑ **Fig. 18.12** Dublin Airport.

→ **Fig. 18.13** Dublin Port.

Attractions

- The region has many **historical sites**, including Dublin Castle, and **national monuments** at Glendalough, County Wicklow, and Newgrange, County Meath.
- **Cultural heritage sites** include the National Gallery and the National Museum. Dublin is a UNESCO city of literature, in recognition of its literary heritage (Samuel Beckett, James Joyce, J.M. Synge, W.B. Yeats, etc.).
- Venues providing **entertainment** include the Temple Bar area and a range of theatres such as the Abbey and the Gate.
- **Shopping** in central Dublin and peripheral shopping centres (e.g. Dundrum Centre, Kildare Village) have boosted the GDA's attractiveness as a retail centre, especially for the domestic visitor sector.
- Other visitor attractions include the Guinness Storehouse, Dublin Zoo and the Irish National Stud in County Kildare.

Activity-based tourism

- Visitors interested in **outdoor activities** are well-served with forest walks and hillwalking trails in the Wicklow Mountains and water sports in Dublin Bay.
- **Golfing** enthusiasts can access golf links and parkland courses, such as Portmarnock and the K Club.

Event-based tourism

A number of activities contribute to the tourism sector on a year-round basis. These include **sporting events** (e.g. horse racing at the Curragh, Fairyhouse and Leopardstown; the All-Ireland Finals and other GAA games at Croke Park; the Six Nations, Champions Cup rugby and international football games at the Aviva Stadium) and **concerts** (e.g. 3Arena, Slane Castle and Croke Park). **Festivals** such as St Patrick's Day, the Bram Stoker Halloween Festival and the New Year Festival have helped to make Dublin a year-round destination for visitors.

The promotion of **city breaks and business tourism** have also helped to boost visitor numbers during the **off-peak season**. Delegates attending the Dublin Convention Centre contribute to hotels, bars, restaurants and tourist attractions, and Dublin is included in the 'Top 15' listing for convention destinations by the International Congress and Conventions Association (Fig. 18.14).

↑ **Fig. 18.14** Dublin Convention Centre.

Government support

The **Department of Transport, Tourism and Sport** is responsible for the development of the tourism sector. A number of tourism agencies, operating under the remit of the Department, have responsibility for tourism development in the region. These include **Fáilte Ireland**, which promotes domestic tourism, grades and inspects **accommodation** and operates tourist information offices in the GDA, and **Tourism Ireland**, a national body responsible for promoting Ireland and the Greater Dublin Area as a tourist destination in overseas markets. The **Office of Public Works** maintains and provides staff for visitor attractions including Newgrange, Kilmainham Gaol, and the Casino at Marino. The government provides direct financial support for locally-based tourism projects and **LEADER** companies, which are directly involved in supporting small-scale developments.

Landscapes

Chapter 19: A Peripheral Irish Region – The Western Region

The **Ireland's Ancient East** campaign was launched in 2016 (**Fig. 18.15**). Modelled on the success of the **Wild Atlantic Way**, the initiative aims to increase visitor numbers by promoting the region's rich and varied historical heritage.

The Irish government's decision to remove **airport tax** in 2014 has also been effective in boosting the tourism sector in the region.

Challenges facing the tourist industry

Brexit

There is huge **uncertainty** about the impact Britain leaving the EU will have on tourism. Overall tourist numbers are generally expected to **decline**. Changes to the exchange rate may mean Ireland will be a **more expensive destination**, and UK visitors will have **lower spending budgets**.

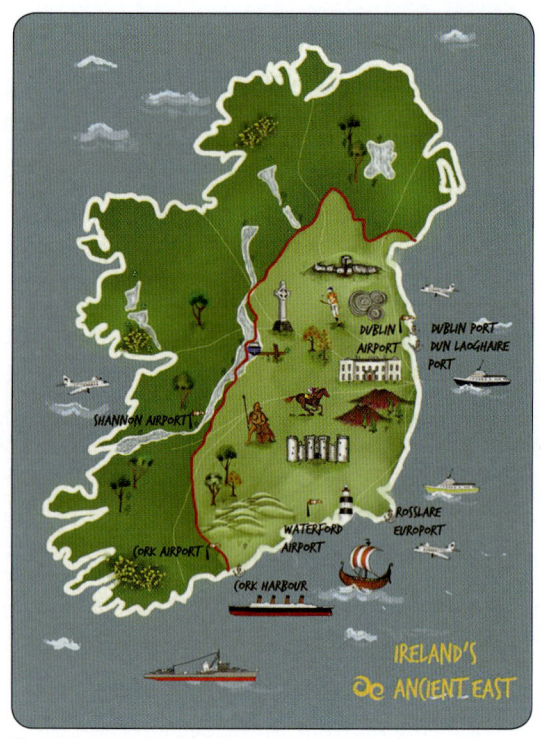

↑ **Fig. 18.15** Ireland's Ancient East promotional map.

Hotel accommodation

Hotel construction was halted during the economic downturn of 2008–2014, resulting in a **shortage of hotel rooms**. While new hotels have been constructed since, it is estimated that by 2020 there will be a shortfall of over 1,000 hotel rooms in Dublin.

Competition

All costs – accommodation, food, drink, transport, etc. – need to be controlled so that tourism offers **value for money** for visitors. A shortage of hotel rooms has contributed to higher room rates in Dublin city. Excessive rates and utility charges, along with the increasing cost of wages for suitably qualified staff, are forcing businesses to increase their prices.

Changes to VAT rates

During the economic downturn, the VAT rate for the tourism sector was reduced to 9% to stimulate activity. In 2019, the government restored the rate to 13.5%. There are concerns that this increase will have a negative impact.

Transport

KEYWORDS	
network	congestion
cycle paths	population

With a **population** of over 1.9 million, the Greater Dublin Area needs a **well-developed and efficient transport network**. A number of factors have contributed to the development of transport in the region.

18 A Core Irish Region – The Greater Dublin Area

Physical factors

The **low-lying, level relief** has enabled the construction of a well-developed **transport infrastructure** (Fig. 18.16).

- An extensive **network of motorways** links the city with other parts of Ireland, while the M50 motorway provides a circular route around the city.
- Dublin's key location at the **lowest bridging point** on the River Liffey meant that it developed port functions early in its history, and it is now a major commercial and passenger port.
- Dublin Airport, located on **lowland** to the north of the city, continues to expand.

↑ **Fig. 18.16** Motorways and National Primary routes serving Dublin.

Political factors

Through the **European Regional Development Fund** the EU provided funding for infrastructural projects. The **National Development Plan 2000–2006** was responsible for major improvements to the GDA's **transportation infrastructure**, which included:

- the construction of the Dublin Port Tunnel;
- upgrades to the M50 and the introduction of barrier-free tolling;
- the construction of Terminal 2 at Dublin Airport.

Under the Irish government's **Transport 21 Initiative 2005–2011**, bus fleets were upgraded, the number of quality bus corridors was increased, and Park and Ride facilities were introduced at a number of locations, including the Red Cow interchange.

Public transport

Dublin is served by a variety of **public transport** types.

- The **DART** train service links the city centre with Howth and Malahide to the north and Greystones to the south.
- The **Luas** tram services provide links within Dublin, Dún Laoghaire-Rathdown and South Dublin County.
- **Commuter trains** link Dublin with Drogheda, Dundalk, Maynooth, Portlaoise, Arklow, Gorey and Wexford.
- The **Phoenix Park Tunnel** allows Kildare commuter trains to travel to Connolly and Pearse stations.
- **Dublin Bus and Bus Éireann** are partly state-owned companies that operate the public bus transport system. (In recent years, private operators have been given permission to operate some routes.) In 2017, Dublin Bus carried over 137 million passengers.

Bicycles

The provision of **cycle paths** and the introduction of the **Dublin Bike Sharing Scheme** in 2009 have contributed to ongoing use of bicycles for leisure and transportation. By 2024, it is planned that the GDA will have increased its cycle network to over 2,840 km.

Landscapes

Transport problems: traffic congestion

As Dublin city expanded, the provision of **public transport infrastructure** in newly-developed estates was neglected. This has forced people to rely on their cars when travelling around the region, resulting in a major traffic **congestion** problem.

Solutions

Since the mid-1990s, the Irish **government's transport policy** has been aimed at **reducing the growth in car travel**. Dublin needs a fast, reliable and efficient public transport system in order to reduce traffic volume.

The **Greater Dublin Area Transport Strategy 2016–2035** aims to deliver effective and sustainable movement of people and goods within the region. Among its proposals are the **construction of a 'Metro North'** to link the city with Dublin Airport, the **'Metro South'** which will terminate near Ranelagh, and **extensions of the Luas tram network** to Lucan, Finglas and Bray. There are also proposals to limit cross-city car flow as a way of directing motorists away from the city centre, reducing traffic volume. So far, there are no proposals to introduce **congestion charges**.

EXAM LINK (OL)

Tertiary Economic Activities – Irish Region (40 marks)

Answer each of the following with reference to an Irish region that you have studied.

(i) Name one tertiary economic activity that contributes to the economy of this region.
(ii) Explain the advantages that this region has for the development of the tertiary economic activity named in part (i) above.
(iii) Describe one challenge faced by this tertiary economic activity in this region.

2018, Q4B

Marking Scheme:
(i) 4 marks
(ii) 9 SRPs × 3 marks
(iii) 3 SRPs × 3 marks

EXAM LINK (HL)

Tertiary Activity in Ireland (30 marks)

Account for the development of tourism or transport in an Irish region that you have studied.

2015, Q4C

Marking Scheme:
15 SRPs × 2 marks

CHECK YOUR LEARNING

1. List two ways accessibility has helped the development of tourism in the Greater Dublin Area.
2. Explain two ways government policy has influenced the development of tourism in the Greater Dublin Area.
3. Describe some of the issues that are facing tourism in the Greater Dublin Area.
4. Identify three socio-economic factors that have affected the development of transport in the Greater Dublin Area.
5. Describe three ways in which the government/EU has influenced the development of transport in the Greater Dublin Area.
6. Examine some of the issues facing the future development of transport in the Greater Dublin Area.

Human Processes

Population density

The average **population density** for the Republic of Ireland in 2016 was 70 persons per km^2. With the exception of County Wicklow, all of the administrative areas of the Greater Dublin Area had densities higher than this (**Tables 18.4** and **18.5**; **Fig. 18.17**).

Population density (per km^2)	1991	2016	% change
Dublin city	4,519	4,810	+4.8
Fingal	341	661	+93.8
South Dublin	937	1,252	+33.6
Dún Laoghaire-Rathdown	1,456	1,707	+17.2

↑ **Table 18.4** Population density Dublin city and County Councils, 1991–2016.

KEYWORDS
population density
urban renewal
migration
distribution
segregation
urban sprawl

SKILLS ACTIVITY
Using graph paper, construct a suitable graph to illustrate the data for 2016 in **Table 18.4**.

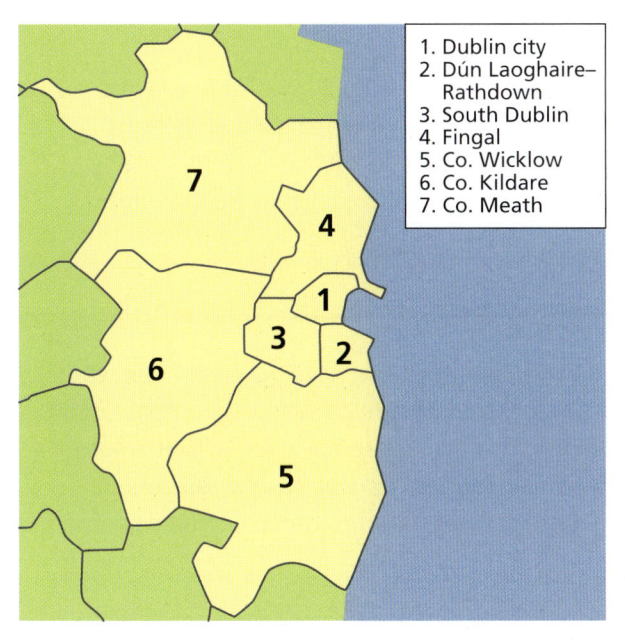

1. Dublin city
2. Dún Laoghaire–Rathdown
3. South Dublin
4. Fingal
5. Co. Wicklow
6. Co. Kildare
7. Co. Meath

← **Fig. 18.17** Greater Dublin administrative areas.

Census data from 1991 and 2016 reveals **population growth** throughout the GDA. This reflects the importance of the region as an economic centre, which attracts **migrants**, the impacts of **natural increase** and the growth and **expansion** of Dublin into surrounding counties.

Population density (per km^2)	1991	2016	% change
Co. Meath	45	83	+84.4
Co. Kildare	72	131	+81.9
Co. Wicklow	48	70	+45.8

↑ **Table 18.5** Population density in counties bordering Dublin, 1991–2016.

Population distribution

Within the region, population is generally concentrated within urban areas. **Planning restrictions** on housing developments in rural areas has meant the percentage change of people living in urban areas is much greater than rural areas. The 2016 census revealed a population increase of 16.6% in Maynooth, County Kildare, while Navan in County Meath experienced a 5.7% increase. Conversely, the relief, harsher climate and poor transport infrastructure result in the upland areas of County Wicklow having low concentrations of population.

Landscapes

Changes over time

Dublin city

The population of Dublin city and county has **fluctuated** since the 1960s. In 1971, the city had a population of 567,900; by 1991 it had fallen to 478,389. Two reasons for the decline were de-industrialisation and the construction of modern housing estates in the suburbs.

The 2016 census showed population had increased to 553,165. Factors contributing to this increase included:

- **urban renewal** and **redevelopment** projects, which increased the amount of housing available in the city;
- **large-scale construction** of apartments within the city area;
- **migration** and **natural increase**.

County Dublin

In 1991, County Dublin had a population of 546,915. By 2016, this figure had risen to 792,237. **Migration** and a **higher birth rate** (due to the younger age profile of the new residents) are two reasons for this. With an increase of 8% between 2011 and 2016, the local authority area of Fingal showed the largest percentage national increase.

Counties Kildare, Wicklow and Meath

Since 1991, the counties making up the Greater Dublin Area have experienced major population change. Counties Meath and Kildare both saw their populations increase by over 80%, while County Wicklow's increased by over 46%. Increasing property prices in the Dublin region forced people to move to new residential developments constructed within these counties during the **Celtic Tiger** boom.

Population density (per km²)	1991	2016	% change
Dublin city	478,389	553,165	+15.6%
Fingal	152,766	296,214	+48.4%
South Dublin County	208,739	278,749	+25.1%
Dún Laoghaire-Rathdown	185,410	217,274	+17.1%
Co. Meath	105,370	194,942	+85.0%
Co. Kildare	122,656	222,130	+81.1%
Co. Wicklow	97,265	142,332	+46.3%

↑ **Table 18.6** Population data for the GDA, 1991–2016.

De-industrialisation: The decline and closure of industries.

Urban renewal: Improving city areas by demolishing older buildings and constructing a variety of new commercial and residential units.

In 1994, Dublin County was divided into three administrative units – Fingal, South County Dublin and Dún Laoghaire-Rathdown.

DID YOU KNOW?
The population of Ireland in 1991 was 3,525,719. The 2016 census showed the Irish population had grown to 4,757,976.

SKILLS ACTIVITY

Using data in **Table 18.6**:
- draw a suitable graph to illustrate the percentage change in population density for Dublin city, Fingal, South Dublin County and Dún Laoghaire-Rathdown;
- draw a suitable graph to illustrate the percentage change in population density for counties Meath, Kildare and Wicklow.

CHECK YOUR LEARNING

Study Table 18.6 and answer the following questions.
1. Which county showed the greatest percentage change between 1991 and 2016?
2. Explain two reasons for this increase.

Social segregation

Affluent areas of South Dublin (e.g. Dalkey, Ranelagh) are characterised by expensive properties, a white-collar and professional workforce, private schools with high attainment rates, and low crime rates. In contrast, **inner-city areas** are marked by high unemployment rates, crime and drug-related activities and poor attainment rates in schools. **Public housing estates** in areas such as Jobstown experience high levels of unemployment, antisocial behaviour, higher crime statistics and high school drop-out rates.

↑ **Fig. 18.18** Parnell Street, central Dublin.

Migration

The **economic growth during the Celtic Tiger** years attracted migrants from within Ireland, the UK, the rest of the EU, especially the new accession states (notably Poland), and from some non-EU countries.

As a result of this migration, Dublin has seen major changes in the fabric of some areas of the city. For example, the **Parnell Street** area has become a focus of Chinese shops and restaurants, while the opening of mosques serving Dublin's Islamic community shows increasing religious diversity (**Figs 18.18**, **18.19**).

↑ **Fig. 18.19** Islamic Cultural Centre of Ireland, Clonskeagh.

Urban sprawl

Corruption, demand for housing and industrial zoned land and a **lack of co-ordinated planning** have resulted in **urban sprawl** across the GDA, the impacts of which will dominate planning in the future (**Fig. 18.20**). Adamstown in Dublin West represented a fresh approach to this problem. Planned for 25,000 residents, it would include schools, a community centre, a swimming pool, shops and a transport hub. Due to the **economic downturn** in 2008, only about **20% of the project was completed**. Construction of new housing resumed in 2017, but there is a severe lack of services and amenities in the area.

Commuter town: A town where people live but travel out of to go to their place of work.

MAP OF DUBLIN 1948

MAP OF DUBLIN 2015

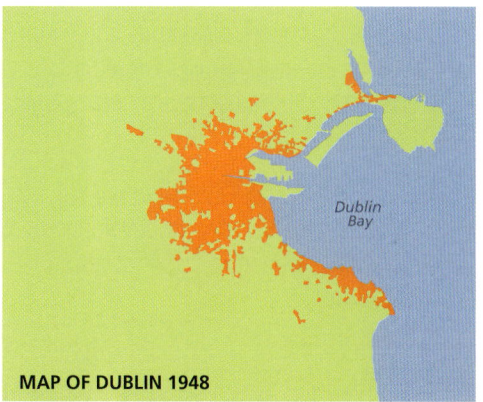

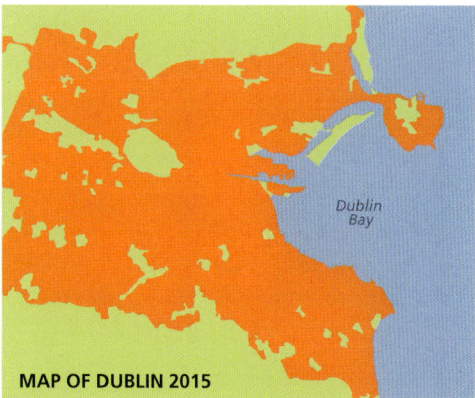

↑ **Fig. 18.20** Urban sprawl in Dublin, 1948–2015.

EXAM LINK (HL)

Population in Ireland (30 marks)

Account for the distribution of population throughout an Irish region that you have studied.

2012, Q4C

Marking Scheme: 15 SRPs × 2 marks

CHECK YOUR LEARNING

1. Outline some impacts of migration on the Greater Dublin Area.
2. Explain social segregation.

Landscapes

CASE STUDY: THE GROWTH OF DUBLIN CITY

KEYWORDS
- hinterland
- expansion
- urban sprawl
- segregation
- decline
- renewal
- employment
- history
- planning

The origins of Dublin date back to the establishment of a monastic settlement in the 6th century. However, it was with the arrival of the Vikings in the 9th century that the city as we know it today began to evolve.

Location

From its early years, a number of physical factors influenced Dublin's growth and development. Expansion to the east was limited by the **Irish Sea**, while the upland relief of the **Wicklow Mountains** formed a natural barrier to the south. The large expanses of lowland to the west, north and north-west allowed Dublin to grow outwards. The River Liffey, flowing through the lowland, was a natural obstacle bisecting the region, but the construction of bridges helped to overcome this (**Fig. 18.21**).

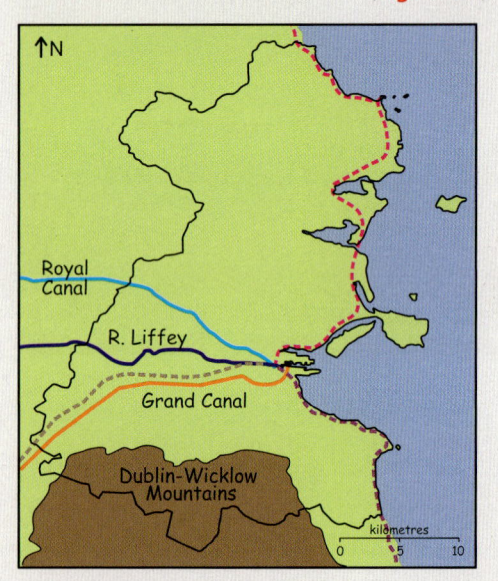

In the **18th and 19th centuries, canals** (the Grand and Royal) were constructed on lowland to the west, facilitating the transportation of raw materials and manufactured goods to and from many parts of Ireland.

In the **20th century**, the lowland relief also allowed the development of an excellent **motorway network**, featuring flyovers and bridges.

The **rich agricultural hinterland** surrounding the city supplied the raw materials for a wide range of food processing industries, offering employment and attracting settlement.

Dublin's location at the **lowest bridging point** on the River Liffey meant the city soon developed into a **major port**. Maritime-related activities provided employment and attracted settlement.

↑ **Fig. 18.21** Sketch map showing physical and transport factors influencing the development of Dublin.

Railways
- - - Belfast
- - - Rosslare
- - - Cork and Galway

6TH CENTURY
An early Christian monastic settlement was founded on the banks of the Liffey.

9TH CENTURY
The Vikings established Dublin as a trading centre.

12TH CENTURY
From the 12th century, the city was the centre of British Rule in Ireland.

18TH CENTURY
As the city prospered and expanded, large Georgian squares and streets were developed (Fig. 18.22).

19TH CENTURY
The Act of Union in 1800 had a disastrous impact on the city with many of the great houses turned into tenements. These were to be a blight on the city well into the 1960s.

The opening of the Dublin and Kingstown rail link in 1834 opened up the south city area to development, while the Malahide link opened in 1884 facilitating northward **expansion**.

20TH CENTURY
Rapid **expansion** led to the development of new suburbs (e.g. Tallaght) and the beginning of **urban sprawl**.

Socio-economic factors

Migration

In the 1970s, the population of Dublin grew rapidly due to natural increase and **immigration** from other parts of the country. Low-density housing estates were developed along the **urban fringe** to cater for this increase, but many had poor or no transport links with the city (e.g. **Tallaght**). As these housing estates were either private or public, a pattern of **social segregation** evolved.

The development of these estates along the edges of the city began the process of **urban sprawl**, which has continued into the 21st century.

↑ **Fig. 18.22** Georgian buildings, central Dublin.

During the **Celtic Tiger** years (1994–2007), **immigration** from the new EU accession states and other non-EU countries led to a further population increase. Increased housing demand **inflated property prices**, forcing people to move from the city centre to cheaper developments in the outer fringe, expanding the city and leading to continuing **urban sprawl** (e.g. **Swords**, **Fingal**).

The influx of migrants has had a major social impact on the city, which has evolved into a **multicultural city** that's home to many ethnic groups, cultures and languages.

> **DID YOU KNOW?**
> The word 'Dublin' comes from the Gaelic *dubh linn*, meaning black pool. The eponymous pool was located where the River Poddle joined the River Liffey near Dublin Castle.

Economic growth

Dublin became the **seat of government** when the Irish Free State was established in 1921. **Employment** in the civil service attracted people from all over the country, while many traditional industries located within the city remained important employers for city residents (e.g. Jacobs).

The increase of FDI following membership of the EEC, the creation of the EU Single Market and Ireland's low **corporation tax rate** all resulted in an increase in manufacturing and service industries within the region from the 1980s onwards. Industrial estates catering for the growing industrial sector were built along the margins of the city, further contributing to **urban sprawl**.

Rapid **expansion** during the Celtic Tiger years saw the city undergo structural changes as new business quarters and clusters developed along the outskirts (e.g. East Point Business Park).

The number of **apartments** throughout the inner city and suburbs also increased as population grew, resulting in higher population densities.

The creation of new public spaces such as the **Grand Canal Docks** and **Smithfield** has somewhat enhanced the city (Figs 18.23, 18.24).

↑ **Fig. 18.23** Grand Canal Docks, central Dublin.

↑ **Fig. 18.24** Smithfield.

Landscapes

Fig. 18.25 ESB offices, Fitzwilliam Street.

Inner city population decline

The **early 1970s** brought changes to the inner city. The switch to containerisation at Dublin Port and the closure or relocation of many traditional industries led to **unemployment** and **population decline** in the **inner-city** areas. Tenements with substandard conditions were demolished and former residents moved to new public housing (e.g. Ballymun).

The change of land use from residential to office also caused **population decline**. During this period, many fine Georgian buildings were destroyed to make way for office blocks (**Fig. 18.25**). In Fitzwilliam Street, in the centre of what had been Dublin's longest Georgian streetscape, 16 Georgian houses were demolished and a modern office block constructed for the ESB (though this site is now being redeveloped).

Urban renewal and regeneration

In the 1980s, **government-supported schemes** were introduced to tackle decaying and derelict properties.

The **Custom House Docks Development Authority** was set up to oversee development in the dockland area. The creation of the **International Financial Services Centre** and a mix of residential, social and commercial developments have completely transformed the area. The **Grand Canal Docks** area is now home to the Bord Gáis Energy Theatre and a variety of residential and commercial properties.

The **Gas Works brownfield site** in East Dublin has seen major residential and office development, while plans have been submitted for the construction of up to 3,500 apartments and other developments on the former **Dublin Glass Bottle site** in the Poolbeg area (**Fig. 18.26**).

Fig. 18.26 Dublin Glass Bottle site, Poolbeg.

Chapter 30: Urban Growth Problems

Urban renewal projects include the **Historic Area Rejuvenation Plan**, which redeveloped Smithfield, the north-east inner city area and the Liberties. Successful **regeneration projects** in Fatima Mansions and Ballymun involved local input into planning and design. As part of the urban renewal programme, enterprise centres were developed to encourage business start-ups and provide employment for inner-city communities (e.g. **Grand Canal Street**).

Growth challenges

To tackle continuing **urban sprawl**, local and national **planning strategies** must address the imbalance between growth in the Dublin region and the rest of the country. Other issues facing authorities include:

- low-density development;
- currently existing unsustainable travel patterns;
- developing a low or carbon neutral city;
- the promotion of social inclusion;
- the integration of ethnic communities into the fabric of the city.

Enterprise centre: A site with numerous small units that can accommodate start-up businesses and has on-site administration and support services.

Brownfield site: Land on which large industrial or commercial buildings were located but has either been redeveloped or is awaiting development.

Greenfield site: A site that has not yet been built on.

18 A Core Irish Region – The Greater Dublin Area

EXAM LINK (OL)

Urban Growth in Ireland (30 marks)

Describe and explain reasons for the growth of any Irish urban area that you have studied.

2014, Q4C

Marking Scheme:
Naming an urban area = 3 marks
Description and explanation: 9 SRPs × 3 marks

CHECK YOUR LEARNING

1. List three different important periods in the growth of Dublin.
2. Identify three physical factors which influenced Dublin's development.
3. List three economic factors which impacted on Dublin's growth.
4. Explain three different ways migration has affected the growth of Dublin.
5. List three different areas that future planning for Dublin will have to address.

EXAMINATION QUESTIONS

ORDINARY LEVEL

Long Question

1. Urban Growth

Explain the reasons for the growth of any urban area that you have studied.

2016, Part Two, Section 1, Q5C (30 marks)

Marking Scheme:
Explanation = 10 SRPs × 3 marks
Allow an urban area named for 1 SRP

HIGHER LEVEL

Long Question

2. Population in Ireland

Account for the distribution of population throughout an Irish region that you have studied.

2012, Part Two, Section 1, Q4C (30 marks)

Marking Scheme:
Cause identified = 2 marks
Impact identified = 2 marks
Examination = 13 SRPs × 2 marks

Landscapes

Revision Summary

Physical processes

- Climate – cool temperate oceanic – summer 15°C winter 5°C – easterly winter winds – long growing season
- Relief and drainage – Caledonian mountains NE–SW – mineral deposits – glaciation – rivers Liffey, Tolka, Dargle, Boyne
- Soil – fertile lowlands – brown earth – alluvial – boulder clay – infertile uplands – podzol – gley

Tertiary economic activities

Tourism

- Accessibility – airport (31.5 m passengers in 2018) – port (cruise ships, ferries) – rail – road
- Attractions: cultural (National Museums) – historical (Kilmainham Gaol) – entertainment (Temple Bar) – activities (hiking)
- Events: sport (GAA) – festivals (St Patrick's Day) – business conventions – concerts
- Government – Fáilte Ireland – Ireland's Ancient East – no airport tax – financial support
- Challenges: accommodation shortage – competition forcing prices up – Brexit – VAT

Transport

- Physical – location at Liffey bridging point – low-lying relief supports transport infrastructure
- Political – ERDF funding from EU – Transport 21 upgrades to buses
- Range of internal public transport – promotion of bicycle use
- Problem of traffic congestion – poor links from city to urban fringe
- Solution – Greater Dublin Area Transport Strategy 2016–2035 – Metro North and South – Luas extension – possibility of congestion charges

Primary economic activities: agriculture

Physical factors

- Cool temperate oceanic climate – mild winters and warm summers – moderating sea influence – little frost – arable farming on fertile lowlands – grass growing and pastoral farming on infertile uplands
- Well-drained lowlands – use of machinery in arable farming – increase in commercial farming
- Low precipitation means little leaching of soil in lowlands, good for arable farming – high precipitation on uplands means extensive leaching, poor soils suited to grazing and peat harvesting

Socio-economic factors

- Farm size and income above average – investment and efficiency are high
- Outdoor forage crops used for fodder, reduce winter costs
- Younger farmers keen to modernise industry – use of technology and machinery

Markets and infrastructure

- Market size 1.9 million people – largest in Ireland
- Supplies individuals and secondary sector
- Developed transport infrastructure increases shelf life – increased value of produce
- Brexit could limit EU market

Political factors

- EU provides funding through CAP – access to Single European Market – rewards for ecological and environmental consideration

Primary economic activities: other

- Fishing – national and EU investment – overfishing and resulting quotas led to decline in landings – polluted water limits aquaculture
- Forestry – poor soil limits upland agriculture, allows forestry – employment in logging, sawmills, tourism
- Minerals – lead and zinc – Tara Mines
- Energy – offshore wind farm at Arklow, expansion opposed – hydroelectric power produced from Liffey

Secondary economic activities

Physical factors

- Raw materials related to climate and relief – barley (Guinness) – dairy (Cadbury) – meat and horticulture (food processing plants) – water (pharmaceuticals)
- Fish processing – artisan foods – forestry products

Socio-economic factors

- Labour force – graduates from third-level institutes – technology and R&D
- English-speaking – attracts US investment
- Skilled migrants from EU – multilingual – good quality of life

Transport

- Airport and port – international trade
- RoRo – in development – links with Netherlands and Belgium to bypass UK ports post-Brexit
- Rail and road links – good internal transport network
- Public transport within city – allows easy commuting for workers – poor links to urban fringe lead to traffic congestion

Markets

- Local market 1.9 m – Northern Ireland 1.8 m – Single European Market 500 m
- Transport infrastructure – road, rail, sea and air – attracts outside investment
- Multiplier effect
- Enterprise Ireland support

Political factors

- Low corporation tax – attracts investment
- National support from IDA and Enterprise Ireland

Challenges

- Brexit – exchange rate – Northern Irish border issue – exports to UK threatened
- Low corporation tax – issue of competition in EU

18 A Core Irish Region – The Greater Dublin Area

Human processes	Case study: The growth of Dublin	
Population density • Kildare and Dublin above average 70 ppkm², Wicklow below (access) • Growth 1991–2016 due to economic growth – migration – natural increase – population spread • Concentrated in urban areas – planning restrictions **Changes over time** • Dublin city – highest in 1971 – down in 1991, de-industrialisation – up in 2016, urban renewal and migration • Co. Dublin – increasing – migration – younger profile of new residents – high birth rates • Counties Kildare and Wicklow – big increase – high property prices in Dublin force people out **Social segregation** • South Dublin – affluent population – property expensive – low crime – white collar • Inner city – public housing – high unemployment – crime – drop-out rate high **Migration** • Attracted by Celtic Tiger boom – EU, UK, rest of world • Multicultural city centre **Urban sprawl** • Demand for housing and industrial land – lack of co-ordinated planning • Adamstown, West Dublin – housing, facilities, transport hub – abandoned at 20% completion 2008–17 due to economic crash	**Location** • Mountains to south, sea to east, so growth to north and west • River Liffey bridging point and port • Lowlands – canals and motorways – large industrial estates • Hinterland – agriculture – employment in primary and secondary sectors **History** • 6th C monastery – 9th C Viking trading centre – 12th C seat of British rule – 20th C independent capital, EU **Migration** • 1970s internal immigration – low density estates – poor transport links – social segregation – urban sprawl • Migration from EU states – non-EU states – demand for housing – inflated property prices – forced from city to fringe – urban sprawl – multiculturalism **Economic growth** • 1921 seat of government – civil service jobs attracted internal migrants – traditional industries for locals • EU membership, low corporation tax attracted FDI – manufacturing and service industries at urban fringe • Celtic Tiger – business parks – new apartment blocks in centre – higher population density – new public spaces	**Inner city population decline** • Containerisation at port – relocation of traditional industries – unemployment and population decline • Tenements demolished – residents moved to new public housing estates • Changing land use residential–office **Urban renewal** • IFSC – docklands developed – modern commercial and business hub • Gas Works East Dublin – residential • HARP – Smithfield – Liberties • Fatima Mansions and Ballymun – local input into planning and design **Growth challenges** • National strategies to rebalance growth between Dublin and rest of country • Low-density development – unsustainable travel patterns – environmental concerns – integration of ethnic minority communities

19 A PERIPHERAL IRISH REGION – THE WESTERN REGION

KEYWORDS
- peripheral
- cool temperate oceanic climate
- relief rain
- frontal rain
- Caledonian folding
- igneous
- metamorphic
- limestone
- glaciation
- peat soils
- blanket bogs
- leaching
- podzols
- gley soils
- brown earth soils
- loam soils

Peripheral region: A less economically developed region.

LEARNING INTENTIONS

Syllabus Links: 2.2

By the end of this chapter I will be able to:
- draw an outline map of Ireland showing the Western Region, and show and name different types of features;
- explain how physical processes have shaped the landscape of this region;
- compare the impact of physical processes on this region with a core Irish region;
- describe the factors that have influenced the development of primary, secondary and tertiary activities in the region;
- describe and explain the human processes that have influenced the population of the region;
- compare the factors that have influenced the development of economic activities in this region with those in a core Irish region.

The Western Region is part of the **Northern and Western Regional Assembly**, one of three regional assemblies in Ireland. Classified as a **peripheral** region, it consists of the counties of Galway, Mayo and Roscommon (Figs 19.1–19.2). While this region accounts for 20% of the Republic of Ireland's land area, it is home to just 10% of the population.

↓ **Fig. 19.1** The Western Region and the Greater Dublin Area.

Sketch Map of the Western Region

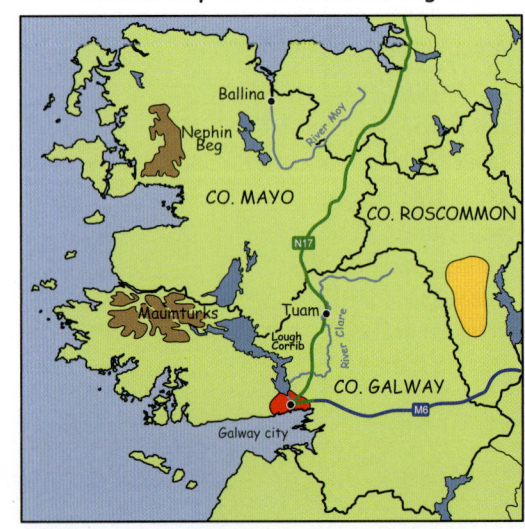

Key for Sketch Map of the Western Region
- Agricultural area
- Industrial area
- Upland area
- Urban centre

↑ **Fig. 19.2** Sketch map of the Western Region.

290

Physical Processes

Climate

The Western Region has a **cool temperate oceanic climate**. Its main characteristics include:

- warm summer temperatures averaging 15°C and mild winter temperatures averaging 6°C due to the influence of warm **North Atlantic Drift** waters (Table 19.1);
- the **prevailing moisture-laden south-westerly winds** bring annual precipitation of 1,500–2,000 mm (Table 19.2); when they meet the uplands, **relief rain** is formed (Fig. 19.3);
- **Atlantic depressions** bringing **frontal rainfall** and cloudy conditions. As a result, the region has approximately 250 rainy days per year and receives an average of just three hours of sunshine per day.

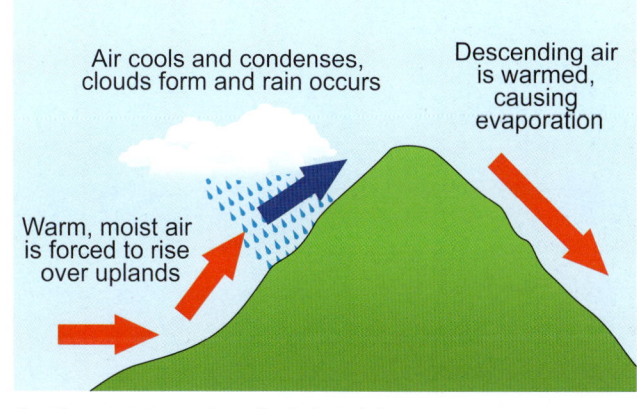

↑ **Fig. 19.3** Formation of relief rainfall.

	Jan	Feb	Mar	Apr	May	Jun	Jul	Aug	Sep	Oct	Nov	Dec
Mean temperature (°C)	6.1	4.9	5.5	8.8	12.1	14.5	15.0	14.3	12.3	10.8	8.4	8.4
Total rainfall (mm)	228.3	123.6	87.4	81.4	67.4	40.1	64.6	135.2	93.9	135.1	147.5	152.3

↑ **Table 19.1** Climate data for Belmullet, 2018 (Met Éireann).

2016	2017	2018
1183.3 mm	1243.1 mm	1356.5 mm

← **Table 19.2** Total annual rainfall at Belmullet (Met Éireann).

> **SKILLS ACTIVITY**
>
> Using graph paper, draw a suitable graph to illustrate the precipitation data from January to June in Table 19.1.

Relief and drainage

Upland areas in the Western Region include the **Maumturks**, County Galway, and the **Nephin Beg Mountains**, County Mayo (Figs 19.4, 19.5). These mountain ranges were formed during the **Caledonian folding period** over 400 million years ago, when magma intruded into folds in the earth's crust and cooled slowly to form **igneous** (granite) and **metamorphic** (quartzite) rocks. **Mineral deposits**, such as the gold deposits discovered at Croagh Patrick, County Mayo in 1989, were formed by volcanic gases.

> **Chapter 17:** The Concept of a Region
> **Chapter 18:** A Core Irish Region – The Greater Dublin Area

← **Fig 19.4** The Maumturk Mountains.

Landscapes

→ Fig 19.5 Relief map of the Western Region.

Carboniferous limestone underlies the lowlands of eastern Galway, Mayo and Roscommon. The lowlands of south Galway contain numerous **karst features**, including **limestone** caves and **turloughs**. These areas are prone to flooding when periods of rainfall cause the water table to rise.

The coastal areas of the Western Region contain numerous bays, inlets and cliffs formed by **marine erosion**, e.g. Galway Bay (**Fig. 19.6**). Long stretches of beaches are the result of **marine deposition**.

> **Turloughs:** Seasonal lakes formed by a rising water table.

→ Fig 19.6 The coastal landscape of the Western Region.

During the **Pleistocene glaciation**, ice eroded the uplands, leaving exposed slopes.

- Features of **glacial erosion** include cirques (e.g. **Lough Nadirkmore, County Mayo**) and U-shaped valleys (e.g. **Lough Inagh Valley, County Galway**).
- Features of **glacial deposition** include granite **erratics** on the Aran Islands, **drumlins** at Clew Bay and **boulder clay** deposits throughout the lowlands of southern County Galway.

The main rivers draining the region are the **River Moy** in County Mayo, the **Corrib** and **Clare** in Galway and the **Shannon** in Roscommon. Major lakes include **Lough Corrib** and **Lough Mask** in County Galway, and **Lough Conn** in County Mayo.

> Chapter 6: Weathering Processes and Landforms
> Chapter 10: Glaciation and Glacial Processes

Soils

High levels of precipitation result in the formation of wet, acidic **peat soils**, which form **blanket bogs** on the uplands of counties Galway and Mayo. Heavy rainfall also results in **leaching** and the formation of **hardpans** in **podzol** soils, impairing drainage. These in turn contribute towards the formation of **gley soils**, which form as a result of poor drainage and waterlogging on lowland boulder clay deposits, e.g. around Clew Bay.

Humus-rich **brown earth soils** formed under the vegetation cover of deciduous trees, and are found in the eastern lowland areas of counties Galway and Roscommon.

Loam soils, consisting of sand, silt and clay, are found in the east of the region where the land is relatively well-drained.

CHECK YOUR LEARNING

1. List one difference between rainfall in the Western Region and the Greater Dublin Area region.
2. Give one reason for this difference.
3. Describe four characteristics of a cool temperate oceanic climate.
4. Name three glacial features found in the Western Region.
5. List the main soil types occurring in this region.
6. Explain the following terms: leaching, blanket bogs.

SKILLS ACTIVITY

Draw an outline map of Ireland showing the Western Region. Include the following:

- two named urban centres;
- a named feature of relief (upland or lowland);
- a numbered road;
- another communication link;
- two features of drainage.

EXAM TIP

Remember, you can always use the map of Ireland shown at the bottom of the OS map to assist you when drawing sketch maps of Irish regions.

Primary Economic Activities

KEYWORDS

arable	migration	aquaculture
rain shadow	Common Agricultural Policy	Common Fisheries Policy
pastoral		Bord Iascaigh Mhara
upland relief	LEADER programme	Corrib Gas Field
podzols	continental shelf	wind farms

Primary economic activities involve the extraction and use of land and sea resources such as agriculture, fishing, forestry, mining and energy – important activities for the economies of **peripheral** regions.

Agriculture

Agriculture plays a significant role in the economy of the Western Region. A number of factors have influenced its development.

Physical factors

Climate

- The **cool temperate oceanic climate** experienced by the Western Region limits agricultural production. High levels of **cloud cover** limits sunshine to an average of three hours per day, hindering the growth and ripening of arable crops. Higher precipitation levels due to **relief rain** leads to **fungal disease** and reduces both the window for harvesting and the value of cereal crops, which is based on moisture content.

Landscapes

- As a result, **arable farming** only comprises 2% of the region's agricultural activity, and that occurs mainly in eastern areas where the **rain shadow effect** results in less cloud cover, lower precipitation rates and better growing conditions.
- The local climate is suited to grass growing, making **pastoral farming** the most common agricultural activity. Poor weather conditions in winter make it necessary to keep cattle indoors for long periods. This means farmers have to pay for more fodder, making it unprofitable to keep cattle for longer than two years. Instead, the animals are sold to farmers in eastern and southern counties to be fattened for sale.

> **Arable farming:** The growing of cereal crops, such as wheat and barley, or tillage crops, such as potatoes or sugar beet.
>
> **Pastoral farming:** Rearing animals (beef cattle, dairy cows, sheep, etc.).
>
> **Fodder:** Silage/hay saved during the summer to provide winter feed for animals.

Relief and drainage

- **Upland relief** with steep slopes, exposure to strong winds, lower temperatures and **relief rain** limit the scope of agriculture in many parts of the Western Region (e.g. **Connemara Mountains**).
- **Arable farming** is unsuited to these areas as:
  - the use of machinery is difficult and dangerous on **steep slopes**;
  - **igneous** and **metamorphic** rocks found on the slopes weather slowly, limiting the mineral content of their soils;
  - large amounts of **relief rainfall** have led to **soil erosion**.
- As a result, **sheep rearing** is the only activity suited to the rough grazing found on exposed **upper slopes** (Fig. 19.7).

→ Fig 19.7 Rough grazing.

- On the **lower slopes**, grass growth supports the **pastoral farming** of cattle, while some **arable farming** of barley, wheat and oats is possible on the lowlands of counties Galway and Roscommon. However, these lowlands are susceptible to summer **flooding** from the River Shannon, which can negatively impact the production of winter fodder.

Soil

- High levels of precipitation have led to the **leaching** of nutrients from soils. Thin, infertile **podzols** have formed, inhibiting agricultural production.
- Poor-quality **gley** and **peat soils** are better suited to **rough grazing and forestry** than arable farming, but **overgrazing** by large numbers of sheep has contributed to **soil erosion**, further limiting agriculture.
- **Dairy farming** is possible in the east of the region where the **loam soils** are well drained.

> **Hectare:** A measurement of land area: 10,000 m² or 2.5 acres.

Socio-economic factors

Small fragmented holdings

Historically, farming in the region has been characterised by **small holdings** and **subsistent farming** practices. While farm sizes have grown by about one-third since 1990, they're still significantly smaller than those in the rest of Ireland. With an **average size of 24.8 hectares**, farm operations are too small to justify the capital investment required for modern commercial agriculture – new farm buildings, technology and machinery.

The restricted output and limited income have led to an **out-migration** of younger farmers, who see little future in agriculture. Of those remaining in full-time farming, approximately **60% are over 55 years of age**. These older farmers are less likely to expand their operations or embrace new farming practices, making them less productive.

Today, approximately 50% of farmers in the region require **off-farm income** in order to survive. Farming part-time supplements the money they earn elsewhere, and allows them to maintain the family tradition of farming the land.

> **DID YOU KNOW?**
> The average size of a farm in Ireland is 32.4 hectares, but the Census of Agriculture 2010 revealed that over 50% of farms in the Western Region were less than 19 hectares in size.

Markets and infrastructure

Low **population density** in the Western Region means there's a **limited local market** for agricultural produce. As a result, the main markets for Western Region produce are the east coast of Ireland, the United Kingdom and the EU. This brings a number of problems for farmers.

- Getting produce to market incurs **extra transport costs**.
- **Poorly-developed communications** within the region means products are slower in getting to the market. For perishable products like meat and dairy, this results in a **shorter shelf life**, thus reducing the value of the product.
- The **declining value of sterling** brought about by the UK's '**Brexit**' referendum in 2016 has been felt sharply by farmers supplying livestock to local marts. There has been a reduction in the number of Northern Irish cattle and sheep dealers crossing the border, as they are getting **less value for money** in the Republic of Ireland. With competition for buying at the local markets reduced, farmers in the Western Region now receive lower prices for their livestock.

Political factors

Support from the European Union **Common Agricultural Policy (CAP)** has been instrumental in the survival of agriculture in the Western Region. It is estimated that just 15% of farms in the region would be able to keep going without the support of the following CAP payments:

- The **European Agricultural Guaranteed Fund** provides direct support payments to farmers through the **single farm payment**.
- Farmers with poor-quality soils, high mountainous land or poor drainage have benefitted from a **'Disadvantaged Area' grant payment**.
- The European Agricultural Fund for Rural Development supported the **Rural Environmental Protection Scheme (REPS)**, which gave financial support to farmers who farmed in an environmentally friendly way, for example, not cutting hedgerows during nesting season. This scheme was replaced by the **Green, Low-Carbon, Agri-Environment Scheme**, which addresses the issue of farming's contribution to greenhouse gases.

Landscapes

'Open farms' provide visitors with an opportunity to see farm animals along with traditional and modern farm activities in a safe environment. They also host group events such as school tours and children's parties.

DID YOU KNOW?
The CAP has resulted in higher agricultural productivity and farm incomes, and a stable, affordable and safe supply of food in Europe.

- The **LEADER Programme** helps farmers to develop alternative income streams, for example, 'open farms' (Fig. 19.8).

One of the biggest challenges facing agriculture in the Western Region is the UK's exit from the EU. As the UK provides **€8 billion to CAP** funding at present, this is likely to mean a cut in funds to all CAP projects in the coming years.

↑ **Fig 19.8** The LEADER Programme supports rural communities.

EXAM LINK (OL)

Agriculture in an Irish Region (40 marks)

Name one Irish region that you have studied and answer each of the following questions.

(i) Name two types of agriculture practised in this region.
(ii) Explain the advantages that this region has for the development of agriculture.
(iii) Describe the challenges faced by agriculture in this region.

2013, Q6B

Marking Scheme:
Named Irish region = 2 marks
(i) Two types named × 1 mark
(ii) Advantages explained = 6 SRPs × 3 marks
(iii) Challenges described = 6 SRPs × 3 marks

EXAM LINK (HL)

Agriculture in Ireland (30 marks)

Account for the development of agriculture in an Irish region that you have studied with reference to any two of the following factors.

Relief   Climate   Markets

2014, Q6C

Marking Scheme:
Factor 1 = 8 SRPs × 2 marks
Factor 2 = 7 SRPs × 2 marks
Allow 2 SRPs for examples of types of agriculture

CHECK YOUR LEARNING

1. Identify three physical factors that influence the development of agriculture in the Western Region.
2. Describe five socio-economic factors that affect the development of agriculture in the Western Region.
3. Outline three ways in which national government and EU policies have affected agricultural development in the Western Region.
4. Name the main types of farming practised in the Western Region.

Fishing

The development of the fishing industry in the Western Region of Ireland is a result of the interaction of a number of factors.

Physical factors

The Western Region has many **natural advantages** that support the development of the fishing industry. Its indented coastline provides **sheltered inlets and bays** suitable for the development of ports, while the shallow waters of the **continental shelf** are easily penetrable by sunlight, resulting in abundant supplies of **plankton**. This has attracted many different species, leading to fertile fishing grounds. The warm **North Atlantic Drift** contributes to plankton growth and keeps ports ice-free in winter.

Continental shelf: Shallow seabed at the edge of a continent.

Plankton: Microscopic organisms in salt water.

Socio-economic factors

The poor agricultural potential of the region meant that fishing has traditionally been an important economic activity, providing both an income and a food source.

Political factors

Government policy

The Irish government has supported the fishing industry by providing **grants** for port improvements (e.g. **Rossaveal, County Galway**) and also promoting the development of **fish processing** and **aquaculture** as important sources of employment.

EU policy

The **Common Fisheries Policy (CFP)** has influenced the development of the fishing industry through regulations and supports.

Country quotas based on the **Total Allowable Catch (TAC)** were initially fixed every year. These have now been replaced by a **Maximum Sustainable Yield**.

The CFP also introduces controls on commercial fishing, including regulation of net mesh size and the recording of all fish catches and landings.

Unfortunately, overfishing and regulations have led to reduced catches, income and employment. To counteract this, the **European Fisheries Fund** has allocated **€148 million** (from 2014 to 2020) to support the Irish fishing fleet, the fish processing sector, aquaculture and coastal communities dependent on the fishing industry.

↓ **Fig 19.9** Fish farming on the Western coast.

Aquaculture

Natural advantages such as sheltered inlets and pollution-free waters have supported the growth of aquaculture in the Western Region (**Fig. 19.9**). Government body **Bord Iascaigh Mhara** also provides **funding and training** for start-ups. Sea trout, salmon, mussels and scallops are the main products of aquaculture in the region; **Clew Bay, County Mayo**, produces salmon and abalone while **Galway Bay** is famous for its oysters.

Landscapes

In 2017, the total value of aquaculture products from Counties Galway and Mayo was €69 million.

Many community and environmental groups increasingly oppose local aquaculture projects due to:
- the negative impacts caused by the **accumulation of waste** feed and faecal debris beneath fish cages;
- **infectious diseases** from farmed fish spreading to the wild population;
- the negative impacts of installations on the visual **landscape**.

Forestry

A number of factors support the growth of forestry in the Western Region, including a climate with mild temperatures and sufficient rainfall for tree growth, and the availability of land which has little agricultural potential.

Forestry in upland areas is confined to the **lower slopes**, as the upper slopes are too exposed. Forestry is also found in **sheltered areas and cut-away bogs**. Forests are mainly **coniferous**, with Sitka spruce and Norway spruce the most common species (**Fig. 19.10**). Most of the region's forests are **state-owned** and managed by **Coillte**, but in recent years, government policy and EU grants have led to **increased private ownership**.

↑ **Fig 19.10** A coniferous plantation.

Mining and energy

The **Corrib Gas Field** off the coast of County Mayo was discovered in 1996. The project was **initially opposed by locals** who had concerns regarding the onshore refinery, the safety of the pipeline carrying the gas to it, and the impact of the project on marine ecology.

Gas began to flow in December 2015, and the field currently supplies up to **60% of the national gas requirement**. It is expected to remain a vital part of Ireland's energy infrastructure for the next 15 years.

Renewable energy

The conditions in the Western Region are excellent for the generation of **wind energy**. The **frequency and strength** of winds has supported the building and growth of numerous **wind farms** in counties Galway, Mayo and Roscommon, though the resulting noise pollution and damage to local scenery has led to local opposition in some cases.

Conditions along the western seaboard are also ideal for generating **wave energy**, and there is ongoing research into methods of harnessing it.

CHECK YOUR LEARNING

1. Describe three physical factors that influence the development of the fishing industry in the Western Region.
2. List three impacts the EU has had on fishing in the Western Region.
3. Outline two advantages the Western Region has for aquaculture.
4. Describe any two issues facing aquaculture in the Western Region.

Secondary Economic Activities

Secondary economic activities involve the **processing of raw materials** and the **manufacture of goods**. A number of factors have influenced their development in the Western Region.

Physical factors

Raw materials

The harsh climate, upland terrain and poor-quality soils of the Western Region have traditionally led to low agricultural output. In the past, this left local food processing and textile industries with a **limited supply of locally-produced raw materials**. Unable to source the required bulky raw materials (e.g. **cattle, milk, wool**) from other areas due to poorly-developed local transport infrastructure and high transport costs, industries were **unable to expand** and couldn't afford to modernise. After Ireland joined the EU in 1973, **protectionist policies** ended and many companies were forced to close, as they couldn't compete with cheaper products from other member states.

For many years, **fish processing** industries have provided an important source of employment in coastal communities (e.g. **Connemara Seafood, Westport**). The warm, clean, plankton-rich waters of the Atlantic Ocean support fertile fishing grounds and large catches, but **overfishing and the introduction of the CFP** have resulted in smaller catches of wild fish. In recent years, however, **aquaculture** has grown rapidly in sheltered inlets and bays, providing valuable raw materials for local processing companies. Seaweed is harvested for use in health supplements and food (e.g. **Connemara Organic Seaweed**; Fig. 19.11).

> **KEYWORDS**
> raw materials
> manufacture
> brain drain
> broadband
> markets
> FDI
> IDA
> Enterprise Ireland
> Údarás na Gaeltachta
> ERDF
> life sciences

↑ **Fig 19.11** Seaweed harvesting.

Socio-economic factors

Labour force

In the past, a limited provision of third-level educational facilities in the Western Region meant many **young people migrated** out of the region to further their education and develop skills, causing a **brain drain**. A lack of employment opportunities meant few returned. Most of those who remained were **older and unskilled**, making the region unattractive for industries just starting up.

> **Brain drain:** The migration of highly trained or qualified people from a region.

Markets

A **low population density** means there's a limited local market for goods manufactured in the Western Region. As a result, the **main markets** are the **GDA**, the **United Kingdom** and the **EU Single Market**.

Sea cargo is the cheapest form of transport for goods to the British and EU markets, but Galway Port is unable to accommodate boats with a capacity greater than 6,000 tonnes.

Most goods have to be transported out of the region by road or rail, but the **local transport network is poorly developed**, as the **upland relief** of the region means the construction of roads and railway lines is difficult and expensive. Many parts of the region are **isolated**, so transport delays and **higher costs** in getting goods to various markets make the region **less competitive**.

Low demand saw a **contraction of the rail network** in the second half of the 20th century. This restricted the option for cheaper freight movement by rail.

More recently, **Brexit** and the **falling value of sterling** have meant a reduction in exports from all parts of Ireland, including the Western Region.

Poor telecommunication coverage in many parts of the region has also impacted the **marketing** of goods produced in the region.

Political factors

Government support

The national corporation tax rate of 12.5% is being used as a stimulus to market the region as a location for **foreign direct investment (FDI)**.

The **Industrial Development Authority (IDA)** attracts investment to the region by:
- actively promoting the advantages for industry in the region;
- constructing fully serviced industrial estates in urban areas of the region;
- providing capital and training support grants.

Enterprise Ireland provides support for **Irish entrepreneurs** in developing business plans, facilitating leadership and management capability, and helping enterprises to connect with buyers and access overseas markets.

Údarás na Gaeltachta attracts **investment into the Gaeltacht areas** of the region. It has built industrial estates (e.g. **Inverin, County Galway**) and provides a wide variety of supports, including grants for employment, equipment and training.

EU support

Having **Objective 2 Status** entitles the Western Region to access **European Regional and Structural funds**. The Objective 2 Programme aims to promote socio-economic development in declining rural areas and depressed areas dependent upon fisheries.

Funding from the **European Regional Development Fund (ERDF)** has been used to improve transport infrastructure (e.g. the M6) and to provide education and training for the local labour force.

Negative sentiment towards the Western Region combined with the attractiveness of the Greater Dublin Area led to difficulty in attracting outside investment.

Foreign direct investment (FDI): Multinational companies set up manufacturing plants/research and development facilities in other countries. Attractions include tax concessions, cheaper labour, market access, etc.

DID YOU KNOW? In 2017, IDA client companies employed 23,286 people in IT, life sciences and the services sectors throughout the Western Region.

19 A Peripheral Irish Region – The Western Region

CASE STUDY: GALWAY – A MANUFACTURING CENTRE

Today, Galway has developed as the major centre for **manufacturing** in the region. Galway's attractiveness as an industrial location is based on the following.

Labour force

FDI has been attracted to the region by a **young, productive, highly skilled workforce**. Galway has developed as an international centre of excellence for manufacturing and research in the **medical and biomedical sectors (life sciences)** as a result of work being done at the National University of Ireland Galway (**NUIG**) and Galway-Mayo Institute of Technology (**GMIT**) and research centres such as the Regenerative Medicine Institute and the National Centre for Biomedical Engineering Science (**Fig. 19.12**).

↑ Fig 19.12 Galway-Mayo Institute of Technology.

Most of the companies establishing in Galway are US multinationals. Galway's **English-speaking workforce** has made it easier for American managers to communicate their needs and ideas with those developing and later working in these facilities. **Immigration** and local education means the workforce also has a strong and diverse range of **multilingual skills**, vital for the areas of sales, distribution and technical support.

Galway also offers a good **quality of life** to employees. This is especially important for those who relocate from other countries.

Infrastructure

A reliable, high-speed, high-capacity **motorway** has been developed linking Galway to ports and airports in Dublin (M6) as part of various national development plans.

There has been significant investment in the modern digital telecommunications infrastructure with Galway now benefitting from a state-of-the-art **fibre optic network**. This is vital for industries operating in a global economy.

To attract **foreign direct investment**, the **Industrial Development Authority** has developed a number of fully serviced **industrial estates** with advance factory units around Galway city.

Examples of industry in the Western Region

Medical devices	Pharmaceuticals	Food processing	Construction materials
Harmac, Castlerea	Allergan, Westport	Coca-Cola, Ballina	Logstrup Ireland, Tuam
Boston Scientific, Galway	Alkermes, Athlone	Arramara Teo, Galway	FDK, Ballaghaderreen
Medtronic, Galway			
Transitions Optical, Tuam			
Baxter Healthcare, Castlebar			

301

Landscapes

Challenges facing manufacturing in the region

The provision of high-speed **broadband** throughout the Western Region is seen as vital in supporting existing facilities, and also in encouraging new investment. **Poor broadband service** across much of the region makes it difficult to promote the region as a suitable location for **modern industries**. The Western Region is hoping to benefit from the government's **National Broadband Strategy**, which aims to provide a high-speed service in all areas of the country. However, delays in the implementation of the plan mean broadband speeds are still very slow in parts of the region.

EXAM LINK (OL)

Secondary Economic Activity in an Irish Region (40 marks)

Answer each of the following questions with reference to an Irish region that you have studied.

(i) Name one example of a secondary economic activity in this region.

(ii) Explain the advantages that this region has for the development of this secondary economic activity.

(iii) Describe one challenge faced by this secondary economic activity in this region.

2018, Q4B

Marking Scheme:
(i) Activity named = 4 marks
(ii) Advantages = 9 SRPs × 3 marks
   Allow one SRP for a named region
(iii) One challenge = 3 SRPs × 3 marks

EXAM LINK (HL)

Secondary Economic Activity (30 marks)

Examine the impact of each of the following on the development of secondary economic activity in an Irish region that you have studied.

Raw materials   Markets

2018, Q5C

Marking Scheme:
Region named = 2 marks
Explanation = 14 SRPs × 2 marks
Raw materials = 7 SRPs
Markets = 7 SRPs

CHECK YOUR LEARNING

1. List three ways raw materials have influenced the development of manufacturing industry in the Western Region.
2. Name and explain four socio-economic factors that have affected industrial development in the Western Region.
3. Outline four ways in which the Irish government supports the development of manufacturing industry in the Western Region.
4. Describe three reasons why Galway city has developed as a manufacturing centre.
5. List some of the main types of manufacturing carried on in the Western Region.
6. Identify one problem facing manufacturing industry in the Western Region.

Tertiary Economic Activities

KEYWORDS		
attractions	Fáilte Ireland	accessibility
accommodation	Tourism Ireland	costs
sport	Wild Atlantic Way	seasonality
recreation	challenges	

A lack of economic development within **peripheral** regions make them unattractive for tertiary activities such as financial services. Two tertiary activities are, however, common to all **peripheral** regions: **tourism** and **transport**.

Tourism

County	Overseas visitors	Value (€ m)	Domestic visitors	Value (€ m)
Galway	1,673,000	589	1,024,000	247
Mayo	324,000	78	503,000	108
Roscommon	54,000	27	130,000	18
Total	2,051,000	€694 m	1,657,000	€373 m

← **Table 19.3** Visitors and spend by county in the Western Region, 2017.

Tourism is vital as a source of income and employment for the Western Region. Over **3.7 million visitors** generated over **€1 billion** for the region in 2017 (**Table 19.3**). The following factors influence its development.

Attractions

Physical, historical and cultural landscapes

The physical landscape of rugged **mountains** such as the **Twelve Bens**, **glacial landscapes** such as **Killary Harbour** and the indented coastline with **steep cliffs and inlets** makes the Western Region uniquely attractive for visitors (**Fig. 19.13**). Islands such as the **Aran Islands, County Galway**, and **Inishturk, County Mayo**, provide visitors with the unique experience of remote island living.

> **DID YOU KNOW?**
> In 2017, the Western Region generated 14% of total earnings from overseas visitors and 19.5% from domestic visitors.

↑ **Fig 19.13** The Twelve Bens.

Fig 19.14 Dún Aengus, Inishmore.

The historical landscape is rich with **antiquities**, many dating back as far as Neolithic times. Two important sites are:
- the **Ceidé Fields** in County Mayo, the oldest known field systems in the world, dating to around 3000 BC;
- the stone fort at **Dún Aengus** on Inishmore (**Fig. 19.14**).

Summer language courses in Gaeltacht areas of Connemara and Mayo attract over 20,000 students each year, making them an important economic contributor to households providing **accommodation**, and to the cultural landscape of the region as a whole.

Religious sites, including **Knock Shrine**, **Croagh Patrick** and **Kylemore Abbey**, are also major attractions.

Sporting and recreational facilities

The region offers a wide variety of activities including:
- **Fishing**: The Western Region's many rivers and lakes (e.g. **Lough Corrib, County Galway, River Moy, County Mayo**) offer freshwater fishing and the coast provides sea fishing;
- **Surface water sports**: Ideal wind and wave conditions in the region have seen the growth of **sea-based recreational activities**, including surfing, windsurfing and kite surfing (e.g. **Keem Strand**, Achill, County Mayo);
- The rugged landscape provides the ideal backdrop for **hill walking and pony trekking**. The **Great Western Greenway** running from Westport to Achill is the longest off-road walking and cycling trail in Ireland;
- **Galway Race Week**, held every summer, is of huge importance to the sporting and tourism calendar;
- The increasing success of **Connacht Rugby** has seen plans submitted for the re-development of its sports ground, increasing its capacity to 12,000 spectators (December 2018).

19 A Peripheral Irish Region – The Western Region

Government support

Tourism is **labour-intensive**, providing employment in **peripheral** regions where such opportunities can be limited. It brings direct employment to those working in hotels and other accommodation sectors, visitor attractions, activity centres, restaurants, National Parks and a host of other tourism-related businesses, and indirectly provides a market for local agricultural and fish products.

The **Department of Transport, Tourism and Sport** is responsible for the development of the tourism sector. It supports a number of agencies including:

- The National Tourism Development Authority (**Fáilte Ireland**) is a public body that is tasked to support the tourism industry and to sustain Ireland as a high-quality and competitive tourism destination. Fáilte Ireland has roles in the development of tourism product, destination development, quality assurance, training, development and research. They also operate a year-round integrated marketing campaign to encourage people living on the island of Ireland to holiday in Ireland;
- **Tourism Ireland** markets the entire island of Ireland (north and south) overseas as a holiday and business tourism destination;
- the Government **Office of Public Works** maintains and provides staff at national monument tourist attractions in the region;
- through EU initiative **LEADER programmes**: the government provides support for rural tourism by supporting capital investment in innovative tourism projects, marketing, networking, events and festivals, and providing training and mentoring.

The **Department of Education and Skills** monitors the provision of tourism related courses in third-level institutions in the region (e.g. **GMIT**). Graduates from these courses are vital to the continued growth and expansion of tourism related activities in the region.

LEADER programme: *Liaison entre actions de développement de l'économie rurale,* an EU initiative which promotes rural development by providing support for a variety of local projects.

↑ **Fig 19.15** The official Wild Atlantic Way trademark logo.

The Wild Atlantic Way

Launched in 2014, the **Wild Atlantic Way** initiative has had major success in the development of tourism in the Western Region (Fig. 19.15). The initiative was launched by **Fáilte Ireland** to **'achieve greater visibility for the west coast of Ireland in overseas tourist markets'**.

The initiative incorporates, amongst other things, the comprehensive signposting of the Wild Atlantic Way, the development of 173 Discovery Points and 15 Signature Discovery Points along the route and the development of Visitor Experience Development Plans for each region, aligning public agency resources and plans. A **Wild Atlantic Way passport**, a memento of the visitor's journey along the Wild Atlantic Way, has also been launched; visitors can 'collect' stamps for each Discovery Point they visit (Fig. 19.16).

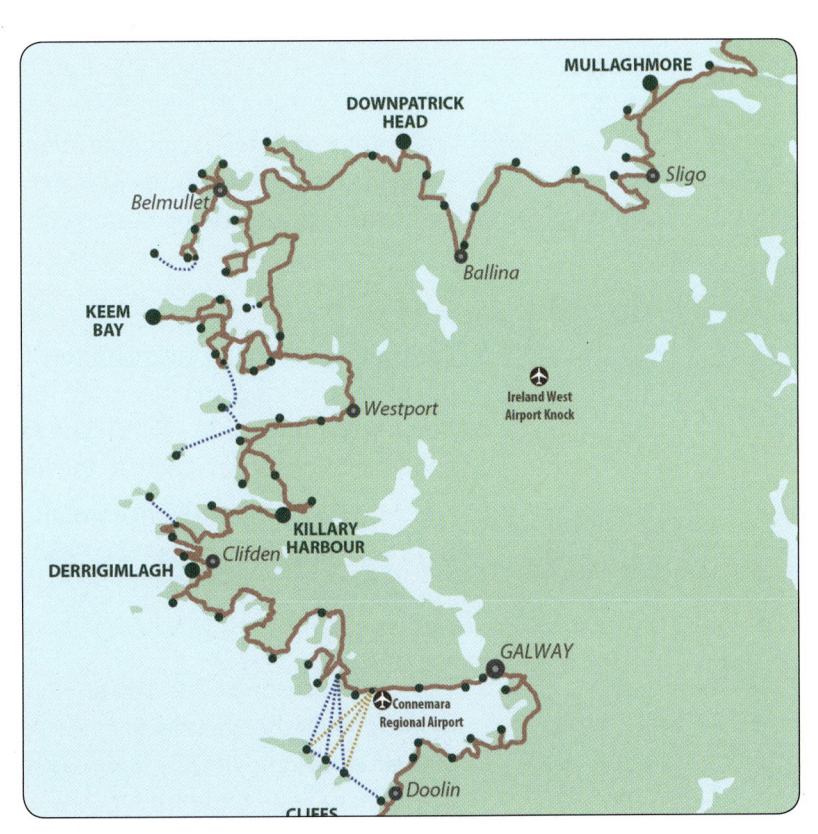

↑ **Fig 19.16** The Wild Atlantic Way runs through the Western Region.

Challenges facing the development of tourism

Accessibility

Of the 9 million overseas visitors to Ireland in 2017, only **1.6 million (18%)** visited the Western Region. The majority of tourists enter Ireland via the east of the country through Dublin Airport and Port, so to encourage people to visit the Western Region, access to and promotion of the region need to be improved. The proposed provision of cruise ship facilities at a redeveloped **Galway Port** is one initiative designed to increase visitor numbers, but an increase in volume of flights to the airport at Knock should also be a priority (Fig. 19.17). Roads and transport infrastructure within the region need major upgrades, but many hope that improving the **tourist attractions** within the region will also attract visitors. The new owners of **Westport House in County Mayo** are hopeful that the proposed development of an outdoor concert venue and other improvements will see visitor numbers rise from 130,000 to 1 million annually.

→ **Fig 19.17** Ireland West Airport, Knock.

Accommodation

A **shortage of hotel accommodation** throughout the region is an issue which results in a reduced number of overnight stays by tourists in the region. It also limits the capacity for increasing visitor growth to the region.

Costs

Controlling costs and giving visitors value for money is essential if tourist numbers are to be sustained and increased. **Increasing labour costs** and the shortage of **hotel accommodation** – which has seen room rates in the region increase – will continue to impact on costs to the industry.

The decision by the Irish government to **restore the VAT rate** from 9% to 13% in 2019 will also affect costs.

Seasonality

The tourist season in the Western Region is mostly confined to the **summer months** when the weather is better; counties Galway and Mayo receive over 25% of their visitor total in July and August. In recent years, increasing numbers of events have been organised for the winter months, attracting more tourism during the **off-peak season**. Examples include Connemara Sea Week, Galway Halloween Festival, Galway Christmas Market, and Light Up Galway City.

19 A Peripheral Irish Region – The Western Region

Transport

The **development** of the **transport network** in the Western Region has been influenced by a number of factors.

Physical factors

Relief

The **upland relief** of the Western Region is criss-crossed by a **network** of regional and local roads. This has resulted in roads that have steep slopes, sharp bends and narrow winding sections. If visitor numbers were to increase, the region's second- and third-class roads could not cope with **modern traffic volumes**.

The upland relief has also limited the development of rail transport.

Drainage

Poor drainage often results in **compromised foundations and surfaces**, for example, potholes, while flooding affects many low-lying roads in the region.

Socio-economic factors

Population density

Low population density in the region means that the provision of public transport is **not commercially viable** (Fig. 19.18).

In the 1960s and 1970s, the railway service underwent major **rationalisation** that resulted in **line closures**, reducing rail services. Today, Galway, Castlebar and Westport are all linked to Dublin by rail. In 2010, the **Limerick–Galway** rail link was **reopened**, and low demand for the service initially led to a slow growth in passenger numbers. Data for 2018, however, indicates a growth in numbers of people using the service, especially between Ennis and Athenry.

Regional and local roads are often the sole means of access for local economic activity and are vital to social and community functions (Fig. 19.19). Responsibility for the maintenance, upgrading and renovation of local roads lies with local and national authorities, but low population densities in areas served by these roads often result in these repairs being neglected.

KEYWORDS
relief
network
drainage
population density
development

Population density: The average number of people living in a unit of area, e.g. a square kilometre.

↑ **Fig 19.18** The Western Region has a low population density.

↑ **Fig 19.19** Roads in the Western Region can be of poor quality.

While an increase in the number of destinations linking with **Ireland West Airport at Knock** means that passenger numbers are increasing (over 770,000 people passed through the airport in 2018), the fact that it **serves a small catchment area** means that total passenger numbers are still insufficient for the airport to function without the help of state and EU funding.

Air and ferry services to the offshore islands, vital to the social and economic lives of islanders, are also supported by government funding.

Politics

Government involvement includes the **provision, maintenance, upgrading and planning for future transport needs**. The road network is maintained by local authorities and Transport Infrastructure Ireland.

The **ERDF** plays a vital role in providing funding for infrastructural projects designed to reduce regional inequality, for example, the **M17 Gort to Tuam motorway**, which opened in 2017.

The long-proposed but delayed **Western Rail Corridor** would result in direct rail connections between Galway and Sligo. Supporters of the project claim that its freight potential will attract manufacturers to the Western Region, while opponents cite **costs** involved in construction and the viability of the service due to lack of demand.

In 2015, the **European Commission's** inclusion of Ireland West Airport at Knock in **Ireland's Regional Airports Programme** permitted state financial support.

Future developments

The semi-state-owned **Galway Harbour Company** has proposed the **development of a new port at Galway Harbour** to accommodate the world's largest cargo ships and cruise liners. Plans are also in place to upgrade road and rail access to the harbour.

The **Galway City Ring Road** project will see the construction of a primary road around the northern fringes of the city and a new bridge over the River Corrib. Designed to **alleviate traffic congestion** in the city and **provide direct access to business parks**, the project – which has been approved by the Irish government – is awaiting planning approval.

The **N59** – one of the major roads in the Western Region – is a scenic route along the coastline that travels through areas of outstanding natural beauty. Upgrades to the road have experienced long delays due to environmental concerns.

In 2018, **Project Ireland 2040**, a government plan incorporating National Development Plan 2027, was unveiled. Transport initiatives under this plan relating to the Western Region include:

- the creation of the **Atlantic Road Corridor**, a high-quality road network linking Cork, Limerick, Galway and Sligo;
- funding for the **Galway City Ring Road**;
- the development of **Park and Ride sites** in Galway;
- **upgrades to rail infrastructure** to improve travel times between Galway and Dublin.

19 A Peripheral Irish Region – The Western Region

> **EXAM LINK (OL)**
>
> Tertiary Economic Activities – Irish Region (40 marks)
>
> Answer each of the following with reference to an Irish region that you have studied.
> (i) Name one tertiary economic activity that contributes to the economy of this region.
> (ii) Explain the advantages that this region has for the development of the tertiary economic activity named in part (i) above.
> (iii) Describe one challenge faced by this tertiary economic activity in this region.
>
> **2017, Q4B**
>
> **Marking Scheme:**
> (i) 4 marks
> (ii) 9 SRPs × 3 marks
> (iii) 3 SRPs × 3 marks

> **EXAM LINK (HL)**
>
> Tertiary Activity in Ireland (30 marks)
>
> Account for the development of tourism or transport in an Irish region that you have studied.
>
> **2015, Q4C**
>
> **Marking Scheme:**
> 15 SRPs × 2 marks

> **CHECK YOUR LEARNING**
>
> 1. Identify two ways tourism contributes to the economy of the Western Region.
> 2. Outline four different factors that have influenced tourism development in this region.
> 3. Describe two challenges facing the development of tourism in the region.
> 4. Name three factors that have impacted on transport in the Western Region.
> 5. List two ways transport has been affected by government policy.
> 6. Name any three transport projects for the region outlined in Project Transport Ireland 2040.

Human Processes

The Western Region covers almost 20% of the land area in Ireland, but contains only 10% of the total population.

Population dynamics

Density

The 2016 census recorded the average **population density** for the Republic of Ireland as **70 persons per km²**. All three counties in the Western Region have figures below the national average (Table 19.4).

County	Persons per km²
Galway	42.40
Mayo	23.35
Roscommon	25.33

← **Table 19.4** Population density in the Western Region (Census 2016).

Galway city had a density of **54.2 persons per km²**, indicating its importance as an economic centre. Variations also occur within each county with higher densities occurring in coastal and lowland areas where most towns and villages are located.

KEYWORDS

population density
depopulation
migration
population structure
Gaeltacht

Landscapes

County	Rural dwellers (% of total population)
Galway	54
Mayo	71
Roscommon	73

↑ **Table 19.5** Percentage of rural dwellers in the Western Region by county (Census 2016).

Distribution

The 2016 census also showed that 37% of the national population lives in rural areas. In the Western Region, however, an average of 66% of the population is classified as rural (**Table 19.5**).

Population distribution is uneven throughout the region. Upland areas of Galway and Mayo have low concentrations of people due to physical factors including **relief**, **climate** and **soils**, and **socio-economic factors** such as isolation and the lack of employment opportunities. The lowlands of Roscommon favour settlement, but lower concentrations occur in areas near the River Shannon that are prone to flooding. All areas of this region have experienced rural **depopulation** caused by lack of employment and the impact of economic downturns.

Having a high percentage of dispersed rural dwellers creates problems for the provision and support of services such as post offices, schools and transport services. Increasing closures and rationalisation of services has increased a sense of isolation, and with the closure of rural Garda stations, concern about increasing crime rates has grown.

Migration

Migration has had a major impact on population distribution within the Western Region. The Great Famine of 1847 began a process of **out-migration** that continued up to the 1990s.

In the early 2000s, natural increase and **immigration** associated with the Celtic Tiger economic boom contributed to population growth and a reversal of the **out-migration** trend. The figures for County Galway also reflect the outward expansion of Galway city during this period (**Table 19.6**).

Between 2007 and 2011, the aftermath of the economic crash led to increased **out-migration**, which slowed population growth in the region. While the recovery since 2012 has brought significant population growth in Galway city and county, only modest growth was recorded in County Roscommon, and County Mayo is still experiencing a decline in population.

Overall, the population of the Western Region declined from 1,082,676 in 1841 to 453,413 in 2016.

	2002	2006	2011	2016
Galway city	65,832	72,414	75,414	79,504
Co. Galway	143,245	159,256	175,127	179,048
Co. Mayo	117,446	123,839	130,552	130,425
Co. Roscommon	53,774	58,768	64,065	64,436
Total	380,297	414,277	445,158	453,413

→ **Table 19.6** Population of the Western Region, selected years (CSO).

CHECK YOUR LEARNING

Study Table 19.6 and answer the following questions:
1. Which county recorded the greatest increase in 2006?
2. Which county recorded the smallest increase in 2006?
3. In 2016, which county recorded a decrease?
4. Give one reason for this.

The impact of **migration** on the Western Region can be seen in the **population structure**. According to the 2016 census:

- the percentage of **old dependents** nationally is 20.4%;
- all three counties in the Western Region have a higher than average percentage of old dependents: 23.15% in County Galway, 28.3% in County Mayo and 26.8% in Roscommon;
- the percentage of old dependents in Galway city is 15.6% which reflects its larger productive sector due to its role as the centre of economic activity for the region.

There is also a long-established trend of **rural-to-urban migration** within the Western Region. **Pull factors** include economic and educational opportunities in urban centres, while poor quality of life and isolation act as **push factors**, encouraging people to leave their rural homes. **Rural depopulation** has resulted in abandoned farms and houses, reduced public services, and the closure of Garda stations, banks, post offices and schools (Fig. 19.20).

The Western Region has, like many other parts of Ireland, recently been attracting migrants from new EU member states such as Poland, Lithuania and Latvia, giving the population figures a slight boost. Census 2016 data showed County Galway had a Polish population of over 7,000. This flow of migrants has contributed to Galway city's increasingly **multicultural** profile.

Old dependency ratio: Proportion of older dependents (people older than 64) to the working age population (between the ages of 15–64). It can be presented as a percentage.

↑ **Fig 19.20** Rural depopulation leads to homes being abandoned.

Language

According to the 2016 census, the total population of **Gaeltacht** areas in Ireland was 96,090. The combined populations of the Galway Gaeltacht – 50,570 – and the Mayo Gaeltacht – 9,340 – meant that these two areas accounted for almost 60% of the total population of Gaeltacht areas.

The census revealed that in Gaeltacht areas daily usage of Irish outside the education system is declining, lending weight to the fears for the survival of the language. The growth of Galway has meant that **the city has extended into Gaeltacht areas**. People moving to these new areas are often not Irish speakers, which is leading to a fall in the language usage (Table 19.7).

One response to this was a proposal, as part of the Galway City Development Plan, to set up an **urban Gaeltacht** – a small housing estate with properties for sale exclusively to Irish speakers. The proposal has not yet been acted upon, and is unlikely to be due to concerns over discrimination.

Gaeltacht areas	2011	2016
Galway city	636	646
Co. Galway	10,085	9,445
Co. Mayo	1,172	895

← **Table 19.7** Census data on daily language usage outside the education system, Western Region (Census 2011, Census 2016).

Support for Gaeltacht areas under **Project Ireland 2040** includes a proposed investment of €178 million. This would include a €105 million investment through **Údarás na Gaeltachta**, creating approximately 1,000 jobs within the Gaeltacht annually, and €27 million to improve marine infrastructure for Inis Oírr, Inis Meáin and Oileán Thoraí.

Chapter 24: The Complexity of Regions II

Landscapes

KEYWORDS

Galway
migration
urban renewal
planning
tax relief
rural-to-urban
economic decline

Urbanisation

Census 2016 showed that 63% of Ireland's total population lived in urban areas. In the Western Region, however, the number of urban dwellers is much lower than the national average (Table 19.8).

County	Urban population (%)	Urban centres (pop. 5,000+)	Urban centres (pop. 500+)
Galway	46	4	21
Mayo	28	3	18
Roscommon	27	1	16

↑ **Table 19.8** Urban population in Ireland's Western Region (Census 2016).

The pattern of urbanisation in the Western Region is one of **small towns and urban centres**. Across the three counties, there are just 55 urban centres with a population greater than 500, while only eight have a population of over 5,000 people.

Galway city is the **largest urban centre** in the region with a population of 79,504 (Census 2016; Fig. 19.21). Even with the economic downturn in 2008, population growth has continued, driven by **immigration**, reflecting Galway's role as the main centre of employment for the region. Other important urban centres include Westport, Castlebar, Ballina, Tuam and Roscommon town.

↑ **Fig 19.21** Galway city centre.

Tax relief under **Section 23 of the Planning and Development Act 2000** resulted in the initiation of **rural and urban renewal** projects. Towns in the region began to improve as new houses and apartments were constructed, but there is evidence of **poor planning** in some of these developments, for example, homes being constructed on floodplains.

Economic decline has had a serious negative impact on urban areas. Businesses have closed, unemployment has risen and buildings are unoccupied and becoming derelict. Unfinished housing estates are a blight in some areas, such as Ballina and Loughrea.

EXAM LINK (HL)

Population in Ireland (30 marks)

Account for the distribution of population throughout an Irish region that you have studied.

2012, Q4C

Marking Scheme:
15 SRPs × 2 marks

CHECK YOUR LEARNING

1. Describe the pattern of population distribution in the Western Region.
2. List five factors which have had an impact on this pattern.
3. Identify three changes to population in the Western Region that have occurred over time.
4. Name three reasons why population in the Western Region is concentrated in and around Galway city.

EXAMINATION QUESTIONS

ORDINARY LEVEL

Long Question

1. Contrasting Regions in Ireland

Draw a sketch map of Ireland. On it, show and name the following:
- Two contrasting regions in Ireland.
- A named town or city in each region.
- A named river in each region.

2013, Part Two, Section 1, Q4A (30 marks)

Marking Scheme:
6 SRPs × 4 marks
Sketch map of Ireland outline = 6 marks graded

19 A Peripheral Irish Region – The Western Region

HIGHER LEVEL

Long Question

2. Agriculture in Ireland

Contrast the development of agriculture in two Irish regions that you have studied.

2011, Part Two, Section 1, Q4B (30 marks)

Marking Scheme:
Clearly stated contrasts = 2 + 2 marks
Discussion = 13 SRPs × 2 marks

Revision Summary

Physical Processes

Climate
- Cool temperate oceanic climate – summer av. 15°C – winter av. 6°C due to North Atlantic Drift
- Prevailing moisture laden SW winds – high precipitation levels 1,500–2,000 mm
- Uplands cause relief rain
- Atlantic depressions – frontal rainfall, cloudy conditions. 250 rainy days p.a.

Relief
- Upland areas: Maumturks, Co. Galway; Nephin Beg Mountains, Co. Mayo
- Caledonian folding period – magma formed igneous granite and metamorphic quartzite rocks
- Mineral deposits formed from volcanic gases, e.g. gold deposits, Croagh Patrick
- Carboniferous limestone – east Galway, Mayo, Roscommon
- Karst features – limestone caves and turloughs – south Galway
- Marine erosion – cliffs, bays along coast, e.g. Galway Bay; Marine deposition – beaches
- Glacial erosion: cirques, e.g. Lough Nadirkmore, Co. Mayo; U-shaped valley: Lough Inagh Valley, Co. Galway
- Glacial deposition: granite erratics, Aran Islands; drumlins, Clew Bay; boulder clay deposits, lowlands south Galway

Drainage
- Main rivers: Moy, Co. Mayo; Corrib and Clare, Co. Galway; Shannon, Co Roscommon
- Lakes: Lough Corrib, Lough Mask Co. Galway; Lough Conn, Co. Mayo.

Soils
- **High precipitation levels – peat soils form** blanket bogs on uplands of Galway, Mayo
- **Leaching** forms **podzols** – impaired drainage – and contributes to **gley soils** on lowland boulder clay deposits, e.g. Clew Bay
- Humus-rich **brown earth soils** – eastern lowland areas of Co. Galway and Roscommon
- **Loam soils** (sand, silt and clay) – well-drained east

Primary Economic Activities: Agriculture

Physical factor: climate
- High levels of cloud cover – precipitation (relief rain) causes fungal disease – not suitable for **arable** (cereal) crops
- Arable farming is 2% of agricultural activity and mainly in the east – better conditions
- Climate suited to grass growing, pastoral farming important
- Rainfall in winter – cattle indoors, expensive fodder, unprofitable to keep cattle after 2 years

Physical factor: relief and drainage
- Upland relief – steep slopes, exposed to strong winds, lower temperatures, relief rain – limit agriculture, e.g. Connemara
- Unsuited to arable farming – cannot use machinery; resistant rocks, low mineral content in soils; soil erosion
- Uplands suited to sheep rearing
- Lower slopes: grass, pastoral farming; arable farming on lowlands of Co. Galway and Roscommon
- Lowlands prone to summer flooding – River Shannon – negative impact on winter fodder production

Physical factor: soil
- High precipitation – **leaching**
- Infertile podzols limit agricultural production
- Gley and peat soils overgrazed – soil erosion
- Well-drained loam soils in the east – dairy farming possible

Socio-economic factor: small fragmented holdings
- Farm sizes too small for modern commercial agriculture
- Restricted output, limited income – out-migration of young farmers
- 60% of full-time farmers over 55 yrs – less productive, unlikely to expand or innovate
- 50% farmers need off-farm income to survive

Socio-economic factor: markets and infrastructure
- Low population density – limited local market for agricultural produce
- Main markets: east coast of Ireland, UK, EU – problems: extra transport costs; poor infrastructure and short shelf-life reduces product value; Brexit

Political factors
- 85% of farms rely on CAP payments
- European Agricultural Guaranteed Fund
- Disadvantaged area grant supports farmers with poor-quality soils, poor drainage, mountainous land
- REPS support for environmentally friendly farming – replaced by GLAS
- LEADER programme – supports alternative income streams, e.g. 'open farms'

313

Landscapes

Primary Economic Activities: Other

Fishing
- **Physical factors:** indented coastline – Continental shelf North Atlantic Drift
- **Socio-economic factors:** poor agricultural sector; fishing important income and food source
- Political factors: Government policy and grants – EU policy: **CFP**, Maximum Sustainable Yield, European Fisheries Fund
- Aquaculture: Natural advantages – BIM – opposition due to waste, infectious disease

Forestry
- Climate – mild temperatures, sufficient rainfall
- Land with little agricultural potential
- Distribution: lower upland slopes – upper slopes too exposed; sheltered areas and cut-away bogs
- Coniferous: Sitka spruce, Norway spruce
- Most managed by **Coillte**; private ownership increasing – EU grants

Mining and energy
- Corrib Gas Field 1996: gas flow Dec. 2015 – supplies 60% of Ireland's gas needs; 15 years life
- Opposition: concerns about onshore refinery, pipeline safety, impact on marine ecology

Renewable energy
- Wind energy: excellent conditions – wind farms Co. Galway, Mayo and Roscommon. Opposition: noise pollution, impact on scenery
- Wave energy: excellent conditions – ongoing research

Secondary Economic Activities

Physical factor: raw materials
- Harsh climate, upland terrain, poor-quality soils – low agricultural output
- Local industries – short supply of locally-produced raw materials – unable to expand and modernise
- Poor transport, high costs – sourcing bulky raw materials difficult
- EU membership 1973: end of protectionist policies, many companies close
- Fish processing industries important Connemara Seafood, Westport but CFP, overfishing – smaller catches
- Aquaculture – rapid growth: raw materials for local processing; seaweed

Socio-economic factor: labour force
- Limited third-level education – migration of young – brain drain – older, unskilled workforce unattractive for industries

Socio-economic factor: markets
- Low population – limited local market
- Main markets: GDA, UK, EU Single Market
- Sea cargo cheapest but Galway Port limited to boats under 6,000 t.
- Local transport network poorly developed; upland relief – construction difficult
- Isolation – delays, higher costs – less competitive
- Reduced rail network restricts cheaper freight movement by rail
- Brexit uncertainty – reduction in exports
- Poor telecommunication coverage impacts marketing

Political factors: government support
- Corporation tax rate of 12.5% attractive for Foreign Direct Investment (FDI)
- IDA: promotion; serviced industrial estates; capital and training support grants
- Enterprise Ireland: support for Irish entrepreneurs
- Údarás na Gaeltacht – industrial estates, e.g. Inverin Co Galway; financial support

Political factors: EU support
- Objective 2 Status – access European Regional and Structural funds to promote industrial development.
- ERDF funding – improve transport infrastructure, e.g. M6; education and training for local labour force

Tertiary Economic Activities: Tourism

Attractions
- Physical landscape: mountains – Twelve Bens; glacial landscapes – Killary Harbour; indented coastline, steep cliffs and inlets; islands – Aran Islands, Co. Galway, Inishturk, Co. Mayo
- Historical landscape: Ceidé Fields, Co. Mayo; Dun Aengus, Inishmore; Gaeltact areas
- Religious sites: Knock shrine, Croagh Patrick, Kylemore Abbey
- Sporting and recreational facilities: fishing – surface water sports – hill walking and pony trekking – Galway Race Week – Connacht Rugby Sportsground development

Government support
- Fáilte Ireland promotes domestic tourism; grades, inspects accommodation; tourist information offices
- Tourism Ireland promotes in overseas markets
- OPW staffs national monument tourist attractions
- LEADER programmes support rural tourism
- Department of Education and Skills – tourism-related courses in third level colleges
- Wild Atlantic Way – launched 2014, major success

Challenges to tourism
- Accessibility: entry via the east – Dublin Airport and Port – strategies: better access and promotion, increase range of tourism products
- Shortage of hotel accommodation limits capacity for increasing visitor growth
- Pressure to offer value for money – increasing labour costs and room rate increases – VAT increase from 9% to 13% in 2019

Seasonality
- Confined to summer months – increasing events for off-peak season, e.g. Galway Christmas Market

Tertiary Economic Activities: Transport

Physical factors
- Upland relief – steep slopes, sharp bends and narrow sections prevent development of comprehensive road and rail network
- Poor drainage – sinking foundations and surfaces, e.g. pot holes, flooding

Socio-economic factors
- Low population density – public transport not commercially viable; road repairs often neglected
- Galway, Castlebar, Westport rail links to Dublin; 2010 Limerick–Galway rail link reopened
- Air transport: Knock Airport passenger numbers increasing but insufficient to function without funding
- Air and ferry services to offshore islands supported by government funding

Political factors
- Government: transport provision, maintenance, upgrading, planning
- Road network maintenance: local authorities, Transport Infrastructure Ireland
- ERDF funds infrastructural projects designed to reduce regional inequality – M17 Gort to Tuam
- Delayed Western Rail Corridor – direct rail link Galway–Sligo – freight potential vs construction costs and viability
- State financial support for Ireland West Airport, European Commission 2015

Future developments
- Development of a new port at Galway Harbour
- Upgrading of road and rail access to the port
- Galway City Ring Road and new bridge over River Corrib
- Upgrades to N59
- Transport initiatives under Project Ireland 2040

Human Processes

Population dynamics
- Below state average population density; higher densities in coastal and lowland areas – favourable for farming, better access, employment; less people in lowland areas
- Rural depopulation – low employment, economic downturn – affected all areas
- Migration: major impact in population distribution in West – high percentage of old dependents; rural-to-urban migration trend

Language
- 60% of total Gaeltacht population in Galway and Mayo
- Daily usage of Irish outside school in decline – concerns for survival of language
- Galway city expansion into Gaeltacht areas – new residents often not Irish speakers
- Galway city Development Plan – urban Gaeltacht
- Project Ireland 2040 – proposed investment of €178m in Gaeltacht

Urbanisation
- Galway city largest urban centre in the region
- Continued population growth, in-migration, main centre of employment
- Westport, Castlebar, Ballina, Tuam, Roscommon town also important urban centres

20 A CORE EUROPEAN REGION – THE PARIS BASIN

LEARNING INTENTIONS
Syllabus Links: 2.2

By the end of this chapter I will be able to:
- draw an outline map of the region, showing and naming different features;
- explain how physical processes have shaped the landscape of this region;
- describe the factors that have influenced the development of primary, secondary and tertiary activities in the region;
- describe and explain the human processes that have influenced the population of the region;
- examine the development of one urban area in the region.

The Paris Basin is a **core economic region** and a major centre of economic activity in France and within the EU (**Figs 20.1, 20.2**).

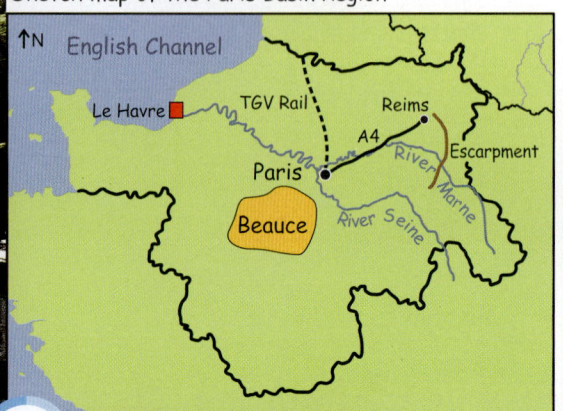

Fig. 20.1 The Paris Basin region.

Sketch map of the Paris Basin Region

Key for Sketch Map of the Paris Basin Region
- Industrial area
- Agricultural area
- Urban centre
- --- TGV rail link Paris–Reims
- Relief feature
- Road link
- River

Fig. 20.2 Sketch map of the Paris Basin region.

20 A Core European Region – The Paris Basin

Physical Processes

Climate

The west and north-west of the Paris Basin region experience a **cool temperate oceanic climate**, influenced by the prevailing south-westerly winds. The main characteristics of this climate are average summer temperatures of 19°C and average winter temperatures of 5°C, while the annual precipitation averages at 700 mm.

The east of the region, however, is influenced by weather patterns pushing in from the continent to the east, resulting in a **cool temperate continental climate**. Summers are warmer with an average summer temperature of 24°C, while winters are colder, averaging 2°C. This eastern part of the region experiences **convectional rainfall**, which brings around 600 mm of precipitation each year, most of which falls during the summer months.

A **transitional climate** is experienced in the zone where the oceanic and continental climates meet.

KEYWORDS

cool temperate continental climate
cool temperate oceanic climate
North European Plain
syncline
sedimentary
escarpments

Chapter 18: A Core Irish Region – The Greater Dublin Area

	Jan	Feb	Mar	Apr	May	Jun	Jul	Aug	Sep	Oct	Nov	Dec
Mean temperature (°C)	3.3	4.2	7.8	10.8	14.3	17.5	19.4	19.1	16.4	11.6	7.2	4.2
Mean precipitation (mm)	54	46	50	44	58	56	53	51	56	57	58	54

↑ Table 20.1 Average monthly temperature and precipitation, Paris (Climate-Data.Org).

Relief

The Paris Basin is part of the **North European Plain**. It is a **syncline** composed of different strata of **sedimentary** rocks. In the east of the region, the underlying sedimentary layers are exposed and form **escarpments**, such as those seen in the **Île-de-France** area.

Drainage

The **River Seine** flows in a north-westerly direction through Paris and into the sea at Le Havre, while the **Marne** and **Somme** rivers flow into the English Channel. The region's **gently sloping relief** allows rivers to drain away any excess water, so preventing flooding. The underlying **permeable sedimentary** rocks also help with drainage and prevent the land becoming waterlogged (Fig. 20.3).

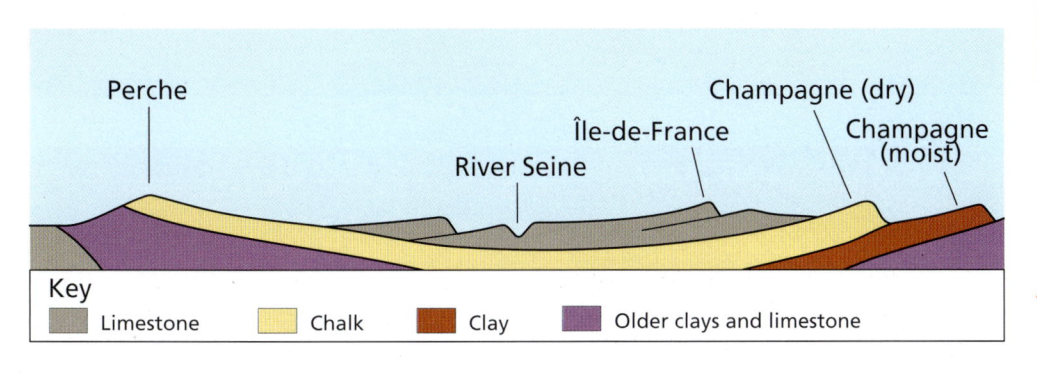

SKILLS ACTIVITY

Construct a climograph to illustrate the precipitation and temperature data for July to December presented in Table 20.1.

Syncline: Land feature formed when layers of rock slope inwards from the edges.

Escarpment: A steep slope separating two relatively gentle slopes or flat areas.

← Fig. 20.3 Geological cross-section of the Paris Basin.

Key: Limestone, Chalk, Clay, Older clays and limestone

Perche — River Seine — Île-de-France — Champagne (dry) — Champagne (moist)

317

Landscapes

Limon soils: Glacial soils deposited during and after the Ice Ages by winds blowing southwards from the ice fields.

Soils

A wide variety of soils have formed in the region (Fig. 20.4). **Limon** soils formed from wind-blown glacial deposits can be found in Île-de-France, while **outwash sands and gravels** deposited by fluvio-glaciation are found in the south of the region at Sologne. **Alluvial clays** form along the banks of the three main rivers (the **Seine**, the **Marne** and the **Somme**), and **boulder clays**, deposited during the last Ice Age, are found in Brie. In Champagne, the underlying **chalk** is covered with a thin layer of well-drained topsoil, which requires frequent nutrient renewal through fertilisers (Fig. 20.5).

SKILLS ACTIVITY

Draw an outline map of the Paris Basin region showing:
- two named urban centres;
- a named feature of relief (upland or lowland);
- a numbered road;
- another communication link;
- an industrial area;
- an area of agricultural production;
- two features of drainage.

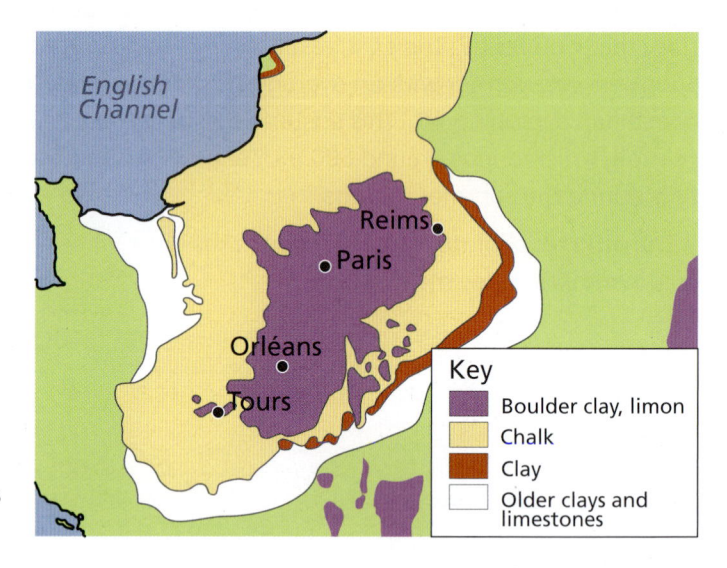

→ **Fig. 20.4** Main soil types in the Paris Basin.

Key:
- Boulder clay, limon
- Chalk
- Clay
- Older clays and limestones

→ **Fig. 20.5** Chalk soils, Champagne.

CHECK YOUR LEARNING

1. Name the two main types of climate found in the Paris Basin region.
2. Describe two characteristics of each one.
3. Name four different soil types found here.
4. Explain the following terms: escarpment, syncline, limon.

Primary Economic Activities

Agriculture

A number of factors have combined to make agriculture an important primary economic activity in the Paris Basin region.

Physical factors

Climate

The **cool temperate oceanic climate** with its mild winters, warm summers and abundant precipitation throughout the year provides ideal conditions for **grass-growing**. As a result, **pastoral farming** is a common form of agriculture in the western parts of the Paris Basin. **Dairy farming** and the rearing of **beef cattle** is commonly found in Brie and Normandy. The Île-de-France breed of sheep, which is native to the region, also thrives in the cool temperate oceanic climate.

To the east of the region, the **cool temperate continental climate** provides a **long growing season** of over 280 days a year. Warm temperatures, **long hours of sunshine** and **convectional rains** are ideal for ripening **arable crops**. **Specialised production** in Beauce has resulted in the highest wheat output per hectare in the EU. Located near the northern limit of grape vine cultivation, the climate in eastern parts of the Paris Basin helps to produce grapes with a high acid content – ideal for the production of Champagne.

Relief

The Paris Basin is part of the **North European Plain**, which is characterised by large expanses of gently sloping **lowlands**. This **relief** supports the widespread use of agricultural machinery, so a well-developed **commercial arable farming** sector has evolved (Fig. 20.6). Ploughing, sowing and spraying is efficiently carried out by single-driver machinery, which reduces labour costs and raises profits. Large, flat fields are also suited to combine harvesters, resulting in the production of cereals such as wheat and barley.

← Fig. 20.6 Farmland, Île-de-France.

Escarpments and the permeable nature of the underlying bedrock (e.g. limestone and sandstone) provides effective drainage throughout the region. Land is productive, as crops are aerated, leading to larger outputs of **arable** crops, including wheat, barley, sugar beet and rapeseed.

The **southerly slopes** of the Champagne region provide ideal conditions for **viticulture** – the growing of grapes. The slopes are well-drained, reducing the possibility of vines sitting in soil that's too wet and heavy. The angle of the slope is important to ensure the vines planted on them can get a maximum amount of sunlight exposure during the day, which in turn helps reduce the risk of frost.

KEYWORDS
pastoral
arable
lowland
horticulture
machinery
markets
energy

DID YOU KNOW?
Approximately 6% of the world's wheat comes from the Paris Basin.

DID YOU KNOW?
Only sparkling wine made in the Champagne area can be called Champagne.

Soils

The variety of soils contributes to a varied pattern of agriculture in different farming regions known as *pays*:

- **calcium-rich** soils in Normandy support **pastoral farming** and **bloodstock** rearing;
- **limon** soils in the Île-de-France are extremely fertile: wheat, barley, maize and sugar beet are produced in this region, widely known as the 'granary of France';
- **boulder clay** soils found in Brie are suited to grass-growing, supporting **pastoral farming**;
- **chalk** soils in the Champagne region are well-suited to viticulture;
- **outwash sands and gravels** in the south around Fontainebleau are generally infertile and devoted to **forestry**.

Socio-economic factors

Efficient commercialised farms

Averaging 400 hectares in size, farms in the Paris Basin are the largest of any EU region. These large, easily accessible fields support the use of **large modern machinery**, reducing labour costs and maximising productivity and profits. This has facilitated the growth of **'specialised' commercial cereal farming** of wheat in the region.

Farmers in the region are generally **young and well-educated**, and employ **progressive farming methods** including modern machinery and new technologies. Moreover, younger farmers tend to be more adaptable to changing market tastes, such as the recent increase in demand for organic vegetables. As a result, farm outputs in the Paris Basin are higher with **incomes 40% higher than the national average**, providing farmers with a good standard of living and surplus cash to reinvest in their farms or in their communities.

Markets

The Paris Basin's population of **24 million people** constitutes the largest – and most affluent – market in France. This has stimulated the growth of the **horticulture** sector, notably the intensive production of **'*primeurs*'** both outdoor and under glass on the farms surrounding Paris.

Primeurs: Early fruit and vegetables, which command a higher market price.

Paris is the world's number one city destination for **tourism**, and the large volume of visitors creates a huge demand for **regional food**, including meat, cheese, vegetables and wine. The region is also home to many of the state's biggest food and drinks **processing** industries (e.g. Pernod-Ricard), which consistently require large volumes of raw materials.

The Paris Basin is close to the **economic core** of Europe where there is a large concentration of **urban centres**, constituting a market in excess of 170 million people.

A well-developed road and rail **transport network** enable the speedy shipment of produce to **French and mainland EU markets**. This is important for two reasons: firstly, it **limits the cost of transporting** agricultural produce, and secondly, it allows a long **shelf life** for perishable products, making them more valuable.

The port at Le Havre facilitates the export of agricultural produce to **global markets**.

Political factors

EU support

The larger and more commercial farms of this region benefitted greatly from the Guidance Section of the **Common Agricultural Policy**, which provided grants for farm improvements through investment in machinery and buildings. This has led to increased farm output and higher profits.

EU membership gives farmers access to the **European Single Market** of 500 million people.

Energy

There is a small amount of **fossil fuel** production in France; the presence of shale oil deposits allows for the possibility of extraction by **fracking**. However, **opposition** from environmentalists may make extraction impossible.

In reality, France relies on **nuclear power** for the production of over 75% of its electricity, 10% of which is produced in the Paris Basin.

Île-de-France is becoming a leader in the production of **geothermal energy** – approximately 80% of the country's supply is produced in the region.

EXAM LINK (OL)

Agriculture in a European Region (40 marks)

Answer each of the following questions with reference to a European region that you have studied.

(i) Name two examples of agricultural activity practised in this region.

(ii) Discuss how any two of the following factors influence the development of agriculture in this region.

Climate   Relief and soils   Markets

2018, Q6B

Marking Scheme:
(i) Two examples named × 2 marks each
(ii) Factor 1 = 6 SRPs × 3 marks
Factor 2 = 6 SRPs × 3 marks
Allow a named region for one SRP

EXAM LINK (HL)

Agriculture in Europe (30 marks)

Account for the development of agriculture in a European region that you have studied, with reference to any two of the following factors.

Relief   Markets   Climate

2012, Q4B

Marking Scheme:
Factor 1 = 8 SRPs × 2 marks
Factor 2 = 7 SRPs × 2 marks

CHECK YOUR LEARNING

1. Outline three physical factors which have influenced the development of agriculture in the Paris Basin region.
2. List four different types of agricultural activity pursued in the Paris Basin region.
3. Outline three socio-economic factors influencing agricultural development in the Paris Basin region. Describe the impact any one of them has had on agriculture.

Landscapes

KEYWORDS
raw materials
agriculture
food processing
labour force
defence
consumer industries
markets
government policy

Secondary Economic Activities

Many factors have contributed to the development of the Paris Basin region as a **core industrial area**.

Physical factors

Raw materials

Traditional industries in the Paris Basin have developed on the back of a rich supply of locally-produced **raw materials**.

The **textile industry** owed its development to the availability of raw materials, such as wool from sheep reared in Île-de-France. Today, **competition** from lower-cost producers, predominantly in South-east Asia, has resulted in a much smaller textile industry in the region, based predominantly on small production units.

During the 20th century, **motor car manufacturers** flocked to the Paris Basin, attracted by the **iron and steel** produced in the neighbouring Nord region. However, many of these heavy industries have now ceased production in France and moved to lower-cost locations in eastern Asia.

The Paris Basin's **temperate climate**, **lowland relief** and **fertile soils** support a wide variety of **agricultural activity**. The abundance of local produce requiring minimal transportation has allowed a range of **food processing** industries to thrive.

The underlying soft chalk around Reims and Epernay has enabled the creation of cellars where temperature and humidity levels remain constant, essential for the production of Champagne (Fig. 20.7).

Flour from **wheat** produced in Beauce is used to supply **bakeries and confectionery manufacturers**, while local **barley** supplies the **brewing** industry.

Milk produced in Brie supplies raw materials for a wide range of industries, including **cheese** production (e.g. **Brie** and **Camembert**; Fig. 20.8) and **yoghurt-based probiotic drinks** (e.g. **Danone**).

Apples grown in Normandy support a well-established **cider** industry, while **rapeseed** grown to the north of Paris is used in the production of **edible oils and bio-diesel**.

↑ **Fig. 20.7** Champagne cellars, Épernay.

↑ **Fig. 20.8** Cheeses from the Île-de-France area.

Socio-economic factors

Labour force

The Paris Basin has a **highly skilled labour force**, which attracts industries requiring a variety of skill sets.

The universities, technical universities and institutes of technology supplying skilled graduates have contributed to Paris's status as a **centre for science and technology**. Graduates of higher education institutes in Paris (e.g. the **Sorbonne**, the **University of Pierre and Marie Curie**) often go on to work in research and product development for manufacturing industries, such as medical technologies. This concentration of manufacturing has also attracted **skilled migrants** from elsewhere in France and across the EU. This has further enhanced the labour profile of the region and attracted the **defence and commercial aerospace** industries (e.g. **Airbus, Élancourt, Paris**; Fig. 20.9) as well as IT, electronics, biotech and pharmaceutical industries (e.g. **Sanofi, Vitry-sur-Seine**).

↑ **Fig. 20.9** Airbus Industries, Elancourt.

The local population of the Paris Basin also provides a large pool of **lower-skilled workers** for industries with minimum skills requirements and in-house training.

Paris's excellent **public transport systems** allow the local labour force to move efficiently throughout the region. High-speed **TGV** trains also make it possible for workers to commute long distances on a daily basis (e.g. **Lyons**).

Transport infrastructure

An **efficient transport network** is vital for the transport of raw materials and manufactured products, especially perishable food products. As a nodal point, Paris is the focus of the French **road and rail systems** (Fig. 20.10). This allows raw materials to be transported quickly and inexpensively to industries located within the Paris Basin region.

The rail network provides linkage with internal **French markets**, **European markets** and through the **Eurotunnel** with the United Kingdom. High-speed **TGV** (Fig. 20.11) trains benefit the region by extending the market area without extending transportation times, while **reduced journey times** for workers contribute to **increased productivity**.

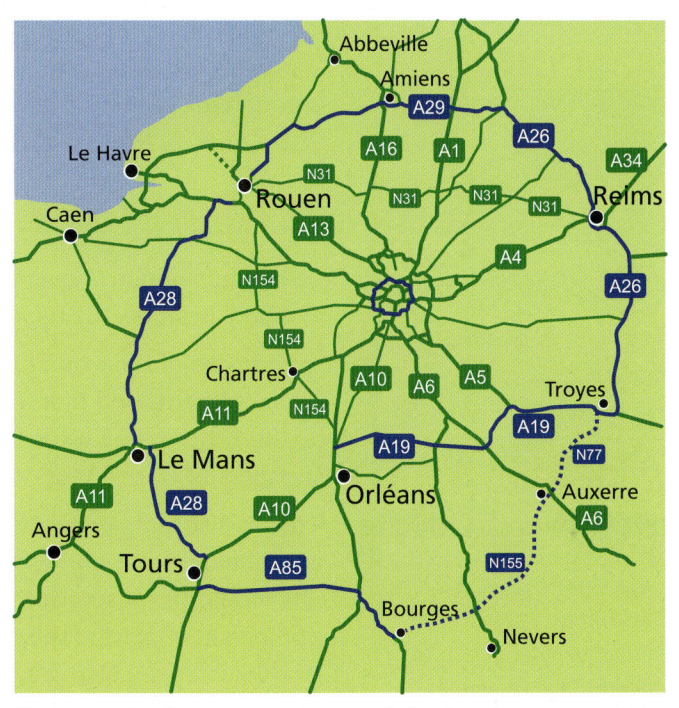

↑ **Fig. 20.10** The Paris Basin has a well-developed road network.

Transport node: A focus of different transport types.

← **Fig. 20.11** TGV high-speed train.

Landscapes

The wide and easily navigable **River Seine** links the Paris Basin region to **Le Havre**, France's largest container port, providing a **cheap mode of transportation** for heavy industries requiring bulky raw materials (**Figs 20.12, 20.13**). The Le Havre industrial centre has also attracted port-related industries, including **oil refineries** and **chemical** and **petrochemical industries**.

→ **Fig. 20.12** The River Seine.

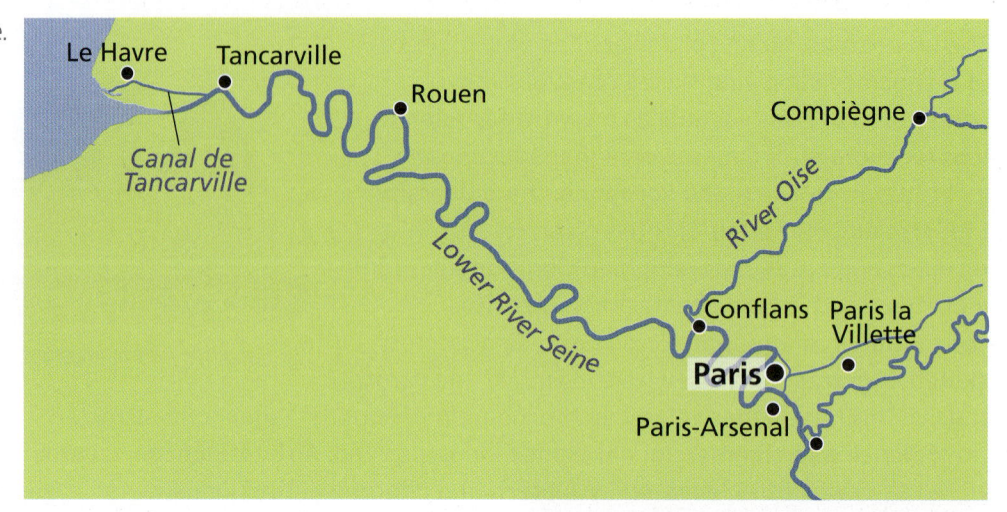

Deindustrialisation: The closure of industry, especially heavy industry, due to competition, falling demand and relocation.

The **banks of the River Seine** were once home to heavy industries that transported bulky raw materials by barge (e.g. **Renault's Billancourt plant**). However, increased **competition** from low-cost centres in Eastern Europe and Eastern Asia has led to significant **deindustrialisation**. Today, barges still carry raw materials and finished goods through the region's canal network (e.g. **Canal du Nord**).

↑ **Fig. 20.13** Le Havre port, France.

Markets

With a population of over **24 million people** and an average income 10% above the national average, the region supports a wide range of **consumer industries**.

Paris is one of the world's **fashion** capitals and is home to **famous design houses** such as **Chanel** and **Dior**. The growth of the textile industry can be traced back to the 17th century when Louis XIV moved the royal court to Versailles, and the demand for clothing for nobles and courtiers stimulated the growth of the industry.

Paris is also a major centre for **cosmetics development** (e.g. **L'Oreal**), and so many personal care companies are based around Chartres that the town has earned the nickname **'Cosmetics Valley'**. The **multiplier effect** comes into play here, as companies supplying the cosmetics companies with materials such as chemicals or packaging are also drawn to the area.

Multiplier effect: One industry can support and promote other industries, which supply it with components, packaging or raw materials. Workers' wages also support jobs in the local economy, through shops, bars, restaurants, etc.

The well-developed agricultural sector supports a market for a wide range of **agri-business**, including fertiliser manufacturing (e.g. **Grandpuits**) and machinery.

Defence industries in the region rely on the French government for contracts to supply **aircraft and defence systems** (e.g. **Nexter Systems**, Versailles).

The large population has made Paris an important **publishing** centre with a number of national newspapers – including **Le Monde** and **Le Figaro** – based in the city, which is also home to over 150 book publishing companies.

The region's central location and excellent transportation links allow manufacturing industries to access the **EU Single Market** of over 500 million people.

Government policy

In the 1960s and 1970s, **traditional industries** such as engineering and textiles went into **decline** in the Paris Basin. This was the result of a number of factors, including the **global economic downturn** caused by the oil crisis of the early 1970s. **Rising labour costs** forced manufacturers to move to lower-cost areas, while previous governments had moved industry away from Paris to try to balance regional economic disparities.

Government incentives to support industrial development in the region included the development of **technopoles** – clusters of manufacturing facilities with formal links to third-level institutions, ensuring a skilled labour pool (e.g. **Saclay; Fig. 20.14**). **Research and development facilities, land banks** and an excellent **transport infrastructure** attract inward investment. In the 1960s, the government developed five **new towns** in the suburbs of Paris to stimulate economic growth (e.g. **Cergy-Pointoise**). The new towns have been successful in attracting a variety of firms providing a large quantity of jobs in IT, life sciences and other high-skilled industries.

> **EXAM TIP**
> Exam candidates should be able to compare the development of economic activities in this region with their development in the Mezzogiorno (Chapter 21).

> **DID YOU KNOW?**
> During the oil crisis of 1973, the price of oil rose from $3 to $12 a barrel.

Challenges facing the manufacturing industry

Employers in France face very high levels of **payroll tax**, which has resulted in manufacturers moving their operations to lower-cost locations outside of France.

With the exception of Malta, France's 33.4% rate of corporation tax is the highest in the EU. This makes it very difficult for France to compete with lower-tax areas when trying to attract foreign direct investment.

→ **Fig. 20.14** Saclay technopole, Paris.

EXAM LINK (OL)

European Region (40 marks)

Describe the development of manufacturing industry in a European region (not in Ireland) which you have studied.

2010, Q5B

Marking Scheme:
Name of region (not in Ireland) = 4 marks
Description = 12 SRPs × 3 marks

EXAM LINK (HL)

Manufacturing in a European Region (30 marks)

Account for the development of manufacturing in a European region that you have studied.

2015, Q5B

Marking Scheme:
Examination = 15 SRPs × 2 marks
Credit 2 SRPs for examples of manufacturing

CHECK YOUR LEARNING

1. Name four ways raw materials produced in the Paris Basin support the manufacturing industry.
2. List three socio-economic factors that influenced the development of manufacturing in the Paris Basin region. Explain two ways each one has affected industrial development.
3. Name two ways government policy impacted on manufacturing in the Paris Basin region.
4. Describe one challenge facing the manufacturing industry in the Paris Basin region.

Landscapes

Tertiary Economic Activities

Over 80% of the workforce in the Paris Basin is involved in the tertiary sector, employed in services including government, retail, banking and finance, tourism and transport.

> **KEYWORDS**
> accessibility
> attractions
> employment
> public transport
> terrorist attacks

Tourism

Tourism is a year-round activity that is hugely significant to the economy of the Paris Basin region. In 2017, tourism contributed over **€21 billion** to the local economy, and 18.4% of the labour force was employed in tourism-related activities. Paris is the **world's most popular tourist destination**, a status achieved due to a number of interdependent factors.

Accessibility

Thanks to its central location within France, the Paris Basin has an **excellent road network**. A range of **high-speed TGV trains** link the region with the rest of France and other EU countries, while the Eurostar and Eurotunnel provide direct train services to and from Great Britain.

Large ports at Le Havre and Cherbourg facilitate **passenger ferries** and **cruise liners**.

Paris is also a global **air transportation** hub: Charles de Gaulle Airport is the number one passenger and freight airport in Europe, Le Bourget Airport is popular for business travel and Beauvais Airport to the east of Paris is widely used by low-cost airlines.

The region itself is served by an excellent internal **transport network**, including the **Metro** (subway), **RER** and **suburban trains**, as well as buses and trams, allowing tourists to visit multiple sites and to spread their area of spending.

Attractions

Paris is famous for its historical sites and architecture, including **Notre Dame Cathedral** and the **Eiffel Tower**. Within the greater Paris area there are also attractions including **World War II D-Day landing sites** and cemeteries, the Palace at **Versailles** and the Gothic cathedrals at **Reims** and **Chartres**.

The **Louvre** and the **Musée d'Orsay** are at the top of the city's list of **cultural attractions**, while **Disneyland Paris** is an incredibly popular recreational attraction (**Fig. 20.15**). The theme park's location – 35 minutes to the east of Paris – gives it access to a potential catchment of over 17 million people, and it provides **direct and indirect employment** to over 55,000 people.

→ **Fig. 20.15** Disneyland Paris.

20 A Core European Region – The Paris Basin

Paris is also a **major commercial centre** with many large shops and department stores. It attracts many wealthy visitors due to its reputation for high-end goods and fashion (e.g. designer stores along the **Champs Élysées**), as well as business people (approximately 10 million annually) attending conventions and trade fairs.

Paris is an important player in **events-based tourism** and hosts many national and international sporting fixtures and cultural events, including the **Six Nations** rugby tournament, the **Tour de France** and **Paris Fashion Week**.

Challenge for tourism – terror attacks

Paris has been the target of a number of violent **terrorist attacks** in recent years. The resulting deaths and injuries – and their extensive media coverage – have had an impact on visitor numbers. Following the November 2015 attacks, hotel cancellations exceeded 55%. The effects of terrorist incidents are usually short term; after the Paris attacks, the government and tourism interests worked together on an active promotion campaign. Social media was used to challenge false news and negative messaging and, by 2017, visitor numbers had recovered.

Transport

The Paris region needs a **well-developed transport network** to serve its huge **population**. Road and rail services link the region internally, while externally they provide links to the rest of France and Europe. Factors contributing to transport development include:

Physical factors

The **lowland relief** of the Paris Basin was well-suited to the **construction of canals** in the 17th and 18th centuries, and later allowed the development of a **rail network** which radiates outwards from Paris to destinations across France and Europe.

Gentle gradients served the development of **roads and motorways**, resulting in a well-developed road transport infrastructure radiating outward to all areas of France and Europe, with Paris again acting as a **node**.

The ease of navigability of the **River Seine** even allowed the city to develop **port functions**. Large ocean-going vessels docked at Le Havre with raw materials that were then transferred to barges for onward shipment to Paris. Today, the Port de Paris, a joint venture between the ports of Le Havre, Rouen and Paris, is Europe's fifth largest in terms of volume of trade, and has extensive container and storage facilities.

Socio-economic factors

With a **population exceeding 24 million** people distributed over a wide area, an efficient road network and a well-developed **public transport** system is essential to the region.

- The **Paris Metro** has 16 lines, over 300 stations and serves an urban area of four million people (**Fig. 20.16**).
- The **RER** connects the suburbs to the city centre.
- The **high population density** and the demand for speedy connections has led to the development of the **TGV** high-speed rail network, linking Paris with all regions of France and surrounding countries, including Belgium and Germany (**Fig. 20.17**).

KEYWORDS
River Seine
relief
public transport
population density
TGV
congestion
planning
Grand Paris Transport Plan

↑ **Fig. 20.16** The Paris Metro.

Landscapes

→ **Fig. 20.17** The rail network connecting Paris to the rest of France and surrounding countries.

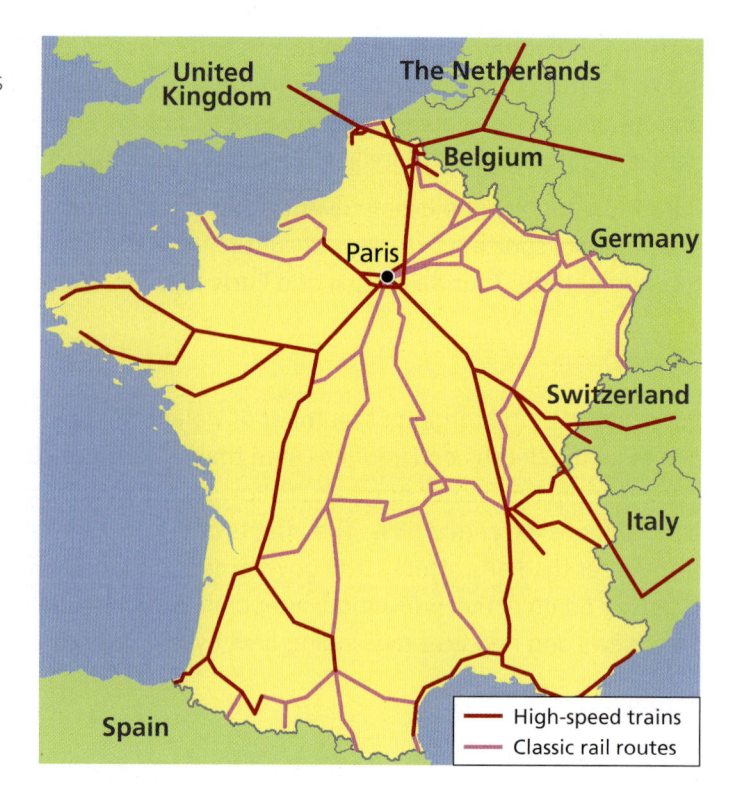

EXAM LINK (OL)

Tertiary Economic Activities – European Region (30 marks)

Discuss the development of two tertiary economic activities in a European region that you have studied.

2018, Q5B

> **Marking Scheme:**
> Two activities named × 3 marks
> Activity 1 = 4 SRPs × 3 marks
> Activity 2 = 4 SRPs × 3 marks
> Credit a named region for 1 SRP

- **Designated bus lanes**, often physically separated from the street by low walls, have been constructed to provide an efficient public bus services and reduce traffic volumes.
- The **Vélib** public bicycle-sharing scheme provides over 20,000 bikes at more than 1,800 stations. The city also has more than 500 km of designated cycle routes.
- The road network is a vital element in the social and economic fabric of the region. As with most cities, **traffic congestion** is a huge problem. **Orbital roads**, including the Peripherique and Superperipherique, have been constructed to direct traffic flow away from the centre.

EXAM LINK (HL)

Tertiary Economic Activity – European Region (30 marks)

Account for the development of one tertiary economic activity in a European region (not in Ireland) that you have studied.

2017, Q4B

> **Marking Scheme:**
> Examination = 15 SRPs × 2 marks

Political factors

National government and local authorities play a vital role in transport provision, maintenance and future **planning** in the Paris Basin region. The Transport Syndicate of Île-de-France is the state agency responsible for all modes of ground transport, and oversees financing, organisation and **planning**. Finance comes from tax and revenue from **public transport** fares. The EU – through the **European Regional Development Fund** – also provides funding for some transport initiatives.

Planning for the future

In 2016, the **Métropole du Grand Paris** was established. This is a new administrative body which will be responsible for the co-ordination of transport, housing and **urban** planning throughout the region.

Its proposed **Grand Paris Transport Plan** includes:

- the modernisation of the current transport network at a cost of over €25 billion;
- the provision of over 200 km of new railway tracks and 70 new train stations;
- the development of a section of automated Metro providing a 24-hour service. The route will link seven economic zones and travel at speeds of up to 60 km/hr. When completed (planned for 2030), expected use will be over two million passengers a day.

20 A Core European Region – The Paris Basin

> **CHECK YOUR LEARNING**
>
> 1. Explain three factors that have contributed to tourism development in the Paris Basin region. Give two SRPs, explaining each one.
> 2. Describe one issue affecting tourism development in the Paris Basin region.
> 3. List three socio-economic factors which influenced transport development in the Paris Basin region. Give two SRPs to explain each one.
> 4. Describe two proposed improvements to transport in the Paris Basin region.

Human Processes

Population density

Paris is the **most densely populated city in Europe**. Within the Paris Basin region, **population density** ranges from 677 per km² (Île-de-France) to 20,000 per km² (city centre).

Birth rate

A decline in the **birth rate** in France in the 1970s and 1980s was reversed in the 1990s, thanks to government incentives including maternity and paternity leave and subsidised day care.

However, in 2011, birth rates in Paris began to decline again, reflecting a national trend. The **total fertility rate (TFR)** for France fell from 2.01 in 2012 to 1.88 in 2017. The **economic recession**, cut backs to **government supports** and a **lack of childcare facilities** in the Paris area due to very high demand contributed to this decline. However, higher birth rates among migrant populations have helped to offset decline in the region.

Population distribution

Paris is a **primate city** consisting of three concentric zones (Fig. 20.18). At the centre lies the **city** of Paris (population 2 million), then the **suburbs** (*unité urbaine*; population 10.5 million) and at the outer extent, **Île-de-France** (population 12 million). Altogether, they account for over 37% of the total population of France.

Changes over time

The main reasons for the **growth in population** in any city are **natural increase** and **migration**.

In 1921, the city recorded its highest ever population at 2.9 million people. Between the years 1954–1999, each census taken showed a trend of **population decline**.

One of the main factors contributing to this decline was **migration** from the city centre into the suburbs. Causes of this migration included:

- **deindustrialisation**, leading to job losses;
- increases to **rent** following urban redevelopment;
- change in **land use** from residential to commercial.

KEYWORDS
primate city
natural increase
migration
deindustrialisation
colonies
integration

↓ **Fig. 20.18** The structure of Paris: 1 = city, 2 = suburbs, 3 = Île-de-France.

Total fertility rate (TFR): The number of children a woman could have during her childbearing years. A replacement rate of two is necessary to sustain population numbers.

329

Migration

Migration has had a major impact on the population structure of the Paris Basin region. **Internal migration** in the post-World War II period saw people move out from the less-developed, lower-density *diagonale du vide* ('empty diagonal'; Fig. 20.19) area of France to Paris in search of **employment**.

During the 1960s, strong economic growth requiring additional labour led to France recruiting labour from its former North African **colonies**, for example, **Morocco** and **Tunisia**. These migrants moved into areas that had been vacated by people moving to the outer suburbs. Nowadays, these areas (*banlieues*) have an overall appearance of neglect and suffer from **lack of investment and employment opportunities**. They are characterised by high-rise apartment blocks, many of which are in poor condition (Fig. 20.20).

↑ Fig. 20.19 The *diagonale du vide*.

Banlieue: A city suburb.

Lack of **integration, cultural differences, poor employment prospects, isolation and growing dissatisfaction** eventually led to civil disturbances between the migrants and the native population of Paris. Following the riots in Clichy-sous-Bois in 2005, the government started addressing these issues and invested millions of euros to improve the *banlieues*. However, following the **2008 financial crisis**, spending in this area has greatly reduced and improvements halted.

↑ Fig. 20.20 Apartment block in the *banlieues*.

High rates of unemployment among young Muslims and the **failure of integration policies** have led to instances of **radicalisation** and subsequent attacks carried out by Islamic extremists. There has been increasing opposition among French society to migration, leading to the rise of the far-right nationalist Front National (now National Rally) political party.

The Paris Basin region has also seen **immigration** from other EU countries. After the 2004 EU enlargement, the number of migrants from the Baltic States and former Soviet bloc countries increased.

The *gilets jaunes* movement

In November 2018, **mass demonstrations** began in Paris in response to rising fuel prices, increasing cost of living and claims that government tax reforms were impacting negatively on the working and middle classes. The demonstrators wore the fluorescent yellow vests associated with manual labourers, and the protest, which lasted for months, became known as the **'gilets jaunes'** (yellow vests)

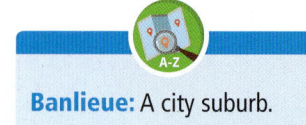

movement. As the demonstrations went on, many developed into violent riots with participants causing damage to commercial properties and the historic monument, the Arc de Triomphe.

In response to the protests, the French government proposed changes to the minimum wage and the removal of overtime charges and taxes. By February 2019, the numbers of *gilets jaunes* had declined but protests were still widespread.

Urbanisation

As the population of Paris grew, the city spread into the surrounding towns and beyond. In the 1960s, the building of the **five new towns** was designed to contain this **sprawl**. The new towns of St Quentin-en-Yvelines, Evry, Senart, Marne-la-Valée and Cergy-Pontoise are **self-contained** with residential housing, employment, services and recreational elements for their inhabitants (**Fig. 20.21**).

Between 1960 and 1980, huge **high-rise apartment blocks** called *grands ensembles* were constructed in suburban areas to house the increasing population. Eventually, those who could afford to move out of these blocks did so, leaving behind lower-income tenants. This marked the beginning of the economic and social decline of the *grands ensembles*, and today, many of them are synonymous with poorer immigrant families.

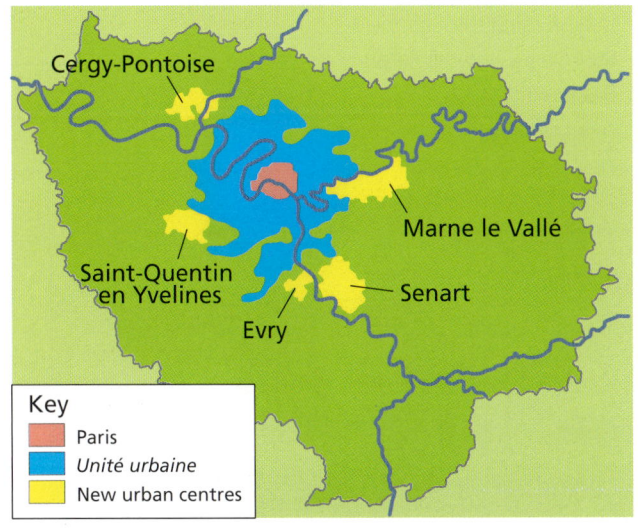

Fig. 20.21 The five new towns constructed in the 1960s.

In 2016, the **Métropole du Grand Paris** came into effect. It is hoped that this will begin to put in place strategies that result in **greater integration** within the region.

CHECK YOUR LEARNING

1. List three facts about population distribution in the Paris Basin region.
2. Identify three ways population in the Paris Basin region has changed over time.
3. List two changes that birth rates have experienced.
4. List three ways migration has impacted on population growth in the Paris region.
5. Describe three issues that have arisen as a result of migration in the region.

CASE STUDY: THE GROWTH OF THE CITY OF PARIS

Paris is the **primate city** of France, and the Paris region is currently home to more than 37% of the total French population.

Location

Paris developed at a **bridging point on the River Seine**. The city lies at the heart of a large, synclinal basin with gently rolling slopes. This **gentle relief** facilitated the construction of a well-developed **transport network** and Paris developed as a **nodal site** and a focus of major transport modes within France.

The **River Seine** links Paris with the coastal port of Le Havre, and contributed to the city's growth as a **centre of manufacturing and employment**. Bulk cargoes were shipped by barge to manufacturing plants that grew up along the banks of the river (e.g. **Renault**). These plants then used the **Seine** to export manufactured goods.

KEYWORDS

primate
nodal site
transport
relief
urban sprawl
monarchy
suburbs
deindustrialisation
radicalisation

331

Landscapes

> The European Industrial Core is a geographical concentration of manufacturing industries, extending from Rotterdam in the Netherlands to Milan, Italy, passing through the Ruhr Valley and the Paris Basin region.

Paris's central location and transport links to the industrial core of Europe has allowed manufacturing industry to access the large markets there.

The **lowland relief** allowed the city to expand and grow without any physical constraints and facilitated the development of a number of airports, which have contributed to the economic growth of the city. However, this has also contributed to **urban sprawl**.

History

The Palace of Versailles, built in the 17th century, was the centre of power of the French **monarchy** and led to the evolution of Paris as a capital city.

In 1854, at the direction of Napoleon III, **Baron Haussmann** created a grand architectural and structural plan for Paris. This involved the creation of **wide boulevards** of similar size and design (e.g. **Champs Élysées**; Fig. 20.22) to give the city a distinctive style. While successful in this respect, the Haussmann plan also led to the demolition of hundreds of buildings and displacement of 300,000 people.

The city limits were extended to accommodate the displaced, and parks and recreation areas were later developed, leading to the creation of the Bois de Boulogne and the Bois de Vincennes.

↑ **Fig. 20.22** The Champs Elysees.

Socio-economic factors

Migration

After World War II, **economic growth stimulated immigration**, leading to **population increase**. To cater for this, huge apartment blocks, *grands ensembles*, were constructed in the **suburbs** (*banlieues*; Fig. 20.23). Migration within the Paris Basin region has also affected the growth of the city of Paris. The increased cost of housing in the more fashionable city areas forced people who couldn't afford it to move into the **suburbs** where costs were lower, and **urban sprawl** now became a feature of Paris's growth.

↑ **Fig. 20.23** The 'Grand Assemble' apartment block in the banlieues.

Deindustrialisation

Deindustrialisation in the 1970s had a negative impact on areas of the city, resulting in abandoned brownfield sites and out-migration to the suburbs. Lower-income families who could not afford to move were left behind in these now run-down areas.

Redevelopment

The redevelopment of declining areas became an important element in the growth of the city. Initiated in the late 1950s, the **La Defense** project oversaw the development of a major business centre providing office accommodation, open space and the signature **Grande Arche** (Fig. 20.24). Today, it is the location of the headquarters of a variety of **financial and commercial companies**, including **BNP Paribas**.

↑ **Fig. 20.24** La Defense.

Around La Defense, low and middle-income residential areas benefit little from the employment opportunities offered; the 150,000 people employed here commute to and from the suburbs. The area shuts down after five in the evening and at the weekends.

Economic activity

Paris is an important economic and financial centre, and the growth of economic activities in the city have led to **population growth**. Among the factors contributing to this economic growth are the supply of raw materials from the farms of the Paris Basin, the well-developed transport infrastructure and the role of Paris as the seat of national government in France. As the executive centre of the country, Paris's civil service provides thousands of well-paid jobs and creates demand for accommodation, contributing to residential growth.

Political factors

National and local government have unsurprisingly played a key role in the development of Paris. The government *Schéma Directeur* ('Blueprint') plan for Paris, introduced in the 1960s, dealt with issues including urban decay, the deterioration of the city's historic buildings, regeneration of poorer suburbs and urban sprawl.

The regeneration of apartment blocks in the city led to **gentrification**, which increased property prices and forced people who could no longer afford to live there to move to the suburbs where prices were lower.

Five new urban centres were constructed to provide housing, as well as employment, open space and facilities for the new residents thereby reducing the necessity for travel into Paris, so helping to tackle traffic congestion.

The city limits of Paris have more or less remained the same since the mid-1800s. However, the creation of the **Grand Metropole Du Paris** in 2016 provided a new administrative structure with responsibility for co-ordinating housing, planning and transport policy in the city and the inner and outer suburbs.

Paris has some of the most affluent and some of the most deprived areas in France. The problems associated with disadvantage can be seen in the poorer suburbs with their **overcrowding, poor housing** and **lack of economic opportunities**. These have contributed to increasing **radicalisation** and tensions. The attacks of 2015 make it imperative that the problems of disadvantage and lack of opportunity are addressed.

CHECK YOUR LEARNING

1. Describe two ways physical factors have influenced the growth of Paris.
2. List tree ways socio-economic factors have impacted on the growth of Paris.
3. Outline three impacts migration has had on the growth of Paris.
4. List two ways government policy has affected the city's growth. Explain each one.

EXAM LINK (HL)

Urban Development (30 marks)

Examine how two of the following factors have influenced the development of any urban area that you have studied.

- Transport
- Location
- Primary economic activity

2016, Q6C

Marking Scheme:
Named urban area = 2 marks
Factor 1 examination = 7 SRPs × 2 marks
Factor 2 examination = 7 SRPs × 2 marks

EXAM LINK (OL)

Urban Growth in a European Region (30 marks)

Discuss the reasons for the growth of an urban area in a European region (not in Ireland) that you have studied.

2018, Q4C

Marking Scheme:
Discussion = 10 SRPs × 3 marks
Credit a named urban area for 1 SRP

Landscapes

EXAMINATION QUESTIONS
ORDINARY LEVEL

Long Question

1. Economic Activity in a European Region

Name a European region (not in Ireland) that you have studied and explain any two of the following.

- The importance of transport to this region
- The reasons why tourists are attracted to this region
- The type of farming practised in this region
- The reasons for the development of industry in this region.

Marking Scheme:
Naming the region = 1 mark
Activity 1 explained = 7 SRPs × 3 marks
Activity 2 explained = 6 SRPs × 3 marks

2014, Part Two, Section 1, Q4B (40 marks)

HIGHER LEVEL

Long Questions

2. European Regions

Examine the importance of relief to the economic development of any two contrasting European regions (not in Ireland) that you have studied.

Marking Scheme:
Examination of region 1 = 8 SRPs × 2 marks
Examination of region 2 = 7 SRPs × 2 marks

2014, Part Two, Section 1, Q5B (30 marks)

3. Economic Activities

Examine how any two of the factors listed below have influenced the development of one urban area in a European region (not in Ireland) that you have studied.

Transport   Location   Primary economic activity

Marking Scheme:
Urban area named = 2 marks
Examination of factor 1 = 7 SRPs × 2 marks
Examination of factor 2 = 7 SRPs × 2 marks

2012, Part Two, Section 1, Q5C (30 marks)

Revision Summary

Physical Processes

Climate
- West, NW: cool temperate oceanic climate; av. 19°C Summer, 5°C Winter; precipitation 710 mm
- East: cool temperate continental climate; av. 24°C Summer, 2°C Winter; precipitation 620mm
- Transitional climate in zones where oceanic and continental climates meet

Relief
- Paris Basin part of North European Plain – syncline of strata of sedimentary rocks
- Île-de-France – example of exposed sedimentary layers – escarpments

Drainage
- Rivers: Seine – flows into the sea at Le Havre; Marne and Somme: flow into English Channel
- Gently sloping relief – rivers drain away excess water, prevents flooding
- Underlying permeable sedimentary rocks prevent waterlogging

Soils
- Limon soils in Île-de-France
- Outwash sands and gravels in South (Sologne)
- Alluvial clays at banks of Seine, Marne and Somme; boulder clays in Brie
- Well-drained topsoil over underlying chalk (Champagne)

Primary Economic Activities: Energy
- Little fossil fuel
- Reliance on nuclear power
- Geothermal energy production in Île-de-France

Primary Economic Activities: Agriculture

Physical factor: Climate
- Cool temperate oceanic climate in west ideal for grass-growing and pastoral farming
- Cool temperate continental climate in east ideal for arable crops

Physical factor: relief
- Gently sloping lowlands of Paris Basin (North European Plain) and large flat fields – ideal for agricultural machinery – high productivity and profits
- Good drainage from escarpments and permeable bedrock – productive land, large outputs of arable crops
- Well-drained southerly slopes of Champagne – ideal for viticulture

Physical factor: soils
- Calcium-rich: Normandy – pastoral farming, bloodstock rearing
- Limon: Île-de-France – wheat, barley, maize and sugarbeet
- Boulder clay: Brie – grass-growing, pastoral farming
- Chalk: Champagne – viticulture
- Outwash sands and gravel: south and Fontainebleau – infertile, best for forestry

Socio-economic factor: farms and farmers
- Paris Basin – largest farms in EU region, highly productive and profitable, specialised commercial cereal farming of wheat
- Farmers: young and well-educated, use progressive methods and modern machinery, adapt to market tastes; income 40% higher than national average

Socio-economic factor: markets
- Paris Basin – largest market in France (24 mn people) – growth in horticulture
- Paris – tourism drives big demand for regional food; large food and drink industry
- Paris Basin close to economic core of Europe – market of 170 mn people
- Well-developed road and rail transport network – fast shipment, low transport costs, long shelf-life of produce
- Le Havre port – export to global markets

Political factor: EU support
- Common Agricultural Policy grants for farm improvements – investment in machinery – higher outputs and profits
- EU membership – access to Single European Market

Secondary Economic Activities

Physical factors
- Rich supply of locally-produced raw materials – textiles (wool); iron and steel manufacturing; food processing; wine and champagne; bakery and confectionery (flour); brewing (barley); cheese production, yoghurt drinks (milk); cider (apples); edible oils and bio-diesel (rapeseed)
- Lower cost industry locations in Asia have threatened some local industries

Socio-economic factor: labour force
- Paris Basin – mix of highly skilled labour force and pool of lower-skilled workers attracts industry; good transport system – workers can travel efficiently

Socio-economic factor: transport
- Excellent transport network – raw materials and produce transported quickly and cheaply
- Rail links to French and European markets extend market area
- River Seine links Paris Basin to Le Havre – cheap transport for bulky materials

Socio-economic factor: markets
- Paris – fashion capital, textile industry
- Cosmetics and personal care companies – multiplier effect
- Agribusiness (fertiliser manufacturing)
- Defence and aircraft industry
- Newspaper and book publishing hub
- Skilled labour force

Government policy
- Incentives to support industrial development (technopoles)
- Development of five new towns in Paris suburbs in 1960s (Cergy-Pointoise) attracted high-skilled industries

Challenge facing the manufacturing industry
- High payroll tax
- Highest corporation tax in the EU – hard to attract foreign investment

Tertiary Economic Activities: Tourism

- Year-round activity worth approx. €21 bn to local economy. World's top tourist destination.

Accessibility
- Central location – excellent road network – TGV – Eurostar and Eurotunnel – large ports – global air transportation hub – internal transport network (Metro, RER, trains, buses and trams)

Attractions
- Historical sites and architecture, e.g. Notre Dame Cathedral, Eiffel Tower
- Cultural attractions, e.g. the Louvre
- Recreation, e.g. Disneyland Paris
- Shopping, e.g. Champs Elysees
- Sporting fixtures, e.g. Tour de France

Challenge for tourism
- Terror attacks

Tertiary Economic Activities: Transport

Physical factors
- Lowland relief ideal for development of canals and rail network
- Gentle gradients good for roads and motorways
- Ease of navigability of River Seine – development of port functions

Socio-economic factors
- Large population distributed over wide area requires efficient public transport system: Paris Metro – RER – TGV – bus lanes – Velib bicycle scheme and cycle routes – road network and orbital roads to control traffic congestion

Political factors
- Government play vital role in transport provision, maintenance and planning – Syndicate of Île-de-France
- ERDF also provides funding

Planning for the future
- Grand Paris Transport Plan: modernisation of transport network; provision of 200 km new railway and 70 new stations; 24-hr automated Metro to link 7 economic zones

Human Processes

- Paris – most densely populated city in Europe
- Birth rate declining since 2011; higher birth rates among migrants help offset decline
- Paris is a primate city – Paris, suburbs and Île-de-France = 37% total population
- Changes over time: Population growth = natural increase and migration. Pattern of population decline in city 1954-1999, mainly due to migration to suburbs

- Impact of migration and Gilets jaunes movement
- Urbanisation: spread of city in 1960s – building of five new towns and high-rise apartment blocks (grands ensembles) in suburbs – now house poorer immigrant families – Metropole du Grand Paris aims for integration in the region

21 A PERIPHERAL EUROPEAN REGION – THE MEZZOGIORNO

LEARNING INTENTIONS

Syllabus Link: 2.2

By the end of this chapter I will be able to:
- draw an outline map of Italy showing the Mezzogiorno, and show and name different types of features;
- explain how physical processes have shaped the landscape of this region;
- compare the impact of physical processes on this region with a core European region;
- describe the factors that have influenced the development of primary, secondary and tertiary activities in the region;
- describe and explain the human processes that have influenced the population of the region;
- compare the factors that have influenced the development of economic activities in this region with those in a core European region.

Incorporating the provinces of **Abruzzo, Basilicata, Calabria, Campania, Molise, Puglia** and the islands of **Sicily** and **Sardinia**, the Mezzogiorno comprises almost 40% of the land area of Italy and contains one-third of the total Italian population of 60.8 million (**Figs 21.1–21.3**). It is an example of a **peripheral** region.

↑ **Fig. 21.1** The Paris Basin and the Mezzogiorno.

337

Landscapes

↑ Fig. 21.2 A political map of the Mezzogiorno.

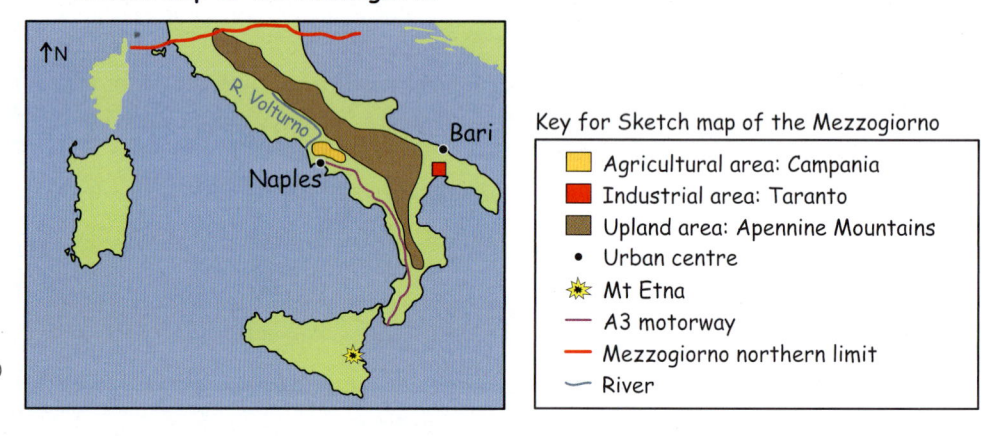

→ Fig. 21.3 Sketch map of the Mezzogiorno.

KEYWORDS

Mediterranean climate
relief
drainage
soils

Physical Processes

Climate

The Mezzogiorno has a **Mediterranean climate**, with hot summers with an average temperature of 29°C, and warm winters averaging 14°C. Annual precipitation is between 600 and 1,000 mm, with minimal amounts during the summer. Convectional rainfall is most common in the summer months.

The factors influencing this climate include the following:

- the region lies at a **latitude** approximately 40°N of the equator, so the summer sun is high, resulting in high temperatures;
- in summer, the dry north-east trade winds dominate;
- the hot **Sirocco** winds that blow in from the Sahara Desert bring extreme temperatures (40°C) and severe drought conditions;
- in winter, the south-westerly winds prevail, carrying Atlantic depressions, which bring precipitation.

	Jan	Feb	Mar	Apr	May	Jun	Jul	Aug	Sep	Oct	Nov	Dec
Mean temperature (°C)	8.6	9.2	10.9	13.3	17.2	21.0	23.3	23.6	21.0	17.0	13.0	9.9
Mean precipitation (mm)	100	84	76	68	44	29	21	37	71	112	141	111

↑ Table 21.1 Average monthly temperature and precipitation, Naples (Climate-Data.Org).

21 A Peripheral European Region – The Mezzogiorno

Relief

The **Apennine Mountains**, which are predominantly composed of sedimentary limestone, sandstone and shale, cover 85% of the land (Fig. 21.4). They were formed during the **Alpine folding** movement when the African and Eurasian plates converged.

Seismic activity is common along the entire length of the Apennines, making the region prone to earthquakes (e.g. **Umbria**, magnitude 5.5, October 2016). Volcanic mineral springs (*terme*) can also be found at several locations (e.g. **Terme di Agnano, Campania**).

Coastal lowland areas are found along the east coast in **Puglia** and **Metaponto** in Basilicata, and on the west coast in **Campania**. In the past, coastal dunes prevented streams from reaching the sea. This led to the formation of **marshes**, which were breeding grounds for **malaria**-carrying mosquitos.

SKILLS ACTIVITY

Draw an outline map of the Mezzogiorno region showing:
- two named urban centres;
- a named feature of relief (upland or lowland);
- a numbered road;
- another communication link;
- two features of drainage.

Drainage

The presence of **permeable** limestone limits the number of surface rivers draining the region. The two main rivers are the **Volturno** and the **Agri**. Water volumes are very low in summer, while heavy winter rains can cause flooding.

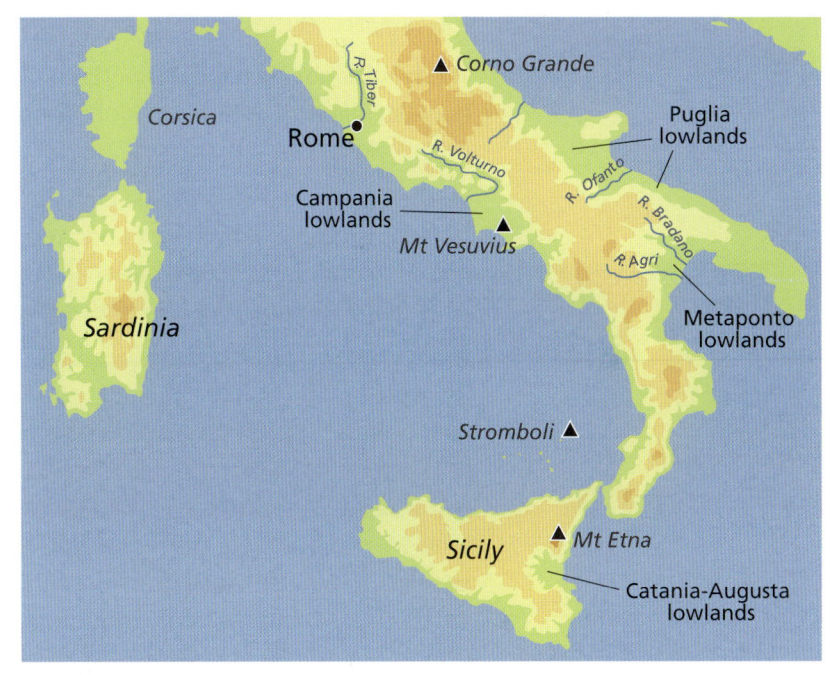

Soils

- **Terra rossa**: Formed when limestone is **weathered**, these well-drained, red clay soils occur widely throughout the region.
- **Volcanic soils**: These occur at the base of Mount Vesuvius in Campania, and Mount Etna in Sicily (Fig. 21.5).
- **Alluvial soils**: These are formed by the rivers depositing eroded material from the upland slopes. They are found on the floodplains of the Volturno and Agri rivers and on the coastal lowlands of Campania, Foggia, and Catania and Augusta in Sicily.

↑ **Fig. 21.4** Relief map of the Mezzogiorno.

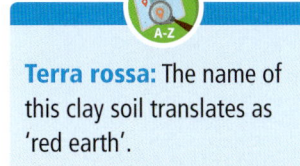

→ **Fig. 21.5** Past eruptions of Mount Vesuvius have provided parts of the Mezzogiorno with fertile volcanic soils.

Terra rossa: The name of this clay soil translates as 'red earth'.

Chapter 1 Plate Tectonics
Chapter 2 Volcanic Activity
Chapter 3 Earthquake Activity

CHECK YOUR LEARNING

1. Explain the factors that contribute to a Mediterranean climate.
2. Outline the main characteristics of a Mediterranean climate.
3. List three soil types found in the Mezzogiorno region.

Landscapes

KEYWORDS
agriculture
soil erosion
mechanisation
subsistence
irrigation
Cassa per il Mezzogiorno
Common Agricultural Policy (CAP)
forestry
fishing
aquaculture
insolation
energy

Primary Economic Activities

Compared to economically developed regions, the economies of peripheral regions have a greater dependency on primary activities.

Agriculture

A combination of factors has resulted in the agricultural sector being poorly developed in peninsular Italy.

Physical factors

Climate

The summer drought, which is a characteristic of the Mezzogiorno's **Mediterranean climate**, has had a major impact on the pattern of agriculture that has evolved in this region.

The **traditional agricultural pattern** of planting winter wheat so that it can be harvested in May (before the onset of high summer temperatures) is still practised on upland farms.

Farmers in the region produce crops that are suited to the dry summers. The **olive** tree, for example, has a thick bark and waxy leaves that allows it to survive the drought conditions. **Vines**, grown in the region since the Ancient Roman Empire, have long tap roots that can reach deep water sources. **Citrus fruit** trees (lemons, limes and oranges) are also well adapted to the dry summer conditions.

Irrigation systems have been developed in coastal lowland areas such as the Metaponto. This, combined with long hours of sunshine, has contributed to the development of horticulture in the region, so farms can now produce vegetables and soft fruits at a commercial level (Fig. 21.6). Supplies of irrigation water in Campania provide mud baths for the **water buffalo** whose milk is used to produce Mozzarella cheese. However, limited grass growth due to the summer drought means that pastoral farming is limited to **goat and sheep rearing** on the upland slopes.

→ **Fig. 21.6** Commercial farming in the Metaponto.

Heavy convectional rain in summer can lead to flash flooding, landslides and **soil erosion**, resulting in the loss of crops.

Climate change, including higher average summer temperatures, is likely to have an impact on evaporation rates, reducing water supplies for irrigation, thus causing problems for production.

Relief

Over 85% of the land area of the Mezzogiorno is classed as upland. This severely limits the agricultural potential of the region.

The steep upland slopes have limited the **mechanisation** of agriculture that has occurred elsewhere in Italy. This means there is little commercial farming and low outputs.

Heavy winter rains and convectional showers in summer lead to rapid run-off from the steep slopes. This causes **soil erosion**, reducing the agricultural potential of the land and damaging existing crops.

The steep relief means that transport infrastructure in the Mezzogiorno region is quite poorly developed. Difficulty and delays in getting produce to local markets means that many farmers are self-sufficient, and **subsistence farming** is widespread in the upland areas.

The lower hillsides, however, being more accessible and less steep than the higher slopes, have been **terraced** and produce winter wheat, citrus fruits, olives, vines and vegetables (Fig. 21.7).

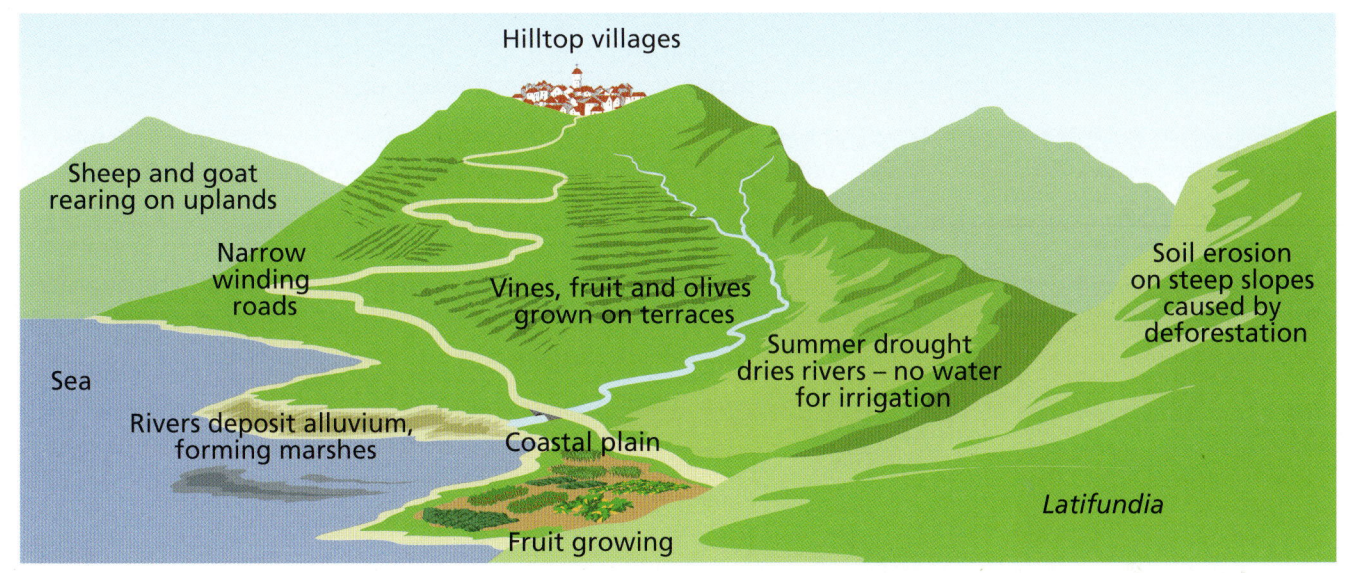

Subsistence farming: Farming where no surplus is produced.

Fig. 21.7 The traditional pattern of agriculture in the Mezzogiorno.

The limestone underlying the Mezzogiorno is **permeable**, which means that water percolates quickly into the lower soil layers. Water, therefore, is only accessible to plants with long tap roots.

In the past, soil that washed onto lowland areas caused river mouths to silt up, creating **malarial marshes**. These coastal marshes have now been drained and irrigated, and today they are used for commercial agriculture (e.g. **Campania**). Production is concentrated on soft fruits and citrus fruits.

In the irrigated coastal lowlands, salad vegetables and soft fruits are produced for export and for the local tourist market (e.g. **Metaponto, Basilicata**).

Soils

The rich volcanic soils of the **Campania** area around Naples are used in the production of fruit (e.g. **apricots, figs, citrus fruits**). The San Marzano tomato, regarded as the best variety of tomato, originates in this region. Campania is also a wine-producing region, with vines grown in volcanic soils on the slopes of Mount Vesuvius (Fig. 21.8).

Fig. 21.8 Vine cultivation on the lower slopes of Mount Vesuvius.

Landscapes

The *terra rossa* soils in **Abruzzo** and **Puglia** have good drainage, making them suitable for vine cultivation, too.

Irrigation on the fertile alluvial soils of the coastal lowlands has made them important horticultural areas.

In the past, **deforestation** of the uplands and **overgrazing** by sheep both led to extensive **soil erosion**, which today severely limits their agricultural potential.

Socio-economic factors

Land ownership

Up until the 1950s, over 75% of agricultural land was owned by absentee landlords who had little interest in the land. They divided their large estates (*latifundia*) into 3–5 hectare plots (*minifundia*), which were rented to peasant farmers (*braccianti*). Farming in the region was subsistent in nature, as the *braccianti* had to hand over almost 60% of their produce to the landlords as rent. With little – if any – surplus income, and with no guarantee that they would get to keep the land from one year to the next, *braccianti* made very few improvements to their holdings. A pattern of extensive traditional farming evolved, based on rearing sheep and goats and producing wheat, olives and grapes (**Fig. 21.9**). Traditional labour-intensive farming methods were maintained, leading to very low outputs.

Absentee landlord: A person not living near or farming the land they own.

Extensive farming: The cultivation of crops or the rearing of animals (sheep/goats) using small amounts of inputs including capital, labour and fertilisers.

The *braccianti's* limited incomes led to an out-migration of younger farmers who saw little future in agriculture. Older farmers remained, but they were unable to expand their operations and less likely to embrace new farming practices.

Markets

Before the 1950s, commercial farming was not at all viable in upland areas of the Mezzogiorno, as the low population density meant a limited local market existed for agricultural produce. Low average incomes and high rates of unemployment also resulted in a limited demand for local produce, so **subsistence farming** was the norm.

Fig. 21.9 Sheep and goats grazing in the Abruzzo province.

The poorly developed local road network inhibited agricultural development, as upland farmers were isolated from lowland market centres of population. Perishable products were slower getting to the market, resulting in a shorter shelf-life, which reduced the value of the product. This meant that the rich markets of the north of Italy and the rest of Europe were effectively inaccessible to the upland farmers.

In the lowland areas, higher population densities provided a market for the horticultural produce of the region. Farmers with land around urban centres such as **Naples** and **Palermo** profited from being able to supply them.

A number of economic developments led to increased demand for agricultural produce; the growth of tourism to the region has increased the demand from local **hotels and restaurants**. The **food processing** industry has grown due to improved access to national and European markets. The production of canned and peeled **tomatoes** has stimulated tomato production throughout the region (e.g. **Foggia**, **Puglia**) even though most of the canning plants are located in Campania. Improved **wine** quality and the growing reputation of wines from Campania, Puglia and Sicily has led to increased demand and stimulated production.

The Cassa per il Mezzogiorno

The **Cassa per il Mezzogiorno** was an integrated plan set up by the government of Italy in the 1950s to develop the economy of the region.

Agricultural improvements

Infrastructure: The new **Autostrada del Sol** motorway linking Milan with Naples, along with improvements to the rail infrastructure, allowed produce from the region to access the rich urban markets of the north of Italy and Europe.

Land reform: The *latifundia* were bought by the government and divided among former *bracciani*, who used long-term, low-interest loans to buy their plots.

Irrigation: To cope with the summer drought, new aqueducts and wells were built to supply water for irrigation. Farmers could now take advantage of the warm climate and produce vegetables, fruits and flowers to sell in the affluent markets to the north.

Co-operatives: Co-operatives were set up to supply seeds and fertilisers, and organise the harvesting, processing and marketing of the region's produce.

Land reclamation: Hillsides were re-afforested to help reduce soil erosion. Coastal marshes were also drained for agricultural production (e.g. **Metaponto, Basilicata**).

> The Comunità Montana is a public body, set up in 1971, to support farming in the more remote mountainous areas of the south. It provides grants to construct farm buildings, install small irrigation schemes and plant trees to reduce soil erosion.

Evaluation

- The agricultural improvements led to increases in agricultural output and farmers' incomes. Farm sizes, however, are too small to provide a commercial return for farmers and many remain at subsistence level.
- Seasonal overproduction has resulted in prices collapsing for certain produce (e.g. **tomatoes**).
- The mechanisation of farming led to job losses and increased unemployment.
- Costly maintenance of the irrigation systems increased production costs and reduced profits (**Fig. 21.10**).
- The coastal lowland areas benefitted more than the upland areas, increasing the income gap between them.

Fig. 21.10 Irrigation systems proved useful but costly for farmers in the Mezzogiorno.

EU

When the Cassa ended in 1984, the EU continued to support agricultural development in the region. The **Common Agricultural Policy** provides farmers with direct payments that are of vital importance to their incomes. The **LEADER Programme** supports agri-projects such as artisan food production (e.g. **Carmasciano cheese, Campania**). The programme also supports projects that help to improve the quality of life in rural areas (e.g. the extension of **broadband in Basilicata**).

Challenges facing agriculture

Despite the changes brought about by the Cassa and EU policies, young farmers are still abandoning the Mezzogiorno's farms, as their holdings are too small and unproductive to make a living. Average farm incomes in the region are still 50% lower than the EU average.

Forestry

During the 19th century, most of the region's natural vegetation (Mediterranean cork, oak and pine) was removed for firewood and to clear the land for agriculture. The inaccessibility of the high upland regions of Basilicata, Calabria and Sicily, however, meant they retained their original cover.

Reforestation of parts of the uplands was undertaken by the Cassa to help prevent **soil erosion**.

Fishing

Favourable factors for fishing include good year-round weather and the availability of naturally sheltered harbours.

Sardines, anchovies and tuna are the main catches supplying local and tourist markets. However, in recent years, the industry has experienced decline due to overfishing.

Aquaculture

Sea bass and European eels are farmed along the coast of Puglia (**Fig. 21.11**), while mussel farming takes place in many locations along the Mezzogiorno's coastline (e.g. **Palermo, Sicily**).

→ **Fig. 21.11** Fish farming along the coast of Puglia.

Energy

Italy is the seventh-largest producer of wind energy in the world: the **Messina-Agrigento** wind farm in Sicily has 124 turbines.

High levels of **insolation** make the region ideal for solar energy production, and the use of domestic solar panels is widespread (**Fig. 21.12**). While most of the potential exists in the south, the main markets are in the north, which increases transmission costs.

Volcanically active zones within the region have the potential for the development of geothermal energy production, but it has yet to be developed.

Insolation: The amount of solar radiation that reaches the earth's surface.

21 A Peripheral European Region – The Mezzogiorno

← **Fig. 21.12** Solar panels in Sicily, Italy.

EXAM LINK (OL)

European Region (40 marks)

With reference to a European region:

(i) Name one primary economic activity that contributes to the economy of this region.

(ii) Explain the advantages that this region has for the development of the primary economic activity named in part (i) above.

(iii) Describe one challenge faced by this primary economic activity in this region.

2016, Q6C

Marking Scheme:
(i) Activity named = 4 marks
(ii) Explanation = 9 SRPs × 3 marks each
(iii) Description = 3 SRPs × 3 marks each

EXAM LINK (HL)

Agriculture in Europe (30 marks)

Account for the development of agriculture in a European region (not in Ireland) with reference to any two of the factors listed.

Relief   Markets   Climate

2014, Q6C

Marking Scheme:
Discussion of factor 1 = 8 SRPs × 2 marks
Discussion of factor 2 = 7 SRPs × 2 marks

CHECK YOUR LEARNING

1. Name three ways climate has influenced the development of agriculture in the Mezzogiorno.
2. List three ways relief has influenced agricultural development in the Mezzogiorno.
3. Name three socio-economic factors that have impacted on the development of agriculture in this region.
4. Describe three positive impacts the Cassa has had on agriculture.
5. Describe three negative impacts the Cassa has had on agriculture.

345

Landscapes

KEYWORDS
raw materials
transition
entrepreneur
disposable income
consumer-based industries
Cassa per il Mezzogiorno
European Regional Development Fund (ERDF)
European Social Fund (ESF)
manufacturing

Secondary Economic Activities

Manufacturing

Manufacturing in the Mezzogiorno has been slow to develop, especially compared to its neighbouring regions. This lack of development is due to the interaction of a number of different factors.

Physical factors

Raw materials

The Mezzogiorno was left behind when other regions' economies **transitioned** from agriculture to industry in the mid-19th century. Local supplies of coal and iron ore were very small, limiting the production of steel that was needed to build machines, railways and other industrial infrastructure.

Industrial development was further hindered in the 20th century, as the region didn't have the necessary supply of **raw materials** to produce the vast amounts of energy required for manufacturing. Supplies of oil found in Sicily and gas found in Basilicata, Sicily and Puglia were small and unable to support large-scale energy production. While hydro-electric power (HEP) was rapidly developing in the north of Italy, opportunities to develop it in the Mezzogiorno were hindered by low levels of rainfall, high evaporation rates and the permeable nature of the underlying limestone.

Industrial development based on **food processing** occurred in the coastal lowlands where agriculture was most developed or close to ports to facilitate the importation of the necessary raw materials. Industries that did develop were typically small in scale. Local supplies of olives supported small-scale olive oil production (**Fig. 21.13**). **Tomatoes** grown in **Puglia** and **Campania** were used in the production of tinned tomatoes and tomato paste. Poor-quality wine was produced for local consumption or for sale to France and Germany as a blending wine.

→ **Fig. 21.13** Olive groves in the Mezzogiorno.

Locally quarried limestone provided one of the raw materials for the iron and steel industry (e.g. **Palermo**). Cheap transport of bulky raw materials by sea led to the development of the iron and steel industry at a number of ports including **Taranto**. Importation of crude oil to ports such as **Bari** allowed the development of oil refining and petro-chemical industries.

Socio-economic factors

Labour

A small supply of local skilled labour discouraged many **entrepreneurs** from investing in the Mezzogiorno.

This region has a history of **low levels of educational achievement**, with many students failing to finish their second-level schooling. With very few high-quality third-level institutions available locally, those who wished to further their education and develop skills had to leave the region. Once equipped with their new skills, few of those who left returned.

There has been a **brain drain** from the region, as many skilled people have left the Mezzogiorno for the north of Italy and the USA in search of a better quality of life. Approximately one million people, mostly young and well educated, left the region between 2000 and 2017. The remaining workforce had a limited education, poor skill-sets and a reputation for low levels of productivity, making it more difficult to attract industries.

Naples, the largest urban area in Campania, has the greatest concentration of **manufacturing** (Fig. 21.14). This has led to immigration and the presence of a workforce with a tradition of working in industry.

Markets

Up until the 1950s, poorly developed local markets restricted the growth of manufacturing in the region. Low population density, **high unemployment levels** and **disposable incomes 40% below** the national average left the region unattractive to **consumer-based industries**. Uneven population distribution also led to fragmentation of the local market.

The high distribution costs of manufactured goods to the rich north and EU markets also restricted industrial development in the past. A poor-quality road network with steep, winding courses resulted in longer journey times for container-carrying HGVs (Fig. 21.15). The steep relief contributes to rock falls that can cause road closures, leading to disruption and delays. **Rail transport** is well suited to the transport of bulky raw materials, however, **difficult terrain** in the Mezzogiorno resulted in a low-density rail network with large sections of track having speed restrictions.

Most industrial development occurred in **coastal areas** where the **lowland relief** meant a better transport infrastructure. Coastal ports also offered low-cost access to markets in the Middle East, North Africa and North America. Engineering industries manufacturing iron and steel products, such as pipes for Middle-Eastern and North African oil fields, were established in **Taranto**. The agricultural sector supports industries specialising in fertilisers, irrigation equipment and farm machinery (e.g. **Bari** and **Naples**).

Campania, with its high population density (**Naples**), constitutes the largest consumer market in the region and supports motor car manufacture (e.g. **Alfa Romeo**).

Lack of investment

A lack of **indigenous entrepreneurs** made the Mezzogiorno dependent on outside investment for industrial development. Competing with the north, with its many locational advantages for the manufacturing industry, proved difficult, and resulted in slow and limited industrial growth.

Fig. 21.14 Naples has a high concentration of secondary economic activity.

Fig. 21.15 A winding road in Calabria.

At present, the Mezzogiorno accounts for just over 10% of Italy's annual exports of €400 billion.

Landscapes

Fig. 21.16 The port of Taranto.

The Cassa per il Mezzogiorno: Industry

A number of strategies were employed by the **Cassa per il Mezzogiorno** in the 1950s to improve the industrial sector and to reduce the north–south economic divide.

Transport infrastructure

The **Autostrada del Sol** motorway opened up access between the Mezzogiorno and the rich markets of the north of Italy and Europe. Better access meant lower transport costs, which made the region more attractive to outside investment.

Improvements to facilities at ports such as **Bari** and **Taranto** allowed more efficient import of raw materials and export of finished goods, increasing their attractiveness as industrial locations (**Fig. 21.16**).

Growth poles

A number of centres were designated as growth poles. '**Engine firms**', such as iron and steel production and oil refinery, were located here. The presence of these industries would stimulate development by attracting related industries such as **engineering** and **the manufacture of chemicals**.

The industrial triangle of **Bari**, **Brindisi** and **Taranto** consists of three growth poles. **Catania**, **Augusta** and **Syracuse** form another triangle on the island of Sicily (**Fig. 21.17**).

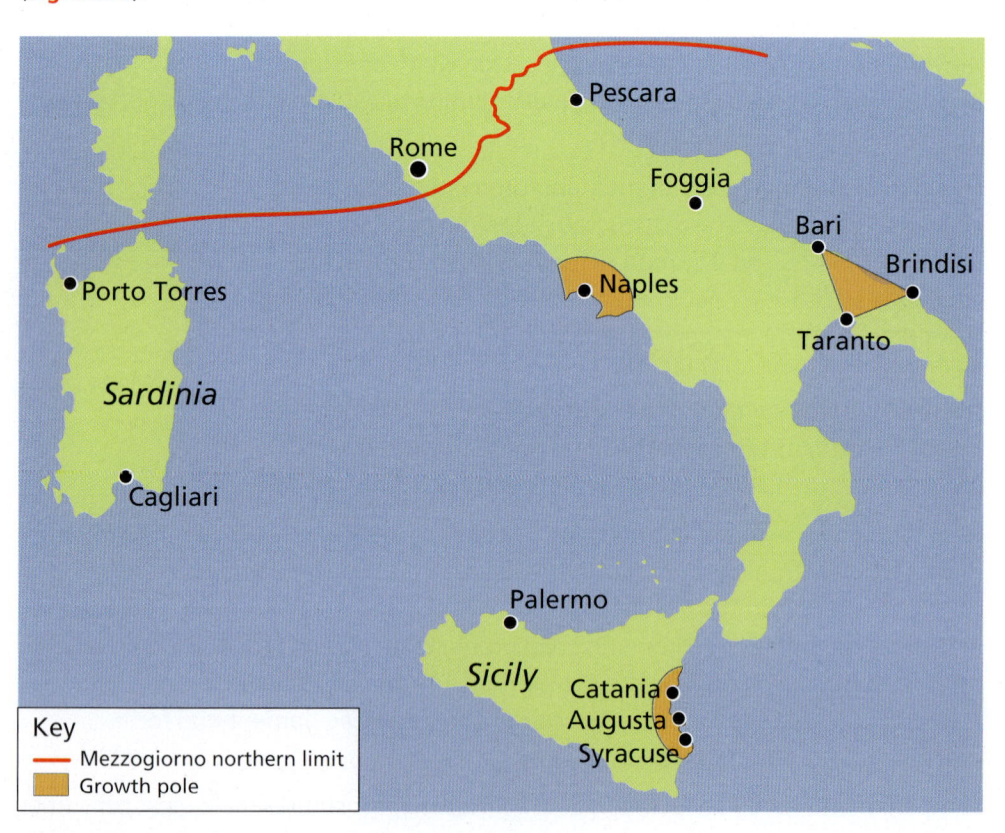

Fig. 21.17 Industrial growth centres.

Investment

The Cassa directed state-controlled industries to locate 40% (later increased to 80%) of new investment in the south.

Other incentives included tax breaks, capital grants and advance factories on industrial estates.

Former agricultural workers were provided with training and further education to increase the skilled labour pool.

Evaluation

Many of the industries, such as oil refining and steel manufacturing, were **capital intensive**, highly automated and did not provide large numbers of jobs. These industries are referred to as '**cathedrals in the desert**' (Fig. 21.18).

Starting in 1992, in response to a government financial crisis, many state companies were **privatised**, making the 80% investment rule unenforceable. The industrial centres, offering higher wages, competed with local industries for skilled labour. As a result, the smaller local industries were forced to close.

As most of the profits made in the Mezzogiorno were **repatriated** back to the north of Italy, this meant the loss of money that could have been re-invested in the region.

Cathedral in the desert: A waste of money; a building with no surrounding infrastructure.

European Union

Having a **GDP** 25% lower than the European average qualifies the Mezzogiorno region for monetary support from the **European Regional Development Fund (ERDF)** and the **European Social Fund (ESF)**. Between 2014 and 2020, the provinces of Campania, Puglia, Basilicata, Calabria and Sicily have been allocated over **€22 billion** to support projects designed to reduce regional disparities.

↑ **Fig. 21.18** Oil refinery, Gela, Sicily, a 'cathedral in the desert'.

European Regional Development Fund: An EU fund that supports developments to correct social and economic imbalance between regions.

Manufacturing industry today

Unemployment levels in the Mezzogiorno are almost twice as high as the national average. The south attracted only 10% of all foreign direct investment (FDI) into Italy between 2009 and 2017. A long history of corruption in the region is a major deterrent for outside investors.

EU funding and foreign investment, however, has made **Puglia** a leader in **solar energy** product manufacture.

EXAM LINK (OL)

European Region (40 marks)

Describe the development of manufacturing industry in a European region (not in Ireland) which you have studied. Clearly state the name of the region in your answer.

2010, Q5B

Marking Scheme:
Named region = 4 marks
Examination = 12 SRPs × 3 marks

EXAM LINK (HL)

Manufacturing in a European Region (30 marks)

Account for the development of manufacturing in a European region (not in Ireland) that you have studied.

2015, Q5B

Marking Scheme:
Examination = 15 SRPs × 2 marks

CHECK YOUR LEARNING

1. Name three physical factors that have impacted on industrial development in the Mezzogiorno.
2. Name three socio-economic factors that have impacted on industrial growth in the region.
3. List three ways the Cassa impacted the industrial sector in the Mezzogiorno.
4. On an outline map, show and name three industrial areas in this region.
5. Name three successes the Cassa had in promoting secondary activities in the Mezzogiorno.

Landscapes

Tertiary Economic Activities

Tourism

Tourism is an important activity in a region lacking economic opportunities. A number of different factors have influenced the development of tourism in the Mezzogiorno.

Physical factors

Climate: The Mediterranean climate with its hot, dry summer attracts visitors from northern Italy and from all over Europe.

Landscape: The varied landscape of rugged mountains and coastal cliffs (e.g. **Amalfi Coast**), and long stretches of sandy beaches on the **Adriatic Coast** are major attractions. The interior uplands provide opportunities for activity-based recreation, e.g. hiking.

Geology: The volcanoes of Mount Vesuvius, Mount Etna and Stromboli are major attractions. Natural **thermal spas** attract health tourists to Abruzzo, Campania and Puglia.

Cultural and historical factors

The Mezzogiorno contains many historical centres and archaeological sites, including:
- Ancient Greek temples at locations such as **Paestum** on the Amalfi Coast (**Fig. 21.19**);
- remnants of the Roman cities of **Herculaneum** and **Pompeii** covered by ash from the eruption of Mount Vesuvius in AD 79 (**Fig. 21.20**).

KEYWORDS
tourism
thermal spas
government
ERDF
direct employment
indirect employment

DID YOU KNOW?
25% of Italy's UNESCO heritage sites are located in the Mezzogiorno.

↑ **Fig. 21.19** Temple of Athena, Paestum.

↑ **Fig. 21.20** Remains of the city of Pompeii.

Government and EU policy

The **Cassa per il Mezzogiorno** identified the important role tourism has to play in the economic growth of the Mezzogiorno. Today, the improved road transport infrastructure has made the region more accessible, and over 70% of the region's visitors now come from central and northern Italy. The Cassa also funded improvements to the **rail network**; Naples was linked with Rome via high-speed train. Transport links within the region were upgraded, enabling visitors to access more remote areas and to spread the economic benefits of tourism.

Improvements to **air transport** included new airport terminals and upgraded facilities at **Bari** and **Catania** in Sicily (**Fig. 21.21**). Today, these and other airports in

21 A Peripheral European Region – The Mezzogiorno

the south are served by low-cost airlines **easyJet** and **Ryanair**. Passenger numbers to all southern airports have increased. Funding was also provided for improvements to **cruise-ship terminals** in Naples, Bari and Messina.

The **ERDF** aided the construction of tourist facilities (e.g. **hotels** and **visitor centres**), while the **ESF** has provided training and upskilling for those working in the tourism sector.

Benefits of tourism

Increased tourist numbers have brought many benefits to the Mezzogiorno, including:

↑ **Fig. 21.21** Catania Airport, Sicily.

- **direct employment** in hotels, restaurants, shops and transport;
- **indirect employment** in other tertiary activities such as banking;
- a bigger market for produce of the region, which has stimulated the **agriculture** sector;
- revenues that have been used to preserve and restore **historic sites** such as Pompeii.

Challenges facing tourism

Many jobs in tourism are **seasonal**, meaning employment is often insecure. Attempts to generate year-round tourism include the development of ski centres on the slopes of Mount Etna.

Many tourism businesses are family-run operations that need to embrace new technologies (e.g. websites with booking facilities) to help them to access markets. Provision of Wi-Fi would help to improve the product they offer.

CHECK YOUR LEARNING

1. Name three reasons why the Mezzogiorno attracts tourists.
2. List two ways the Cassa helped the development of tourism in the region.
3. Name two ways the EU supports the development of tourism in the Mezzogiorno.
4. Describe any three benefits of tourism to the region.
5. Name any two challenges facing tourism development in the region.

Transport

Prior to the 1950s, a number of factors had influenced the development of transport in the Mezzogiorno.

Physical factors

Gentler gradients contributed to the development of good road and rail networks on the coastal lowlands, especially in **Campania**.

Steep gradients, valleys and gorges in the upland regions were major challenges, and tunnel and bridge construction added greatly to costs.

The narrow, winding roads with steep gradients made journey times longer, and were not suited to heavy goods vehicle (HGV) traffic.

KEYWORDS

investment
population density
Autostrada del Sol
Autostrada del Mediterraneo
Trans-European Transport Network (TEN-T)

351

Landslides caused by tectonic activity and heavy convectional rain in summer can cause damage to transport installations; this can take a long time to repair and can disrupt travel patterns.

Socio-economic factor: Population density

Low population densities in the uplands made the provision of public transport services expensive, and government subsidies were needed to support them.

Political factors

This peripheral region had seen a lack of government **investment** in upgrading and modernising the transport networks for many years. However, the implementation of the **Cassa**, and later the policies of the **ERDF**, brought much-needed **investment** to the Mezzogiorno's infrastructure.

Improvements

Government

The **Cassa** allocated over €2.5 billion in improvements to the road network, including the construction of the 700 km-long **Autostrada del Sol** motorway, an arterial road connecting the Mezzogiorno with the northern markets.

The EU

When the Cassa ended in 1984, the **ERDF** continued to support infrastructural improvements. Between 2000 and 2006, over €27 billion of ERDF funding was allocated to projects in the region. Improvements to transport included:

- **Roads:** The **A3 Salerno-Reggio Calabria motorway**, known as the **Autostrada del Mediterraneo**, was completed in December 2016 (Fig. 21.22). Trans-Apennine routes were improved and upgraded, for example, the **A16** had climbing lanes added. Cost issues have prevented construction of the long-proposed bridge project linking Sicily to the mainland via the Strait of Messina.

- **Rail:** The **ERDF** supported rail electrification, enabling higher speeds. High-speed trains now link Rome with Naples and Salerno, while the east coast is linked with the west via the Bari-Foggia–North Naples railway.

- **Ports: Bari** port was upgraded; three separate docks for cruise ships, passenger ferries and freight traffic were constructed (Fig. 21.23). **Taranto** port had its container and freight facilities improved. **Naples** port will see further investment of over €115 million to include dredging and the reorganisation of the road and rail infrastructure.

- **Airports:** Improvements included the construction of new terminals (e.g. **Cagliari**) and the upgrading of the air traffic control systems serving the region.

↑ **Fig. 21.22** Part of the A3 Salerno-Reggio Calabria motorway.

↑ **Fig. 21.23** A cruise ship in the port of Bari.

Future developments

ERDF funding for the region for the period 2014 to 2020 will amount to **€22.2 billion**. The main emphasis of this funding will be modernisation of the rail network, including:

- increasing train frequency, reducing travel times and increasing use of railways for freight transport;
- the **TEN-T Connecting Europe project**, which has 11 designated rail corridors covering the EU, including the **Scandinavian-Mediterranean Transport Corridor** which runs from the Baltic regions through Central Europe to the ports of southern Italy. The TEN-T project is designed to create an **integrated** European transport network for passengers and freight.

EXAM LINK (OL)

Tertiary Economic Activities – European Region (30 marks)
Discuss the development of two tertiary economic activities in a European region.
2018, Q5B

Marking Scheme:
Two activities named = 6 marks
Activity 1 discussed = 4 SRPs × 3 marks
Activity 2 discussed = 4 SRPs × 3 marks
Credit a named region for one SRP

EXAM LINK (HL)

Tertiary Economic Activity – European Region (30 marks)
Account for the development of one tertiary economic activity in a European region (not in Ireland).
2017, Q4B

Marking Scheme:
Examination = 15 SRPs × 2 marks

CHECK YOUR LEARNING

1. Name three factors that have influenced the development of transport in the Mezzogiorno.
2. List four improvements that have been made to the transport infrastructure of the Mezzogiorno.
3. Name one improvement planned for transport in the Mezzogiorno.

Human Processes

Population

In 2016, Italy's population numbered 60.6 million, of which 20.8 million (34%, or one-third) lived in the Mezzogiorno and the islands of Sicily and Sardinia.

Birth rate

In 1970, Italy recorded a national **birth rate** of **16.8 births** per 1,000. By 2017, the rate had reduced to **7.7 births** per 1,000. Higher-than-average rates were recorded in **Sicily** (8.3), **Campania** (8.6) and **Calabria** (8.1). All other regions recorded rates lower than the national average, with **Sardinia** the lowest at **6.3**. These lower birth rates reflected the impact of **migration** and the loss of younger age groups.

KEYWORDS
birth rate
migration
population density
uneven
population distribution
relief
rural depopulation
organised crime
urbanisation

Landscapes

Population density

According to the Italian National Institute of Statistics, the national average population density in 2017 was 201 persons per km². The provinces of **Campania** and **Puglia** were the only ones with densities above the national average (Table 21.2).

	Abruzzo	Basilicata	Calabria	Campania	Molise	Puglia	Sardinia	Sicily
Mean temperature (°C)	123	57	130	428	70	209	69	196

↑ **Table 21.2** Population density by province, 2017 (ISTAT).

SKILLS ACTIVITY
Construct a suitable graph to illustrate the data in **Table 21.2**.

Population distribution

The relief of the Mezzogiorno has contributed to an **uneven population distribution pattern**.

Relief

The lowland province of Campania had a population density of 428 persons per km², while the upland province of Molise (over 90% upland) had a density of 70 per km².

The Apennine Mountains dominate much of the Mezzogiorno, and because of the upland relief, many areas have historically had poor agricultural potential, poor transport infrastructure and poor access, resulting in low population densities.

The highest population densities can be found on the coastal lowlands of the peninsula and the islands of Sicily and Sardinia, where favourable geographical factors (e.g. lowland relief, accessibility) resulted in higher population densities.

Migration

→ **Fig. 21.24** Nova Siri, a hilltop village in Basilicata.

Within the Mezzogiorno, **internal migration** has had a major impact on population distribution. A pattern of movement from interior upland areas such as Abruzzo to coastal lowlands has evolved.

In the past, hilltop village settlements were scattered throughout the uplands (**Fig. 21.24**). These were home to subsistence farmers who farmed the small plots created by the subdivision of large estates (*latifundia*) surrounding the villages. These smaller plots supported a large number of farmers and their families in upland areas.

In the 1950s, changes to the structure of farming as a result of the **Cassa** impacted on the distribution of population. The *latifundia* were nationalised and divided into larger plots. By increasing farm size, the overall number of farms was reduced. This meant farming now supported fewer people. Lack of economic opportunity in upland areas led to out-migration, **resulting in rural depopulation** and abandoned villages. Damage and destruction caused by earthquakes have also resulted in villages being abandoned.

21 A Peripheral European Region – The Mezzogiorno

← **Fig. 21.25** The port of Catania, Sicily.

The draining of coastal malarial swamps under the Cassa meant that these areas were now suitable for agriculture and settlement and attracted migrants from the uplands.

Under the Cassa's industrial strategy, growth poles centred on ports were developed (e.g. **Catania**, **Sicily** and **Taranto**, **Puglia**; **Fig. 21.25**) and the employment opportunities they offered attracted settlement.

Population distribution has also been affected by tourism development. Both Sicily and Sardinia have high population densities in coastal regions, while the upland interior has very low densities. Declining farm incomes and the growth of tourism-related employment on the coast are two reasons for this.

Emigration

Another migration pattern involved movement from the Mezzogiorno to the richer north of Italy, central Europe and the USA. Between the years 2001 and 2013, the **net migration** figure from the south to the north was over 700,000 people, while the global diaspora of Italians runs into tens of millions, and these migrants now comprise an important ethnic element in the population of the USA and Australia.

During the economic downturn between 2007 and 2017, over 70% of the almost one million jobs lost in the Italian economy were lost in the south.

Migration has meant the loss of younger, more dynamic people from the region. This has impacted on the structure of population, increasing the old-age dependency ratio.

Forecasts suggest that, over the next 50 years, the south of Italy could lose over four million people through out-migration.

> **DID YOU KNOW?**
> There are 15.7 million Italian-Americans in the USA. They account for almost 6% of the population of the USA, and 14% of the population of New York.

Immigration

In recent years, a pattern of inward migration to the region has also become established. The changing political and economic situation in various African countries (e.g. **Eritrea**, on the east coast of Africa) has compelled people to seek a better life in Europe (**Fig. 21.26**). Estimates suggest that since 2013, over 690,000 **migrants** and refugees have landed in the south of Italy.

→ **Fig. 21.26** Migration routes from North Africa to Italy.

355

Landscapes

While some urban centres have embraced migrant resettlement as a way of revitalising their dwindling communities, others are opposed to it and have called for the EU to tackle the problem (Fig. 21.27).

The Italian island of **Lampedusa** is one of the main landing points for migrants: it is only 460 km from Libya.

The number of migrants on this route has substantially decreased from **181,436 in 2016** to **23,370 in 2018**.

Chapter 27 Migration

→ **Fig. 21.27** Rescue of migrants crossing from Libya to the Mediterranean.

EXAM LINK (HL)

Population in a European Region (30 marks)

Account for the distribution of population throughout a European region (not in Ireland) that you have studied.

2013, Q5C

Marking Scheme:
15 SRPs × 2 marks

Organised crime

The activities of **organised crime groups** such as **Cosa Nostra** in Sicily impact on private investment. Racketeering, intimidation, criminal gangs and corrupt practices make the region unattractive to outside investors. Criminal involvement in road infrastructure projects led to the use of substandard materials, which, in turn, has led to a crumbling infrastructure.

Urbanisation

In January 2015, the province of Naples was replaced by the Metropolitan City of Naples. With a population of over three million, it dominates the urban geography of the region. The

→ **Fig. 21.28** Sketch map of the main urban centres of the Mezzogiorno.

356

city has long suffered from overcrowding, high unemployment, run-down districts and the influence of the **Camorra Mafia**.

In the province of Calabria, the main town of **Reggio Calabria** is a port and tourist resort, with a number of food processing industries providing employment for locals.

In Sicily, **Greater Palermo** has a population of over 1.2 million people. In the east of Sicily, **Catania**, with a population of over 300,000, is the largest city. As an industrial and tourist centre, Catania attracts workers from the rural inland, contributing to its growth.

With a population of over 200,000 people, **Taranto** in Puglia province is the main urban centre in the south. In Puglia, the coastal towns of **Bari** (300,000 people) and **Brindisi** (89,000 people) are the main centres of population.

EXAM LINK (HL)

Population in a European Region (30 marks)

Account for the distribution of population throughout a European region (not in Ireland) that you have studied.

2013, Q5C

Marking Scheme:
Examination = 15 SRPs × 2 marks

CHECK YOUR LEARNING

1. Name six ways in which the population distribution of the Mezzogiorno has changed over time.
2. List four ways in which migration has impacted on population distribution in the region.

EXAMINATION QUESTIONS

ORDINARY LEVEL

Long Question

1. Economic Activities – European Region

Explain the development of any two of the following with reference to a European region (not in Ireland) that you have studied.

- The reasons why tourists are attracted to the region
- The importance of manufacturing to the region
- The development of transport in the region.

Marking Scheme:
Region named = 1 mark
Activity 1 = 7 SRPs × 3 marks
Activity 2 = 6 SRPs × 3 marks

2017, Part Two, Section 1, Q5B (40 marks)

HIGHER LEVEL

Long Question

2. Primary Economic Activity – Agriculture

Explain the impact of climate on the development of agriculture in two contrasting European regions (not in Ireland) that you have studied.

Marking Scheme:
Examination of region 1 = 8 SRPs × 2 marks
Examination of region 2 = 7 SRPs × 2 marks

2018, Part Two, Section 1, Q4C (30 marks)

Landscapes

Revision Summary

Physical Processes

Climate
- Mediterranean climate; hot summers av. 29°C, warm winters av. 14°C
- Precipitation 600–1,000 mm, minimal in summer – convectional
- Latitude – 40°N: high summer sun, high temperatures
- Hot sirocco winds from Sahara Desert can bring extreme temperatures
- SW winds in winter – Atlantic depressions – precipitation

Relief
- Apennine Mountains – sedimentary limestone, sandstone, shale – covers 85% of land, formed during Alpine folding
- Seismic activity common in Apennines – earthquakes, e.g. Umbria
- Volcanic mineral springs – e.g. Terme di Agnano, Campania
- Coastal lowlands: Puglia, Metaponto in east; Campania in west – coastal dunes creating malarial marshes

Drainage
- Permeable limestone limits surface drainage
- Volturno and Agri rivers – low in summer but potential flooding in winter

Soils
- *Terra rossa*: weathered limestone – well-drained, red clay soils – occur widely
- Volcanic soils: base of Mt Vesuvius and Mt Etna
- Alluvial soils: river deposits of eroded material from upland slopes – floodplains of Volturno and Agri rivers, lowlands of Campania, Puglia, Catania and Augusta

Primary Economic Activities: Agriculture

Climate
- Mediterranean climate – summer drought dries rivers, no water for irrigation
- Traditional agriculture pattern on upland farms
- Farm crops suited to dry summers – olive trees, vines, citrus fruit
- Irrigation systems and plentiful sunshine in coastal lowlands – commercial horticulture
- Pastoral farming limited to goat and sheep rearing on uplands
- Heavy summer rain – flooding, landslides, soil erosion – loss of crops

Relief
- 85% is upland – limits mechanisation and potential for commercial farming
- Soil erosion from heavy winter rain, convectional summer showers – damage crops
- Steep relief – poor transportation; subsistence farming widespread
- Lower hillsides – vines, fruit and olives grown on terraces
- Irrigated coastal lowlands – commercial fruit growing

Soils
- Rich volcanic soils in Campania – fruit and wine production
- *Terra rossa* soils in Abruzzo and Puglia – vine cultivation
- Alluvial soil irrigation on lowlands – horticulture
- Soil erosion from deforestation and overgrazing – limited agricultural potential

Socio-economic factors: land ownership
- History of absentee landlords – pattern of traditional farming using labour-intensive methods
- Limited income – out-migration of young farmers

Socio-economic factors: Markets
- Pre-1950: commercial farming not viable in uplands – low population, low income, poor road network
- Higher population in lowlands – market for horticultural produce
- Growth of tourism and food processing industries, improved access to European markets – increased demand for agricultural produce

Il Cassa per il Mezzogiorno
- Improved road (**Autostrada del Sol** motorway) and rail network
- Land ownership reform – co-operatives
- Irrigation systems to facilitate fruit and vegetable farming
- Land reclamation – hillsides re-afforested, coastal marshes drained

Results
- Farms still too small and unproductive – subsistence
- Seasonal overproduction – price collapse
- Mechanisation – increased unemployment
- Irrigation maintenance, higher production costs = reduced profit
- Increased income gap between lowlands and uplands

EU
- Common Agricultural Policy – direct payments to farmers
- LEADER Programme – supports agri- and rural improvement projects

Primary Economic Activities: Other

Forestry
- Clearing in 19th century
- Reforestation by the Cassa

Fishing
- Good weather and sheltered harbours – plentiful catch for local and tourist markets
- Threat of decline – overfishing

Energy
- World's seventh-largest **wind energy** producer: **Messina-Agrigent**o wind farm – 124 turbines
- High levels of **insolation** – ideal for **solar energy**
- Potential for geothermal energy production

Secondary Economic Activities: Manufacturing

Physical factors
- Industrial development hindered by lack of raw materials for production (coal, iron ore) or energy (oil, gas)
- Small-scale food processing industries successful in coastal lowlands or close to ports (olive oil, tinned tomatoes, blending wine)

Socio-economic factors: Labour
- Brain drain and low education – small supply of skilled labour – unattractive to industries
- Naples – largest urban area in Campania, industrious workforce

Socio-economic factors: Markets
- Pre-1950: high unemployment, low disposable income – unattractive to consumer-based industries
- Steep relief, poor infrastructure and high distribution costs limited industry
- Industrial development limited to coastal lowland areas
- Campania – largest consumer market

Socio-economic factors: Lack of investment
- Dependent on outside investment – slow and limited growth

Il Cassa per il Mezzogiorno
- Autostrada del Sol lowered transport costs
- Improved port facilities increased potential as industrial site
- Designated growth poles attracted industry
- Industrial triangles: Bari–Brindisi–Taranto; Catania–Augusta–Syracuse
- State-controlled industries moved to south
- Training and education
- Evaluation: Cathedrals in the desert, privatisation in 1990s

EU
- GDP – 25% less than EU average
- Support from ERDF, ESF

Tertiary Economic Activities: Tourism

Physical factors
- Mediterranean climate
- Varied landscape – mountains and beaches
- Geology – volcanoes, thermal spas

Cultural and historical factors
- Ancient Greek temples (**Paestum**)
- **Herculaneum** and **Pompeii**

Government and EU Policy
- Improved road and rail infrastructure by the Cassa
- New and upgraded airport terminals
- Funding for cruise-ship terminals
- ERDF-funded tourist facilities
- ESF-funded training

Benefits and challenges
- Direct and indirect employment – increased markets – revenue
- Seasonal employment insecure

Tertiary Economic Activities: Transport

Physical factors
- Lowlands: gentle gradients – good road and rail networks
- Upland: steep gradients, valleys, gorges – challenge
- Landslides – disruptive, costly to repair damage

Socio-economic factor
- Low population density – public transport expensive

Political factors
- Cassa improved road networks
- ERDF: funded roads (**Autostrada del Mediterraneo**), rail, port and airport upgrades; further plans to modernise railway (TEN-T project)

Human Processes

Population
- Population (2016): total 60.6 m, 20.8 m in Mezzogiorno
- Birth rate: 16.8 per 1,000 (1970) – 7.7 per 1,000 (2017) – reflects migration of young people
- Population density – av. 201 persons per km²
- Uneven population distribution – lower density in upland areas; highest densities in coastal lowlands
- Pattern of internal migration from uplands to increased economic opportunities of lowlands
- Tourism-related employment – higher population densities in Sicily and Sardinia

Migration
- Migration to richer north, central Europe, USA; loss of younger, more dynamic people
- Migrant and refugee numbers increasing – 690,000 since 2013

Organised crime
- Cosa Nostra, Sicily
- Negative impact on private investment
- Mafia involvement in infrastructure – poor materials

Urbanisation
- Metropolitan City of Naples (2015): overcrowding, unemployment Camorra Mafia
- Reggio Calabria: port, tourist resort, food processing industries
- Sicily (Catania, Greater Palermo): industry and tourism attracts workers
- Urban centres in Taranto, Puglia, Bari, Brindisi

22 A CONTINENTAL/ SUBCONTINENTAL REGION – INDIA

LEARNING INTENTIONS — Syllabus Link: 2.2

By the end of this chapter I will be able to:
- draw an outline map of the Indian subcontinent, showing and naming different features;
- explain how physical processes have shaped the landscape of this region;
- describe the factors that have influenced the development of primary, secondary and tertiary activities of the region;
- describe and explain the human processes that have influenced the population of the region;
- examine the development of one urban area in the region.

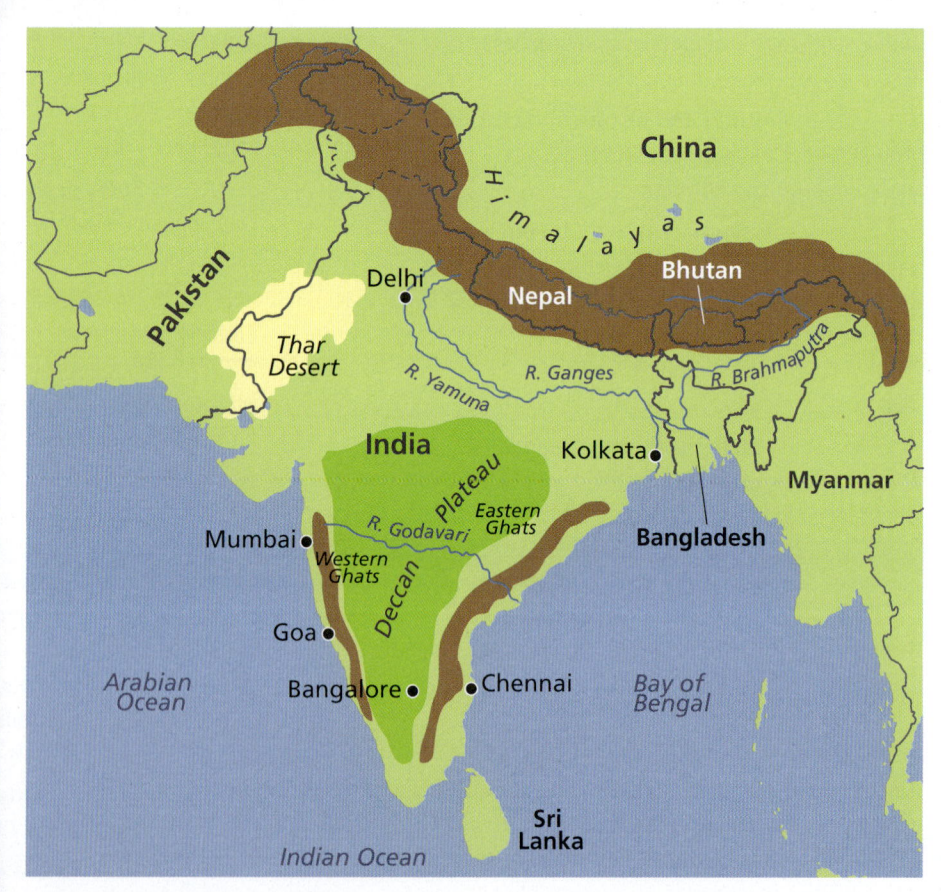

↑ **Fig. 22.1** The Indian subcontinent.

With over 1.2 billion people, India is the second most populous country in the world (after China). It is composed of 29 states that elect their own governments, and seven union territories ruled by a central government (**Figs 22.1–22.3**). It is bordered by a number of countries including Pakistan, Bhutan, Nepal, Myanmar (Burma) and Bangladesh, and has an extensive coastline.

22 A Continental/Subcontinental Region – India

Sketch Map of the Indian Subcontinental Region

↑ **Fig. 22.2** Political map of the Indian subcontinent.

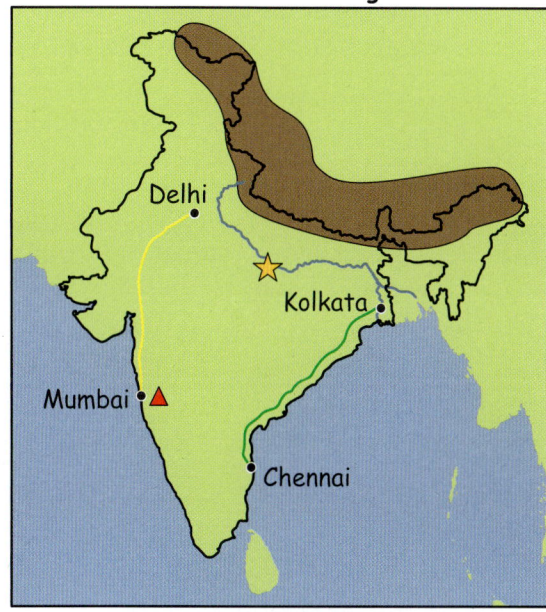

→ **Fig. 22.3** Sketch map of India.

Key for Sketch Map of the Indian Subcontinental Region
- ★ Agricultural area: Ganges Plain
- ▲ Industrial area: Mumbai
- ▬ Upland area: Himalayas
- • Urban centre
- — Ganges
- — Chennai–Kolkata Railway
- — National Highway 48 Mumbai–Delhi

Physical Processes

Climate

There are a variety of climates on the Indian subcontinent, including: tropical wet and dry (**savannah**), semi-arid, desert, mountain and tropical wet (**monsoon**).

Originating from the Arabic word *mausim*, meaning season, the **monsoon climate** is influenced by the seasonal changing **pressure patterns** and their effect on the prevailing winds. The two main seasons are:

- **Cool, dry season, October–February:** Low temperatures over the continental land mass (Tibetan Plateau) result in the formation of high pressure (Fig. 22.4(a)).

In this season, **dry winds blow from land to sea**. This is the monsoon dry season over most of India. However, the north-east trade winds travelling over the Bay of Bengal evaporate moisture from the Indian Ocean and bring precipitation to the southern peninsula and Sri Lanka. This is known as the **retreating monsoon** (Fig. 22.4(b)).

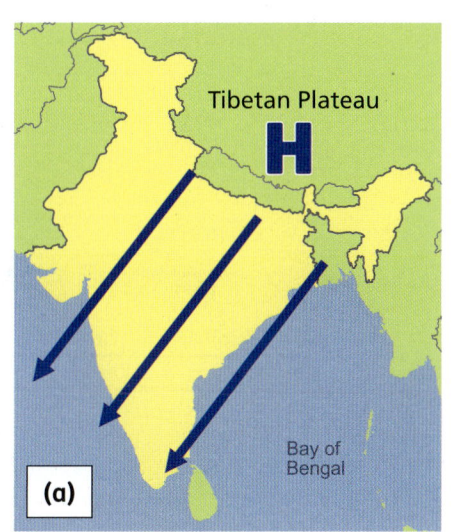

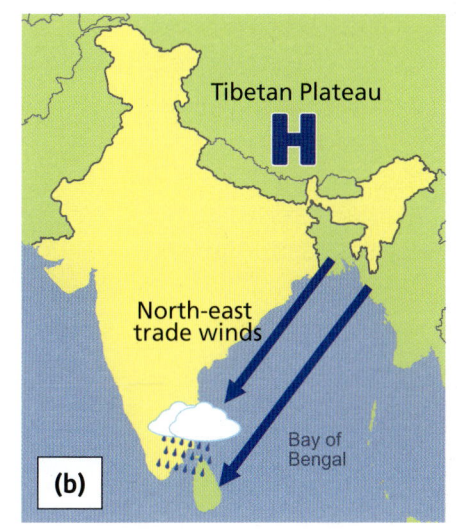

KEYWORDS
pressure patterns
dry
relief
soils

↑ **Fig. 22.4** The cool dry season: (a) the high pressure pattern; (b) the retreating monsoon.

361

Landscapes

- From **March to May**, conditions are generally dry. Temperatures begin to rise, heating the land mass, and forming areas of low pressure.
- **Hot, wet season, June–September:** High temperatures create low pressure, drawing the rain-bearing trade winds inland (Fig. 22.5). This is the wet season. In north-east India, the Himalayas act as a barrier and cause relief rain.

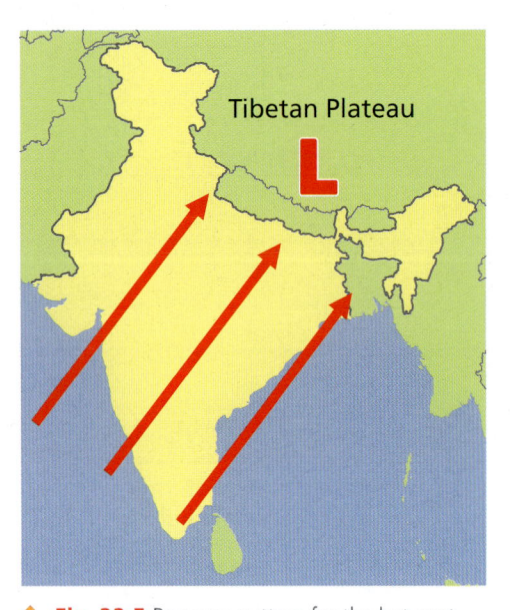

↑ **Fig. 22.5** Pressure pattern for the hot, wet season in India.

↑ **Fig. 22.6** High temperatures and low pressure bring heavy rains to much of India in the summer.

	Jan	Feb	Mar	Apr	May	Jun	Jul	Aug	Sep	Oct	Nov	Dec
Mean temperature (°C)	19.5	22	27	29.9	30.4	29.7	28.7	28.6	28.9	27.4	23.3	19.5
Mean precipitation (mm)	14	22	28	51	126	301	375	339	305	141	26	7

↑ **Table 22.1** Average monthly temperature and precipitation, Kolkata (Climate-Data.Org).

SKILLS ACTIVITY
Construct a suitable graph to illustrate the precipitation data from April to October in **Table 22.1**.

DID YOU KNOW?
During the monsoon season in India, it is common to see a mouse on the back of the frog. They do this to escape the floodwaters.

Relief and drainage

The Indian subcontinent contains a number of different physical regions with distinctive landscapes and drainage patterns.

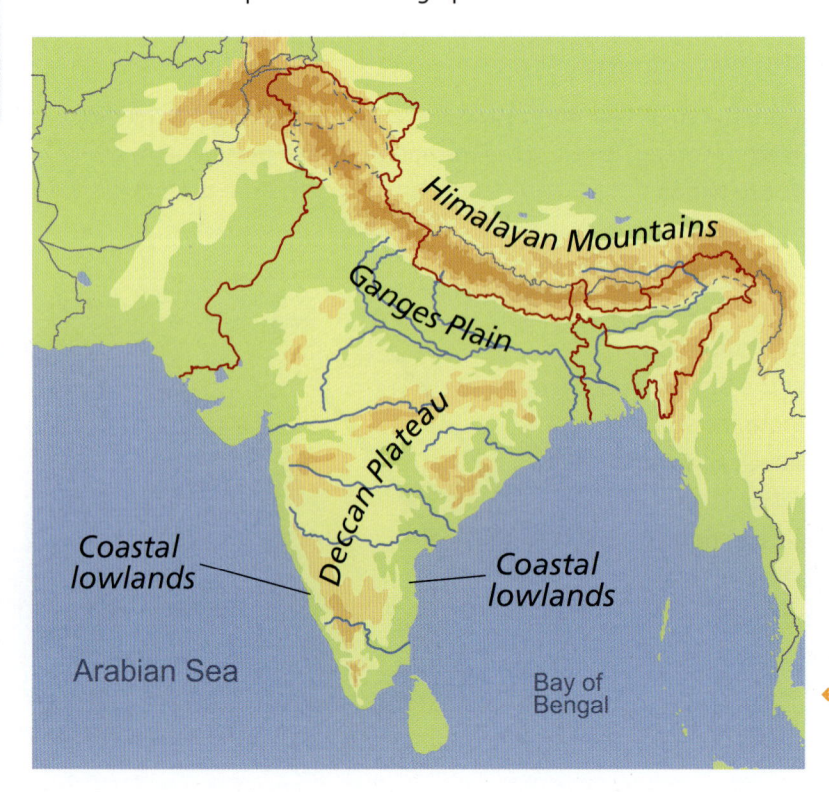

← **Fig. 22.7** The physical regions of India.

Himalayan Mountains

Extending over 2,500 km in length, the Himalayan Mountains are the world's tallest mountain range (Mount Everest on the China–Nepal border peaks at 8,848 m; Fig. 22.7). Their formation began 40–50 million years ago, when the Indian and Eurasian continental plates converged. Ongoing tectonic activity still causes frequent earthquakes and landslides. Some of the highest peaks are covered in snow all year, and the range contains active glaciers (Fig. 22.8).

The Ganges Plain (Northern Plain)

The **Ganges Plain** extends across northern India, from the Thar Desert in the west to the Ganges Delta in the east (Fig. 22.9). It is drained by the Ganges and its many tributaries, which originate in the Himalayas (e.g. the **Yamuna River**). Melting spring snow over the centuries caused flooding and led to the deposition of **alluvium** on the plain. In the east, the plain extends from the foothills of the mountains to the delta area on the **Bay of Bengal**, where the Ganges divides into distributaries (e.g. the **Hooghly River**).

↑ **Fig. 22.8** The Himalayas.

Chapter 1 Plate Tectonics
Chapter 10 Glaciation and Glacial Processes

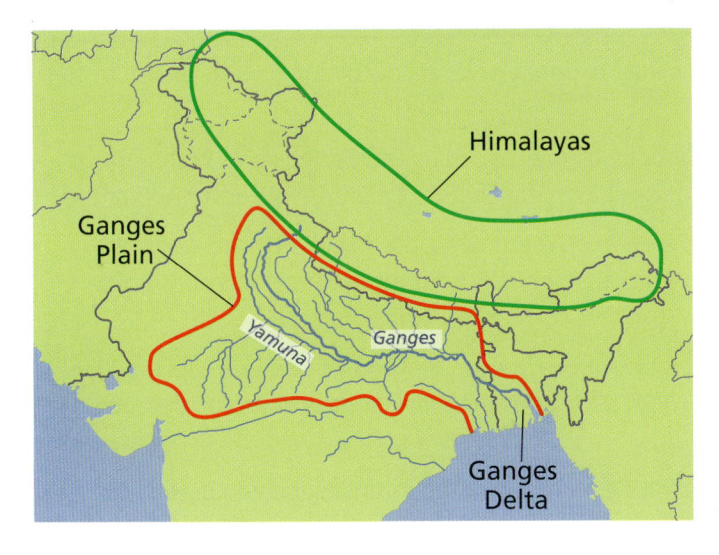

← **Fig. 22.9** The Ganges Plain.

DID YOU KNOW?
The Ganges Plain covers 630 million acres, or 2.5 million km².

The Deccan Plateau

Lying to the south of the Ganges Plain, the triangular-shaped **Deccan Plateau** is bordered by the **Western and Eastern Ghat Mountains**. Lava flows from tectonic activity formed large expanses of **basalt**, creating a plateau. Drainage here is dominated by eastward-flowing rivers.

Coastal plains

The **Eastern Coastal Plain** lies between the Eastern Ghats and the Bay of Bengal, and contains the deltas of three main rivers – the Godavari, the Krishna and the Kaveri.

The **Western Coastal Plain**, extending from the Western Ghats to the Arabian Sea, has short, fast-flowing rivers.

Landscapes

SKILLS ACTIVITY

Draw an outline map of the Indian subcontinent showing:
- two named urban centres;
- a named feature of relief (upland or lowland);
- a numbered road and one other communications link;
- an industrial area;
- an agricultural area;
- two features of drainage.

Soils

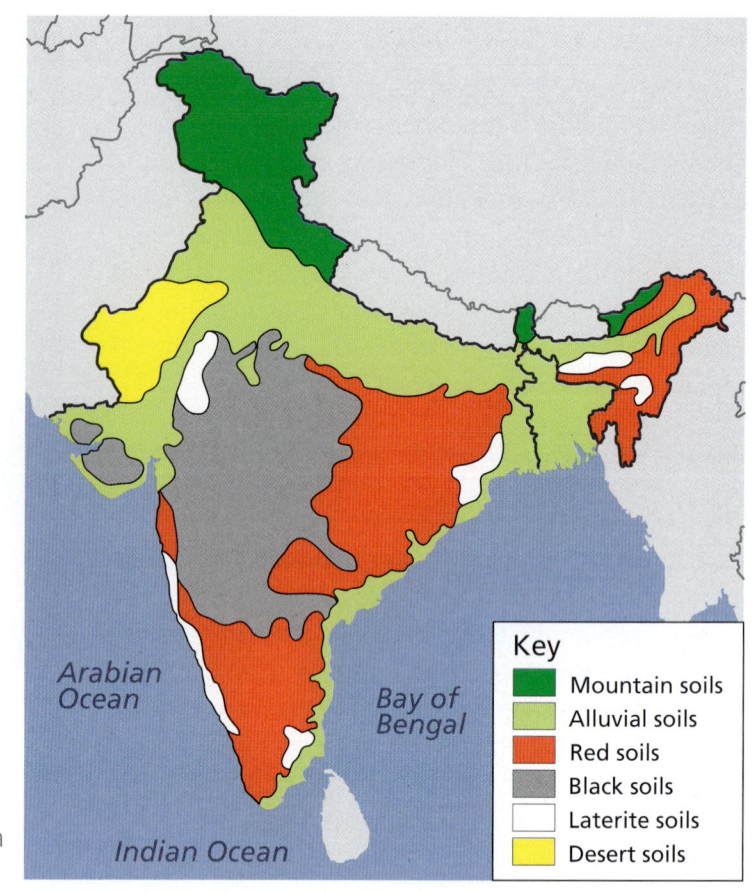

→ Fig. 22.10 The main soil types in India.

The Indian subcontinent is a vast expanse of land containing a wide variety of soil types (Fig. 22.10).

Alluvial soils: Deposited annually by rivers such as the Ganges and Brahmaputra, alluvial soils occur in the Ganges Plain, the Eastern Coastal Plain and river valleys.

Black soils: Black soils, also known as **regur soils**, are formed by the weathering of basalt in the Deccan Plateau. The high clay content means these soils hold moisture very well.

Red soils: Found over large areas of the Deccan Plateau, red soils are formed by the weathering of igneous rocks such as granite, and metamorphic rocks such as gneiss.

Laterite soils: Laterite soils form as a result of the intense leaching associated with the **monsoon climate**. This leaching removes all minerals, except for iron and aluminium compounds, which give the soils their distinctive red colour. Laterite soils occur in the Western Ghats, Eastern Ghats, West Bengal and Assam.

Desert soils: Lack of moisture and humus make desert soils infertile. These are found in the Thar Desert, in the west of India.

Chapter 5 Rocks

CHECK YOUR LEARNING

1. Describe the main characteristics of a monsoon climate.
2. Draw a sketch map showing and naming the main relief divisions of India.
3. Outline the main physical characteristics of each region.
4. Name four different types of soils found on the Indian subcontinent.
5. Describe the main characteristics of each type of soil.

Primary Economic Activities

Over 54% of the Indian population is involved in primary economic activity, including agriculture, fishing, forestry and mining.

Agriculture

The development of agriculture is the result of the interaction of many factors.

Physical factors

Climate

The agricultural cycle in India is influenced by the **monsoon climate**.

Crops that require monsoon rains to grow are planted in June and harvested in early November. These are called *kharif*, or 'summer' crops, and include rice, cotton and millet.

Rabi, or 'winter' crops, which require less water, are planted in November and harvested in March. These include wheat and barley.

Because it's so dependent on the monsoon, the harvest can be affected when the rains come late or early, or if they are irregular and unreliable. Monsoon flooding can also cause crop losses.

Two crops are particularly well suited to this type of climate:
- **Rice** needs an average temperature of 25°C and a lot of water in order to grow. Seedlings planted under water on paddy fields are weeded and thinned as they grow. Before harvesting, the water is drained. Basmati is one type of rice produced on the Ganges Plain.
- **Tea** requires temperatures between 20°C and 30°C and between 1,500 mm and 3,000 mm of rain per year to grow. Tea plants prefer well-drained slopes, and are cultivated on large plantations in north-east India (**Fig. 22.11**). Assam and Darjeeling are two tea-producing areas.

Over much of the Deccan Plateau, however, rainfall levels are low. **Irrigation** comes from water in the numerous river valleys where crops such as rice and cotton are produced (e.g. the **Godavari River valley**).

In **Rajasthan**, in the west, very low levels of precipitation result in **drought** conditions, so farmers have to rely completely on **irrigation**. **Pilot programmes** are underway to encourage the growing of citrus fruits and vegetables using water-economising technology (e.g. **polytunnels**).

KEYWORDS

agriculture
monsoon climate
irrigation
soil
Green Revolution
forestry
fishing
aquaculture
mining
energy

Millet: A cereal grass crop with small seeds that are used as a foodstuff and as livestock fodder.

← Fig. 22.11 Tea plantations, Assam.

Landscapes

Fig. 22.12 Valley terraces, Himalayas.

Relief

Areas of gently sloping land in the Lower Himalayas form upland pastures, where mixed crop and livestock farming takes place (e.g. cattle, buffalo and goat farming in **Himachal Pradesh**).

Throughout most of the Himalayas, agriculture has to contend with steeply sloping valleys, soil run-off and landslides, but the construction of **terraces** along the lower slopes allows the **subsistence production** of crops such as wheat and rice (Fig. 22.12).

South-facing slopes provide very favourable growing conditions for fruit crops and vegetables.

Crops can also be grown on the floodplains of valley floors.

The lowland relief of the Ganges Plain facilitates the flooding of **paddy fields** for rice cultivations.

Double cropping – involving the planting of wheat after the rice crop has been harvested – ensures **year-round land use** and continuous production.

Low-lying land in the Ganges Deltas is suitable for **intensive** levels of farming, though it has to cope with severe flooding in the monsoon season.

The narrow Western Coastal Plain is not as vital for agricultural production as the broader eastern area, but rivers such as the Krishna have formed **deltas** that are intensively farmed, mostly for rice.

Soils

A wide variety of soil in India allows the cultivation of a wide range of crops.

Alluvial soils: In the Himalayas, alluvial soil deposits along valley floors support subsistence agriculture. The deep alluvial soil covering on the Ganges Plain makes it the most productive agricultural region in India. The Ganges and Brahmaputra rivers in the Eastern Coastal Plain have also deposited alluvial soils, and this has contributed to a well-developed agricultural sector in this region (e.g. rice, sugar cane and jute).

Black soils: Their ability to retain moisture makes black soils well suited to the production of cotton. Maharashtra in west-central India is a major producer.

Red soils: Red soils have low amounts of organic matter but can be used for wheat and millet production.

Laterite soils: A high acidic content and poor water retention makes laterite soils unsuited to agriculture.

Desert soils: Lack of moisture and humus make desert soils infertile, but a high potash content means that, with irrigation, these soils can be productive.

Potash: A potassium compound created from the ashes of burnt wood, which helps crops to grow.

Socio-economic factors

The population of over 1.2 billion people means agriculture is primarily geared to food production, most of which is consumed internally.

Subsistence agriculture, where farmers cultivate and harvest crops on small plots of land, is the most common form. Most of the produce is consumed by the family, leaving little to sell in local markets (Fig. 22.13).

Labour-intensive activities, such as rice production and tea harvesting, provide a source of employment and income for many rural dwellers (Figs 22.14, 22.15).

Population growth is placing huge pressure on the agricultural sector, which must produce food and provide employment. To achieve both, more land is needed for agriculture. However, as urbanisation increases, land availability for agriculture is reduced.

Increased **mechanisation** may improve output, but it has a negative impact on rural employment (Fig. 22.16).

↑ **Fig. 22.13** Traditional farming methods.

↑ **Fig. 22.14** Rice planting.

↑ **Fig. 22.15** Tea harvesting, Assam.

↑ **Fig. 22.16** Mechanisation of agriculture.

The variety of **spices** used in Indian cuisine results in widespread spice production. Examples include cardamom from Kerala and chili from West Bengal (Fig. 22.17).

Cattle production and exports of beef are very important. India is the second largest world exporter of beef. Hindu objections to the slaughter of cattle has resulted in the farming of water buffalo for their meat, which is known as *carabeef*.

The Green Revolution

The **Green Revolution** describes the changes brought to the production of staple crops such as rice through the use of high-yielding, pest-resistant seed varieties, fertilisers and pesticides. Initiated in the 1970s, its aims included:

- increasing food supply for a rapidly growing population;
- the introduction of modern farming methods and farmer education programmes;
- the improvement of economic conditions through the employment created by dam and irrigation construction projects;
- the hope that the hydroelectric power these dams produced would encourage industrialisation and improve living conditions.

↑ **Fig. 22.17** Indian spices.

Achievements

High-yielding crop varieties resulted in increased food production, so famine was no longer a threat. **Surplus** production meant commercial trading in crops could take place, earning income for farmers.

Failures

Increased **mechanisation** reduced the need for labourers, forcing many to migrate to the cities. The **rising cost of inputs** (seeds, fertilisers and pesticides) meant that many small farmers who could not keep up repayments lost their holdings.

Challenge facing agriculture

Land ownership

- Unequal ownership of land means subsistence farming is common.
- Farmers renting land have little or no security of tenure.
- These farmers have no incentive to improve farming, so output levels remain low.

> **DID YOU KNOW?**
> Aproximately 24.4% of India's land surface is covered in forests and trees. A festival of trees – Van Mahotsav – is celebrated by Indian people every July.

Forestry

The government, which owns over 95% of forestry, has initiated numerous projects aimed at developing **sustainable** forestry, the designation of protected forest zones and reforestation. Clearance of land for agriculture is one of the main causes of **deforestation**.

The main types of forest include:
- tropical rain forests (**Western Ghats** and **Assam**), which produce hardwoods including ebony and mahogany;
- tropical deciduous forests (**monsoon forests**, **Himalayan foothills**), which produce teak, sandalwood and bamboo.

Forestry provides **raw materials** for the construction industry, paper and pulp manufacturing, and for wood-based industries such as plywood and veneer manufacture. (**Fig. 22.18**)

Fig. 22.18 Forests form an integral part of India's landscape, industry and culture.

Fishing

With a coastline of over 8,000 km, numerous estuaries, lagoons, inland canals, reservoirs and lakes, India has ideal conditions for fishing and aquaculture. A number of major fishing ports are located around the coast (e.g. **Kochi** and **Chennai**). Fishing provides employment and food.

Aquaculture

Overfishing and reduction in catches has led to major growth in aquaculture. Ideal climatic conditions and physical locations have led to India becoming a major global producer, supplying both home and export markets (e.g. **freshwater prawns in Andhra Pradesh**).

Mining and energy

India has the third-largest coal reserves in the world (**Fig. 22.19**). **Coal** is used for domestic consumption and in coal-fired power stations. **Orissa** in the east of the country is a major coal-mining area.

Iron ore, once a major raw material produced in India, has declined in importance due to falling global prices and government concerns about illegal mining and environmental damage. One of the largest copper mines in India is at **Khetri** in Rajasthan.

Suitable sites along rivers flowing from the **Himalayas** and the **Deccan Plateau** give enormous potential for **hydroelectric power**; dual-purpose dams constructed for irrigation projects currently supply a significant proportion of the area's renewable energy.

Nuclear energy is the fourth most important energy source in India. However, opposition to the construction of new installations is increasing.

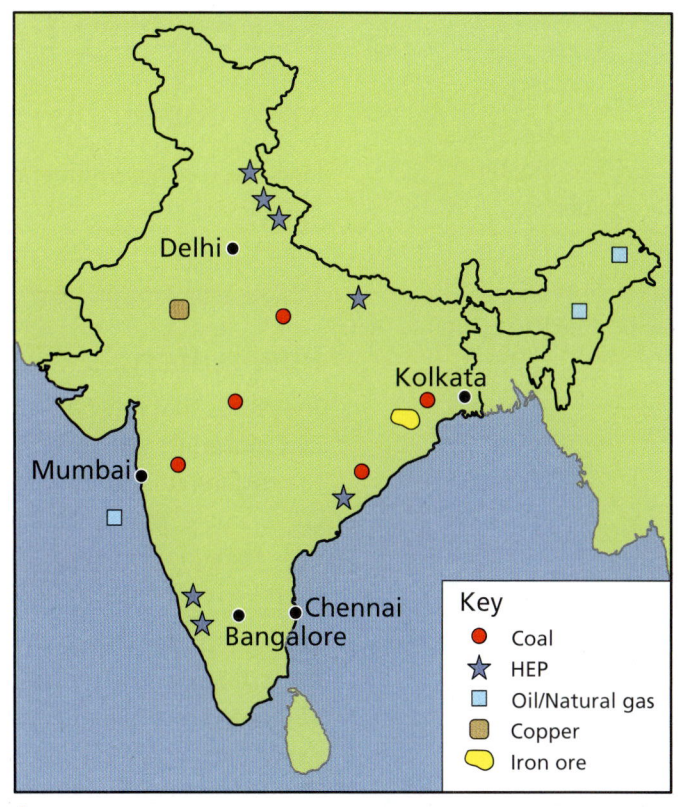

Fig. 22.19 Energy and mineral resources.

EXAM LINK (OL)

Agriculture – Continental/Subcontinental Region (30 marks)

Explain how two of the factors listed below influence the development of agriculture in a continental/subcontinental region that you have studied.

Climate   Relief and soils   Markets

2017, Q4C

Marking Scheme:
Explanation of factor 1 = 5 SRPs × 3 marks
Explanation of factor 2 = 5 SRPs × 3 marks

EXAM LINK (HL)

Agriculture in a Continental/Subcontinental Region (30 marks)

Account for the development of agriculture in a continental/subcontinental region with reference to any two of the following factors.

Soil   Relief   Climate

2016, Q5B

Marking Scheme:
Account of factor 1 = 8 SRPs × 2 marks
Account of factor 2 = 7 SRPs × 2 marks

CHECK YOUR LEARNING

1. Name four ways climate has affected the development of agriculture in India.
2. List four ways relief has impacted on agricultural development.
3. Describe four ways soil has influenced the development of agriculture.
4. Name four socio-economic factors that have affected the development of agriculture.
5. Name three aims of the Green Revolution.
6. Explain one challenge facing agriculture in India.

KEYWORDS

raw materials
weight-losing
labour
infrastructure
Special Economic Zone
foreign direct
Make in India

Secondary Economic Activities

Manufacturing

Many factors have influenced the development of the manufacturing industry in India.

Physical factors

Raw materials

Industries that rely on **weight-losing raw materials** will generally locate in the regions close to the raw materials. For example, the iron and steel industry uses coal and iron ore, which are reduced during the manufacturing process.

Coal deposits in **Orissa** state and in north-eastern India have resulted in the growth of a wide range of industries that use coal – including iron and steel, and fertiliser production (e.g. **Jharkhand, West Bengal**) – on sites surrounding the coal mines.

Iron ore deposits have given rise to the development of iron and steel manufacturing. The **TATA plant at Jamshedpur** in Orissa, for example, is located close to iron ore and coal deposits (**Fig. 22.20**).

↑ **Fig. 22.20** TATA steel plant, Jamshedpur.

Weight-losing manufacturing: A process where the weight of the final product is less than the weight of the raw materials that go into making it.

Copper deposits at **Khetri**, in the western state of Rajasthan, support copper smelting that supplies copper to a variety of engineering industries (e.g. cable manufacture).

Sugar cane is another weight-losing crop, so sugar production plants are located close to producing regions (e.g. **Maharashtra**).

Cotton does not reduce in weight or volume during the manufacturing process, and therefore proximity to raw materials is not such an important factor for the location of cotton mills. What is important is the **proximity to the market** – large urban centres such as **Mumbai** are important textile manufacturing centres.

Jute, grown in **West Bengal**, supplies the raw material to numerous jute mills in the region. The industry is centred on **Kolkata**, due to the presence of a huge, predominantly immigrant labour pool from surrounding Indian states and Bangladesh.

Hydroelectric power is used by electrometallurgical industries. For example, aluminium is manufactured by Hindalco Industries using power from the **Hirakud Dam in Orrisa** state.

Electrometallurgical industry: Uses electricity to perform a number of processes in the production of metals.

Socio-economic factors

Labour

With a population of over 1.2 billion, the Indian manufacturing industry has access to a huge labour pool.

Urban areas are centres of labour supply – this has resulted in industrial concentrations in cities such as **Mumbai** and **Kolkata**. Lower labour costs and an availability of skilled English-speaking workers has proved attractive to foreign multinational corporations (e.g. **Mitsubishi**).

Increased participation in **third-level education** and **scientific research** has created a highly-skilled labour force that has attracted a wide range of industries. **Bangalore** is home to a number of third-level institutions including the prestigious **Indian Institute of Science**. As a result of the skilled work force it produces, the city's industries include **aeronautics** and it is a major centre for **IT** (Fig. 22.21).

The **pharmaceutical** industry in India is widely distributed, and Indian companies in production centres like **Mumbai** and **Chennai** specialise in the production of low-cost generic medicines.

Fig. 22.21 Bagalore is one of India's industrial centres.

Restrictive labour laws in some states apply to companies of more than 100 employees. Smaller textile plants with fewer than 100 employees can avoid these laws, but are unable to compete with huge plants in China.

Infrastructure

When manufacturing industry is located in areas close to raw materials, an efficient **transport infrastructure** is vital in getting the product to market while keeping the **distribution costs** low. The same rule applies where raw materials are transported to manufacturing plants.

Where the transport network was poorly developed in upland areas, industry was mainly small cottage-type production (e.g. **Himalayas**).

Lowland areas are well suited to the development of transport networks for the rapid transport of **perishable** raw materials. The wide range of food processing plants on the Ganges Plain are due to this.

During **colonial** times, Britain established three main **ports** to serve as export points for raw materials and points of import for manufactured goods. These ports were **Kolkata**, **Mumbai** and **Madras**. Today, these nodal port cities are major manufacturing and export centres (Fig. 22.22).

The **railways** were also constructed under British rule. They were designed to get raw materials to ports and back to Great Britain to factories where they were processed. The processed goods were then exported back to India for sale. As a result, the British contribution to early industrial development was minimal.

Transport infrastructure development creates demand for construction materials such as iron, steel and cement while the supply of rolling stock to the railways supports engineering.

Railways allowed for the transport of bulky manufactured goods from plants located near to raw materials (e.g. the **iron and steel industry** in **Orissa**.

Major improvements to the road networks include the **Golden Quadrilateral** that links the main cities of **Chennai**, **Kolkata**, **Delhi** and **Mumbai**. By providing efficient access to markets by HGVs, it has allowed manufacturing industry to locate in smaller urban centres.

Fig. 22.22 Chennai Port.

Landscapes

Fig. 22.23 Clothing manufacture is an important industry in India.

Markets

India's population of over 1.2 billion has significant market potential, and is capable of supporting a wide range of consumer industries, including clothing manufacture (Fig. 22.23). Different income levels, however, lead to differences in levels of demand and consumption between urban and rural areas.

Local markets in rural areas support a variety of small-scale manufacturing activities.

Multinational corporations wishing to gain access to the vast market have established manufacturing plants throughout the subcontinent (e.g. **Samsung, New Delhi**).

The major **urban centres** such as Delhi and Mumbai have attracted a wide range of consumer industries including textiles and food processing (e.g. **Nestle, Coca-Cola**).

Increasing affluence among the wealthier classes in India has led to increased demand for **cars** (e.g. **the TATA motor plant, Gujarat**; Fig. 22.24) and other technology. In 2017, mobile phone production in India totalled 11 million units.

Association of South-East Asian Nations (ASEAN): A political and economic organisation comprised of ten South-East Asian countries.

← Fig. 22.24 TATA motor plant, Gujarat.

Membership of the **ASEAN** Free Trade area gives India access to Asian markets. A free trade agreement with the EU has yet to be agreed, but in 2017, the value of India's exports to the EU was over €44 billion.

Government

The Make in India campaign was launched by the government in 2014, with the key aim of developing strategies to reduce red tape and regulations, making it easier to conduct business.

State-owned enterprises can be found in most sectors of India's economy, but many are inefficient and end up losing money.

Industrial parks have been developed in every state, and over 200 **Special Economic Zones**, within which companies are exempt from customs and excise duties, have been set up. The **Falta Special Economic Zone in Kolkata** includes companies manufacturing textiles, solar cells, pharmaceuticals and electronics.

To attract international manufacturing and services, the Indian government is planning a number of **industrial corridors**. The proposed Delhi–Mumbai Industrial Corridor, costing €900 billion, will extend over 1,400 km and will contain 24 smart cities, all linked by high-speed train.

Industrial corridor: Area containing a variety of transport infrastructures which has been targeted for industrial development.

Smart city: A smart city uses ICT to monitor and control services such as waste disposal, lighting, transport and water supply to ensure a more efficient and sustainable city.

Foreign direct investment was first allowed in the Indian market in 1991. Since then, there has been an influx of foreign companies investing in India. All of the major multinationals are represented, including manufacturing giants such as **IBM** and **Coca-Cola**. They not only provide employment in their own facilities, but the production and logistical links that develop between them and local Indian companies (via the **multiplier effect**) have also increased employment. Other manufacturers have been attracted as part of the **Make in India** campaign, and produce items for export (e.g. **Kia, General Motors**).

Challenge facing manufacturing: Energy production

- As the economy expands, demand for electricity has increased, but it is not matched by supply.
- Increasing affluence has also led to a growth in domestic electricity consumption.
- Power outages, interrupting manufacturing, occur when demand exceeds supply.

EXAM LINK (OL)

Manufacturing in a Continental/Subcontinental Region (30 marks)

Describe and explain the development of manufacturing in a continental/subcontinental region that you have studied.

2016, Q6B

Marking Scheme:
Description/explanation = 10 SRPs × 3 marks
Credit a named region for 1 SRP

EXAM LINK (HL)

Secondary Economic Activity – Continental/Subcontinental Region (30 marks)

Examine the development of secondary economic activity in a continental/subcontinental region that you have studied, with reference to two of the following factors.

Markets   Infrastructure
Government policy   Raw materials

2017, Q6B

Marking Scheme:
Examination of factor 1 = 8 SRPs × 2 marks
Examination of factor 2 = 7 SRPs × 2 marks

CHECK YOUR LEARNING

1. Name four ways raw materials have influenced the development of manufacturing in India.
2. List four ways labour has influenced Indian industrial development.
3. Describe four ways transport has influenced the development of industry.
4. Explain four ways markets have impacted on Indian industrial development.
5. List four ways government policy has affected industrial development.
6. Explain one challenge facing the manufacturing industry in India.

Tertiary Economic Activities

Tourism

A number of different factors have contributed to the development of tourism in India.

Physical factors

Accessibility

India has over 50 national airports and 12 **international airports**, allowing foreign tourists good access to the country. The Indian **railway** system helps tourists to move around the country.

KEYWORDS

accessibility
climate
eco-tourism
landscapes
religion
pollution

Landscapes

Climate
The **variety of climates** in India makes it possible for tourists to experience a wide range of natural environments, including the snow-capped Himalayas, the sandy expanses of the Thar Desert and the tropical rainforests of Assam.

Landscapes
Tourists can avail of a variety of landscape-based activities. The Himalayas provide a perfect backdrop for **trekking** holidays that include options to stay in family homes. Tourists pay the families for accommodation and food, thus bringing the benefits of tourism directly to the local population (Fig. 22.25).

Eco-tourism helps to create employment in remote rural areas and provides funding to protect natural habitats. The economic benefits of **wildlife tourism** to local populations has led to greater awareness of issues concerning the environment as well as increasing conservation. For example, in **Ranthambore Park, Rajasthan**, the tiger population has increased from 48 in 2013 to 85 in 2018 (Fig. 22.26).

↑ **Fig. 22.25** Trekking in the Himalayas.

↑ **Fig. 22.26** Eco-tourism at Ranthambore National Park, Rajasthan.

Socio-economic factors

Historical
India's rich and varied history is reflected in its many historic sites (e.g. the **Taj Mahal, Agra;** Mysore Palace; Amritsar Temple; the royal palaces of Jaipur).

Cultural
As the birthplace of **Buddhism** and **Hinduism**, India attracts visitors who wish to explore these religions. The city of **Varanasi** on the Ganges is regarded as the spiritual capital of India. In 2017, it had almost six million domestic visitors and over 300,000 foreign visitors.

Wellness tourism
India has capitalised on the global increase in 'wellness' tourism. Indian **ashrams** are centres offering a variety of programmes based on yoga, meditation and the quest for enlightenment.

Medical tourism
Due to **rising medical costs** in the developed world, increasing numbers of people are choosing to travel to India for **medical procedures**. The use of modern technologies, high standards and lower costs have contributed to the growth of the medical tourism sector.

Government

The **Indian Tourism Development Corporation** is the government agency responsible for the construction and management of hotels and the promotion of tourism. Its **Incredible India** campaign has had huge success in raising the profile of the country.

Challenges facing tourism

Tourists can often have negative experiences in the major cities:

- visitors are targeted by street beggars (**Fig. 22.27**);
- piles of rotting rubbish generate foul smells and look unattractive;
- traffic congestion results in noise and air pollution.

Fig. 22.27 Street begging in India.

CHECK YOUR LEARNING

1. Name two physical factors that have influenced the development of tourism in India.
2. List four socio-economic factors that have influenced tourism development.
3. Name two ways in which the Indian government influenced tourism development.
4. Explain one challenge facing tourism in India.

Transport

The development of the Indian transport network is due to a number of factors.

Historical factors

From 1850 to 1947, India was a **British colony**. Three main **ports** were established at **Bombay (Mumbai)**, **Calcutta (Kolkata)** and **Madras (Chennai)** to handle imports and exports. **Railways** were constructed to transport raw materials from production areas to these ports for export to Great Britain, while imported manufactured goods could be transported to inland markets.

Physical factors

Relief

While the gentle relief of the **Ganges Plain** facilitated the construction of railway lines, similar construction in the foothills of the Himalayas has been limited by the region's **steep slopes and deep valleys**. In East Bengal, difficulty digging rail foundations in the **deltas** of the Ganges and Brahmaputra resulted in a lower density of railways.

The development of the road network has been affected by the steep **gradients** in mountain regions. Building protection and supports to minimise the impact of **landslides** due to mass movement, and constructing bridges to cross **rivers and gorges**, have also added to cost.

Roads can still be blocked and damaged by landslides due to earth tremors, causing disruption to communications and involving costly repairs.

KEYWORDS

British colony
relief
landslides
flooding
climate
pollution
displacement
rail
congestion
modernisation

The Indian road network extends over four million kilometres, and is the second largest in the world after the USA.

Landscapes

Climate

Flooding associated with the monsoons causes serious problems in relation to transportation. Rural unsurfaced roads become unusable during the wet summer months, while flooding of railway lines interferes with train schedules. Heavy rains can also trigger **landslides**, which cover roads and make them impassable (Figs 22.28, 22.9).

Rajasthan's desert climate means it cannot support many people, and as such it has a low population density. Because of this, the railway network is poorly developed and attracts little investment from the government.

↑ **Fig. 22.28** Monsoon flooding in Mumbai.

→ **Fig. 22.29** A landslide triggered by monsoon rains.

Socio-economic factors

Suburban **commuter transport systems** allow people to access the commercial centres of Indian cities.

Employing over 1.5 million people, the **Indian rail network** is an essential component of the economic and social infrastructure of the country. Indian railway stations are economic ecosystems that support railroad employees and a vast range of activities associated with the informal economy. Mumbai, Delhi and Kolkata are served by metro systems (Fig. 22.30). Mumbai's suburban railway system caters for over seven million passengers daily, but the large number of passengers leads to **overcrowding**.

Informal economy: Also known as the black economy, it refers to people who are not registered and so pay no tax on earnings, e.g. street hawkers, shoe shiners.

→ **Fig. 22.30** The New Delhi Metro.

Air pollution, noise pollution and traffic congestion are all negative consequences of the heavy urban road traffic (Fig. 22.31).

The construction of new roads and railways involves the compulsory purchase of land and can lead to the **displacement** of people in slum areas.

The **domestic air passenger market** is set to rise to 336 million by 2020. Many of India's existing airports will need major upgrades, and predicting where demand will warrant the construction of new airports is difficult.

↑ **Fig. 22.31** Traffic congestion, Bangalore.

Political factors

In response to a shortage of government funding and increased construction costs, **Public Private Partnership** (**PPP**) schemes in India now finance transport infrastructure projects. Current government transport proposals include:

- **Railways:** The development of high-speed rail links between Mumbai and Delhi/Delhi and Kolkata.
- **Ports:** Existing ports will be deepened and bulk material handling facilities and containerisation facilities will be updated.

Public Private Partnerships (PPPs): The public sector (government) and the private sector combine to construct and operate infrastructural projects, for example, bridges, toll roads, schools, etc.

Challenges facing transport: Modernisation of railways

- Major capital investment is needed to improve existing **equipment** and introduce more high-speed trains.
- As major employers, rationalisation and increasing use of technology in the railways will result in **job losses**. This would have serious economic impacts for 'railroad families'.
- Improved **information systems** are needed to provide accurate and up-to-date timetable information.

EXAM LINK (HL)

Tertiary Economic Activity (30 marks)

Account for the development of tourism or transport in a subcontinental region that you have studied.

2018, Q5B

Marking Scheme:
15 SRPs × 2 marks

CHECK YOUR LEARNING

1. Name two ways historical factors have influenced transport development in India.
2. Name two physical factors that have impacted on transport development.
3. Identify two socio-economic factors that have influenced transport development.
4. List two proposals for future transport development in India.
5. Explain one challenge facing transport in India.

Landscapes

KEYWORDS
total fertility rate (TFR)
life expectancy
migration
population distribution
population density
caste system
government
religion
language
urbanisation

Human Processes

Population

Between the 2000 and the 2011 census, the population of India had increased from 1.02 billion to 1.2 billion people. Forecasts for 2050 suggest that, with 1.7 billion residents, India will surpass China to become the world's most populated country.

Density

The national average **population density** in India is 396.7 persons per km^2, however, there are massive variations within the country. The state of Bihar, located on the fertile Ganges Plain, has the highest population density at 1,102 persons per km^2. At the other end of the scale, Arunachal Pradesh, in the Himalayan region of north-east India, has just 17 persons per km^2.

The **total fertility rate (TFR)** in India has declined from 3.83 in 1995 to 2.48 in 2015. In a number of states the TFR has already fallen below 2.0, and by 2020 the TFR for the country is expected to be at replacement level.

Between 2000 and 2015, **life expectancy** figures for men had risen from 61 to 66.9 years, while for women the figure had risen from 63.4 to 69.4 years.

Migration

Statistics suggest that over 20% of India's population is composed of **internal migrants**, of whom 70% are women. Following marriage, women will move to live with their in-laws. Men migrate from rural areas in search of employment. Cities such as **Delhi**, **Mumbai** and **Kolkata** receive large migrant flows from **Uttar Pradesh** and **Bihar**, two states with very high rural population percentages. Migrants who move from one state to another frequently lack proper identification, which leads to all types of exclusion. These migrants can also experience **exploitation** in terms of poor wages and working conditions, and can be forced to live in **slums** (**Fig. 22.32**).

→ **Fig. 22.32** Dharavi slum, Mumbai.

Population distribution

The distribution of population is **uneven** and has been influenced by a number of factors (Fig. 22.33).

Physical

Relief and soils

The **uplands of the Himalayas** have very low concentrations of population due to the harsh nature of the climate and inaccessible conditions (e.g. **Sikkim, 86 per km²**). Along the lower slopes in river valleys and on south-facing valleys, settlement numbers increase.

The **lowland relief** and fertile soils of the Ganges Plain have resulted in very high **population densities** (Fig. 22.34). The state of Uttar Pradesh, with almost 200 million people or 16.5% of the total population, is the most populous state in India.

In West Bengal, the **alluvial soils** of the deltas of the Ganges and Brahmaputra rivers support intense agricultural production and have a high population density.

In the Deccan Plateau, the river valleys with their alluvial soils and water for irrigation support agriculture and are densely populated. The drier **interior uplands** are more **inaccessible** and have lower population densities.

Agricultural potential, fishing and **lowland relief** contribute to high densities in the coastal lowlands of southern India.

Climate

Moving westward along the Ganges Plain, rainfall amounts decrease and in Gujarat and Rajasthan low population concentrations are associated with the **arid** lands of the Thar Desert. The use of irrigation in the Punjab has compensated for a lack of rainfall and results in higher **population densities**.

In many areas of India, tropical rainforests have been removed, however, where they remain, **inaccessibility** contributes to low population density (e.g. **Assam**).

Socio-economic factors

Over 66% of the population of India lives in rural areas, illustrating the important role **agriculture** plays in settlement patterns. Estimates, however, suggest that by 2050, 60% of India's population will be urban.

Greater Mumbai, with over 18 million people, and Delhi, with a population of over 16 million, are the two largest cities in India. As centres of expanding economic activity, they are continuing to grow due to **migration and natural increase**.

Rural-to-urban migration has resulted in the growth and spread of cities such as **Kolkata** and **Chennai**. Very high densities are associated with the slums that have developed on the outskirts of many Indian cities.

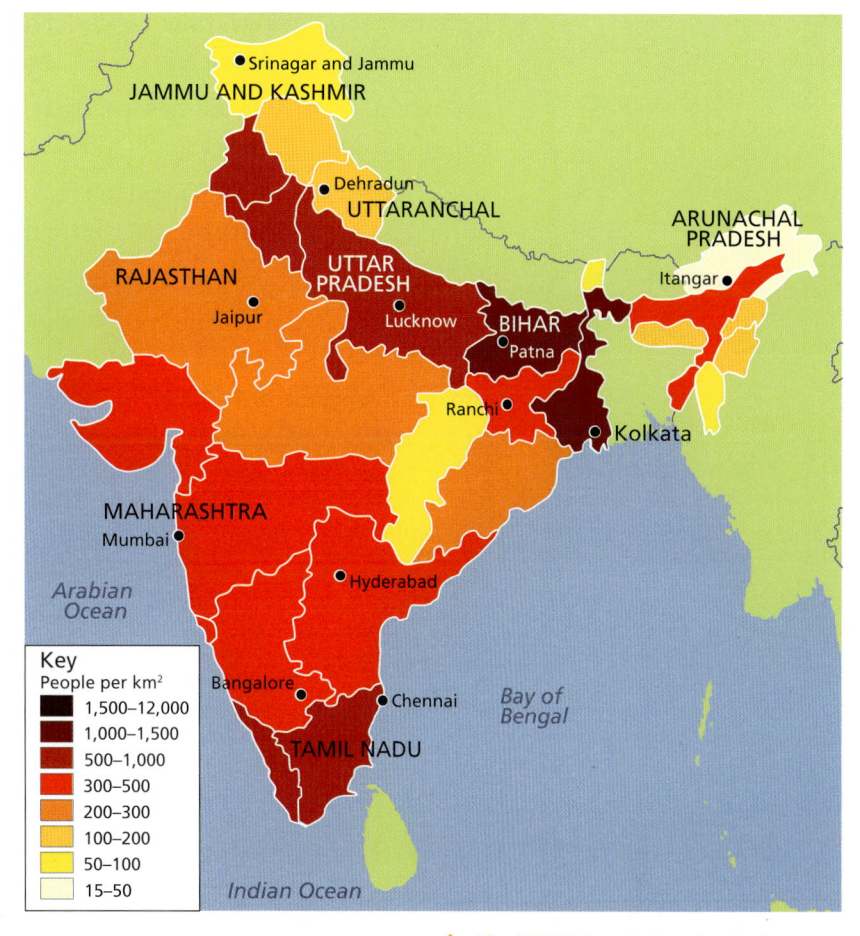

Fig. 22.33 Population density by state.

Fig. 22.34 A satellite image of the Ganges Plain.

Increased **foreign investment** in India has led to a growth in manufacturing in many urban areas, attracting skilled and unskilled migrants (e.g. **Bangalore**).

Deposits of mineral **resources** in **Orissa** have contributed to the development of a manufacturing industry that, in turn, has attracted settlement.

Jute cultivation in **West Bengal** led to the development of the textile industry. This attracted **migrant workers** and contributes to the very high **population density** of this region.

Religion

The main religious breakdown in India is as follows:

Religion	Percentage of population
Hinduism	79.8
Islam	14.2
Christianity	2.3
Sikhism	1.7
Buddhism	0.7
Other and no religion	1.3

↑ **Table 22.2** Religions in India (Indian Census 2011).

Through the rigid **caste system**, Hinduism has had a major impact on human development in India. It led to exploitation, created **social injustices** and gave preferential treatment based on birth rather than merit. The four main castes are:

- Brahmins: occupy key positions as priests and in government and business
- Kshatriyas: land-owners
- Vaishyas: traders, merchants and farmers
- Shudras: peasants and servants

The fifth group, the **Dalits**, live on the fringe of Indian society working in the cremation grounds and cemeteries and as street and sewer cleaners. They are also known as the **untouchables**.

Today, Indian law forbids caste-based discrimination. Positive strategies for addressing the inequality include:

- a reservation policy when accessing educational courses;
- reserved parliament seats.

Today the caste system is still in evidence, especially in rural areas, where inter-caste marriages very rarely take place. Lower castes are also employed by higher castes to do menial and degrading jobs.

Religious tensions

After India gained independence from Great Britain in 1947, the number of Muslims living in India was greatly reduced. The slaughter of cattle for the production of beef, which is opposed by Hindu teaching, is permitted in Islamic teaching. Efforts by Hindus to enforce a total ban on the slaughter of cattle have met with opposition from local and international meat processing industries.

Sikhs, who make up over 65% of the population in Punjab, are seeking the formation of an independent state.

Caste system: A class structure that is determined by birth.

In 1947, after the Indian subcontinent gained independence from Britain, it was divided into two independent states – India, which had a Hindu majority, and Pakistan, with a Muslim majority. This is known as the Partition of India. East Pakistan later became independent, and was renamed Bangladesh (1971).

Language

The **Indian Constitution** officially recognises 23 languages, though the national government uses just two official languages: **English** and **Hindi**. The print media produces over 80,000 newspapers across the country, over 32,000 of which are printed in Hindi and over 11,000 in English. The national radio broadcaster **All India Radio** operates over 400 radio stations, broadcasting in more than 20 different languages.

Urbanisation

The number of Indian cities with a population of one million or greater is expected to rise from 53 in 2011 to 87 by 2031. To monitor, oversee and control urban growth, the national government issues directives through **five-year plans**, and has introduced legislation relating to urban planning and the redevelopment of inner-city areas.

Within cities, the main areas that need to be addressed are housing provision, safe drinking water, improved sanitation, waste collection and disposal, improvements to transport infrastructure and tackling traffic congestion.

EXAM LINK (HL)

Population Distribution – Continental/Subcontinental Region (30 marks)

Account for the distribution of population throughout a continental/subcontinental region (not in Europe) that you have studied.
2017, Q5B

Marking Scheme:
Examination = 15 SRPs × 2 marks

CHECK YOUR LEARNING

1. Name four ways in which relief and soil have influenced population distribution in India.
2. List two ways in which climate has impacted on population distribution.
3. Name four socio-economic factors that influence population distribution.
4. Describe two characteristics of religion in India.

CASE STUDY: THE GROWTH OF KOLKATA

The Kolkata metropolitan area has a population of over 14 million and an average **population density** of 7,480 per km² (**Fig. 22.35**). The growth of the city has been influenced by a number of factors.

North Kolkata: oldest area, high density, narrow alleys
Esplanade: CBD
Maidan: central park
South Kolkata: affluent residential area
East Kolkata: industrial and residential growth (Salt Lake City)
Barrackpore: municipality within Kolkata
Howrah: west side of the Hoogly River, newer suburbs, most of the suburban slums located here
Southern and northern suburbs: increasing urbanisation

↑ **Fig. 22.35** Map of Kolkata.

Historical factors

In 1772, the British made Calcutta (an Anglicised spelling of Kolkata) their administrative capital and built a number of imposing buildings (**Fig 22.36**). The development of the railways linked Kolkata with the interior. Port facilities and warehouses were constructed along both banks of the Hoogly River, south of the colonial heart of the city, expanding its role as a primary port for the export of raw materials such as cotton and jute to Britain. The port also handled large quantities of manufactured goods from Britain.

↑ **Fig. 22.36** Queen Victoria Memorial Hall in Kolkata was built during British rule.

Landscapes

> **DID YOU KNOW?**
> In 2001, the city's name was changed from the Anglicised Calcutta back to Kolkata as part of a continuing national movement to remove links with the British colonial past. Likewise, in 1996, Bombay's name changed to Mumbai.

When the British moved the capital to Delhi in 1911, there was a huge loss of the civil service employment and the tertiary sector declined.

Following **Independence** and the **Partition of India** in 1947, a flood of Hindu migrants leaving the newly created Muslim majority state of East Pakistan poured into the city, leading to a rapid expansion of slums.

Independence affected the industrial economy. With the creation of **East Pakistan**, Kolkata lost most of its jute-supplying areas, leading to a loss of manufacturing. In 1971, the war between West Pakistan and East Pakistan, which eventually led to the formation of **Bangladesh**, led to further migration and slum expansions.

Physical factors

Kolkata grew up on the eastern banks of the **Hoogly River**, one of the distributaries of the Ganges. This linked it to the sea and allowed it to later develop important port functions.

The surrounding lowlands presented no physical barriers to growth and expansion.

Socio-economic factors

Migration has played a significant role in the growth and expansion of Kolkata. **Slums** developed to house the workers attracted by the availability of employment in the jute mills and other industries (Fig. 22.37). The older slums are located within the city, while newer ones on the outskirts occupy lands that have been targeted for redevelopment. Attempts at **slum clearance** often lead to protests.

The population of central Kolkata has declined, while the suburban population has increased. **De-industrialisation** in the centre during the 1970s and 1980s, and the movement of the middle classes to new suburban housing, contributed to this.

The city continues to expand due to increasing population and industrial growth. The slums on the outer fringes are growing as new migrants, attracted by the possible economic opportunities that Kolkata has to offer, continue to arrive. Commuter transport services, including suburban trains and a north–south metro allowing people to travel from outer suburbs, have also contributed to the expansion of the city (Fig. 22.38).

Bidhannagar, known by locals as **Salt Lake City** because it was built on a reclaimed salt marsh, is an example of a new town constructed in the east of Kolkata (Fig. 22.39).

The growth of Kolkata has seen huge increases in traffic volumes that has led to increasing **traffic congestion** and pollution (Fig. 22.40). This congestion, along with overcrowded conditions on trains and buses, resulted in many workers employed in the new **industrial zones** in the east of city moving to newly built apartments in these zones to reduce commuting.

↑ **Fig. 22.37** A slum in Howrah in the west of the city.

↑ **Fig. 22.38** The Kolkata Metro.

↑ **Fig. 22.39** Bidhannagar (Salt Lake City).

In the 1990s, following the relaxing of rules on **FDI**, Kolkata experienced huge inflows of investment. New industrial estates grew up on the eastern side of the city, and the **Falta Export Zone** was built to the south.

Howrah, on the west side of the Hoogly River, is undergoing major industrial and residential development that will be further stimulated by the proposed metro extension.

Government

Stretches of the riverfront have been redeveloped with landscaped walkways and recreational spaces (Fig. 22.41).

Plans announced in 2015 for a **smart city** at the northern boundary of the Kolkata metropolitan area will bring industrial, residential and commercial developments to the area.

The city of Kolkata still suffers from a negative image associated with **poverty**, **overcrowding** and **congestion**. The state and municipal authorities are keen to project an image of a new vibrancy that will attract inward investment.

↑ **Fig. 22.40** Traffic congestion, Kolkata.

↑ **Fig. 22.41** Millennium River Park, Kolkata.

CHECK YOUR LEARNING

1. Explain two ways in which historical factors have influenced the growth of Kolkata.
2. Describe one impact that migration has had on the city.
3. Name two problems that the city is currently facing.
4. Outline some of the factors contributing to urban sprawl in Kolkata.
5. Describe any two government proposals for future growth.

EXAM LINK (OL)

Urban Growth in a Continental/Subcontinental Region (30 marks)

Describe and explain the reasons for the growth of an urban area in a continental/subcontinental region (not in Europe) that you have studied.

2017, Q5C

Marking Scheme:
Description/explanation = 10 SRPs × 3 marks

EXAM LINK (HL)

Urban Development (30 marks)

Examine the factors that have influenced the development of one urban area in a continental/subcontinental region (not in Europe) that you have studied.

2018, Q6B

Marking Scheme:
Examination = 15 SRPs × 2 marks

EXAMINATION QUESTIONS
ORDINARY LEVEL

Long Question

1. Economic Activities – Continental/Subcontinental Region

Explain any two of the following with reference to a continental/subcontinental region (not in Europe) that you have studied.

- The factors influencing agriculture in the region
- The importance of manufacturing to the region
- The reasons why tourists are attracted to the region.

Marking Scheme:
Two activities named = 3 marks each
Activity 1 = 4 SRPs × 3 marks
Activity 2 = 4 SRPs × 3 marks

2018, Part Two, Section 1, Q5C (30 marks)

HIGHER LEVEL

Long Question

2. Urban Development

Examine the factors that have influenced the development of one urban area in a continental/subcontinental region (not in Europe) that you have studied.

Marking Scheme:
Examination = 15 SRPs × 2 marks

2018, Part Two, Section 1, Q6B (30 marks)

3. Agriculture in a Continental/Subcontinental Region

Explain the development of agriculture in a continental/subcontinental region (not in Europe) that you have studied, with reference to any two of the following factors.

- Soils
- Markets
- Relief.

Marking Scheme:
Discussion of factor 1 = 8 SRPs × 2 marks
Discussion of factor 2 = 7 SRPs × 2 marks

2013, Part Two, Section 1, Q5B (30 marks)

Revision Summary

Physical Processes

Climate
- Varied: savannah, semi-arid, desert, mountain, monsoon
- Cool, dry season, Oct–Feb: low temperatures, high pressure, dry winds from land to sea; retreating monsoon (southern peninsula, Sri Lanka)
- Hot, wet season, June–Sept: high temperatures, low pressure – rain-bearing trade winds

Relief and drainage
- **Himalayan Mountains:** 2,500 km – world's tallest mountain range – formed 40–50 mn years ago – frequent earthquakes and landslides – snow on high peaks, active glaciers
- **Ganges Plain:** Thar Desert to Ganges Delta – drained by the Ganges – melting snow, flooding – alluvium deposits – divides into distributaries at Bay of Bengal
- **Deccan Plateau:** South of Ganges Plain, bordered by Ghats – basalt plateau formed from lava – drainage by eastward-flowing rivers
- **Coastal lowlands:** Eastern Coastal Plain, three main rivers – Western Coastal Plain, short, fast rivers

Soils
- Alluvial soils: annual river deposits; Ganges Plain, Eastern Coastal Plain, river valleys
- Black soils (regur soils): weathering of basalt in Deccan Plateau; high clay content – moisture retention
- Red soils: weathering of igneous rocks; Deccan Plateau
- Laterite soils: leaching activity of monsoon climate strip minerals except iron, aluminium; Western Ghats, Eastern Ghats, West Bengal, Assam
- Desert soils: dry, infertile; Thar Desert

Primary Economic Activities: Other

Forestry
- Raw materials for construction industry
- Tropical rain forests (Western Ghats, Assam): hardwoods
- Tropical deciduous forests (monsoon forests, Himalayan foothills): teak, sandalwood, bamboo
- Clearance for agriculture – deforestation
- Government-led projects for sustainable forestry, protected zones, reforestation

Fishing
- Major fishing ports (Kochi, Chennai)
- Provides employment and food
- Overfishing – growth in aquaculture – global producer (prawns)

Mining and energy
- Coal: domestic use, power stations (Orissa)
- Iron ore: decline – falling prices and environmental concerns; Khetri copper mine
- Hydroelectric power: potential sites along Himalayan rivers and Deccan Plateau
- Nuclear energy: important but opposition increasing

Primary Economic Activities: Agriculture

Physical factors: climate
- Monsoon climate influences agricultural cycle
- Summer crops (kharif) June–Nov.: rice, cotton, millet
- Winter crops (Rabi) Nov.–March: wheat, barley
- Rice and tea – well-suited to monsoon climate
- Deccan Plateau – low rainfall – irrigation from river valleys

Physical factors: relief
- Lower Himalayas: gentle slopes – mixed crop and livestock farming (Himachal Pradesh)
- Himalayas: steep valleys, soil runoff, landslides; terrace subsistence farming on lower slopes
- South-facing slopes – ideal for fruit crops and vegetables
- Flood plains of valleys – suitable for crops
- Lowlands Ganges Plain – flooding, good for rice
- Double cropping (wheat after rice)
- Low land in Ganges Deltas – intensive farming, some flooding
- Western Coastal Plain – deltas farmed

Physical factors: soils
- Alluvial soils: support subsistence farming; covers Ganges Plain – most productive in India
- Black soils: moisture retaining, ideal for cotton farming (Maharashtra)
- Red soils: low mineral content – wheat, millet production
- Laterite soils: acidic, low moisture – unsuitable for agriculture
- Desert soils: infertile; high potash content – potential

Socio-economic factors
- Population 1.2 bn – agriculture for food production
- Subsistence agriculture common; excess sold in markets
- Rice production, tea harvesting – labour intensive – jobs and income
- Population growth – more land required
- Mechanisation – increase output but reduce employment
- Widespread spice production
- Second-largest world exporter of beef; Hindu objections – farming water buffalo

Green Revolution
- 1970s – use of high-yielding, pest-resistant seeds, fertilisers and pesticides to increase food supply
- Educate farmers, introduce modern methods
- Dam and irrigation projects to increase employment
- Production of hydroelectric power – industrialisation, improved living
- **Result:** increased food production; surplus sold – income – mechanisation – reduced employment – migration – higher input costs – small farmers struggled

Challenges facing agriculture
- **Land ownership:** unequal ownership – subsistence farming – renting – no security, no incentive to improve

Landscapes

Secondary Economic Activities: Manufacturing

Physical factors
- Weight-losing raw materials attract manufacturing industry to locate close by
- Coal deposits (Orissa, NE) – growth of iron, steel, fertiliser industries nearby
- Iron ore deposits – iron and steel manufacturing (TATA, Jamshedpur)
- Copper deposits (Khetri, Rajasthan) – engineering industries
- Sugar cane – production plants (Maharashtra)
- Cotton mills – close to textile manufacturing market (Mumbai)
- Jute (grown in West Bengal) supplies mills in Kolkata
- Hydroelectric power (Hirakud Dam, Orrisa) supplies electrometallurgical industries

Socio-economic factors: labour
- Huge labour pool – 1.2 bn
- Urban industrial concentrations – Mumbai, Kolkata
- Low labour costs, skilled English-speaking workers – attractive to foreign multinationals (Mitsubishi)
- Third-level education, science centres – skilled workforce – aeronautics and IT industries
- Pharmaceutical production centres (Mumbai, Chennai)
- Restrictive labour laws reduce competition

Socio-economic factors: infrastructure
- Transport infrastructure vital for reliable and low-cost distribution of raw materials
- Upland: poor transport – cottage-type production (Himalayas)
- Lowland: rapid transport networks good for perishable materials – food processing on Ganges Plain
- Ports: Kolkata, Mumbai, Madras: major manufacturing and export centres
- Railways: transport of bulky manufactured goods (iron, steel)
- Roads: Golden Quadrilateral links main cities; HGVs – possible for industries to locate in smaller urban centres

Socio-economic factors: markets
- Population 1.2 bn – huge market potential
- Rural areas: local markets, small industries
- Multinational plants – seek access to market
- Urban centres (Delhi, Mumbai) – large consumer industries (Nestle, Coca-Cola)
- Increasing affluence – bigger demand for cars and technology
- ASEAN India Free Trade area – access to Asian markets
- Exports to EU – €44 bn

Socio-economic factors: government
- Many state-owned enterprises – inefficient, non-profitable
- Industrial parks; 200 Special Economic Zones
- Plans for industrial corridors to attract international industry
- Foreign direct investment since 1991 – large multinationals
- Make in India campaign 2014 – simplify business

Challenges facing manufacturing
- Demand for energy from manufacturing and domestic usage outstrips supply
- Power outages

Tertiary Economic Activities: Tourism

Physical factors
- **Accessibility:** good access – 50 national, 12 international airports – railway system provides links
- **Climate:** variety: snow-capped Himalayas, sandy Thar Desert, Assam tropical rainforests
- **Landscapes:** trekking in Himalayas, stay with local family – eco-tourism – employment for remote areas, funding for natural habitats, greater awareness of environmental issues

Socio-economic factors
- Historical sites (Taj Mahal, Agra)
- Cultural interest – Buddhist, Hindu religions, Varanasi spiritual capital
- Wellness tourism – ashrams
- Medical tourism: lower-cost medical procedures

Government
- Indian Tourism Development Corporation – Incredible India campaign

Challenges facing tourism
- Street beggars – rotting rubbish – traffic congestion, noise and air pollution

Tertiary Economic Activities: Transport

Historical factors
- 1850–1947: British colony – Britain built three main ports (Bombay, Calcutta, Madras) as export and import points and railways to carry raw materials

Physical factors: relief
- Gentle relief of Ganges Plain – railway lines
- Steep slopes and valleys in Himalayas limit rail construction
- Deltas of Ganges, Brahmaputra – less railways
- Steep gradients of mountains limit road network and building protection increases cost
- Landslides – road blockages, disruption, costly repairs

Physical factors: climate
- Monsoon flooding – rural roads unusable, railways disrupted, landslides block roads
- Desert climate, Rajasthan – low population, poor railway network, little investment

Socio-economic factors
- Commuter transport systems – access to commercial centres
- Indian rail network employs 1.5 mn – support formal and informal economies
- Heavy urban road traffic – congestion, air and noise pollution
- Land for new roads – displacement of people in slums
- Planned upgrade of airports

Political factors
- Public Private Partnership (PPP) schemes finance transport projects, e.g. high-speed rail between Mumbai, Delhi and Kolkata; upgrading of ports

Challenges facing transport
- Major capital investment needed
- Upgrades will result in job losses – economic impacts
- Improved information systems needed

Human Processes

Population density
- Over 1.2 bn; forecast to become world's most populated country by 2050
- Av. population density = 396.7 persons per km²
- TFR declining 3.83 (1995) – 2.48 (2015)
- Life expectancy risen to 69.4 (women), 66.9 (men)

Migration
- After marriage, women move to live with in-laws
- Men migrate to urban centres in search of employment
- Exploitation – poor wages and conditions, live in slums

Population distribution: physical factors
- **Uplands of Himalayas**: harsh climate, inaccessible – low population; numbers increase in lower slopes
- **Ganges Plain**: lowland relief, fertile soils – high population densities
- **West Bengal**: good agricultural conditions – high population density
- **Deccan Plateau**: river valleys densely populated; interior uplands lower population
- **Coastal lowlands**: agricultural potential, fishing, lowland relief – high population
- **Gujarat and Rajasthan**: arid conditions – lower population density
- **Punjab**: use of irrigation, higher population
- **Tropical rainforests**: inaccessible – low population

Population distribution: socio-economic factors
- 66% population – rural – importance of agriculture
- Two largest cities: Mumbi (18 mn), Delhi (16 mn)
- Rural-urban migration – spread of cities (Kolkata, Chennai)
- Slums around cities – high density
- Increased foreign investment – increase in migrants (Bangalore)
- Mineral resources, manufacturing in Orissa – attracts settlement
- Jute cultivation, textile industry (West Bengal) – migrant workers, high population

Religion
- Hinduism, Islam, Christianity, Sikhism, Buddhism
- Caste system – exploitation – social injustices
- Caste-based discrimination now against the law but evidence remains in rural areas
- Independence from GB 1947 – fewer Muslims in India – tensions over slaughter of cattle
- Sikhs (65% Punjab population) seek independent status

Language
- 23 languages officially recognised; 2 official languages: English, Hindi

Urbanisation
- Government legislation and directives on urban planning to control urban growth
- Main issues: housing, drinking water, sanitation, waste, transport, traffic congestion

23 THE COMPLEXITY OF REGIONS I

> **LEARNING INTENTIONS** — Syllabus Links: 2.3
>
> By the end of this chapter I will be able to:
> - describe how economic, political and cultural activities interact within a region;
> - explain the implications of cultural groups interacting within political regions;
> - describe and evaluate issues relating to economic union, political union, sovereignty and their likely impact on the future development of the EU.

KEYWORDS
Anglo-Irish Treaty
Good Friday Agreement
smuggling
border
Troubles
Partition
Special EU Programmes Body
INTERREG
hinterland
Brexit

The Interaction of Economic, Political and Cultural Activities in a Region

The study of regions illustrates the geographical complexity of the interaction between economic, cultural and physical processes.

CASE STUDY: THE REPUBLIC OF IRELAND AND NORTHERN IRELAND

The **Anglo-Irish Treaty** of 1921 ended the Irish War of Independence and divided the island of Ireland into two distinct political states: the Irish Free State (later the Republic of Ireland) and Northern Ireland (**Figs 23.1, 23.2**). Northern Ireland viewed the Free State as a threat to its existence and was eager to maintain strong economic, political and cultural links with Great Britain, while the Irish Free State was opposed to partition. Interaction between the governments was therefore minimal both at the administrative and political level. However, the two states soon formed strong links in terms of sporting and cultural activities. Since the **Good Friday Agreement** in 1998, interaction between the two regions at all levels has changed greatly.

↓ **Fig. 23.2** The six counties of Northern Ireland and the border counties of the Republic.

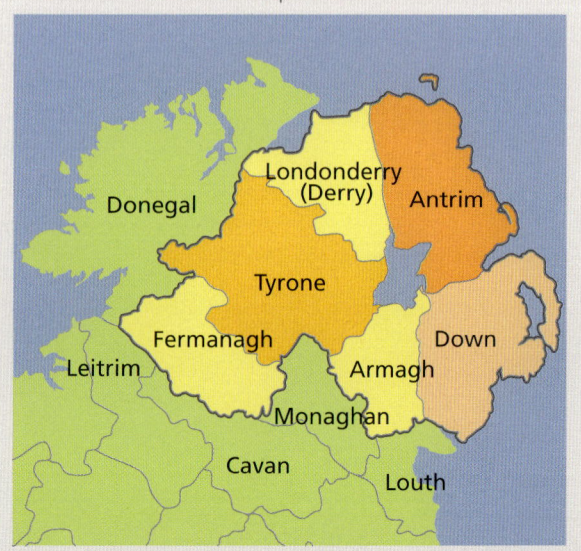

← **Fig. 23.1** Northern Ireland and the Republic of Ireland.

Economic interaction

In 1923, **customs posts** were set up along the border, where goods being traded between North and South were inspected and **customs levies** charged. People **smuggling** goods over the border to avoid the payment of duties soon became a problem for law enforcement and customs officers on both sides.

This new border cut off many towns on both sides from their natural hinterland; long-established economic connections were weakened and business declined.

Throughout the **Troubles (1968–1998)**, border controls, military checkpoints and road blockages (minor roads that had no permanent control posts) by Northern authorities led to increased difficulty and costs in the **cross-border movement** of goods and people.

Declining numbers of international visitors and a huge reduction in visitors travelling from the South to the North had a negative impact on the Northern Irish tourism sector.

The **Belfast Agreement**, more commonly known as the **Good Friday Agreement** was signed in 1998 and provided for the creation of a number of bodies and initiatives to improve economic interaction, including **InterTradeIreland** and **Tourism Ireland** (**Fig. 23.3**). According to InterTradeIreland, the total value of cross-border trade in 2017 was over €7 billion. Agriculture-related activity forms a substantial part of this trade.

↑ **Fig. 23.3** The Good Friday Agreement supported North–South tourism and trade initiatives.

Political interaction

After the Partition of Ireland in 1921, both parliaments operated independently of each other and with minimal interaction. It was not until 1965 that the first ever meeting between an Irish Taoiseach and the Prime Minister of Northern Ireland took place. During the **Troubles**, suspicion and mistrust on both sides discouraged political dialogue.

The Good Friday Agreement 1998 consisted of three strands:

- **Strand 1: Internal arrangements** – a Northern Ireland Assembly was created and a power-sharing executive established (**Fig. 23.4**);
- **Strand 2: North–South relationships** – the North–South Ministerial Council was established and a number of North–South implementation bodies were created (**Fig. 23.5**);
- **Strand 3: East–West relationships** – the British–Irish Council and the British–Irish Intergovernmental Conference involving Northern Ireland, England, Scotland, Wales and the Republic were established.

Under the Good Friday Agreement, the North–South Ministerial Council led to political interaction at the highest government levels.

The **Special EU Programmes Body**, which manages cross-border EU Structural Funds programmes under the **Peace Initiatives** (currently Peace IV), and **INTERREG** programmes, which support cross-border projects in the EU, have also contributed to increased political interaction.

↑ **Fig. 23.4** Northern Ireland Parliament, Stormont.

↑ **Fig. 23.5** Irish Parliament, Leinster House.

Landscapes

Cultural interaction

The border cut communities off from each other and separated towns and villages from their natural hinterland. Opportunities for **social interaction** that activities such as shopping, going to pubs and dances had provided in the past were lost.

The **GAA** had been formed on a 32-county basis. However, participants came almost exclusively from the **Nationalist** side, and cross-border travel to games usually involved one community only (**Fig. 23.6**).

↑ **Fig. 23.6** Sport has contributed to North–South cultural interaction.

Members of the Irish **rugby** team are drawn from both North and South, and support and involvement in rugby crosses religious and political divisions. Many northern **Unionists** saw no contradiction in travelling to Dublin to support Ireland's rugby team while strongly opposing greater economic or political interaction.

Religion

The Presbyterian, Roman Catholic and Anglican churches have an all-Ireland structure that enables links and allows cross-border ecumenical initiatives to be developed. The **Orange Order**, a Protestant organisation, has a number of groups (lodges) in the Republic (**Fig. 23.7**).

Music

Comhaltas Ceoltóirí Éireann is an all-Ireland organisation promoting Irish music. County, provincial and all-Ireland Fleadhs are important elements in North–South cultural interaction.

↑ **Fig. 23.7** Orange Order parade, Rossnowlagh, Co. Donegal, 2016.

Brexit

The United Kingdom's decision to leave the EU will have major implications for North–South interaction. There is great uncertainty about the future and the outcome of the negotiations. Issues such as the **border, movement of goods and people, trade, the implications for funding and support of EU initiatives** under the Special EU Programmes Body will have to be addressed.

Chapter 17 The Concept of a Region

EXAM LINK (HL)

Economic, Political and Cultural Activities (30 marks)
Examine the interaction between economic, political and/or cultural activities in any region that you have studied.
2013, Q6C

Marking Scheme:
Examination = 15 SRPs × 2 marks

CHECK YOUR LEARNING

1. Name three different types of North–South economic interactions.
2. Identify four different cultural interactions between the North and South.

The Interaction of Different Cultural Groups and Political Regions

Throughout history, smaller regions have been annexed to form larger political units. While many of these became assimilated, others have nurtured separate identities and are seeking their independence. Catalonia in Spain is an example of such a region.

CASE STUDY: CATALONIA, SPAIN

Introduction

In Spain, **Galicia**, the **Basque region** and **Catalonia** are three of 17 **autonomous** regions that are governed by the National Constitution but have their own devolved powers (Statutes of Autonomy; **Fig. 23.8**). The Constitution recognises the existence of different nationalities, languages and regions, but clearly states that the **unity** of Spain as a country cannot be destroyed.

KEYWORDS		
autonomous	Catalan nationalism	austerity
Spanish Civil War	independence referendum	implications

Historical background

Catalonia has been a part of Spain since the 15th century. When Spain became a republic in 1931, Catalonia was given broad autonomy but after the **Spanish Civil War** (1936–1939), General Franco revoked autonomy, suppressed **Catalan nationalism** and restricted the use of the Catalan language.

Full autonomy was restored in 1979 with the establishment of the **autonomous community** of Catalonia. While Catalonia has long campaigned for independence, calls for action began to increase as the **economic recession** of the late 2000s took hold (**Fig. 23.9**).

The **Catalan independence referendum**, held on 1 October 2017, was declared illegal by Spain's constitutional court. The organisers claimed a voter support of 90%, however, voter turnout was only 43% as most supporters of union with Spain **boycotted** the vote.

↑ **Fig. 23.8** Map showing Galicia, the Basque region and Catalonia.

On 27 October 2017, after declaring independence, the Catalan parliament was **dissolved** by the Spanish government and an election called for December. The Catalan 'president' and four others fled to Belgium, accused of rebellion, and two ex-ministers were imprisoned in Spain.

The election resulted in an overall majority for pro-independence parties, who won 70 of the 135 seats.

In June 2018, after ending direct control from the central government in Madrid, Catalan nationalists regained control of the parliament of the region.

The trial of former ministers of the regional government for their roles in the independence referendum began in Madrid in February 2019.

Economic arguments for independence

> Population of Catalonia: 7.5 million
> Population of Ireland: 4.7 million

All of Spain's autonomous regions **remit taxes** collected back to the central government in Madrid. During the recession in the late 2000s, **austerity** measures forced the national government to reduce contributions to Catalonia and other regions.

Angered by the perception that the poorer regions were getting more while the government of Catalonia was forced to cut spending (e.g. reduced health services), support for independence began to grow.

Supporters claim an independent Catalonia would be ranked **10th in the EU** in terms of **GDP per capita** and 15th in terms of population.

Economic arguments against independence

Following the unlawful referendum in 2017 and amid fears of secession, over 1,300 companies moved their headquarters to other parts of Spain to secure **free market access** to Spain and the EU. This suggests that outflows of capital and a slowdown of inward investment is highly likely if Catalan independence became a reality.

Setting up an independent state would include paying the cost of services currently provided by the national government, e.g. social welfare, and the state would therefore be forced to borrow large sums of money in order to meet these costs.

Cultural arguments

All education in the region is carried out in the **Catalan language**. In 2013, a new national law stated that parents' desire for greater use of Spanish in schools must be granted. Catalans have viewed this as an attack on their culture. They insist that central government is attempting to destroy their culture and language, and that independence is the only way to ensure their survival.

Implications of independence

To cover the cost of setting up an independent Catalonia, the new government would have to borrow money, however, lenders would be reluctant to loan money given the uncertainty surrounding the new state's **economic and political viability**.

Once independent, Catalonia says it would apply for **EU membership**. This would not be easy as the approval of all member states will be required, and Spain would almost definitely oppose it.

Other EU countries facing issues with **nationalism** would likely oppose the application because of the **implications** this would have for other regions seeking independence (e.g. **Flanders, Belgium**).

Fig. 23.9 Pro-independence rally, Barcelona, October 2017.

In 2019, the Catalan government's demands for a referendum or an advance towards a republic continued, though the national government in Madrid says that such questions cannot even be discussed, let alone negotiated.

CHECK YOUR LEARNING

1. Draw an outline map of Spain showing and naming two regions of nationalities.
2. Give three economic arguments in favour of Catalan independence.
3. Give two economic arguments for opposing Catalan independence.
4. Name two implications of Catalan independence.

The Future of Europe and the European Union

Future development of the EU will involve proposals for greater political and economic **integration** between member states and the addition of new member states. Greater integration and enlargement face political and economic challenges and concerns about **sovereignty**.

Political union

Greater **political union** has been an expressed aim of the EU, however, what form it might take has still not been defined. Two possible choices are:

- **supranational** union, where the EU would have the greatest power;
- **intergovernmental** union, where member states would create EU regulations.

Tensions have always existed between those members seeking an ever-closer union and those preferring the intergovernmental model. A number of issues – notably the transfer of greater decision-making power from individual governments to the European Commission – have caused division among members, making the dream of greater political union seem more remote.

The refugee crisis

In 2015, over one million **refugees and migrants** entered the EU. Responses to the crisis saw actions being taken by individual countries rather than an EU-wide response (**Fig. 23.10**).

Front-line states such as Italy and Greece – where the majority of refugees enter Europe – claim they are overburdened because of the **Dublin Regulation**, and are not being supported by other member countries. Germany's decision in 2016 that it would no longer apply the Dublin Regulation to Syrian asylum seekers was seen as abandoning agreed procedures and failing to consider the **implications** for the wider EU. The move created political tensions between member countries.

The crisis is threatening the **Schengen Area**, which consists of 26 European states that have removed controls and checks at their mutual borders. Some countries including Germany, Austria, Denmark and Sweden, have instituted temporary internal borders (**Fig. 23.11**).

Efforts to establish EU-wide redistribution and resettlement programmes are opposed by some members who object to being forced to participate in them.

Chapter 24 The Complexity of Regions II

KEYWORDS

integration
sovereignty
political union
refugee
Dublin Regulation
Schengen Area
Eurozone
Brexit
solidarity

Dublin Regulation: This EU law declares that the first state in which a person seeks asylum is usually responsible for processing their claim.

← Fig. 23.10 March supporting refugees, London 2016.

Landscapes

Fig. 23.11 Migrants cross into Hungary through an unfinished border, 2015.

The rise of Eurosceptic parties

In recent years, economic stagnation, youth unemployment, austerity measures, the Eurozone crisis, a perceived '**democratic deficit**' and heightened fears about migrants have led to growth in support for **Eurosceptic** parties (e.g. the **National Rally party** – *Le Rassemblement National* – in France).

Many governments fear that accepting more asylum seekers and refugees could increase support for far-right, anti-EU, anti-immigrant political parties. Islamist fundamentalist terror attacks in London, Barcelona and Paris have increased opposition to migrants from Muslim-majority countries.

Democratic deficit: A term to describe the way institutions suffer from a lack of democracy and are not accessible to ordinary citizens.

Eurosceptic: Someone opposed to participation in the European Union.

Europhile: A supporter of participation in the European Union.

Brexit

Further EU political union will require major constitutional changes and necessitate the holding of referendums in some member states. The UK's **Brexit** referendum result highlighted a number of concerns including **migration policy**, **the free movement of peoples** and **the democratic deficit** (Fig. 23.12). All of these issues must be addressed by the EU before proceeding with further political integration.

→ Fig. 23.12 UK referendum Leave campaign poster.

Lack of trust

The migration crisis and the effects of economic collapse in Greece have led to increased ill feeling and a lack of trust among member states.

The principle of EU **solidarity**, with members supporting each other, seemed to some to be absent in the approach taken to **Greece and its economic crisis**, where policies appeared to be punishing it for past mistakes.

The dominant position of **Germany** throughout the Eurozone crisis was also seen by some as evidence of the claim that political union will lead to the richer states dominating and shaping Europe according to their interests.

CHECK YOUR LEARNING

1. Name two issues that are affecting proposals for greater political union.
2. Identify three problems the refugee crisis has caused.
3. Explain the following terms: democratic deficit, Eurosceptic.

Challenges to the Economic Union

Economic achievements

Some of the economic achievements of the EU include increased prosperity, capital transfers between rich and poor regions and the creation of the single market for goods and services. Steps towards greater economic union include the introduction of the **euro currency** and the creation of the **European Central Bank** (Fig. 23.13).

Economic challenges

The **Eurozone debt crisis of 2008** presented a serious threat to European economies and to the single currency (Fig. 23.14). New strategies to deal with the problems included the creation of a number of bodies and policies.

- The **European Support Mechanism (ESM)** supports countries in financial difficulties;
- The **Fiscal Compact** was designed to prevent countries from getting into debt. Members agree to have their domestic budgets examined. This is viewed by some as an important step on the road to full economic unity, and by others as evidence of the erosion of economic independence.

The proposal for a **fiscal union** by 2025 – in which decisions about the collection and spending of taxes are made by common institutions shared by the participating governments – is supported by those who claim it will impose strict control on government spending and will bring strength and stability. This union would theoretically be run by a Finance Ministry with full powers and proper democratic oversight.

Opponents of the proposal believe that solutions to economic issues should be tailored to the needs of individual countries rather than being based on an EU-wide policy.

KEYWORDS

euro
European Support Mechanism (ESM)
Fiscal Compact
fiscal union
Brexit

↑ **Fig. 23.13** The European Central Bank.

Fiscal: Revenue that the government collects through taxes.

Enlargement

Opposition to increased membership is growing in some countries as there is a feeling that the EU cannot afford the **cost** of these new member states.

Budgetary waste

Each year, the EU Court of Auditors reports instances where EU funds have been mismanaged and misappropriated. **Wastage of money** is particularly frustrating for many citizens given that within their countries **EU-promoted austerity packages** have reduced their living standards.

Brexit

The loss to the EU budget when the UK leaves the EU will be over €10 billion. This shortfall will have **implications for all budgets** including the Common Agricultural Policy and the European Regional Development Fund.

The population of the EU will be reduced from 508 million people to 444 million people, reducing the size of the Single Market.

Political uncertainty creates **economic uncertainty**, impacting on growth within the EU. Brexit has shocked the European Union and its full economic effects will only evolve as the UK negotiates its departure and finally leaves.

The European Parliament rotates between Strasbourg and Brussels. It sits for four days in each month in Strasbourg. This rotation is estimated to cost €114 million every year.

Landscapes

CHECK YOUR LEARNING

1. Name two initiatives towards economic union in the EU.
2. List one argument for and one against fiscal union.
3. Name two issues affecting greater economic union.

KEYWORDS

Eurozone crisis
Troika
austerity

Sovereignty

Sovereignty is the right a state has to govern itself without interference from outside. Within the European Union, common passports and driving licences are viewed by some as evidence of a loss of sovereignty.

Eurosceptics believe that too much decision-making power is now centred in Brussels.

The response to the **Eurozone crisis** raised concerns about a loss of sovereignty. The **Troika**, which consisted of the **European Commission**, the **European Central Bank** and the **International Monetary Fund**, set out strict conditions that would apply to any financial assistance given to governments during the crisis. In Ireland the government was forced along a path of spending cuts, increased taxation and revenue collection. In Greece, similar **austerity** measures led to great hardship and political unrest.

The impact of austerity programmes has led to the rise of **Eurosceptic** political parties opposed to the erosion of national sovereignty.

↑ **Fig. 23.14** Anti-austerity protest, Athens 2015.

In some cases, countries can negotiate opt-outs from proposed legislation or treaties, for example, Ireland and the UK opted out of the Schengen Agreement.

Revelations regarding **tax evasion** strategies by multinational companies have resulted in the EU promising to take more central control of **corporation tax** policy. This will have major implications for Ireland's corporate tax rate and our sovereign right to set these rates.

National governments and the media can be accused of using Brussels as a **scapegoat** and blaming it for having to implement unpopular policies. Irish government spokespersons claimed that it was directives from Brussels that forced them to introduce water charges.

Often the prospect of fines from Brussels for repeated failure to comply with directives is given more attention than the failure of governments to comply in the first instance.

EXAM LINK (HL)

European Union (30 marks)

Discuss the potential challenges facing the future development of the European Union with reference to factors such as political union, economic union and sovereignty.

2018, Q6C

Marking Scheme:
Potential challenges identified = 2 marks + 2 marks
Discussion = 13 SRPs × 2 marks

CHECK YOUR LEARNING

1. Explain the term sovereignty.
2. List four issues relating to sovereignty in the context of the EU.

EXAMINATION QUESTIONS
HIGHER LEVEL

Long Question

1. Economic, Political and Cultural Activities

Examine the interaction between economic, political and/or cultural activities in any region that you have studied.

2013, Part Two, Section 1, Q6C (30 marks)

Marking Scheme:
Examination = 15 SRPs × 2 marks
Credit two named examples of interaction = 2 marks each

Revision Summary

Economic, Political, Cultural Interaction Case Study: Ireland	Interaction of Cultural Groups and Political Regions Case Study: Catalonia, Spain
• **Anglo-Irish Treaty 1921** ends War of Independence – Republic and Northern Ireland • NI – links with GB; Republic opposed partition – interaction minimal • **1998 Good Friday Agreement** – increased interaction **Economic interaction** • 1923 customs posts at border – custom levies – smuggling • Troubles (1968–1998) – checkpoints, road blockages made cross-border movement difficult • Tourism industry affected • Belfast Agreement (Good Friday Agreement) 1998 – improvements in economic interaction: InterTradeIreland, Tourism Ireland **Political interaction** • Anglo-Irish Treaty 1921: Independent parliaments North and South • 1965: First meeting of Taoiseach and Prime Minister NI • Troubles: suspicion – no interaction • Good Friday Agreement 1998 – three strands: internal arrangements; North–South relationships; East–West relationships • Special EU Programmes Body, Peace Initiatives, INTERREG support cross-border projects **Cultural interaction** • Border – divided communities • Sport: GAA – 32-county but mostly nationalist; rugby – support from nationalists and unionists • Religion: all-Ireland structure; cross-border initiatives • Music: all-Ireland Comhaltas Ceoltóirí Éireann, Fleadhs • Brexit: impact on North–South interaction	• Catalonia autonomy 1931; revoked after Spanish Civil War (1936–1939); restored 1979 • 17 autonomous regions include Galicia, Basque region, Catalonia • Constitution – recognises nationalities, languages and regions but Spain must remain united • Increased calls for independence in 2000s – economic recession • Illegal Catalan Independence referendum 2017 – election, majority for pro-independence • 2018 Catalan nationalists regain control of region **Economic arguments for independence** • Autonomous regions remit taxes to Madrid • Recession 2000s – Madrid reduces money to Catalonia – forced cuts – support for independence • Independency – higher EU ranking (GDP, population) **Economic arguments against independence** • Unlawful referendum 2017 – company hqs moved out – outflow of capital, slow inward investment • Est. independent state – huge financial costs **Cultural arguments** • All education in Catalan • 2013 national law to use Spanish in schools – viewed as attack on Catalan culture • Independence – survival of culture and language **Implications of independence** • Set-up cost – borrowing – but lenders uncertain about viability • EU membership likely opposed by Spain • Implications for independence demands in other countries

Future of Europe and EU

Political union
- Options: supranational union; intergovernmental union
- Divisions on where balance of power should rest

Refugee crisis
- 2015: 1m refugees and migrants enter EU
- Response to crisis individual, not EU-wide – political tensions
- Schengen Area (26 European states) – temporary internal borders
- Opposition to EU-wide resettlement programmes

Rise of Eurosceptics
- Triggers: economic stagnation, youth unemployment, austerity, Eurozone crisis, democratic deficit
- Govt fears increased support for refugees = support for far-right, anti-EU, anti-immigration parties
- Concerns highlighted in Brexit referendum result

Lack of trust
- Greek situation – lack of EU solidarity – ill feeling
- German dominance in Eurozone crisis – mistrust

Challenges to the EU

Economic achievements
- Increased prosperity
- Capital transfers between rich and poor regions
- Single market
- Euro currency, European Central Bank

Economic challenges
- Eurozone debt crisis 2008 – threat to EU economies
- Strategies: ESM; Fiscal Compact
- Proposal for a fiscal union by 2025 – support divided

Enlargement
- Growing opposition to increased membership – cost concerns

Budgetary waste
- Mismanagement of EU funds
- Vexing for those countries with EU-promoted austerity packages

Brexit
- Loss of 8 bn to EU budget – implications
- Reduced EU population – reduced Single Market
- Political uncertainty – economic uncertainty

Sovereignty

- The right of a state to govern itself without interference
- Common passports and driving licences viewed as loss of sovereignty
- Eurozone crisis response – concerns: strict financial conditions by the Troika (impact on Ireland and Greece)
- Threats to sovereignty: austerity programmes; increased EU control on corporation tax
- EU used as scapegoat for unpopular policies (water charges) and fines

24 THE COMPLEXITY OF REGIONS II

LEARNING INTENTIONS
Syllabus Links: 2.4

By the end of this chapter I will be able to:
- describe the causes and impacts of changes to the boundaries and extent of language regions;
- describe the ways in which changes to political boundaries can impact on cultural groups;
- identify and name on maps and tables the countries and stages of EU enlargement;
- outline the stages in the development and expansion of the EU;
- explain how EU enlargement has impacted on member countries.

Changes in the Boundaries and Extent of Language Regions

For language regions to survive, the language of that region (e.g. **Irish** in the Gaeltacht) must be in everyday use. Immigration in response to positive economic conditions can dilute the number of native speakers and put pressure on the language. This often leads to tensions, as was the case with the migration of French speakers into areas of Brussels, which is located in Flemish-speaking Flanders. Out-migration due to negative economic conditions reduces the numbers of speakers causing the region to reduce in extent (e.g. **the Gaeltacht**).

KEYWORDS
Gaeltacht
extent
Great Famine
migration
usage
government

CASE STUDY: GAELTACHT REGIONS

The **Gaeltacht** is an example of a **language region** whose extent and boundaries have changed over time.

Defining the extent of the Gaeltacht areas is a process that began in 1926 with the **Gaeltacht Commission**. It was not until the 1950s that the Gaeltacht was clearly defined in spatial terms. It consisted of areas along the western seaboard including **Counties Donegal, Mayo, Galway, Kerry** and on the south coast **Ring in County Waterford**. Since then, **Ráth Cairn** and **Baile Ghib in Co. Meath, West Muskerry in Co. Cork** and **Brandon** and **Cloghane in west Co. Kerry** have been added (Fig. 24.1).

Population and migration

The Gaeltacht areas were severely impacted by the **Great Famine** of 1847–1849, when death and migration led to large population decline. Since then, **migration** has had a continuous impact on the demographics of the Gaeltacht.

Between 2006 and 2011, the population of Gaeltacht areas increased by over 6,000. However, the 2016 census revealed that in the period 2011–2016, population had declined by over 1,000.

↑ Fig. 24.1 Gaeltacht areas.

Population increase does not necessarily translate into an increase in the number of Irish speakers. The largest increases in population in the Gaeltacht have been in Galway, where the population residing in the Gaeltacht has expanded by 9.9% (4,472 people). This is due to the growth of **Galway city**, and it is important to note that many of the new residents are not **native Irish speakers**.

The populations of the Gaeltacht areas of Donegal and Mayo are in decline, and a task force has been set up to address the issue in the **Iveragh Peninsula, Co. Kerry**. The **Mayo Gaeltacht** has seen continual population decline since the 1960s; its current population of 9,340 is 29.6% lower than it was in 1966 (14,762). The main cause of this decline is **out-migration** due to lack of **jobs** and **investment** in Gaeltacht areas.

> **Irish Language Networks:** Areas that have achieved sufficient community and state support for the Irish language (e.g. Loughrea, Co. Galway; Ennis, Co. Clare; Clondalkin, Dublin). Foras na Gaeilge has responsibility for the preparation and implementation of language plans.
>
> **Foras na Gaeilge:** A North–South language body set up under the Good Friday Agreement with the aim of promoting the Irish language.
>
> **Gaeltacht Service Towns:** Towns situated in or adjacent to Gaeltacht Language Planning Areas that have a population of least 1,000 and that play a significant role in providing public services, recreational, social and commercial facilities to the Gaeltacht community (e.g. Daingean Uí Chúis, Tralee and Caherciveen, Co. Kerry).

Language use

Daily language usage within Gaeltacht areas also defines the extent of those areas. RTÉ Radió na Gaeltachta, established in 1972, and TG4, established in 1996, have helped to reduce the impact of English-language stations on daily Irish language usage (Fig. 24.2).

However, the 2016 census revealed that the number of people in Gaeltacht areas recorded as **daily speakers** has decreased from 23,175 in 2011 to 20,586 in 2016. The decline in language usage and the increasing use of English has added urgency to the need to ensure the survival of the language as an everyday medium.

↑ **Fig. 24.2** TG4 studios Baile na hAbhann, Co. Galway.

Changing boundaries of the Gaeltacht

The Gaeltacht Act was passed in 2012. Two of its most important goals were to define Gaeltacht areas by **linguistic criteria** instead of geographic area, and to focus **language planning** at a community level.

Under the act, Gaeltacht areas were re-designated as Gaeltacht Language Planning Areas. Twenty-six of these areas were identified, and with the support of **Údarás na Gaeltachta**, these areas were expected to devise language plans to ensure that the Irish language would be supported as the community and family language of the area (Fig. 24.3). Irish language planning officers would be appointed to oversee implementation of the plans. By early 2019, 13 Gaeltacht language plans had been generated and 10 language planning officers had been appointed.

The act also set out devices for the creation and implementation of language plans for areas located outside the existing Gaeltacht. These would help the areas achieve statutory recognition as either **Irish Language Networks** or as **Gaeltacht Service Towns**.

→ **Fig. 24.3** Gaeltacht signage.

Another government initiative, **Investing in Our Culture, Language and Heritage 2018–2027**, proposes the allocation of €105 million for Údarás Na Gaeltachta to invest in **job creation**. Providing secure employment will help to stabilise and, in the long term, strengthen populations in these peripheral areas.

> Chapter 17:
> The Concept of a Region
> Chapter 19:
> A Peripheral Irish Region – The Western Region

CHECK YOUR LEARNING

1. Name three Gaeltacht regions in Ireland.
2. Outline some of the changes to population that have occurred in Gaeltacht regions.
3. How did the 2012 Gaeltacht Act change the way Gaeltacht areas will be designated in future?
4. Explain the term Irish Language Networks and name two examples.
5. What are Gaeltacht Service Towns? Name any two.
6. Outline some of the proposals contained in the recent 2018–2027 government initiative.

Urban Growth and the Expansion of Cities

In 2014, 54% of the global population lived in urban areas, and the figure is expected to reach 60% by 2050. Urban areas are growing and expanding, and this presents many challenges for the people living in those areas.

Case studies examining the growth of urban areas can be found in *Chapter 18: A Core Irish Region – The Greater Dublin Area*, *Chapter 20: A Core European Region – The Paris Basin* and *Chapter 22: A Continental/Subcontinental Region – India*.

> Chapter 18:
> A Core Irish Region – The Greater Dublin Area
> Chapter 20
> A Core European Region – The Paris Basin
> Chapter 22:
> A Continental/Subcontinental Region – India

Changes in Political Boundaries and Their Impact on Cultural Groups

Throughout history, political boundaries have changed as territory was lost and gained by different states. Adjusting to these changing boundaries presented huge challenges for the people living in the affected areas.

KEYWORDS

Iron Curtain	Berlin Wall	brain drain
East Germany	reunification	centrally planned
West Germany	migration	

CASE STUDY: THE REUNIFICATION OF GERMANY

After the end of World War II, Europe was divided by the **Iron Curtain**. Germany, having lost the war, was divided into two separate sections – East and West – with Russia controlling **East Germany** and France, the USA and the UK controlling **West Germany**. The city of Berlin, located in East Germany, was divided into sections controlled by France, Great Britain, the USA and Russia respectively. In 1961, the **Berlin Wall** was erected to stop people escaping from the Russian-controlled East to the West.

When the Berlin Wall 'fell' in 1989, the process of **reunification** of the two former states began. While they shared a common language, the process had socio-economic and cultural impacts for the populations of East and West Germany.

> The Iron Curtain, which existed from 1946 to 1989, refers to the border between Western Europe and the communist countries of Eastern Europe.

Landscapes

Fig. 24.4 East and West Germany.

Fig. 24.5 Opening of the Berlin Wall, 1989.

Fig. 24.6 Abandoned chemical plant Rüdersdorf, former East Germany.

Fascist state: A state where government controls all aspects of life, and opposition is not tolerated.

Socio-economic impacts

There was a mass migration to the West in the immediate aftermath of reunification. In 2010, it was estimated that over two million people had left the former East Germany.

This **brain drain** impacted on **population structure**, leaving behind an ageing population who had to come to terms with the total collapse of their state and its workings.

In the East, subsidised crèches provided free care for babies, while kindergartens were provided free of charge for all children over four. Following reunification, the introduction of the West German model, where people pay for **childcare**, meant increased costs for East German families.

In the East, women were encouraged to participate in the workforce, and it was normal for **mothers** to work outside the home while rearing families. In the West, mothers were more likely to stay at home to raise their children. The newly unified Germany posed challenges for women in preserving their former roles.

Reunification is estimated to have cost the German economy the equivalent of over €1.3 trillion.

West Germany had an **open market economy** with no barriers to economic activities. East Germany, on the other hand, was a **centrally planned communist economy**, where all economic activity was state-owned and controlled, with state subsidies and guaranteed full employment. The transformation from a planned economy to a free, open market system had a catastrophic effect on the industrial sector. All subsidies and protections were removed and all state-controlled factories were sold. Many people lost their jobs when plants were closed or modernised. The **removal of state subsidies** and protections in the agricultural sector resulted in over 700,000 agricultural labourers losing their jobs. By 1994, unemployment rates in the East had reached 14%.

After almost 30 years, the economy of the area that previously formed East Germany has improved, but unemployment is higher than the former West Germany, and average wages are about 10% lower. **Productivity** is also lower than in the former West Germany.

Cultural impacts

East Germany was in existence for 40 years. During that time, the citizens developed their own cultural characteristics and also developed ideas about West Germany. For them, West Germany was the enemy.

The citizens of West Germany also developed their own cultural characteristics and regarded East Germany as a **fascist state**.

402

In former East Germany, the state controlled most aspects of life. The secret police (**STASI**) exerted huge influence and people were encouraged to spy and report on each other.

The new system of government meant that people now had to come to terms with being in control of their own lives with new freedoms, but also without the supports they had become accustomed to.

Many former East Germans felt some elements of their former way of life should have been kept to prevent them from feeling that the 'new' Germany contained nothing of them.

In the former East Germany, many regard their Western counterparts as selfish and arrogant, while some of the West Germans regard those in the East as being very demanding and never satisfied.

After almost 30 years, cultural differences still exist. The term *Ostalgie* (*Ost*, meaning east, + *Nostalgie*, meaning nostalgia) is used to describe nostalgia for aspects of life in East Germany, and it is finding expression in a growing market for food products associated with the former East Germany.

CHECK YOUR LEARNING

1. Name one economic difference between West and East Germany before reunification.
2. Name five socio-economic impacts of reunification.
3. List four cultural impacts of reunification.

The Development of the European Union

The European Union is an example of a region whose boundaries have changed over time. When Croatia joined the EU on 1 July 2013, it became the 28th member of a union with a population of over 506 million, 24 official languages and an area of 4 million km². Since its founding, a series of treaties enabled the EU:

- to introduce policies leading to greater cooperation and integration;
- to adapt to increasing membership;
- to increase economic activity;
- to make the operation of the institutions more efficient.

KEYWORDS

European Coal and Steel Community (ECSC)

European Economic Community (EEC)

European Atomic Energy Community (Euratom)

European Union (EU) treaties

Beginnings

The formation of the **European Coal and Steel Community (ECSC)** by the **Treaty of Paris** in 1952 began a process that ultimately led to the formation of the European Union. The six **member states** – Belgium, France, Italy, Luxembourg, Netherlands and West Germany – agreed to allow the **tariff-free movement** of coal, steel and iron ore between them.

In 1957, these states signed further treaties that established the **European Economic Community (EEC)** and the **European Atomic Energy Community (Euratom)**. The EEC formed a customs union and common market based on the principles of free movement of people, goods, services and capital, and Euratom was created to ensure the peaceful use of nuclear energy.

In 1967, the **Treaty of Brussels** merged all three communities (ECSC, EEC, Euratom) and their institutions to form the **European Community**.

Landscapes

EU treaties

Paris Treaty — Established the ECSC (1952)

Treaty of Rome — Established EEC and EURATOM (1957)

Brussels Treaty — Merged ECSC-EEC-EURATOM to form EUROPEAN COMMUNITY (1967)

Single European Act — Set deadline of 1 January 1993 for SINGLE MARKET (1986)

Maastricht Treaty (1992)
- Name changed to EUROPEAN UNION
- Framework for Monetary Union
- Euro
- Increased parliament powers

Amsterdam Treaty — Governments devolved powers and criminal law, foreign and security policy to European Parliament (1997)

Nice Treaty (2000)
- European Parliament and Commission increased in size
- Future enlargement

Lisbon Treaty (2009)
- European Parliament increased power
- Exit clause
- Democratic deficit addressed Citizen's Initiatives

↑ **Fig. 24.7** EU treaties.

CHECK YOUR LEARNING

1. Name the six members of the European Coal and Steel Community.
2. Give the names of the treaties that addressed the following:
   - The Single Market
   - The introduction of the euro
   - The Exit Clause.

KEYWORDS

Common Agricultural Policy (CAP)

Common Fisheries Policy (CFP)

European Central Bank (ECB)

Eurozone

Schengen Area

Environmental Action Programme (EAP)

Chapter 17: The Concept of a Region
Chapter 19: A Peripheral Irish Region – The Western Region

EU Policy Development

The introduction of a variety of different policies contributed to the development of the EU.

Economic policies

The **Common Agricultural Policy (CAP)** provides supports to improve farmers' incomes, increase production and achieve security of food supply.

The **Common Fisheries Policy (CFP)** supports the fishing industry by preserving fish stocks through quotas and a system of Maximun Sustainable Yields (MSY).

Cohesion Policy is an EU strategy aimed at reducing differences in development levels between regions. Projects are funded under the **European Social Fund**, the **Cohesion Fund** and the **European Regional Development Fund (ERDF)**.

Since 1975, the ERDF has provided funding for infrastructural development designed to promote economic growth in peripheral regions (e.g. the **Mezzogiorno**), areas experiencing industrial decline (e.g. the **Sambre Meuse Valley**) and border areas (e.g. **Northern Ireland** and the **Republic**).

→ **Fig. 24.8** The ERDF funds regional development within EU member states.

EUROPEAN UNION European Regional Development Fund

The euro

On 1 January 2002, 12 of the 15 EU members began using **the euro** as a common currency. Denmark, Sweden and the UK decided not to join the Eurozone. Since its introduction, membership has grown to 19. The **European Central Bank (ECB)** oversees the currency by:

- setting interest rates;
- regulating inflation;
- ensuring national authorities supervise financial institutions.

↑ **Fig. 24.9** The euro was introduced in 2002.

Advantages of the common currency	Disadvantages of the common currency
Currency exchange fluctuations that existed when each country had its own currency have gone	Some claim that unfamiliarity with exchange rates meant prices rose when the euro was introduced
People in member countries are able to compare prices	Individual countries could no longer adjust their interest rates in response to economic difficulties
The euro reduced trading costs and stimulated economic activity	National governments surrendered decision-making to the ECB

The Stability and Growth Pact was designed to ensure member states behaved in a financially responsible way. Spending could not exceed 3% of GDP, while government debt could not exceed 60% of GDP.

Social policies

The EU has initiated **policies** and **directives** (laws) affecting areas such as education and training, travel, employment, working conditions and healthcare.

The **European Social Fund** provides funding for a variety of skills and education programmes that help people to return to education, learn and develop new skills and to start new businesses.

The **Schengen Agreement**, made in 1985, removed internal borders between member states and created a single external border at which immigration checking would take place. Belgium, France, Germany, Luxembourg and the Netherlands were the initial participants, but there are now 26 European countries in the **Schengen Area**.

Workers' rights

EU legislation is now in place relating to working hours, part-time work, safer **working conditions and workplace discrimination**. **Mutual recognition of qualifications** has made it easier for graduates to work in member countries.

The European Globalisation Adjustment Fund provides support for workers made redundant as a result of changing global trade patterns, when large companies shut down or production is moved outside the EU.

Social security and healthcare

There is now coordination to ensure that when people move to work in other EU countries, **pension contributions** and **social security benefits** are protected.

EU citizens visiting other member states for short periods can receive basic and emergency care with a **European Health Insurance Card (EHIC)**.

↑ **Fig. 24.10** An EHIC card.

Landscapes

Environmental policies

In 1973, the EU adopted the **Environmental Action Programme (EAP)**. The associated legislation now covers areas such as birds and wildlife habitats, special areas of conservation, air quality, and waste management. It also includes the **Water Framework Directive**, which aims to ensure cleaner rivers, lakes, groundwater and coastal beaches in member states.

Key EU environmental targets to be met by 2030 include:

- at least 40% cuts in **greenhouse gas emissions** (from 1990 levels);
- at least 32% share for **renewable energy**;
- at least 32.5% improvement in **energy efficiency**.

By providing information for agencies involved in developing, implementing and evaluating environmental policy, the **European Environmental Agency** helps the EU and its member states make informed decisions about improving the environment (Fig. 24.11).

→ **Fig. 24.11** The European Environmental Agency advises the EU on environmental policy.

European Environment Agency

CHECK YOUR LEARNING

1. List three economic policies that have contributed to the development of the EU.
2. Name three examples of social change that have been introduced by the EU.
3. List three EU environmental targets.

EU Enlargement

→ **Fig. 24.12** Map showing EU enlargements.

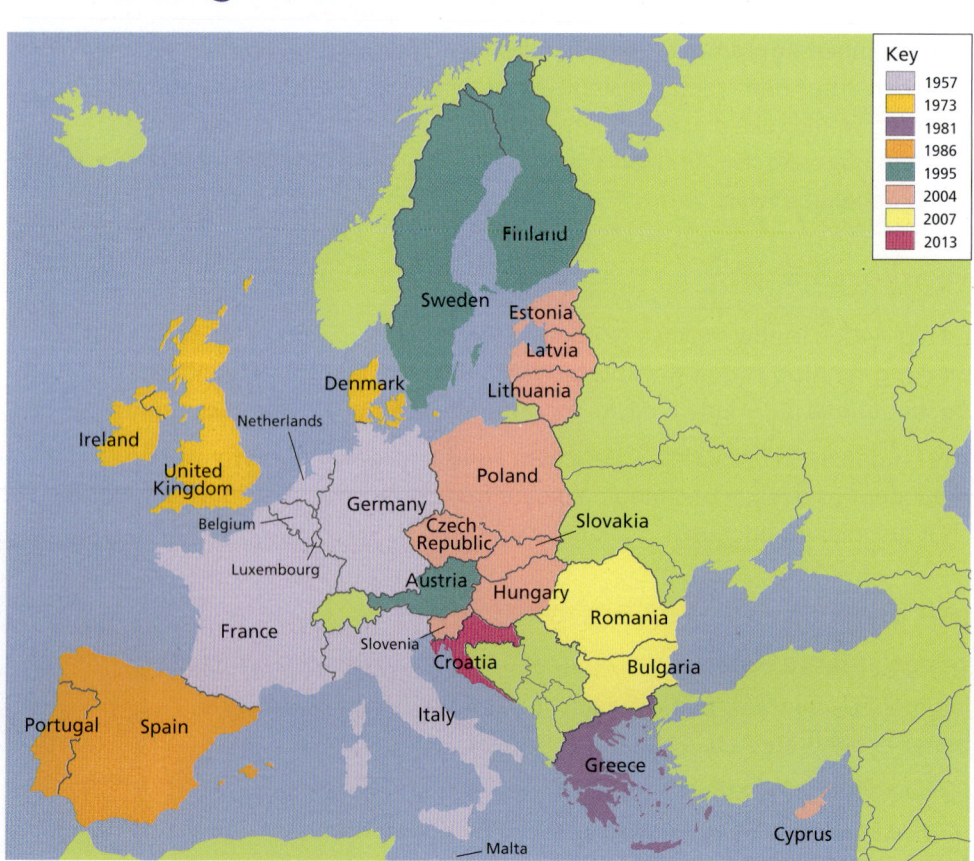

406

Enlargements

This list shows how the original six member countries became 28. The number in brackets shows the total number of member states at that time.

- **1973:** Denmark, Ireland and the United Kingdom (9)
- **1981:** Greece (10)
- **1986:** Spain and Portugal (12)
- **1989:** *West and East Germany reunite*
- **1995:** Austria, Finland and Sweden (15)
- **2004:** Cyprus, Czech Republic (Czechia), Estonia, Hungary, Latvia, Lithuania, Malta, Poland, Slovakia and Slovenia (25)
- **2007:** Bulgaria and Romania (27)
- **2013:** Croatia (28)

Becoming a member of the EU

Applicant countries must:
- have a market economy based on supply and demand with minimum government control;
- meet standards for democracy, justice and human rights.

After a successful application, an applicant country becomes a **candidate country**, and begins a period of negotiations. Before joining the EU, the candidate country has to implement all existing EU legislation.

New members are also expected to join the single currency, the euro.

Future enlargement

Candidate countries still negotiating or waiting to begin negotiations:
- Albania
- Bosnia and Herzegovina
- Montenegro
- Serbia
- Republic of North Macedonia

Kosovo

Kosovo has been recognised by the EU as a potential candidate, but Serbia and five EU member states don't recognise it as an independent country. Kosovo declared independence from Serbia in 2008.

Leaving the EU

Article 50 of the Treaty on European Union states that:

> Any Member State may decide to withdraw from the Union in accordance with its own constitutional requirements.
>
> A Member State which decides to withdraw must notify the European Council of its intention. The Union shall then negotiate and conclude an agreement with that State, which sets out the arrangements for its withdrawal, taking account of the framework for its future relationship with the Union.
>
> EU treaties shall cease to apply to the State in question from the start date of the withdrawal agreement or failing that two years after notification unless the European Council, in agreement with the Member State concerned, unanimously decides to extend this period.
>
> If a State which has withdrawn from the Union asks to rejoin, its application will subject to the same membership criteria for all new applicants.

Landscapes

EXAM LINK (OL)

European Union Expansion (40 marks)
(i) Name two countries that joined the European Union since 2000.
(ii) Explain the advantages of European Union expansion for Ireland.
(iii) Explain the disadvantages of European Union expansion for Ireland.
2017, Q6B

Marking Scheme:
(i) 2 marks + 2 marks
(ii) Explanation = 6 SRPs × 3 marks
(iii) Explanation = 6 SRPs × 3 marks

CHECK YOUR LEARNING

1. When did Ireland join the EU?
2. Name one other country that joined with Ireland.
3. In which year did the largest number of new members join? Name any three of those.
4. Identify two conditions for membership of the EU.

KEYWORDS
refugee
solidarity
migration
austerity
communism

Factors That Have Influenced EU Development and Enlargement

External factors

The collapse of communism

The fall of the Berlin Wall in 1989 led to the reunification of Germany. The total collapse of communism resulted in the largest expansion in the European Union's history when eight former members of the Soviet Bloc joined in 2004.

The refugee crisis

The flood of refugees from **conflict zones** such as Syria has placed major strains on the EU. More than one million migrants and refugees entered Europe in 2015.

A lack of willingness to take a quota of refugees, the closing of borders and the lack of support for Greece and Italy, which are in the front line of the influx, indicate a move away from cooperation and solidarity between the members.

Increased opposition to migrants in many member countries has seen a growth in support for **right-wing political parties**.

→ **Fig. 24.13** Migrant flows into Europe.

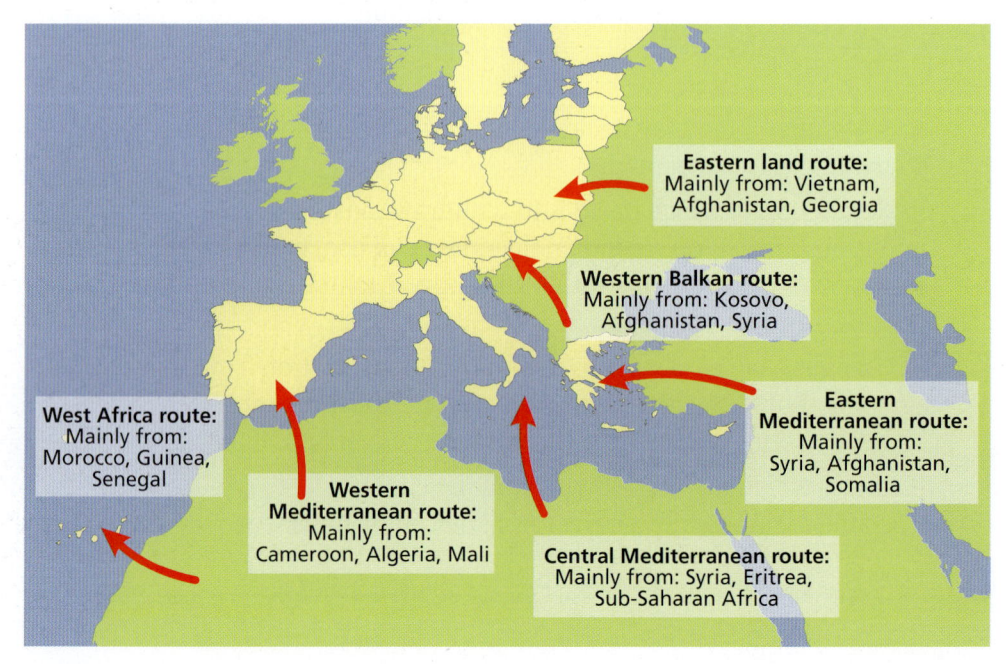

Internal factors

The Eurozone crisis

In 2008, Portugal, Ireland, Cyprus, Greece and Spain experienced serious financial difficulties when the global economic crash hit Europe (**Fig. 24.14**). The crisis highlighted how borrowings by some governments had gone out of control, and the lack of proper banking supervision within the Eurozone.

Tackling the difficulties became the responsibility of the **Troika** – the European Central Bank, the International Monetary Fund and the European Stability Facility – who designed **Economic Adjustment Programmes** for the countries that found themselves in difficulty. The countries involved had to agree to austerity programmes designed to reduce government spending and increase revenue by increasing taxation.

Fig. 24.14 The Eurozone crisis

Ireland exited its programme in 2013.

Terrorism

Terrorist attacks in Paris, London, Brussels, Madrid and other European cities have resulted in calls for an examination of the **free movement of people**. A return of border checks would deal a huge blow to the concept of free movement of peoples within the European Union.

> **CHECK YOUR LEARNING**
>
> 1. Name two external factors that have affected the development and expansion of the EU. Explain one factor.
> 2. Name two internal factors that have affected the development and expansion of the EU. Explain one factor.

Impacts of enlargement

The increased EU population has meant a **larger internal market** that stimulates economic activity and increases prosperity. However, expansion also increases the cost of running the EU and has caused some member states to complain about **increasing contributions** (e.g. the United Kingdom).

The Eastern European states that joined the EU in 2004 are classified as **poorly developed**, and require major funding through the ERDF and ESF. Many other member states have seen their status redefined and receive less EU funding (e.g. Ireland).

The eastern expansion of the EU has resulted in a huge **migration** westward from the poorer accession states. The population of Latvia declined by 700,000 between 1990 and 2016. Migration has changed the population structures of some countries as most migrants come from the younger productive sectors of the population (e.g. Romania).

Fig. 24.15 A protest against alleged human rights violations in Turkey, London

Future enlargement

There are major concerns around **Turkey** becoming a member of the EU. Issues include the Turkish occupied part of Cyprus, concerns about Turkish human rights and the inability of the EU to absorb another 80 million people (**Fig. 24.15**).

In 2014, the EU signed Association Agreements with **Georgia**, **Moldova** and **Ukraine** that recognised the 'European perspective' of all three countries.

Increasing opposition to enlargement and the growth of right-wing political parties will undoubtedly slow down the process of enlargement.

Landscapes

Impacts of Brexit on the EU

Membership will be reduced to 27 countries and the **total population will decline** from 512 million to 446 million.

The **EU budget** will be affected, with the loss of Britain's annual net contribution of €10 billion.

The size of the **European Parliament** will be reduced. Of Britain's 73 seats, 27 will be redistributed and 46 retained for future enlargements.

Northern Ireland and the Republic have seen huge growth in cross-border economic, political, social and cultural activities. The reimposition of a **hard border** will do untold damage to the normalisation of relationships between the two regions.

The **pattern of trade** between the EU and Britain will be changed, and the **common travel area** between Ireland and Britain is in doubt. Rights and guarantees for EU citizens living in Britain and UK citizens living in Europe will need to be addressed.

↑ **Fig. 24.16** The UK's exit from the EU will impact on the union's parliament, budget, trade patterns and freedom of movement.

Chapter 23
The Complexity of Regions I

CHECK YOUR LEARNING

1. Name three impacts of EU expansion.
2. Name four issues raised by Brexit.
3. List one problem affecting EU enlargement.

CASE STUDY: THE IMPACT OF AN ENLARGED EU MEMBERSHIP ON IRELAND

Between 2004 and 2013, 13 new countries joined the EU, bringing total membership to 28. Enlarged membership has had **socio-economic and political impacts** on Ireland.

KEYWORDS

integration	education	foreign direct investment (FDI)
perceptions	competition	skilled labour

Socio-economic impacts

Integration

Ireland, the UK and Sweden did not put any **entry restrictions** on people from states that joined the EU in 2014 and 2017. At this time, Ireland was in a period of economic expansion and labour shortages, so it began to witness huge inflows of migrants from countries such as Poland, Latvia and Lithuania. In 2006, over 90,000 Polish citizens applied for PPS numbers. The huge influx of migrants during this period had a major impact on the structure of Irish society and presented many challenges.

Tensions often arose as there was a **perception** that migrants were undercutting Irish workers by charging lower rates for jobs. Some people had the impression that migrants were abusing the benefits system and costing the state money.

The **educational system** was affected when workers were joined by their families. Extra resources had to be provided in schools to help students who did not speak English.

Market

EU enlargement provided Ireland with increased **export** market potential. In 2004, Ireland's trade with Poland amounted to €259 million; by 2016, the figure was €3.4 billion.

Increased market size resulted in increased output and employment opportunities.

Competition for labour

Lower labour costs in the accession states resulted in the eastward movement of manufacturing immediately after the EU enlargement. In 2009, computer manufacturer **Dell** closed its facility in Limerick and moved manufacturing to Lodz in Poland, resulting in the loss of 1,900 Irish jobs.

After accession, and continuing to this day, Ireland faced increasing competition for **foreign direct investment (FDI)** from member states with lower labour costs (e.g. **Czech Republic**).

The accession of the new member states coincided with a period of rapid growth in the Irish economy. Strong demand for labour and higher earning potential made Ireland an attractive destination and created a large labour pool of skilled and unskilled workers. This labour pool attracted FDI into Ireland.

Polish, Latvian and Lithuanian workers took up employment in all sectors. **Tax contributions** through PAYE on their incomes and VAT on purchases and services contributed to state revenues, which funded government spending.

Remittances sent back by workers to their home countries meant a loss of money to the economy. Estimates suggest that between 2004 and 2011 over €5 billion was repatriated back to Poland.

Political impacts

The political effects of enlargement relate to European structures and how the EU works.

As the EU enlarged, so did the number of representatives in the **European Parliament**. The **Lisbon Treaty** limited the number of MEPs to 751, so some countries with smaller populations were faced with reducing the number of MEPs.

Ireland's **allocation of MEPs** was reduced from 15 to 11, while the number of constituencies reduced from four to three. Critics say that these changes have led to the EU becoming less democratic.

> **EXAM LINK (OL)**
>
> European Union Expansion (30 marks)
>
> **Describe and explain the impacts of European Union expansion on Ireland.**
>
> **2015, Q6B**
>
> **Marking Scheme:**
> Description and explanation
> = 10 SRPs × 3 marks

> **EXAM LINK (HL)**
>
> European Union (30 marks)
>
> **Examine the impact of the expansion of the European Union on member states, with reference to both economic and social impacts.**
>
> **2016, Q4B**
>
> **Marking Scheme:**
> Economic impact identified = 2 marks
> Social impact identified = 2 marks
> Examination = 13 SRPs × 2 marks

> **CHECK YOUR LEARNING**
>
> 1. Name five socio-economic impacts of increased EU membership on Ireland. Briefly explain each one.
> 2. List two political impacts of EU enlargement.

Landscapes

EXAMINATION QUESTIONS
ORDINARY LEVEL

Long Question

1. European Union Expansion
   (i) Name two countries that joined the European Union since 2000.
   (ii) Explain the advantages of European Union expansion for Ireland.
   (iii) Explain the disadvantages of European Union expansion for Ireland.

Marking Scheme:
 (i) Two valid countries × 2 marks
 (ii) Advantages = 6 SRPs × 3 marks
 (iii) Disadvantages = 6 SRPs × 3 marks

2017, Part Two, Section 1, Q6B (40 marks)

2. European Union

Examine the map opposite showing the Eurozone area in 2015 and answer each of the following questions.

Year of joining the Eurozone area	
1999	Austria, Belgium, Finland, France, Germany, Ireland, Italy, Luxembourg, the Netherlands, Portugal, Spain
2001	Greece
2007	Slovenia
2008	Cyprus, Malta
2009	Slovakia
2011	Estonia
2014	Latvia
2015	Lithuania

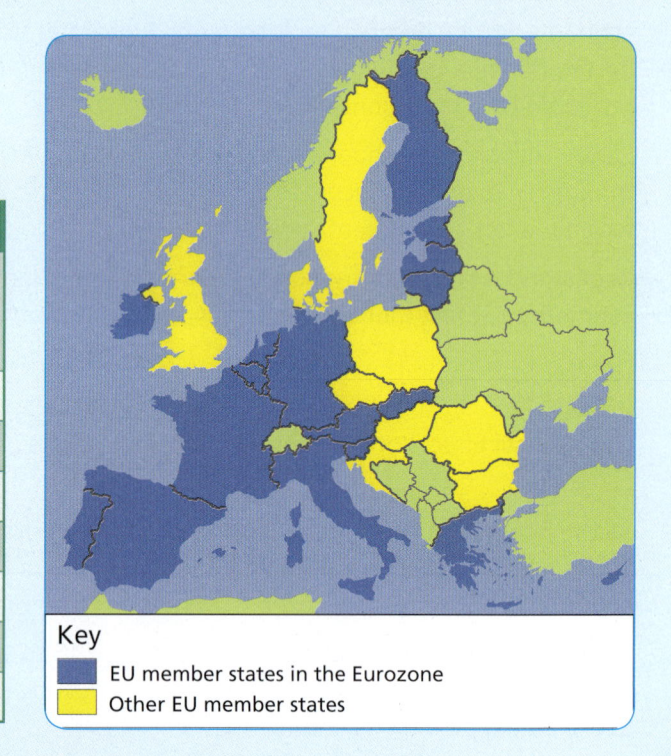

Key
- EU member states in the Eurozone
- Other EU member states

   (i) In what year did Ireland join the Eurozone area and how many countries including Ireland joined that year?
   (ii) Name two European Union (EU) member states not in the Eurozone area in 2015.
   (iii) Calculate the total number of European Union member states in the Eurozone area in 2015.
   (iv) Explain briefly two advantages of being part of the Eurozone area.

Marking Scheme:
 (i) 3 marks + 3 marks
 (ii) 2 × 3 marks
 (iii) 6 marks
 (iv) Advantage 1 = 2 × 3 marks
      Advantage 2 = 2 × 3 marks

2016, Part Two, Section 1, Q5A (30 marks)

412

HIGHER LEVEL

Short Question

3. European Union

Examine the map of Europe opposite showing the member states of the European Union and indicate whether each of the following statements is true or false, by circling the correct option in each case.

(i) Only six countries joined the European Union in 2004.

True   False

Belgium joined the European Union in the same year as the Netherlands.

True   False

Denmark joined the European Union in 1971.

True   False

(ii) Slovakia joined the European Union in 2013.

True   False

Marking Scheme:
4 × 2 marks

2015, Part One, Q3 (8 marks)

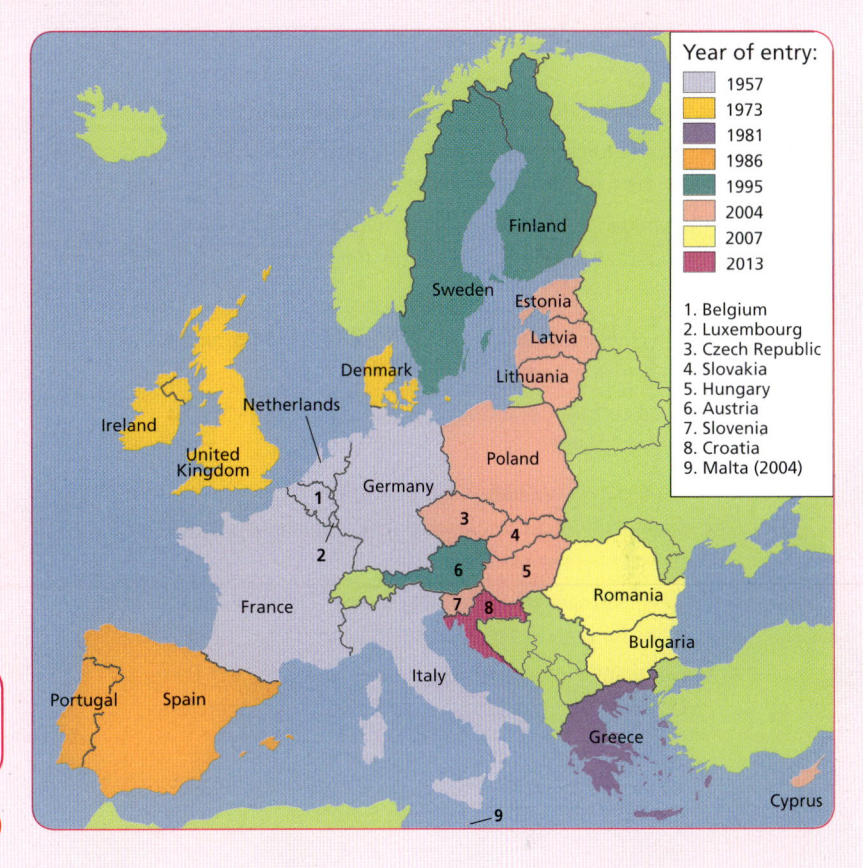

Long Question

4. Complexity of Regions

Number of daily Irish speakers in selected Gaeltacht areas 2011 and 2016

Gaeltacht Area	2011	2016
County Kerry	2,500	2,000
County Donegal	7,000	5,900
County Mayo	1,100	900

Examine the table above and answer each of the following questions.

(i) Using graph paper, draw a suitable graph to illustrate this data.

(ii) Explain briefly one strategy that could be used to address the decline in the number of daily Irish speakers in Gaeltacht areas.

2018, Part Two, Section 1, Q6A (20 marks)

Marking Scheme:
(i) Bar chart: title = 2 marks; axes named = 2 × 1 mark
Pie chart: title = 2 marks; circle and centred = 2 marks
6 items illustrated = 6 × 2 marks
(ii) Any valid brief explanation = 2 marks + 2 marks

Revision Summary

Changes in Boundaries and Extent of Language Regions Case Study: Gaeltacht Regions

- Areas: Donegal; Mayo; Galway; Kerry; Ring in Waterford; Ráth Cairn, Baile Ghib Meath; West Muskerry, Cork; Brandon, Cloghane, Kerry
- Survival – language spoken daily
- Immigration and out-migration – fewer native speakers

Population and migration
- Population decline: Great Famine, migration
- Population increase 2006–2011 – growth of Galway city, many not native speakers
- Donegal and Mayo Gaeltacht areas in decline – out-migration, lack of jobs and investment

Language use
- RTÉ Raidió na Gaeltachta (1972); TG4 (1996) promote daily Irish usage
- 2016 census: decline in daily Irish speakers, increased use of English

Changing boundaries
- Gaeltacht Act 2012 – areas defined by linguistics, not geography; community-focused
- Gaeltacht Language Planning Areas – devise language plans for daily usage in community
- Language plans for Irish Language Networks, e.g. Ennis, Co. Clare and Gaeltacht Service Towns, e.g. Caherciveen, Co. Kerry
- Govt initiative: Investing in Our Culture, Language and Heritage 2018–2027 – €105mn for jobs in peripheral areas

Urban Growth and the Expansion of Cities

- 60% global population living in urban areas by 2050
- Expansion of urban areas – challenges

Impact of Changes in Political Boundaries Case Study: Reunification of Germany

- End World War II: Germany divided – East and West
- 1961 Berlin Wall – stop movement East to West
- 1989: Fall of Berlin Wall – socio-economic, cultural impacts

Socio-economic impacts
- Mass migration to West
- East – brain drain; ageing population; West German childcare policies – increased costs
- Different roles of women – East (workers), West (home-makers) – problems
- Cost of reunification €1.3 trillion
- Change from planned economy to free, open market – industrial catastrophe in East
- Former East German economy still recovering

Cultural impacts
- East Germany: own culture, saw West as the enemy
- West Germany: own culture; saw East as fascist
- Unification: new freedoms, less supports – cultural differences – East seen as demanding; West as arrogant
- *Ostalgie*

Development of EU

- Paris Treaty 1952: ECSC – beginning of EU – tariff-free movement of coal, steel, iron ore
- Six members ECSC: Belgium, France, Italy, Luxembourg, Netherlands, West Germany
- Treaty of Rome 1957: EEC (customs union; common market); Euratom (peaceful use of nuclear energy)
- Brussels Treaty 1967: ECSC, EED, Euratom merge – European community
- Single European Act 1986: Single Market by 1993
- Maastricht Treaty: EU; framework for euro
- Amsterdam Treaty: European Parliament
- Nice Treaty: expansion European Parliament
- Lisbon Treaty: Exit clause

EU Policy Development

Economic policies
- CAP supports farmers – CFP supports fishing
- Cohesion Fund, ESF, ERDF: reduce differences in development levels

Euro
- Jan 2002: 12 of 15 EU members; now 19 members
- Controlled by ECB
- Positive: no exchange rates; price comparisons; reduced trading costs
- Negatives: price increases; no control over interest rates; ECB has control
- Stability and Growth Pact: financial responsibility

Social policies
- Education, travel, employment, healthcare
- ESF: education and business funding
- Schengen Agreement
- EU laws on working conditions; recognition of qualifications
- European Globalisation Adjustment Fund
- Pension and social security protection
- Basic and emergency healthcare – EHIC

Environmental policies
- EAP, Water Framework Directive
- EU targets 2030: 40% cut in greenhouse gases; 32% renewable energy; 32.5% improved energy efficiency
- European Environmental Agency – helps with decision-making

EU Membership

- Members increased from 6 to 28 by 2013
- Applications pending from four countries
- Ireland, UK and Denmark joined in 1973
- Applicant countries: meet criteria – applicant – candidate – negotiations – implementation of EU laws
- Article 50: terms of exiting EU

EU Enlargement

External factors
- Collapse of communism – largest expansion EU history
- Refugee crisis – opposition to quotas, border closures; lack of support for Greece, Italy = reduced EU solidarity

Internal factors: Eurozone crisis
- 2008: Portugal, Ireland, Cyprus, Greece, Spain – financial crisis
- Troika – Economic Adjustment Programmes – austerity programmes
- Ireland exited austerity in 2013

Terrorism
- Attacks Paris, London, Brussels, Madrid – question free movement of people

Impacts of enlargement
- Larger internal market – economic prosperity
- Higher running costs
- Poorly developed Eastern European states receive more funding
- Westward migration from poorer accession states – changes to population structures
- Future expansion – opposition, growth of right-wing politics

Impacts of Brexit
- 27 countries, population loss of 66mn
- Budget loss of €10 bn
- EU parliament: Britain 73 seats – 27 redistributed, 46 retained
- Relationship NI and Republic
- Trade agreements between EU and Britain
- Common travel area Britain–Ireland in doubt
- Rights of EU citizens in Britain and vice-versa

ELECTIVE UNIT 5
PATTERNS AND PROCESSES IN THE HUMAN ENVIRONMENT

CHAPTER 25 POPULATION CHANGES OVER TIME AND SPACE 417
CHAPTER 26 POPULATION AND HUMAN DEVELOPMENT 440
CHAPTER 27 MIGRATION 459
CHAPTER 28 SETTLEMENT 481
CHAPTER 29 URBAN LAND USE AND PLANNING 500
CHAPTER 30 URBAN GROWTH PROBLEMS 519

25 POPULATION CHANGES OVER TIME AND SPACE

LEARNING INTENTIONS
Syllabus Links: 5.1

By the end of this chapter I will be able to:
- understand that world population is dynamic;
- identify and explain the factors affecting population density and distribution;
- describe and explain the factors that affect the structure and the rates of population growth;
- interpret and explain the Demographic Transition Model and population pyramids;
- identify and explain the impact of life expectancy and fertility rates on population growth.

KEYWORDS
dynamic
population distribution
uneven
dense
sparse

Sparsely populated: When there is little settlement in an area.

Densely populated: When lots of settlement is present.

Dynamic: Something that is constantly changing.

World population is **dynamic** and is in a state of constant change in terms of **distribution** and **density**.

Population Distribution

Population distribution refers to the pattern of human settlement. Global population distribution is **uneven**, with areas of high, medium and low concentrations (Figs 25.1, 25.2)

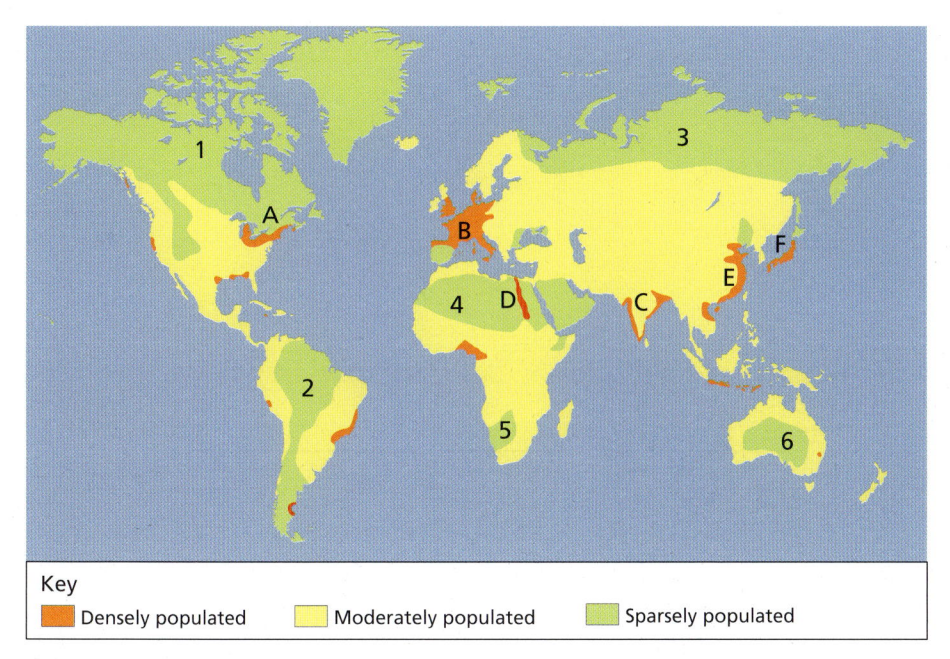

	Sparsely populated areas
1	Northern Canada
2	Amazon Basin
3	Northern Russia
4	Sahara Desert
5	South-West Africa
6	Central Australia

	Densely populated areas
A	Eastern USA
B	Central Europe
C	Indian Sub-Continent
D	Nile Valley
E	Eastern China
F	Japan

Key: Densely populated | Moderately populated | Sparsely populated

↑ **Fig. 25.1** Map of the world showing global population distribution.

417

Landscapes

→ **Fig. 25.2** Bar chart showing global population distribution in 2017, by continent.

Continent	Share of the global population
Asia	59.63%
Africa	16.59%
Europe	9.89%
Latin America and the Caribbean	8.53%
Northern America	4.8%
Oceania	0.56%

KEYWORDS

climate
altitude
soils
water
urbanisation
colonialism
manufacturing

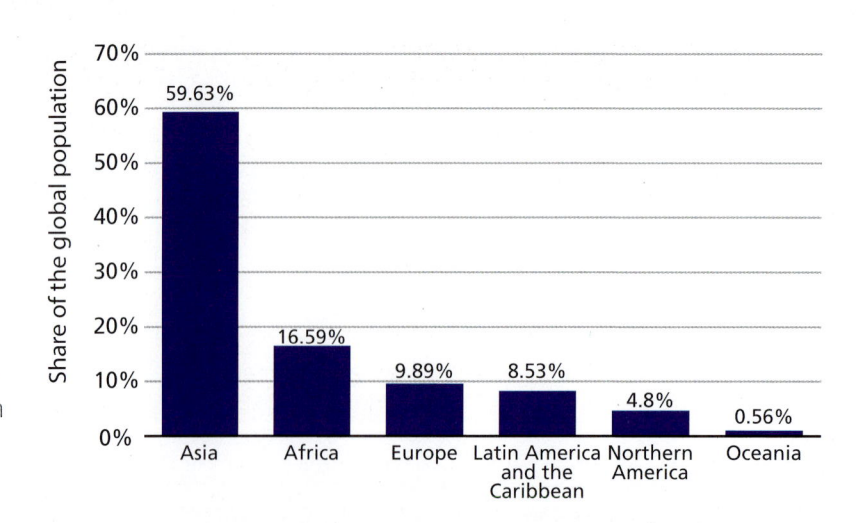

Factors that influence population distribution

Physical factors

Climate: The mid-latitudes of 20°–60°, where climate is more suitable, show the highest population densities. Areas of low density therefore include more northerly and southerly latitudes (e.g. **Northern Canada**) and equatorial regions (**tropical rainforests of Brazil**, areas of **desert**).

Altitude: Between 50% and 60% of all settlement occurs below 300 metres. Upland areas are unattractive due to lower temperatures, poor soils and inaccessibility (e.g. **Apennines-Mezzogiorno**; **Himalayas, India**), while lowland areas have more favourable conditions (e.g. **Paris Basin, France**).

Soils: Fertile soil conditions contribute to well-developed agriculture capable of supporting settlement (e.g. **Ganges Plain, India**).

Water: The availability of water for domestic and agricultural consumption results in high population densities in river valleys (e.g. **Nile Valley, Egypt**).

Socio-economic factors

As centres of economic activity, cities encourage **migration** leading to increasing concentrations of population in urban areas (e.g. **Kolkata, India; Fig. 25.3**). This is known as **urbanisation**. Estimates suggest that by 2030, 60% of the global population will live in urban areas.

→ **Fig. 25.3** Map of the world showing the predicted top 20 cities by population in 2025.

Resources: The coal-mining regions of Europe became major industrial centres and attracted settlement (e.g. **Sambre Meuse Valley, Belgium**). Areas with fertile soils attract settlement (e.g. **Paris Basin, France**).

CHECK YOUR LEARNING

1. Name any four cities located in Asia.
2. Identify two cities in: Africa, North America, South America.

Historical factors

Colonialism: The development of major **ports** to facilitate the export of raw materials and the import of **manufactured goods** during the colonial period resulted in urban growth and concentration of population in coastal areas of many colonies (e.g. **India**).

Population Density

Population density is an average measurement of the number of people in an area. It is calculated by dividing the number of people by the area and is expressed in either square kilometres (km²) or square miles (ml²).

Population density formula: $\dfrac{\text{number of people}}{\text{land area ml}^2/\text{km}^2}$

DID YOU KNOW?
90% of the global population live on 10% of the land.

Almost 40% of the world's land has little settlement.

The average population density of the earth is 14.36 per km².

CHECK YOUR LEARNING

1. Name three factors that influence population distribution.
2. Identify (i) a densely populated (ii) a sparsely populated European region.
3. Identify (i) a densely populated (ii) a sparsely populated area in a subcontinental region.

CASE STUDY: IRELAND – POPULATION DISTRIBUTION AND DENSITY

Ireland has an **uneven** distribution of population.

Areas of low density include:

- **upland areas**, where a combination of difficult landscape, extreme climatic conditions and infertile soils discouraged settlement (e.g. the **Western Region**; **Fig. 25.4**);
- **fertile areas**, such as the **Golden Vale**, where larger farms mean less settlement;
- **offshore islands**, where extreme conditions and isolation have led to continuous population decline (e.g. the **Aran Islands**).

KEYWORDS

emigration
recession
population density
population structure
net migration
life expectancy
dependency ratio
total fertility rate (TFR)

→ Fig. 25.4 Connemara upland areas have a low population density.

Areas of high density include:

- **urban centres**, such as the large cities of **Dublin**, **Cork**, **Galway** and **Limerick**, and smaller centres, such as **Athlone** and **Drogheda**, which are all centres of economic activity supporting settlement;
- **coastal lowlands** where there is fertile soil and **relief** favoured settlement. These areas extend from **Kerry to Donegal**. According to the 2016 census, 40% or 1.9 million people in Ireland lived within 5 km of the coast. In these areas, historical factors such as continued farm subdivision led to multiple **smallholdings**, each with separate dwellings;
- **urban centres** that have grown up on **rivers** (e.g. **Kilkenny**; Fig. 25.5) or settlement that has occurred along river valleys due to historical and geographical factors (e.g. bridging points or alluvial soils);
- **ports** that grew up at the mouth of large rivers, which became centres of economic activity and attracted settlement (e.g. **Waterford**).

↑ **Fig. 25.5** Kilkenny city on the River Nore.

EXAM LINK (HL)

Population Density and Distribution (30 marks)

Describe and explain, using examples you have studied, the difference between the terms 'population density' and 'population distribution'.

2008, Q10C

Marking Scheme:
Explanation of terms = 2 × 2 marks
Examples = 2 × 2 marks
Explanation of difference = 11 SRPs × 2 marks

Chapter 18
A Core Irish Region – The Greater Dublin Area
Chapter 19
A Peripheral Irish Region – The Western Region

CHECK YOUR LEARNING

1. Name three areas of low population density. List two reasons for this.
2. Name three areas of high population density. List two reasons for this.

Changes in population growth over time

In 1841, the recorded population of Ireland was over 6.5 million people. By the 1871 census, it was down to 4,053,187 – a decline of almost 2.5 million. This demonstrated the impact of death and **emigration** due to the Great Famine.

- The 1961 population of **2,818,341** was the lowest recorded since Independence and reflected the impact of migration in the 1950s.
- The removal of protectionist policies in the 1960s led to a more open economy. Employment increased, migration declined and population numbers grew.

Census year	Population totals	% change
1961	2,818,341	−5.6
1971	2,978,248	3.3
1979	3,368,217	13.1
1981	3,443,405	2.2
1986	3,540,643	2.8
1991	3,525,719	−0.4
1996	3,626,087	2.8
2002	3,917,203	8.0
2006	4,239,848	8.2
2011	4,588,252	8.2
2016	4,761,865	3.8

↑ **Table 25.1** Selected Irish census data

- EEC membership in 1973 led to increased investment, growing employment and reduced migration.
- The 13.1% increase between 1971 and 1979 was due to natural increase and positive net migration.
- The 4% decrease between 1986 and 1991 reflects the economic downturn of the 1980s.
- The mid-1990s to the mid-2000s saw major economic growth that contributed to population increases.
- EU expansion eastwards increased migrant numbers to Ireland from Poland and the Baltic states (e.g. **Latvia**).
- The economic downturn of 2008 led to a period of **recession** and **outmigration**. Estimates suggest a negative net migration of 140,000 for the period 2008 to 2014.
- Census 2016 shows positive net migration, the first since 2009.

> A census has been taken 17 times since Independence. It is traditionally taken on a Sunday in April.
>
> Since 1951, the census has been held at five-year intervals in years ending in 1 and 6.

CHECK YOUR LEARNING

Study Table 25.1 and answer the following questions:
1. Which year recorded the lowest totals?
2. Which year recorded the highest totals?
3. Which year recorded the highest percentage change? Give two reasons for this.
4. Which year recorded the lowest percentage change? Give two reasons for this.

Changes in population distribution

Between 1926 and 2016, Leinster was the only province to increase its overall percentage of population. Much of the increase is associated with the growth of the Greater Dublin Area. **Connacht** recorded the greatest decrease, reflecting a **lack of economic growth** and the impact of **migration**. Decreases in Ulster were due to economic decline and the impact of the border.

	1926	1956	2006	2016
Munster	32	30	28	27
Leinster	39	46	54	55
Connacht	19	16	12	12
Ulster	10	8	6	6

↑ **Table 25.2** Census data showing % of total population for selected years by province

CHECK YOUR LEARNING

1. Name and explain two reasons why the percentage of population in Connacht declined between 1926 and 2016.
2. Suggest two reasons why Ulster recorded declines between 1926 and 2006.
3. Name two reasons for population changes in Leinster.

The **Greater Dublin Area** has experienced huge population growth, reflecting its importance as the main centre of economic activity on the island. In 2016, 40% of the population of the country lived in this region, up from 38% in 2011.

Changes in population density

In 1966, **51%** of the population of Ireland was classified as **rural**. This had fallen to **37%** by 2016. The 2016 census recorded a national population density of **70 per km^2** (2006: 62 per km^2). The increase reflects the population growth during the Celtic Tiger years.

Areas of economic disadvantage have lower densities. Density in County Leitrim is **20 per km^2**, while Dublin city and suburbs show a density of **3,678** per km^2.

Chapter 27: Migration

Changes in population structure

1986 census age groups
- 0–14: 29%
- 15–64: 60%
- 65+: 11%

2016 census age groups
- 0–14: 21%
- 15–64: 65%
- 65+: 13%

↑ **Fig. 25.6** Age groups, selected censuses.

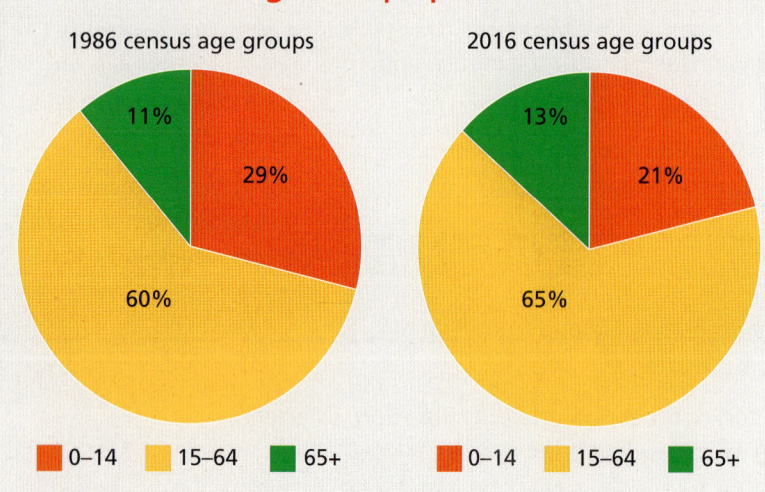

Changes in **population structure** between 1986 and 2016 are shown in **Figure 25.6**.

The main changes illustrated are:
- a decrease in the **0–14** group, indicating falling birth rates;

and percentage increases in:
- the **15–64** age group, showing the impact of natural increase and **positive net migration**;
- **65+** category, indicating increasing **life expectancy** and an ageing population.

Changes to the different age categories impact on the **dependency ratio**. The 2016 census shows a figure of 52.7 dependents for every 100 workers. This is an increase on the 2006 figure of 45.8, reflecting the impact of **negative net migration** caused by the economic downturn of 2008. Rural areas tend to have higher ratios due to **outmigration** of the younger age groups.

EXAM LINK (HL)

Population Characteristics, Ireland (30 marks)

Describe and explain how the characteristics of Ireland's population have changed since the 1950s.

2018, Q12B

Marking Scheme:
Change identified = 2 marks
Description/explanation = 13 SRPs × 2 marks

Chapter 18: A Core Irish Region – The Greater Dublin Area
Chapter 19: A Peripheral Irish Region – The Western Region

CHECK YOUR LEARNING

Study Figure 25.6 and answer the following questions:
1. Describe the main changes in each of the age groups for the years shown.
2. Name one reason for each change.

Birth rate

The 1950 birth rate of 21.4 per 1,000 had declined to 13.7 in 2016. The **total fertility rate** for Ireland had also declined from 3.85 in 1970 to 1.9 in 2016. Reasons for both changes include the changing **status of women** and **family planning**.

Life expectancy

In 1960, the average life expectancies were 67.9 years for men and 71.57 years for women. In 2016, due to socio-economic advances, the figures were 78.7 years for men and 83.2 years for women.

Total fertility rate (TFR): The total number of children that each woman could give birth to should she live to the end of her childbearing years.

CHECK YOUR LEARNING

1. Explain the term dependency ratio.
2. Why do dependency ratios tend to be higher in rural areas?
3. Explain the term TFR.
4. List two reasons for the decline in the TFR in Ireland.
5. Suggest one reason why life expectancy has increased in Ireland.

CASE STUDY: THE MEZZOGIORNO – POPULATION DISTRIBUTION AND DENSITY

Population distribution

KEYWORDS		
uneven	uplands	urban centres
rural depopulation	migration	tourism
Cassa	growth poles	birth rate

The estimated population of Italy in 2017 (ISTAT) was 61 million, of which 34% or 21 million lived in the south. The Mezzogiorno has an **uneven population distribution**, with the highest concentrations occurring on the coastal lowlands of the peninsula and on the coastal lowlands of the islands of Sicily and Sardinia. The distribution pattern is the result of a number of factors.

Physical factors

Due to the presence of the Apennines, many of the Mezzogiorno's provinces have very high percentages of uplands (e.g. **Basilicata, 92%; Fig. 25.7**). These uplands have very poor economic potential and a pattern of **rural depopulation** has resulted in abandoned villages.

↑ **Fig. 25.7** Map showing relief and population densities for the provinces of the Mezzogiorno.

In the past, the many small farms in the uplands supported a sizeable rural population. Changes to the land holding structure by the **Cassa**, which increased the size of farms, had the effect of reducing the number of farmers. The uplands were unattractive for settlement due to poor infrastructure and a lack of economic opportunity.

Cassa: Cassa per il Mezzogiorno, a development fund for Southern Italy.

Provinces with coastal lowlands have a higher population density (e.g. **Campania**). These lowlands are centres of economic activity with cities and towns. The lowland **relief** facilitated agriculture, communications and industrial development.

Socio-economic factors

Internal migration has had a major impact on population distribution throughout the region. Draining of coastal lowlands by the **Cassa** removed malarial swamps, making these areas attractive for settlement and also improving their agricultural potential. In **Puglia**, the Metaponto lowlands developed as a centre for commercial horticulture, offering employment and attracting settlement.

The creation of a number of **growth poles** centred on **ports** in coastal areas was part of the industrial strategy of the **Cassa**. They attracted workers to areas such as **Catania**, **Augusta** and **Syracuse** in Sicily.

The **urban centres** in the region – **Bari**, **Brindisi**, **Taranto**, **Palermo** and **Naples** – all have coastal locations and higher population densities due to a variety of economic activities providing employment.

In response to a lack of economic opportunity, a pattern of **external migration** from the south to the north has continued for many years. Estimates suggest that between 2001 and 2013, over 700,000 people left the south of Italy.

The growth of **tourism** has also impacted on population distribution. Employment in coastal resorts has attracted settlement to these areas. In Sardinia, coastal populations have increased, while inland numbers have severely declined.

Landscapes

Since 2013, over 690,000 mostly **African migrants** have landed in the south of Italy. Some **urban centres** in the region have embraced migrant resettlement as a way of revitalising their dying communities. In **Sutera** in interior Sicily, migrants were housed in abandoned properties. Local families assisted with integration and asylum applications, and the children of these migrants have boosted declining numbers in the local school.

Population density

In 2017 the estimated national average population density was 201 per km². Only two of the provinces in the Mezzogiorno have higher totals, they are **Campania at 428 per km²** and **Puglia at 209 per km²**. The city of Naples, with a population of over 3 million, is the major centre for secondary and tertiary economic activities in Campania and is the main reason for the high figure there. Over 90% of Molise is classed as upland, and as a result its population density is only 70 per km² (**Fig. 25.8**).

↑ **Fig. 25.8** Over 90% of Molise is classed as upland.

> Chapter 21
> A European Peripheral Region – The Mezzogiorno

Birth and **fertility rates** in the south are declining. All provinces in the region recorded negative population growth for the year 2017. **Migration** continues to change the **population structure**, reducing the percentages of younger people.

Fertility rate: Average number of births per 1,000 women aged between 15 and 44 years.

CHECK YOUR LEARNING

1. What percentage of the Italian population live in the Mezzogiorno?
2. Name one physical factor that influences population distribution.
3. List three socio-economic factors that influence population distribution in the Mezzogiorno.
4. Identify one area within the region with a high population density. Name two reasons for this.

KEYWORDS

Malthus
population explosion
total fertility rate (TFR)
mortality rate
social engineering
replacement level
one-child policy
pro-natalist policy

Global Population Growth Patterns

The ability of our world to sustain a population began to occupy the minds of scholars during the 18th century. **Thomas Malthus** suggested that famine and other natural disasters were esssential in order to prevent world popuation exceeding food supply. In the 20th century, global advances in sanitation and medicine saw a decline in death rates and rapid increases in population (**Fig. 25.9**). This '**population explosion**' has led to debate about what will happen to population numbers in the 21st century: will they keep rising? And if they do, what are the implications for humankind?

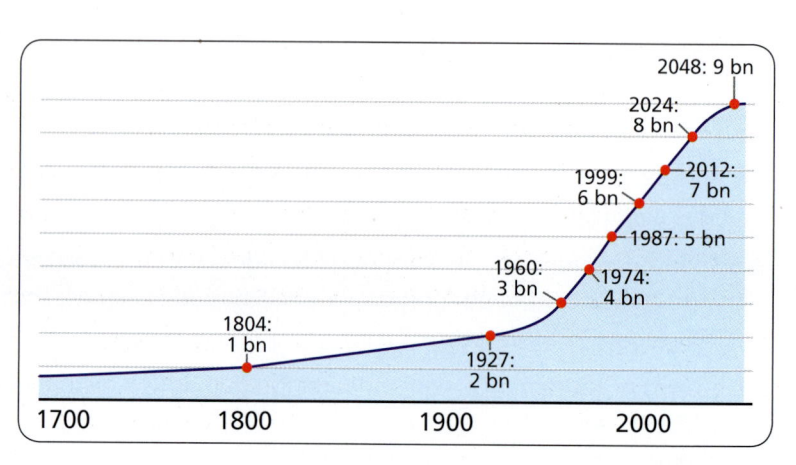

→ **Fig. 25.9** World population growth since 1700 in billions (United Nations World Population Prospects).

- 1804: 1 bn
- 1927: 2 bn
- 1960: 3 bn
- 1974: 4 bn
- 1987: 5 bn
- 1999: 6 bn
- 2012: 7 bn
- 2024: 8 bn
- 2048: 9 bn

424

25 Population Changes Over Time and Space

> **CHECK YOUR LEARNING**
>
> Study Figure 25.9 and answer the following questions:
> 1. How many years did it take for the population to double from 1 to 2 billion?
> 2. How many years did it take for the population to double from 2 to 4 billion?
> 3. When is the global population expected to reach 9 billion?
> 4. What is this rapid population growth called?

Globally and regionally, population is influenced by **birth rates**, **total fertility rates**, **mortality rates** and **migration**.

Total fertilty rates (TFR)

The TFR required to keep population levels stable from generation to generation is referred to as the **replacement level** and is currently estimated at **2.1**. In 2018, the global average TFR was **2.4**, indicating global population is increasing (Source: Population Reference Bureau). In parts of the developed world, for example **Italy**, the rate has fallen below replacement levels. While some developing world countries are experiencing decline, for example, **Brazil** with a rate of 1.75, TFR rates in the developing world are generally high.

Social engineering: Strategies used by governments to try to encourage or limit population growth.

Future trends

Predicting global population numbers involves examining the impacts of changing **fertility rates**. Continuing high rates will see population increase. However, economic and social factors can cause fertility rates to decline, leading to decreasing population.

> **CHECK YOUR LEARNING**
>
> 1. Explain the term replacement level.
> 2. Name one possible impact that changing fertility rates will have on population.

CASE STUDY: CHINA'S ONE-CHILD POLICY

Key points of China's one-child policy

- Introduced in 1979 as the Chinese population edged closer to 1 billion, it decreed that China's Han majority could only have **one child** per couple.
- Contraceptives and **family planning** were widely available.
- **Financial incentives** to encourage compliance included monthly allowances; compliant parents also had the first choice for government jobs.
- Families who did not comply were **fined** and in some cases **forced abortions** were carried out.
- In wealthy cities such as Shanghai, people could easily afford penalties for a second or third child.

↑ Fig. 25.10 China's one-child policy.

425

Impacts of the policy

- The rate of natural increase fell from 14.35 births per 1,000 in 1980 to 4.5 per 1,000 in 2017.
- A bias for male children that resulted in the aborting of female foetuses has led to a serious gender imbalance – **118 males to every 100 females** – with implications for future marriage rates and other social considerations.
- Declining births since 1980 has led to a decrease in the 15–64 age group, resulting in **labour shortages**.
- There is a shortage of young relatives to care for and support the ageing population.

2013: end of one-child policy

- In 2013, in response to the negative impacts experienced, the one-child policy was relaxed and having a second child was actively encouraged by the government.
- In 2016, the number of new births totalled 17.8 million, the highest since 1993.
- China will require an increasing labour supply in the coming years if it is to continue to grow economically. To ensure this, the government will now have to introduce **pro-natalist policies** to keep the TFR at replacement level.

Pro-natalist policies: Policies designed to encourage people to have children.

CHECK YOUR LEARNING

1. List three key points about China's one-child policy.
2. Name three impacts of this policy.

CASE STUDY: FRANCE PRO-NATALIST POLICIES

The **code de la famille**, introduced in France in 1939, was a series of pro-child policies designed to increase the fertility rate. The main elements include:

- **maternity leave**, with full pay, from 20 weeks to 40 weeks, depending on the number of children the woman already has;
- government-subsidised **child care**, crèches, day-nurseries, full tax benefits to parents until the youngest child reaches 18.

In spite of these policies, the TFR continues to decline. It fell from **1.96 in 2015** to **1.88 in 2017**, but France still has one of the highest rates in the EU.

KEYWORDS
maternity leave
child care

CHECK YOUR LEARNING

1. Name two strategies employed by the French government to increase TFR rates.

The Demographic Transition Model

The Demographic Transition Model (Population Cycle) uses historical population data to identify the different stages countries move through as social and economic changes impact on **birth** and **death rates** (Fig. 25.11). The current model has five stages. Countries with populations in Stages 2 and 3 are in the developing world, while developed world countries are in Stages 4 and 5. Progression from one stage to the next is related to how economic and social factors impact on birth and death rates.

KEYWORDS
birth rate
death rate
natural increase
natural decrease
Eurocentric
senile stage

25 Population Changes Over Time and Space

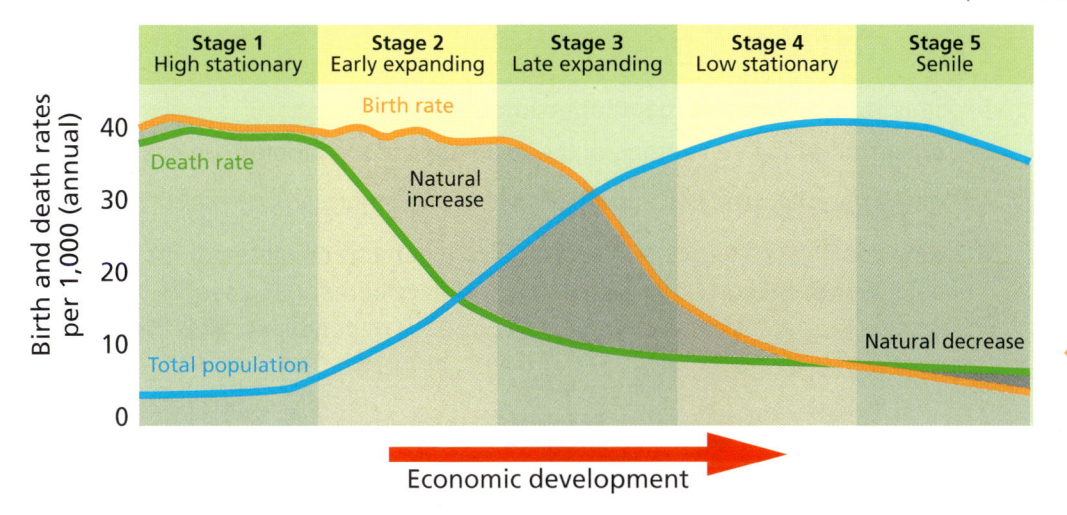

← Fig. 25.11 The Demographic Transition Model (Population Cycle).

Stage 1: High stationary stage

This stage applied to most of the world prior to the industrial revolution; birth rates and death rates are both high. Famine, wars and pandemics cause the death rate to fluctuate and overall population numbers remain low. No countries today are classified as belonging to this stage.

Stage 2: Early expanding stage

Due to improved basic **healthcare** (especially for children), improved sanitation and food production, the death rate falls rapidly. Birth rates are still high, resulting in a rapid increase in population. Today, many Less Economically Developed Counties (LEDCs) are in Stage 2 (e.g. **Chad**, **Afghanistan**).

Stage 3: Late expanding stage

Birth rates begin to decline due to a number of factors including the improved **status of women**. The death rate continues to decline but the rate reduces. Population growth continues but at a slower rate. Countries in this stage include **India** and **Morocco**.

Stage 4: Low stationary stage

Birth and death rates have declined and are almost equal. Economic and social advances and a well-educated population have resulted in reduced family size. Examples of countries in this stage include **Canada** and **Ireland**.

Stage 5: Senile stage

The birth rate continues to decline while the death rate is stable. Total population is declining. Countries in this stage include **Japan** and **Germany**.

CHECK YOUR LEARNING

1. List two differences between birth rates in Stages 2 and 4.
2. Explain two reasons for these differences.
3. List three reasons why birth rates decline in Stage 3.
4. Outline any two evaluations of this model.

Birth rate: The number of births per 1,000 of population.

Death rate: The number of deaths per 1,000 of population, also known as mortality rate.

Natural increase: The annual number of births exceeds the number of deaths.

Natural decrease: The annual number of deaths exceeds the number of births.

Life expectancy: The average number of years a person can expect to live.

Pandemic: A disease outbreak that covers a large area.

Evaluation

- Critics claim that this model is **Eurocentric** and its application to the developing world countries is limited.
- The model does not show the impacts of **migration**.

427

Landscapes

KEYWORDS

age profiles
gender profiles
population pyramid
dependency ratio
dependent sector
active sector

Population Structure

Two important elements of **population structure** are:
- **age profiles:** the percentage of the population in the different age categories;
- **gender profiles:** the percentage of males and females in each category.

This data can be used to create a graph called a **population pyramid.** The shape of a population pyramid can indicate the stage of development of a country, while the information it contains can be used to calculate the **dependency ratio** (Fig. 25.12).

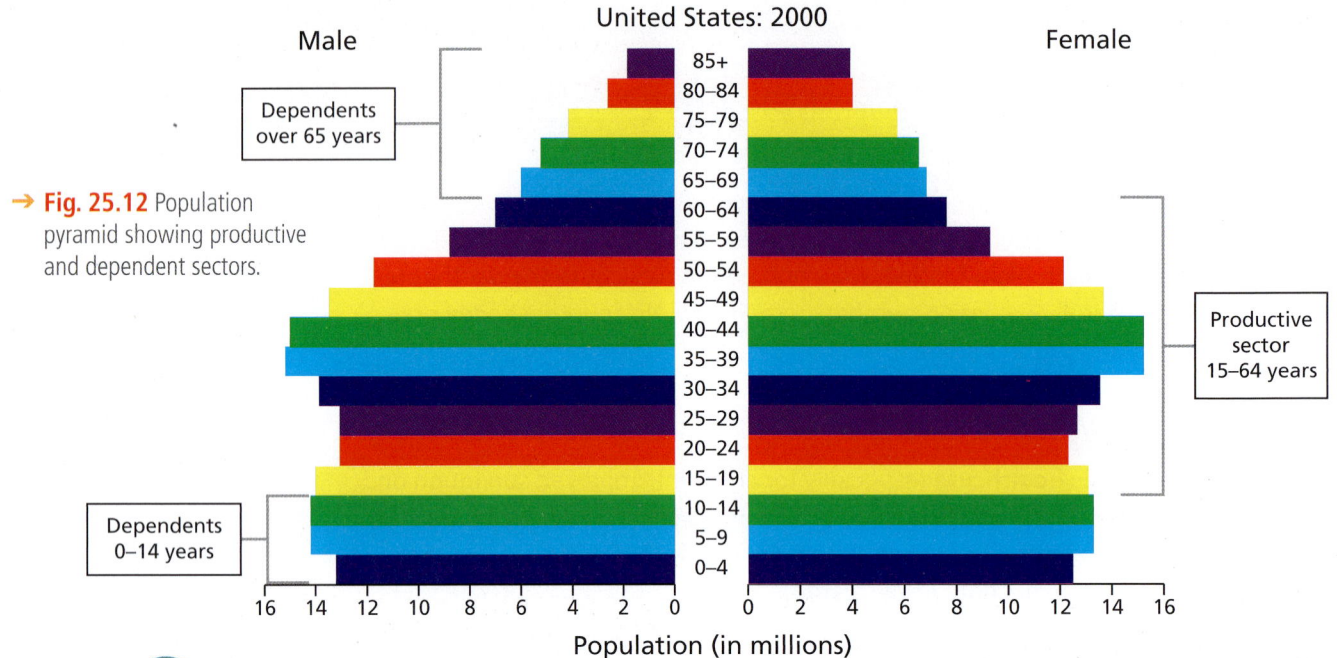

United States: 2000

Male | Female

Dependents over 65 years

→ **Fig. 25.12** Population pyramid showing productive and dependent sectors.

Productive sector 15–64 years

Dependents 0–14 years

Population (in millions)

Dependency ratio: The ratio of the dependent sector to the active sector in an economy.

Dependent sector: Those aged between 0 and 14 years and over 65.

Active sector: Those aged between 15 and 64 years.

How to calculate the dependency ratio using 2011 Irish census data:

Dependent sector	1,514,983
Active sector	3,073,269

$$\frac{\text{dependent sector}}{\text{active sector}} \times \frac{1,514,983}{3,073,269} \times \frac{100}{1} = 49.2$$

This means that in 2011, for every 100 people at work there were 49.2 dependents.

It can also be expressed as a percentage 49.2%.

CHECK YOUR LEARNING

1. Using the data in Table 25.3, calculate the dependency ratio in Ireland for 2016.

   → **Table 25.3** 2016 census data for Ireland.

Dependent sector	1,006,552
Active sector	3,117,746

KEYWORDS

expansive
stationary
constrictive
demographic anomaly

Population pyramids

Population pyramids are constructed to show population structure. There are three main types of population pyramids.

428

Expansive

Expansive population pyramids are associated with **developing** nations with **high fertility rates**. The wide base indicates high birth rates. Progressing upwards, each group decreases in size indicating lower than average life expectancies (e.g. **Afghanistan**; **Fig. 25.13(a)**).

→ **Fig. 25.13(a)** Population Pyramid, Afghanistan (Stage 2 Demographic Transition Model).

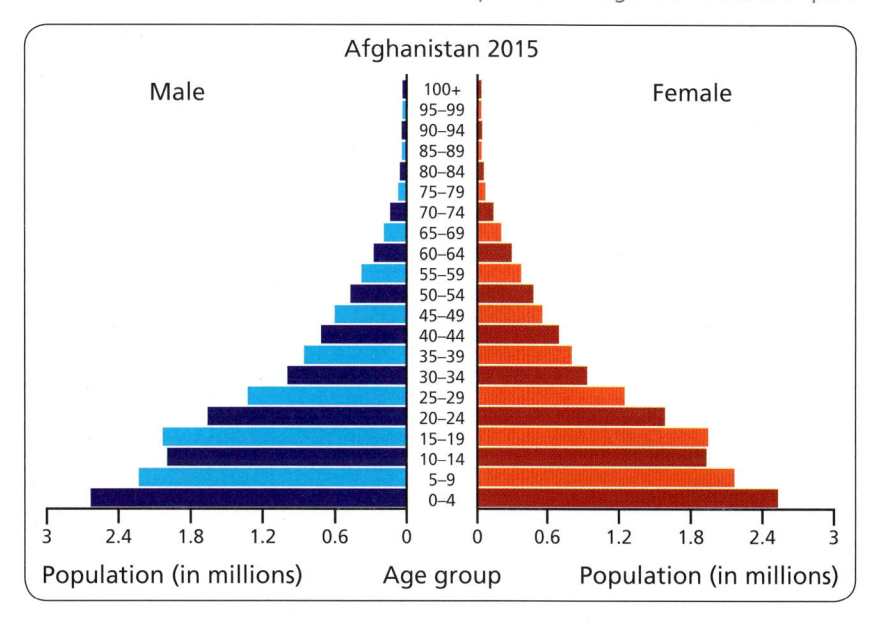

Stationary

Stationary population pyramids show a stable population with almost equal proportions in each group to the mid-age groups (e.g. **Morocco**; **Fig. 25.13(b)**).

→ **Fig. 25.13(b)** Population Pyramid, Morocco (Stage 3 Demographic Transition Model).

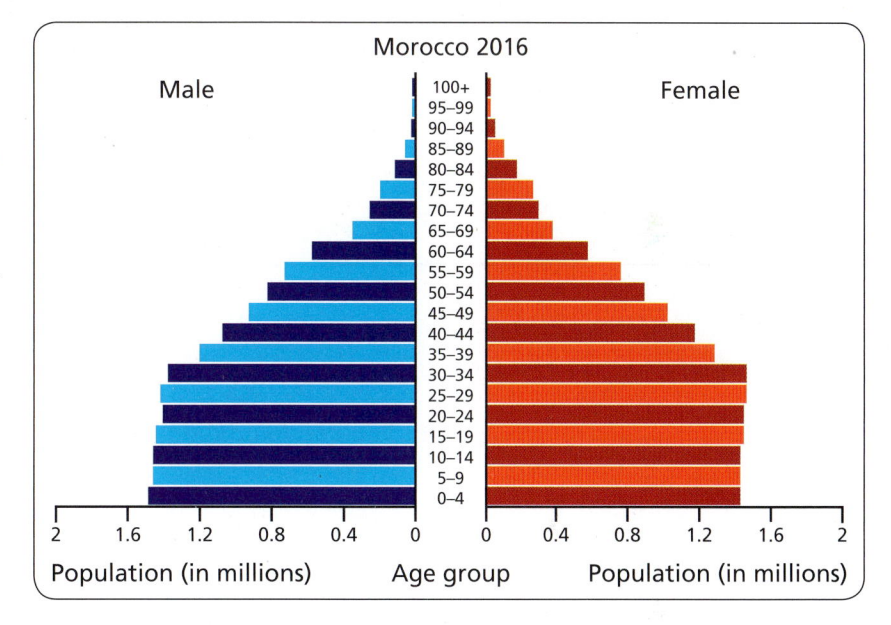

Constrictive

Constrictive population pyramids have narrow bases indicating **falling birth rates**. They are associated with countries with higher levels of economic growth and well-developed health and social services (e.g. **Italy**; **Fig. 25.13(c)**).

→ **Fig. 25.13(c)** Population Pyramid, Italy (Stage 5 Demographic Transition Model).

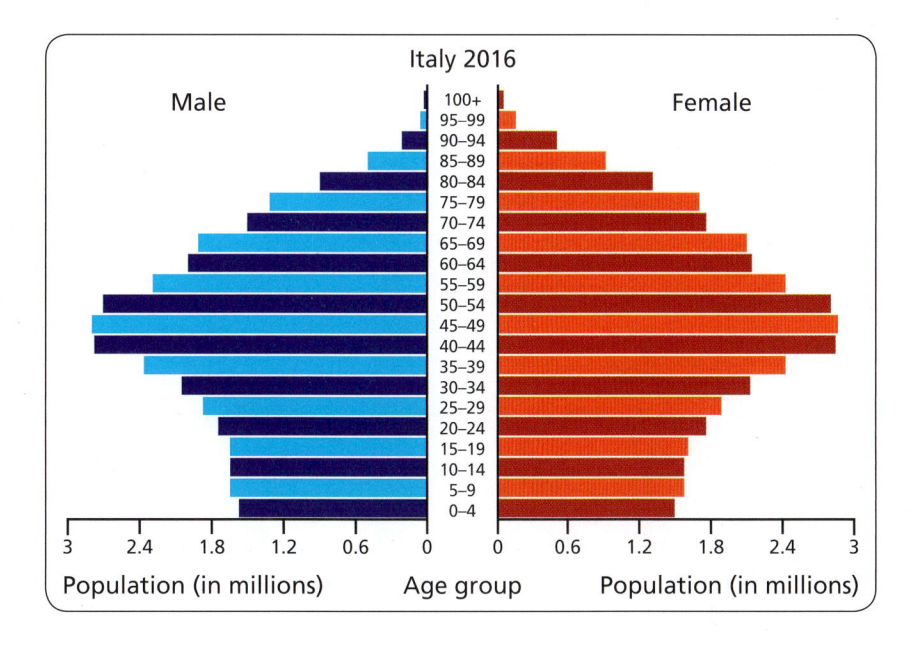

Landscapes

Reading population pyramids

- Wide base = high birth rate
- Narrow base = falling birth rate
- Concave shape = high death rate
- Convex shape = low death rate
- The percentages of females to males should be relatively the same (symmetrical)
- Moving upwards, the percentage of females will be greater due to higher female **life expectancy**
- A bulge in the side shows a **demographic anomaly**, for example, baby boom, impact of **migration** (Fig. 25.14)

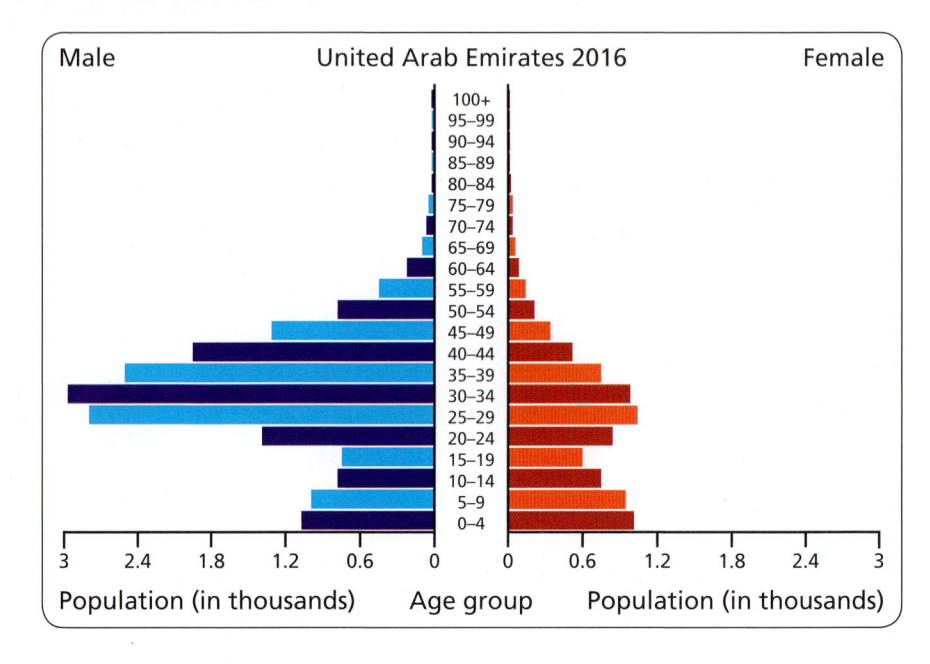

Demographic anomaly: When the expected population pattern does not occur.

→ **Fig. 25.14** Population Pyramid, United Arab Emirates. This pyramid shows an anomaly in the ratio of males to females. Total males between 20 and 54 far exceed female totals. The large number of male migrant workers present in the country explains this.

Uses of population pyramids

Governments and local authorities use population pyramids to predict healthcare requirements for the elderly and demand for housing and schools, and to inform **taxation** policy to cope with increasing dependents.

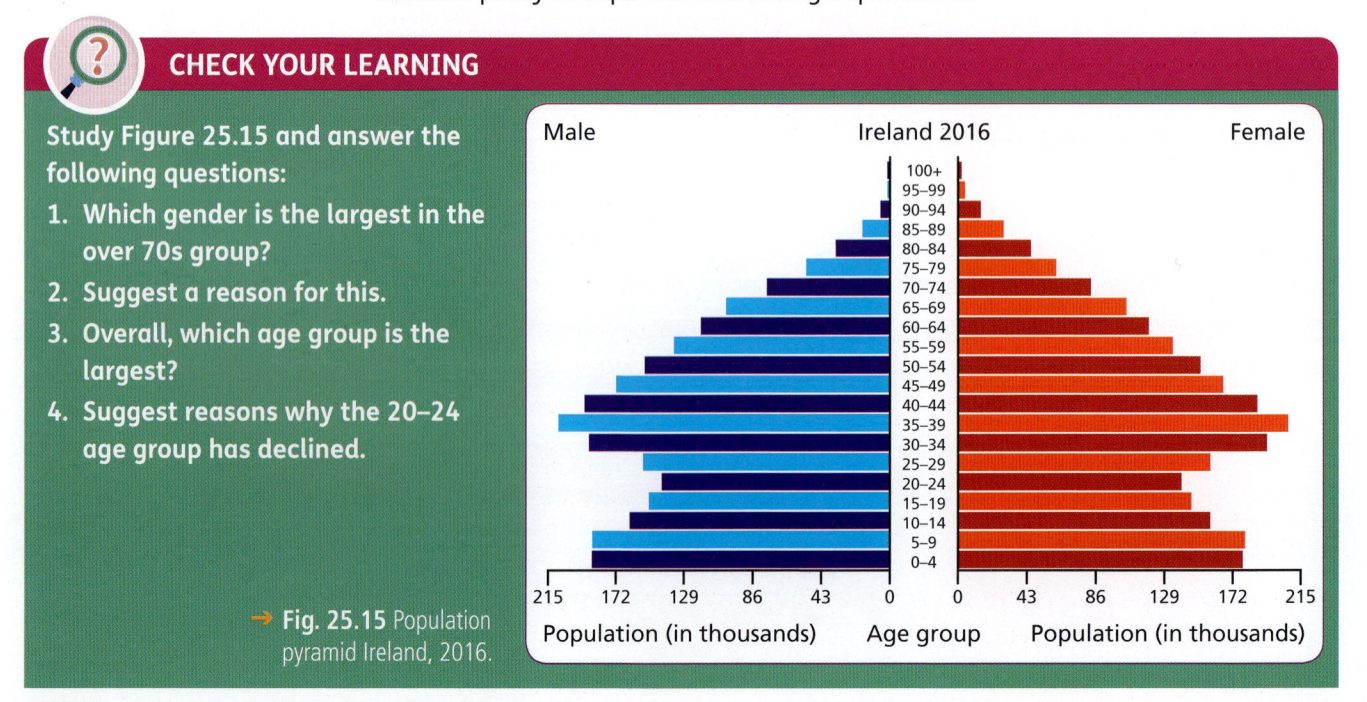

CHECK YOUR LEARNING

Study Figure 25.15 and answer the following questions:
1. Which gender is the largest in the over 70s group?
2. Suggest a reason for this.
3. Overall, which age group is the largest?
4. Suggest reasons why the 20–24 age group has declined.

→ **Fig. 25.15** Population pyramid Ireland, 2016.

Fig. 25.16(a)

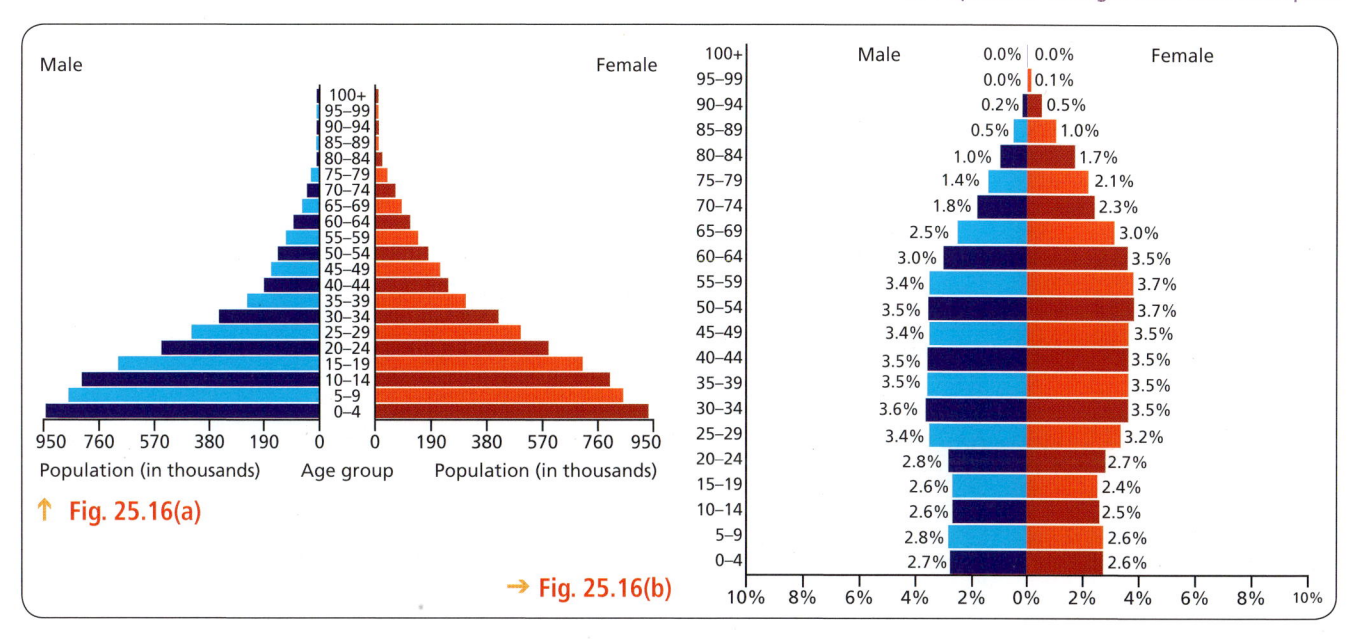

Fig. 25.16(b)

CHECK YOUR LEARNING

Study Figure 25.16 and answer the following questions:
1. Pyramids A and B in Figure 25.16 represent data for the United States and Chad. Identify which is which.
2. Identify the type of pyramid each one is.
3. Name two trends shown in pyramid A.
4. Name two trends shown in pyramid B.
5. Which pyramid would you associate with Stage 2 of the Demographic Transition Model?

The Impact of Fertility Rates on Population Structure

Population structure refers to the composition of the population and includes the numbers in the different age groups, as well as the number of males and females.

Fertility rates in developed countries

In developed countries, **total fertility rates** tend to be low, and in many cases they fall below **replacement level**. Factors contributing to this include:

Socio-economic factors

- Increasing educational opportunities have resulted in women pursuing careers and delaying marriage and motherhood. The average age for women marrying in Ireland in 1977 was 24; in 2015 it was 33.
- Increased percentages of women in the workforce have impacted on family size – this impacts on **child care costs**.
- Greater access to **family planning** has resulted in reduced family sizes.
- The cost of rearing children, including education, impacts on family size.

Role of governments

- Provision of state pensions ensures economic security in old age, thus reducing the need for large families.
- **Government incentives** to reverse **falling fertility rates** include allowances, increased maternity leave and the introduction of paternity leave (e.g. **France**).

KEYWORDS
cost
family planning
government
population decline
status of women

Landscapes

The changing status of women in Ireland
In the 1970s, women working in the civil service and many private companies were forced to resign when they got married.

In the 1981 census, 55% of women over the age of 15 classed themselves as 'looking after home/family', compared with just 17.5% in 2011.

Impacts

- The population will decline.
- The labour supply will decrease.
- A declining workforce will result in lower tax revenues.
- An increasing **dependency ratio** presents socio-economic challenges, e.g. supporting health and social care requirements.

CHECK YOUR LEARNING

1. Name and explain three reasons why fertility rates are low in developed countries.
2. Name three countries with low fertility rates.
3. Name two impacts low fertility rates have on a country.

Fertility rates in developing countries

KEYWORDS
infant mortality rates   poverty   status of women
family planning   social welfare

Infant mortality: Number of deaths of children under one year per 1,000 of population.

Child mortality: Number of deaths of children under five years per 1,000 of population.

Maternal mortality: Number of deaths of mothers while pregnant or within 40 days of birth.

Crude death rate: Total number of deaths per 1,000 of population.

In developing countries, **total fertility rates** tend to be high. Factors contributing to this include:

Socio-economic factors

- Early marriages mean longer years of child-bearing and contribute to higher **fertility rates** (e.g. **Bangladesh**).
- High **infant mortality rates** due to poor maternity services mean women have more children to ensure some survive.
- Poverty contributes to a lack of **family planning**.
- In some patriarchal societies, women lack power and have little say in birth control (e.g. **South Sudan**).
- In many societies, there is a cultural acceptance of large families (e.g. **Niger**).
- Children are a source of labour on the land or can contribute to the family's income through a variety of unskilled jobs (e.g. **Chad**).
- Lack of social welfare means parents depend on their children as they grow older (e.g. **India**).

↓ **Fig. 25.17** A family planning poster from Kenya.

Impacts

- An increasing population puts pressure on housing and employment (e.g. **Bangladesh**).
- As population increases, so too does demand for food and resources, which can lead to overpopulation (e.g. **Chad**).
- Poorly developed economies face challenges providing immunisation programmes, healthcare and education (e.g. **Kenya; Fig. 25.17**).

> **CHECK YOUR LEARNING**
>
> 1. Name and explain three reasons why fertility rates are higher in developing countries.
> 2. Name three countries with high fertility rates.
> 3. Name two impacts of high fertility rates.

The Impact of Mortality Rates and Life Expectancy on Population Structure

Mortality rates and life expectancy in developed countries

As a country advances economically, better living conditions and health services result in decreasing **infant**, **maternal** and **general mortality rates**, as well as increased **life expectancy** and changes to the population structure.

Impacts

Increasing **life expectancy** leads to ageing populations. This presents challenges including:

- as people live longer, the percentage of old-age dependents will increase;
- an ageing population puts greater demand on hospitals, for example, a winter flu outbreak;
- there is an increased need for **healthcare** workers and facilities, such as nursing homes and day care centres;
- increasing diagnoses of age-related dementia have implications for provision of long-term care.

Planning for an ageing population

Governments have to plan for ageing populations. Possible strategies include:

- mandatory participation in pension schemes by all workers to provide for their retirement;
- increasing the pension entitlement age; it is currently 66 but in 2028 it will rise to 68;
- examination of compulsory **retirement ages** with a view to increasing them;
- introduction of gradual retirement strategies, where people can work reduced hours and not have to fully retire;
- changing attitudes to ageing – **The National Positive Ageing Strategy (Ireland) 2013** outlines a number of objectives, including identifying any barriers preventing people as they age from accessing continued employment and training opportunities (Fig. 25.18).

KEYWORDS
mortality rates
life expectancy
population structure
healthcare
planning

↑ Fig. 25.18 Age Friendly Ireland logo.

Landscapes

CASE STUDY: JAPAN – IMPACT OF AN AGEING POPULATION

CHECK YOUR LEARNING

Study Figure 25.19. List one change in each of the population sectors between 1950 and 2010.
1. 0–14
2. 15–64
3. 65+

→ **Fig. 25.19** Population pyramids Japan 1950–2050.

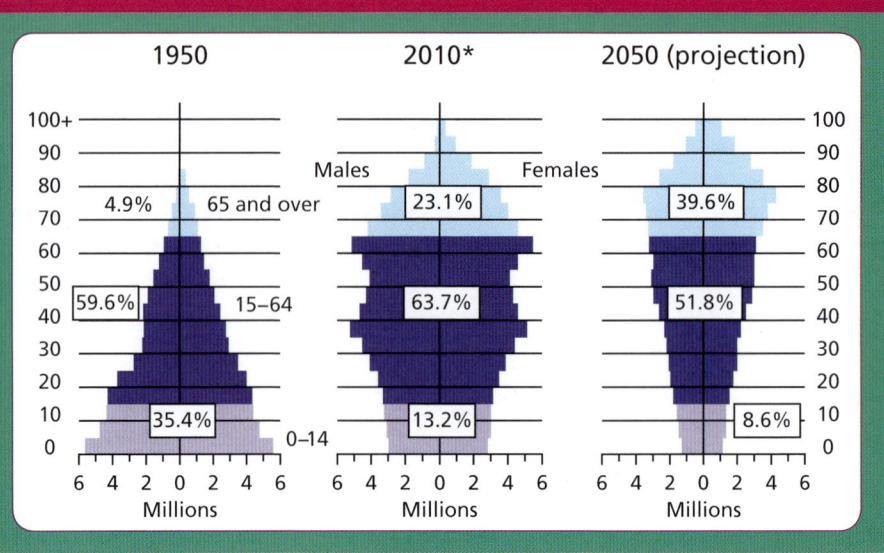

1950 — 65 and over: 4.9%; 15–64: 59.6%; 0–14: 35.4%
2010* — 65 and over: 23.1%; 15–64: 63.7%; 0–14: 13.2%
2050 (projection) — 65 and over: 39.6%; 15–64: 51.8%; 0–14: 8.6%

KEYWORDS
life expectancy
economic impact
government finances
government expenditure
labour shortages
dependency ratio
automation
technology

In 2017, Japan had an **average life expectancy** of 87 years, and 28% of the population were aged over 64. By 2050, estimates suggest that will increase to 40% of the population. Genetic, social and lifestyle factors along with diet and high standards of living all account for increased life expectancy.

Economic impacts

- The funding of pensions places huge demand on **government finances** and has led to increased public debt.
- The cost of nursing homes, home-care services and health workers increases **government expenditure**.
- **Labour shortages** exist in all sectors of the economy – Tokyo has almost twice as many job vacancies as applicants.
- Increased **dependency ratio**: in 2016, every 100 workers supported 65.29 dependents. This is up from 43.56 in 1990.

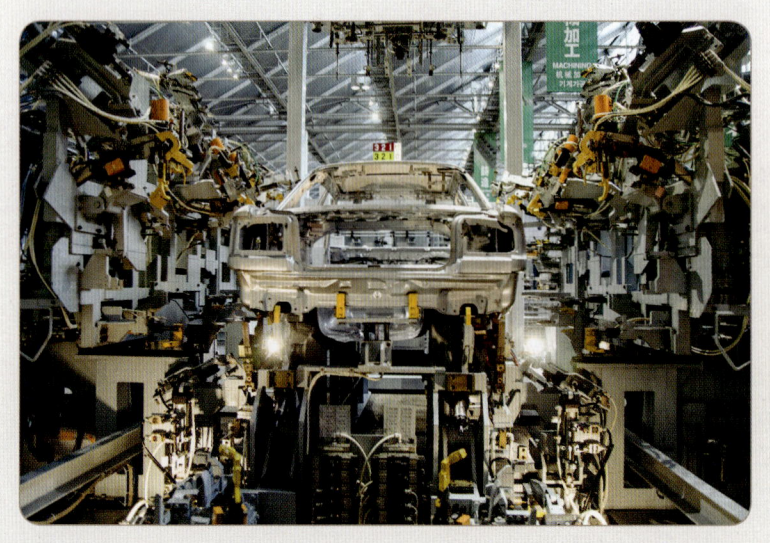

Responses

- **Government policies** aimed at increasing birth rates include a variety of financial supports, shorter working hours and an overtime limit of 24 hours a month.
- **Automation:** There is increasing use of robots in factories to cope with the declining labour force (Fig. 25.20).

← **Fig. 25.20** An automated car plant in Japan.

Technology

Many of Japan's high-tech industries have responded to issues arising from the changing demographics (Fig. 25.21). Responses include:

- drone technology that can be used to deliver medicines to people in remote rural areas;
- domestic robots to assist older people in their homes.

→ **Fig. 25.21** Robotic vacuum cleaners are programmed to move around a room and pick up dust and dirt without the need for human operation. They can be scheduled to clean, or operated via remote control.

EXAM LINK (OL)

Population (30 marks)

By the year 2031 there will be nearly one million people over the age of 65 in Ireland. That will have been an increase of more than 86% since 2016.

Discuss the challenges associated with an ageing population and how this ageing population can be planned for.

2018, Q11B

Marking Scheme:
Discussion = 11 SRPs × 3 marks

CHECK YOUR LEARNING

1. Why are mortality rates low in developed countries?
2. Why are life expectancy rates high in developed countries?
3. Name two impacts an ageing population will have on a country.
4. Name three steps governments can take to plan for an ageing population.
5. List two ways Japan has responded to its ageing population structure.

Mortality rates and life expectancy in developing countries

Infant and **maternal mortality rates** in developing countries are higher than in more developed countries. Reasons for this include:

- poor families cannot afford even the most basic **healthcare** (e.g. **Malawi**);
- **malnutrition** contributes to more than half of child deaths after the first month of birth (e.g. **South Sudan**);
- governments lack funds to invest in health services, particularly maternity and neonatal services;
- people cannot afford the **cost** of medicines for the treatment of illnesses;
- the spread of **HIV/AIDS** due to lack of education and the high **cost** of retroviral drugs to treat this disease prevents governments from buying them (e.g. **Uganda**).

KEYWORDS

mortality rate
healthcare
malnutrition
costs
HIV/AIDS
government
life expectancy

Socio-economic impacts

High **infant mortality rates** lead to high birth rates to ensure survival of children to look after parents (e.g. **Mali, Afghanistan**; Fig. 25.2). High birth rates contribute to increasing populations, causing pressure on resources.

Continuing decline in **adult mortality rates** due to improving **healthcare** has led to **increased life expectancy**. Impacts of this include:

↑ **Fig. 25.22** Families in Mali tend to be very large.

- financial problems for governments in areas such as elderly **healthcare** provision;
- supporting and caring for older people becomes the responsibility of extended families and non-governmental organisations.

CHECK YOUR LEARNING

1. Explain the following three terms: infant mortality, child mortality, maternal mortality.
2. Name two reasons why infant mortality rates are high in developing countries.
3. List one impact of high infant mortality rates.
4. Name two impacts of increased life expectancy in developing countries.

EXAMINATION QUESTIONS
ORDINARY LEVEL

Long Questions

1. Population Dynamics

Life expectancy at birth in 2015 (amended from www.hdr.undp.org)

Country	Life Expectancy
Afghanistan	60 years
Ireland	81 years
Mali	58 years
Brazil	75 years
Sudan	64 years

Examine the table above showing life expectancy at birth for selected countries in 2015 and answer each of the following questions.

(i) Using graph paper, draw a suitable graph to illustrate this data.

(ii) In your answer book, state two ways that life expectancy could be increased in countries such as Mali and Sudan.

Marking Scheme:

(i) Graph paper = 3 marks
Vertical axis labelled/Circle = 3 marks graded (3/1/0)
Horizontal axis labelled/Centred = 3 marks graded (3/1/0)
Five items × 3 marks graded (3/1/0) = 15 marks. Subtotal 24 marks

(ii) Two valid statements × 3 marks each = 6 marks

Total 30 marks

2017, Part Two, Section 2, Q10A (30 marks)

HIGHER LEVEL

Long Questions

2. Demographic Transition Model (20 marks)

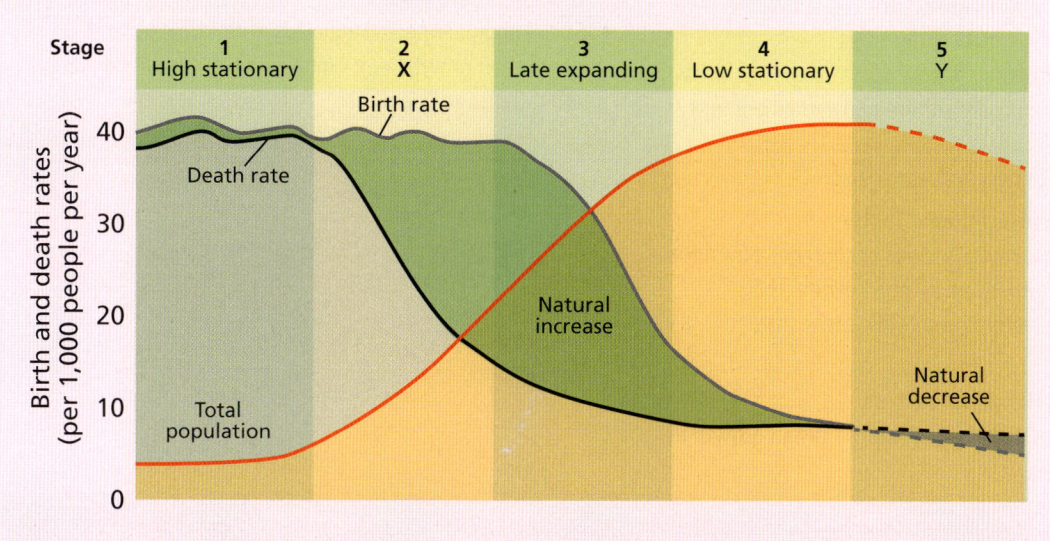

The Demographic Transition Model

| Stage | 1 High stationary | 2 X | 3 Late expanding | 4 Low stationary | 5 Y |

Birth and death rates (per 1,000 people per year): Birth rate, Death rate, Natural increase, Total population, Natural decrease

Examine the diagram above showing the Demographic Transition Model and answer each of the following questions.

(i) In which stage of the Demographic Transition Model is the total population at its lowest?

(ii) Name X, Stage 2 and name an example of a country in this stage.

(iii) Name Y, Stage 5 and name an example of a country in this stage.

(iv) Explain briefly one problem facing countries in Stage 5 of the Demographic Transition Model.

(v) Explain briefly what is meant by natural increase.

Marking Scheme:
(i) 4 marks
(ii) 2 marks + 2 marks
(iii) 2 marks + 2 marks
(iv) Any valid explanation = 4 marks
(v) Any valid explanation = 4 marks

2014, Part Two, Section 2, Q11A (20 marks)

Revision Summary

Population Distribution

- Population density = Average measurement of people in an area per km² or ml²
- Pattern of human settlement – dynamic

Physical factors
- Climate: mid-latitudes – highest densities
- Altitude: 50-60% settlement below 300 m, e.g. Paris Basin
- Soils: Fertile soils support agriculture and settlement, e.g. Ganges
- Water: high density in river valleys, e.g. Nile

Socio-economic factors
- Migration: economic activity in cities encourages migration – higher population – urbanisation, e.g. Kolkata, India
- Resources: industrial centres and fertile areas attract settlement

Historical factors
- Colonialism: Ports for export and import – urban growth in coastal areas of colonies

Global Population Growth Patterns

- Influenced by birth rates, total fertility rates, mortality rates, migration
- Advances in sanitation and medicine – 20th century population explosion
- Social engineering strategies used to increase/limit population growth, e.g. China's one child policy, France's pro-natalist policies

Demographic Transition Model

- Measures impact of social and economic changes on population
- **Stage 1:** High stationary – high birth and death rates; famine, wars, pandemics
- **Stage 2:** Early expanding – high birth rate, lower death rate - improved healthcare, sanitation, food production (LEDCs - Afghanistan)
- **Stage 3:** Late expanding – declining birth rates, slower death rate, slow population growth, e.g. India
- **Stage 4:** Low stationary – birth and death rates almost equal; reduced family size, e.g. Ireland, Canada
- **Stage 5:** Senile – declining birth rate, stable death rate, e.g. Japan, Germany

Population Structure

- Age profiles, gender profiles – data - population pyramid

Population pyramids
- Pyramid shows development stage, dependency ratio
- Used to predict healthcare requirements, taxation and social needs
- **Expansive:** Developing nations, high fertility rates, high birth rates, low life expectancy, e.g. Afghanistan
- **Stationary:** stable population, almost equal in age groups to mid-age level, e.g. Morocco
- **Constrictive:** falling birth rates, countries with high economic growth, good health and social services, e.g. Italy
- **Demographic anomaly:** difference in expected population pattern, e.g. baby boom, migration

Fertility Rates: Developed Countries

- Low TFR, may fall below replacement level

Socio-economic factors
- Education opportunities for women - delay in marriage and motherhood
- Women in workforce – high childcare costs – reduced family size
- Family planning access – smaller families
- Costs of child-rearing impacts on family size

Role of governments
- State pensions – security in old age, less need for large families
- Incentives to reverse falling fertility rates

Impacts
- Population decline
- Decreasing labour supply
- Lower tax revenues
- Increasing dependency ratio

Fertility Rates: Developing Countries

- High TFR

Socio-economic factors
- Early marriages, longer child-bearing years, e.g. Bangladesh
- High infant mortality
- Poverty – lack of family planning
- Low status of women, little say in birth control
- Large families part of culture, e.g. Niger
- Children contribute to labour force, e.g. South Sudan
- Parents depend on children in old age

Impacts
- Pressure on housing and employment, e.g. Bangladesh
- Increased demand for food and resources – overpopulation, e.g. Chad
- Immunisation, healthcare, education – challenge, e.g. Kenya

Mortality Rates: Developed Countries	**Mortality Rates: Developing Countries**
• Decreasing infant, maternal and general mortality rates, increased life expectancy – changes to population structure **Impacts** • Increasing life expectancy – ageing population • Higher percentage of old age dependents • Increased need for healthcare facilities • Increasing age-related conditions, long-term care **Planning for ageing population** • Mandatory pension schemes • Raising pension entitlement age • Review of compulsory retirement ages • Gradual retirement • Changing attitudes, e.g. National Positive Ageing Strategy (Ireland) 2013	• Higher infant and mortality rates • Basic healthcare unaffordable, e.g. Malawi • Malnutrition – child deaths, e.g. Malawi • No healthcare funding • Medicines unaffordable • Drugs to treat HIV/AIDS – unaffordable, e.g. Uganda **Socio-economic impacts** • High infant mortality rates – high birth rates, e.g. Mali – pressure on resources • Decline in adult mortality – increased life expectancy – healthcare provision costly, family care of older people

26 POPULATION AND HUMAN DEVELOPMENT

KEYWORDS
human development
carrying capacity
underpopulation
overpopulation
optimum population

LEARNING INTENTIONS
Syllabus Links: 5.2

By the end of this chapter I will be able to:
- describe and explain how overpopulation can result from resource development;
- show how society and culture can contribute to overpopulation;
- explain the impact of income levels on overpopulation;
- identify and explain the impact of technology on overpopulation;
- explain how population growth impacts on human development.

The UN Development Programme defines the basic objective of human development as the creation of an enabling environment where people have a decent standard of living, access to education and live long and healthy lives. Population characteristics including size and density, birth rate and mortality rate impact on the rates and levels of human development experienced around the world.

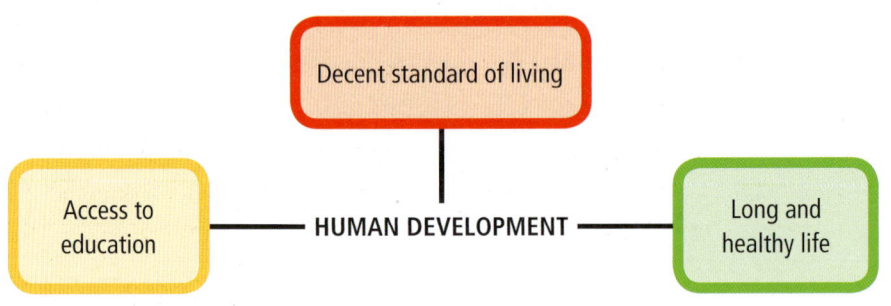

Fig. 26.1 The objectives of human development, according to the UN Development Programme.

A region's ability to support its population is called its **carrying capacity**. The carrying capacity is influenced by the size of the population and the resources the region possesses, for example, fertile land, water and technology.

When a region's resources are capable of supporting population numbers in excess of their current values, the region is underpopulated. Such regions attract inward migration (e.g. **Australia**).

When the resources of a region are not sufficient to support its population, the region is described as **overpopulated** (e.g. **the Sahel, Africa**).

The carrying capacity of a region can change. Declining population, increased food production, economic growth and new farming methods can all increase the carrying capacity.

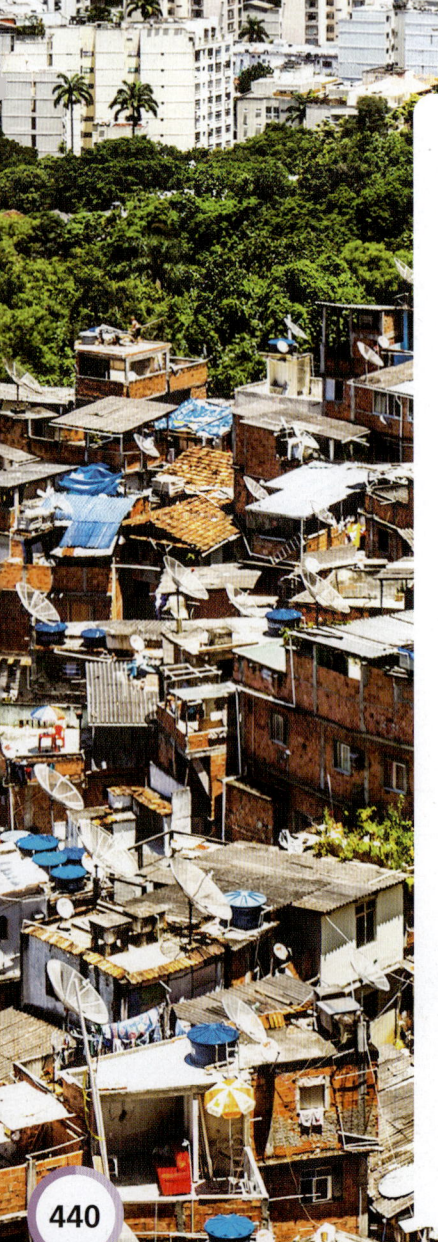

Increasing population, famine, war, political unrest, economic recession and climate change can reduce the carrying capacity of a region.

Where the resources and population of a region are balanced, it is referred to as **optimum population**.

> **CHECK YOUR LEARNING**
>
> 1. Explain the following terms: overpopulation, underpopulation, optimum population.
> 2. What is carrying capacity?
> 3. Identify two factors that would decrease carrying capacity.
> 4. Name two factors that would increase carrying capacity.

The Impact of Resource Development on Population

Global populations are increasing, however, global resources are finite. Improved levels of knowledge have resulted in increased productivity in terms of resources, for example, food production. However, poor resource management has led to problems in many areas, resulting in overpopulation.

Overpopulation

Overpopulation is usually the result of the interplay of a number of different factors, including:

- **over-exploitation of resources**, which can occur in response to human pressure and as a result of unsustainable activities;
- **increasing population** caused by high total fertility rates and/or migration.

KEYWORDS
climate
desertification
gullying
population growth
deforestation
soil erosion
overgrazing
over-cultivation
zai pits
solar ovens

CASE STUDY: OVERPOPULATION – THE SAHEL

The Sahel region of Africa is an example of how resource depletion combined with increasing population results in overpopulation.

Extending for over 5,400 km, the Sahel lies to the south of the Sahara Desert, and extends from Senegal on the Atlantic Ocean through **Mauritania**, **Mali**, **Burkina Faso**, **Niger**, **Chad** and **Sudan** to **Ethiopia** and **Eritrea** on the Red Sea.

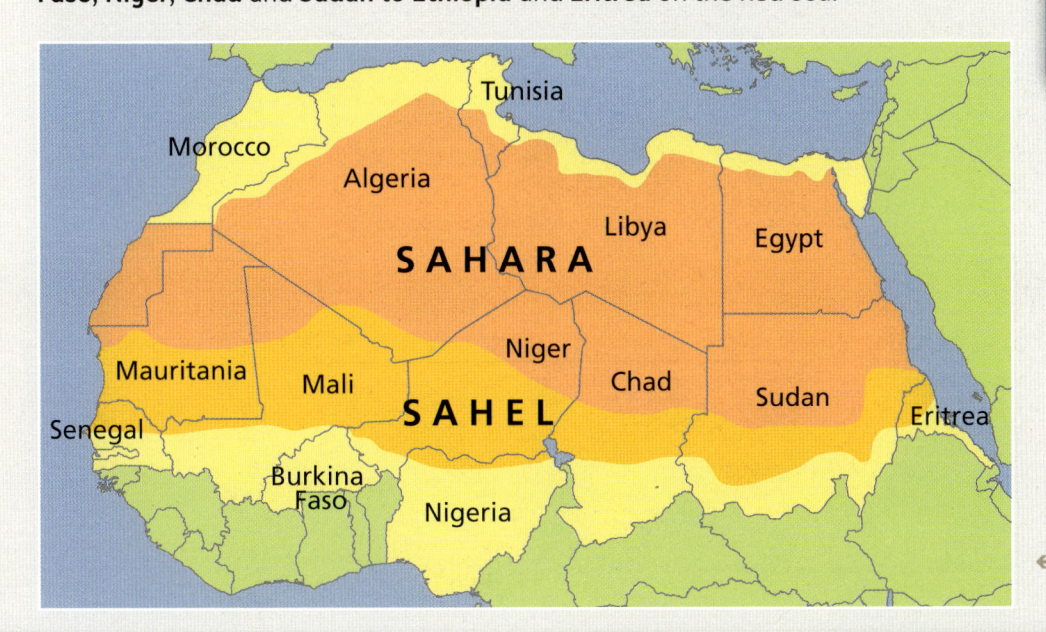

DID YOU KNOW?
The word *sahel* derives from the Arabic word for shore, and the area known as the Sahel is on the edge – or shore – of the Sahara.

← Fig. 26.2 Map of the Sahel.

Landscapes

Causes and impacts of overpopulation

Climate

The Sahel has a **tropical semi-arid climate** with seasonal variations in rainfall and temperature. It receives 200–600 mm of rainfall a year, most of which falls between May and September (**Fig. 26.3**). Most of the rain falls in the south; rainfall levels quickly decline as one moves northwards towards the northernmost edge of the Sahel. The rainfall pattern shows great variation from year to year and from decade to decade.

Desertification: The expansion of desert into surrounding areas.

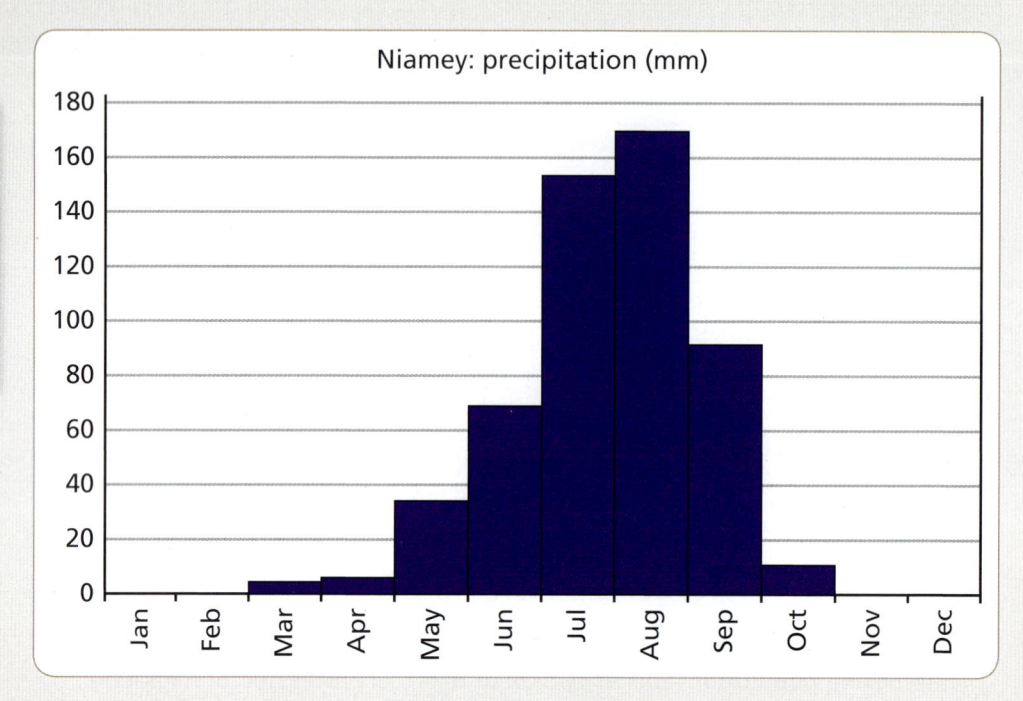

Gullying: Rainwater erodes deep channels into the soil.

→ **Fig. 26.3** Annual precipitation Niamey, Niger (Allmetsat.com).

Unpredictable rainfall patterns can result in:
- extended periods of drought, leading to food shortages and famine;
- reduced water levels in rivers and lakes, which impacts on food supplies (e.g. **Lake Chad**);
- crop failure, animal deaths, loss of life and forced migration.

During the rainy season, intense run-off causes **gullying** and soil erosion, which contribute to **desertification** (Fig. 26.4).

→ **Fig. 26.4** Gullying in the Sahel.

Climate change

Among the impacts of climate change on the Sahel region are temperature increases 1.5 times higher than the global average and an increasingly unpredictable rainfall pattern. It is estimated that 95% of farmed land in the Sahel is rain-fed, so longer dry seasons, water shortages and the negative effects of higher temperatures on evaporation rates will seriously impact on food production.

At the same time, high rates of population growth will mean increased demand for food. These pressures will likely lead to increased conflict and famine, resulting in migration north towards a region that is already receiving high numbers of refugees and migrants.

Climate change will also impact on agricultural output, resulting in increasing **food insecurity**.

> **Food insecurity:** When sufficient quantities of nutritious food are not regularly available.

Population growth

The countries of the Sahel are in the **early expanding stage** of the **Demographic Transition Model** (Stage 2) and have high fertility rates, birth rates and rates of population growth (Tables 26.1, 26.2). The rapid expansion of population will continue until economic development in these countries elevates them to Stage 3 – the late expanding stage – of the Demographic Transition Model when birth rates begin to decline.

A growing population means increased demand for limited resources such as food, water, fuel and land. It can also result in unsustainable practices like deforestation, over-cultivation and overgrazing, which lead to soil degradation, soil erosion and desertification.

> Chapter 25: Population Changes Over Time and Space

	Mali	Niger	Chad
2017	19	21	15
Projected 2050	45	68	35

← **Table 26.1** Population in millions for selected countries of the Sahel (UN).

	Mali	Niger	Chad	Sudan
Birth rate/1,000	44.4	37.3	36.1	28.5
Total fertility rate (TFR)	5.95	5.13	4.45	3.68
Infant mortality/1,000	100	71	87	50
% population growth rate	2.96	2.44	1.8	1.69

← **Table 26.2** Demographic data for selected countries of the Sahel, 2016 (World Bank).

Deforestation

Population growth increases the demand for wood. Wood is used for building shelters and grain storage units, as firewood for cooking and for the production of charcoal, which is sold to provide income (Figs 26.5, 26.6).

↑ **Fig. 26.5** Wood is used to make grain stores.

↑ **Fig. 26.6** Burning wood to make charcoal.

Landscapes

> Soil erosion is the process where upper fertile layers of soil are removed by wind and rain. Deforestation and the removal of natural vegetation leads to the destruction of the root network, causing the soil to be unstable and prone to being removed.

This increased demand contributes to soil erosion and desertification, as tree removal destroys the root network that stabilises the soil. Desertification reduces the land area available for food production. It also removes wind breaks that reduce the ability of the wind to carry the soil.

An increasing population means increased demand for food. Shrubs and trees are cleared to provide land for arable farming, but this removes the vegetation barriers that break the force of winds, reducing their ability to erode soil.

Soil erosion and desertification

Tree and vegetation removal destroy the root network that stabilise the soil. Unconsolidated soil is washed away during the rainy season, while during the dry season it can be eroded through wind erosion (**Fig. 26.7**). Formerly fertile land is transformed into desert, reducing the land area available for food production. With less land available, farmers increase the pressure they place on more productive land, causing many areas to be overgrazed and over-cultivated.

Overgrazing

The importance of cattle as a sign of wealth in the culture of this region has resulted in an increase in numbers well beyond the **carrying capacity**. Increased numbers of cattle not only contribute to vegetation removal but also an increased demand for water. As a result, more wells are dug, leading to reduced groundwater levels. During droughts, fodder and water shortages lead to animal deaths.

↑ **Fig. 26.7** A dust storm in the Sahel.

Over-cultivation

Over-cultivation has led to **soil erosion** and **reduced soil fertility** in many areas. The natural vegetation, whose **root networks** stabilises the soil, is cleared for crop cultivation. Over-cultivation occurs because:

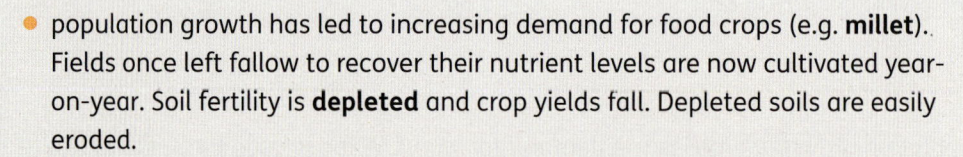

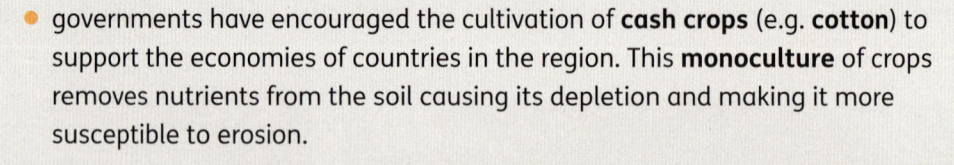

- population growth has led to increasing demand for food crops (e.g. **millet**). Fields once left fallow to recover their nutrient levels are now cultivated year-on-year. Soil fertility is **depleted** and crop yields fall. Depleted soils are easily eroded.

> **Monoculture:** Using the same land area to grow the same crops year after year.

- governments have encouraged the cultivation of **cash crops** (e.g. **cotton**) to support the economies of countries in the region. This **monoculture** of crops removes nutrients from the soil causing its depletion and making it more susceptible to erosion.

Conflict

Across the region, **armed conflicts** have displaced many people from their homes. Food production and harvests in conflict areas are disrupted, while insecurity and fear have led to forced migration. As the borders between the countries are so porous, conflicts in one country can lead to refugee flows into neighbouring ones, increasing population and demand for scarce resources in these receiving countries.

Violence and intimidation by **Boko Haram** Islamists in Northeast Nigeria have resulted in over three million Nigerians being internally displaced, and over 300,000 refugees have fled to neighbouring states of **Cameroon**, **Chad** and **Niger**.

Solutions

The Sahel region has become the focus of many international aid and environmental agencies. These agencies are involved in education programmes for farmers and environmental rehabilitation projects. Initiatives include:

- **Zai pits:** At the start of the rainy season, seeds are planted into holes filled with compost and manure (Fig. 26.8). The concentration of nutrients and water around the seeds leads to increased output and better food security.

← **Fig. 26.8** Zai pits in the Sahel.

- **The Great Green Wall:** This is a project involving 11 countries in the sub-Saharan Africa region. Trees and plants will be grown along an 8,000 km stretch. The aims of the project include: food production, a response to climate change and a reduction in outmigration.

- **Solar ovens:** By reducing the demand for firewood, simple low-cost solar ovens reduce the rate of deforestation (Fig. 26.9).

← **Fig. 26.9** Solar ovens.

CHECK YOUR LEARNING

1. Name any four countries located in the Sahel.
2. Describe the climate of the region.
3. List three causes of overpopulation.
4. Name three impacts of overpopulation.
5. Identify three solutions to the problem.

EXAM LINK (OL)

Overpopulation (30 marks)

(i) Explain briefly what is meant by the term overpopulation.

(ii) Describe and explain the causes and effects of overpopulation with reference to example(s) that you have studied.

2016, Q12B

Marking Scheme:

(i) Explanation = 2 SRPs × 3 marks

(ii) One cause stated = 3 marks

One effect stated = 3 marks

One example stated = 3 marks

Description/explanation = 5 SRPs × 3 marks

EXAM LINK (HL)

Overpopulation (30 marks)

Describe and explain the causes and effects of overpopulation, with reference to examples that you have studied.

2015, Q10C

Marking Scheme:

Cause identified = 2 marks

Effect identified = 2 marks

Examples = 2 + 2 marks

Description/explanation = 11 SRPs × 2 marks

The Impact of Society and Culture on Population

KEYWORDS		
customs	patriarchal	poverty
climate	fertility rate	conflict
food insecurity	birth rate	war
population growth	infant mortality	

The **structures** and **customs** found in some societies can contribute to high birth rates, leading to increasing population numbers and, in the absence of sufficient resources such as food, clean water and shelter, can result in **overpopulation**.

CASE STUDY: OVERPOPULATION – SOUTH SUDAN

South Sudan is a landlocked country located in East Africa (**Figs 26.10, 26.11**). It became independent from Sudan in 2011 following a long-running civil war, though unrest is still ongoing. South Sudan has **a tropical climate**, with **a wet season** extending from April to November, followed by **a dry season**. With little irrigation available, food production depends on the annual rains. Food produced during the wet season has to last through the dry season.

↑ Fig. 26.10 A map of Africa showing South Sudan.

↑ Fig. 26.11 A map of South Sudan.

Climate

The climate of South Sudan contributes to **food insecurity**, which is one of the characteristics of overpopulation. South Sudan has a tropical climate, with a wet season extending from April to November followed by a dry season (**Fig. 26.12**). With little irrigation, agriculture is rain-fed and the production of food depends on the annual rains. Food produced during the wet season has to last through the dry season. Depending on the harvest and storage conditions, food supplies can become scarce before the new crops are harvested. Shortage leads to rising prices, which contribute to food insecurity. Relief agencies have to step in to ensure relief food supplies reach the most vulnerable.

Drought is not the only climatic condition that causes food insecurity. If the annual rains are late then planting will be late, and before the crops are fully mature the dry season will have arrived. Lack of rainwater during the crucial growing season can lead to reduced yields and loss of harvest.

During the rainy season, **heavy rainfall** can cause major problems. The run-off, which can carry human and animal waste, floods wells and waterholes, causing drinking water to become contaminated, which leads to the spread of disease. Flooding of toilets in camps set up to house internally displaced people leads to unsanitary conditions, the spread of disease and increased mortality rates.

Unsurfaced clay roads turn to mud during the heavy rains, making them inaccessible. This makes the distribution of food supplies to the most vulnerable much more difficult.

↑ **Fig. 26.12(a)** The rainy season in South Sudan.

↑ **Fig. 26.12 (b)** The dry season in South Sudan.

Causes of overpopulation

Population growth
The population of South Sudan is just over 12 million, with over 80% of the total population living in rural areas. In 2017, the country had an annual population growth rate of 2.8%. Continuing high population growth rates increase demand for already limited resources and can lead to overpopulation.

Status of women
South Sudan is a **patriarchal society** where decisions that will impact on women are all made by men. Women have no right to property ownership and lack autonomy. **Arranged marriages** are common, and there is no law regarding the minimum age for marriage: over 52% of girls are married by the age of 18. Early marriage increases the potential number of children a woman will bear in her lifetime. In 2017, South Sudan had a **total fertility rate** (TFR) of 5.06 and a **birth rate** of 35.5 per 1,000. These high rates will ensure continued population growth and pressure on food, land and water resources.

Infant mortality
High rates of **infant mortality** contribute to further births as families try to ensure the survival of children to look after them in old age. In 2017, South Sudan had an **infant mortality rate** of 58.1 per 1,000 births, while the rate for Ireland was 3.6 per 1,000 births.

Poverty

Over 80% of the population of South Sudan live in rural areas and rely on **subsistence agriculture** and cattle rearing. Lack of monetary income means people cannot afford healthcare, and at the end of the dry season when food is scarce, prices rise and become unaffordable, leading to **food insecurity**.

Conflict

Government and opposition forces in South Sudan have been in conflict since 2013, and up to 300,000 people have been killed as a direct result of the fighting. Over four million people have been forced from their homes, 2.2 million of whom are **internally displaced** and living in refugee camps. Over two million refugees have flooded into neighbouring countries, e.g. **Uganda**. While a ceasefire and peace accord were signed in August 2018, there are concerns that the fragile peace may not hold.

War has greatly impacted on food production. People have been forced to flee areas of fighting, abandoning fertile farms, which results in food shortages. Estimates suggest that over seven million people are in need of **humanitarian** assistance. During the war, clinics, health centres and schools were destroyed, as were clean water supplies.

In the more remote regions of the country, conflict between armed groups is ongoing. Threats and attacks on aid workers have meant aid agencies have had to withdraw, resulting in a loss of humanitarian assistance to the 1.5 million people living in these areas.

> **Humanitarian assistance:** Aid and support that helps save lives, reduce human suffering and maintain human dignity by providing clean water, food, shelter, etc.

Future

Cultural attitudes towards women and girls are slowly changing. More families are sending girls to formal schools and ensuring that they delay early marriage and complete their education. The Irish Loreto Sisters opened a girls' secondary boarding school in Rumbek in 2006. Continued growth has created a compound consisting of a day primary school for over 500 boys and girls, and a secondary boarding school accommodating over 200 girls. While the government has undertaken to ensure that 25% of all government jobs are allocated to women, lack of education has prevented them being given meaningful jobs. Schools such as the Loreto Rumbek School are contributing to change, but with such strong patriarchal attitudes towards the status of women, change will be slow.

↑ **Fig. 26.13** Loreto School Rumbek, South Sudan.

CHECK YOUR LEARNING

1. Explain the following terms: infant mortality rate, total fertility rate, patriarchal society.
2. Identify four different ways in which society and culture can affect birth rates. Explain each one.

The Impact of Income Levels on Population

In many developing countries, a large percentage of the population is located in rural areas where economic opportunities are very limited. Many work as farm labourers, relying on subsistence agriculture for food supply. Low-income levels in these rural areas are often in stark contrast with those in urban areas, where better employment opportunities exist. The difference between rural and urban incomes has resulted in increased migration to urban areas, where problems with overpopulation have emerged.

KEYWORDS

subsistence agriculture
per capita income
rural poverty
status of women
population growth
migration
density
overcrowding
slums
pollution
traffic congestion

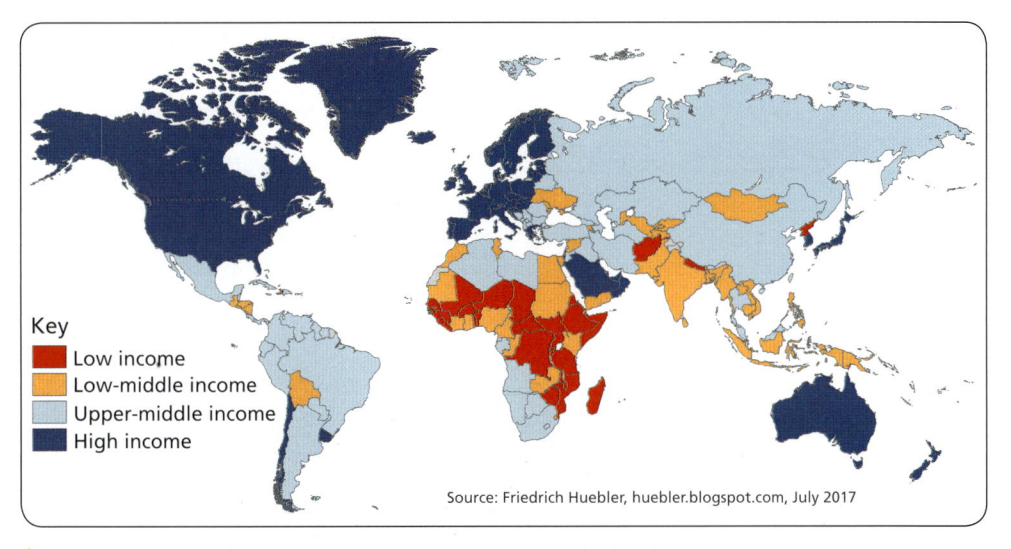

↑ **Fig. 26.14** Map of the world showing countries by income level, 2016.

SKILLS ACTIVITY

Using the information in **Figure 26.14**, identify and name three different countries from each category.

CASE STUDY: MUMBAI, INDIA

Located in the Indian state of Maharashtra, the city of Mumbai and its extensive suburbs have a combined population of over 21 million people. Mumbai is the location of a wide variety of manufacturing industries, including shipbuilding, and a range of service industries. With higher per capita incomes, this economic hub has attracted migrants from the poorer rural parts of Maharashtra and the surrounding states, which has resulted in overpopulation in the city.

Causes of overpopulation in Mumbai

Rural poverty

In rural areas of Maharashtra, incomes are very low and levels of poverty are high. Industries are often small-scale cottage industries employing only a few people. Agricultural work and day labouring jobs are the most common type of work available, but the agriculture sector is not able to provide sufficient employment for the growing population. With **increasing mechanisation** in agriculture, the employment potential of this sector is decreasing. Poverty can contribute to **higher birth rates**, as children have an earning potential as day labourers or in the unregulated economic sectors.

↑ **Fig. 26.15** Location of Mumbai in India.

Per capita income: This is the average income earned per person in a year and it is calculated by dividing the total income in a country by its total population.

Status of women

The lack of **empowerment** among women in many rural areas results in a lack of formal education and early arranged marriages, which contribute to higher **total fertility** and **birth rates**. The rate of population growth in rural areas is therefore very high, and population increase puts further pressure on limited resources.

Migration

The combination of **push factors** caused by rural poverty and **the pull factors** of employment, improved income levels, services and the prospect of a better life have resulted in **rural-to-urban migration** to Mumbai.

Impacts on Mumbai

Population density

The increase in population in Mumbai has led to increased urbanisation. However, the coastal location of the city means that there are a limited number of areas for expansion. This has led to a population density of over 29,000 people per km^2; Bangalore has a density of 4,381 people per km^2.

Chapter 22: A Continental/Subcontinental Region – India
Chapter 30: Urban Growth Problems

Overcrowding and slums

A lack of sufficient housing to meet demand has led to increased property and rental prices. Unskilled migrants have no option but to live in **slums**.

Estimates suggest that over **42% of the population of Mumbai live in slums** (approx. 9 million people). **Unemployment** rates are high, and poor living conditions can contribute to poor health outcomes for the inhabitants.

Communal toilets and a build-up of domestic rubbish contaminate water and spread **disease**. During the monsoon, contaminated water floods living quarters, causing further spread of disease. **Life expectancy** in the Govandi slum in the north-east of the city is 39.4 years, while the average for Mumbai is 68 years.

↑ **Fig. 26.16** A crowded railway station in Mumbai.

↑ **Fig. 26.17** A slum in Mumbai.

Education is beyond the reach of many children in slums, who are forced into **child labour** to supplement family income. This can involve trawling through rubbish in search of recyclable materials, begging and petty crime.

Pollution

Within Mumbai, higher levels of income and the growing affluence of the middle classes have contributed to increased car ownership. This has resulted in increasing levels of pollutants, especially nitrogen oxide, and has contributed to an increase in respiratory diseases.

Slum dwellers living beside waste tips are exposed to harmful substances, including chemicals and bacteria, which can cause serious illness and death.

Traffic congestion

The increasing population of Mumbai has placed extreme pressure on the transport infrastructure. Increased car ownership has led to traffic jams. Poorer migrants have to rely on the public transport system, and the overcrowded trains and buses indicate that the transport resources are insufficient to cope with the large population.

> **CHECK YOUR LEARNING**
> 1. List two reasons why people move to Mumbai from rural areas.
> 2. Name four impacts of overpopulation on the city of Mumbai.
> 3. Describe any two impacts of overpopulation on Mumbai.

The Impact of Technology on Population

Technological advances since the 19th century have increased **food production**, led to improved **nutrition** and increased **life expectancy**. Medical advances have also improved **mortality rates**. These factors have led to an increasing global population.

While improved food resources can increase the carrying capacity of areas, population growth will lead to increased pressure on resources, which can reduce the carrying capacity.

Two areas where technological advances have impacted on population are **agriculture** and **healthcare**.

Agriculture

The **Green Revolution** describes the technological changes that have been brought to agriculture since the late 1960s. The combined impacts of all these advances – farming practices, machinery, research and development, genetically modified crop varieties, irrigation – has been an increase in yields and quality of food.

KEYWORDS
food production
nutrition
life expectancy
mortality rate
agriculture
healthcare
machinery
medical research
irrigation
birth rate
dependency ratio
Demographic Transition Model
population momentum
fertility rate
carrying capacity

↑ **Fig. 26.18** The mechanisation of agriculture.

↑ **Fig. 26.19** Traditional farming methods.

451

New technologies in relation to food processing and storage have also contributed to more secure food supplies.

- **Machinery:** Increased mechanisation has contributed to more efficient agriculture and increased outputs.
- **Artificial fertilisers:** These add nutrients to the soil and improve crop yields.
- **Biotechnology:** New higher-yielding crop varieties have been developed, that produce more seeds and are capable of withstanding drought.
- **Genetically modified organisms (GMOs):** GMOs have been developed, with properties including higher yields and resistance to disease and pests.

Advantages of GMOs	Disadvantages of GMOs
• More food can be produced using less land. • Reduced need for pesticides.	• High cost means developing countries benefit less from them. • Unknown possible health impacts.

- **Pest control herbicides/fungicides:** The development of these has helped to decrease damage to crops and to increase yields.
- **Storage:** Improved methods of food storage have increased food security in many countries that have to cope with dry seasons (e.g. **Niger**, **Ethiopia**).

The impact of climate change

Increased levels of carbon dioxide due to technological advances in society have contributed to climate change. This is reflected in droughts and rising sea levels. Climate change has serious implications for the carrying capacity of many regions of the world. In the **Mekong Delta, Vietnam**, rising sea levels are causing saltwater intrusion into the paddy fields.

→ **Fig. 26.20** Rice farmer, Vietnam.

Irrigation

Improved irrigation technology has led to increased food production in areas of the world where precipitation is unreliable. However, there are a number of negatives to this technology.

Aquifer: An underground layer of permeable rock that contains water.

Water pumped up from aquifers: As aquifers need a long time to replenish their supplies, depletion of their water supplies will have serious consequences for food production and domestic consumption.

Water diverted from rivers: Diverting water threatens fish populations that are a vital source of food for many communities, thus reducing the carrying capacity of these areas (e.g. the destruction of fishing in the **Aral Sea**).

→ **Fig. 26.21** An irrigation scheme in Jordan.

Evaluation

The cost associated with many of these new technologies has meant their impacts and benefits in developing countries have been limited.

- Many farmers cannot afford machinery.
- Fertilisers are too expensive.
- The cost of modern irrigation techniques is prohibitive.
- Increased mechanisation results in unemployment in rural areas, leading to outmigration to already overpopulated cities (e.g. **Kolkata**).

While global food supply has increased, food distribution is still a major issue, with many developing countries still experiencing food shortages due to crop failures.

Healthcare

Global advances in medicines, healthcare and living conditions have been responsible for reductions in **mortality rates** and increases in **life expectancy**. However, the stage of economic development of a country will result in differences in these rates.

> **Chapter 25:** Population Changes Over Time and Space

Developed countries

In developed countries, advanced healthcare systems have resulted in increased life expectancy. Improvements in medical diagnostics, medicines and medical research have all contributed to better health outcomes for people who are able to afford them in private facilities, or who can access them in public state-run hospitals (**Fig. 26.22**).

While life expectancy is increasing, improved family planning has contributed to a reduction in the TFR (e.g. **Germany 1.45**, **Australia 1.77**) and falling birth rates. This results in ageing populations and increasing dependency ratios.

↑ **Fig. 26.22** A paediatric hospital in Melbourne, Australia.

Developing countries

Most developing countries are in Stages 2 and 3 of the **Demographic Transition Model**. While death rates in these countries are declining, birth rates are still very high, resulting in continued population increase. This is called **population momentum** and refers to the fact that high fertility rates in the past and increased life expectancy mean that there are more women of reproductive age in the world today. This has resulted in continuing high birth rates, increasing populations, increased pressure on carrying capacity and the potential for overpopulation (e.g. **Nigeria**, **Indonesia**).

Poorly developed and financed healthcare systems result in poor neonatal services and **higher infant mortality rates**.

High levels of disease and infection due to **poor living conditions**, contaminated water supplies and a lack of proper sanitation all contribute to higher mortality rates and a lower life expectancy.

A lack of **government funding** means there is limited availability of new technologies, while extreme poverty prevents people from accessing medicines and treatments.

Social and **cultural influences**, along with cost implications, have resulted in family planning practices being less widespread.

Medical advancements in the treatment of diseases is ongoing, and research into **HIV/AIDS** and **Ebola** have resulted in treatments that have had major impacts.

HIV/AIDS

Since the **HIV/AIDS** pandemic started in 1983, more than 70 million people have been infected and over 35 million people have died. The African continent accounts for more than 15 million of that total. Improvements in treatments have led to a dramatic reduction in deaths, and now more people are living with the disease than are dying from it.

In the period 2005–2016, global AIDS-related deaths have fallen from 1.9 million to 1 million. New drug treatments have greatly reduced the viral load in those affected, resulting in them being unable to transmit the disease.

HIV/AIDS has had a dramatic impact on many African countries where thousands of sufferers are unable to work or to attend school. Caring for the many thousands of orphans poses huge challenges for countries lacking resources (e.g. **Kenya, Uganda**).

The cost of new drug treatments presents a challenge for many countries. **UNAIDS** (the joint United Nations Programme on AIDS) estimates that over €22 billion will be required for the HIV/AIDS response in low- and middle-income countries in 2020.

Ebola

The Ebola virus is transmitted to people from wild animals and spreads in the human population through human-to-human transmission. The 2014–2016 outbreak began in Guinea in West Africa and spread across land borders to Sierra Leone and Liberia. Outbreaks were recorded in major urban and rural areas and over 11,000 deaths were recorded. An experimental Ebola vaccine proved highly protective against the deadly virus in a major trial in Guinea.

> **HIV/AIDS**
> When the human immune system is infected by the Human Immunodeficiency Virus (HIV), it is weakened and loses its ability to protect against infection and disease.
>
> Acquired Immunodeficiency Syndrome – AIDS – is associated with very advanced stages of HIV, when multiple infections are present.

> **Ebola**
> Ebola is a highly infectious disease that results in fever and internal bleeding. The virus is thought to be transmitted when humans eat the meat of infected animals. A number of vaccines are in the development stage.

CHECK YOUR LEARNING

1. Name four technological advances that have impacted on agricultural production.
2. Have the impacts of new technologies been evenly distributed around the world? Explain your answer.
3. Explain the term GMO and describe any two advantages and two disadvantages of them.
4. Explain the term population momentum.
5. Describe two ways in which medical advances have influenced population growth.

The Impact of Population Change on Rates of Human Development

KEYWORDS
Human Development Index
life expectancy
literacy rates
education provision
living standards

The Demographic Transition Model shows that, as a country develops economically, death rates decline. Increasing and decreasing population totals have socio-economic and political impacts. The UN Human Development Index (HDI) lists 188 countries and uses data on **life expectancy**, **literacy rates**,

education provision and **living standards**. The index ranges from 0 to 1 and the categories are: very high, high, medium and low (Table 26.3). The HDI ranking shows a close correlation between low index levels and areas of the world with growing populations. It suggests such growth has a negative impact on human development. In many developing countries, rapid population growth presents many challenges and some opportunities.

Category	HDI
Very high	0.8–0.999
High	0.7–0.799
Medium	0.6–0.699
Low	0.1–0.599

↑ **Table 26.3** Human Development Index categories.

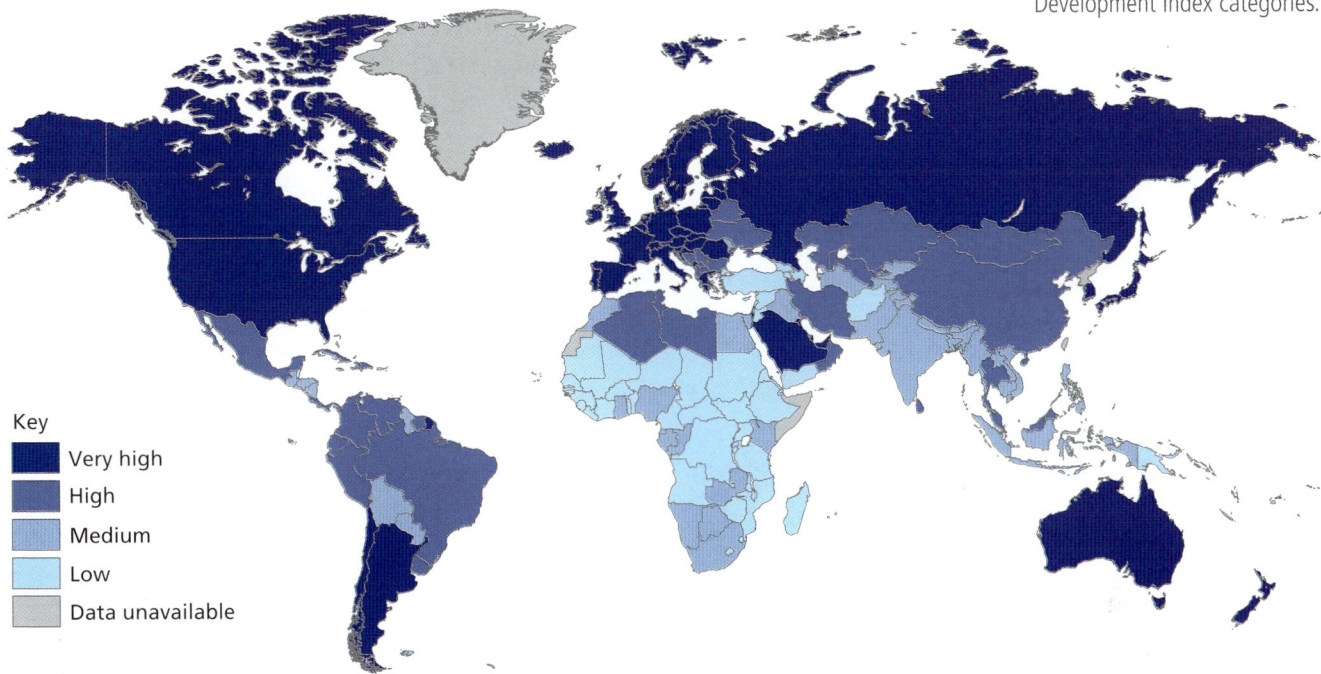

↑ **Fig. 26.23** Map of the world showing categories of Human Development Index (2013 data).

CHECK YOUR LEARNING

Study Figure 26.23 and answer the following questions:
1. Name three countries from each of the HDI categories.
2. What data is used to compile this index?
3. List two reasons why many African countries are in the low category of this index.
4. Name one country in the very high category and one in the low.

HDI rank	Country	HDI index	Life expectancy at birth	Expected years of schooling	Per capita income (US$)
1	Norway	0.953	82.3	17.9	68,012
4	Ireland	0.938	81.6	19.6	53,754
74	Mexico	0.774	77.3	14.0	16,944
113	Philippines	0.699	69.2	12.6	9,154
157	Nigeria	0.532	53.9	10.0	5,231
187	South Sudan	0.388	57.3	4.9	963

↑ **Table 26.4** HDI ranking and data for selected countries (UN, 2018).

SKILLS ACTIVITY

Draw a suitable graph to illustrate the HDI index for the countries shown in Table 26.4.

CHECK YOUR LEARNING

Study Table 26.4 and answer the following questions:
1. List three differences between Ireland and South Sudan.
2. Explain two reasons for any one difference.

Landscapes

KEYWORDS

rural-to-urban migration
governments
poverty
employment
food production
income
brain drain
newly industrialised countries (NICs)
multinational corporations (MNCs)
environment

The Impact of Population Growth on Human Development

Developing countries

Socio-economic impacts

Increasing populations in rural areas lead to rural-to-urban migration, causing cities to become overpopulated as the city's resources cannot support such an increase in population. This leads to poor living conditions in slums on the outskirts of urban centres (e.g. **Mumbai, India**).

Governments in many poorer countries have to focus investment in urban centres, where large numbers of people are concentrated, in order to limit unrest and opposition to the government (e.g. **Abuja, Nigeria**).

Rapid population growth forces families to spend a large part of whatever income they have on rearing their children. There is no scope for savings that would contribute to financial security.

Poverty leads to high rates of child labour, preventing children from accessing education (e.g. **Pakistan**) and thus from getting high-skilled, highly paid jobs.

An increasing population puts pressure on employment. A lack of economic opportunity results in economic migrants (e.g. **sub-Saharan Africans cross the Mediterranean**, hoping for a better life in Europe).

An increasing population puts pressure on food production. Inadequate food supplies result in undernourishment and decreased productivity, leading to less income to save and invest (e.g. **Bangladesh**).

A lack of investment in healthcare forces many newly qualified nurses and doctors to emigrate in search of work. This brain drain impacts hugely on these countries (e.g. **healthcare workers from the Philippines** moving to the Irish healthcare system).

In newly industrialised countries (NICs), increasing population has actually proved to be of great economic benefit. Cheap labour supplies have attracted multinational corporation (MNC) investment and have made these countries powerhouses of manufacturing (e.g. **Taiwan, South Korea**).

Environment

Continued population expansion in countries such as India and China will see an increased demand for and consumption of fossil fuels. Increasing use of coal in power stations will further contribute to global air pollution and increased carbon dioxide emissions, which will impact on climate change.

Increased population results in increased pressure on ecologically sensitive areas. Rainforests are being cleared to provide farmland for cattle rearing and the growing of crops. Population growth in India has led to the threat of extinction of some species (e.g. the **Indian tiger**), while in China population growth has endangered the survival of the **Giant Panda**.

Newly industrialised countries (NICs): Countries whose economies have recently changed from an agricultural base to a manufacturing one.

CHECK YOUR LEARNING

1. Name four impacts of population growth on human development in developing countries.
2. Briefly explain each one.

456

Developed countries

Developed countries are experiencing declines in birth rates, ageing populations, declining populations and increasing dependency ratios (e.g. **Japan**, **Italy**). These changes in population will have a number of socio-economic impacts.

An ageing population means an increase in the number of people drawing a state pension. This means that the government will have to use more of its budget to pay for pensions.

An increase in the mandatory retirement age is one of the ways governments have of dealing with the cost implications of pension provision. In 2014, the Irish Government raised the age limit for the state pension from 65 to 66, and indicated that it would rise to 67 in 2021 and 68 in 2028. Moreover, pension rates will have to match inflation, otherwise older people will face financial hardship. Other EU countries are proposing to link the retirement age to life expectancy rates (e.g. **Finland**).

A decreasing number of people of working age means a reduced skilled labour pool, which could pose difficulties for employers and create problems in attracting inward investment (e.g. **Germany**). Tax revenue will be reduced as the productive sector shrinks, creating **budget deficits**. The shortfall will dictate spending cuts or increased taxation, raising the cost of living (e.g. **Japan**).

There will be increased expenditure on **health** including care facilities for older people, medical supplies and healthcare staff (e.g. **Italy**).

> **Chapter 25:** Population Changes Over Time and Space

CHECK YOUR LEARNING

1. List three changes that are occurring in the populations of developed countries.
2. Explain how each one of these changes will impact on human development in these countries.

EXAMINATION QUESTIONS

ORDINARY LEVEL

Long Questions

1. Population Dynamics

Explain how any three of the following factors influence population.

Resources   Society and culture   Income levels   Technology

2017, Part Two, Section 2, Q11C (30 marks)

Marking Scheme:
Factor 1 = 4 SRPs × 3 marks
Factor 2 = 3 SRPs × 3 marks
Factor 3 = 3 SRPs × 3 marks

HIGHER LEVEL

Long Questions

2. Dynamics of Population

Examine the impact of any one of the following factors on levels of population growth, with reference to example(s) that you have studied.

Development of resources   Income levels
Society and culture   Technology

2017, Part Two, Section 2, Q11C (30 marks)

Marking Scheme:
Impact on population growth identified = 2 marks
Example of location = 2 marks
Examination = 13 SRPs × 2 marks

Revision Summary

Overpopulation and Human Development

Population and Resources
- Objective of development – create enabling environment
- Carrying capacity: a region's ability to support its population (resources)
- Resources in excess of population needs – underpopulated, e.g. Australia
- Resources insufficient for region – overpopulated, e.g. Sahel, Africa
- Carrying capacity increases (economic growth) or decreases (war, famine)
- Balanced resources and population = optimum population
- Overpopulation: over-exploitation of resources – increasing population (TFR, migration)

Case Study: The Sahel
- Resource depletion + increasing population = overpopulation
- Causes and impacts: tropical semi-arid = drought, crop failure, famine, soil erosion – unpredictable rainfall = soil erosion, desertification – climate change = impact food production
- Population growth: early expanding stage – increased demand on resources – deforestation = soil erosion; over-cultivation = reduced yields, overgrazing = fodder shortages – political instability = disruption of food production, refugees
- Solutions: zai pits, Great Green Wall, solar ovens

Impact of Income Levels on Population
- Migration to urban areas – better opportunities – overpopulation

Case Study: Mumbai, India
- Causes:
  1. Rural poverty: small-scale cottage industries, increasing mechanisation – little employment; high birth rate
  2. Status of women: lack of empowerment – high TFR
  3. Rural-to-urban migration to Mumbai
- Impacts:
  1. Increased population density
  2. Increased poverty – slums – disease, high unemployment, low life expectancy, child labour
  3. Increasing pollution – respiratory disease
  4. Traffic congestion

Impact of Technology on Population: Agriculture
- **Green revolution:** increased yields, quality, more secure food supplies – mechanisation – artificial fertilisers – biotechnology – GMOs – pest control – storage
- Irrigation: helpful where precipitation unreliable – aquifers take long time to replenish; using river water threatens fish population

Evaluation
- High costs – impacts limited
- Mechanisation – unemployment in rural areas – outmigration
- Food distribution still a problem

Society and Culture: Impact on Population

Case Study: South Sudan
- Climate: tropical – wet season, dry season
- Little irrigation, rain-fed food production – food insecurity, overpopulation
- Population growth: high growth rate
- Status of women: patriarchal society – arranged marriages, high TFR
- High infant mortality rates – more children for social security
- Poverty: 80% rely on subsistence agriculture, food insecurity
- Conflict: internal displacement – refugee camps; agricultural cycle disrupted
- Future: patriarchal attitudes towards women changing slowly

Impact of Technology on Population: Health

Developing world
- Population momentum – high birth rate, continued population increase
- Poorly developed health systems – high infant mortality rate
- Poor living conditions – disease, infection
- Lack of govt funding – poor prevented from medicines, treatment
- Social/cultural issues – family planning not widespread
- Treatment of HIV/AIDS and Ebola

Developed world
- Advanced healthcare systems – longer life expectancy
- Medical research, better health outcomes
- Improved family planning – TFR reduced – ageing population

Impact of Population Growth on Human Development

Developing world
- Rural-to-urban migration – overpopulated cities, poor living conditions
- Govt investment is urban-focused
- No scope for saving
- Poverty – child labour, poor education
- Pressure on employment – economic migrants
- NICs – cheap labour pool attracts multinationals
- Pressure on food production – inadequate supplies
- Lack of investment – brain drain – healthcare workers emigrate
- Increased demand for fossil fuels – impact on climate change
- Ecological implications – clearing of rainforests; endangered species

Developed world
- Declining birth rates, ageing population, declining populations, increasing dependency ratios
- Ageing population: cost implications of state pension
- Reduced skilled labour pool
- Reduced tax revenue – budget deficits – spending cuts/taxation
- Elderly healthcare costs

27 MIGRATION

LEARNING INTENTIONS
Syllabus Links: 5.3

By the end of this chapter I will be able to:
- identify and explain the impacts of migration on donor and receiver regions;
- describe the changing patterns of migration in Ireland;
- explain how rural-to-urban migration affects the developed and developing regions of the world;
- outline and explain Irish and EU migration policies;
- identify and explain ethnic, racial and religious issues that can arise from migration.

DID YOU KNOW?
The UN estimates that in 2017 the number of international migrants was 257.7 million people – 3.34% of the global population.

Since prehistoric times, migration has featured in global population dynamics. Reasons for internal and international migration are varied and include economic, social and political factors. The imbalance in economic activities within and between countries is one of the major drivers of migration, with push factors operating in donor regions and pull factors in host regions.

Push factors – donor regions	Pull factors – receiver/host regions
Overpopulation: where the resources of an area can no longer support the population (e.g. the **Sahel region**)	Underpopulation: areas where labour shortages exist (e.g. **Canada**)
Poor economic opportunities result in low wages and unemployment (e.g. the **Mezzogiorno**)	Highly developed economies with a variety of economic activities and employments (e.g. **Paris**)
Lack of services: health and education (e.g. rural areas of **India**)	Large range of services: health and education (e.g. **Galway**)
Conflict and political unrest (e.g. **Syria**)	Higher incomes and a better standard of living (e.g. **Brussels**)
Natural disasters and famine (e.g. **Darfur**)	Freedom from persecution (e.g. **Europe**)

Push factors: Considerations that cause people to leave a region known as the donor region.

Pull factors: Considerations that draw people to a region known as the receiver or host region.

Migration: The long-term movement of people from one place to another.

Barriers to migration include:

Financial: The costs involved in travel and resettling can prevent people from moving.

Legal: The requirements for visas and work permits can result in people being denied permission to move to a new country.

Personal: Family ties can prevent people from leaving their country of origin.

CHECK YOUR LEARNING
1. Name two pull factors and explain how each one operates.
2. Name two push factors and explain how each one operates.
3. Identify any three barriers to migration.

Migration and Donor Regions

KEYWORDS		
safety valve	skills	brain drain
remittances	gender imbalance	donor
resources	quality of life	

Push factors operating in donor regions result in out-migration, which has both positive and negative impacts.

Positive socio-economic impacts

Safety valve: Migration can be a **safety valve** that acts to reduce the numbers of unemployed people.

Migrants send **remittances** back to their families in their country of origin. Global estimates for 2016 suggest that this amounted to $575 billion. At $62.7 billion, India was the largest recipient.

Resources: Overpopulation triggers migration and the out-movement can relieve pressure on resources such as food and healthcare.

Skills: Migrants may return with **new skills**. Many Polish migrants who have settled in Ireland since the Celtic Tiger are now returning home with enhanced skills that are supporting current economic growth in Poland.

Negative socio-economic impacts

Gender imbalance: Female migrants outnumber male migrants in Europe and Northern America, while in Africa and Western Asia, migrants are predominantly male. This imbalance impacts on marriage rates and leads to changes in the population structure (e.g. the **Mezzogiorno**).

Quality of life: Sport and recreation activities suffer as a result of decreased numbers of participants (e.g. GAA and sports clubs in the West of Ireland).

Brain drain: As education improves in many developing countries, the migrant profile changes. The cost of education and the potential contribution to the donor country is lost when skilled IT graduates, doctors and nurses migrate in search of a better life (e.g. **Pakistan**). Since the 1980s, Ireland has lost skilled graduates in various disciplines during recessionary cycles.

Depopulation: A decline in population leaves abandoned homes and farms, and the loss of economic activities.

Emigration: Moving out of a place.

Immigration: Moving into a place.

International migration: Moving to another country.

Internal migration: Movement within one's country.

Internally displaced person: A person who has been forced to move from their home to a safe location within their own country.

Rural-to-urban migration: Moving from a rural area to a city.

Counter-urbanisation: Movement from urban areas to rural areas.

Forced migration: Governments force people to move (e.g. Jewish people in World War II) or war, famine and political unrest push people out (e.g. the Syrian civil war).

Voluntary migration: The choice to move is made by the migrant (e.g. Ireland to the United Kingdom).

Remittances: Money sent by migrants to their home country.

CHECK YOUR LEARNING

1. Explain the following terms: forced migration, voluntary migration, internally displaced person, counter-urbanisation.
2. Explain the following terms: remittances, resources, brain drain.
3. Name two examples of donor regions.
4. Describe three positive impacts of migration on donor regions.
5. Explain three negative impacts of migration on donor regions.

Migration and Host Regions

Pull factors that operate in host regions attract migrants and can have both positive and negative impacts.

Positive socio-economic impacts

The presence of people from many different cultural backgrounds leads to **cultural enrichment** and the creation of a multiracial society. With proper integration strategies, the society is enhanced.

The arrival of young, skilled workers can address existing **labour shortages** (e.g. **Australia**). Semi-skilled and non-skilled workers also contribute to different economic activities, for example in hotels and restaurants (e.g. **Killarney**). By addressing labour shortages in an economy, migration can enable **economic growth** to be sustained (e.g. **Dubai**).

Migrants' spending supports consumer industries and tertiary activities such as retail and leisure. **Government revenues** benefit from income taxes, VAT and sales taxes.

Migrant entrepreneurs can create employment and also build trade links with their countries of origin (e.g. **Chinatown, San Francisco, USA**; Figs 27.1, 27.2).

KEYWORDS

pull factors
cultural enrichment
integration policies
labour shortage
economic growth
consumer industries
government revenues
birth rates
wages
reliance

↑ **Fig. 27.1** Chinatown, San Francisco.

↑ **Fig. 27.2** An African supermarket in Paris.

Negative socio-economic impacts

Birth rates among migrants tend to be higher than the native population, putting pressure on the maternity services (e.g. **Dublin**). Migrants place extra demands on **social services**, including housing and welfare. Far-right parties in Europe claim that growing demand by migrants for these services has resulted in decreased levels of services for nationals (e.g. **France**).

Cultural and religious tensions can arise resulting in **discrimination** and **attacks based on religion or race**. A lack of proper **integration policies** can lead to increasing racial tensions and anti-migrant sentiment (e.g. **Belgium**).

↑ **Fig. 27.3** Horticulture in California relies on Mexican migrants.

Undercutting of **wage rates** can occur because migrant workers are prepared to work for lower rates. This can become a source of tension.

Some sectors of the economy can develop a reliance on migrant workers (e.g. **Mexican migrants in California** working in the horticulture sector; Fig. 27.3).

Chapter 20: A Core European Region – The Paris Basin
Chapter 22: A Continental/Subcontinental Region – India

CHECK YOUR LEARNING

1. Name two examples of receiver regions.
2. List three benefits migration brings to receiver regions.
3. List three negative impacts of migration on receiver regions.

Landscapes

KEYWORDS
- recession
- rural-to-urban migration
- agriculture
- skills
- tariffs
- Single European Market
- Celtic Tiger

Recession: A period when economic activity declines.

Net migration: The number of people coming into a country, minus the number of people leaving.

Positive net migration: More people are entering than leaving.

Negative net migration: More people are leaving than entering.

Changing Migration Patterns in Ireland

Migration flows

Beginning with the **1847 famine**, out-migration has had a constant impact on the population of Ireland. Since Independence in 1921, cycles of migration have been closely linked to economic conditions within the country. Periods of recession see emigration increase, while periods of economic growth result in immigration. Rural-to-urban migration is an ongoing process (**Fig. 27.4**).

1950s
Agriculture employed over 40% of the working population. However, poor income on small farms, especially in the West of Ireland, and a lack of employment due to low levels of government investment in new industries, meant levels of emigration were high. During this era, over **400,000** people emigrated, most of them to the UK. The vast majority of these had a basic education and lacked skills.

1960s
In 1961, the population of Ireland was **2,818,341**, the lowest since the foundation of the State. However, in the early years of this era, economic policy changed, export tariffs were removed and Foreign Direct Investment (FDI) was encouraged. Economic growth meant employment rose and emigration decreased. Between 1961 and 1971, net migration had reduced from **212,003 to 53,906**.

1970s
In 1973, Ireland joined the EEC and a period of economic expansion followed – emigration reduced and immigration increased. By the end of the era, however, a number of combined factors, including the oil crisis of 1973–1974, resulted in economic decline and recession. Net migration measured over **104,000** people during this period.

1980s
The baby boom of the 1960s meant a huge growth in the labour market during this period. However, poor global economic conditions led to recession and many manufacturing facilities in Ireland closed. The unemployment rate reached 17%. Over **200,000** people emigrated during this period, with more than 60% going to the UK. This time, the profile of the emigrants had changed and highly skilled graduates were lost.

1990s
The creation of the Single European Market in 1993 lead to increased FDI. The economy expanded and employment in all sectors increased. Between 1993 and 2001, unemployment declined from 15.9% to 3.6%, resulting in labour shortages.

2004
When the EU enlarged in 2004, under the free movement of people within the EU, citizens from the new member states came to live and work in Ireland. Figure 27.4 shows that approximately **150,000 migrants** entered Ireland in 2007. That figure includes returning Irish who had emigrated during the 1980s.

2007
Economic expansion during the early years of the Celtic Tiger era, increasing employment and shortages in the labour market fuelled immigration. In 2007, a net inward migration figure of **104,800** people was recorded.

2008

The global banking crisis triggered an economic recession in 2008. The construction industry collapsed and falling global demand for goods caused the closure of foreign plants and increasing unemployment. The rate of unemployment rose from 6.1% in 2008 to 14.7% in 2012. Outward migration, mainly to the UK, Australia, Canada and the USA, was once again a feature of Irish demographics.

2012–2016

Economic recovery saw unemployment decrease.

2017

In July 2017, the unemployment rate was down to 6.4%. Census 2016 showed a positive net migration of **3,100** – the first increase since 2009.

2017–2018

Continued economic growth resulted in increased employment. Unemployment rates fell from 14.7% in 2012 to 5.8% in 2018. Out-migration fell, while returning and new migrants meant a net increase of **33,900** from April 2017 to April 2018, giving the highest positive net migration figure since 2008.

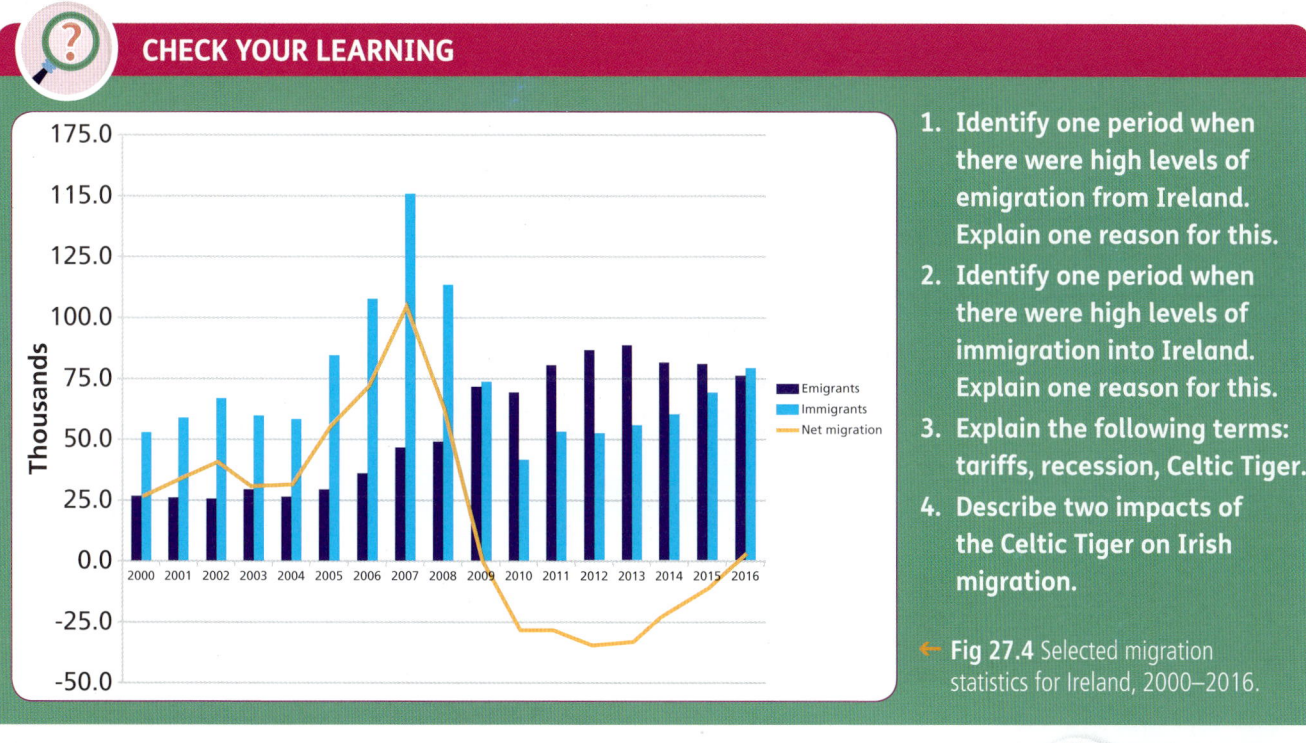

CHECK YOUR LEARNING

1. Identify one period when there were high levels of emigration from Ireland. Explain one reason for this.
2. Identify one period when there were high levels of immigration into Ireland. Explain one reason for this.
3. Explain the following terms: tariffs, recession, Celtic Tiger.
4. Describe two impacts of the Celtic Tiger on Irish migration.

Fig 27.4 Selected migration statistics for Ireland, 2000–2016.

Year	Immigration	Emigration	Net Migration
2010	41,800	69,200	−27,500
2011	53,300	80,600	−27,400
2012	52,700	87,100	−34,400
2013	55,900	89,000	−33,100

Table 27.1 Migration data 2010–2013 showing the impact of the collapse of the Celtic Tiger (CSO).

SKILLS ACTIVITY

Using the information in **Table 27.1**, draw a suitable graph to illustrate the data for outward migration.

CHECK YOUR LEARNING

Study Table 27.1 and answer the following questions:
1. Which year recorded the lowest emigrant numbers?
2. Which year recorded the highest number of immigrants?
3. Suggest two reasons why people emigrate from Ireland.
4. Which year recorded the highest figures for net migration?
5. Which year recorded the lowest figure for net migration?
6. Suggest two reasons why people immigrate into Ireland.

Landscapes

> **EXAM LINK (OL)**
>
> **Patterns in Migration (40 marks)**
> (i) Explain two reasons why people immigrated (moved in) to Ireland in recent times (early 2000s).
> (ii) Explain two reasons why in 2013 people were emigrating (moving out) of Ireland in large numbers.
>
> **2013, Q12C**
>
> **Marking Scheme:**
> (i) Name two reasons = 2 × 1 mark
>   Explanation = 3 SRPs × 3 marks for each reason
> (ii) Name two reasons = 2 × 1 mark
>   Explanation = 3 SRPs × 3 marks for each reason

> **EXAM LINK (HL)**
>
> **Patterns of Migration (30 marks)**
> Describe and explain changes in the patterns of migration into and out of Ireland since the 1950s.
> **2018, Q12B**
>
> **Marking Scheme:**
> Changing patterns identified into Ireland = 2 marks
> Changing patterns identified out of Ireland = 2 marks
> Examination = 13 SRPs × 2 marks

CASE STUDY: IRELAND AS A RECEIVER/HOST REGION

KEYWORDS
EU enlargement
Celtic Tiger
purchasing power
remittances
attitudes
integration
government
racism
exploitation
education
people trafficking
security

The enlargement of the EU in 2004 coincided with the **Celtic Tiger** period of major economic expansion that attracted migrant flows from the new EU states. Census 2016 revealed that 11.6% of the population were **non-Irish**. Polish people made up the largest group, followed by people from the UK (**Fig. 27.5**).

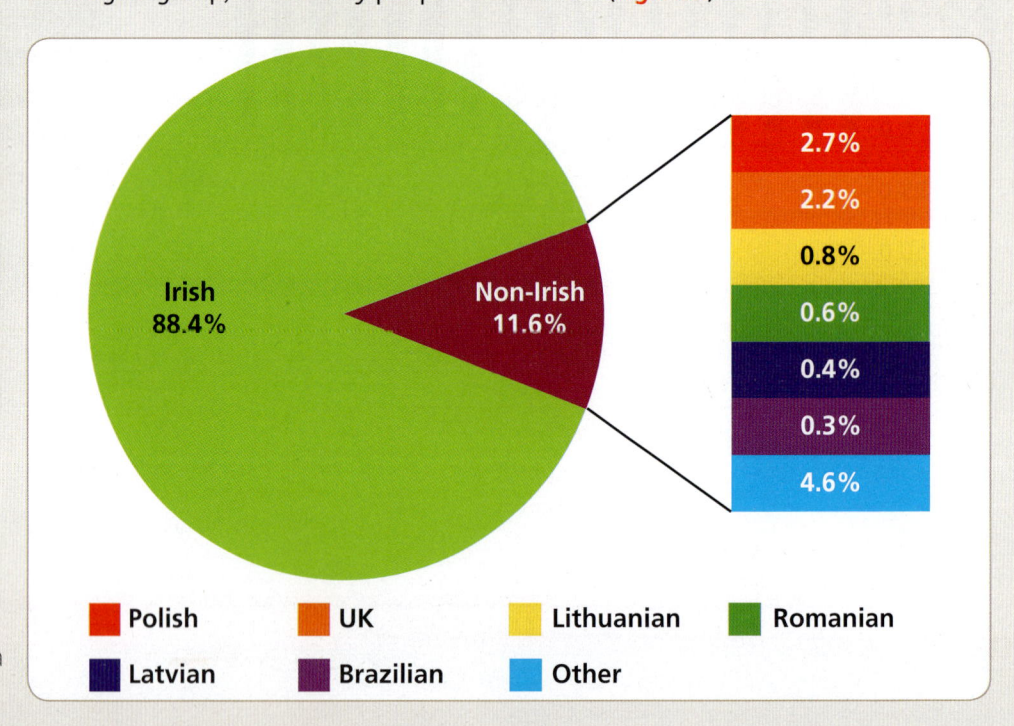

Irish 88.4%
Non-Irish 11.6%

2.7% Polish
2.2% UK
0.8% Lithuanian
0.6% Romanian
0.4% Latvian
0.3% Brazilian
4.6% Other

→ **Fig. 27.5** Census data on nationality, 2016.

The inflow of migrants into Ireland has had both positive and negative socio-economic impacts.

Positive socio-economic impacts

Migration from the new EU accession states brought **skilled, multilingual workers** to the country, which contributed to global companies such as Google and Facebook deciding to locate operations in Dublin. The construction boom attracted **skilled and semi-skilled tradespeople** from Poland and Lithuania, helping to solve skills and labour shortages during a period of rapid economic expansion.

Migrants contribute to **government revenues** through income tax contributions and VAT paid on the purchase of consumer goods.

Further contributions to the economy include increased **purchasing power**, leading to growth in the retail and recreational sector of the economy and the purchasing/rental of accommodation.

Migrants help to fill **employment gaps** in a variety of sectors including the hospitality sector and horticulture (e.g. **Temple Bar, Dublin**; Fig. 27.6).

Migrants settling in smaller towns and villages **increase population**, which helps to maintain the level of services such as local schools.

Fig. 27.6 Migrants are important to the horticultural sector.

Cultural diversity is reflected in ethnic shops and restaurants. Some areas develop a distinct cultural character (e.g. **Parnell Street – Dublin's Chinatown**).

Negative socio-economic impacts

Migrant **remittances** mean a loss of money to the economy. In 2017, migrants transferred €785 million out of Ireland to family members in their home countries.

As economic conditions have changed, so have **attitudes** towards migrants. The Economic and Social Research Institute survey on changing attitudes to migrants between 2002 and 2014 revealed that, while in 2000 attitudes were very positive, the economic recession of 2008 coincided with an increase in negative attitudes. This is possibly due to migrants being seen as competition for employment.

Migrant flows put pressure on **services**, including demand for housing and accommodation. Migrants are usually young and as such have a high birth rate; this increase in the number of births put pressure on maternity services.

Integration difficulties can present themselves. Ireland had to adjust to large numbers of migrants and their families who had little command of English. Schools often need to provide language support teachers and classes, which can put a strain on resources.

Government departments had to produce information leaflets in a variety of European languages, while the court system needed the services of translators, increasing costs.

There has been an increase in **racism** and **racially-motivated crimes**. Irish people take an active part in a number of international campaigns to increase awareness of the issue, and the Garda Racial Intercultural and Diversity Office engages with minority communities to build trust and encourages reporting of crime (Fig. 27.7).

Workers who lack English language skills, and who are not familiar with worker's rights and labour laws, can be subjected to **exploitation**.

In the area of **education**, Catholic Church ownership and management of many schools, at both primary and secondary level, limits choice for migrants who are not members of this faith.

Fig. 27.7 The European Network Against Racism – Ireland.

Landscapes

People trafficking: The use of force or deception in moving migrants to countries where they can be exploited for labour (e.g. sex trade).

In more recent years, increasing terror attacks in Europe and the growing threat caused by Islamist fundamentalism has increased the need for increased monitoring by **security services**. In Ireland, a number of convictions for organising financial support for Islamist terrorist groups have been secured.

Instances of **people trafficking** have increased in Ireland, with organised crime often playing a major role in its organisation (Fig. 27.8).

→ **Fig. 27.8** Blue Blindfold Campaign: don't close your eyes to human trafficking.

EXAM LINK (OL)

Migration – Ireland (40 marks)

Migration takes place due to push factors and pull factors.
(i) Name one push factor and one pull factor associated with migration in Ireland.
(ii) Discuss the positive impacts of migration on Ireland.
(iii) Discuss the negative impacts of migration on Ireland.

2018, Q10C

Marking Scheme:
(i) 2 marks + 2 marks
(ii) 6 SRPs × 3 marks
(iii) 6 SRPs × 3 marks

CHECK YOUR LEARNING

1. Identify four ways in-migration has impacted on Ireland.
2. Outline some of the measures that have been taken to support migrant integration.
3. Explain the following terms: remittances, racism, multicultural.

KEYWORDS
push factors
mechanisation
unemployment
services
population structure
birth rates
property prices
urban sprawl

Rural-to-Urban Migration in the Developed World

In 2016, global estimates suggested that 54.5% of the population lived in urban areas and that this would rise to 60% by 2030. Rates of growth differ between developed and developing countries, so estimates suggest that, by 2030, urban dwellers will number 3.9 billion in developing countries, and 1 billion in developed countries.

The pattern of out-migration from rural areas that began during the **Industrial Revolution** has continued to the present day. Economic and social factors are the main forces driving people out of rural areas and attracting them to urban areas. Like all migration flows, this will impact on the donor rural areas and urban host areas.

Chapter 20:
A European Core Region
– The Paris Basin

466

CASE STUDY: RURAL-TO-URBAN MIGRATION IN THE DEVELOPED WORLD – IRELAND

In 1946, 63% of the Irish population lived in rural areas. By 2016, this figure had fallen to 37%. Push factors contributing to this included:
- increased mechanisation reduced employment in the agricultural sector;
- high rates of rural unemployment due to a lack of investment by government;
- underdeveloped infrastructure and a lack of services and facilities.

Within all the Irish provinces, rural populations show decline, while urban centres are increasing. According to Census 2016, nationally there were 41 towns with a population of over 10,000 (**Table 27.2**). The distribution of these towns shows the west–east divide in terms of rural-to-urban migration.

Connaught	Leinster	Munster	Ulster
3	27	9	2

↑ **Table 27.2** Towns with over 10,000 inhabitants by province (Census 2016)

Socio-economic impacts on donor regions

Counties such as **Mayo** along the western seaboard and **Leitrim** in the border area have been affected by **rural depopulation**.

Migration in Ireland tends to be age selective, and this impacts on the **population structure**; the 2016 Census showed Counties Mayo and Kerry as having the highest average age at 40.2 years.

The **dependency ratio** also increases. The 2016 census showed that while the **national average dependency ratio** was 52.7%, the figure for Leitrim was 62.6%.

The younger age profile of those who leave leads to a **decline in birth rates**. In 2016, while the average **birth rate** for Ireland was 13.7 per 1,000, rates in Co. Mayo were 12.1 per 1,000.

The **brain drain of skilled people moving away from rural areas** results in the lack of a skilled labour force, making it difficult to attract inward investment.

Rural depopulation has resulted in abandoned homes and farms, while falling enrolments in schools and colleges can lead to the loss of teachers, and the amalgamation and closure of schools (**Fig. 27.9**).

It also leads to a reduction in the **local purchasing power**, causing banks, post offices and businesses to close down (**Fig. 27.10**).

A declining population can also result in poorly supported **public transport** services being reduced or discontinued, thus increasing rural isolation.

↑ **Fig. 27.9** Rural depopulation leads to abandoned homes.

↑ **Fig. 27.10** Derelict shop in Co. Kilkenny.

Chapter 19:
A Peripheral Irish Region – The Western Region

CHECK YOUR LEARNING

1. Describe two push factors that lead to rural depopulation.
2. Explain two pull factors that lead to urban migration.
3. What is the dependency ratio?
4. Explain why the dependency ratio is higher in counties that experience out-migration.
5. Explain two economic and two social impacts of rural decline.

Landscapes

Chapter 18: A Core Irish Region – The Greater Dublin Area

Socio-economic impacts on receiver/host areas

While all urban areas in Ireland have seen inflows of people, the greatest increase has taken place in the Greater Dublin Area (GDA). A variety of economic and social pull factors have contributed to this. Census 2016 showed the Greater Dublin Area as having 44% of the total population of the Republic of Ireland.

The population will increase and as migration is age-selective, the **population structure** will change. The average age will tend to be lower due to the influx of younger people.

Census 2016 showed that the counties with the lowest average ages were in the GDA, including Kildare at 34.9 years.

Younger average ages mean **higher birth rates**. In 2016, Fingal in Dublin had a rate of 17 per 1,000, while the national rate was 13.9 per 1,000.

An increased population leads to increasing pressure on schools, hospitals and other services (e.g. **National Children's Hospital**).

An increased demand for housing in the city causes property prices to rise, forcing people to move out into the surrounding counties where homes are more affordable (e.g. **Co. Kildare**; Fig. 27.11). This has led to **urban sprawl** and has impacted on rural areas in the GDA.

A lack of development of proper public transport facilities in these new residential areas has led to a huge dependence on motor transport, resulting in major traffic congestion (e.g. **M50**).

The labour pool attracts industry and contributes to the growth of economic activities. Many major international companies have their headquarters or manufacturing facilities in the GDA (e.g. **Microsoft**).

An increased demand for housing results in housing shortages and leads to increases in rents.

↑ **Fig. 27.11** Rural-to-urban migration increases housing demand.

EXAM LINK (OL)

Migration – Rural-Urban (40 marks)
(i) Explain the reasons why people migrate from rural areas to urban areas.
(ii) Explain the problems experienced in urban areas as a result of this migration.
2017, Q11B

Marking Scheme:
(i) Two reasons identified = 3 marks + 2 marks
Explanation = 5 SRPs × 3 marks
(ii) Two problems identified = 3 marks + 2 marks
Explanation = 5 SRPs × 3 marks

EXAM TIP

A question on rural-to-urban migration appeared at Ordinary Level in 2011, 2013, 2014, 2016 and 2017.

EXAM LINK (HL)

Migration (30 marks)
With reference to a developed region you have studied, explain the impact of rural-to-urban migration on donor and receiver regions.
2014, Q10C

Marking Scheme:
Named developed region = 2 marks
Impact on donor region = 2 marks
Impact on receiver region = 2 marks
Examination = 12 SRPs × 2 marks

CHECK YOUR LEARNING

1. Describe some of the impacts of rural-to-urban migration on the population of Dublin.
2. List any two economic impacts of this type of migration.
3. Outline any three social impacts of this type of migration.

Rural-to-Urban Migration in the Developing World

In today's world, cities in developing countries are experiencing the most rapid growth of all urban areas, and the movement of people from rural to urban areas is projected to continue into the future (Table 27.3).

Year	Urban	Rural
2018	55%	45%
2050	68%	32%

← Table 27.3 Global rural-to-urban population percentages (UN)

The ten cities projected to become megacities by 2030 are all located in developing countries (e.g. **Bogota, Colombia**). Natural increase and rural-to-urban migration are the two main drivers of this growth. **Push factors** driving people from rural areas include:

- landholding inequality;
- mechanisation of agriculture causing job losses;
- poor living conditions – no electricity, poor sanitation;
- poor provision of services including education and health.

KEYWORDS
push factors
landholding
mechanisation
services
conditions
megacities
depopulation
population structure
child labour
migration pattern

Megacity: A very large city with a population in excess of 10 million people.

CASE STUDY: RURAL-TO-URBAN MIGRATION IN THE DEVELOPING WORLD – INDIA

In 1960, 18% of India's population was classed as urban. By 2017, it had risen to 34% and it continues to rise. Indian cities attract migrants as they hold the possibility of finding employment and earning an income (e.g. **Mumbai**; Fig. 27.12). There is a greater availability of medical and educational facilities, but, above all, they offer the possibility of breaking out of the cycle of poverty (Fig. 27.13).

For many migrants who move to urban areas, the reality turns out to be poorly paid jobs and very poor living conditions (Fig. 27.14).

Rural-to-urban migration can be short term – for example, after the harvest period when there is little work, people migrate to supplement income – or it can be permanent.

Socio-economic impacts on rural areas

Rural depopulation is occurring throughout India. As rural-to-urban migration is age- and gender-specific in the country, it is mostly young men who leave their rural homes to find work in the city.

The **population structure** in the rural areas changes, with a higher percentage of women, young children and older adults remaining.

Children are forced to find whatever work they can to supplement family income (**child labour**), as many fathers and younger men in the family have left for the city. Attendance at school is therefore impossible for some children, and a lack of education severely impacts on their future prospects.

A **pattern of migration** can begin when one family member has moved to the city and the immediate and extended family is encouraged to follow.

↑ Fig. 27.12 Downtown Mumbai – pull factors draw migrants to Indian cities.

↑ Fig. 27.13 Push factors force migrants out of rural areas in India.

↑ Fig. 27.14 Dharavi slum, Mumbai.

Landscapes

Impacts on urban areas

Chapter 22: A Continental/Subcontinental Region – India
Chapter 26: Population Growth and Human Development
Chapter 30: Urban Growth Problems

Detailed material on **Kolkata** can be found in Chapters 22 and 30, and on **Mumbai** in Chapter 26. Table 27.4 below will allow you to research material from these chapters and to provide relevant information for this topic.

Social	Services	Economic	Environment
Overcrowding (slums)	Poor sanitation	Lack of employment	Air pollution
Crime (including prostitution)	Lack of rubbish collection	Exploitation of workers	Traffic congestion
Violence and opposition towards migrants	Lack of clean water	Informal economy	
Disease and poor health		Lack of electricity	

↑ **Table 27.4** The impacts of rural-to-urban migration on urban areas in developing countries.

CHECK YOUR LEARNING

1. Describe the impact of rural-to-urban migration on developing world cities using the following four headings (give three SRPs for each heading): Social, Services, Economic, Environment.

European Union Immigration Policies

KEYWORDS
birth rates
ageing population
legal immigration
illegal immigration
labour shortages
work permits
EU/EEA
Blue Card
Schengen Area

In many EU countries, declining birth rates and ageing populations are leading to labour and skills shortages. EU migration policies aim to:

- manage legal immigration so as to address labour and skills shortages;
- control irregular immigration;
- deal with refugees and asylum seekers.

Each member country has its own procedures and requirements regarding **work permits for non-EU/EEA nationals**. The **European Economic Area** (EEA) is made up of **EU member states**, along with **Norway, Liechtenstein and Iceland**.

However, **EU-wide** rules apply to highly qualified workers, researchers, students and seasonal workers who are not citizens of the EU but wish to work there. These rules also allow citizens of non-member countries who are legally staying in an EU country to bring their family members to live with them and to become long-term residents.

The EU Blue Card scheme is designed to attract professionals and highly qualified workers from outside the European Union (Fig. 27.15). Ireland, Denmark and the United Kingdom do not participate in this scheme. Conditions for applicants include a valid work contract or binding job offer for highly qualified employment of at least one year's duration.

Card holders have free movement within the Schengen Area, and are offered favourable conditions for bringing their families over to join them (Fig. 27.16).

↑ **Fig. 27.15** The EU Blue Card Scheme.

27 Migration

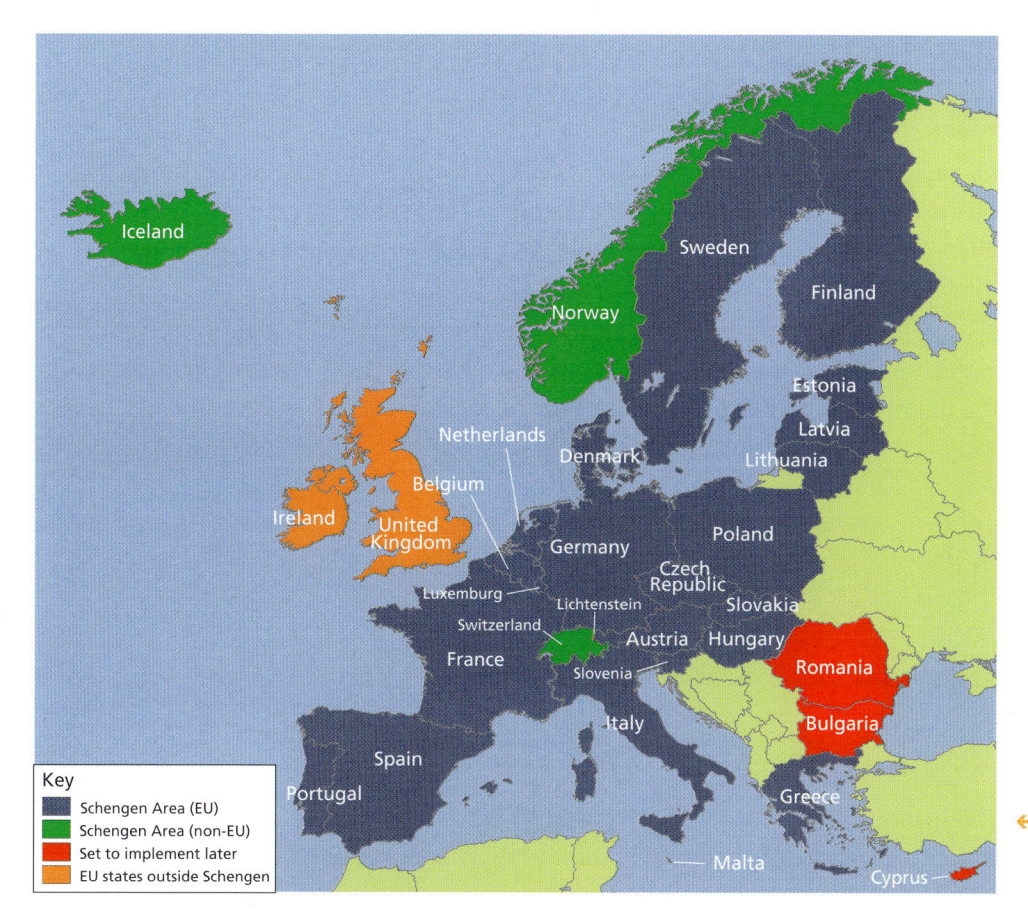

Fig. 27.16 Map of Europe showing Schengen and non-Schengen countries.

The Schengen Convention permits anyone legally present in one of the participating countries to travel to any of the participating countries without having any border checks. The Schengen Area currently consists of 26 European countries. Ireland and the United Kingdom are not members.

CHECK YOUR LEARNING

1. Name two EU countries that are not part of the Schengen Area.
2. Name three non-EU countries that are part of the Schengen Area.

Irish immigration policies

The EU Single Market allows people to move freely within the **European Economic Area (EEA)**. Policies were needed to deal with migrants who wish to come to Ireland from outside this area.

Any employment opportunities occurring in Ireland must first be offered to suitably skilled Irish and other EEA nationals. If no suitable candidate is found, then the position may be offered to a non-EEA national.

There are nine different permit types, one of which is **the Critical Skills Employment Permit**, which is aimed at attracting skilled migrants and applies to all occupations on the **Highly Skilled Eligible Occupations List**. The applicant must have secured a two-year job offer with a minimum annual pay of over €60,000.

KEYWORDS

European Economic Area (EEA)

Critical Skills Employment Permit

Highly Skilled Occupations List

skills shortages

Highly Skilled Eligible Occupations List: This list describes occupations that are of vital importance to our economy but are in short supply within the labour market (e.g. radiographers, midwives).

CHECK YOUR LEARNING

1. Explain the following terms: Blue Card, EEA.
2. Describe three aims of the EU's current migration policies.
3. Name any one Irish permit type and briefly describe it.

471

Asylum Seekers and Refugees in the European Union

> **KEYWORDS**
> asylum seeker
> refugee
> Dublin Regulation

Refugee: A person who crosses an international border to escape from persecution, violence or conflict.

Asylum seeker: A person who is awaiting determination of refugee status.

Frontline countries: The countries where asylum seekers first arrive (e.g. Italy).

An **asylum seeker** is someone who is seeking to be recognised as a **refugee**. The EU **Common European Asylum System (CEAS)** is a set of EU laws, completed in 2005, that set out minimum standards and procedures for asylum applications and the treatment of asylum seekers and refugees.

One important element of this **Common System** is the **Dublin Regulation**. This states that the responsibility for registering and examining asylum claims lies with the member state that played the greatest part in the applicant's entry into the EU; usually the first member state entered.

CHECK YOUR LEARNING

1. Explain the following terms: asylum seeker, refugee.
2. What does the Dublin Regulation state?

Asylum seekers and refugees in Ireland

> **KEYWORDS**
> International Protection Office
> direct provision
> Reception and Integration Agency (RIA)
> employment

The **International Protection Office (IPO)** processes applications for asylum in Ireland. Applicants are housed in **Direct Provision Centres** where the **Reception and Integration Agency (RIA)** provides accommodation, welfare support, healthcare and weekly allowances of €19.10 per adult and €15.60 per child processed.

Asylum seekers must comply with the laws of the country and reside or remain at the accommodation centre allocated to them. Those who fulfil certain requirements may seek employment or may start their own business while their application is processed.

If refugee status is granted, the person will have the right to live and work in Ireland and to have certain family members live with them. If denied, the applicant may have the right to appeal. If this fails deportation orders are issued. In 2017, 40 deportation orders were issued.

The European Migrant Crisis

Chapter 23: The Complexity of Regions I

> **KEYWORDS**
> frontline countries
> routes
> trafficking
> migrant flows
> asylum policies
> opposition
> push factors
> quota

During 2015, more than 1.2 million people applied for asylum in the EU. Under the Dublin Regulation, **frontline countries** such as Greece and Italy became responsible for handling the vast majority of asylum claims, putting huge strains on their services.

The three main migration routes that have seen the greatest flows are:

- **Eastern Mediterranean:** The majority of people using this route were escaping conflicts in Syria, Afghanistan and Iraq.
- **Central Mediterranean:** Migrants on this route come from sub-Saharan Africa and depart from Libya.

- **Western Mediterranean:** Migrants from West African and sub-Saharan countries use this route (Fig. 27.17).

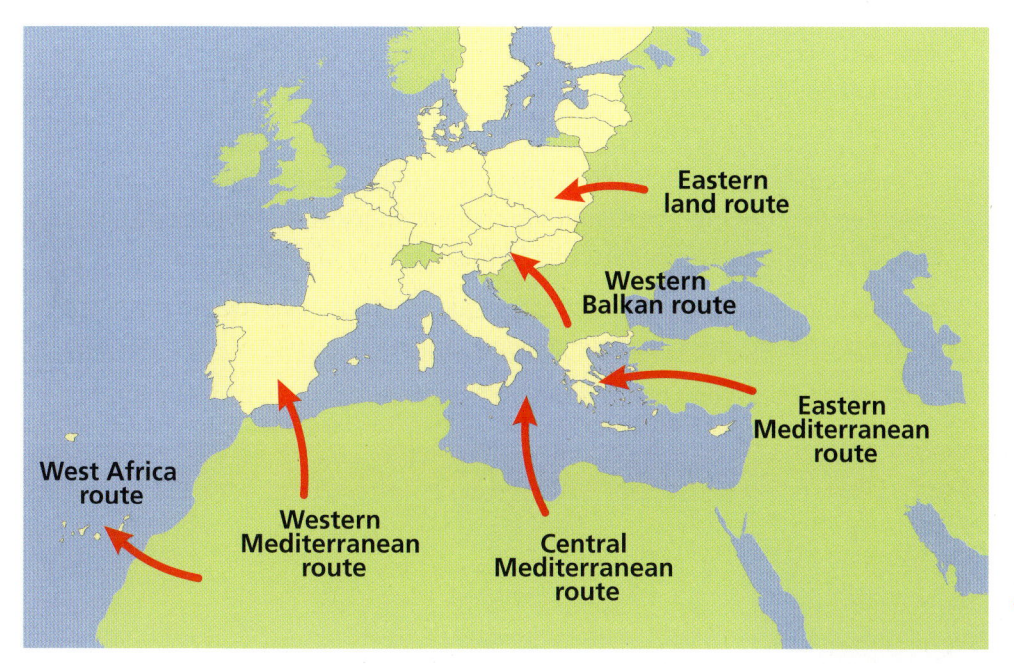

Fig. 27.17 Map of main migrant routes to Europe.

FRONTEX – The European Border and Coastguard Agency: The role of this agency is to co-ordinate co-operation between member states in managing their external borders.

Trafficking migrants can be very lucrative, and because the migrant smugglers use poorly maintained inflatable boats, and fill them with as many people as they can, there have been many deaths by drowning during crossings. The Central Mediterranean route has seen the highest number of deaths, as it is the longest sea crossing (Fig. 27.18).

Migrant flows

The number of migrants arriving in the EU from Africa and the Middle East has been in decline since 2015. This is due to a number of reasons, including:

- EU and Italian funds have helped to upgrade and improve the Libyan coastguard.
- Changes in border operations in Niger, which is a major collecting station on the migrant route.
- Under a 2016 Joint Action Plan, all new irregular migrants crossing from Turkey to the Greek islands are returned to Turkey. For every Syrian returned under the agreement, another Syrian already registered in Turkey will be resettled in the EU.

Fig. 27.18 Irish Naval Service personnel assisting migrants as they cross the Mediterranean.

Migrant smuggling: The illegal movement of people across borders purely for profit.

Impacts

Some countries have temporarily reinstalled **border controls**, threatening free movement of people under the Schengen Agreement (e.g. **Hungary**; Fig. 27.19).

Many countries opposed to being forced to accept refugee quotas are threatening a Europe-wide solution to the crisis (e.g. **Slovakia**).

Support for **right-wing political parties** opposed to migration has increased, with some demanding the repatriation of all migrants (e.g. **Austria**).

Fig. 27.19 Border fence Hungary, 2015.

Landscapes

Responses

At a meeting of 27 EU members in June 2018, agreed responses included:

- Rescued Mediterranean migrants would be sent to '**control centres**' in other member countries that volunteer to have them, relieving the pressure on frontline countries such as Italy;
- At these centres, once identified, genuine asylum seekers will be allocated and resettled to other member countries on a voluntary basis – those designated **irregular** migrants will be returned to their country of origin;
- Increased **investment** in sub-Saharan Africa is required to reduce the push factor caused by lack of economic opportunity;
- A reform of EU **asylum** policy is needed, particularly the Dublin Regulation.

CHECK YOUR LEARNING

1. Name two frontline countries in the EU.
2. What impact do the increased migrant flows have on the frontline countries?
3. Identify the three main routes used by asylum seekers to get to Europe.
4. Name two reasons why migrants want to come to Europe.
5. Name the Irish agency responsible for asylum seekers.
6. Explain what is meant by direct provision.
7. Briefly explain the 2016 Joint Action Plan.
8. Describe three impacts that the migrant crisis has had on the European Union.
9. Outline three strategies to be taken to address this crisis.

CASE STUDY: GERMANY AND THE MIGRANT CRISIS

KEYWORDS
open border
integration
language
training
attitudes
anti-immigrant
security
labour shortages

In 2015, Germany adopted an '**open border**' policy, taking in 890,000 refugees and receiving 476,649 formal applications for political asylum (**Fig. 27.20**). Other EU states opposed this action, as it completely disrupted the agreed asylum protocols.

The German government implemented strategies to promote economic and social **integration**. One key strategy is the nine-month 'integration course' for migrants, which includes 600 contact hours of German-language instruction and inputs on German society and culture.

To help improve employment opportunities, the government supported 100,000 placements in **job-related language training courses** for refugees. By March 2017, over 450,000 refugees had been linked up with German job centres and public employment agencies.

→ Fig. 27.20 Migrants arriving in Munich in 2015 react to welcoming Germans.

Impacts

In 2016, spending on **integration** measures reached €5.3 billion.

When the refugees first arrived, they were greeted by an outpouring of sympathy, however, a number of Islamist-led terrorist attacks carried out by asylum seekers have caused **attitudes** to change.

At the moment there is little support for further intakes of refugees and **anti-immigration movements** are exploiting increasing **security fears**. However, when the contribution that migrants can make to **labour shortages** are recognised, attitudes may change.

CHECK YOUR LEARNING

1. How many migrants arrived in Germany in 2015?
2. Describe any three ways that Germany has attempted to integrate the migrants.
3. Describe some of the problems the migrants faced.
4. Explain some of the benefits of the migrant inflow.
5. What was the attitude of Germans to migrants in 2015? How and why has that attitude changed?

EXAM LINK (HL)

Migration (30 marks)

Discuss how recent trends in migration are impacting on migration policy in Europe.

2018, Q10C

Marking Scheme:
Impact on migration policy identified = 2 marks
Discussion = 14 SRPs × 2 marks

Issues That Can Arise from Migration

KEYWORDS

language	ghettoisation	far-right
racism	tension	white supremacists
ethnic	profiling	radicalisation
melting pot	discrimination	conflict
values	sport	terrorism

Ethnic: Sharing a common and distinctive culture, religion or language (e.g. Indian, Arab).

Xenophobia: A fear or hatred of people from other countries or cultures.

Salad bowl: All the cultures maintain their individual traits, just like the ingredients in a salad.

Melting pot: Where people of different ethnic backgrounds gradually blend together forming a single society.

With increasing migration, more countries are becoming multi-ethnic and face the challenges of accommodating and integrating migrants of different races, religions, languages and cultures. Many have put in place legal, social and economic structures to ensure that problems relating to ethnicity, race and religion are managed. The reality, however, is that instances of xenophobia and racism have been increasing in many countries.

Ethnic issues

When people migrate they bring their language, culture, traditions and religious practices with them. Adjusting to the new society can cause problems. Some countries attempt to integrate migrants by creating a **melting pot**. Other countries adopt a **multicultural** or **salad bowl** approach, where migrants maintain their individual cultural identities.

Landscapes

Fig. 27.21 A polling booth in the USA.

Fig. 27.22 The existing border wall at Tijuana on the Mexican–US border.

In California and Texas, USA, **dual Spanish and English-language signs** in government offices and public transport are visible signs of a large Mexican immigrant population (Fig. 27.21). With many businesses catering for this community and the development of Spanish language media, the Mexican population are able to function with very little English language usage. Many Americans object to this, believing that people who live in the USA should speak English.

Tensions between native populations and ethnic minority groups are growing in many countries. The pledge by Donald Trump to **build a wall** to keep out illegal immigrants found support among many Americans during the 2016 Presidential Election (Fig. 27.22). Hungary and other European countries have installed border fences. In Europe, entry of migrants is opposed by right-wing political groups who claim migrant values are not **European values**. These groups believe that rather than adapt, the migrants want to mould Europe to their own cultural identity.

The **ghettoisation** and marginalisation of racial groups in some countries shows the failure of integration policies (e.g. **France** and **Belgium**). There can also be ethnic tensions within migrant groups. In some American cities, gang violence between different Hispanic groups is frequently reported on by local and national media.

Racial issues

Racial profiling, where people are stopped by police or other authorities because of the colour of their skin or another racial characteristic, is a very real issue in many countries.

Increasing security risks posed by Islamist fundamentalists have led to increasing **discriminatory policing** of Middle-Eastern migrants in many European countries.

Racially-based **employment discrimination** includes non-recognition of foreign qualifications, exploitation and low wages.

In sport, racist comments about football players by spectators have been increasing. Strong anti-racist policies within sporting organisations have been designed to tackle this (Fig. 27.23).

Far right: Political terminology for extremely conservative and nationalist viewpoints. The Nazi Party was a far-right political party.

Stereotype: A prejudiced, simplified idea or opinion about a person or race.

Within Europe, support for far-right parties that oppose migrants and promote racist policies is growing (e.g. France's **National Rally** party).

In the USA, **white supremacist movements** believe that people of European descent are superior to people from non-European regions, and support and promote racist ideas (e.g. the **Ku Klux Klan**). The attacks on mosques in Christchurch, New Zealand in March 2019 have been also linked to white supremacist ideology.

Fig. 27.23 UEFA's anti-racism campaign.

As support for these movements grows, mainstream political parties and governments face increasing difficulties in preventing the rise of racial tensions, forcing some to adopt policies that limit migration.

Religious issues

For many migrants, religion is a huge part of their cultural identity. Western European society has become more **secular**, with declining church attendances and minimal integration of religion into state matters. Migrants, especially Muslims with their religious distinctiveness in terms of dress, tend to stand out. A lack of integration has led to increasing religious intolerance.

In some countries, issues have arisen around religious dress codes. Many European states have moved to outlaw Muslim headwear in public (e.g. **France**; the **Netherlands**).

As the number of migrants of the Islamic faith increased, the lack of proper integration policies in some Western European countries led to the increasing isolation of Muslim communities (e.g. **France**). Poor social conditions, unemployment and poverty resulted in some of the young people in these areas becoming radicalised and resorting to violent actions that they claim are in the name of Islam. Radicalisation has inspired terrorist attacks, which, in turn, led to growing Islamophobia (e.g. following the bombing in **Manchester**, 2017).

Conflicts can also arise where migrants within a country are from different religious sects (e.g. **Sunni and Shia Muslims**).

The travel ban on citizens from certain Muslim majority countries introduced in the USA in 2017 is seen by many as blatant religious discrimination (**Fig. 27.24**).

Migrants to Middle-Eastern countries such as Saudi Arabia must conform to the strict Islamic rules governing life there. Strict rules govern dress and public behaviour and the consumption of alcohol is banned. Many European migrants have fallen foul of these regulations and faced imprisonment and public punishment.

> **Radicalisation:** The process where individuals or groups adopt extreme political, religious or social beliefs and use extreme methods to have these adopted.
>
> **Islamophobia:** A dislike or fear of anyone who is a follower of Islam.

← **Fig. 27.24** Protesting against American government immigration policies.

CHECK YOUR LEARNING

1. Explain the following terms: ethnic, racism, xenophobia, salad bowl, melting pot.
2. Describe, providing examples, any five ethnic issues that arise as a result of migration.
3. Describe, providing examples, any five racial issues that arise due to migration.
4. Explain the following terms: radicalisation, Islamophobia.
5. Outline, providing examples, any five religious issues than can result from migration.

Landscapes

EXAMINATION QUESTIONS
ORDINARY LEVEL

Long Questions

1. Migration

Examine the graph on the right showing the number of migrants rescued by the Irish Naval Service in the Mediterranean and answer each of the following questions.

Number of Migrants Rescued by the Irish Naval Service in the Mediterranean

Month	No. of Migrants Rescued
May (2015)	501
June (2015)	2231
July (2015)	1633
August (2015)	901
September (2015)	329
October (2015)	562
November (2015)	437
May (2016)	522
June (2016)	621
July (2016)	191

*There were no Irish Naval vessels deployed in the Mediterranean from December 2015 to April 2016

AMENDED FROM DEFENCE FORCES IRELAND

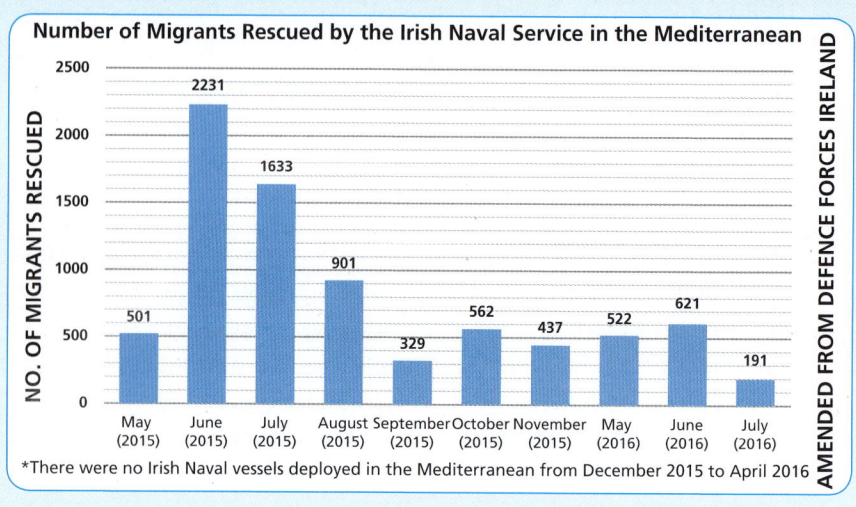

(i) How many migrants were rescued in May 2015 and how many migrants were rescued in May 2016?

(ii) Calculate the total number of migrants rescued in 2016 in the three months of May, June and July combined.

(iii) Name two pull factors that result in people migrating to Europe.

(iv) Explain briefly one of the pull factors named in part (iii) above.

(v) Explain briefly one positive impact for the European Union of receiving these migrants.

2017, Part Two, Section 2, Q12A (30 marks)

Marking Scheme:
(i) 3 marks + 3 marks
(ii) 6 marks
(iii) Two factors × 3 marks
(iv) Brief explanation = 2 SRPs × 3 marks
(v) Brief explanation = 2 SRPs × 3 marks

HIGHER LEVEL

Long Questions

2. Migration

Examine how ethnic and religious issues can arise as a result of migration.

2017, Part Two, Section 2, Q12B (30 marks)

Marking Scheme:
Ethnic issue identified = 2 marks
Religious issue identified = 2 marks
Examination = 13 SRPs × 2 marks

3. Irish Migration

Examine the graph of Irish migration opposite and answer each of the following questions.

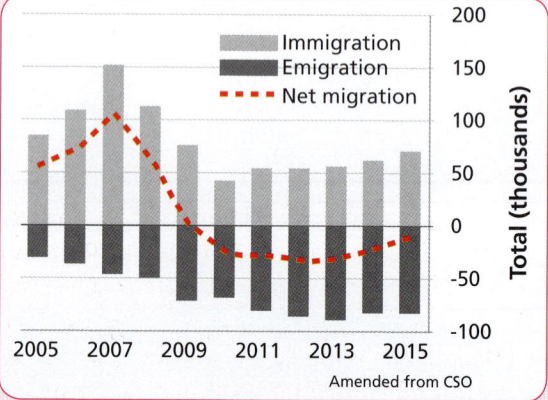

(i) In which year was the number of people immigrating equal to the number of people emigrating?

(ii) When did immigration exceed emigration by more than 100,000?

(iii) In which years was emigration greater than immigration?

(iv) Explain briefly one reason why immigration declined between 2007 and 2010.

(v) Explain briefly the term net migration.

(vi) Name two barriers to migration.

Amended from CSO

2017, Part 2, Section 2, Q11A (20 marks)

478

Revision Summary

Donor Regions Push Factors	Receiver Regions Pull Factors	Barriers to Migration
• Overpopulation • Low wages/unemployment • Lack of services • Political unrest • Natural disasters	• Underpopulation, labour shortages • Highly developed economies • Large range of services • Higher incomes • Freedom from persecution	• Financial – resettling costs prohibitive • Legal, e.g. visas, work permits • Personal – family ties

Impacts on Donor Regions	Impacts on Host Regions	Case Study: Ireland as Receiver Region
Positive impacts • Safety valve to reduce unemployment • Migrant remittances to home country • Migrants return home with new skills • Pressure relieved on resources **Negative impacts** • Gender imbalance – more female migrants – affects population structure • Quality of life – decreased numbers in local sports and activities • Brain drain – loss of skilled workers • Depopulation – abandoned homes and farms	**Positive impacts** • Cultural enrichment, multiracial society • Add to labour pool – enable economic growth • Increased spending – higher revenues • Migrant entrepreneurs – create employment, build trade links **Negative impacts** • Higher birth rates – extra pressure on services • Extra demands on social services, e.g. housing, welfare • Discrimination – cultural and religious tensions • Lack of integration policies – racial tensions • Undercutting of wage rates – tension • Over-reliance on migrant workers in some sectors	**Positive impacts** • Skilled, multilingual workforce – attractive for global companies • Skilled, semi-skilled tradespeople solve labour shortages • Increased contributions to govt revenues • Increased purchasing power – growth in retail, recreation, accommodation sectors • Fill employment gaps, e.g. horticulture, hospitality • Maintain services in small towns • Cultural diversity **Negative impacts** • Migrant remittances – loss of money to economy • Racism – seen as competition for employment • Pressure on services, e.g. housing • Strain on school management, e.g. language support teachers • Increasing costs of translators, multi-lingual information • Racism and racially motivated crimes • Exploitation of vulnerable workers • Threat of terrorism • Increase in people trafficking

Rural-to-Urban Migration

Developed World Case Study: Ireland	Developing World Case Study: India
Impacts on donor regions • Rural depopulation – e.g. Mayo • Higher-than-average age impacts population structure and dependency ratio – declining birth rate • Brain drain – lack of skilled labour force, investment unattractive • Falling school enrolments • Loss of services • Business closures **Impacts on receiver regions** • Population increases, esp. GDA • Average age is lower – higher birth rates – pressure on schools, hospitals and services • Increased demand for housing – urban sprawl – rents rise • Traffic congestion • Labour pool attracts industry – economic growth	**Impacts on donor regions** • Rural depopulation, mostly young men • Population structure changes – women, young children, older adults • Child labour to supplement family income – lack of education, poor prospects • Pattern of migration **Impacts on receiver regions** • Overcrowding (slums) • Crime and violence • Poor living conditions • Poorly paid jobs/lack of employment • Exploitation • Air pollution, traffic congestion

Landscapes

Irish Immigration Policies	European Migrant Crisis	EU Immigration Policies
• Irish and EEA citizens prioritised for jobs • Nine permit types • Critical Skills Employment Permit – applies to Highly Skilled Eligible Occupations List **Asylum seekers in Ireland** • IPO processes applications • Applicants housed in Direct Provision Centres • RIA – accommodation, welfare support, healthcare, allowances • Refugee status – right to live in Ireland, some family members may join them	• 2015 – 1.2 m applicants for asylum in EU • Dublin Regulation • Trafficking – lucrative – many deaths • Migrant flows in decline – upgrading of Libyan coastguard – border controls in Niger – 2016 Joint Action Plan **Impacts** • Temporary border controls in Schengen regions • Opposition to refugee quotas • Increased support for right-wing political parties **Responses** • Control centres in other member countries for rescued Mediterranean migrants • Genuine asylum seekers allocated and resettled • Irregular migrants returned • Investment in Sub-Saharan Africa needed – reduce push factor • Reform of Dublin Regulation, EU asylum policy	• To address labour & skills shortages • Control irregular migration • Deal with refugees and asylum seekers • Work permits particular to each country • Blue Card Scheme: acceptance of highly qualified non-EU citizens within Schengen area; Ireland, Denmark, UK do not participate **Asylum seekers and refugees** • CEAS 2005 – EU laws for asylum application procedures, treatment of asylum seekers • Dublin Regulation – responsibility for asylum claim with state that played biggest part in entry • Application denial – appeal – deportation order **Case Study: Germany** • 2015 – open border policy – 890,000 refugees • German govt – language and culture integration courses for migrants • Refugees linked up with German job centres, employment agencies • **Impacts:** cost – terrorist attacks by some asylum seekers – changing attitudes – anti-immigrant sentiments

Issues Arising from Migration

Ethnic	Racial	Religious
• Migrants bring own language, culture, traditions, religion • Attempts to integrate – melting pot or multicultural/salad bowl • USA – dual Spanish and English signs facilitate Mexican immigrants – objections • Mounting tensions between natives and migrants – build a wall (USA); border fences (Europe) • Failure of integration policies – marginalisation (France, Belgium) • Ethnic tensions within migrant groups – gang violence	• Racial profiling an issue in many countries • Security risks by certain groups – discriminatory policing • Racially-based employment discrimination • Sport – rise in racist taunts • Europe – growing support for far-right politics • USA – white supremacist movements, e.g. Ku Klux Klan • Political parties and govt forced to adopt policies to limit migration	• Migrants – religion part of cultural identity; Western Europe – increasingly secular • Lack of integration – radicalisation, violence • Terror attacks – growing Islamophobia • Religious dress code – issues • Conflicts between migrants of different sects • USA travel ban – religious discrimination • Migrants to Middle East must conform to strict Islamic rules

28 SETTLEMENT

> **LEARNING INTENTIONS** — Syllabus Links: 5.4
>
> By the end of this chapter I will be able to:
> - explain the concepts of site situation and function and how they relate to settlements;
> - describe how Irish settlements evolved;
> - identify and explain rural settlement patterns and types and how they are represented on a map;
> - describe planning strategies for rural Ireland;
> - describe how the functions and services of an urban area can change over time;
> - explain Central Place Theory and urban hierarchy.

Development of Settlements

Introduction

Many Irish settlements began to develop before and during the Early Christian period. During this time, travel and transport was by boat, foot, horseback and horse-drawn cart. As rivers were major obstacles, shallow crossing places or fords became the focus of roads. These, in turn, led to the development of settlements. The Gaelic word for ford, **áth**, is an important element in many Irish place names (e.g. **Athlone**).

Most Irish towns originated with the arrival of the Normans in the 12th century. Factors that influenced the siting of settlements during that period included access to water and protection from attack.

Settlements became market centres to which those living in the surrounding area brought their produce to be traded. They also attracted inhabitants. In this way, towns evolved and grew.

Factors that led to the evolution of modern-day urban centres at particular sites include the following.

Geographical factors

Relief

Most settlements favour lowlands below 200 metres. Reasons for this include suitable climatic conditions and gentle gradients that allow infrastructural development. Very steep slopes and upland areas were generally avoided.

Rivers

Rivers not only provided fresh water and a food supply, they were also a source of power and were used for transportation by boat.

Fords or shallow crossing places developed into bridging points. These became nodal sites for roads and paths across the area.

Settlement generally avoids wet point sites. These are sites that are liable to flood. Dry point sites are elevated sites near rivers that are not likely to be flooded.

KEYWORDS
- áth
- aspect
- site
- dry/wet point site
- rivers

Site: The immediate land on which a settlement is located.

Nodal site: Intersection or converging point of multiple roads.

Defence

On lowlands, isolated hills or ridges gave a defensive element to protect settlements by creating a barrier between the attackers and the settlement.

Aspect and shelter

Warmer south-facing slopes and sites sheltered from exposure to harsh winds were preferred sites for settlements.

Economic factors
Resources

A fertile agricultural hinterland provided food that was sold in local settlements, contributing to their market function. Fishing contributed to the growth of settlements in coastal areas. Later, industries processing these raw materials developed (e.g. **brewing**; Fig. 28.1).

Fig. 28.1 The Smithwick's Brewery in Kilkenny is the oldest brewery in Ireland.

Trade

Settlements often developed where trade and communication points met, along river valleys or natural passes, at bridging points and at nodal sites.

Historical factors

Castles were symbols of the power and authority of the local lord. Their bawns, surrounded by walls, offered a secure place for people to retreat to in times of attack (e.g. **Trim, Co. Meath**; Fig. 28.2).

During the plantation period, planned towns were developed by landlords to provide homes for estate workers (e.g. **Malcolmson family, Portlaw, Co. Waterford**).

Fig. 28.2 Trim Castle in Co. Meath.

Agrarian: Relating to land cultivation.

Plantations: The granting of large tracts of land in Ireland to loyal British settlers during the 16th and 17th centuries.

Situation

Situation refers to the location of a settlement in relation to its **surroundings**. Fertile lowland areas supported agriculture, while lowland relief led to the development of transport routes. **Natural routes** – valleys, gaps through uplands – contributed to the development of nodal sites. Uplands also provided shelter and natural defence.

CHECK YOUR LEARNING

1. Explain the following terms: site, situation, áth, wet point site, dry point site, aspect.
2. Name three factors that influenced the site of urban settlements. Explain each factor.

28 Settlement

CASE STUDY: SAMPLE EXAM QUESTION

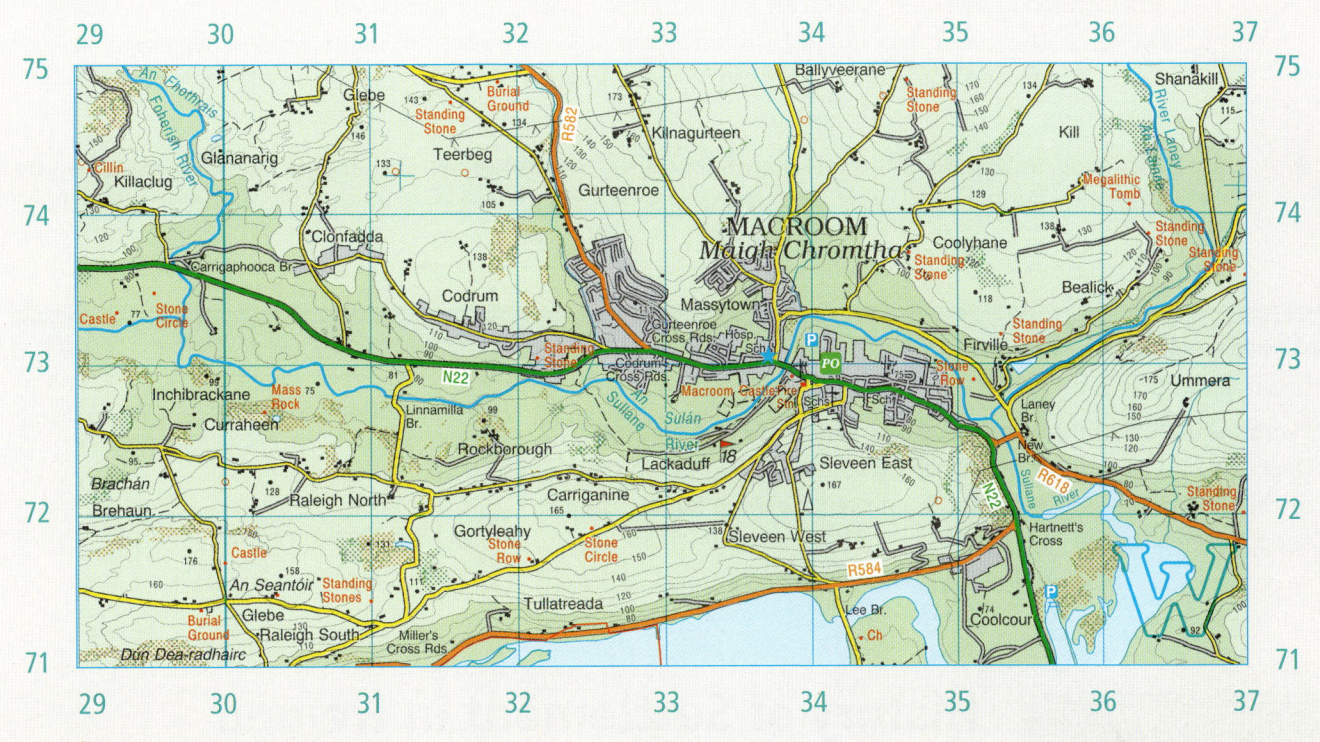

↑ **Fig. 28.3** OS map of Macroom, Co. Cork.

Urban Settlement (30 marks)

Examine the 1:50,000 Ordnance Survey map of Macroom above. Answer the following question using evidence from the Ordnance Survey map and the legend on page 171 to support your answer.

Explain three reasons why the town of Macroom developed at its present location.

2017, Higher Level, Q12C

> **Marking Scheme:**
> Three reasons × 10 marks each
> For each reason:
>   Reason stated = 2 marks
>   OS map evidence = 2 marks
>   Examination = 3 SRPs × 2 marks

Sample Answer:

River Sullane

The town of Macroom in County Cork is located between two meanders in the valley of the River Sullane (W 340 734). The river would have been an important source of fresh water and food in the early days of the settlement.

River flooding had an impact on the development of the town and settlement avoided wet point sites (W 325 725, W 345 733).

The bridging point of the river (W 338 729) was a major factor in the development of Macroom. Roads and routes from the surrounding hinterland became focused on this crossing point and contributed to it becoming a market centre for the area.

Relief

Macroom developed on sloping land north and south of the River Sullane. The southerly aspect of the northern slope, which catches more sunlight than the southern slope, is a possible reason why there is greater development on this side. The gentler slopes associated with the northern side also favoured greater settlement here. The very steep slopes at W 337 725 on the southern side have been avoided.

The elevated land on both sides of the valley (W 327 735; 111 metres OD) gave suitable dry point sites, avoiding risk of flooding.

Landscapes

Historical

The location of Macroom Castle (W 338 729) at a strategic position on sloping land in a narrow section of the river valley suggests that it was a defensive site. The castle would have provided protection for the early inhabitants of the town and the security it offered would have attracted settlement.

The lands and estate of the castle would have supported workers and tradesmen who settled nearby. This contributed to the development and growth of economic activities and settlement expansion.

EXAM LINK (OL)

Urban Development (30 marks)
Examine the 1:50,000 Ordnance Survey map of Sligo on page 182. Describe and explain three reasons why the town of Sligo developed at this location, using evidence from the Ordnance Survey map to support each reason.
2018, Q12B

Marking Scheme:
Three reasons × 10 marks
For each reason:
OS map evidence = 1 mark
Explanation = 3 SRPs × 3 marks

KEYWORDS
Neolithic
Megalithic
Bronze Age
fulacht fiadh
Iron Age
forts
early Christian
round towers

History of Settlement in Ireland

The Irish landscape contains evidence of a long history of settlement in the form of antiquities and monuments.

Prehistoric settlement

Neolithic period: 4000 BC–2500 BC

Around 4000 BC, new settlers with a knowledge of farming and the domestication of animals arrived in Ireland. This resulted in the development of permanent settlements. While there is little evidence of Neolithic wooden dwellings, remains of burial sites in the form of megalithic tombs are found throughout the country (**Figs 28.4–28.6**).

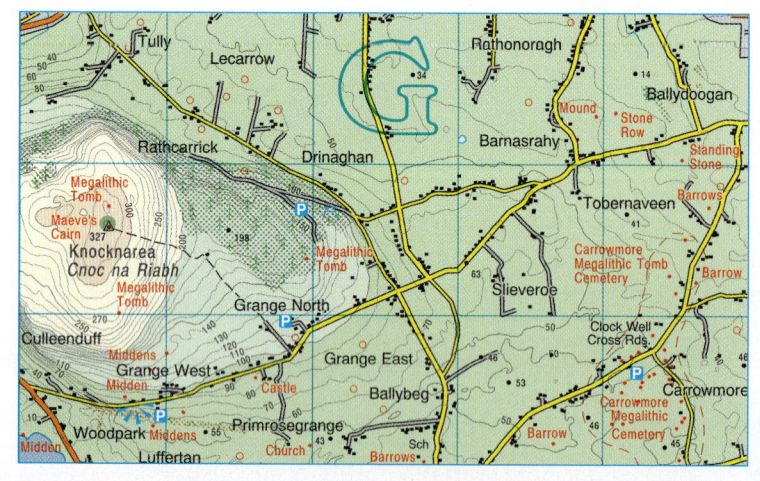

Fig. 28.4 OS map of Sligo showing Carrowmore megalithic cemetery.

Fig. 28.5 Queen Maeve's Cairn, Knocknarea, Co. Sligo.

Fig. 28.6 Carrowmore megalithic cemetery, Co. Sligo.

484

Megalithic tombs

Megalithic monuments are associated with burials. Examples include **court cairns**, **passage tombs** and **portal dolmens** constructed using large stones and covered with a mound of stones called a **cairn**.

Large groups of passage tombs occur in **Carrowmore Cemetery** in Co. Sligo. Some passage tombs contain megalithic art, while others such as **Newgrange** in Co. Meath have astronomical alignments. **Barrows** are mounds that may cover megalithic tombs.

> It is impossible to be precise as to the function of prehistoric monuments. Questions as to whether they had a religious significance, social significance or were calendars to record the annual seasonal change are all valid. Their construction, however, does indicate the presence of a structured, stable and settled society.

Bronze Age: 2500 BC–500 BC

The development of bronze, an alloy of tin and copper, led to the creation of better tools and weapons. Using bronze axes, lowland forests were cleared and more permanent settlements developed.

Fulacht fiadh

Usually located near streams or in areas where the water table was high, this cooking place consisted of a stone-lined pit that filled with water (Fig. 28.7). Nearby fires heated stones that were then transferred to the pit to heat the water. Meat wrapped in straw was placed in the pits. Continuous transfer of heated stones meant the meat slowly cooked.

← **Fig. 28.7(a)** A fulacht fiadh on an OS map.

↑ **Fig. 28.7(b)** Fulacht fiadh, Drombeg, Co. Cork.

Iron Age: 500 BC–AD 500

The Iron Age period marked the arrival of the Celts into Ireland, who brought with them their knowledge of iron working. The built landscape is marked by Celtic settlements whose main focus was the provision of security and protection from attack.

Forts

Ring forts were circular enclosures surrounded by up to three earthen banks (Fig. 28.8). An entrance was cut through the banks and there were often underground storage chambers called **souterrains**. In western areas and areas where soil was scarce, the banks were made of stone. Dún, caiseal, ráth and lios are names associated with these and many have been absorbed into Irish place names (e.g. **Dundalk, Cashel, Raheny, Lismore**). Used for habitation and protection of livestock, the larger forts may have had a socio-religious function.

← **Fig. 28.8(a)** A ring fort on an OS map.

↑ **Fig. 28.8(b)** A ring fort.

485

Promontory: A high point of land or rock projecting into a body of water.

Promontory forts were built in coastal areas on promontories or headlands. They were surrounded on three sides by the sea and had banks constructed on the landward side, as this was the only approach that had to be defended (**Fig. 28.9**).

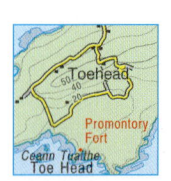

↑ **Fig. 28.9(a)** Promontory fort on an OS map.

↑ **Fig. 28.9(b)** A promontory fort, Aran Islands.

CHECK YOUR LEARNING

1. Identify the three main prehistoric phases.
2. Name and describe one antiquity associated with each prehistoric phase.

Early Christian period: 5th century–8th century

Monasteries and round towers

Monasteries were surrounded by stone walls and had round towers (**Fig. 28.10**). The towers were originally bell towers, but when Viking raids began, they were adapted to protect valuable items and relics. Monasteries were often built near rivers and lakes, which provided food and water. Settlements often developed around monasteries.

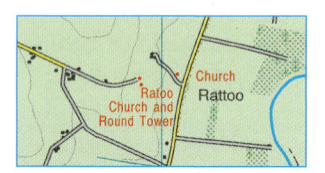

↑ **Fig. 28.10(a)** A round tower on an OS map.

↑ **Fig. 28.10(b)** Ratoo round tower, Co. Kerry.

KEYWORDS

castle
motte and bailey
bawn
abbeys
priories
monasteries
plantation
new towns
defensive

Norman period: 12th century

Castles

The arrival of the Normans had a marked impact on the Irish landscape. As invaders, they were quick to establish defensive structures to protect against attack from the native Irish. **Motte and bailey** castles were soon followed by stone-built castles. The castles had surrounding walls enclosing an open area or **bawn**. They were often sited in strategic locations, such as controlling an entry to natural routes or gaps and at crossing points on rivers. Settlements grew up around these castles in response to the security they offered. Many of them were located beside rivers that offered a water supply, food supply and a transport route (e.g. **Caher Castle, Co. Tipperary**; **Fig. 28.11**).

↑ **Fig. 28.11(a)** Caher Castle, Co. Tipperary on an OS map.

28 Settlement

← **Fig. 28.11(b)** Caher Castle at a bridging point on the River Suir.

Medieval priories, abbeys and monasteries

Priories, abbeys and monasteries were established by the religious orders in the 13th century (e.g. **Cistercian Order**, **Franciscan Order**). They were often located near rivers that provided water, food and water power for mills (**Fig. 28.12**). Some monasteries became very wealthy and controlled lots of land. Place names with **manach** (monk) may indicate lands once owned by the monasteries (e.g. **Baile na Manach/Monkstown**). Very often, settlements grew up around these religious sites.

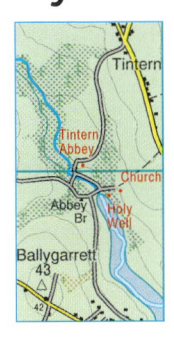

← **Fig. 28.12(a)** Tintern Abbey, Co. Wexford on an OS map.

↑ **Fig. 28.12(b)** Tintern Abbey, Co. Wexford.

Plantations

During the plantations of the 17th century, settlers from England were given large estates in Ireland. The owners of many of these estates designed and built large houses and villages to house their estate workers and tenants.

Evidence of this period shown on OS maps include: **fortified towers**, place names containing '**lot**' (planters were given land in varying sized lots), **court, park, demesne** or **house (ho)** and names possibly linked to landlords (e.g. **Philipstown**).

New towns

Shannon in County Clare was the first new town built since Independence. It was designed to provide homes for workers in the Shannon Free Zone industrial estate. Construction began in the 1960s.

The rapid growth of Dublin in the 1970s led to the development of a number of new towns including **Tallaght, Lucan, Clondalkin** and **Blanchardstown**. A poor transport infrastructure serving these areas has contributed to traffic congestion.

In 2004, construction of **Adamstown** in Dublin began. It is planned that the new town will have a population of 25,000. Better planning is evident in the provision of a rail link with the city centre.

EXAM TIP

Statement–Evidence–Explanation

When answering questions relating to historic settlement on Ordnance Survey maps, you should choose **three examples dating from different historic periods**. For each one you must name the example, give a six-figure grid reference and write three SRPs that refer to the era, site and function.

487

Landscapes

EXAM LINK (OL)

Historic Settlement (30 marks)

Examine the 1:50,000 Ordnance Survey map of Macroom on page 188.
  (i) Name and give a six-figure grid reference for the location of three different examples of historic settlement evident on the Ordnance Survey map.
  (ii) Describe each of the three historic settlements named in part (i) above.

2017, Q10B

> **Marking Scheme:**
>   (i) 3 named × 2 marks each
>   3 located × 2 marks graded (2/1/0) = 6 marks
>   (ii) Description = 2 SRPs × 3 marks each = 18 marks

EXAM LINK (HL)

Phases of Historical Settlement (30 marks)

Examine the 1:50,000 Ordnance Survey map of Kenmare on page 194.
  (i) Name three different phases of historical settlement evident on the map.
  (ii) Name and locate, using six-figure grid references, examples of each of the three named phases of historical settlement.
  (iii) Explain briefly each of the three phases.

2015, Q12C

> **Marking Scheme:**
>   (i) Name = 3 × 2 marks
>   (ii) Examples of each phase = 3 × 2 marks
>   Location of examples = 3 × 2 marks
>   (iii) Explain = 3 × 2 + 2 marks

CHECK YOUR LEARNING

1. Describe some of the impacts that the arrival of the Normans had on the Irish landscape.
2. What evidence can be found on OS maps of the effects of the plantations?

CASE STUDY: SAMPLE EXAM QUESTION

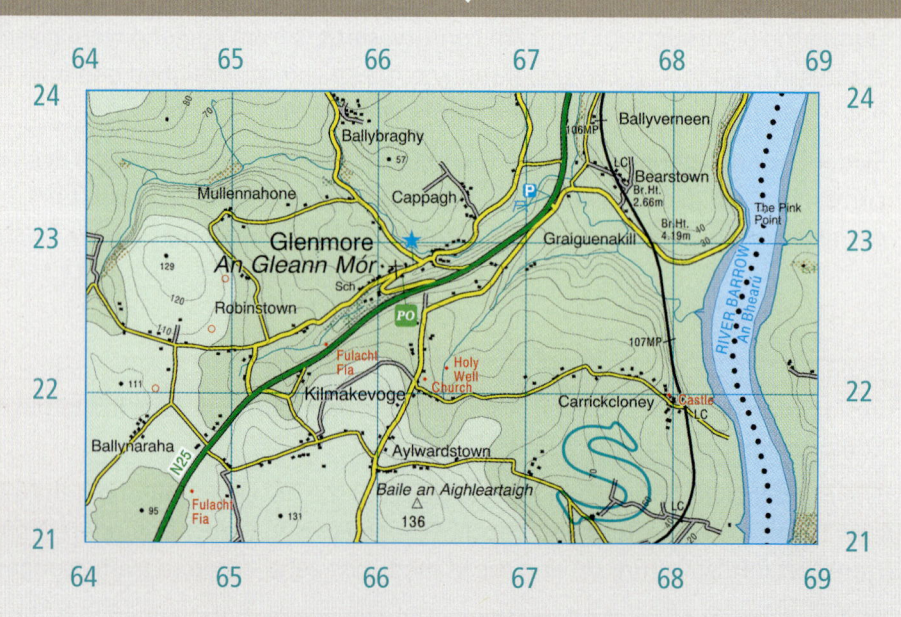

→ **Fig. 28.13** OS map extract, Co. Wexford.

The Ordnance Survey map extract above reveals a long history of settlement in the Wexford area. Examine this statement, using map evidence, with reference to any three different aspects of historic settlement.

488

Sample Answer:

Fulacht fiadh, S 656 224

Dating from the Bronze Age (2500 BC–500 BC), these stone-lined pits were cooking sites. This site is located at an elevation of 60 metres near a river that probably provided the water for cooking. A fire was used to heat stones that were then transferred to the pit to heat the water. The fulacht fiadh is evidence that there was a permanent settlement here during the Bronze Age.

Ring fort, S 648 227

These circular enclosures date from the Iron Age and are associated with the Celts. They were surrounded by one or more banks on which wooden palisades or fences were placed. They were used for habitation, defence and also to protect livestock from raids. This example is located at 110 metres on gently sloping land, which made construction easier and gave a commanding view over the area. Underground chambers called souterrains that were used for food storage and possibly protection occur in these forts.

Castle, S 680 220

When the Normans arrived in the 12th century, they built castles as symbols of their control and domination. This castle is located approximately 40 metres above the surrounding landscape, giving it a strategic height advantage, while the upland to the west provides shelter. The river, approximately half a kilometre to the east of the castle, was a source of water and food, and was possibly used as a mode of transport. It also formed an important defensive element for the castle.

Rural Settlement Patterns

There are four main types of rural settlement pattern.

Dispersed settlement

Dispersed settlement develops in areas where agriculture is an important primary activity. Farm dwellings are surrounded by farmland and separated from each other. Access to the farmhouses can be from main roads or via third-class roads or passages. In areas where the land is fertile, average farm size is larger, so greater distances separate dwellings giving a lower settlement density (Fig. 28.14).

Linear settlement

Linear settlement is also called **ribbon development** and it can be found on approach roads to towns and along sections of rural roads (Fig. 28.15). This pattern evolved for a number of reasons:

- **Availability of sites:** Farmers could earn extra income by selling plots of land that had road frontage and were suitable for development.
- **Services:** Most services, including water and electricity, run parallel to roads so sites along them had access to these essential services.
- **Scenery:** In coastal areas, development often occurred parallel to the coast, to give scenic views for as many people as possible. Linear development is not sustainable and planning regulations now discourage it.

KEYWORDS

dispersed
linear
ribbon
nucleated
absence

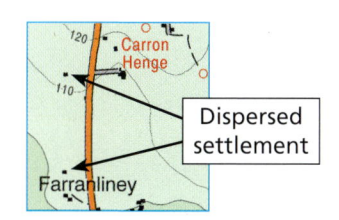

↑ **Fig. 28.14** Dispersed settlement on an OS map.

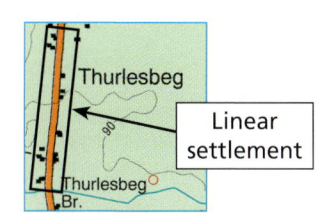

↑ **Fig. 28.15** Linear settlement on an OS map.

Landscapes

The Rundale System
Under the Rundale System, farmland that had been jointly held by a number of tenants was divided into infield, with better-quality land, and outfield, where poorer-quality land was located.

Nucleated settlement

Nucleated settlements can range in size from a cluster of dwellings to a small settlement or village. They have all grown up around a **central point** (Fig. 28.16).

The **Rundale System** of farming gave rise to the development of nucleated settlements called **clachans**. Cottages were clustered into clachans in the better infield, while poorer outfield areas and mountain slopes were used for rough grazing.

Nucleated settlements also developed as a result of historical factors, for example, around castles that provided protection.

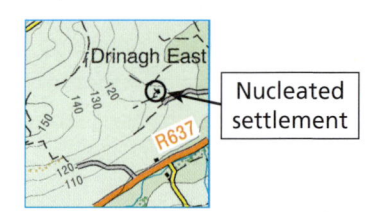

↑ **Fig. 28.16** An OS map showing nucleated settlement.

Absence of settlement

Upland areas have a very low density of settlement (Fig. 28.17). Reasons for this include:

- harsher climates, lower temperatures and exposure to strong winds;
- they tend to have poor soil covering, making farming difficult and unprofitable, which discouraged farm settlements;
- steep slopes make areas inaccessible and isolated, as construction of roads is difficult and expensive.

River flood plains also have low population densities due to the possibility of seasonal flooding (Fig. 28.18).

↑ **Fig. 28.17** An OS map showing absence of settlement on upland.

→ **Fig. 28.18** An OS map showing absence of settlement on a flood plain.

EXAM LINK (OL)
Rural Settlement Patterns

Examine the 1:50,000 Ordnance Survey map of Westport on page 191.

(i) Name three different rural settlement patterns evident on the map and give a six-figure grid reference for the location of an example of each.

(ii) Explain each of the three rural settlement patterns named.

2016, Q12C

Marking Scheme:
(i) Named = 4 marks + 3 marks + 3 marks
Located = 3 references × 4 marks
(ii) Each pattern = 2 SRPs × 3 marks

EXAM TIP
Include simple annotated diagrams of the types of settlement patterns in your answer.

CHECK YOUR LEARNING
1. Name four different settlement patterns.
2. Give two descriptions of each one.

490

Rural Planning

Proper planning is essential to ensure sustainable development and to safeguard the environment. There is plenty of evidence of poor planning practices around the country, for example, ribbon development and building on flood plains. The Planning and Development Act 2000 introduced new structures to the planning process. Local authorities were mandated to draft **county** and **local development plans** that would:

- clearly set out a framework to ensure the development of new housing is encouraged and facilitated in the correct locations;
- ensure a sufficient supply of zoned and serviced land exists;
- set out clear policies and objectives where new housing is to be allowed on unzoned lands in villages and open countryside.

One-off housing is now subject to very strict conditions. Generally, sites cannot be in an open field, or in elevated or exposed locations, and ribbon development is not permitted. The design of homes is subject to very strict guidelines.

County development plans

County development plans have to define the location and extent of three possible rural area types, the type of development to be encouraged in each, and rules and regulations governing any such development (**Fig. 28.19**).

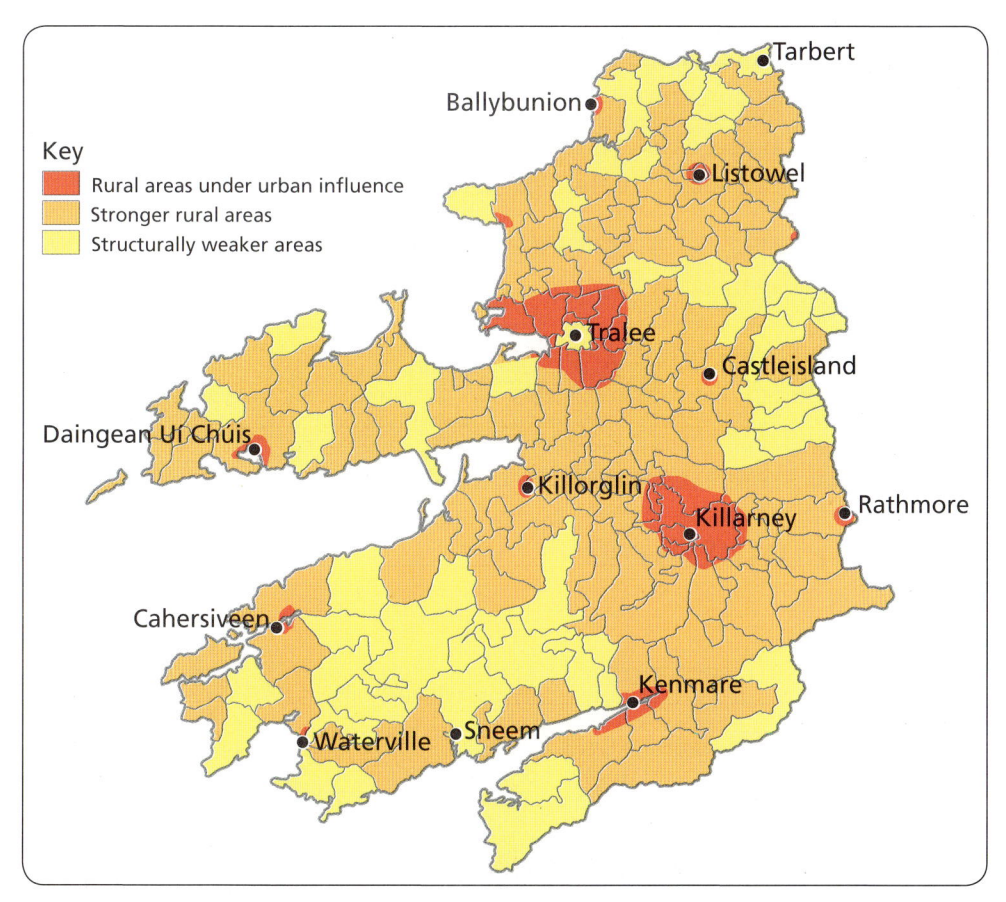

↑ **Fig. 28.19** Co. Kerry Development Plan, showing the three different types of rural areas.

Type 1: Rural areas under strong urban influence

These areas are close to large towns and cities. Reasons for this strong influence include short commuting distance and the availability of more affordable housing.

Strategies should direct new developments to serviced land in existing towns and villages whose character must be protected.

KEYWORDS

Planning and Development Act 2000
development plans
one-off housing
'locals only'

A 'locals only' clause had previously applied to one-off housing. This meant that the person wishing to build had to prove established links with the area, either through family or employment. However, a ruling by the European Court of Justice in 2017 declared the 'locals only' condition in planning permission to be against the principle of free movement of people. This means that this restriction can no longer apply and will have major implications for planning policies in county plans. New guidelines have yet to be published but it is likely that new rules may result in a total ban for everyone on house construction in highly protected areas.

Ribbon development: Where five or more houses exist on any one side of a given 250 metres of road frontage.

Serviced land: Land that has roads, mains water, sewers and electricity.

Type 2: Stronger rural areas

These areas have a strong agricultural base with well-developed towns and villages surrounded by rural areas. Appropriate development should occur in villages and small towns. Serviced land should be provided in these locations.

Type 3: Structurally weaker rural areas

These areas have weak economic potential and experience population decline. Where possible, any demand for permanent housing should be facilitated in accordance with planning guidelines. Tourism-related developments that can capitalise on the potential of the natural and cultural landscapes are to be encouraged.

In all of the three areas, one-off housing, where appropriate and subject to strict conditions, is permitted.

County Wicklow Development Plan – Rural housing

Being a part of the Greater Dublin Area, the plan for Wicklow states that the entire county can be **considered an area under strong urban influence**. Some of its rural development aims include:

- urban generated development, including housing, shall not be permitted in the **rural areas** of the county, other than in **rural settlements** deemed suitable for such development;
- ensuring water quality and the natural and cultural heritage of rural areas are protected to support quality of life and economic vitality;
- accommodating necessary rural development, including rural housing and ensuring that it is subject to the highest standards of siting and design.

SKILLS ACTIVITY

Using the internet, check the county development for your county and:

- name one example of each rural area identified;
- name three identified goals in relation to rural housing contained in the plan;
- investigate the conditions attached to one-off housing in any one of the rural areas.

CHECK YOUR LEARNING

1. Name the three different types of rural areas outlined in county development plans.
2. Describe the characteristics of each rural area type.
3. Explain the term one-off housing.
4. What is ribbon development, and why do planning authorities oppose it?

Urban Functions

Function

Every settlement provides a number of services and activities for its inhabitants and for the surrounding hinterland. The number and type of functions vary with settlement size. They also change over time.

Commercial	Shop, supermarket, large car park …
Educational	University, college, school …
Industrial	Industrial estate …
Open space	Picnic area, park …
Port	Dockland, harbour, marina …
Recreational	Sports ground, cycle path, golf course …
Religious	Church, mosque, graveyard …
Residential	Housing estate …
Services	Post office, Garda station, hospital …
Tourism	Tourist office, youth hostel, camp and caravan site …
Transport	Roads, bus station, train station, port …

↑ **Table 28.1** Urban functions.

Aerial photographs

Some examination questions on urban functions are based on aerial photographs. Interpreting evidence of functions requires the **identification, location (using accepted notation) and explanation** of at least three different functions based on evidence shown in the photograph.

Chapter 13: Aerial Photographs

EXAM LINK (HL)

Urban Functions (30 marks)

Name, locate (using accepted notation) and explain three different urban functions evident on the aerial photograph of Westport on page 207.

2016, Q10B

Marking Scheme:
Three different urban functions × 10 marks each
For each urban function:
- Function named = 2 marks
- Function located = 2 marks
- Function explained = 3 SRPs × 2 marks

Changing Functions and Services of an Urban Centre

The origins of most urban centres in Ireland can be dated back to the Normans in the 12th century. Since then, changing socio-economic influences have resulted in changes to their functions and to the services they provide. Limerick city is an example of such an urban centre.

CASE STUDY: LIMERICK

Defensive function

The city of Limerick, which was founded by the Vikings in the 10th century, expanded during the Norman period. In the 13th century, King's Island, beside the strategic lowest bridging point on the River Shannon, became the site of King John's Castle (**Fig. 28.20**). All movements along and across the river were monitored and controlled from the castle. Englishtown grew up on the island where the castle provided protection. Extensive city walls with numerous gates also formed part of the defensive structures associated with the growth and development of the city during the medieval period. Over time, the need for defensive structures disappeared. Today, much of the city wall has disappeared, while the restored King John's Castle is a major tourist attraction.

KEYWORDS
- castle
- city walls
- defensive
- port
- Foynes
- food processing
- industry
- life sciences
- technology

← **Fig. 28.20** King John's Castle, Limerick.

Port function

Since Viking times, port functions have been important in the economy of Limerick. Surrounded by the agricultural heartland of the Golden Vale, it was an important point of export for the agricultural produce of the region (e.g. **beef**, **pork**, **butter**).

Goods manufactured in the city also formed an important element of the export trade. Imports consisted of raw materials and coal. Canal, and later rail transport, meant goods could be transported to and from Dublin.

Port functions have changed over time. In the 1970s, coal imports greatly declined and the increasing size of ships caused problems in Limerick Port. Further down the Shannon, the deep-water berth at **Foynes** is capable of handling the larger ships and its trade has expanded, while Limerick Port traffic has been impacted. Many of the warehouses and port buildings that once lined the docks lie derelict or have been adapted for commercial and residential use. The future of the port is uncertain, however, the land in this area has enormous development potential for mixed residential–commercial use and recreational activities (Fig. 28.21).

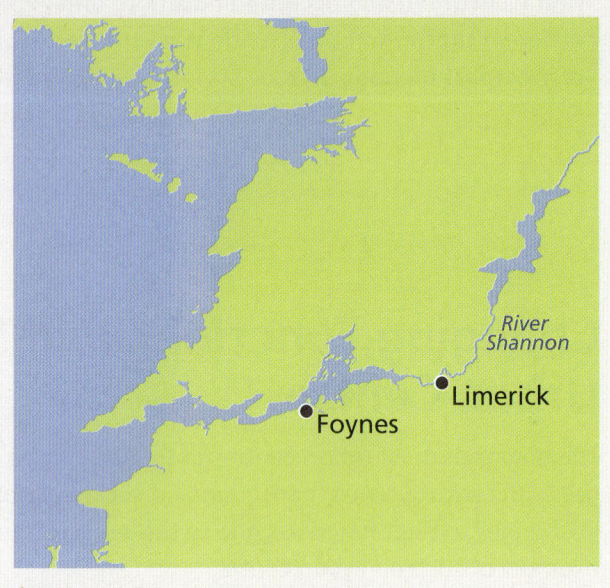

↑ **Fig. 28.21** Map of the Shannon Estuary.

Industrial function

Up until the 1970s, food processing industries were important employers in the city. They processed the raw materials supplied by the large farms in the surrounding Golden Vale (e.g. **ham** and **leather making**).

Imported and homegrown wheat supported the flour milling industry, which, in turn, led to a significant confectionery sector. The clothing industry was also a large employer. However, this and other traditional industries suffered great decline, with the removal of protectionist tariffs in the 1960s, and competition when Ireland joined the European Economic Community in 1973.

Foreign direct investment led to industrial growth and in 1990, **Dell** computer manufactures set up a major facility in Limerick. In 2009, Dell announced the closure of their plant, with the loss of 1,900 direct jobs.

Today, the industrial sector in Limerick is based on ICT, life sciences, engineering and knowledge-based industries. Numerous industrial estates and business parks have developed in locations with good access to the road infrastructure (e.g. **National Technology Park, Raheen Business Park**; Fig. 28.22).

↑ **Fig. 28.22** Raheen Business Park, Limerick.

EXAM LINK (OL)

Urban Functions (30 marks)

Describe and explain how the functions and services of urban areas change over time, with reference to example(s) that you have studied.

2014, Q10B

Marking Scheme:
Example = 3 marks
Description/explanation = 9 SRPs x 3 marks each

28 Settlement

> **EXAM LINK (HL)**
> Changing Urban Functions (30 marks)
> **Examine how the functions of urban centres can change over time, with reference to Irish example(s).**
> 2014, Q10B
>
> **Marking Scheme:**
> Functions identified = 2 + 2 marks
> Example of Irish urban centre = 2 marks
> Examination = 12 SRPs × 2 marks

> **CHECK YOUR LEARNING**
> 1. Explain three functions of Limerick that have changed over time.
> 2. Describe the reason for each of these changes.

Central Place Theory

KEYWORDS		
central place	threshold	hierarchy
range	hinterland	

In 1933, German geographer **Walter Christaller** proposed a theory to describe the relationship between **settlement size**, **distribution** and **functions**.

In developing his model, Christaller made the following assumptions:
- the existence of a flat, limitless plain;
- an evenly spread rural population with equal purchasing power;
- even distribution of resources;
- equal transport costs in all directions.

He defined a **central place** as an urban centre, varying in size from small villages to large cities, providing goods and services to a surrounding area or **hinterland** (e.g. **Killarney, Co. Kerry; Clifden, Co. Galway; Naples, Italy**).

Central Place Theory states that two main concepts – range and threshold – will govern the number, size and distribution of settlements.

Range: This is the maximum distance people are prepared to travel to either purchase goods or to avail of a service. Those used every day will have a shorter range than those used less frequently.

Threshold: This is the minimum number of people required to make a service profitable. If goods and services are in regular demand, they do not need a large number of people to sustain them (e.g. **local shops**).

Hinterland: This is the area surrounding the central place and availing of its services. Its size will be determined by the size of the central place and the types and variety of functions it provides (e.g. **Dublin** has a large hinterland). In his model, Christaller envisaged hexagonal shaped hinterlands that prevented overlapping (Fig. 28.23).

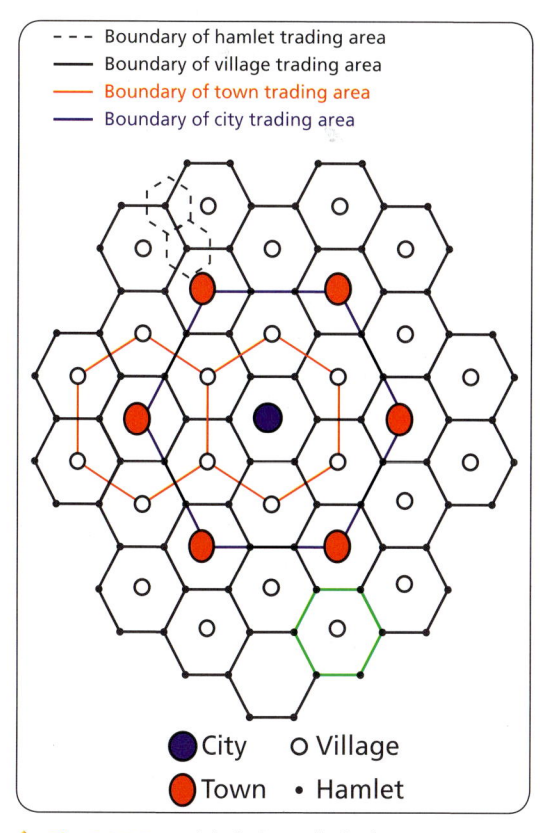

↑ **Fig. 28.23** Model of Christaller's Theory.

495

The variety and types of goods and services can be classified into three main categories.

Low-order goods and services: These are required by people on a regular or often daily basis (e.g. **bread**). They are purchased from shops and premises located close to where people live.

Medium-order goods and services: These are not availed of as frequently and so people will be prepared to travel to access them (e.g. **supermarkets**, **cinemas**).

High-order goods and services: These are the luxuries that people do not purchase regularly. They need a large population to survive and are located in larger towns and cities. They include goods and services in large department stores and shopping centres (e.g. **Blanchardstown Centre, Dublin**).

Evaluation

Christaller based his theory on a number of assumptions that exist in very few places (e.g. **polders** in the Netherlands).

His theory helps our understanding of:
- the relationship between higher- and lower-order central places;
- the location of retail services in urban areas.

Issues include:
- increasing wealth and mobility mean that rural populations can now travel further to avail of all services;
- people's shopping patterns can vary as they do not always go to the nearest centre.

> **DID YOU KNOW?**
> According to Census 2016, Co. Tipperary had:
> **28** central places with a population of less than **500**;
> **5** central places with a population greater than **5,000**.

Urban hierarchy

Christaller proposed that central places can be comparatively ranked in terms of **size** and the **range of functions and services** they provide to form a pyramid-shaped urban hierarchy model (**Fig. 28.24**).

As you go up the pyramid:
- settlement and population size **increases**;
- the number of settlements at each level **decreases**;
- the number and variety of goods and services **increases**;
- the hinterland of each settlement **increases**.

Urban hierarchy: Ranking of towns according to size and the number and types of services and functions they have access to.

Conurbation: A region comprising a number of cities, large towns and other urban areas.

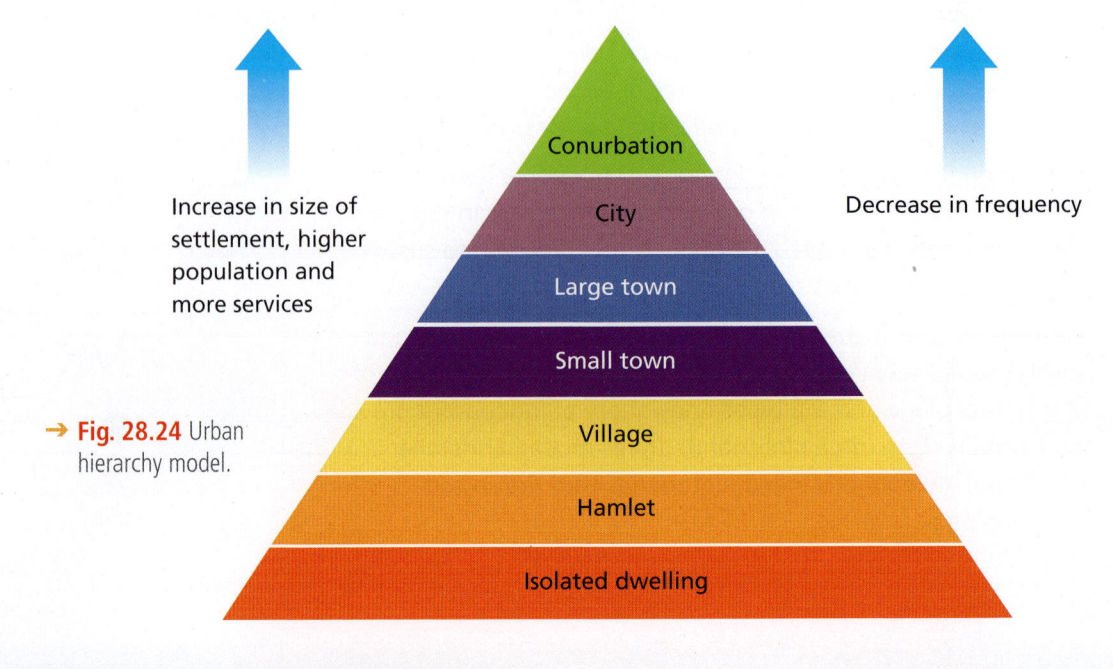

→ **Fig. 28.24** Urban hierarchy model.

Increase in size of settlement, higher population and more services

Decrease in frequency

Pyramid levels (top to bottom):
- Conurbation
- City
- Large town
- Small town
- Village
- Hamlet
- Isolated dwelling

EXAM LINK (HL)

Central Place Theory (30 marks)

Describe and explain Central Place Theory with reference to example(s) that you have studied.

2016, Q12B

Marking Scheme:
Example = 2 marks
Description/explanation = 14 SRPs × 2 marks

CHECK YOUR LEARNING

1. Explain the following terms: range, threshold, hinterland.
2. What is a central place? Name two examples.
3. Name and give examples of the three different categories of services a central place provides.
4. Explain the term urban hierarchy.
5. Describe any three characteristics of the pyramid model of urban hierarchy.
6. Explain two evaluations of Central Place Theory.

EXAMINATION QUESTIONS

ORDINARY LEVEL

Long Question

1. Urban Development

Examine the 1:50,000 Ordnance Survey map of Sligo on page 182.

Describe and explain three reasons why the town of Sligo developed at this location, using evidence from the Ordnance Survey map to support each reason.

2018, Part Two, Section 2, Q12B (30 marks)

Marking Scheme:
Three reasons × 10 marks
For each reason:
  Ordnance Survey map evidence = 1 mark
  Description/explanation = 3 SRPs × 3 marks
  At least one SRP for explanation

HIGHER LEVEL

Long Question

2. Urban Settlement

Examine the 1:50,000 Ordnance Survey map of Kenmare on page 194.

Transport and routeways have played a role in the growth and development of the town of Kenmare historically and to the present day.

Discuss this statement, using evidence from the Ordnance Survey map to support your answer.

2015, Part Two, Section 2, Q11B (30 marks)

Marking Scheme:
Map evidence = 2 marks
Discussion = 14 SRPs × 2 marks

Revision Summary

Development of Settlements

- Early Christian settlements – rivers focus of roads (áth)
- Normans – siting influenced by access to water, protection from attack
- Market centres for surrounding areas – growth – towns

Geographical factors
- Relief: lowland favoured – infrastructure, climate
- Rivers: water, food, power, transport
- Defensive: hills/ridges provide barrier to attack
- Aspect/shelter: south-facing slopes preferred

Economic factors
- Resources: fertile agricultural land, fishing, raw materials
- Trade at communication points – bridges and nodal sites

Historical factors
- Castle bawns – secure retreat in attack
- Plantation – settlements to provide homes for estate workers

Situation
- Location in relation to surroundings
- Fertile lowland – agriculture, transport routes
- Natural routes – nodal sites
- Upland – shelter and defence

Settlement History Ireland

Prehistoric
- Neolithic 4000–2500 BC – settlers with experience of farming and animals – permanent settlements – megalithic tombs and burial sites: court cairns, passage tombs, portal dolmens

Bronze Age 2500–500 BC
- Better tools and weapons – lowland forests cleared for permanent settlements – fulacht fiadh

Iron Age 500 BC–AD 500
- Arrival of Celts – settlement focus on security and defence
- Forts: ring forts (surrounded by banks), promontory forts (coastal areas)

Early Christian 5th–8th century
- Monasteries, round towers – built near rivers and lakes – attracted settlement

Normans 12th century
- Invaders – built defensive structures – motte and bailey castles, stone castles – sited near rivers, natural routes, crossing points – security of castles – attractive settlement points

Priories, abbeys, monasteries
- Established 13th century by religious orders – located near rivers – food, water, power – attractive for settlements

Plantations 17th century
- English settlers given large estates – built villages to house workers – fortified towers, place names with 'lot', 'court', 'park'

New towns
- Shannon, Co. Clare – first new town since Independence
- 1970s – new towns due to growth of Dublin – Tallaght, Lucan
- 2004 – Adamstown

Rural Settlement Patterns

Dispersed
- Develops where agriculture is primary activity
- Separated farm dwellings surrounded by farmland

Linear
- Ribbon development
- Approach roads to towns; rural roads
- Available sites; access to services; scenic views

Nucleated
- Range in size – cluster of dwellings to village
- Central point
- Rundale system of farming – nucleated clachans
- Historical factors – around castles for protection

Absence
- Upland: harsher climates, poor soil covering, inaccessible
- River flood plains: flooding risk

Rural Planning

- Essential for sustainable development
- National Development Plan, National Spatial strategy – new planning structures for county and local developments
- One-off housing – strict conditions

County development plans
- Must define location and extent of three possible rural area types and give recommendations:
  - Rural areas under strong urban influence
  - Stronger rural areas
  - Structurally weaker rural areas

Urban Functions

- Commercial – educational – industrial – open space – port – recreational – religious – residential – services – tourism – transport

Changing Urban Functions Case Study: Limerick

Defensive

- Founded by Vikings 10th century, expanded by Normans
- King's Island, King John's Castle – monitoring and control point – Englishtown – defensive structures – now tourist attraction

Port

- Important in economy of Limerick since Vikings
- Export point for goods of Golden Vale; import of raw materials; canal and road links
- 1970s – coal imports decline; port unsuitable for new larger ships
- Future uncertain

Industrial

- Until 1970s – processing of raw materials from Golden Vale – local employment
- Removal of tariffs and EEC membership – industry decline
- FDI – industrial growth in 1990s
- Today, industry is ICT, life sciences, engineering, knowledge-based
- Development of industrial estates

Central Place Theory

- 1933 Walter Christaller
- Theory: range and threshold govern number, size and distribution of settlements
- Range – max. distance for travel
- Threshold – min. people for sustainability
- Hinterland – surrounding area
- Variety of goods/services: low order (daily needs), medium order, high order (luxury)

Evaluation

- Assumptions exist in few places
- Helps explain the relationship between high- and low-order centres.
- Explains the location of retail services in urban areas
- Issues: now have greater mobility, shopping patterns vary

Urban hierarchy

- Pyramid model: towns ranked in order of size and functions
- Isolated dwelling at base
- Rising upwards = increasing settlement size, population, goods and services, size of hinterland

29 URBAN LAND USE AND PLANNING

LEARNING INTENTIONS
Syllabus Links: 5.5

By the end of this chapter I will be able to:
- identify and explain the variety of land use zones within the modern city;
- outline how urban land use theories can explain the layout of urban areas;
- describe and explain how changes in land use occur and the planning issues relating to changes from industrial, residential and commercial land use;
- explain changing land values and social stratification within cities;
- identify and explain how expanding cities put pressures on rural land use.

KEYWORDS
Central Business District (CBD)
commercial
transport
residential
industrial
recreational

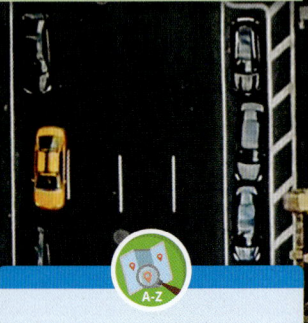

Land use zone: Division of land used for a specific purpose, e.g. residential zone, commercial zone.

Land Use Zones

All urban settlements have a variety of land use zones.

Commercial

The **Central Business District (CBD)** is where the main transport elements in a city – roads, bus routes, mass transit systems – converge, making it very accessible. As a result, the CBD has the greatest concentration of commercial activities including retail, restaurants and services (e.g. **Champs-Élysées, Paris**), in the city. As space is limited, land values and rents are high, so buildings are multi-use and high-rise, with retail on the ground floor and offices and apartments on the upper floors (e.g. **Chicago, USA**; Fig. 29.1). Retail centres have also developed in suburban areas and along the urban fringe, where a well-developed transport infrastructure gives excellent access.

↑ **Fig. 29.1** Mixed-use buildings, Chicago CBD.

Residential

Residential is the most widespread land use and consists of different types including public, private, detached, terraced and apartment blocks. Land costs determine densities, with city centres having high-density apartment blocks (e.g. **Central Park, New York**), while in the suburbs where land is cheaper, lower densities occur. High-density apartment blocks can also be found in suburban areas in response to limiting urban sprawl (e.g. **Sandyford, Dublin**; Fig. 29.2).

↑ **Fig. 29.2** Apartments in Sandyford, Dublin.

Industrial

In the past, industrial land use was associated with areas bordering the CBD. Congestion, lack of space and other factors have resulted in industrial zones moving out to the suburbs. Cheaper land, better transport infrastructure and less traffic congestion have attracted industry. The old industrial brownfield sites have been redeveloped to commercial, residential and recreational land use (e.g. **Titanic Quarter, Belfast**; Figs 29.3, 29.4).

↑ **Fig. 29.3** A brownfield site in San Francisco.

Transport

Transport allows people living in the commuter belt to travel in and out of the city. This type of land use is of vital importance to the commercial and residential life of a city. Transport use includes roads, railways, bus corridors, tram lines and their associated stations and, in the case of some cities, ferry ports (e.g. **New York**). In more recent times, cycle lanes have become an important form of land use in order to reduce congestion and respond to increasing CO_2 emissions.

↑ **Fig. 29.4** An industrial estate in Dublin.

Recreational

Parks and open spaces, both large and small, form an important open space element for recreation activities (Fig. 29.5). They also contribute to improved environmental conditions.

↑ **Fig. 29.5** Weaver Park, Cork Street, Dublin.

↑ **Fig. 29.6** Phoenix Park.

CHECK YOUR LEARNING

1. Identify five different land uses associated with urban areas.
2. List two reasons why the CBD of a city has a high percentage of commercial land use.
3. Why are buildings in the CBD taller than in other areas?

CASE STUDY: LAND USE ZONES IN DUBLIN

Commercial

The **CBD**, the core of commercial activities, spans the River Liffey extending from Parnell Street through O'Connell Street, Henry Street and south to Grafton Street (**Fig. 29.7**). With bus, DART and LUAS services, it is the most **accessible** city area. Buildings are **multi-storey** and **multifunctional**. Ground floor use is mainly retail and commercial, while upper floors have different uses, including offices and apartments. It is the zone with highest land and rent values. Grafton Street is Ireland's most expensive street. Commercial land use is also associated with shopping centres and business parks in the urban fringe that have large areas for parking and excellent road access. (e.g. **Liffey Valley**).

↑ **Fig. 29.7** Grafton Street, Dublin CBD.

Residential

In Dublin, residential land use is divided in terms of **density** and **type**. Generally, inner-city areas have higher densities due to land costs and a lack of space. Local authority housing in the inner city consists of flat complexes with very little open space. Expansion in the post-war period led to lower-density developments in areas such as **Marino** (**Fig. 29.8**) and **Crumlin**, consisting of terraced housing with front and back gardens. Middle-class housing with large front and rear gardens is associated with areas such as **Terenure**, while **Howth** and **Dalkey** are examples of more affluent areas with expensive residences. In more recent years, in response to rising land prices and increasing demand, higher-density apartment complexes have been built throughout the Dublin area.

↑ **Fig. 29.8** Middle-class housing in Marino, Dublin.

Industrial

As with most developed world cities, manufacturing in Dublin has moved to **suburban** sites. This is known as **deindustrialisation**. The Guinness Brewery is one of the last manufacturing industries remaining close to the CBD. Brownfield sites associated with abandoned industrial sites have been redeveloped (e.g. **Dublin Docklands**). In the Poolbeg Strategic Zone, the site of a glassmaking plant is one of the last major brownfield sites in Dublin awaiting redevelopment. Today, industry is located in industrial estates close to the major roads on the urban fringe (e.g. **Grange Castle**) and surrounding counties of the **GDA** (e.g. **Intel, Leixlip, Co. Kildare**). Large land banks, good transport infrastructure and government policy have all contributed to this.

Transport

Roads and streets are the largest transport land use in the city. The **M50** is part of an extensive motorway network surrounding the city, however, in the CBD a narrow street pattern causes traffic flow problems. Transport land use also includes mainline railway stations at **Heuston** and **Connolly**; DART commuter stations such as **Pearse**; and the **LUAS Red and Green** routes. **Quality Bus Corridors** and **LUAS Park and Ride** facilities at **Red Cow** and other stations are newer transport land uses designed to promote the use of public transport. The promotion of cycling as a clean form of transport has led to increased cycle lanes and paths throughout the city (e.g. **S2S Sutton to Sandycove**).

Recreation

Parks and open spaces are important for people living and working in Dublin. City centre spaces such as **St Stephen's Green** and **Merrion Square** are very accessible. Other parks such as **St Anne's** in Clontarf serve larger areas and provide playing pitches. **Phoenix Park** is the largest urban park in Europe, while **Weaver Park** in the Liberties area is a smaller open space.

> **EXAM LINK (HL)**
> Urban Land Use (30 marks)
> **Describe and explain the land use zones in any city that you have studied.**
> 2017, Q11B
>
> **Marking Scheme:**
> Land use zones identified = 2 + 2 marks
> City named = 2 marks
> Description/explanation = 12 SRPs × 2 marks each

CHECK YOUR LEARNING

1. Describe three different characteristics of any four land uses found in Dublin.

Urban Land Use Theories

Urban land use theories attempt to explain the layout of urban areas. Using data collected from studies carried out primarily in the USA, simplified models have been created that attempt to explain how land use patterns evolve in cities. Three theories relating to this topic are discussed below.

E.W. Burgess's concentric zone theory, 1920

Based on the city of Chicago, E.W. Burgess's model identified **five different zones** arranged in a series of concentric rings varying in size (**Fig. 29.9**). The theory stated that land values were highest in the CBD and decreased with outward movement. Better housing and increased affluence were associated with zones farthest away from the CBD.

KEYWORDS

Burgess concentric zone theory
CBD
zone of transition
public transport
railways
residential
sector theory

The Burgess Model
- CBD
- Zone of Transition
- Working-class Residential Zone
- Middle-class Residential Zone
- Upper-class Residential Zone

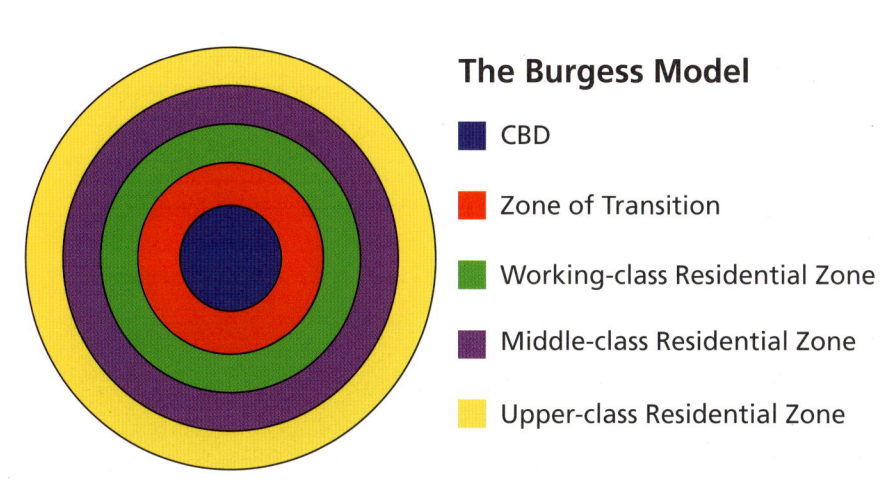

← Fig. 29.9 Burgess' concentric zone model, 1920

503

1. CBD (Central Business District)

The CBD was located at the centre of the city where excellent transport networks made it accessible to commuters. It was the commercial core and contained department stores, entertainment and business activities. High land costs resulted in skyscrapers that allowed high-density usage of the space (Fig. 29.10).

↑ **Fig. 29.10** The CBD Chicago in 1927.

2. Zone of transition

The zone of transition had manufacturing industries and transport infrastructure, especially railways. Poor-quality, high-density housing accommodated newly arrived migrants who worked in the nearby factories. This zone was constantly changing as some factories were expanding, while others were moving out. The CBD also expanded into this zone.

3. Residential zone (working class)

Located near zones 1 and 2, the zones of major employment, this was a low-cost location for working-class people, many of whom were second-generation migrants. Population density was high and people mostly rented accommodation.

4. Residential zone (middle class)

In this zone, homes were bigger with more garden space around them. Land prices were lower and there were more open spaces for parks and recreational use. This was the middle-class area, which had very high levels of home ownership. Transport links, especially rail, allowed people to commute to the CBD.

5. Residential zone (upper class)

This zone contained very large houses on expansive plots (Fig. 29.11). Located farthest from the CBD, in the days before widespread use of cars, residents here relied on rail transport, so most of these zones were located close to railway stations.

Evaluation

This model was developed at a time when most people used public transport; it did not consider the impact of car ownership on the development of a city. It mainly focused on American cities and has limited applicability elsewhere. It was based primarily on residential land use and shows strong social stratification.

↑ **Fig. 29.11** A house in zone 5, Evanston, Chicago.

CHECK YOUR LEARNING

1. Name the main zones described in the concentric zone theory.
2. Describe the main characteristics of each zone.
3. What does the theory state about land values?
4. Give three evaluations of the theory.

Hoyt's sector theory, 1939

Developing ideas from Burgess's theory, Hoyt's sector theory proposed that cities would:

- develop in a series of sectors;
- expand outwards from the CBD in wedge shapes containing different activities.

The theory highlighted the importance of transportation routes, especially railroads, in the development of these sectors (Fig. 29.12).

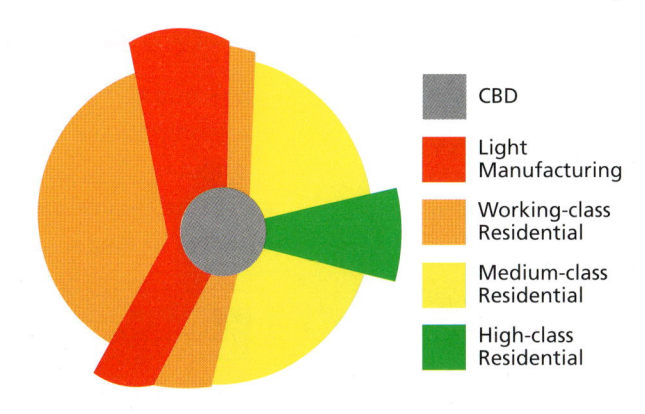

↑ Fig. 29.12 Hoyt's sector theory model, 1939.

1. CBD (Central Business District)

Consisting of partial rings and sectors, this zone was the commercial heart of the city and a focus of transport routes, which made it very accessible.

2. Light manufacturing

This zone radiated out from the centre and was related to the presence of rail transport and its impact on attracting industry. Residential land use in this zone was made up of poor-quality housing for the workers in nearby factories.

3. Working-class residential

The closeness of this zone to the factories in zone 2 attracted workers who could not afford the cost of travel. High population densities and low-rental, poor-quality housing were found here (Fig. 29.13).

↑ Fig. 29.13 Zone 3 dock workers' cottages, Dublin.

4. Middle-class residential

Located away from the industrial zone and consisting of better housing and living conditions, this was the largest residential area where middle-income groups who could afford the cost of travel lived.

5. Upper-class residential

This is where the wealthiest people lived and commuted daily to the CBD. Houses were large with lots of land around them (Fig. 29.14).

↑ Fig. 29.14 Zone 5 upper-class residential housing, Monkstown, Dublin.

Evaluation

This model was based on a far greater sample than the concentric zone theory. It showed how land uses such as industry impacted on the type of residential location. However, the theory only considered the impact of railways, and not private cars.

CHECK YOUR LEARNING

1. Describe two ways that cities would develop according to Hoyt's sector theory.
2. Name the five zones associated with the theory.
3. Describe one characteristic of each zone.
4. Explain one evaluation of Hoyt's sector theory.

Landscapes

KEYWORDS
nuclei
business districts
land values
social stratification
attract
linkages
repel
developing world cities
government policy

Harris and Ullman's multiple nuclei theory, 1945

Harris and Ullman's theory takes ideas from both Burgess and Hoyt. A number of assumptions were made, including: land is not flat in all areas; there is even distribution of resources and of people in residential areas; transportation costs are even. **The theory suggested that cities grow from a number of different business districts or nuclei rather than a single CBD (Fig. 29.15).**

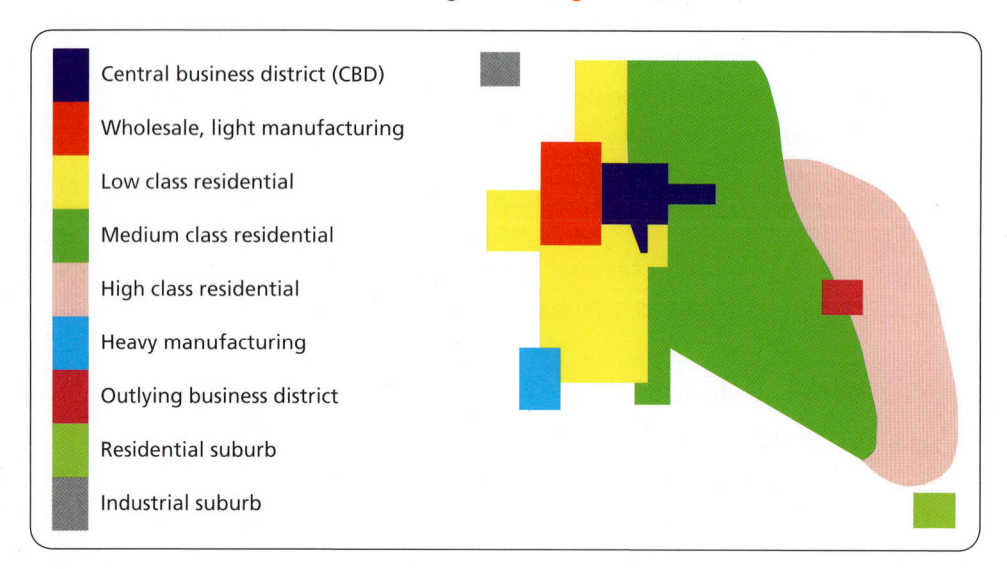

- Central business district (CBD)
- Wholesale, light manufacturing
- Low class residential
- Medium class residential
- High class residential
- Heavy manufacturing
- Outlying business district
- Residential suburb
- Industrial suburb

→ **Fig. 29.15** Harris and Ullman's multiple nuclei theory model, 1945.

Key elements

The **CBD** located at the very centre of the multiple nuclei model is **easily accessed** by a variety of transport types.

The model also contains **eight other nuclei**, around which activities such as wholesale, industry and housing are established. This was based on the idea that increased car ownership gives **greater freedom of movement**, allowing the development of different specialised business districts (e.g. business parks, shopping centres).

With lower land values, the **suburbs** developed as **industrial** areas.

The model also shows strong evidence of **social stratification**, with separate working-, middle- and upper-class residential zones.

According to the model, some land uses **attract** each other: zone 3 – working-class residential – was close to zones 2 and 6 – light and heavy manufacturing. Similar types of industries and services will locate close to each other where they can benefit from linkages and the presence of services such as printing and packaging.

Land uses can also **repel** each other; zone 5 – upper-class residential – is placed far away from zones 2 and 6 – light and heavy manufacturing.

According to this model, **population density** and **land values** both decline with distance from the nuclei.

Evaluation

This theory does not consider **government policy** in relation to urban regeneration and controlling urban sprawl.

The theory is not relevant for cities in **developing countries**. In Rio de Janeiro and São Paulo, Brazil, favelas (slums) grow right beside zones of upper-class housing on the slopes overlooking the city centres (Fig. 29.16).

← **Fig. 29.16** Favela, Rio de Janeiro, Brazil.

29 Urban Land Use and Planning

CHECK YOUR LEARNING

1. What is the main proposition of the multiple nuclei theory?
2. Outline any three elements of the theory.
3. Give two evaluations of the multiple nuclei theory.

CASE STUDY: MULTIPLE NUCLEI THEORY AND DUBLIN

In accordance with the multiple nuclei theory, the CBD is located in the centre of Dublin. It is the commercial, business and entertainment core of the city. The CBD is the area that is most accessible by public transport, with bus stations, railway stations, and DART and LUAS stops.

Brownfield sites in the manufacturing zone have been redeveloped. The former gasworks site in the Docklands has a variety of commercial, residential and recreational services (e.g. **Bord Gáis Energy Theatre**).

Availability of cheaper land in **greenfield** sites at the outer edges of the city has resulted in the location of numerous industrial zones (e.g. **Citywest**).

↑ **Fig. 29.17** Dublin Airport Logistics Park.

The area around Dublin Airport is a good example of land uses attracting other land uses. Hotels have been built to accommodate visitors and a number of transport and courier companies are located here (**Fig. 29.17**).

Examples of working-class residential housing can be found near the CBD. However, many of these have been upgraded, with older flat complexes demolished and replaced with apartment blocks and townhouses (e.g. **Summerhill**). Because of their proximity to the city centre, many of the dockers' cottages and workers' houses have been upgraded and what was once classed lower-class residential now contains professional residents (e.g. **Docklands**). In inner-city areas, **urban renewal**, **planning regulations** relating to affordable and social housing, and **gentrification** have resulted in the mixing of residential types.

↑ **Fig. 29.18** Liffey Valley Shopping Centre, Dublin.

The location of similar services can be seen around the **Four Courts**, where solicitors' offices and a variety of legal services are located. The area around the new Criminal Courts of Justice will attract law-related activities, contributing to its regeneration.

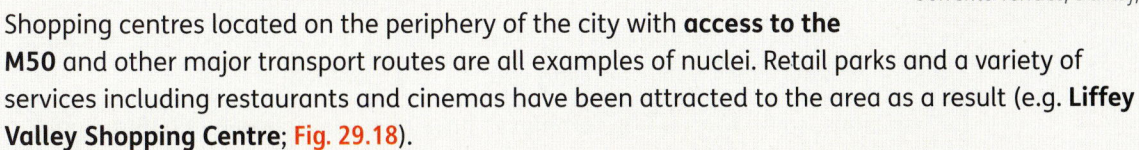

↑ **Fig. 29.19** Upper-class housing, Sorrento Terrace, Dalkey, Dublin.

Shopping centres located on the periphery of the city with **access to the M50** and other major transport routes are all examples of nuclei. Retail parks and a variety of services including restaurants and cinemas have been attracted to the area as a result (e.g. **Liffey Valley Shopping Centre**; **Fig. 29.18**).

The model shows upper-class residential areas are relatively far from the CBD, and areas of this type in Dublin (e.g. **Howth** and **Dalkey**; **Fig. 29.19**) conform to the model.

CHECK YOUR LEARNING

1. Name any five zones identified in the multiple nuclei model.
2. Explain three assumptions upon which the multiple nuclei theory was based.
3. Name any six key elements of the theory.
4. Explain two evaluations of the multiple nuclei theory.
5. Describe five ways in which the multiple nuclei theory can be applied to the development of Dublin.

Landscapes

KEYWORDS
segregation
stratification
housing policy
renewal

Social Stratification in Cities

Within cities, people with similar income levels and educational achievements tend to live in the same areas. This pattern of segregation has evolved over a long period of time, and is referred to as social stratification. There are a number of indicators of social stratification.

Housing type

Those on higher incomes live in large houses on large sites, often protected by high walls and security gates. Often located in elevated or coastal sites, property prices here are very high (e.g. **Malibu, California**; Fig. 29.20). In many cities, downtown, high-rise apartment blocks are also associated with high net earners (e.g. **Central Park, New York**).

Middle-income families live in more modest houses, with smaller front and back gardens. In Dublin, this type of housing is associated with older suburbs such as **Terenure** and newer suburbs such as **Castleknock**.

↑ **Fig. 29.20** Exclusive residences in Malibu, California.

Lower-income housing in American cities is found in developments known as **projects**, while many European cities also have distinct areas of lower-income housing (e.g. **Clichy-sous-Bois, Paris**; Fig. 29.21). Areas of lower-income housing tend to be less well maintained, are subject to higher rates of vandalism and have very few higher-order services located within them.

↑ **Fig. 29.21** Public housing project in Los Angeles, USA.

Chapter 20: A Core European Region – The Paris Basin

Ireland

In Ireland, local authority housing constructed since the 1950s was associated with areas of lower income. Housing policy resulted in the development of large areas to house low-income families, leading to clearly defined social segregation (e.g. **Moyross, Limerick; Knocknaheeny, Cork**). During the 1940s and 1950s, Dublin Corporation cleared inner-city tenements and built four- and five-storey blocks of flats at various locations in the city centre. In Dublin, the northside–southside divide is based on the fact that the southside has greater concentrations of middle- and upper-class housing (e.g. **Sandymount**), while the northside has large areas of working-class public housing estates (e.g. **Coolock**).

In Irish cities, some former flat complexes have been demolished (e.g. **Blackpool Flats, Cork**), while others have undergone renewal or been replaced by modern housing units (e.g. **Fatima Mansions, Dublin**). Urban renewal has changed some areas; places that were once associated with lower-income housing have a mix of lower- and middle-income residents (e.g. **Cork St, Dublin**). New policies on social housing attempt to ensure that new housing developments have an affordable housing element within them, thus reducing social segregation.

Education

Lower-income areas have a lower rate of progression to third-level colleges than middle and higher-income areas. Annual feeder schools tables published by Irish newspapers highlight this.

CHECK YOUR LEARNING

1. Explain the term social stratification.
2. Describe three indicators of social stratification.

Changes in Land Use

KEYWORDS
zoning, re-zoning, brownfield sites, containerisation, gentrification, greenfield sites, International Financial Services Centre

Cities are constantly evolving, which results in the continuing change of land use both within urban areas and on their fringes. In order to ensure orderly growth, city authorities draw up development plans that will allow certain types of development in different areas. This is called **zoning**. Over time, development plans need to be changed. These changes may involve **re-zoning** or changing the land use zones to other uses.

- Manufacturing industry has moved from central locations to the outskirts of cities, leaving brownfield sites.
- Changes to how ports operate – **RoRo**, **containerisation** – have led to major changes in land once associated with port activities.
- Inner-city locations have undergone regeneration, resulting in changing land use. The social structure of these areas has also changed through **gentrification**.
- **Greenfield sites** in the outskirts of cities that were once agricultural zones have been rezoned and now have residential, commercial and industrial uses.

RoRo: An abbreviation of roll-on roll-off, where trucks carrying containers drive on to ferries to travel between ports.

Containerisation: Goods and raw materials in containers are moved by ship and truck.

Gentrification: The process where more affluent residents replace the original working-class population.

CASE STUDY: CHANGING LAND USE IN URBAN AREAS – DUBLIN'S DOCKLANDS

Dublin Port developed as the major port for the country (Fig. 29.22). Land use associated with the Docklands included **warehouses and storage areas for imported coal and gasworks, which used some of this coal to manufacture gas** (e.g. **Dublin Gas Company**). **Transport land** use to allow movement of goods included harbours for the Royal and Grand canals, as well as railway lines and rail depots (e.g. **Point Depot**). Port-related employment attracted many workers and working-class residential land use, with small, poor-quality houses developed.

↑ **Fig. 29.22** Sir John Rogerson's Quay, Dublin Port, in the early 1900s.

Changing times for Dublin port and docks

The development of RoRo and containerisation in the 1950s, and the increased use of mechanical cranes, led to job losses in the Docklands (Fig. 29.23).

Reclamation of land closer to the sea allowed port activities to relocate to deeper water, leaving abandoned warehouses behind.

The piping of natural gas from Kinsale to Dublin in 1978 led to the closure of the Dublin Gas Company's manufacturing facility.

↑ **Fig. 29.23** Containerisation led to job losses.

Landscapes

Renewal and redevelopment

The first step that led to extensive land use changes in the Docklands was the creation of the **International Financial Services Centre (IFSC)** (Fig. 29.24). This was constructed in two phases between 1988 and 2000. Land on which bonded warehouses storing tobacco and spirits once stood became the site of office blocks, which housed international financial institutions and employed 14,000 workers.

Fig. 29.24 International Financial Services Centre, Dublin.

The Dublin Docklands Development Authority (DDDA) 1997–2005

The DDDA was responsible for the development of an area of 520 hectares, spanning both sides of the river. The area has been transformed and now has mixed land use.

Changed land use

Commercial

Large numbers of office complexes and hotels have been constructed (Fig. 29.25). Bars, shops and restaurants have opened on the ground floors of multi-use buildings. The **Central Bank** relocated from Dame Street to this area, while the **Convention Centre** attracts large numbers of visitors.

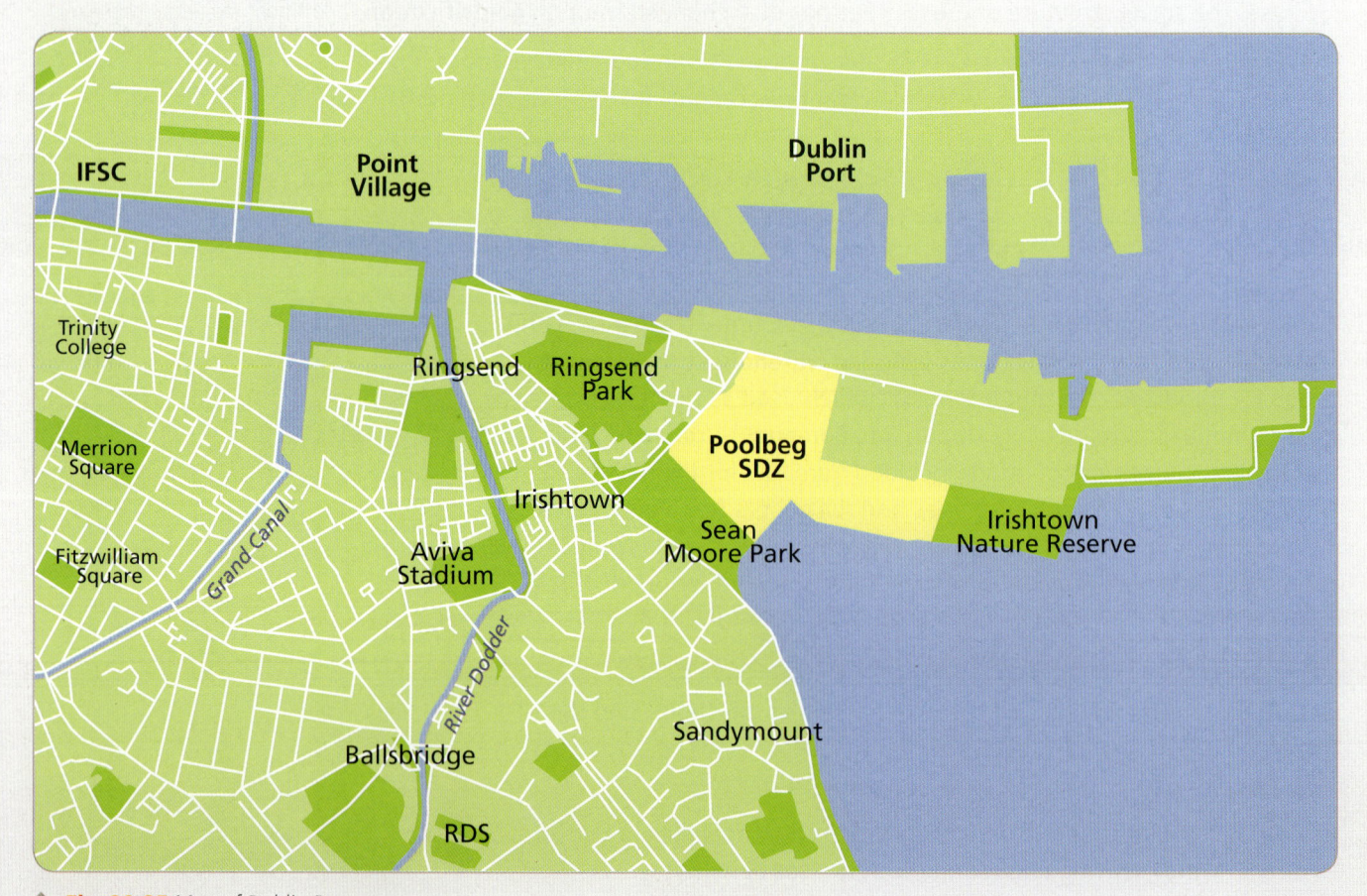

Fig. 29.25 Map of Dublin Port area.

Recreational

The **Bord Gáis Energy Theatre** in Grand Canal Docks and the **3Arena** in the former railway depot at the Point are examples of recreational land use (**Fig. 29.26**). Warehouses have been removed and walkways created along the River Liffey. The planting of trees and the installation of sculptures have greatly enhanced the visual appearance of the area (**Figs 29.27**, **29.28**).

Transport

The **LUAS Docklands** extension connects with the LUAS network. Designated **bus corridors** have also been created. Cycle paths and walkways have been laid down, and bike stations for the **Dublin Bike Scheme** have opened at many locations throughout the Docklands. New bridges – the Samuel Beckett Bridge and the pedestrian Seán O'Casey Bridge – have also been constructed.

Residential

Formerly an area of high-density, working-class homes, the change of land use to high-density, modern apartments designed to house middle-class professionals working in the area was not without its problems. Social and affordable housing was to comprise 20% of all residential development in the area, but reports in 2019 reveal that only 1% of designated social housing in the Docklands has been supplied. In spite of efforts at social integration, many local residents feel excluded from most of the employment on offer in the area.

Educational

The **National College of Ireland**, which offers graduate and postgraduate courses, moved to a new campus in the Docklands.

Cultural

EPIC, The Irish Emigration Museum, is located in the vaults of the Custom House Quarter Building.

Changing land use will continue within the Docklands. There are plans to construct 3,000 homes and provide commercial space for up to 8,000 workers in the **Poolbeg Peninsula**, a designated **Strategic Development Zone**.

↑ **Fig. 29.26** Bord Gáis Energy Theatre, Dublin.

↑ **Fig. 29.27** Famine commemorative sculpture, Custom House Quay, Dublin.

↑ **Fig. 29.28** Recreational land use, Liffey Linear Park, Dublin.

EXAM LINK (OL)

Urban Land Use (30 marks)
(i) Name one urban area that you have studied and name any two land uses in this urban area.
(ii) Describe and explain how land use in this urban area has changed over time.

2018, Q10B

Marking Scheme:
(i) Urban area named = 3 marks
Two land uses named × 3 marks
(ii) Description/explanation = 7 SRPs × 3 marks

Strategic Development Zone: An area of land designated to contain developments of economic or social importance to the State.

Landscapes

EXAM LINK (HL)

Urban Development (30 marks)
Examine how urban centres change over time with reference to example(s) that you have studied.
2016, Q12C

Marking Scheme:
Change identified = 2 marks
Example = 2 marks
Examination = 13 SRPs × 2 marks

CHECK YOUR LEARNING

1. Name four land uses present in Dublin Port up to the 1970s.
2. Explain four changes that affected land use in Dublin Docklands.
3. Name one major planning initiative that changed land use in this area.
4. Explain four land use changes that occurred as a result of this initiative.

Planning Issues Arising from Changes in Land Use

KEYWORDS		
repellent land use	health risks	traffic congestion
EU policy	pollution	waste management

As cities evolve, land **re-zoning** and land use changes can lead to objections from residents and local business owners.

CASE STUDY: THE POOLBEG INCINERATOR, DUBLIN

The proposed **change of land use** to build an incinerator in the Docklands is an example of a land use that is **repellent** to residential land use. There was major opposition from local residents to the proposal. Objections were based on both environmental and social concerns, as well as the economic impact of the development on the value of nearby properties.

In 2007, planning permission for the incinerator was applied for. Supporters of the project argued that with new EU directives Ireland was running out of landfill and the proposed **waste-to-energy plant** supplying electricity and local heating was the norm across the EU.

↑ **Fig. 29.29** The Poolbeg Incinerator in Ringsend, Dublin.

29 Urban Land Use and Planning

Objections to the project included the following:
- By 2007, recycling rates had grown to 40% – continued increases in recycling would greatly reduce the amount of waste to be disposed.
- Dublin alone could not possibly create enough waste to feed the incinerator, and within 10 years the plant would be burning more than half of Ireland's residual waste.
- Waste-carrying lorries would have to access the facility daily, resulting in congestion and noise pollution.
- Road infrastructure would need to be upgraded to cope with increased traffic volumes.
- Concern about health risks caused by the release of pollutants and independent monitoring of the plant were also highlighted.

In spite of all the protests, the facility was built and opened in 2017 (**Fig. 29.29**). The proposed istrict heating scheme to distribute the energy generated by the burning of the waste has yet to be put in place and critics say it will be many years before it is.

CHECK YOUR LEARNING

1. List three arguments in favour of the Poolbeg Incinerator.
2. Name three objections to the development.
3. Working in small groups, prepare presentations supporting and opposing the incineration process.

Land Values in Cities

Within cities, land values fluctuate over time and change from area to area. The general pattern is that values fall with increasing distance from the CBD. There can also be secondary peaks associated with suburban business cores such as shopping centres and retail parks.

The bid rent theory

The bid rent theory attempts to explain the distribution of retail, commercial and industrial activities. **Land cost** and **distance from the CBD** are its two key elements. Land users all compete for the most accessible land within the CBD. The more accessible an area is, the greater the number of possible customers in that area. Locating here (the **Peak Land Value Intersection**) should mean a business will be profitable. The price that different land users are willing to pay for land is known as the **bid rent**.

- People will be willing to pay more for a location in the CBD.
- Limited land makes city centres the most expensive.
- Constructing high-rise buildings makes maximum use of a site.
- People will pay less for land farther away from the CBD.

KEYWORDS

peak land value
bid rent theory
Peak Land Value Intersection

During the Celtic Tiger years, land values in the Greater Dublin Area reached extraordinary levels and during the downturn that followed, land prices fell dramatically. Since the economic recovery, prices are once again rising.

Peak Land Value Intersection: The point in a CBD or at a suburban road intersection where land values are at a maximum.

CHECK YOUR LEARNING

1. Describe two ways that land values affect land use in urban areas.

Landscapes

KEYWORDS
footfall
commercial
business centre
suburban areas

How Land Values Influence Land Use in Modern Cities

Retail

High rents are associated with the CBD, where potential customer numbers (**footfall**) are highest. High-order services with large thresholds are found here (e.g. **department stores;** Fig. 29.30). High rents mean that stores have many floors to maximise their square footage. Other high-order services that need direct access from the street, such as jewellery stores and mobile phone stores, will also locate in this area (e.g. **Henry Street, Dublin; Patrick Street, Cork**)

↑ **Fig. 29.30** Arnotts Department Store, Henry Street, Dublin.

Fast food outlets, bars, restaurants and hotels can be found throughout the CBD. They rely on large volumes of customers and are willing to pay the high rents associated with these locations.

Away from the CBD, footfall will decrease, resulting in declining land values. The bid rents that retail activities are prepared to pay in these areas will therefore be lower.

Commercial

By locating on the ground floors of buildings in the CBD, banks and building societies are accessible to their customers (e.g. **Shop Street, Galway**). However, the introduction of online banking and the consequent fall in people visiting banks have resulted in many closures.

On the edge of the CBD where office space is cheaper, you will find architectural, accountancy, legal and medical consultants (e.g. **Merrion Square, Dublin**). Within the CBD, some of these services will also be found on the upper floors of buildings where rents are not as high. Large office buildings are also located near the edge of the CBD where rents are lower (e.g. **Google offices, Barrow Street, Dublin**).

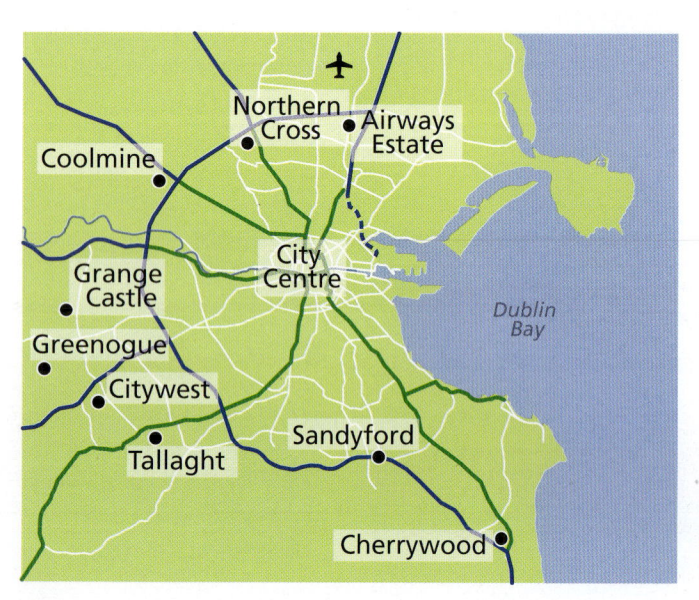

Industry

Modern industry requires locations with good transport access and land for buildings, car parking and loading and unloading, so it locates on the outskirts of cities (Fig. 29.31). Here, large sites are available, rents are lower and there is access to an efficient transport network (e.g. **Raheen Business Park, Limerick**).

← **Fig. 29.31** Business and industrial parks on the outskirts of Dublin city.

Suburban areas

Generally, land prices tend to decrease with distance from the CBD. However, outer areas can have peaks where land values are high. The development of business centres, such as shopping centres and retail parks located on good transport routes, leads to the creation of local secondary peaks with high land values (e.g. **Blanchardstown Shopping Centre, Dublin**; **Mahon Point Shopping Centre, Cork**; Fig. 29.32).

↑ **Fig. 29.32** The Mahon Point Shopping Centre in Cork is located beside the Cork South Ring Road.

CHECK YOUR LEARNING

1. Explain two ways in which land values affect retail activities in urban areas.
2. Describe two ways in which commercial activities are affected by land values.

Expanding Cities and the Pressure on Rural Land Use

KEYWORDS
agriculture
environment
social
heritage

As urban areas expand, land use in surrounding rural areas changes, as residential and commercial developments are constructed. Some of the impacts of this expansion are discussed below.

Agriculture

New roads can result in **divided farms**, cutting off parts of them and making the transfer of machinery and livestock difficult.

Re-zoning of agricultural land to residential land use increases the value of land. Farmers who wish to expand their farms have to pay **inflated prices** and cannot compete with developers.

The **high land prices** can also put pressure on farmers to sell their land and get out of farming, thereby reducing the land area for agriculture and negatively impacting output. In North Co. Dublin, housing is now located on the sites of former glasshouses used for horticulture.

Environment

Illegal dumping of waste can occur in fields and along roadsides near new residential developments.

Loss of habitat threatens the survival of some species. Some areas have become isolated from each other, preventing the movement of animals, impacting on mating and endangering some species.

Most motorway construction is accompanied by extensive **tree planting** along the margin. This, in some way, compensates for the loss of other habitats.

Social

Overdevelopment destroys the **distinctive character** of rural villages and small towns. New planning regulations associated with county plans mean that new developments have to be sensitive to the local built environment.

Many of the new residents in these areas commute daily to work in the city centre or nearby business nodes, resulting in **increased traffic volume**.

Increased residential land use increases population and results in increasing demand for **school places**. This can lead to the enlargement of existing schools and/or the construction of new ones.

Heritage

Built heritage sites can be destroyed to make way for road projects, for example, **Carrickmines Castle** in Dublin is surrounded by the M50.

The construction of motorways can lead to the destruction of heritage (**Fig. 29.33**), while the proximity of proposed motorways to important heritage sites can lead to major objections, e.g. M3 motorway near **Tara, Co. Meath**.

↑ **Fig. 29.33** Motorway construction can destroy heritage.

Sometimes, preparatory work on road projects can lead to archaeological discoveries. In 2003, work on the N25 Waterford bypass led to the discovery of an important Viking settlement at **Woodstown**.

Culture

Instead of using local place names, generic names with no link to the area are used (e.g. **Oak Manor**).

CHECK YOUR LEARNING

1. Explain three impacts of urban expansion on agriculture.
2. Explain three environmental impacts of urban expansion.
3. Describe three social impacts of urban expansion on rural areas.
4. Outline three ways in which urban expansion can impact on heritage in rural areas.

EXAMINATION QUESTIONS

ORDINARY LEVEL

Long Questions

1. Urban Land Use
  (i) Name one urban area that you have studied and name any two land uses in this urban area.
  (ii) Describe and explain how land use in this urban area has changed over time.

2018, Part Two, Section 2, Q10B (30 marks)

Marking Scheme:
(i) Urban area named = 3 marks
   Two land uses named × 3 marks
(ii) Description/explanation =
   7 SRPs × 3 marks

HIGHER LEVEL

Long Questions

2. Urban Expansion
As cities grow and expand they impact on the surrounding rural areas.
Discuss this statement with reference to example(s) that you have studied.

2018, Part Two, Section 2, Q12C (30 marks)

Marking Scheme:
Impact identified = 2 marks
Example = 2 marks
Discussion = 13 SRPs × 2 marks

Revision Summary

Donor Regions Push Factors	Receiver Regions Pull Factors	Barriers to Migration
• Overpopulation • Low wages/unemployment • Lack of services • Political unrest • Natural disasters	• Underpopulation, labour shortages • Highly developed economies • Large range of services • Higher incomes • Freedom from persecution	• Financial – resettling costs prohibitive • Legal, e.g. visas, work permits • Personal – family ties

Impacts on Donor Regions	Impacts on Host Regions	Case Study: Ireland as Receiver Region
Positive impacts • Safety valve to reduce unemployment • Migrant remittances to home country • Migrants return home with new skills • Pressure relieved on resources **Negative impacts** • Gender imbalance – more female migrants – affects population structure • Quality of life – decreased numbers in local sports and activities • Brain drain – loss of skilled workers • Depopulation – abandoned homes and farms	**Positive impacts** • Cultural enrichment, multiracial society • Add to labour pool – enable economic growth • Increased spending – higher revenues • Migrant entrepreneurs – create employment, build trade links **Negative impacts** • Higher birth rates – extra pressure on services • Extra demands on social services, e.g. housing, welfare • Discrimination – cultural and religious tensions • Lack of integration policies – racial tensions • Undercutting of wage rates – tension • Over-reliance on migrant workers in some sectors	**Positive impacts** • Skilled, multilingual workforce – attractive for global companies • Skilled, semi-skilled tradespeople solve labour shortages • Increased contributions to govt revenues • Increased purchasing power – growth in retail, recreation, accommodation sectors • Fill employment gaps, e.g. horticulture, hospitality • Maintain services in small towns • Cultural diversity **Negative impacts** • Migrant remittances – loss of money to economy • Racism – seen as competition for employment • Pressure on services, e.g. housing • Strain on school management, e.g. language support teachers • Increasing costs of translators, multi-lingual information • Racism and racially motivated crimes • Exploitation of vulnerable workers • Threat of terrorism • Increase in people trafficking

Rural-to-Urban Migration

Developed World Case Study: Ireland	Developing World Case Study: India
Impacts on donor regions • Rural depopulation – e.g. Mayo • Higher-than-average age impacts population structure and dependency ratio – declining birth rate • Brain drain – lack of skilled labour force, investment unattractive • Falling school enrolments • Loss of services • Business closures **Impacts on receiver regions** • Population increases, esp. GDA • Average age is lower – higher birth rates – pressure on schools, hospitals and services • Increased demand for housing – urban sprawl – rents rise • Traffic congestion • Labour pool attracts industry – economic growth	**Impacts on donor regions** • Rural depopulation, mostly young men • Population structure changes – women, young children, older adults • Child labour to supplement family income – lack of education, poor prospects • Pattern of migration **Impacts on receiver regions** • Overcrowding (slums) • Crime and violence • Poor living conditions • Poorly paid jobs/lack of employment • Exploitation • Air pollution, traffic congestion

Landscapes

Social Stratification

Housing type
- Higher incomes – large private homes in coastal sites
- Middle income – modest homes in suburbs
- Lower income – projects/distinct areas, neglected, few high-order services

Ireland
- Lower income – local authority housing estates, flat complexes – clear social segregation
- North–South divide, Dublin – working-class housing vs middle- and upper-class housing
- Urban renewal – mixed social structure
- New policies on social housing aim to reduce social segregation

Changes in Land Use
- Cities – Continual change of land use
- Manufacturing moved from centre to outskirts
- Ports evolve – RoRo, containerisation
- Inner city renewal and gentrification
- Urban spread – agricultural land now residential, commercial, industrial

Case Study: Dublin Docklands
- Port land use: warehouses, storage, transport, rail depots, gas works, dockers housing
- 1950s RoRo and containerisation – job losses
- Reclamation of land close to sea – relocation of port facilities – abandoned warehouses

Redevelopment
- 1998–2000 IFSC commercial offices, hotels, retail
- 1997–2005 DDDA – mixed land use both sides of river
  1. Recreational: 3Arena, Bord Gáis Theatre, river walk
  2. Transport: LUAS Docklands extension, bus corridors, cycle paths, walkways, bridges
  3. Residential: Middle-class, high-density apartments, locals excluded
  4. Educational – National College of Ireland
  5. Cultural – EPIC (The Irish Emigration Museum)
- Continuation of land use change – Strategic Development Zone

Planning Issues
- Cities constantly evolving – land-use changes – objections

Case study: Poolbeg Incinerator, Dublin
- 2007 planning permission sought for waste-to-energy plant
- Supporters: EU regulations would reduce landfill, incineration EU norm
- Objections: increased recycling; country-wide waste; traffic volumes; lack of infrastructure; health and safety
- Opened 2017 – heating scheme not yet in place

Land Values in Cities
- Fluctuate with time and between areas
- Bid rent theory – explains distribution of retail, commercial and industrial activity
- Key elements: land cost, distance from CBD
- Accessibility + many customers = Peak Land Value Intersection = profit
- Bid rent higher if close to CBD, city centre expensive, high-rise

Influence on Land Use in Cities

Retail
- CBD – high footfall, high rents
- Attract large department stores, fast food outlets, bars
- High-rise to maximise square footage
- Street access stores, e.g. mobile phones

Commercial
- Banks on ground floors of buildings in CBD
- Edge of CBD – cheaper office space – consultants, large office buildings, e.g. Google

Industry
- Outskirts – large sites, low rents, good transport access
- Industrial estates

Suburban areas
- Peaks of high land value – shopping centres, retail parks on good transport routes, e.g. Mahon Point, Cork

Expanding Cities – Rural Land Use Pressure

Agriculture
- Roads bisect farms – moving machinery and livestock difficult
- Re-zoning agricultural land – increases land value – too expensive for farmers

Environment
- Illegal dumping
- Loss of habitat – endangered species
- Tree planning – some compensation

Social
- Overdevelopment – destroys character of rural villages
- Commuters increase traffic volumes
- Increasing population – demand for more schools

Heritage
- Built heritage sites destroyed
- Integrity of heritage sites compromised
- Archaeological discoveries during preparatory work

Culture
- Use of generic place names with no link to the area

30 URBAN GROWTH PROBLEMS

LEARNING INTENTIONS
Syllabus Links: 5.6

By the end of this chapter I will be able to:
- identify and explain the causes and impacts of traffic movement and congestion;
- describe and explain the causes and impacts of urban sprawl;
- outline issues facing heritage in urban areas;
- describe planning strategies to deal with urban decay and renewal;
- explain issues around the absence of community;
- identify and explain problems caused by the growth of developing world cities;
- identify issues relating to cities of the future.

Around the world, the growth and expansion of urban centres result in issues that impact on how those cities function.

Traffic Flow and Congestion

Traffic movement and congestion have become major issues in all the cities of the world.

Causes

Urban sprawl is pushing residential zones and the **commuter belt** further out and away from the Central Business District (CBD) of cities.

Public transport networks are limited in extent and capacity, so people have no choice but to use their cars to commute to the CBD and other business cores within cities.

Huge volumes of traffic at rush hour, a lack of capacity on roads, and **narrow streets** all contribute to the problem.

Impacts

Socio-economic

Longer journey times result in increased fuel consumption, adding to transport costs and increasing production costs.

Delays result in increased **stress levels** for workers, impairing their health and work performance.

Early departures and late arrival home for workers results in a lack of quality family time.

KEYWORDS
commuter belt
public transport
narrow streets
fuel consumption
delays
family time
toxic fumes
congestion charges
carpooling
bus lanes
cycle lanes
rush hour

519

Environmental

Traffic exhaust fumes (nitrogen oxide) lead to **air pollution** and result in respiratory diseases.

Solutions

The long-term solution to traffic congestion is to get people to leave their cars and to use **cheap, reliable public transport systems**.

Congestion charges discourage vehicles entering certain zones at peak traffic times (e.g. **London Congestion Charge**; Fig. 30.1).

Designated high-occupancy lanes and **carpooling** reduce the number of single occupant cars (Figs 30.2, 30.3).

Bus lanes and **smart traffic signals** improve journey times, encouraging greater bus usage.

Cycle lanes and bike rental schemes reduce car volumes and are increasingly becoming part of the global urban transport landscape (e.g. **Rome**).

> **DID YOU KNOW?**
> Motorist have to pay around €13 just to enter the London Central Zone during peak traffic times.

Fig. 30.1 The London Congestion Charge.

Fig. 30.2 A high-occupancy lane on a busy Los Angeles highway.

Fig. 30.3 A high-occupancy vehicle (HOV) lane.

High-occupancy vehicle: A vehicle containing multiple people.

CHECK YOUR LEARNING

1. Explain three causes of traffic congestion.
2. Name three impacts of traffic congestion.
3. Describe three solutions to this problem.

30 Urban Growth Problems

CASE STUDY: TRAFFIC CONGESTION IN DUBLIN

In 2016, the Greater Dublin Area had a population of just over 1.9 million, or over 40% of the population of Ireland. It had a registered car ownership of over 660,000.

Causes of congestion

Continuing **urban sprawl** means people live further away from their places of work. Increased **car ownership** has resulted in increased traffic flows to the CBD and to other business and commercial nuclei (e.g. **commuters travelling from Meath, Kildare, Wicklow**).

Failure to supply an efficient **public transport system** serving the newly developed suburban estates around the city leave commuters with no alternative but to use private cars (e.g. **Swords**).

The **road infrastructure** is not able to cope with peak volumes of traffic (e.g. **M50**). A large percentage of the traffic is directed from main arteries on to city roads where bottlenecks occur (**M1, M7**; **Figs 30.4, 30.5**).

The city bus network has very few **cross-city services**. This forces commuters to take multiple buses and makes public transport an unattractive alternative to a private car.

The morning school run causes increased congestion. In 1981, 20% of primary school students and 8% of secondary school students were driven to school. In 2016, the figures were 59.8% and 41.9%, respectively.

KEYWORDS
- urban sprawl
- car ownership
- public transport
- roads
- bottlenecks
- cross-city services
- school run
- LUAS
- Leap Cards
- Quality Bus Corridors
- orbital routes

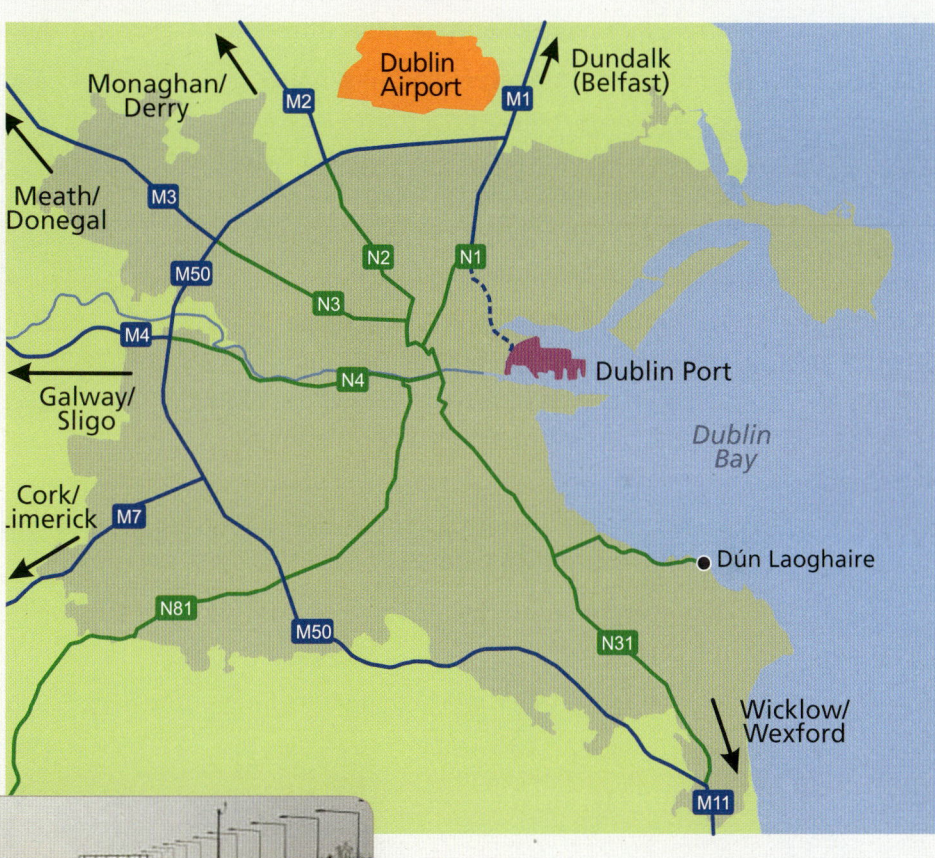

↑ **Fig. 30.4** Map showing the main roads into Dublin city.

← **Fig. 30.5** Traffic congestion on the M50.

521

Landscapes

Solutions

A number of measures designed to improve the efficiency and availability of public transport have been or are in the process of being implemented. These improvements will make public transport more attractive and encourage people to leave their cars at home, thus reducing traffic volume.

- The **LUAS** is contributing to reduced traffic volumes. In 2018, LUAS lines carried over 41 million passengers (Fig. 30.6).
- The introduction of an **integrated ticketing** scheme called **Leap Card** in 2011 allows users to move between **Dublin Bus**, **DART** and **LUAS** services.
- **Quality Bus Corridors** have improved journey times, making bus transport more attractive.
- A proposed overhaul of Dublin Bus routes will introduce more **orbital routes** travelling between suburbs, while **Busconnects Dublin 2018** proposes building a network of new bus corridors on the busiest routes to make bus journeys faster and more reliable.
- The growth of the **Dublin Bike Scheme** and an active programme of cycle path construction will encourage greater use of this environmentally friendly transport method (Fig. 30.7).

↑ Fig. 30.6 A LUAS tram.

↑ Fig. 30.7 The Dublin Bike Scheme.

The **Greater Dublin Area Transport Strategy 2016–2035** will inform transport planning into the future. Among its provisions are:

- **new overground rail link**: a train link from Sandyford to Swords, connecting Dublin Airport to the city centre;
- **extending the LUAS**: bringing the tram lines out to Bray, Finglas and Poolbeg.

CHECK YOUR LEARNING

1. Explain four causes of traffic congestion in Dublin.
2. Describe three strategies to solve this problem.

EXAM LINK (OL)

Traffic in Urban Areas (40 marks)
(i) Name one city where traffic congestion is a problem.
(ii) Explain the reasons why traffic congestion occurs in this city.
(iii) Describe one solution to traffic congestion.
2015, Q11B

Marking Scheme:
City named = 4 marks
Explanation = 9 SRPs × 3 marks
One solution described = 3 SRPs × 3 marks

Urban Sprawl

KEYWORDS		
low density	green belt	National Planning Framework
re-zoning	property prices	
urban fringe	co-ordinated planning	regional economic engines
greenfield site	high density	regeneration

Urban sprawl occurs when poorly planned, car-dependent, **low-density, residential and commercial developments** spread out over large areas on the outskirts of cities. Examples of urban sprawl include **Brussels** and **Los Angeles**.

CASE STUDY: URBAN SPRAWL IN DUBLIN

Causes

Dublin is Ireland's **primate city** and is the major centre of economic activity in the country. In the 1970s, in response to improving economic conditions, the city began to grow rapidly. Dublin's population almost doubled in 10 years, from 1 million in 1971 to 1.9 million in 1981.

In response to poor housing conditions in the inner city and a general lack of housing, city authorities **re-zoned** huge areas of agricultural land on the **urban fringe** for residential and industrial use. Low-density housing estates with large open spaces were developed and the spread of the city began (e.g. **Tallaght**; Fig. 30.8).

Manufacturing units in the city moved to **greenfield sites** on the urban fringe, where cheap land and little traffic congestion were the main attractions (e.g. **Jacobs**).

Corrupt planning practices led to **green belts** between **Tallaght**, **Lucan** and **Clondalkin** being re-zoned and lost.

Increased housing demand during the Celtic Tiger fuelled increases in **property prices**. People were forced to move outwards from the GDA, where house prices were more competitive and where new residential developments were being constructed.

As the Greater Dublin Area is governed by various different local authorities, there was a lack of **co-ordinated planning** to address the problems.

↑ Fig. 30.8 Brookfield Estate, Tallaght, 2009.

Solutions

The development of **Clongriffin** (Fig. 30.9) on Dublin's northside is an example a of high-density development with rail links, while the larger development at **Adamstown** (Fig. 30.10), a contained urban area with services and direct rail links with the CBD, are positive steps to tackling the problem. By 2040, it is estimated that the population of Ireland will have increased by 1 million people, with up to 75% of this increase focused on the GDA.

↑ Fig. 30.9 Clongriffin, Dublin.

→ Fig. 30.10 Adamstown, Dublin.

Landscapes

Urban sprawl will continue in the GDA unless a number of **national** and **local** strategies are adopted. These include:

- The **National Planning Framework (NPF)** proposes a 50:50 distribution of growth between the Eastern and Midland region, and the Southern and Northern and Western regions. It is planned that **Cork**, **Galway**, **Limerick** and **Waterford** will attract greater foreign direct investment to become '**regional economic engines**'.
- Increased building height and density in Dublin; the re-development of underutilised, vacant or abandoned sites in urban areas for housing; and effective urban renewal and regeneration will increase residential land use within cities. €2 billion will be allocated towards urban regeneration.

Chapter 18: A Core Irish Region – The Greater Dublin Area
Chapter 29: Urban Land Use and Planning

CHECK YOUR LEARNING

1. What is urban sprawl?
2. Explain two impacts of urban sprawl.
3. Name one city that has experienced this problem.
4. Explain any four causes of urban sprawl in that city.
5. Describe two ways of tackling urban sprawl in that city.

EXAM LINK (OL)

Urban Sprawl (40 marks)
(i) Name one city where urban sprawl has occurred.
(ii) Explain the reasons why urban sprawl has occurred in this city.
(iii) Describe one solution to urban sprawl.

2017, Q10C

Marking Scheme:
Named city = 4 marks
Explanation = 9 SRPs × 3 marks
One solution described = 3 SRPs × 3 marks

KEYWORDS
development
preservation
Heritage Act 1995
Heritage Council
Record of Protected Structures (RPS)
conservation areas
Planning and Development Act 2000
fines
Wood Quay
Georgian Dublin
Carrickmines Castle

Heritage in Urban Areas

Urban areas contain heritage sites below the surface and in the built environment. The conflict between development and preservation is one confronting all city authorities. In Ireland, our complex relationship with historic buildings and a lack of proper legislation have resulted in heritage destruction. In more recent years, however, there have been major changes.

Protection of heritage

The **Heritage Act 1995** established the **Heritage Council** to advise and make recommendations to local authorities in relation to planning applications and their impact on heritage. Under the **Local Government Planning and Development Act 2000**, planning authorities are obliged in their development plans to:

- create a Record of Protected Structures (RPS) and outline objectives for their protection;
- designate architectural conservation areas and strategies preserving their character.

EU law relating to the preservation of heritage has also forced local authorities to address the issue.

Other government initiatives include a grants scheme to help with the repair and upkeep of protected structures.

CASE STUDY: HERITAGE ISSUES IN DUBLIN

Dublin City Council now has a list of protected structures and architectural conservation areas. Strict guidelines also apply to developments.

The preservation of older buildings is dependent on their suitability for use in commercial, cultural and/or social contexts. They can be difficult and expensive to adapt for newer use and as a result many of them have been allowed to fall into serious disrepair. The Planning and Development Act of 2000 now **empowers authorities to compel owners to maintain properties or else face prosecution and fines**.

Examples of heritage issues

Wood Quay

In the 1970s, archaeological excavations on Wood Quay in Dublin uncovered remains of an original Viking settlement dating back to the 9th century. In spite of huge protests, the site was covered over and the Dublin Civic Offices were built on the site. Outlines of the houses and sculptures of some of the artefacts found are embedded in the paved areas around Christchurch Cathedral.

Georgian Dublin: Lower Fitzwilliam Street

In the early 1960s, Dublin's longest expanse of Georgian facades was demolished. The 16 Georgian houses on Lower Fitzwilliam Street were replaced by a modern office building (Fig. 30.11). Construction is underway that will result in a more appropriate facade and building.

Fig. 30.11 ESB offices, Lower Fitzwilliam Street, Dublin.

Religious buildings

Changing demographics and falling religious vocations have led to the closure of a number of churches and the sale of former convents. Some churches have been adapted to new functions. St James's Church on James's Street in Dublin houses a distillery, while many old convents have been converted into apartment complexes (Fig. 30.12).

Fig. 30.12 Pearse Lyons Distillery, St James's Church, Dublin.

Carrickmines Castle

Originally built in the Middle Ages to defend the English city of Dublin, the remains of Carrickmines Castle lay in the path of the rerouted M50 motorway. In spite of protests, much of the site is now covered while isolated remnants are surrounded by the road network (Fig. 30.13).

Heritage also relates to the historical, social and cultural environment. The proposal by the Irish Government to only give National Monument status to some of the buildings associated with the 1916 Easter Rising is being strongly opposed by activists who want all of them to be included in the designation.

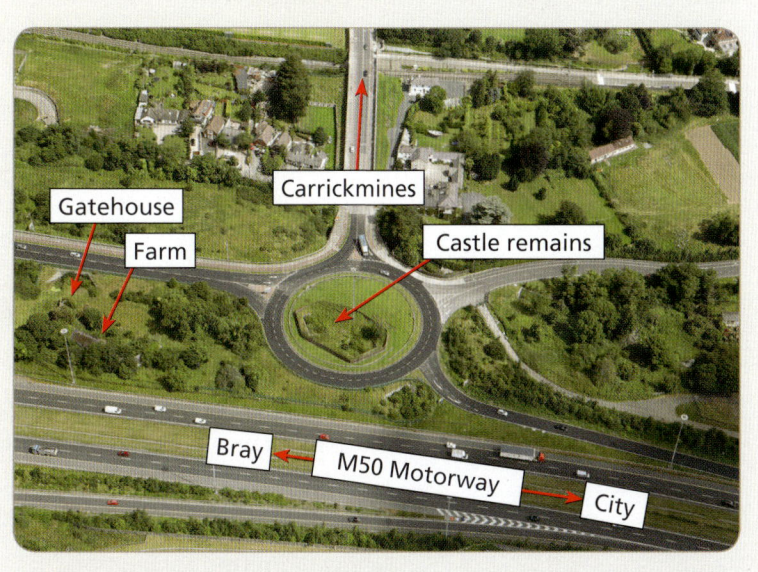

Fig. 30.13 Aerial view of Carrickmines Castle surrounded by motorway.

Landscapes

> **CHECK YOUR LEARNING**
> 1. Name three heritage protection obligations for local authorities under the Planning and Development Act 2000.
> 2. Describe two problems associated with the preservation of older buildings.
> 3. Identify three heritage issues encountered in Dublin.

KEYWORDS
Environmental Protection Agency
south-westerly winds
particulate matter
Air Quality Index
smoky fuels
diesel
respiratory illness
acid rain

Environmental Quality in Urban Areas

In developed countries, environmental issues in urban areas have been addressed and improvements have occurred as a result of changing industrial patterns and stricter legislation. In Ireland, EU and national legislation relating to air, water and noise pollution are in force. **The Environmental Protection Agency (EPA)** is responsible for monitoring levels of pollution, for licencing projects which may impact on the environment and for ensuring compliance with legislation.

Air quality

In Ireland, the prevailing south-westerly winds and a low concentration of heavy industry mean overall air quality is good. In the larger urban centres, air quality has improved since legislation restricting the domestic use of smoky fuels in urban areas was first introduced in 1990. The main source of pollutants continues to be car emissions. Air pollutants include nitrogen dioxide, nitric oxide and sulphur dioxide. **Particulate matter (PM)** refers to the small particles of pollutants present in the air. Using real-time data, the EPA issues an **Air Quality Index** for various areas of the country. On this index, 1 is excellent, while 10 shows very poor air quality.

There are two categories of particulate matter, PM10, which can be seen, and PM2.5, which is not visible to the naked eye.

In smaller urban areas, **smoky fuels** were permitted; however, a full nationwide ban comes into force in autumn 2019. In the meantime, these domestic fuels can cause air quality to deteriorate during cold, calm weather conditions when there is no wind to disperse pollutants.

Recent research has shown **diesel** fuel to be far more polluting than unleaded fuel and there are growing calls for its use to be restricted (**Fig. 30.14**).

↑ **Fig. 30.14** Diesel fuel is far more polluting than unleaded fuel.

Impacts

Air pollution causes **respiratory illnesses** and there is a growing body of evidence to suggest it is a contributory factor in rates of cancer and heart disease.

When sulphur and nitrogen oxide combine with precipitation, **acid rain** is formed. This has a corrosive effect on heritage buildings and on trees and plants associated with open spaces and parks.

The **Air Quality in Ireland 2017** report from the EPA reported that all levels were below permitted EU limits.

30 Urban Growth Problems

CASE STUDY: LOS ANGELES, USA

Since the 1950s, the city of Los Angeles has experienced major problems with air quality when pollution reacts with heat and light to form low-level ozone or smog.

Factors influencing the formation of smog in the Los Angeles area include:
- high levels of traffic pollution due to car dependency;
- industrial-based pollution from oil refineries and power stations;
- the mountains surrounding the city to the north, east and south trap pollutants (Fig. 30.15);
- the warm, sunny climate aids the formation of ozone.

KEYWORDS
smog
car dependency
climate
emission standards
electric vehicles
mountains

← Fig. 30.15 Mountains surrounding Los Angeles trap pollutants.

Impacts

The smog has had a major impact on public health; during periods of high smog levels, vulnerable groups are advised to stay indoors (Fig. 30.16). Economic effects include high healthcare costs and worker absence due to respiratory conditions.

Improvements

Improvements made to tackle the problem include:
- new emission standards for cars and strict enforcement of legislation (e.g. the **Clean Air Act**, 1970);
- reducing nitrogen oxide and sulphur oxide emissions from refineries;
- greater use of electric vehicles, carpools and the sustained promotion of public transport;
- increasing use of renewable energy to reduce use of fossil fuels.

↑ Fig. 30.16 Smog hanging over Los Angeles.

Current situation

While there have been major improvements, high levels of smog can still occur as a result of temperature inversions or brush and forest fire outbreaks.

527

Landscapes

KEYWORDS
Irish Water
contamination
E. coli
cryptosporidium
disinfectants
lead pipes

Water quality

Urban areas require secure supplies of clean, safe water for domestic consumption. In developed countries, domestic water quality and the quality of water in rivers and lakes is carefully monitored. In developing countries, poor-quality water supplies can have a major impact on human health.

In Ireland, most of the public water supply originates as surface water in our lakes, rivers and streams. Sewage treatment plants work to ensure that water entering our rivers and lakes is clean. However, water in these sources can become contaminated by bacteria and parasites from slurry spills and sewage leaks, and heavy rain can lead to discolouration. **Irish Water** is responsible for the production, distribution and monitoring of drinking water, while the EPA has supervisory powers for public water supplies (**Fig. 30.17**). In the major urban areas, water treatment and supply networks are monitored and inspected.

→ **Fig. 30.17** Domestic water for Dublin is cleaned and purified at the Vartry water treatment plant in Co. Wicklow.

Clean water

Sometimes, treatment plant malfunctions can result in domestic water supplies being contaminated by the **E. coli** bacteria and by the microscopic cryptosporidium parasite (e.g. **Galway, 2007**). When this happens, boil water notices are issued in contaminated areas until the source is found and treated. Treatment includes identifying and removing the source of the contamination and repairing equipment.

Under Irish Water's Services Strategic Plan 2015–2040, the use of harmful disinfection products in water treatment plants to remove organic matter from water will be discontinued and replaced by new treatment methods, e.g. using ultraviolet light. With regard to the distribution network, old lead piping systems need to be replaced in order to prevent lead contamination.

Moving forward, upgrading and improving existing infrastructure and planning for future demand are two important areas relating to this vital resource. Proposals to have water pumped from the River Shannon to supply Dublin have been objected to by interest groups in the Shannon Basin.

Chapter 18: A Core Irish Region – The Greater Dublin Area

CHECK YOUR LEARNING

1. Explain two reasons why air quality in Ireland is generally good.
2. Identify the main types and sources of air pollutants found in urban areas.
3. Name three causes of smog in Los Angeles.
4. Explain how domestic water supplies in Ireland can become contaminated.

Urban Planning and Renewal

Cities and towns are constantly changing. Effective planning policies are essential to plan for the future and to ensure that urban areas are good places to live and work. Urban planning strategies have to contend with issues such as **traffic congestion, urban decay, lack of community** and **urban sprawl**. Planning strategies to deal with urban decay include urban redevelopment and urban renewal or regeneration.

Re-development: Redevelopment occurs when sites that are no longer used for activities such as industry or port-related activities are redeveloped for housing, commercial, cultural and recreational activities (e.g. **Dublin Docklands**).

Regeneration: Regeneration involves improving urban areas that have declined, have high levels of unemployment, poor housing conditions and high levels of crime and antisocial behaviour (e.g. **Moyross, Limerick**).

KEYWORDS
re-development
regeneration
antisocial behaviour
transition zones
derelict sites
drugs
unemployment

Urban decay

The models of urban growth show **zones of transition** where economic and social changes occur. These areas become run down and unattractive for residents, business and commercial activities.

Causes

City growth in the early 20th century was associated with a zone of industrial activity located near the CBD. A residential zone developed nearby, housing those who worked in the industries. The social structure that developed in these areas was one of **high-density housing** for low-paid, poorly educated manual labourers living in close-knit communities.

Changing economic conditions caused by local industries either closing or moving to suburban locations led to **deindustrialisation** and the **out-migration** of business and people from these areas. In many American cities, **ghettoes** have developed in these areas (e.g. **Cleveland, Ohio; Fig. 30.18**). In Dublin, the inner-city area of Sean Mac Dermott Street, near O'Connell Street, is an example of an area affected by such changes.

↑ **Fig. 30.18** Abandoned buildings in Cleveland, Ohio.

Chapter 29: Urban Land Use and Planning

Impacts

Visual

Visible signs of neglect – **derelict sites** and **abandoned** and **locked-up businesses** – make the areas unattractive for investment.

Socio-economic

Unemployment rates are high and **long-term unemployment** is a reality for people living in these areas. Low levels of educational achievement limit employment potential.

Poor social and economic conditions contribute to **drug dealing** and consumption, resulting in high rates of violence, crime and antisocial behaviour.

Residents begin to feel overpowered by the **antisocial behaviour** happening around them and often feel abandoned and neglected by local and national authorities.

Landscapes

CASE STUDY: URBAN REGENERATION, FATIMA MANSIONS, DUBLIN

KEYWORDS
employment
community-led
crèche
programme
arts

The public housing scheme known as Fatima Mansions in Dublin's south inner city was completed in 1947. Fifteen blocks, each of four floors, were built to house people from inner-city tenements. In the 1970s, many local factories closed as a result of recession and by the 1980s the area experienced high levels of unemployment and poverty. Fatima Mansions became synonymous with heroin use and drug addiction. Antisocial behaviour and high levels of crime meant that any resident who could afford to move from the area did so. This left behind a marginalised community that faced many years of official neglect (Fig. 30.19).

In 1995, **Fatima Groups United** was formed to campaign for improvements; this finally led to the provision of government and private funds for the regeneration of the area.

Fatima regeneration

The Fatima regeneration project was community-led with high levels of local involvement in all stages of the project.

The project began with the demolition of the blocks and the construction of over 600 social, affordable and private housing units.

↑ **Fig. 30.19** Fatima Mansions before the regeneration.

The F2 Community Centre gives a focus for community, providing a space for social, recreational, cultural and educational activities.

Community employment programmes are directed at the long-term unemployed and education and training workshops help residents to upskill.

The provision of crèche facilities not only enable mothers to return to work, but also provide valuable pre-school education for young children.

The children's day care centre provides a homework club that supports students at primary and secondary level.

A major element of the regeneration scheme was the focus on arts and culture. An arts studio and many cultural events have contributed greatly to this.

Commercial, retail and leisure facilities, including a gym and a football pitch, were also constructed.

Evaluation

The area has gone from being one where the community felt abandoned and powerless to one with a vibrant community spirit, with involvement at all levels, and a strong model of community leadership. Now known as **Herberton apartments**, this housing regeneration scheme has transformed the area physically, economically and socially, and is a model for future regeneration projects (Fig. 30.20).

↑ **Fig. 30.20** Herberton apartments.

CHECK YOUR LEARNING

1. Explain why inner-city areas experience decline and decay.
2. Name two impacts of decline on these areas.
3. Describe three problems that existed in Fatima Mansions.
4. Explain some of the changes regeneration has brought to the area.

Lack of community

One aspect of the growth and change within cities is the movement of people from the centre to the suburbs. This movement results in challenges for the communities in both areas. **Inner-city decline** leads to high levels of unemployment and antisocial behaviour, leading to fear and a sense of abandonment. These areas become run down and many older residents, who either cannot or do not want to move, are left behind. Long-established, tight-knit communities are broken up, leading to isolation, abandonment, fear and loneliness among those who remain. Within these areas, community activists play a very important role, challenging local authorities and government to tackle the problems (e.g. **Dublin's Sheriff Street area**).

People in newer suburban estates can also experience a lack of community. These estates lack a developed community spirit and supports. Sporting and recreational facilities, which only develop as a community becomes established, are often lacking. Planners have to take account of the need to include zoning for services and facilities that will nurture the development of a community spirit (e.g. **childcare facilities and recreational facilities**).

CHECK YOUR LEARNING

1. Identify two issues that lead to a lack of community in urban areas.

Cities in the Developing World

KEYWORDS		
megacity	slums	exhaust
migration	public transport	respiratory
natural increase	rubbish	emission standards
overcrowding	sewage	electric vehicles
traffic congestion	drainage	
bustees	car ownership	

A **megacity** is defined as a city with over 10 million inhabitants. By 2030, it is estimated that of the global total of 41 such cities, 31 will be located in the developing world (e.g. **Cairo, Egypt; Mumbai, India**). The rapid growth of developing world cities is due to migration and natural increase. This growth brings with it a variety of problems and while all cities have similar problems, developing world cities can experience different types and scales. Problems and issues include **overcrowding**, lack of services, **traffic congestion** and pollution.

---

30 Urban Growth Problems

EXAM LINK (HL)

Urban Planning
(30 marks)

Examine the effectiveness of urban planning strategies in solving two of the following urban problems, with reference to any urban area(s) that you have studied.

- Housing
- Transport
- Pollution

2018, Q10B

Marking Scheme:
Example of urban area = 2 marks
Examination of problem 1 = 7 SRPs × 2 marks
Examination of problem 2 = 7 SRPs × 2 marks

Bustee: In India, a slum or a shanty town.

DID YOU KNOW?
Of the 50 most polluted cities in the world, 25 are in China and 10 are in India.

CASE STUDY: KOLKATA, INDIA

The **Kolkata Metropolitan Area** has seen its population increase from 7.42 million in 1971 to over 14 million people in 2017. By the year 2025, it is estimated that the population will exceed 20 million. This rapid expansion has brought many problems.

Overcrowding

Slums and bustees

Slums and **bustees** are visible signs of the overcrowding that Kolkata is experiencing. Older slums in the city centre are more confined and have higher densities than those on the outskirts where they are spreading in an uncontrolled fashion. Slums are lacking in services, are not subject to planning or building regulation and have very narrow streets. The homes are poorly constructed, with very poor light and ventilation, and lack proper latrine facilities (**Fig. 30.21**). Kolkata also has a large community of homeless people who live on the streets.

Fig. 30.21 Slums with an open sewer in Delhi, India.

Public transport

Large volumes of commuters mean that trains, trams and buses are overcrowded and uncomfortable (**Fig. 30.22**).

Lack of services

Rubbish collection

The lack of a properly organised city-wide rubbish collection service contributes to piles of rotting, foul-smelling rubbish. This rubbish causes serious ecological and public health problems (**Fig. 30.23**).

Fig. 30.22 A crowded commuter train, Kolkata, India.

Sewage

The ageing sewer system in the older parts of Kolkata are unable to cope with the increased population. In the slum areas, open surface sewers run along narrow streets and contribute to illness. Floods associated with the monsoon wash raw sewage through slum dwellings spreading diarrhoea, malaria and jaundice.

Fig. 30.23 Lack of services leads to streets not being cleaned.

Drainage

The growth of the city means more concrete surfaces, resulting in more rapid run-off. Kolkata was surrounded by wetlands that absorbed rain water and prevented flooding. The loss of these wetlands has impacted on flooding.

Clean water

Groundwater levels have dropped as more wells are sunk to meet increasing demand for water. Groundwater supplies can be contaminated by leaking sewage pipes and by industrial pollutants. In slum areas, residents have to get their water from public stand posts.

Traffic congestion

As with all global cities, traffic congestion is a recurring problem for Kolkata (**Fig. 30.24**). Among the causes are:

- increasing affluence has resulted in increasing **car ownership**, which puts further pressure on already overcrowded streets;
- increasing **urban sprawl** to the west and north of the city has increased the **commuter belt**;
- a lack of compliance or enforcement of **parking regulations** on narrows streets has reduced the traffic flow;
- homeless street dwellers and hawkers reduce the width of major street junctions, forcing traffic to slow down as it negotiates these intersections;
- **rickshaws** and other vehicles move at slower speed, causing traffic flows to be reduced;
- lack of a modern **traffic signal** system that can be adjusted in real time.

↑ **Fig. 30.24** Traffic congestion, Kolkata.

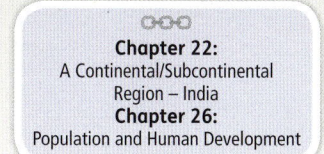

> **Chapter 22:**
> A Continental/Subcontinental Region – India
> **Chapter 26:**
> Population and Human Development

Pollution

After Delhi, Kolkata has the second-highest levels of air pollution in India. The main causes of this pollution are traffic exhaust fumes (50%), industrial activities (48%) and burning fuel for cooking (2%). The severe traffic congestion confounds the problem. In winter, smog forms when temperature inversions trap pollutants (**Fig. 30.25**). Estimates suggest that over 70% of the inhabitants of the city suffer from respiratory complaints. Proposals for tackling this problem include introducing and enforcing emission standards for cars and trucks, increasing use of solar energy and greater use of electric vehicles.

↑ **Fig. 30.25** Pollution causes smog in Kolkata.

EXAM LINK (OL)

Developing World City (40 marks)
  (i) Name one city in the developing world that is rapidly growing.
  (ii) Explain the reasons for the rapid growth of this developing world city.
  (iii) Describe the problems caused by this rapid growth.
  (iv) Explain one solution to these problems.

2017, Q12C

Marking Scheme:
  (i) Developing city named = 4 marks
  (ii) Explanation = 5 SRPs × 3 marks
  (iii) Description = 4 SRPs × 3 marks
  (iv) Explanation = 3 SRPs × 3 marks

Landscapes

> **EXAM LINK (HL)**
>
> **Urban Growth – Developing World City (30 marks)**
>
> **Problems can develop from the growth and expansion of urban centres.**
>
> **Discuss this statement with reference to one developing world city that you have studied.**
>
> 2016, Q11C
>
> **Marking Scheme:**
> Example of developing world city = 2 marks
> Problems identified = 2 + 2 marks
> Discussion = 12 SRPs × 2 marks

> **CHECK YOUR LEARNING**
> 1. Name any two global cities that are rapidly expanding.
> 2. Identify four problems that continued growth has caused in a named developing world city.
> 3. Examine any two of these problems in detail.

KEYWORDS
new cities
carbon footprint
sustainable
hubs
integrated travel
congestion charges
electric vehicles
cycling
smart buildings
street lighting
waste
water
open space
rising sea levels
expansion

The Future of Urbanism

In 2016, 23% of the global population lived in cities with at least one million inhabitants. Within the next 30 years, more than two billion people will move to urban areas. This will involve **existing cities expanding** but it will also result in the creation of **new urban centres**. In China, new cities under construction give an insight into how cities will develop and adapt in the future. Cities will have to continue to reduce their **carbon footprint**, become more sustainable and ensure a good quality of life for citizens. Issues facing cities of the future include **transport** and **environment**.

Transport

Future planning should involve the creation of local hubs where employment and services might be concentrated, reducing the need for people to commute over distance and reducing transport-related emissions. Addressing traffic congestion and achieving zero carbon emissions will dominate transport policy.

Integrated travel: Properly linked-up public transport systems that allow people to change from bus to tram to train using the same payment method lead to greater use (e.g. **Leap Card, Dublin**).

Congestion charging: Charging people for driving on busy roads at peak times will encourage them away from cars and on to public transport.

Electric vehicles: As electric cars are developed, increased charging points and possible hire schemes for small electric vehicles will see greater usage and result in cleaner air (e.g. **Los Angeles**; Fig. 30.26).

→ **Fig. 30.26** Electric vehicles charging.

Cycling and walking: There is increasing awareness of the need to plan for cities where cycling and walking are promoted. Benefits include reduced traffic congestion, better air quality and better health outcomes (Fig. 30.27). Dublin city has begun to put in place a good cycling infrastructure.

Environment

Urban planners will need to reduce the environmental impact of cities.

Buildings: Smart energy-efficient buildings with low carbon footprints will become more common. Homes will have high standards of insulation, solar panels and energy-efficient appliances, and will make greater use of smart technology.

Energy: A move away from fossil fuels will make renewable energy a feature of cities of the future. **Solar energy** and **wind turbines based on innovative designs** will be important elements in providing clean power to cities and helping them to become carbon neutral (Fig. 30.28).

Street lighting: LED and solar-powered lighting will reduce energy consumption.

Urban waste: High levels of recycling and recovery of useful components will reduce urban waste to almost zero.

Water: Treatment of waste water so that it can be reused will help with water conservation.

Food: Cities of the future will encourage inhabitants to produce their own food on allotments, in home gardens, in planters or on rooftops of apartment complexes (Fig. 30.29).

Open space and planting: Parks, open spaces and lakes will play an important role in supporting biodiversity, while design of apartment blocks will incorporate space for trees and plants (e.g. **Bosco Verticale, Milan**; Fig. 30.30).

For many of the world's coastal cities, rising sea levels due to global warming pose a major threat (e.g. **Sydney, London, Tokyo, Bangkok**). Flood defences and flood warning systems will need to be put in place at enormous cost and it is possible that large areas of coastal cities may have to be abandoned altogether.

↑ **Fig. 30.27** Cycle path, New York.

↑ **Fig. 30.28** Solar panels provide energy for electrical vehicle charging points in New York.

↑ **Fig. 30.29** A rooftop garden in Tokyo, Japan.

City carbon footprint: The total amount of carbon released into the atmosphere as a result of all the activities within a city.

Carbon neutral: The amount of carbon dioxide released into the atmosphere is reduced to zero because it is balanced by other actions, e.g. using renewable energy to offset emissions.

← **Fig. 30.30** Bosco Verticale (vertical forest) apartment block, Milan, Italy.

Landscapes

EXAM LINK (HL)

Future Urbanism (30 marks)

Discuss two issues facing cities of the future in the developed world.

2018, Q11C

Marking Scheme:
Two issues identified = 2 marks + 2 marks
Discussion of issue 1 = 7 SRPs × 2 marks
Discussion of issue 2 = 6 SRPs × 2 marks

CHECK YOUR LEARNING

1. Explain the terms: carbon footprint, carbon neutral.
2. Name two issues facing cities in the future.
3. Describe any one of these issues.
4. Explain how global warming may impact on world cities.

EXAMINATION QUESTIONS

ORDINARY LEVEL

Long Questions

1. Urban Problems

(i) Name a developing or a developed city that you have studied.
(ii) Explain two problems arising from the growth of the city named in part (i).
(iii) Describe two solutions to these problems.

2012, Part Two, Section 2, Q11C (40 marks)

Marking Scheme:
City named = 4 marks
Two problems explained = 3 SRPs × 3 marks each
Two solutions explained = 3 SRPs × 3 marks each

HIGHER LEVEL

Long Questions

2. Urban Issues

Discuss any two of the following issues that may arise from the growth of urban settlements.

Heritage issues   Planning issues   Environmental issues.

2017, Part Two, Section 2, Q10C (30 marks)

Marking Scheme:
Discussion of issue 1 = 8 SRPs × 2 marks
Discussion of issue 2 = 7 SRPs × 2 marks

3. Urban Problems

Discuss how the growth of urban centres can lead to any two of the following problems, with reference to example(s) that you have studied.

Traffic congestion   Urban decay   Urban sprawl

2015, Part Two, Section 2, Q10B (30 marks)

Marking Scheme:
Example of urban centre = 2 marks
Discussion of problem 1 = 7 SRPs × 2 marks
Discussion of problem 2 = 7 SRPs × 2 marks

536

Revision Summary

Traffic Congestion

Causes
- Urban sprawl – commuter belt pushed further from CBD
- Limited public transport networks – more cars
- Traffic volumes, rush hour, narrow streets

Impacts
- Socio-economic: longer journey times – costs – stress, less family time
- Environment: exhaust fumes – air pollution, respiratory disease

Solutions
- Efficient public transport system – bus lanes
- Congestion charges
- High-occupancy vehicle lanes – carpooling
- Cycle lanes, bike rental schemes

Case study: Dublin
- Urban sprawl – commuters live further from work
- Increased car ownership
- Poor public transport for suburbs, e.g. Swords
- Road network can't cope with peak times
- Few cross-city bus services – unattractive

Solutions
- Integrated ticketing – Leap Card
- Quality Bus Corridors – new cross-city and orbital bus routes
- Dublin Bike Scheme
- Greater Dublin Area Transport Strategy – new rail links – extension of LUAS

Urban Sprawl
- Poorly planned, low-density, car-dependent developments on outskirts, e.g. Brussels, LA

Case study: Dublin
- 1970s – economic growth, population doubles
- Land on outskirts re-zoned – low-density housing and industry
- Manufacturing units – move to greenfield sites, e.g. Jacobs
- Corrupt planning – loss of green belts
- Celtic Tiger – property prices rise – move outwards
- Lack of co-ordinated planning

Solutions
- High-density development with integrated public transport, e.g. Clongriffin, Adamstown
- NPF – 50:50 growth between regions
- Cork, Galway, Limerick, Waterford – attract FDI – regional economic engines
- Increase building height, urban renewal, infill sites

Heritage in Urban Areas
- Conflict – development and preservation

Protection
- Heritage Act 1995 – Heritage Council
- Planning and Development Act 2000 – Record of Protected Structures; preservation of conservation areas
- EU law – preservation of heritage
- Grant schemes for repair and upkeep

Heritage Issues Case Study: Dublin
- List of protected structures – strict development guidelines
- Planning and Development Act 2000 – owners must maintain listed properties
- Wood Quay – remains of Viking settlement covered over
- Georgian Dublin – demolition of houses on Fitzwilliam St
- Religious buildings converted
- Carrickmines Castle – remains lay in path of M50 – covered
- Moore Street preservation – govt opposition

Urban Environmental Quality

- Ireland – air, water, noise pollution – EU and national legislation
- EPA – monitors pollution levels

Air quality
- Ireland – SW winds, low-level heavy industry – 1990 smoky fuel ban; nationwide in 2019 – good-quality air
- Car emissions – main air pollutant, esp. diesel
- Particulate matter – particles of pollutants in the air
- EPA Air Quality Index – Ireland below permitted EU levels
- Impacts – respiratory disease, cancer, heart disease, acid rain

Case Study: Los Angeles
- Major problems with smog
- Causes: traffic and industrial pollution – surrounding mountains trap pollutants – sunny climate – ozone formation
- Impacts: health issues – costs from respiratory illness

Water quality
- Safe and reliable domestic supplies required
- Ireland's public water – surface water – rivers, lakes, streams
- Sewage treatment plants – clean water entering rivers
- Source contamination – bacteria, parasites from spills, leaks
- Drinking water contamination – E. coli, cryptosporidium – boil notices (Galway 2007)
- Future plans – UV light vs disinfectants, replace lead pipes
- Upgrade distribution network; plan for demand – water supplies from Shannon

Urban Planning and Renewal

- Issues: traffic congestion, urban decay, lack of community, urban sprawl
- Planning strategies: redevelopment, regeneration
- Urban decay: transition zones in urban growth – run-down, unattractive

Causes
- City growth – industrial activity near CBD – high-density housing for workers
- Deindustrialisation, out-migration – ghettoes, run-down inner-city areas

Impacts
- Derelict sites, abandoned businesses – unattractive for business
- High and long-term unemployment
- Drugs, violence, crime, antisocial behaviour
- Feeling of abandonment

Case study: Renewal, Fatima Mansions
- Built to house inner-city residents
- 1980s – high unemployment and poverty
- Fatima Mansions – synonymous with drug problems – antisocial behaviour, crime – marginalised community
- 1995 – Fatima Groups United – funds for regeneration

Fatima regeneration
- Community-led
- Demolition of blocks – social, affordable, private housing
- F2 Community Centre – social, recreational space
- Community employment and training workshops
- Crèche facilities, day-care centre – art and culture facilities – commercial, retail and leisure facilities
- Evaluation: abandoned to vibrant community – strong model of community leadership – physical, economic, social transformation

Lack of community
- City growth – movement to suburbs
- Inner-city decline – high unemployment, antisocial behaviour, fear
- New suburbs – lack community spirit, few community services

Developing World Cities

- Migration, natural increase – rapid growth
- Problems: overcrowding, lack of services, traffic congestion, pollution

Case Study: Kolkata, India
- Overcrowding: slums and bustees, homelessness
- High volume of commuters – public transport overcrowded
- Lack of services – no rubbish collection, old sewer system, contaminated water
- Traffic congestion: increasing car ownership – urban sprawl – increased commuter belt – slack parking regulations – homeless street dwellers – rickshaws and slow vehicles – no modern traffic light system
- Pollution: second-highest air pollution level in India – traffic, industry, cooking fuel – winter smog when temperature inversions trap pollutants – respiratory complaints
- Solutions: emission standards; solar energy, electric vehicles

Future of Urbanism

- Continued growth – expansion of cities, new urban centres
- Environmental, transport and social challenges

Transport
- Local hubs of employment, services – less commuting
- Integrated public transport systems; congestion charges; electric vehicles; promotion of cycling, walking

Environment
- Smart buildings – insulation, solar panels, energy-efficient appliances
- Clean, renewable energy – solar panels, wind turbines
- Street lighting – LED and solar-powered
- Recycling of waste
- Water treatment and conservation
- Sustainable food production – allotments, home gardens
- Focus on open spaces and biodiversity
- Flood defences due to rising sea levels

EXAMINATION GUIDE

Understanding the Question

Before you attempt to answer any question on the paper, you should clearly examine each of the following areas associated with the question:

Area	Example
Topic	Patterns and Processes in the Physical Environment, Regional Geography, Geographical Skills, Patterns and Processes in the Economic Environment or Patterns and Processes in the Human Environment
Section	This is the specific area of the topic being covered, e.g. for the Physical Geography topic, the section could be **plate tectonics**, **rocks**, **rivers**, etc. Sometimes two sections can be combined in one question, e.g. **plate tectonics** and **earthquake activity**.
Factor(s) being examined	This is the exact subject that the examiner wants to test your knowledge of, e.g. the **formation** of a specific rock type, the **processes** involved in the formation of a feature of erosion on the landscape.
Command word	This word tells you what the examiner wants you to do, e.g. **'calculate'**, **'describe'**, **'explain'**, **'list'**, etc.
Additional command word(s)	This informs you that you must take/interpret information from a diagram, a graph, a table, an OS map or an aerial photograph when answering the question, e.g. '**Using** the 1:50,000 Ordnance Survey map and legend …', '**Examine** the diagram …'
Mark allocation	How many marks are awarded for answering the question correctly – anywhere from **1 to 40** at Ordinary Level, or **1 to 30** at Higher Level.

Understanding command words

Understanding the command word is vital in order to achieve a high grade in the Leaving Certificate Geography exam. Command words are **guides** in the question that identify **how the question should be answered**. Once you understand the meaning of the command word, you can identify **what the examiner is looking for**, how they want the question answered and the detail they require.

> **EXAM TIP**
>
> Always highlight the command words at the start of the question when you first read it.

539

Landscapes

List of command words

Account for	→	Give reasons or an explanation for a particular action or event.
Analyse	→	Look closely at the detail; give reasons why or how something is done and the effect that this has.
Assess	→	Decide the importance of something by discussing its strengths and weaknesses.
Calculate	→	Work out the value.
Compare	→	Identify the similarities or differences between two or more things. Say whether any of the shared similarities or differences are more important than others, where possible.
Contrast	→	Stress the differences between associated things, qualities, events or problems. Don't describe all the features of one thing and then all the features of the other – show the differences in one specific feature for both sides together, then move onto the next feature.
Describe	→	Provide a detailed explanation of what or how or why something happens; be precise and avoid vague words or phrases.
Discuss	→	You are expected to build up an argument on a given topic. Using specific examples, give the main reasons both 'for' and 'against', and then come to a conclusion.
Evaluate	→	Present a careful appraisal of the subject, stressing both advantages and limitations.
Examine	→	Look closely at something and discuss its effects in a balanced way in order to come to a conclusion.
Explain	→	Give reasons for how or why something happens, using specific examples.
Identify	→	Pick out what you think is the main reason for something happening.
Illustrate	→	Present information as a figure, diagram or detailed example.
List	→	Write a list, in either single words or phrases. Sometimes the order will be important, but this will be stated in the question.
Name	→	Simply name something, but be very specific – try to avoid vague or general terms where possible.
Outline	→	Give the main points with a brief explanation. Omit minor details and present the information in an organised manner.
Sketch	→	Draw using a pencil.
State	→	Express in clear terms.

Answering the Question

Significant Relevant Points (SRPs)

> **EXAM TIP**
>
> Examiners award 2 marks for each SRP in the Higher Level exam.
>
> Examiners award 3 marks for each SRP in the Ordinary Level exam.

You must be able to organise your answers into **Significant Relevant Points (SRPs)**, as this is the method used to mark the exam. An SRP is a piece of **factual information** that is **relevant to the question** being asked. Well-structured points that include a geographical term with a brief explanation or a relevant example, statistic or fact to the question being asked will be awarded marks for an SRP.

Writing style

When the current Geography syllabus was first introduced, answers for 30-mark Higher Level questions and 30–40-mark Ordinary Level questions were graded on **content** and **structure** (coherence). Essay-style answers with well-structured paragraphs were required for these questions.

While this format continues for the Options section, answers for structured questions in the Physical, Regional and Elective sections can now be broken down into **shorter paragraphs**. Using headings and/or bullet points, key areas of the question can be dealt with separately. It important to note, however, that giving information in bullet points may result in some of the bullets being amalgamated into one SRP if the information in a bullet is not judged to be significant enough on its own.

Diagrams

All diagrams must be relevant to the question being asked and labelled to receive marks. They should:

- be drawn in using a **hard pencil** (HB) as they as they produce clean, sharp lines which are neater in presentation and easier to alter;
- have a **frame**, drawn with the help of a ruler;
- contain a **title**, e.g. 'Sea-floor spreading'.

Fully labelled diagrams with a frame and a title will receive 1 SRP. If the diagram contains additional information not mentioned in the text then it may be awarded an extra SRP. A maximum of 2 SRPs are allocated to labelled diagrams.

Practical Exam Tips

- Do the short questions first. Don't leave blank spaces, and attempt to answer all parts.
- Start with your strongest section, e.g. Physical Geography, as this allows you to continue your good momentum and stay in a positive frame of mind.
- Make sure to answer the question you are asked, not the question you would like to be asked! You can do this by reading the entire question carefully, at least three times, before you start to answer it.
- Start each part of a long question (A, B and C) at the top of a new page in your answer book.
- Number the question you are answering in the left-hand margin of your answer book, e.g. Q3A.
- Don't write in the examiner's section on the right-hand side of the page – this won't be marked!
- All diagrams and sketches need to be fully labelled, be titled and have a frame around them.
- All graphs must be drawn on graph paper.
- If the answer is a figure, always give the unit (e.g. metres) or symbol (e.g. € or %) after the number.
- Grid references must have the sub-zone letter (e.g. L 980 860 or N 797 156).
- Time yourself throughout the exam. Make sure you leave a little bit of time – about five minutes – to go back over your answers and make minor corrections if necessary.

The night before the exam, make sure you have all the materials you'll need:
- A black or blue pen, and a red pen;
- A pencil, a pencil sharpener and an eraser;
- A set of colouring pencils;
- A ruler, a compass and a protractor.

541

Landscapes

Sitting the Ordinary Level Exam

Exam structure

Good time management is vital to achieving a good grade. Before going in to the exam, you should know exactly what questions you need to answer and the recommended time allowed for each one.

Reading through the exam and choosing questions				5 minutes
Part One: Short Questions		**Marks**	**% of exam**	**Time**
Answer 10 of 12 questions		100	20%	40 minutes
Part Two: Long Questions		**Marks**	**% of exam**	**Time**
Section 1: Physical Geography and Regional Geography				
1, 2 or 3	Core Unit 1: Patterns and Processes in the Physical Environment	100	20%	40 minutes
4, 5 or 6	Core Unit 2: Regional Geography	100	20%	40 minutes
Section 2: Electives				
7, 8 or 9 OR 10, 11 or 12	Elective Unit 4: Patterns and Processes in the Economic Environment Elective Unit 5: Patterns and Processes in the Human Environment	100	20%	40 minutes
Reading back over your exam script				5 minutes
Total for the written exam		400	80%	170 minutes
Fieldwork question (submitted prior to the exam)		100	20%	
Overall total		500 marks	100%	

Part One: Short-answer questions (100 marks, 40 minutes)

- There are 12 questions in this section.
- Each question is worth 10 marks.
- At least 10 questions must be attempted. Attempt all 12 questions if the time allows, as your 10 best answers will be counted.
- You can expect the following in this section:
  - 3 or 4 Physical Geography questions;
  - 1 Regional Geography question;
  - 7 or 8 Geographical Skills questions (Ordnance Survey, aerial photograph, weather map, satellite image, graphical and chart interpretation).

EXAM TIP

Read all three parts of every multi-part question before you choose which one to answer.

Part Two: Structured/multi-part questions

Section 1: Core Unit 1 – Patterns and Processes in the Physical Environment (100 marks, 40 minutes)

This section includes long questions 1, 2 and 3. You must choose **one question** and answer **all parts** of that question.

Each question has three parts: A, B and C. Two of these parts are worth 30 marks and should take 12 minutes. The third part is worth 40 marks and should take 16 minutes.

Example: 2018, Part Two, Q2C – Human Interaction with the Rock Cycle (30 marks)

> Discuss how humans interact with the rock cycle with reference to one of the following.
>
> Quarrying   Mining   Oil/Gas exploitation   Geothermal energy production

Understanding the question

- The command word is '**Discuss**': the examiner wants you to build up an argument on a given topic.
- Using specific examples, give the main reasons both '**for**' and '**against**', and then come to a conclusion.
- The **factor** being examined in this question is **human interaction with the rock cycle**.
- **30 marks** are allocated to this question, which means **10 SRPs** are required (worth 3 marks each).

Sample answer

Quarrying is the removal of igneous, sedimentary or metamorphic rocks from open cast mines. ✓ Most of the rock quarried in Ireland today is used in the construction of buildings and transport infrastructure. ✓ Quarry operators use several methods to remove rock depending on the type involved and whether it's going to be used as a dimension stone (sills, curbing, flagstone, etc.) or as an aggregate. ✓

Aggregates such as sand, gravel and stone are taken from quarries located close to highly populated areas due to the high cost of transporting the low value product. ✓ Large blocks of rock are blasted using explosives and the rockpile is then broken into smaller pieces in a crushing machine and before it's washed. ✓ Finally the stone is screened into different sizes, shapes and types to be used in ready-mixed concrete, concrete blocks, bricks, etc. ✓

<u>Positive Impacts of Quarrying:</u>

- Direct employment is created in the operation and maintenance of quarries. Indirect employment opportunities are also created for hauliers, mechanics etc. ✓
- It provides a secure supply of raw materials, free of price fluctuations for local industries such as cement, concrete and glass. ✓

<u>Negative Impacts of Quarrying:</u>

- Quarries can have a negative effect on people's quality of life however as they generate a lot of noise, dust and heavy goods traffic. ✓
- Quarries and their rusting machinery can also take from the beauty of the rural landscape. ✓

KEY
✓ = 1 SRP

10 SRPs ✓ × 3 marks = 30 marks

Landscapes

Example: 2018, Part Two, Q1C – Volcanoes (40 marks)

(i) State what is meant by each of the following types of volcanoes:
   a. Active volcano
   b. Extinct volcano
   c. Dormant volcano

Understanding the question

- The command word is '**State**': the examiner wants you to express something in clear terms.
- 10 marks are allocated for this part of the question – 3 statements at 4 marks + 3 marks + 3 marks.

Sample answer

3 statements ✓ = 10 marks

Active volcanoes are those which erupt regularly, e.g. Mount Etna in Sicily is one of the world's most active volcanoes. ✓ **(4 marks)**

Extinct volcanoes have not erupted in historic times (over 2,000 years), and are not expected to erupt again as they no longer have a magma supply e.g. Lambay Island located off Ireland's east coast was formed by a now extinct volcano. ✓ **(3 marks)**

Dormant (sleeping) volcanoes have not erupted in a long time but scientists believe they could erupt again, e.g. Parcutin, Mexico. ✓ **(3 marks)**

(ii) Describe the negative effects of volcanoes.

Understanding the question

- The command word is '**Describe**': the examiner wants you to provide a detailed explanation of what, how, or why something happens.
- The factor being examined is the **negative effects of volcanoes**.
- 15 marks are allowed for this question, which means 5 SRPs are required at 3 marks each.

Sample answer

5 SRPs ✓ × 3 marks = 15 marks

1. When snow-capped volcanic mountains erupt, lahars (volcanic landslides) are formed from the ash, mud and melting snow. ✓ In 1985, the Nevado del Ruiz erupted in Colombia and the resulting lahar killed over 20,000 people in the town of Armero. ✓

2. Thick clouds of ash emitted from a volcano can block the sun's rays, causing global cooling. ✓

3. On the other hand, global warming can result if the erupting volcano fills the atmosphere with greenhouse gases. ✓

4. When Mount St Helens erupted in 1980, the eruption triggered a landslide, which destroyed 600 square kilometres of trees and killed over 7,000 wild animals, including deer, elk and bears. ✓

(iii) Describe the positive effects of volcanoes.

Understanding the question

- The command word is '**Describe**': the examiner wants you to provide a detailed explanation of what, how, or why something happens.
- The factor being examined is the **positive effects of volcanoes**.
- 15 marks are allowed for this question, which means 5 SRPs are required at 3 marks each.

Sample answer

1. Lava and ash deposited during an eruption breaks down to provide valuable nutrients creating rich fertile soils. ✓ Rich volcanic soils are common in Brazil, the world's leading coffee producer, and in Italy where they are used to produce fruit and vegetables. ✓

2. The dramatic scenery created by volcanic eruptions attract large numbers of people, creating jobs in the tourist industry. ✓ Mount Vesuvius, which erupted and covered the town of Pompeii in 79 AD, is a popular tourist attraction while the volcanic islands of Hawaii are another tourist hot spot. ✓

3. Despite the cool temperatures and short growing season, Iceland is self-sufficient in food production, with crops such as tomatoes, cucumbers and green peppers grown in geothermal greenhouses. ✓

> 5 SRPs ✓ × 3 marks = 15 marks

Section 1: Core Unit 2 – Regional Geography (100 marks, 40 minutes)

This section includes long questions 4, 5 and 6. You must choose **one question** and answer **all parts** of that question.

Each question has three parts: A, B and C. Two of these parts are worth 30 marks and should take 12 minutes. The third part is worth 40 marks and should take 16 minutes.

Example: 2018, Part Two, Q5A – Irish Trade (30 marks)

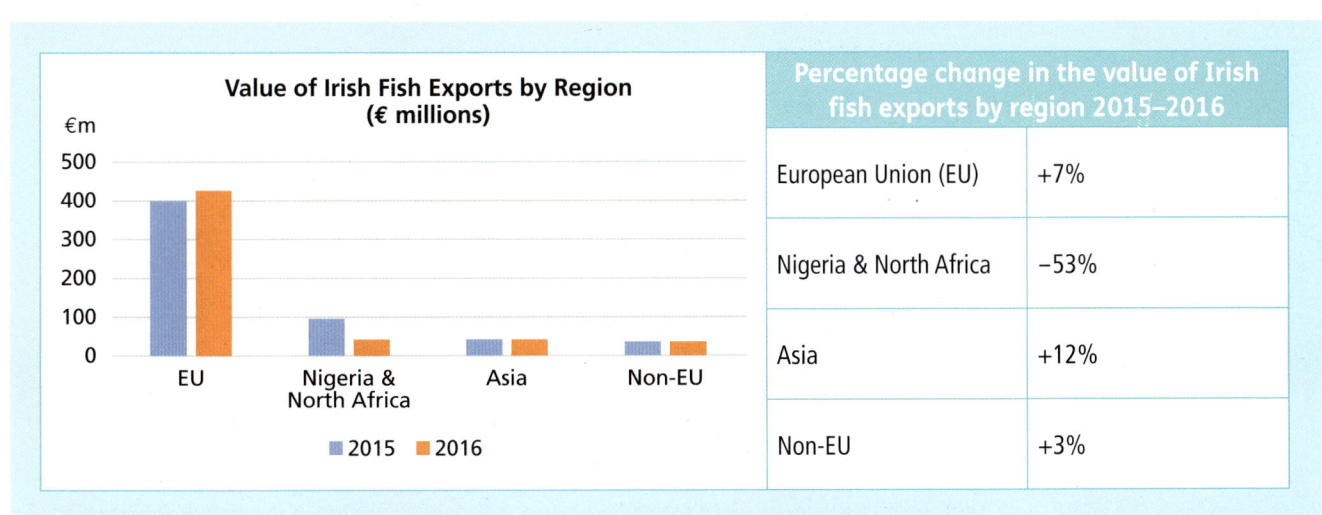

Value of Irish Fish Exports by Region (€ millions)

(Bar chart showing 2015 and 2016 values: EU ~400/~425; Nigeria & North Africa ~90/~40; Asia ~40/~40; Non-EU ~30/~30)

Percentage change in the value of Irish fish exports by region 2015–2016	
European Union (EU)	+7%
Nigeria & North Africa	−53%
Asia	+12%
Non-EU	+3%

Examine the chart and table above and answer each of the following questions.

(i) The greatest value of Irish fish was exported to which region in 2016?

Landscapes

[Region named ✓ × 3 marks = 3 marks]

Sample answer

In 2016, the greatest value of Irish fish was exported to the EU (€420 million approx.). ✓

(ii) Explain briefly one reason why the greatest value of Irish fish was exported to this region.

Understanding the question

- The command word is '**Explain**': the examiner wants you to give a reason for why something happens, using one or more examples.
- As this question needs to be developed, it requires a minimum of 2 SRPs worth 3 marks each.

Sample answer

As a member of the European Union (EU), any goods produced in Ireland have tariff-free access to the huge EU market of over 500 million. ✓ Therefore, fish caught by Irish-owned vessels on the EU market generally costs less than fish caught by vessels outside of the EU, making it more attractive to the customer. ✓

[2 SRPs ✓ × 3 marks = 6 marks]

(iii) The value of Irish fish exports to which region underwent the greatest percentage increase between 2015 and 2016?

Sample answer

Asia had the greatest percentage change, increasing by 12% in value. ✓

[Region named ✓ × 3 marks = 3 marks]

(iv) Calculate the difference (in millions of euro) between the value of fish exports to the European Union and the value of fish exports to Nigeria & North Africa in 2015.

Understanding the question

- The command word is '**Calculate**': the examiner wants you to work out a value.

Sample answer

The difference between the value of fish exports to the European Union (€400 million) and the value of fish exports to Nigeria & North Africa (€100 million) in 2015 is €300 million. ✓ ✓

[Correct answer + working shown = 6 marks]

546

(v) Explain briefly one advantage of exports to the Irish economy.

Understanding the question

- The command word is '**Explain**': the examiner wants you to give reasons for how or why something happens, with examples.
- As this question needs to be developed, it requires a minimum of 2 SRPs worth 3 marks each.

Sample answer

Export-orientated businesses and industries employ a huge percentage of the Irish workforce generating massive tax returns on an annual basis. ✓ *These tax returns enable the Irish government to make large investments in infrastructure and education which in turn attracts more business and industry to the country.* ✓

> When asked to make a calculation from a graph or table, always include the workings that show how you calculated the final figure. You may not receive full marks if you don't show your working.

2 SRPs ✓ × 3 marks = 6 marks

(vi) State two advantages that Ireland has for fishing.

Understanding the question

- The command word is '**State**': the examiner wants you to express something in clear terms.
- The factors being examined are the **advantages that Ireland has for fishing**.
- This question requires 2 SRPs worth 3 marks each.

Sample answer

Two advantages Ireland has for fishing are:
- *The North Atlantic Drift: The warm waters of the North Atlantic Drift provide ideal conditions for the growth of plankton, which is the main source of food for fish.* ✓
- *Ireland's 3,000 km-long coastline has many inlets that provide sheltered, safe conditions for fishing ports such as Castletownbere, Rossaveal and Killybegs to develop and grow.* ✓

2 SRPs ✓ × 3 marks = 6 marks

Example: 2016, Part Two, Q4B – Agriculture in Ireland (40 marks)

(i) Name two types of farming in Ireland.

Understanding the question

- 4 marks are allocated for this question – two types of farming named worth 2 marks each.

Sample answer

Two types of farming carried on in Ireland are arable farming, e.g. the growing of wheat, ✓ *and pastoral farming, e.g. the rearing of beef cattle.* ✓

2 types of farming named ✓ × 2 marks = 4 marks

Landscapes

(ii) Explain how any two of the following factors influence the development of agriculture in an Irish region that you have studied.

Relief and soils   Markets   Climate

Understanding the question

- The command word is '**Explain**': the examiner wants you to give reasons for how something happens, using examples.
- 36 marks are allocated for this question:
  - explanation of factor 1 = 6 SRPs at 3 marks each = 18 marks;
  - explanation of factor 2 = 6 SRPs at 3 marks each = 18 marks;
  - **One SRP is available only if you name the region** (in the examiners' marking scheme, this is written as '**Allow** 1 SRP for ...').

Sample answer

Climate:

6 SRPs ✓ × 3 marks = 18 marks

The cool temperate oceanic climate experienced by the Western Region limits agricultural production. ✓ High annual levels of rainfall prevent the growing of cereal crops, as the soil is too wet for early ploughing to allow seed planting to be carried out. ✓ Damp soils can also cause seeds to rot before germination occurs. ✓

The cool temperate oceanic climate is suited to grass growing with pastoral farming — dairy, beef cattle, sheep — the most common activity. ✓ Poor weather conditions during winter and early spring, however, make it necessary to keep cattle indoors for long periods. ✓ This raises fodder costs, making it unprofitable to keep cattle for longer than two years. Instead, they're sold to farmers in eastern and southern counties to be fattened for sale. ✓

Relief & Soils:

6 SRPs ✓ × 3 marks = 18 marks

Much of the relief of the region consists of uplands with steep slopes where rough grazing of sheep is the main farming activity – Connemara Mountains. ✓ The lowlands of Galway and Roscommon are more suited to the use of machinery so arable farming of barley, wheat and oats occurs there. ✓ These lowlands are susceptible to summer flooding from the River Shannon, however, which can negatively impact on the production of winter fodder such as hay and silage. ✓

High precipitation levels have led to the leaching of nutrients from soils forming thin, infertile podzol soils. ✓ Poor quality gley and peat soils are suited to rough grazing by sheep. ✓ In the east of the region the well-drained loam soils are well suited to dairy farming. ✓

Section 2: Electives (100 marks, 40 minutes)

In this section, you have to choose **one question** from **either** of the electives, and answer all parts of that question. The two electives are:

- Patterns and Processes in the **Economic** Environment – long questions 7, 8 and 9;

  OR

- Patterns and Processes in the **Human** Environment – long questions 10, 11 and 12.

Each question has three parts: A, B and C:

- Two of these parts are worth 30 marks and should take 12 minutes;
- The third part is worth 40 marks and should take 16 minutes.

In the Economic elective, one can expect questions on the following subjects to appear:
- sketch maps of OS maps or aerial photographs;
- tables, which may be used to answer questions or construct a graph;
- economic development;
- European Union policies;
- multinational companies;
- conflict between economic activity and environmental concerns;
- renewable energies.

In the Human elective, one can expect questions on the following subjects to appear:
- sketch maps of OS maps or aerial photographs;
- tables which may be used to answer questions or construct a graph;
- migration;
- urbanisation – planning, land use, trends, issues, etc.
- Dynamics of Population – characteristics, overpopulation, etc.

Examples of these questions can be found on **gillexplore.ie**.

Sitting the Higher Level Exam
Exam structure

Good time management is vital to achieving a good grade. Before going in to the exam, you should know exactly what questions you need to answer and the recommended time allowed for each one.

Reading through the exam and choosing questions				5 minutes
Part One: Short Questions		Marks	% of exam	Time
Answer 10 of 12 questions		80 marks	16%	32 minutes
Part Two: Long Questions		Marks	% of exam	Time
Section 1: Core				
1, 2 or 3	Core Unit 1: Patterns and Processes in the Physical Environment	80 marks	16%	32 minutes
4, 5 or 6	Core Unit 2: Regional Geography	80 marks	16%	32 minutes
Section 2: Electives				
7, 8 or 9 OR 10, 11 or 12	Elective Unit 4: Patterns and Processes in the Economic Environment OR Elective Unit 5: Patterns and Processes in the Human Environment	80 marks	16%	32 minutes
Section 3: Options				
13, 14 or 15 OR 16, 17 or 18 OR 19, 20 or 21 OR 22, 23 or 24	Geoecology Global Interdependence Culture and Identity The Atmosphere-Ocean Environment	80 marks	16%	32 minutes
Reading back over your exam script				5 minutes
Total for the written exam		400	80%	170 minutes
Fieldwork question (submitted prior to the exam)		100	20%	
Overall total		500 marks	100%	

Landscapes

Part One: Short-answer questions (80 marks, 32 minutes)

- There are 12 questions in this section.
- Each question is worth 8 marks.
- At least 10 questions must be attempted. Attempt all 12 questions if the time allows as your 10 best answers will be counted.
- You can expect the following in this section:
    - 3 or 4 Physical Geography questions;
    - 1 Regional Geography question;
    - 7 or 8 Geographical Skills questions (Ordnance Survey, aerial photograph, weather map, satellite image, graphical and chart interpretation).

Part Two: Structured/multi-part questions

Section 1: Core Unit 1 – Patterns and Processes in the Physical Environment (80 marks, 32 minutes)

> **EXAM TIP**
>
> Read all three parts of every multi-part question before you choose which one to answer.

This section includes long questions 1, 2 and 3. You have to choose **one question** and answer **all parts** of that question. Each question is made up of three parts.

Part A is a skill-based question worth 20 marks. You may be asked to draw an OS sketch map, identify a landform or interpret a diagram, aerial photograph, satellite image or OS map. Part A answers should take approximately 6 minutes.

Example: 2014, Part One, Q2A – The Internal Structure of the Earth (20 marks)

Examine the diagram showing the internal structure of the earth and answer the following questions.

Name each of the layers of the earth A, B, C, D, E and F.

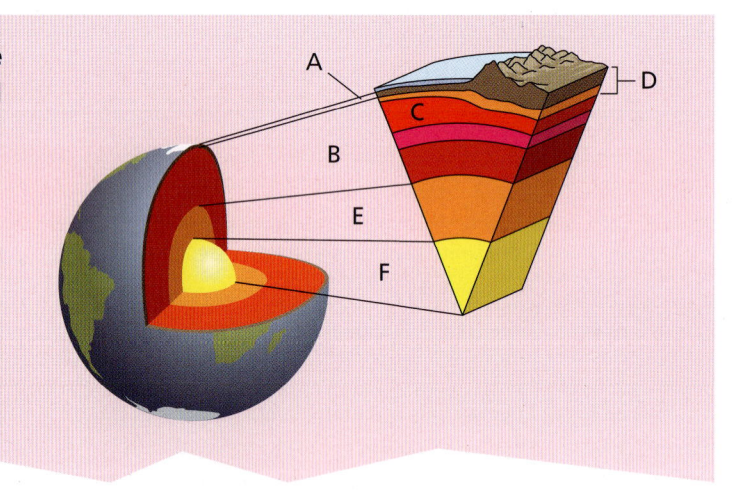

Understanding the question

- The command word is '**Name**': the examiner wants you to simply name something, but be very specific. Try to avoid general or vague terms.
- There are 6 elements to be named and each will receive equal weighting of marks. Typically, when the command word is 'list' or 'name' in this section, you will receive 2 marks for each element – so 6 layers named at 2 marks each for a total of 12 marks.

550

Examination Guide

Sample answer

A = Crust ✓

B = Mantle ✓

C = Asthenosphere ✓

D = Lithosphere ✓

E = Outer core ✓

F = Inner core ✓

6 names ✓ × 2 marks = 12 marks

> **(i)** Describe briefly the main difference between the composition of layer C and layer D.

Understanding the question

- The command word is '**Describe**': the examiner wants you to provide a detailed explanation of what, how or why something happens.
- As this question needs to be developed, it requires a minimum of 2 SRPs worth 2 marks each.

Sample answer

Layer C is a part of the upper mantle composed of semi-molten rock called the asthenosphere. ✓ Layer D is the lithosphere, which consists of solid rock found in the upper mantle and outer crust. ✓

2 SRPs ✓ × 2 marks = 4 marks

> **(ii)** Explain briefly why plates move.

Understanding the question

- The command word is '**Explain**': the examiner wants you to give reasons for how or why something happens.
- As this question needs to be developed, it requires a minimum of 2 SRPs worth 2 marks each.

Sample answer

Tectonic plates float on heavier, semi-molten rock (magma) beneath them in the mantle ✓ They are moved along by convection currents in the molten rock, causing them to collide with, separate from and slide past each other. ✓

2 SRPs ✓ × 2 marks = 4 marks

Parts B and C are 30-mark questions that require short essay-style answers. Each answer requires 15 SRPs, with 2 marks awarded for each SRP. Marks will also be awarded for relevant named examples (2 marks each) and labelled diagrams (maximum of 4 marks). Parts B and C answers should take approximately 13 minutes.

Landscapes

Example: 2014, Part Two, Q2B – Landform Development (30 marks)

Explain the formation of one landform of erosion and one landform of deposition that you have studied.

Understanding the question

- The command word is '**Explain**': the examiner wants you to give reasons for how or why something happens.

- The factor being examined is the **formation** of one landform of **erosion** and one of **deposition**. You will only receive marks for one landform of each process, so don't waste time explaining multiple features of erosion or deposition.

- Once you have named the landform (1 SRP) and given a relevant example (1 SRP), the remaining marks will only be awarded for an explanation of how the landform is formed. Make sure to name and explain the physical processes involved, for example if explaining waterfalls, explain hydraulic action, differential erosion and undercutting and collapse.

- Fully labelled diagrams with a frame and a title will receive 1 SRP. If the diagram contains additional information not mentioned in the text, then it may be awarded an extra SRP. A maximum of 2 SRPs are allocated to labelled diagrams.

- 30 marks are allocated to this question, which means 15 SRPs are required. This will be divided as an 8 SRP/7 SRP split, with one landform requiring 8 SRPs and the other landform requiring 7 SRPs.

Sample answer

V-Shaped Valleys:

V-shaped valleys are formed in the youthful/upper stage of a river. ✓ As the river flows down the steep gradient from the source, it vertically erodes the riverbed using its small volume of water. ✓ The river erodes using the processes of hydraulic action (the force of the moving water) and abrasion (the load carried by the river is used as a tool of erosion). ✓ Due to the upland nature of the area, there is also increased rainfall, while temperatures are more likely to fluctuate above and below freezing point. ✓ As a result, the material on the landscape is weakened and broken down by freeze-thaw action. ✓

Over time, this angular material called scree will break away and move downslope under the influence of gravity (mass movement), gathering in the river channel as a bedload. ✓ The river then uses this load to further erode the river bed by abrasion, deepening the river channel, creating a V-shaped valley. ✓ A V-shaped valley can be found on the youthful stage of the River Slaney. ✓

[8 SRPs ✓ × 2 marks = 16 marks]

Levees:

Levees are formed in the old age/lower stage of a river. ✓ The gentle gradient of the river valley causes the river to slow down and deposit some of its load on the riverbed. The raised riverbed results in the river overflowing its banks following periods of heavy rainfall. As the floodwaters move away from the river channel, it loses its ability to carry its load and deposition occurs. ✓ After heavy rain, the volume of water in the river may get too high to remain within its channel, causing the river to overflow its banks and flood the surrounding land. ✓ As the floodwaters spread out across the floodplain away from the river channel, it loses its ability to carry its load and deposition occurs. ✓ The coarser, heavier material is deposited first on the banks of the river, as the river doesn't have the

[7 SRPs ✓ × 2 marks = 14 marks]

energy to carry it any further, while the lighter sandy alluvium is deposited on the flat land of the floodplain. ✓ Repeated flooding will cause the banks of the river to be raised over the floodplain, forming levees, which act as natural barriers against further flooding. ✓ Levees can be found on the River Blackwater near Fermoy. ✓

Section 1: Core Unit 2 – Regional Geography (80 marks, 32 minutes)

This section includes long questions 4, 5 and 6. You must choose **one question** and answer **all parts** of that question. Each question is made up of three parts:

Part A is a skill-based question worth 20 marks. You may be asked to:

- draw an outline map or graph – it is vital you practise drawing sketch maps of Irish, European and Continental regions, as this question will almost definitely come up;
- interpret information from a graph or passage of text;
- answer a few short questions on Regional Geography.

Part A answers should take approximately 6 minutes.

Example: 2015, Part Two, Q4A – Map Skills (20 marks)

> **Draw an outline map of a European region (not in Ireland) that you have studied.**
> **On it, show and name each of the following:**
> - **A named feature of relief**
> - **A named urban centre**
> - **A named road or rail link**
> - **A named river.**

Understanding the question

- The command word is '**Draw**': the examiner wants you to sketch something using a pencil.
- A map of the European region (the Mezzogiorno or Paris Basin) within the area of its country should be drawn as accurately as possible.
  - Mark in each of the features asked for in the question using a symbol.
  - Name each of the features in a key, linking the name to the symbol used in the diagram.
  - Draw a frame around both the map and the key.
- The map outline is worth a maximum of 4 marks. It must include a full map of the country with the European region clearly identified within this boundary. Marks are awarded as follows:
  - Very accurate = 4 marks
  - Partially accurate = 2 marks
  - Inaccurate = 0 marks
- The features you put on the map are worth a total of 16 marks, which breaks down as 4 features at 4 marks each. Naming the feature will get you 2 of those marks, while showing it on the map will get you the other 2 (or 1, if partially accurate).

Sample answer

Sketch map of the South of Italy

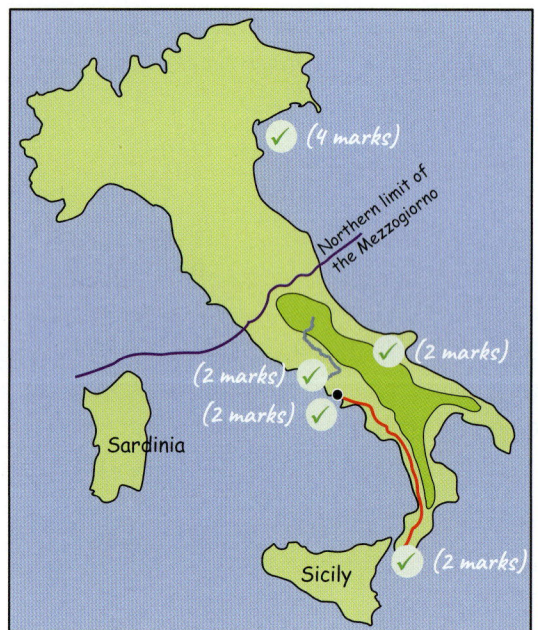

(4 marks) — Northern limit of the Mezzogiorno

(2 marks)
(2 marks)
(2 marks)
Sardinia
Sicily (2 marks)

Key for Sketch map of the South of Italy
- Naples ✓ (2 marks)
- Apennine Mountains ✓ (2 marks)
- A3 motorway ✓ (2 marks)
- Volturno River ✓ (2 marks)

Parts B and C are 30-mark questions that require short essay-style answers. Each answer requires 15 SRPs worth 2 marks each. Marks will also be awarded for relevant named examples (2 marks each). Part B and C answers should take approximately 13 minutes.

Example: 2015, Part Two, Q4B – Industrial Decline (30 marks)

Examine the causes and impacts of industrial decline with reference to any region(s) that you have studied.

Understanding the question

- The command word is '**Examine**': the examiner wants you to look closely at something and discuss its effects in a balanced way in order to come to a conclusion.
- The factors being examined are the **causes and impacts of industrial decline**.
- 30 marks are allocated to this questions, which means 15 SRPs worth 2 marks each are required:
    - Identifying the cause = 2 marks;
    - Identifying the impact = 2 marks;
    - Examination of the causes and impacts = 13 SRPs × 2 marks;
    - 1 SRP will be awarded if a second cause is listed. All other causes need to be explained in detail to receive marks;
    - 1 SRP will be awarded if a second impact is listed. All other causes need to be explained in detail to receive marks;
    - You will be awarded 1 SRP for an example of an industry in decline.
- Be careful here – this answer require discussion of **both** causes **and** effects. Answers with causes only would receive a maximum of 16 marks out of a possible 30. There doesn't have to be a 50/50 split of causes and impacts, but you do need to look at both.

Sample answer

The Sambre-Meuse Valley region in Belgium began to decline in the late 1950s. ✓

<u>Causes of Industrial Decline</u>

One of the main reasons for this was the decline in coal mining. ✓ Many coal mines had become exhausted while in others mining costs increased as pits went deeper. ✓ Cheaper coal imports from Poland and the USA ✓ and competition from oil and gas led to reduced demand for coal from the Sambre-Meuse Valley. ✓

Iron and steel production ✓ also suffered major decline. The increased use of imported coal and iron ore led to the building of modern coastal plants, which had lower costs and higher productivity. ✓ Competition from these plants and competition from lower cost producers, e.g. India, led to falling demand for steel produced in inland plants, which began to close. ✓ A global recession in the 1980s also led to falling demand for steel. ✓

<u>Impacts of Industrial Decline</u>

The decline of these industries had a major economic impact with unemployment increasing. ✓ By the mid-1980s, when the last coal mines closed, an industry that once provided employment for over 100,000 people had disappeared. ✓

The de-industrialisation of the region coincided with the growth of industries such as electronics and petro-chemicals in Flanders in western Belgium. ✓ High unemployment rates in the Sambre-Meuse Valley meant people now migrated to growth areas in Flanders, e.g. Antwerp. ✓

One of the social impacts of the decline was that Wallonia lost its dominant economic position and a region that once attracted migrants was now experiencing out-migration. ✓ This movement of French speakers to the non-French speaking area of Flanders caused tension and problems between Flemish and French speakers. ✓

Coal waste heaps and abandoned industrial plants littered the Sambre-Meuse Valley after it went into industrial decline, resulting in an unattractive, depressed local environment. ✓

> 15 SRPs ✓ × 2 marks = 30 marks

Section 2: Electives (80 marks, 32 minutes)

In this section, you have to choose **one question** from either of the electives, and answer **all parts** of that question. The two electives are:

- Elective Unit 4: Patterns and Processes in the **Economic** Environment – long questions 7, 8 and 9;
- Elective Unit 5: Patterns and Processes in the **Human** Environment – long questions 10, 11 and 12.

Each question is made up of three parts:

Part A is a skill-based question worth 20 marks. You may be asked to:

- draw a sketch map using the OS map or aerial photograph on the exam paper – usually this is a sketch map of the aerial photograph, but not always;
- draw a graph;
- interpret information from a graph, chart or passage of text.

Part A answers should take approximately 6 minutes.

Parts B and C are 30-mark questions that require short essay-style answers. Each answer requires 15 SRPs worth 2 marks each. Marks will also be awarded for relevant named examples (2 marks each). Part B and C answers should take approximately 13 minutes.

In the Economic elective, one can expect questions on the following subjects to appear:
- economic development;
- European Union policies;
- multinational companies;
- conflict between economic activity and environmental concerns;
- renewable energies.

In the Human elective one can expect questions on the following areas to appear:
- migration;
- urbanisation – planning, land use, trends, issues, etc.;
- the dynamics of population – characteristics, overpopulation, etc.

Section 3: Options (80 marks, 32 minutes)

In this section, you must choose **one question** from **any** of the following four options:
- Geoecology – long questions 13, 14 and 15;
- Global Interdependence – long questions 16, 17 and 18;
- Culture and Identity – long questions 19, 20 and 21;
- The Atmosphere-Ocean Environment – long questions 22, 23 and 24.

This section requires one answer, which should be answered in essay-style format. If you don't require 32 minutes to complete the short questions in Section 1, use the surplus time to plan the aspects for this answer.

Students have the choice of discussing three or four key aspects in detail.

	Option 1	Option 2

Aspects
  Identifying aspect
  Examination
	3 aspects × 20 marks
	4 marks
	8 SRPs × 2 marks
		4 aspects × 15 marks
		3 marks
		6 SRPs × 2 marks

Overall coherence	20 marks (graded)	20 marks (graded)
Total	80 marks	80 marks
Note: Allow for up to three examples for 3 SRPs (different examples and in different aspects).		
Note: Allow for up to two labelled illustrations for 2 SRPs (different illustrations and in different aspects).		

When the examiner is awarding the Overall Coherence (OC), they will consider how well you have dealt with the set question. They will use the following set of descriptors:

Marking Descriptors for Overall Coherence		
Type	Marks	Description
Excellent	20	Excellent ability to relate knowledge to set question. Excellent comprehensive response demonstrating detailed knowledge of subject matter.
Very Good	17	Considerable strength in relating the knowledge to the set question. Very good response demonstrating very broad knowledge of the subject matter.
Good	14	Reasonable capacity to relate knowledge appropriately to set question. Good response with worthwhile information. Broad knowledge of the subject matter demonstrated.
Fair	10	Some effort to relate knowledge to set question. Some relevant information presented but insufficient application of information to set question.
Weak	6	Very limited engagement with set question. Identified some relevant information.
Poor	0	Failure to address the question, resulting in a largely irrelevant answer.

Index

A
ablation 149
abrasion 82, 104, 108, 111, 126, 131
   ice 149
absentee landlord 342
active plate margins 65
active sector (ages) 428
administrative regions 250
aerial photographs
   direction 204
   interpreting
      colour and shading 200
      rural land use 203
      time of year 201
      traffic management 202
      urban functions 203
   oblique 199
   sketch map 199
   vertical 198
aftershock 29
aggregate 66
agrarian 482
air mass 213
alluvial fan 113
alluvial soil 267
Alpine folding 47, 49
altostratus clouds 214
Amazon Basin case study
   deforestation 96–97
Amorican folding 47, 48–49
anticline 46
anticyclone 214, 215
aquifer 452
arcuate delta 117
arête 151
arrondissement 252
Association of South-East Asian Nations (ASEAN) 372
asthenosphere 2
attrition 104, 126
avalanche 93

B
backshore 136, 137
backswamp 114
backwash 125, 132
banlieue 330
bar chart 228
   stacked 229
basalt 58
batholith 19
baymouth bar 135
bays 128
beach 136–137
bedload 106
beds (sediment) 117
Belgium case study
   European language region 254–255
   Sambre-Meuse Valley 259–260
      coal mining contraction 259
      environmental impact 260
      iron and steel production decline 259
      redevelopment 260
      socio-economic impact 259
      textile industry decline 259
bergschrund 150
berms 136
bid rent theory 513
bilingual region 255
bird's foot delta 118
birth rate 427
black smokers 19
block mountain 52
blowhole 130
bluff line 114
bogburst 90
Bord Iascaigh Mhara 297
boulder clay 155, 267
braided stream 113
brain drain 299
breccia 62
brownfield site 286
Burgess, E.W. 503
Burren landscape 78–79
bustee 531

C
calderas 17
Caledonian folding 3, 9, 10, 47, 48
carbonation 75, 79, 81
carbonic acid 79
cardinal points 174
caste system 380
castles 486
Catalonia case study 391
   historical background 391
   independence
      cultural arguments 392
      economic argument for and against 392
      implications of 392
cathedral in the desert 349
caves/caverns 82
cavitation 104
cementation 57
Central Business District (CBD) 500, 502, 504, 505, 506, 507
central place theory 495–497
China case study
   one-child policy 425–426
choropleth map 234
Christaller, Walter 495
cinders 16
cirque 150
cirrus cloud 214
cities in the developing world see developing world
city 261
civil rights 256
cliffs 131–132
climatic regions 247–249
climograph 232
clinometer 241
clints 79
coal 62
coastal areas, human interaction 138–139
coastal deposition 133
coastal erosion 126–132
cold front 214
compaction 57
compression (plates) 45
compression (waves) 127, 131
conglomerates 62
containerisation 509
continental crust 1
continental drift 2
continental plate 6, 7
continental shelf 2, 297
continental splitting 8
conurbation 496

convection currents 2, 5
core region 265
core, inner/outer 2
corrosion 104, 126, 127
crest (wave) 125
cross-brace buildings 35
cross-section (OS map) 183–184
cultural groups, changes in political boundaries and impact on 401
cultural regions 253–258
curtains 81
cuspate delta 118
cusps 136
Custom House Docks Development Authority 286

D
Davis, William Morris 167
death rate 427
deforestation 96–97
deindustrialisation 282, 324
deltas 117–118
democratic deficit 394
demographic anomaly 430
Demographic Transition Model 453
dendritic drainage 102
denudation 49, 53, 71
dependency ratio 428
dependent sector 428
deposition 81, 114
depression 213
   weather 215, 249
deranged drainage 104
desertification 442
developing world
   cities in 531–533
dimension stone 66
diurnal temperature range 73
dolines 80
dome structures 53
dripstone features 81
drumlin 157
Dublin case study
   Dublin's Docklands 509–511
      changed land use 510–511
   heritage issues 525
      Carrickmines Castle 525
      Georgian Dublin 525
      religious issues 525
      Wood Quay 525
   land use zones 502–503
   multiple nuclei theory 507
   Poolbeg incinerator 512–513
   traffic congestion in 521–522
   urban regeneration, Fatima Mansions 530
   urban sprawl 523–524
Dublin city case study
   growth of 284–286
      inner city population decline 286
      urban renewal and regeneration 286
Dublin Dockland's Development Authority (DDDA) 510
Dublin Regulation (EU law) 393

E
East African Rift Valley case study 51
Eastern and Midland Regional Assembly 265
Ebola 454
Economic Union, challenges to 395

Brexit 395
   budgetary waste 395
   economic achievements 395
   economic challenges 395
   enlargement 395
Education and Skills, Department of 305
electrometallurgical industry 370
endogenic forces 1
englacial 155
enterprise centre 286
Enterprise Ireland 300
epicentre 29
epoch 147
erosion 48, 49, 57, 59, 61, 63, 71, 111
   differential 108, 128, 152
   geographical cycle 167
   glacial see under glaciation
   headward 109
   lateral 111
   vertical 106, 108
erratics 156
escarpment 317
esker 158–159
EU Cohesion Policy 404
EU Common Agricultural Policy (CAP) 295, 321, 343, 404
EU Common European Asylum System (CEAS) 472
EU Common Fisheries Policy (CFP) 271, 404
EU Environmental Action Programme (EAP) 406
EU Stability and Growth Pact 405
Europe
   and the European Union, future of 393
      Brexit 394
      eurosceptic parties, rise of 394, 396
      political union 393
      refugee crisis 393
      trust, lack of 394
European Agricultural Guaranteed Fund 295
European Atomic Energy Community 403
European Central Bank 395, 396, 405
European Coal and Steel Community (ECSC) 403
European Commission 396
European Economic Area (EEA) 471
European Economic Community (EEC) 403
European Health Insurance Card (EHIC) 405
European migrant crisis 472–474
   impacts 473
   migrant flows 473
   responses 474
European Regional and Structural funds 300
European Regional Development Fund (ERDF) 300, 349, 404
European Single Market 270, 321
European Social Fund 404, 405
European Union
   asylum seekers and refugees in 472
   development of and enlargement 403, 406–410
      economic policy 404
      environmental policies 406

557

EU treaties 404
the euro 405
factors influencing 408
  Brexit 410
  collapse of communism 408
  Eurozone crisis 409
  future enlargement 409
  impacts of 409
  membership, joining/leaving 407
  refugee crisis 408
  social policies 405
  terrorism 409
  workers' rights 405
social security and healthcare 405
European Union immigration policies 470–471
europhile 394
eurosceptic 394
evaporation 81
exfoliation 73
extensive farming 342

F

Fáilte Ireland 277, 305
fascist state 402
Fatima Mansions, urban regenerisation 530
fault
  graben fault 50
  normal 50
  reverse 51
  tear (slip) fault 52
  thrust 51
faulting 4, 5, 9, 19
  fault line/plane/scarp 8, 29, 50
  faulted structures 50
feldspar 76
fertility rate 424, 425
  population structure, impacts on
    in developed countries 431–432
      Government role 431
      socio-economic factors 431
    in developing countries 432
      socio-economic factors 432
fetch (waves) 125
firn 148
fiscal 395
fissures 7, 8, 15
fissure eruptions 18
flocculation 117
floodplains 114–115
fluting 79
fluvial 101
fluvioglaciation 158
focus (earthquake) 29
folding 4, 5, 19
  fold mountains 6, 7, 9, 10, 46, 47
  fold types 46–47
  movements 47–49
  structures/elements 46
food insecurity 443
Foras na Gaeilge 400
forced migration 460
Foreign Direct Investment (FDI) 273, 300
foreshore 136
forts 485–486
fossils 61
France case study
  local government 252–253
  pro-natalist policies 426
freeze-thaw action 72, 77, 149
frontal rain 249
FRONTEX – The European Border and Coastguard Agency 473

fulacht fiadh 485

G

gabions 139
Gaeltacht Commission 399
Gaeltacht language region case study 253–254, 399–401
  changing boundaries of 400–401
  language use 400
  population and migration 399–400
Gaeltacht Service Towns 400
Galway case study
  manufacturing centre 301
  challenges facing 302
gases 16, 20, 34
genetically modified organisms (GMOs) 452
gentrification 509
geo 131
geographic information systems (GIS) 223
geomorphological regions 250
geothermal energy 23–24
Germany case study
  migrant crisis 474–475
Germany, reunification case study 401
  cultural impacts 402–403
  socio-economic impacts 402
geysers 18
gilets jaunes movement 330
glaciation 148
  erosion 149
  glacial ice formation 148
  glacial spillway 158
  glacial valleys 152
  glacier mass balance 148, 149
  ice movement 149
  Midlandian glaciation 148
  Munsterian glaciation 148
  Pleistocene glaciation 147
gley soils 269
gneiss 63
Good Friday/Belfast Agreement 256
gorge 109
Government of Ireland Act 1920 255
granite 59
Greater Dublin Area (GDA) 265
  human processes
    migration 283
    population density and distribution 281
    social segregation 283
    urban sprawl 283
  physical processes 266–267
  primary economic activities
    agriculture 268
    fishing 271
    forestry 271
    renewable energy 271
  secondary economic activities
    manufacturing, challenges facing 275
    physical factors
      artisan foods 272
      fish processing 272
      forestry 273
    political factors
      Government support 274
    socio-economic factors 273–274
  tertiary economic activities
    tourism 276–278
    transport 278–280
Greater Dublin Area (GDA) Transport Strategy 2016–2035 280, 522
Green, Low-Carbon, Agri-Environment Scheme 270

greenfield site 286
grikes 79
gullying (from rainwater) 442

H

Haiti earthquake case study 37–38
haloclasty see salt crystallisation
Harris and Ullman's multiple nuclei theory 1945 506
Harris, Chauncy 506
headlands 128–130
hectare 294
hectopascals 215
Heritage Act 1995 524
Heritage Council 524
heritage, Record of Protected Structures (RPS) 524
Hess, Harry 3–4
Highly Skilled Eligible Occupations List 471
HIV/AIDS 454
horizontal structures 53
horst see block mountain
hotspots 15
Hoyt, Homer 505
human development
  population change on rates of 454–455
  population growth on 456–457
    developed countries 457
    developing countries 456
Human Development Index 455
humanitarian assistance 448
hydration 75
hydraulic action 82, 104, 108, 111, 126, 131
hydrolysis 76, 77
hydrothermal vents 18

I

Ice Age 3
Iceland case study
  geothermal energy 23–24
igneous rocks 57, 58–59, 65
India 360–361
  human processes
    language 381
    population
      density 378
      distribution 379
      socio-economic factors 379–380
    religion 380
    urbanisation 381
  physical processes
    climate 361–362
    relief and drainage 362–363
    soils 364
  primary economic activities
    agriculture 365–368
    Green Revolution 367–368, 451
    physical factors 365–366
    socio-economic factors 366–367
  fishing 368
    aquaculture 368
  forestry 368
  mining and energy 369
  secondary economic activities
    manufacturing 370–372
    challenges facing 373
    physical factors 370–372
  tertiary economic activities
    tourism 373–375
      physical factors 373–374
      socio-economic factors 374
    transport
      challenges; railways modernisation 377

historical factors 375
physical factors 375–376
political factors 377
socio-economic factors 376–377
India case study
  Kolkata expansion 532–533
    overcrowding 532–533
    pollution 533
    traffic congestion 533
  rural-to-urban migration 469–470
Indian Tourism Development Corporation 375
industrial corridor 372
industrial decline regions 258–260
Industrial Development Authority (IDA) 274, 300
Industrial Revolution 258
informal economy 376
insolation 344
interlocking spurs 108
internally displaced person 460
International Monetary Fund (IMF) 396
International Protection Office (IPO) 472
intervisibility 183
Ireland
  asylum seekers and refugees in 472
  changing migration patterns in 462–463
  glaciations 148
  Republic and Northern Ireland 388
    Anglo-Irish Treaty 1921 388
    Belfast Agreement 389
    Brexit 390
    cultural interaction
      music, religion, sport 390
    economic interaction 389
    Good Friday Agreement 388, 389
    INTERREG programmes 389
    InterTradeIreland 389
    political interaction 389
    Tourism Ireland 389
    Troubles (1968–1998) 389
  settlements 484–487
  social stratification in cities 508
Ireland case study
  European Union enlargement
    political impacts 410
    socio-economic impacts 410
  population distribution and density 419–422
  as a receiver/host region 464–466
    socio-economic impacts 464–466
  rural-to-urban migration 467–468
    impacts on donor regions 467
    impacts receiver/host areas 467
Irish Immigration policies 471
Irish Language Networks 400
Irish settlements on OS maps 184–185, 187
Irish Water 528
Irish Water Services Strategic Plan 2015–2040 528
Islamic World
  Sunni and Shia sects 257
Islamic World case study
  region associated with religion 257–258
Islamophobia 477
isobars 215
isohyet 215
isostasy 164
isotach 215
isotherm 215

Index

J
Japan case study
  earthquake/tsunami 38–40
  impact of an ageing population 434–435
  technology 435
jet streams 249
joints (limestone) 61, 72, 74, 75, 76, 77, 78, 79

K
kame 159
kaolin 76
karren 79
karst landscapes 78, 81–82
kettle hole 159
knick points 165
Kolkata, growth of, case study 381–383
  Government 383
  historical factors 381–382
  physical growth 382
  socio-economic 382–383

L
laccolith 19
lagoon 135
lahars 22, 91
Lahinch case study
  coastal protection 138–139
land use zone 500
land use, changes in 509–511
  planning issues 512–513
  rural areas
    pressure on, from expanding cities 515
      agriculture 515
      environment 515
      heritage and culture 515
      social 515–516
land values in cities 513
  influence on land use 514–515
landslide 92
language regions, changes in boundaries and extent of 399
lava 16, 17, 18
leaching 269
LEADER Programme 296, 305, 343
lee slope 157
levee 114, 115
  artificial 121
Limerick case study 493–494
  defensive function 493
  industrial function 494
  port function 494
limestone 60–61
limestone pavements 79
limon soils 318
liquefaction 34, 94
lithification 57, 58, 60
lithosphere 2, 4
local government in 250–251
Local Government planning and Development Act 2000 524
longshore drift 133, 136
lopolith 19
Los Angeles case study
  air quality 527

M
Macroom case study 483–484
magma 4, 8, 14, 15, 19, 23, 48, 57, 58
mantle 2
marble 63

marine delta 117
marram grass 139
meanders 111
  incised (entrenched/ingrown) 165–166
medieval priories, abbeys 487
megacity 469
megalithic tombs 485
megathrust earthquake 30
Mercalli, Guiseppe (Mercalli scale) 33
mesosaurus 2
metamorphic rocks 57, 58, 63–64, 65
meteorology 212, 220–222
  natural disasters 221–222
Mezzogiorno region 337
  human processes
    organised crime 356
    population
      birth rate 353
      density/distribution 354–355
      urbanisation 356–357
  physical processes 338–339
  primary economic activities
    agriculture 340–343
      Cassa per il Mezzogiorno 343
      challenges facing 343
    fishing 344
      aquaculture 344
    forestry 344
  secondary economic activities
    manufacturing 346–349
      Cassa per il Mezzogiorno 348
  tertiary economic activities
    tourism 350–351
      benefits and challenges 351
      cultural and historical factors 350
      Government/EU policy 350–351
      physical factors 350
    transport
      EU support 352
      future developments 353
      improvements 352
      physical factors 351–352
      political factors 352
      socio-economic factor: population 352
Mezzogiorno region case study
  population distribution and density 423–424
    physical factors 423
    socio-economic factors 423–424
Mid-Atlantic Ridge 3, 7–8, 15, 19, 23, 30
mid-ocean ridge 3, 7, 15
Midlandian glaciation see under glaciation
migration 459
  and donor regions 460
    socio-economic impacts 460
  and host regions 461
    socio-economic impacts 461
  issues arising
    ethnic 475–476
    racial 476
    religious 477
  net migration 462
  rural-to-urban in the developed world 466
  rural-to-urban in the developing world 469
Mississippi River case study 119–122
moho 1
Mohorovicic, Andrija 1
monasteries and round towers 486
monoculture 444
moraine 148, 155–156
mort lake 116
mortality rates

child mortality 432
crude death rate 432
infant mortality 432
and life expectancy
  in developed countries 433
  in developing countries 435–436
    socio-economic impacts 436
  maternal mortality 432
movements 47
mudflow 91
multiple nuclei theory 506
  and Dublin 507
multiplier effect 324
Mumbai case study 449–451
  overpopulation
    causes 449–450
    impacts, population density 450–451
Munsterian glaciation see under glaciation

N
National Broadband Strategy 302
National Grid 170
National Planning Framework (NPF) 524
Nevado del Ruiz case study 91
newly industrialised countries (NICs) 456
nimbostratus clouds 214
nivation 150, 152
nodal regions see urban regions
nodal site 481
North Atlantic Drift 249
North European Plain 317, 319
Northern and Western Regional Authority 290
Northern Ireland case study
  region associated with religion 255–256
nuées ardentes 22
nunatak 148

O
occluded front (occlusion) 214
ocean currents 249
ocean trench 5
oceanic climate case study 248–249
oceanic crust 1
oceanic plate 6, 7
Office of Public Works 305
offshore bar 135
old dependency ratio 311
onglacial 155
Orange Order 256
Ordinance Datum (OD) 178
Ordinance Survey Ireland (OSI) 170
orogeny 47
OS map
  area calculation 176–177
  curved line distance 175
  direction 174
  grid reference 172–173
  height calculation 178
  interpretation of 184–187
  legend 171
  scale 172
  slope 179–180
  straight line distance 175
  tourist attractions 186
  urban functions 187
outwash plain 160
overgrazing in the west of 95
oxbow lake 116

oxidation 75

P
Pacific Ring of Fire 4
paired terrace 166
pandemic 427
Pangaea 2–3
parallel drainage 103
Paris Basin 316
  human processes
    birth rate 329
    population characteristics 329
      migration 330–331
      urbanisation 331
  physical processes 317–318
  primary economic activities
    agriculture 319–321
    energy 321
  secondary economic activities
    manufacturing, challenges facing 325
    physical factors 322
    socio-economic factors 323–325
  tertiary economic activities
    tourism 326
      accessibility 326
      attractions 326–327
      terror attacks, challenges from 327
    transport
      future planning 328
      physical factors 327
      socio-economic factors 327–328
Paris case study
  city growth 331–333
    history 332
    location 331–332
    political factors 333
    socio-economic factors 332–333
passive plate margins 65
pater noster lakes 154
peak land value intersection 513
peneplain 167
per capita income 449
percolation 79, 81
peripheral region 290
permafrost 89
permeable rock 267
pie chart 229–230
pillars 81
plankton 297
Planning and Development Act 2000 312
plantations 482
plate boundaries 4, 5
  convergent (destructive) 5–6, 15, 17, 30, 46, 51, 59
  divergent (constructive) 6, 7, 15, 30, 50, 58
  transform 8, 30, 52
Pleistocene glaciation see under glaciation
plucking (ice) 149
plug and feather 66
plutonic features (plutons) 19
plutonic rocks 58
pocket beach 136
podzol soil 267
point bar 111, 112
polar front 213
population
  impact of income levels on 449
  impact of resource development on 441
  impact of society and culture on 446
  impact of technology on 451–454

559

Landscapes

agriculture 451–453
healthcare 453
overpopulation 441
population pyramids 428–431
population structure 428
population change 417 *see also under human development*
population density 307, 419
population distribution 417–418
historical factors 419
physical factors 418
socio-economic factors 418
population cycle, demographic transition model 426–427
population growth patterns, global 424–425
future trends 425
total fertility rates (TFR) 425
potash 366
pressure release (rocks) 74
prevailing winds 248–249
primeurs 320
pro-natalist policies 426
Project Ireland 2040 311
Public Private Partnerships (PPPs) 377
pyramidal peak 151
pyroclastic flow 16

Q

quarrying case study
building materials extraction 66–67
quartzite 64

R

radial drainage 103
radicalisation 477
radon gas 34
rapids 110
Reception and Integration Agency (RIA) 472
recession 462
regions, core/peripheral 261
regolith 88
rejuvenation (rivers) 165
relief rain 248
religious discrimination 256
revetments 120, 122
ribbon lakes 152
Richter, Charles (Richter scale) 32
riffles 111
ripples 136
river
deposition 105
drainage patterns 101–104
erosion 104
processes 104–105
rejuvenation 108
river capture 167
stages
mature, middle valley 111–113
old age, lower valley 114–115
youthful, upper valley 106–110
stream
disappearing stream 80
river of resurgence 80
transportation 105
rock armour 138
rock cycle 57
human interaction with 65
rockfall 93
RoRo (roll-on roll-off) 509
Rosslare case study
Harbour development 140–142
rotational slip 150

Rural Environmental Protection Scheme (REPS) 270, 295
rural planning 491–492
county development plans 491

S

Sahel case study
overpopulation 441–445
causes and impacts of
climate 442
conflict 444
deforestation 443–444
overgrazing and over-cultivation 444
soil erosion and desertification 444
solutions 445
salt crystallisation 74
salt marsh 134
saltation 105
sand bar 135
sand spit 134
sandstone 61–62
satellite imagery 218–223
and GIS 223
meteorology 220
saturation, zone of 81, 82
Saudia Arabia, Kingdom of 257–258
scarp 93
scatter graph 232
Schengen Area/Convention 405, 471
Scoilnet 242
scree 72, 152
sea arch 129
sea cave 129
sea stack/stump 130
sea-floor spreading 3, 7
sedimentary rocks 57, 60–62
seismic waves 32
seismographs/seismic activity 21, 31, 33
seismology 29, 31, 33
settlements
development of 481–484
economic factors 482
geographical factors 481–484
historical factors 482
situation 482
history of in Ireland 484–487
prehistoric settlement
Bronze Age 485
Iron Age 485–486
Neolithic Period 484–485
new towns 487
Norman Period 486–487
rural settlement patterns 489–490
shaft mining 65
shale 62, 75
shearing 45
SIMA 1
sketch map 181
Sligo OS Map 182
slump rotational slide (slumping) 93
smart city 372
social engineering 425
social stratification in cities 508
socio-economic regions 261
soil creep 89
solifluction 90
solution 82, 127
solution/corrosion 104, 105
South Sudan case study
overpopulation 446–448
causes 447–448
climate 446–447
future 448
sovereignty 396

spillways 121
stalactites 81
stalagmites 81
storm beach 137
stoss slope 157
strainmeters 33
strata 61
strategic development zone 511
stratified drift 155
stratovolcano 17
sub-zones 170
subduction 5. 6, 15, 30, 34, 57
subglacial 155
subsistance farming 341
swallow holes 80
swash 125
syncline 46, 317
synoptic chart 215

T

talus slope 93
tectonic activity impact 9–10
tectonic forces 45, 46–47, 53, 88
tectonic plates 2, 4
tephra 16
terra rossa 339
terracettes 89
thermal convection 4
tiltmeters 20, 34
tombolo 135
tor 77
total fertility rate (TFR) 330, 422
Tourism Ireland 305
traction (riverbed) 105
traffic flow and congestion
causes 519
impacts
environmental 520
soco-economic 519
solutions 520
transport (by sea) 133
transport node 323
Transport, Tourism and Sport, Department of 305
trellis drainage 102
trend (line) graph 231
triangle graph 233
tsunami 30
turloughs 80, 292
types of 150

U

U-shaped valley 152
Údarás na Gaeltachta 254, 300, 311
Ullman, Edward L. 506
Ulster Plantation 255
undertow 136
uniclinal structures 53
unstratified drift 155
urban areas/regions 261, 526–528
environmental quality 526–528
air quality 526
water quality 528
heritage in 524–525
urban functions 492–494
urban growth and expansion of cities 401
urban hierarchy 496
urban land use
theories 503–507
E.W. Burgess's concentric zone theory 1920 503
Hoyt's sector theory 1939 505
zones 500–503

urban planning and renewal 282, 529–531
urban decay 529
urban sprawl 523–524
in Dublin 523–524
urbanism, future of 534–535
environment 535
transport 534–535

V

V-shaped valley 107
valley, dry 80
vent eruptions 16
volcanic islands 7–8, 15
volcanic rocks 58
volcanoes 8, 14–17, 20–22

W

warm front 214
waterfalls 108–109
wave refraction 126, 133
wave-cut platform 132
waves 125–126
constructive (spilling) 126, 133, 136
destructive (plunging) 126, 131, 132, 133
weather charts 214
weathering 48, 49, 57, 59, 61, 63, 71
biological 76
chemical 75–76
mechanical 71, 72
weathering landscapes 77
Wegener, Alfred 2, 3
weight-losing manufacturing 370
Western Region (Ireland's) 290
human processes
population dynamics
density 309
distribution 310
language 311
migration 310–311
urbanisation 312
physical processes
climate 291
relief and drainage 291–292
primary economic activities
agriculture 293–295
fishing
aquaculture 297–298
physical factors 297
socio-economic factors 297
forestry 298
mining and energy
renewable energy 298
secondary economic activities
physical factors 299
political factors
Gov./EU support 300
socio-economic factors 299–300
tertiary economic activities
tourism 303
attractions 303–304
development challenges 306
Government support 305
transport
future developments 308
physical factors 307
politics 308
socio-economic factors 307
Wicklow development plan, rural housing 492
Wild Atlantic Way 254, 305
wind radar charts 216
wind rose diagram 216
wing dykes 112